MANAGEMENT INFORMATION SYSTEMS

Concepts, Structure, and Applications

MANAGEMENT INFORMATION SYSTEMS

Concepts, Structure, and Applications

ELIAS M. AWAD

McIntire School of Commerce
University of Virginia

**The Benjamin/Cummings
Publishing Company, Inc.**
Menlo Park, California · Reading,
Massachusetts · Don Mills, Ontario ·
Wokingham, U.K. · Amsterdam ·
Sydney · Singapore · Tokyo · Madrid ·
Bogotá · Santiago · San Juan

To Sandy, Michael, Bruce, and Brenda

Editorial Director: Sally Elliott
Sponsoring Editors: Jake Warde, David Jackson
Production Management: Richard Mason, Bookman Productions
Production Coordinator: Janet Vail
Text and Cover Design: Hal Lockwood, Bookman Productions
Illustrator: Mary Burkhardt
Copy Editor: Victoria Nelson
Composition: Graphic Typesetting Service

The basic text of this book was designed using the Modular Design System, as developed by Wendy Earl and Design Office Bruce Kortebein.

Cover photos (clockwise from left) courtesy Hewlett-Packard Company; courtesy 3M; courtesy Unisys; courtesy Unisys.

Library of Congress Cataloging-in-Publication Data

Awad, Elias M.
  Management information systems : concepts, structure, and applications /
Elias M. Awad.
    p.   cm.
  Includes index.
  ISBN 0-8053-5110-8
  1. Management information systems.   I. Title.
T58.6.A92   1988
658.4'038—dc19

EFGHIJ-DO-89

The Benjamin Cummings Publishing Company, Inc.
2727 Sand Hill Road
Menlo Park, California 94025

Contents

8   The Decision-Making Process   232

PART V
MANAGERIAL CONSIDERATIONS   533

To the Student

You are already a member of a rapidly growing society committed to the use of information systems for productivity and growth. The computer as a sophisticated tool has become an important part of business and personal lifestyle. Ranging in size from the monstrous "number crunching" supercomputer to the desktop portable, the computer has found its niche in both public and private sectors so successfully that few areas remain untouched by today's highly productive information systems.

Consider the following questions:

- Do you know of a more effective way to provide information for decision making than by computer?
- Can you imagine how easy and convenient it is to use the computer for handling boring and time-consuming computational jobs such as payroll and inventory control?
- How could today's corporations compete without reports such as sales analysis and the graphics that show managers how their firm's performance compares with the competition?

This text will introduce you to the concept of the information system—how it is used in business, why it is used, and how the resulting information can affect you. In your first course in management information systems, you are probably anxious to learn about a number of applications that involve the computer. Based on our experience in teaching this course and the demands of industry, this book covers the following relevant areas:

- The computer's role in business
- What computers can and cannot do
- How computers communicate information to the end user
- The way files and databases are structured for end user computing
- How to analyze and design an information system
- How to manage computer professionals and ensure that company personnel make good use of computers.

It is assumed that you, the reader, are more likely to be a user than a designer of an information system. This book, then, is written with the end user in mind, although two or three chapters briefly treat the technical features of system design. To ensure readability and ease of learning, every chapter contains many examples and practical applications. Several important learning aids are also included. For example, each chapter opens with a chapter outline to guide your reading and an *At a Glance* capsule that highlights chapter contents. Each chapter ends with the following:

- A *chapter summary* that reviews the main points of the chapter.
- *Key words* to improve your vocabulary in information systems.
- *Review questions* that reinforce your understanding of the key points of the chapter.
- *Minicases* based on real-life business situations that illustrate the concepts covered in the chapter. Questions at the end of the cases ask you to identify the problem and prescribe solutions based on your reading.
- *Selected references* that offer additional sources of knowledge about the subject.

In preparing this book, we have kept in mind that people, not computers, are the final decision makers. Information systems support human decision making. Although the underlying technology continues to provide more "intelligence" to improve the quality of decision making, humans have the final say in the way businesses and society in general must perform.

Before the manuscript found its way into production, it was tested in the classroom over a two-year period, with successive revisions resulting from student feedback and rapid changes in technology. To those students whose suggestions are reflected in the final draft, I am deeply indebted. And since no information systems book is ever complete, future revisions are inevitable. After having gone through this material, you are invited to share your experience, ideas, or thoughts. Please feel free to write to me at the following address:

ELIAS M. AWAD
McIntire School of Commerce
University of Virginia
Charlottesville, Virginia 22903

To the Instructor

Today's major theme in the human-machine interface is the use of information for competitive advantage. Computer-generated information is both an asset and a weapon that business organizations use to gain competitive advantage in the marketplace. At one time, computers were back-office machines operated by a handful of technicians. In today's information-dependent environment, we find that:

- Computers are mandatory tools for operating a business.
- The right information in the right format available at the right time can make a difference between profit and loss—the success or failure of a business across industries.
- System design and support is now the joint responsibility of management at all levels as well as MIS personnel.
- More and more managers and administrators are becoming computer literate, and systems analysts and designers are gaining a better understanding of the business of the end user. Bridging the formerly enormous gap between users and designers means improved communications and stronger support for information systems in business.
- A surge of telecommunication and networking technology has made it possible for end users to operate applications on their own premises as well as "download" information from the mainframe database directly and economically.
- More and more time is available for the end user to explore creative ways of improving the business as computers take on additional jobs.

New trends, changing technology, and their potential impact on the end user and organizations influenced the writing of this text. Unlike many MIS texts that emphasize heavy-transaction data processing, this volume includes fundamental features of information systems and the state-of-the-art concepts and procedures so vital to management information systems. The following topics are covered:

- End user computing
- MIS planning
- Database concepts and design

- Expert systems and applications
- Managing MIS personnel and career planning
- Decision-making concepts
- How to select hardware and software packages
- Local area networks and telecommunications
- Decision support systems and software
- Analyzing and designing information systems
- Prototyping as a tool
- Fourth-generation languages

Other concepts, topics, and examples illustrate the role of the end user, the use of the personal computer, and the implications of MIS for decision making. Throughout the book, I have tried to keep the material practical, to give examples, and to make concepts easy to understand. Much effort has also been taken to ensure a balance between syntactic and semantic coverage of MIS. This book is neither a "hands-on" nor a theoretical approach to information systems. It draws from established system development concepts and tools to explain how information systems are designed and used in today's organizations. Implementation problems are candidly discussed based on the realities of day-to-day installations. (It is important to point out to the student, for example, that systems can fail not only from faulty design or user resistance to change, but from sheer office politics and lack of top management support.)

This text is designed to be used in one semester or one quarter as a first course in management information systems. No prior programming or data processing background is required, although an understanding of the basics of business or business management is helpful. A summary of hardware and software concepts and developments that normally represent the bulk of a first course in data processing are covered in Chapters 3 and 4, respectively.

This text includes a variety of learning aids:

- A *boxed vignette* at the beginning of each chapter based on a real-life situation that illustrates one or more aspects of the chapter.
- *Tables* and *boxed illustrations* to support concepts or procedures in the chapter.
- A complete *summary* of each chapter.
- *Key words* that are defined in a *glossary* at the end of the book.
- *Review questions.*
- *Application problems* or minicases designed to highlight key issues.
- *Selected references* to provide additional sources of information about the subject matter.

The text is organized around five major areas:

- Two *introductory chapters* that discuss historical developments in MIS, where the field is going, MIS structure classifications, and how MIS is related to decision support and expert systems.

- *Information systems technology* (Chapters 3–7), with special emphasis on how computers work, characteristics of software and how programs are developed, how files and databases are organized, and the concepts of networking and data communications.
- *Decision support and end user computing* (Chapters 8–12), highlighting the procedures behind decision making, the structure and tools of decision systems, the role of end user computing, and the basics and potential of expert systems.
- *Application planning and system development* (Chapters 13–17), beginning with MIS planning and followed by determining the user's information requirements, exploring alternative approaches to hardware and software, and designing and testing the information system.
- *Managerial considerations* (Chapters 18–19), presuming a knowledge of MIS technology, design, and implementation and focusing on how to select, motivate, and manage MIS personnel. Chapter 19 concludes with trends and future directions in management information systems.

Acknowledgments

A book of this magnitude could not have been completed without support. I wish to acknowledge a number of people whose efforts influenced the content and direction of this project. I would like to thank the following reviewers for their helpful recommendations and comments:

Maryam Alavi	University of Houston
Mary Culnan	American University
George Diehr	University of Washington
E. James Dunne	University of Dayton
Jane Fedorowicz	Boston University
Karen A. Forcht	James Madison University
David E. Godderz	Lakewood Community College
Malcolm Gotterer	
Wallace J. Growney	Susquehanna University
Mary Jo Haught	
Cary Hughes	North Texas State University
Ernest A. Kallman	Bentley College
Laurence A. Madeo	University of Missouri at St. Louis
Grover Rodich	Portland State University

I am especially indebted to Professor George Diehr, University of Washington, for his detailed review of the entire manuscript. His constructive comments influenced the makeup of the book and its usefulness to instructors and students. During my stay as a visiting professor at Dartmouth College, my graduate CIS students provided feedback about various aspects of the manuscript.

Special thanks go to Dean William G. Shenkir, McIntire School of Commerce, for providing computer, word processing, and moral support in the preparation of this work. I thank my colleagues, Andy Ruppel and Robert H. Trent, for their contributions to the initial drafts of Chapters 2 and 13, respectively. Donald Burkhard was an effective sounding board on material concerning database concepts and software (Chapter 6). Randy Smith thoroughly reviewed Chapters 3 and 4. Malcolm Gotterer's insightful critiques of Chapters 5 and 6 were very helpful. Mary Jo Haught made invaluable contributions to the discussion of software throughout the text.

I owe a great deal to the team of professionals at Benjamin/Cummings Publishing Company, who have been models of talent and motivation. Sally Elliott, executive editor, adopted the project and provided needed support. Jake Warde, my editor, supervised the reviews and ensured a publishable manuscript. Camille Cusumano transformed Chapters 3 and 4 into readable material. Special words of appreciation to Devra Lerman, editorial assistant, for encouraging creativity and for many hours of work on the illustration program. I thank Vicki Nelson, my copy editor, for a first-class job on the entire manuscript. Richard Mason at Bookman Productions supervised the production of the manuscript under a tight time schedule.

My deepest debt goes to my family, whose patience, support, and family time made this project possible. My son, Bruce, was instrumental in preparing various portions of the manuscript using WordPerfect.

PART I

MIS:
AN INTRODUCTION

MIS: An Overview

Chapter Contents

Existing Information Resources Can Give You the Competitive Edge

IT IS ONE THING for a firm to use information resources strategically for cost leadership or product differentiation. It is another matter to find new ways to use such resources in supporting business strategies. The latter is a trend that is gaining in popularity. New units are being formed within and without MIS departments to do electronic banking, telemarketing videotext and home retailing, point-of-sale development and information retailing and wholesaling. Their objectives are usually to research and pilot-test new and creative ways of extending the services and products of the company by building on existing information resources about customers, buyers or suppliers and extending through information technologies the services offered in new or existing markets.

For example, the Buick division of General Motors Corp. has organized a "Marketing through Technology" department to develop a new information system called Epic to aid in the marketing of its automobiles. Epic is being used by Buick in dealer showrooms, in public areas such as hotels and shopping malls and in homes via videotext services.

In dealer showrooms, the Epic system uses PCs in kiosks that allow a salesman to respond to customer questions about the availability of various models, colors, options, prices and financing terms for Buick cars. If a customer is interested in a particular model, the salesman can use Epic to determine the nearest dealership that has the car, and if the customer is comparison-shopping with other makes of cars in mind, the salesman can, through Epic, use another videotext service, Compuserve, Inc.'s Compuserve, to get data on most makes and models of cars to compare with the Buick model under consideration.

Thus, Epic provides better and more accurate information about the Buick product line to salesmen and customers alike as well as integrates the use of a car locator system for inventory control and an external information service for comparison-shopping. The long-term mission of the Marketing through Technology department is to determine the profitability of using new technologies to extend the reach of information resources in creative directions to enhance the sales effectiveness, inventory control and productivity of the dealer work force.

—*Adapted from Don Marchand and Forest Horton, Jr.,* Computerworld, *May 26, 1986, 79–80.*

AT A GLANCE

In today's knowledge society, information is a critical resource. The wide range of computer and communication technologies provides quality information for management and is the basis for the management information system, or MIS.

MIS is an integrated, computer-based, interactive system that supports operations and decision-making functions at all levels. It serves the organization's functional areas through decision models. Models draw most of their inputs from the database and place the output into it.

MIS, relatively unknown in the 1960s, had its foundations in the early 1970s. Today, having gone through several stages of technological change—from "isolated" computing to today's user-machine interface—it is a backbone for industry and commerce.

Related to MIS are decision support systems (DSS)—the managerial use of computers. DSS represents a step away from the traditional terminal toward the personal computer linked to the mainframe. DSS incorporates expert systems that use rules of logic and a knowledge base to simulate the human expert's thought processes.

By the end of this chapter, you should know:

1. What MIS is and does
2. The stages of MIS development
3. The direction of MIS and DSS
4. The role of the personal computer in MIS development

Introduction

The computer's vast popularity in recent years results from the fact that usable information is the backbone of industry in today's knowledge society. Information is a resource that must be managed and controlled. Two-thirds of the average executive's time is spent processing or communicating information, and well over half of the U.S. workforce is directly engaged in some form of information handling—reports, ad hoc inquiries, spreadsheet analysis, and other functions.

Computers have become an integral part of a company's everyday activities because of the kind of information they generate and their speed of delivery. The use of computers in business dates back to the mid-1950s, when batch-processing applications such as payroll were once the mainstay of computer centers. The role of computers in such activities is now so routine that they are taken virtually for granted.

Today's information resource is used not only for cost reduction but in pursuing business strategies. For example, consider Mobil Oil's strategy to market gasoline in California by installing point-of-sale terminals at gasoline stations for customers to use with the automated teller machines of two major banks. And what about airlines, car rental firms, and hotels working together to offer bonus programs for frequent flyers through computers that track bonus miles and issue awards?

These examples illustrate today's emphasis on information and the *value* of information. The challenge of the 1980s is using information technology to gain *competitive advantage* and extending the limits of the computer to incorporate artificial intelligence as a revolutionary step for decision support. The wide range of computer and communication resources that provides information for decision making makes up today's **management information systems**, or MIS.

In this text, we will focus on MIS as a practical approach to developing information systems in support of decision making. MIS is a broad category of systems. Some activities are highly integrated and "prespecified" for repetitive transaction processing; other activities are customized for specific decision-making tasks. We will also emphasize office automation and the communication network that facilitates clerical support.

Definition

Just what is MIS? What does it do? There is no agreement on a common definition. Terms such as information systems, information services, or information processing systems, often used as synonyms for MIS, refer to an information system that supports transaction processing and management decision-making functions.

MIS, a field of over a quarter century's standing in practice and a subject of research since the late 1960s, is an *integrated, computer-based, user-machine system that provides information for supporting operations and decision-making functions*. Its key elements are:

1. *Integrated* system to serve many users
2. *Computer-based* system that integrates a number of applications through a database
3. *User-machine* interface that gives instant response to ad hoc inquiries
4. *Providing information* to all managerial levels
5. *Support of operations* and decision-making functions

These elements tell us that MIS can be an important organizing medium. Developing a MIS means creating a new environment in which to manage a business. To clarify this point, we will elaborate on each element and discuss the activities that led to the developmental trends in MIS.

Integrated System

If MIS is to provide a new environment for decision making, the applications must be integrated to serve all authorized users. Integration means centralizing files for shared access to information across applications. It also means eliminating redundancies and inconsistencies that are common in traditional files. Individual applications designed with one user in mind are often incompatible with other applications that use the same data. In contrast, a single application integrating common data across users becomes the preferred approach in application design.

Integration of computer-based applications is usually based on a master plan that commits management to MIS development. The plan specifies actions to be taken, standards, and guidelines for installing an information system. Although users may develop their own applications on freestanding microcomputers, a master plan can require that such applications be compatible with the organization's mainframe. Providing diverse applications within integration standards is a trend that promotes user-machine interface and compatibility of files for use by multiple users.

Computer-Based System

A MIS depends heavily on the capabilities and power of the computer used for it. A computer system has four major components: input, processing, output, and secondary storage. As shown in Figure 1.1, data are entered into the central processing unit (CPU) through an input device such as a keyboard. The CPU acts on the data based on an application program stored in the computer's main memory. The resulting

Figure 1.1
Configuration of a large computer system. Data are input and then sent to the central processing unit, which may be at a different location. Information can be output on a high-speed printer. Secondary storage may take the form of magnetic tape or, as shown here, magnetic disk. (Reprinted with permission of Unisys Corporation.)

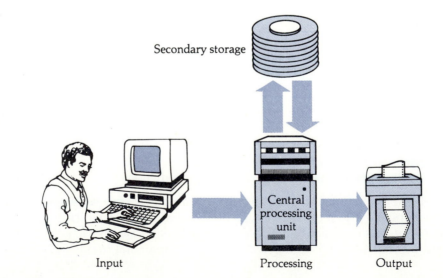

Secondary storage

Central processing unit

Input   Processing   Output

information is produced through a printer in the form of a report. Computer fundamentals are covered in Chapter 3.

Today's computer power makes MIS a reality. The question facing MIS designers, however, is not how much computer power is required, but what applications should be run on the computer. Choice of applications depends on how ready the user is to interface with the computer, cost/benefit aspects, and management support for change.

Because management information systems are computer-based, developing a MIS depends on the right choice of *hardware, software, database, procedures* for computer operation, and MIS *personnel*—analysts, database designers, programmers, computer operators, and support staff. Hardware and software are discussed in Chapters 3 and 4, database concepts and applications in Chapters 5 and 6. MIS personnel requirements are reviewed in Chapter 18.

Using a Database　A major component of MIS is the database. Before it became available, users operated in a conventional file environment. Programs handled data with no data sharing across applications (see Figure 1.2). In a database environment, common data are available to multiple users. Instead of restricting each user or program to managing separate data, users share data across applications. The software, called the **database management system** (DBMS) manages the data as an entity and coordinates data sharing.

Figure 1.2
Conventional and DBMS environment. The DBMS allows shared but selective access to information. Note that only user C has unrestricted access to all data.

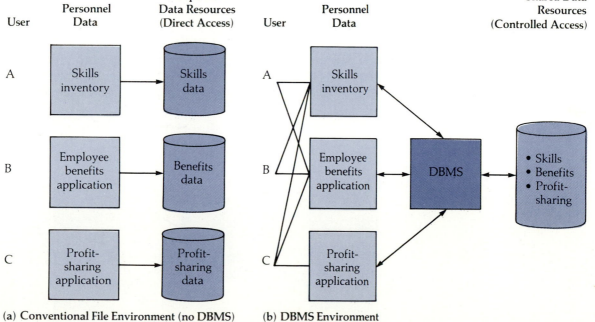

(a) **Conventional File Environment (no DBMS)**　　(b) **DBMS Environment**

As we shall see later in the text, a database is crucial for MIS operation. It stores information as an integrated entity. The goal is to make information access easy, quick, inexpensive, and flexible for the user. This is accomplished by controlling *redundancy*, making the system *user friendly* (easy to learn and use), and ensuring **data independence** (changing hardware or adding new data without having to rewrite existing programs), and data accuracy and integrity.

Managing databases requires a database administrator (DBA) to coordinate data activities and the database. Besides a background in management, the DBA is expected to have the technical knowledge to deal with database designers. For the success of this key role, MIS staff and senior management support is critical.

Using Models   MIS applies decision models for problem solving. A *model* is a near representation of reality. Decision models are oriented to a number of decision-making areas:

1. Evaluation of investment alternatives (e.g., net present value analysis)
2. Data analysis (e.g., sales analysis)
3. Scheduling (e.g., production scheduling)
4. Simulation (e.g., plant expansion planning)

Today's modern manager uses models for studying decision situations. A database provides an interface with the models on a *real-time* basis—that is, processing inquiries or data as they actually occur (see Figure 1.3). Real time is discussed in Chapter 3.

Despite a surge in popularity during the past decade, decision models have not been as effective as they should be. In many cases, they are used on an ad hoc basis. Model outputs stand alone rather than as inputs to other models. Most decision models are also not easily updated and lose their usefulness in a changing decision-making environment. One alternative is to have an integrated database that is compatible with the model. Decision models are discussed in greater detail in Chapter 8.

Figure 1.3
Decision models in a
database framework.

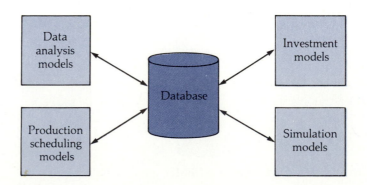

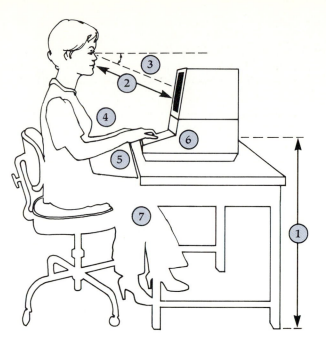

Figure 1.4
A workstation design.
(1) The European rec-
ommendation for the
height of the home-row
keys is 28¼ to 29½
inches. The U.S. mili-
tary standard is 29¼ to
31 inches. (2) The view-
ing distance should be
between 17¼ and 19¾
inches, with a maximum
of 27½ inches. (3) Gen-
erally, the center of the
screen should be at a
position between 10 and
20 degrees below the
horizontal plane
at the operator's eye
height. One researcher
recommends that the
top of the screen be
below eye height, anoth-
er that the top line of
the display be 10 to 15
degrees below the hori-
zontal, with no portion
of the screen at an angle
greater than 40 degrees
below the horizontal.
(4) One researcher rec-
ommends that the angle
between the upper and
lower arms be between
80 and 120 degrees.
(5) The angle of the
wrist should be no
greater than 10 degrees.
(6) The keyboard should
be at or below elbow
height. (7) Do not forget
to provide enough room
for your legs. (From
*Potential Health Hazards
of Video Display
Terminals*).

User-Machine Interface

A critical element in MIS design is the user-machine *interface*, an environment that allows the user to enter a command into the computer and
the computer displays the results on the screen. This face-to-face dialog
improves the user's decision-making potential. Today's computers provide on-line interface between the user and the machine by means of
screen, keyboard or "mouse," menu-driven software, and the physical
design of the system to match human comfort. The last factor falls under
the category of **ergonomics** because it is concerned with comfort, fatigue,
ease of use, and issues that affect the welfare, satisfaction, and performance of people working with user-machine systems. For example, a
built-in swivel under a monitor allows a user wearing bifocals to tilt the
screen for easy reading angle. Similar features apply to the design of
desks, chairs, lighting, etc. (see Figure 1.4). Ergonomics is discussed in
Chapter 11.

The concept of user-machine interface is a major step away from the
days when an end user got reports only through the computer center.
The *end user* is anyone authorized to enter, access, or retrieve data from
a computer facility. In an interface environment, the end user interfaces
with the computer on a real-time basis. Instructions are entered through
a keyboard. The computer may be a freestanding microcomputer or a
mainframe serving multiple users through remote terminals. Response
to inquiries is either displayed on a monitor or printed out in a matter of
seconds.

The user-machine interface has several implications:

1. The user is likely to support a computer if the language or procedure is easy to learn and use.
2. The hardware and software must produce results in time to be used for making decisions.
3. MIS designers must have knowledge of computer technology and the user's business requirements to ensure a successful user-machine interface.

Today's trend in MIS development suggests that the user need not be a computer "hacker" or an expert in information technology. The goal is to design a system that accepts user inquiries in English-like words, processes commands through a menu-driven format, and produces results accurately, quickly, and completely.

MIS: How Did We Get Here?

MIS, developed in the early 1970s, is now a full-fledged business support system. We will first highlight the major stages of technological change in MIS development and how they evolved.

Stages of Technological Change

The five stages of MIS technological change are summarized in Table 1.1.

Isolated Computing   The first stage, **isolated computing**, began in the early 1960s when computers were housed in their own rooms and run by youthful "supermen." The major activities were cost-reducing data processing applications such as payroll and accounts receivable. The computer, viewed as a tool for reducing operating costs, became a savior for many firms. Data processing managers were promoted and rewarded by their organizations.

Despite these feats, the computer was not utilized to its full potential. Management was lax. Controls were lacking. There were no chargebacks of computer costs. Stage 1 kept the pace with the rush to improve the utilization factor.

Consolidated Computing   This stage, **consolidated computing**, represents the mid- to late 1960s, when computer functions were merged into a computer center facility. There was a surge of applications in all functional areas. General ledger, forecasting, and inventory control were typical applications. The rush to complete projects resulted in poor documentation and high maintenance costs caused by program errors. The programming staff grew and total costs began to get out of hand. In most

Table 1.1 Major Stages of Technological Change

Development Stage	Period	Name	Features
1	1960–64	*Isolated Computing* (development of application portfolios)	• Cost-reducing accounting applications • Management lax on full utilization of EDP resources • Rush to use idle capacity later in the stage • No chargebacks of EDP costs to users • EDP managers moving up in the organization *Typical applications:* payroll, accounts receivable, accounts payable, billing
2	1965–69	*Consolidated Computing* (development of EDP organizations)	• Surge of applications in all functional areas • High maintenance and development costs • Poor documentation • High demand for programmers • EDP operations were invisible costs *Typical applications:* general ledger, forecasting, budgeting, inventory control
3	1970–74	*Management Controls and Restraints*	• Freeze on applications—emphasis on control of existing ones • Belt tightening of EDP budgets—no additional funds spent for the EDP function • Move toward centralization of computer processing to save money • Controls and standards enforced • Implemented systems for charging users for EDP resource utilization

(continued)

Table 1.1 Major Stages of Technological Change **(continued)**

Development Stage	Period	Name	Features
4	1975–79	*The Rising Role of the User*	• Restructuring of applications portfolios • Surge of application software packages • Greater involvement of users in EDP activity • Appearance of databases and distributed computing for developing MIS
5	1980–85	*The User-Machine Interface*	• Early 1980s: microcomputers used as "single-thread" or one-application-at-a-time systems; mid-1980s: microcomputers linked to the mainframe through networking technology • User-friendly, ready-to-use, off-the-shelf packages becoming popular • Decision support systems (DSS) beginning to show promise • Word-processing packages becoming popular • Office automation showing promise • Experimental work in expert systems and artificial intelligence on its way • Decreased importance of the application programming function that now overlaps with the database administration function • Structured programming taking a firm foothold in system development; it plays down coding and promotes analysis and design activities. *Typical applications:* DSS—LOTUS 1-2-3, Visicalc, IFPS; database—dBASE III plus, K-Man, POWERBASE; word processing—WORDSTAR, PFS

computer installations, no one knew exactly how much was spent on computer operations.

At the end of the 1960s, organizations began to realize that technological feasibility was not enough to justify further expansion. With no additional funds allocated for data processing, management put a freeze on new applications. This set the tone for stage 3—management controls and restraints.

Management Controls and Restraints   The third stage, management controls and restraints, started in the early 1970s. It was a period of belt tightening; computer centers began to charge users for computer services. Efficiency in computer operations and services became a paramount objective.

Embedded Computing   The fourth stage unfolded in the mid- to late 1970s. The pent-up demand for implementing computer technology and the appearance of application software packages signaled a greater demand for the computer professional. Of significance was the rising role of the user who, by then, was computer literate and could become a partner in the computer processing function. This meant the MIS manager had to evolve from a technician into a manager with interpersonal and administrative skills. The changing profile of the MIS manager is summarized in Table 1.2.

The proliferation of minicomputers, databases, and distributed computing during this stage laid the foundation for MIS. In distributed computing, computer power is provided at the user's level and linked to the mainframe for higher-level processing and reporting. **Embedded computing** allows the end user to access files via a terminal linked to a remote computer. During this stage in MIS development, heavy emphasis was placed on single, ad hoc inquiry into databases for decision making.

The User-Machine Interface   In the early to mid-1980s, emphasis switched to the user-machine interface and MIS was transformed from a formerly *programmer-oriented* transaction support system and from "single-thread" applications such as payroll to *user-oriented* decision support systems (DSS) that handle multiple applications and inquiries. MIS is now a user-oriented, user-friendly, user-driven environment with emphasis on structured programming, ad hoc inquiries, and real-time information access.

Where Is MIS Going?

The goal of MIS is to provide an environment for the support of various organizational and managerial decisions. MIS has been viewed as a "fed-

Table 1.2 Changing Role of the MIS Manager

Attribute	Mid- to late 1950s	Mid- to late 1960s	Mid- to late 1970s	Mid- to late 1980s
Experience	programming	programming/ analysis	programming/ analysis/ project management	analysis/project management/ system development
Education/ training	high-school math	technical degree	bachelor's/ master's	master's
Skills				
a. Technical	card file/batch	batch, on-line	enough to converse with staff	hands-on knowledge of various software
b. Organiza- tional	superclerk	report generator	change agent	leader
Reporting hierarchy	to accounting	to accounting	to VP	to president or executive VP
Loyalties	to computer	to computer department	to organization as a whole	to organization/ profession/ society

eration of subsystems . . . conforming to an overall plan" (Davis and Olson, 1984, 10). The primary extensions of the MIS concept in shaping information systems are decision support systems (DSS), expert systems (ESS), office support systems, and end user computing systems.

Decision Support and Expert Systems

DSS, or the managerial use of computers, is a type of MIS—a computational aid to help managers integrate judgment, experience, and insight for improving their performance as managers. It examines alternatives in semistructured decision-making situations. Using simulation and decision models, the interactive dialog allows trial-and-error search for feasible solutions.

DSS represents a step away from the traditional terminal toward the personal computer (PC) linked to the mainframe. Such an environment encourages users to interface with a computer for addressing "what if" situations in business. More on DSS is found in Chapters 2, 9, and 10.

An **expert system** is one type of artificial intelligence (see Figure 1.5) that allows a novice user to achieve results comparable to those of an "expert" in a specific decision-making area. An expert system transforms

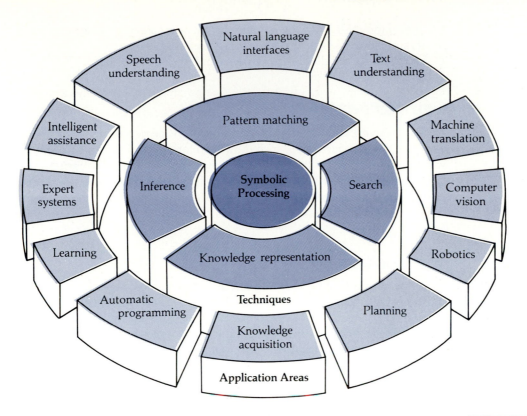

Speech understanding

Natural language interfaces

Text understanding

Intelligent assistance

Pattern matching

Machine translation

Expert systems

Inference

Symbolic Processing

Search

Computer vision

Learning

Knowledge representation

Robotics

Automatic programming

Techniques

Planning

Knowledge acquisition

Application Areas

Figure 1.5
Elements of artificial intelligence. The outer circle allows twelve application areas including expert systems, to be discussed in Chapter 12. The inner circle focuses on four symbolic processing techniques. Each technique deals with one or more application areas.

computers that have always been "dumb" calculators into machines that draw conclusions from a massive database. An *intelligent* terminal is a system with memory, processing capability, and the ability to accept input and produce output. The personal computer is an example of an intelligent terminal. More on terminals is found in Chapters 3 and 11.

Expert systems (arbitrarily called expert support systems or ESS) can also be viewed as one aspect of DSS. Their *knowledge base* and the *decision rules* represent the "expert's" thought processes. For example, a passenger for an airline reservation expert system submits a list of facts such as "I want to fly to Miami from Boston a.m., nonstop, October 9 and stay five days on super saver. I am diabetic, traveling alone." The system searches the knowledge base for various flights, departure times, meals, and fares. An interactive dialog allows a series of questions and answers concerning a special breakfast, car rental, seat selection, and so on. The initial inquiry is generally unstructured because of fragmented or incomplete information. Various strategies are then considered for searching the knowledge base to determine the best fit between an available flight and the passenger's requirements.

An expert system "learns" from each episode and uses it to ask fewer or different questions for a final decision. The user's responses are stored for later interaction with the passenger just as an alert travel agent would understand the likes and dislikes of a frequent flyer using the agency. Expert systems are discussed in detail in Chapter 12.

Office Support Systems

This area covers the day-to-day functions of office personnel—managers and professional personnel, including secretaries. Until recently, the term was restricted to word processing. Today it includes administrative functions such as electronic mail, electronic filing, and processing of images, voice, and data as well as text. An important extension of MIS practice, office support is discussed in Chapter 11.

End User Computing

End user computing has been called different names, including DSS. As the term implies, the objective of this system is to help end users— managers, professionals—to make timely decisions by interacting directly with the computer. To implement this environment, the system must incorporate tools such as query and report generators, electronic spreadsheets (e.g., LOTUS 1-2-3), financial models, statistical analysis programs, and graphic display routines.

End user systems tend to overlap with office support systems. The data generated by a data processing system are presented in graphic or tabular form in reports prepared on the word processor. The reports may also be transmitted to other managers via electronic mail or filed in an electronic filing system for later retrieval.

The trend in MIS is to get closer to the user and expand the information system network to allow transactions to be collected closer to their source. This goal is being achieved by the greater availability of intelligent terminals and the personal computer. The networking cuts paperwork and minimizes reaction time. More on end user computing is found in Chapter 11.

As we have seen, the developments shaping MIS are intertwined but ultimately deliver ad hoc service to the end user. The transition from the *production-consumer* (computer center-user) environment of information delivery to *cooperative computing* by end users and MIS is already here. User-friendly interfaces such as graphics and *windowing*—where various portions of a report or a financial statement (windows) are shown on the computer's monitor (see Chapter 11)—are obvious indicators.

DSS appears to be a step toward supporting the entire process of decision making. The current trend is adopting expert systems that help us extend MIS by adapting the system to the cognitive styles of the end user. The goal is to establish a mutual relationship between the individual manager as a decision maker and the information system.

The Role of the Personal Computer

A major change has taken place in the way managers in the office and factory do their work. Wherever a visitor to a Fortune 1000 firm turns, the personal computer is performing as an aid to personal productivity, a data processing machine, a mainframe and network link, and more. These chores are permanently changing the user's work habits.

The many uses and applications of the personal computer are too numerous to list. The important point is that the personal computer has introduced a new way of doing business. In terms of personal productivity, lap-based or airline portable PCs help get writing, calculating, or other simple work done. These machines are used for word processing, running spreadsheets, and integrated application packages. They also take care of appointments, time management, and the like. Some PCs use modems to transmit information from, say, the user's hotel room to the home office. Data communication is discussed in Chapter 7.

In the early 1980s, the personal computer was mainly used for stand-alone processing without links to the mainframe. This situation is rapidly changing. As microcomputers became more powerful, end users began to inquire about accessing the wealth of information stored on the host computer to improve their decision making—thus the micro-to-mainframe link. With the growing sophistication of end users and their increasing demand for mainframe data, programmers and end users are cooperating in developing new applications by jointly building a prototype that the user then tests. In this way, applications are built more quickly and with better results.

The PC has had a mixed impact on the MIS function in general and MIS managers in particular. Since the PC handles various applications at the user's level, the responsibility for application development is now the user's. On one hand, this has eased the computer center's applications backlog. Yet user-originated applications have caused problems for the MIS manager who must maintain compatibility between PCs and the mainframe. Additional problems resulting from recent attempts at linking the PC to the mainframe are not all solved or even soluble. There are technical, organizational, and security issues that will take time to resolve.

The Rising Tide of Information Management

So far, we have found that MIS is not data processing, although it encompasses certain processing activities. It is not computer science, even though database structure and design require knowledge drawn from computer science. It is not management science, although decision and optimization models are used for decision support. It is not management or human

Figure 1.6
Areas of MIS.

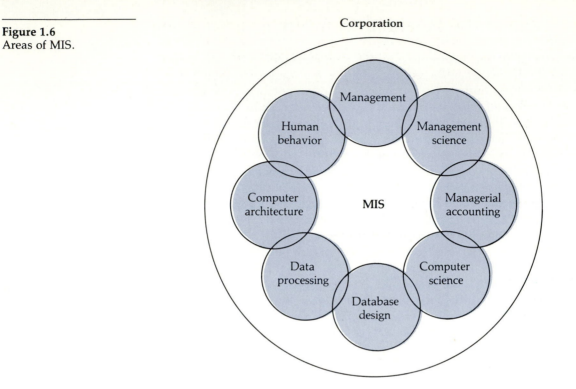

behavior either, although MIS designers need a background in organization behavior for a successful system installation. MIS, in fact, draws from all these areas (see Figure 1.6).

MIS and its heavy reliance on information technology is changing the shape and behavior of organizations. Today's user-machine interface means response time to inquiries in a fraction of a second, where information access and retrieval from high-density databases regardless of distance are almost taken for granted. Yet a gap still exists between technology-driven opportunities and our ability to use them.

Several important factors determine the winners from the losers in the use of information technology in business:

1. *Selecting clear-cut, definable problems.* Most of today's MIS projects start with insufficient understanding of business needs, failure to quantify benefits and costs, and poor presentation of the facts.

2. *Designing effective systems.* There are adequate tools available with existing technology, yet we design new systems that do not reflect user requirements, and cannot be installed without causing serious disruptions or provoking employee resistance to change. It seems obvious that the probability of a successful installation can be enhanced by assigning qualified analysts/designers to the project.

3. *Managing system development.* Well-conceived projects often fail because of poor cost estimates, inexperienced project managers, lack of user involvement, personnel turnover, or inadequate resources. A successful information system requires effective management of project costs and procedures as well as technology.

4. *Building a qualified MIS staff.* The challenge in MIS development is attracting, motivating, and retaining outstanding people in a field where the notion that data processing is the "road to the top" has been largely abandoned. Recent attempts by computer giants such as IBM to finance MIS education in colleges and universities are a positive move to correct this deficiency.

In addition to outside support, staff development includes a well-defined career path, a skills index defining job requirements, a training program linked to the index, and an appraisal process that rewards performance. Once competent staff is secured, high productivity is achieved with each project. System performance, then, is directly related to the appraisal process.

5. *Communicating with users and management.* There are four communication channels in MIS development: a sound business system plan, a means to track and report performance, end user involvement, and end user support. Launching a project with a sound overall plan, executed by a qualified MIS staff with user participation, is a virtual ticket to success in a MIS installation. These factors are addressed in various sections of the text.

MIS Issues and Directions

The ever-changing nature of MIS raises two important managerial issues. In a 1986 Arthur Andersen and Co. survey, 120 senior MIS executives of Fortune 500 firms were surveyed. The most important MIS issue voiced by the respondents was managing end user computing. The high level of importance (76%) placed on end user computing indicates a commitment to apply information technology to decision-making activities. A related factor is the importance of *connectivity* issues such as faster transfer of records from the PC to the mainframe and support for a multiuser environment using the microcomputer.

With information technology changing the ground rules by which businesses compete, another important management issue is finding qualified managers with combined business experience and technical knowledge. For example, should top management rotate managers with MIS professionals? Should career paths be created for those with technical knowledge? Most studies indicate that the transition from technical to business management is not easy. It requires serious preparation and training.

Based on the changes that information technology can make in the organization, there are a number of critical questions that top management should consider in using information technology to gain a competitive edge. For example:

1. Is there enough information technology knowhow in the MIS department to harness new opportunities?
2. What new market opportunities exist in the organization's area of business where strategic use of information technology can be a clear advantage? How should it be pursued?
3. What vulnerability do competitors have resulting from ineffective use of information technology? What is the best way to take advantage of competitive lethargy?

Such questions make it important to consider long-range MIS planning and make a conscious effort to align MIS goals with corporate goals. This is a new MIS role that, if properly carried out, should create closer working relationships between those who utilize the information and the MIS personnel who help generate it. Long-range planning will also provide MIS managers an opportunity to increase their influence and productivity in the organization and bring information management to maturity as a vital corporate asset.

How This Text Is Organized

This book is about management information systems—concepts, technology, and ways to develop and manage information systems in business. Part I provides an overview of MIS. Chapter 1 describes what it is, how it started, where it is going, and related managerial issues. Chapter 2 discusses the different approaches to MIS structure and the relationship among MIS, decision support, and expert systems. The latter two concepts are viewed as types of MIS.

Part II focuses on the technical aspects of MIS—essentially computer fundamentals, database technology, and the communication network that links the database to user terminals for data access and decision making. Chapter 3 is a summary of the computer hardware, with special emphasis on the microcomputer and its role in end user computing. Chapter 4 covers software: what it is, how it is acquired, how programs are developed, and various levels of programming and end user languages with special focus on application development without programming. Chapter 5 describes how files are organized and how data are accessed. Chapter 6 reviews database concepts, with particular emphasis on the relational database, commonly used on the personal computer. Chapter 7 expands on telecommunication concepts—how information is transmitted from one point to another. A special section on local area networks

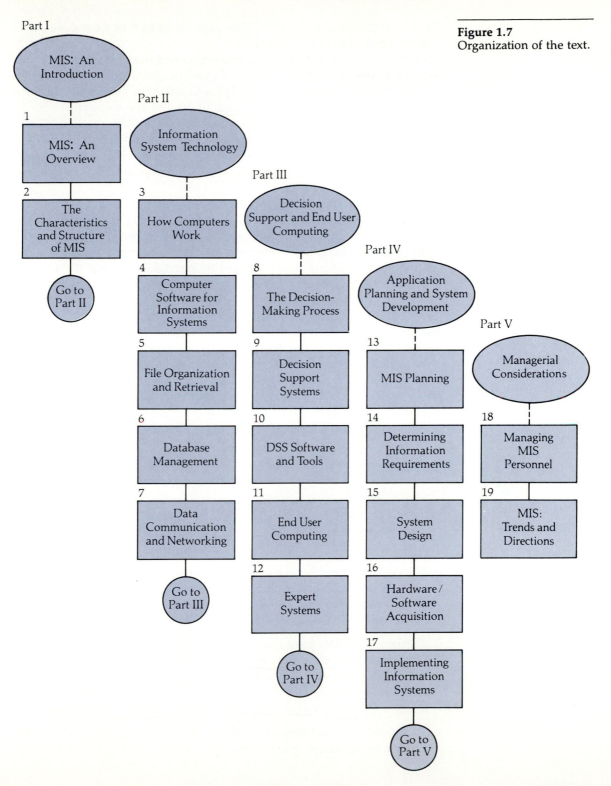

Figure 1.7
Organization of the text.

brings up the microcomputer's growing role as part of a network rather than a stand-alone unit.

Part III addresses the decision-making process and the software available for decision support. Chapter 8 examines how decisions are made and how the computer can be helpful in decision making at different organizational levels. Chapters 9 and 10 discuss the tools and software that support managers in decision situations on an ad hoc basis. Related to decision support is office automation and the role of the intelligent workstation in the user-machine interface, both of which are covered in Chapter 11. The newest approach to decision support, expert systems, is examined in Chapter 12.

Part IV illustrates how an information system is implemented into the organization. The first step is to develop a long-range plan for the installation (Chapter 13). Once the plan is in place, the next step is determining the organization's requirements that can be met through an information system. The detailed analysis is covered in Chapter 14. Chapter 15 illustrates the process of system design. Chapter 16 addresses system acquisition issues as a part of the system development life cycle. Chapter 17 elaborates on a procedure for testing the new system and planning for recovery from a system failure.

Part V centers on management of the computer facility and the personnel that operate the information system (Chapter 18). Chapter 19 reflects retrospectively on the field of MIS and suggests future trends based on today's technology. Figure 1.7 summarizes graphically the organization of the text.

Summary

- MIS is an integrated, computer-based, user-machine system that provides information for supporting operations and management decision-making functions. Integration means centralization of files across applications and elimination of redundancies.

- MIS depends heavily on the computer's processing power. A computer consists of input, processing, output, and secondary storage components for supporting MIS activities. The operating elements are the hardware, software, database, procedures, and MIS personnel.

- A major computer-based aspect of MIS is the database with common data shared by multiple users according to need and prior arrangements. The software that manages the database is the database management system or DBMS. The overall objective is to make access to information easy, quick, inexpensive, and flexible for the user.

- MIS applies various decision models oriented to a number of decision-making areas such as evaluation of investment alternatives, data analysis, scheduling, and simulation. Database provides a constant interface with the models for analysis and solutions.

□ The user-machine interface represents the screen, the keyboard, user-friendly software, menus, and ergonomic features for human comfort. Through the keyboard, the user enters instructions for information access or retrieval. The implication of this interface is that the user can "live" with a user-friendly environment and a system that can produce results for decision making.

□ In fifteen years MIS underwent five major stages of technological change:
   a. *Isolated computing* with focus on cost-reducing accounting applications
   b. *Consolidated computing* with high demand for programmers caused by surge of applications at the cost of poor documentation
   c. *Management controls and restraints,* signified by a freeze on applications and enforcement of controls and standards
   d. *The rising role of the user* and surge in application software, databases, and distributed computing
   e. *The user-machine interface,* exemplified by user-friendly and DSS packages, office automation, and beginning of structured programming

□ The personal computer has introduced a new way of doing business. It started as a stand-alone for specific application processing; today it is being linked to the mainframe, allowing the user to interface with corporate databases for decision making.

□ DSS is a computational aid to help managers integrate judgment, experience, and insight with focus on management performance. It is used in planning and examines alternatives in relatively unstructured decision-making situations.

□ The expert system, an extension of artificial intelligence, is one aspect of DSS with a knowledge base and decision rules for representing the "expert's" thought processes.

□ The trend in MIS is to get closer to the user and expand the information system network to allow transactions to be collected closer to their source. This goal is achieved by the availability of intelligent terminals and the personal computer.

□ There are five important factors in the use of information technology:
   a. Select clear-cut, definable problems.
   b. Use proper tools for designing information systems.
   c. Provide effective management of project costs, procedures, and technology.
   d. Attract, motivate, and retain qualified MIS staff.
   e. Develop effective communication channels with the users at all times.

Key Terms

Consolidated computing

Database management systems
  (DBMS)

Data independence

Embedded computing

Ergonomics

Expert system

Isolated computing

Management information system
  (MIS)

Review Questions

1. What is MIS? Do you agree with the text's definition? Explain.

2. In what way is MIS an integrated system? What role does the micro-computer play in such an integrated environment?

3. Describe briefly the operating elements of MIS. Which elements do you consider most critical? Why?

4. "In a database environment, common data are available and used by several users." Do you agree? Explain.

5. Distinguish between:
   a. Conventional and DBMS environment
   b. Redundancy and data independence
   c. User-machine interface and ergonomics

6. What implications can be drawn from the user-machine interface? Elaborate.

7. Describe the major stages of technological change in MIS development and how they evolved into today's MIS.

8. Distinguish between:
   a. Isolated and consolidated computing
   b. Structured and unstructured decision making
   c. Embedded and distributed computing

9. In what ways did the role of the MIS manager change over the past two decades? Explain.

10. What is a "single-thread" application? How does it differ from applications handled by a decision support system?

11. What is DSS? Carefully discuss the relationships between MIS and DSS.

12. How does DSS differ from expert systems? Explain.

13. What is a knowledge base? How does it differ from a database?

14. Elaborate on the characteristics of office support systems.

15. In what way(s) is MIS changing the shape and behavior of business organizations? Explain in detail.

Application Problems

1. The marketing department of Parker Can Company is considering five new products. It has to evaluate and select the product(s) that best serves the immediate needs of the firm. The firm has several branches scattered throughout the state of Virginia. Because product planning cuts across various organizational functions, what are the key functions involved? What information is required from MIS to help in the evaluation and selection of the new product(s)?

2. Ben Hirsher is the vice president of the MIS division of a large cereal manufacturer. The firm has several plants in the state of Minnesota. The company's MIS has been publicized to be the "computer for all people." Recently, the new executive of the firm called the MIS director and said, "Ben, it's not clear to me how your computer can be a 'computer for all people.' I'd like you to tell me how this is possible."

  In your capacity as Mr. Hirsher, write a three-page memo to support the capabilities and features of MIS in managerial decision making at all levels.

3. Abel, Inc., operates two plants that produce an assortment of electronic games for the home market. The products are sold through department stores on a nationwide basis. The main problem is lack of reliable reports. Inventory reports are generally a week late. Sales executives are growing impatient because decisions cannot be made based on old information. One consequence is poor coordination between the plants. One vice president suggested that manufacturing and sales divisions should be linked through a central computer facility that could help in sales forecasting and planning.

  In view of these problems, you as a consultant were asked to summarize the latest in MIS technology that can be applied to the inventory update problem and improve decision situations in manufacturing and sales. Write a report detailing your plan.

4. Daleiden and Tremaine, Ltd., is a Chicago-based manufacturing company with three plants, four assembly departments, and more than 150 machine centers. The company manufactures a large product line broken down to 126 family groups, representing 9,000 finished goods. Approximately 30 percent of the goods are carried in inventory and the balance is made to order. These 9,000 goods require 18,400 component parts, 11,000 of which are carried in inventory and the balance is made to order.

  The operators are coordinated through a nationwide distribution network with headquarters in Chicago. There are 21 branches and 209 authorized dealers, all of whom carry some inventory.

The company's integrated system has already paid for itself in benefits. Over 75 percent of the orders are delivered according to customer requests, with no delays. However, clerical expenses ran 4.7 percent of sales and cost of products exceeded 25 percent of retail price.

In an effort to improve the company's competitive edge, several cost control areas were given serious consideration:

1. Clerical costs must be reduced to a minimum.
2. Production costs must also be contained—preferably no more than 15 percent of retail.
3. Distribution costs should be reduced without compromising customer service standards.

By 1985, the firm has already upgraded its MIS environment. During the first six months of operation, over 95 percent of customer orders were promptly filled, compared to 75 percent under the older system. The sale/inventory ratio improved 60 percent, whereas clerical costs have also dropped to a palatable 2.7 percent. Product costs, however, dropped only 6 percent.

QUESTIONS

a. What is your general assessment of the firm?
b. How do you evaluate the improvements in customer service and clerical costs? Could this be achieved without the growth rate experienced by the firm?
c. Can you relate production cost changes to MIS? How?
d. Which area in the firm is likely to focus the most on MIS for decision making? Planning? Control? Elaborate.

Selected References

Ackley, Pat and Ackley, Dave. "Can MIS Lead the Push for Productivity?" *Computerworld*, March 11, 1985, ID35–38ff.

Davis, G. B. "Management Information Systems—A Fifteen-Year Perspective." *Data Base*, 13, 4 (Summer 1982), 10–11.

Davis, G. B. and Olson, M. *Management Information Systems: Conceptual Foundations, Structure, and Development.* New York: McGraw-Hill, 1984, 10.

Dickson, G. W., Benbassat, Izak, and King, W. R. "The MIS Area: Problems, Challenges, and Opportunities." *Data Base*, Fall 1982, 7–12.

Gillin, Paul. "Integration: Putting the Pieces Together." *Computerworld*, January 28, 1985, SR 3ff.

Heheshtian, Mahdi. "Personal Computers and the Decision Makers." *Journal of Systems Management*, May 1986, 32–35.

Martin, Herbert and Hartog, Curt. "MIS Rates the Issues." *Datamation*, November 16, 1987, 79–80ff.

Martin, James A. "Getting Information to the End User." *Computerworld*, November 3, 1986, 151ff.

Power, Daniel J. "The Impact of Information Management on the Organization: Two Scenarios." *MIS Quarterly*, September 1983, 13–20.

Roach, John V. "Don't Ignore Micros, or End Users Will Ignore You." *Data Management*, February 1985, 16–19.

Sharizen, Sanford. "Technology: Invader or Protector of Privacy?" *Computerworld*, July 28, 1986, 59–60ff.

Vogel, Douglas R. and Wetherbe, James C. "MIS Research: A Profile of Leading Journals and Universities." *Data Base*, Fall 1984, 3–14.

Zwass, Vladimir. "Management Information Systems—Beyond the Current Paradigm." *Journal of MIS*, 1984, vol. 1, no. 1, 6–7.

The Characteristics and Structure of Management Information Systems

Chapter Contents

A Psychoanalytic Approach to MIS

I AM A PSYCHIATRIST with a prime interest in well people who are working in the worlds of business, government, and education. I think of myself today as a builder of management information systems. It is second nature for a psychoanalyst to ask "Why?"—to wonder about meanings—and so on. Both you and I exist and work to make things better. We exist for the purpose of change. But real change is hard—for any person—for any organization. Today I begin by proposing the following analogy I see between psychoanalysis and the building of information systems:

MIS Design

1. Resistance to changes in established organizational procedures
2. MIS department and user
3. Focus: life and welfare of total organization
4. User participation
5. Management
6. Process of building an MIS
7. Improved management processes
8. Organization with a working MIS

Psychoanalysis

1. Resistance to changes in established mental processes
2. Psychoanalysis and patient
3. Focus: life and welfare of total person
4. Patient participation
5. Ego
6. Psychoanalytic process
7. Improved intrapsychic management
8. Person who has completed a psychoanalysis

What do these analogies suggest to MIS, and does our way of proceeding shed light on your way? My experience recently, as I have become somewhat acquainted with MIS, is that the fundamentals of my own work seem sharper to me. There are certainly gross differences in our fields, but I see basic similarities. First of all, we take enough time, but we establish enough informa-tion before we intervene at all. Timing and pace are also critical in the creation of your management information systems. I suspect that organizations, like individuals, have time-lives of their own. You know that moving too fast or too slowly can add measurably to costs and other difficulties. These moves can affect the quantity and kinds of resistance too, so that optimal design and implementation is prevented.

Second, we ask different things of our users than you do. Implicit here is the idea that somewhere users know what they need and can use. The content and the availability of the changes they ask for is in them. It is not imposed by me. My function is to discover the needs and uncover the means to their best realization.

The MIS literature contains many assertions that it is essential to go beyond the user's statement of requirements in designing a system, but it tells little about how to do this. I suggest that you can in your MIS-appropriate way ask the user to say whatever comes to mind. There will be tangents and wishes, history and important ideas, perhaps different from yours. In my field, we never know at the beginning the extent and variety of deep-rooted untapped potential. I think this fact is another one of our similarities.

Third, we convert resistance into sources of energy and direction. I think it is important to remember that resistance is produced by the same intelligence and competence that produced the need for our services in the first place.

Finally, our successes are not accidental. Neither are our failures. We do not build a new intrapsychic management information system by hit-or-miss techniques. I do not mean that we follow recipes. I am sure that you will never build two identical information systems. I know that I will never conduct two identical analyses.

—*Adapted from a presentation by May Weber, MD, to the Interface Conference, September 1985, San Francisco, CA.*

AT A GLANCE

MIS structure may be described in terms of (1) physical components (hardware, software, personnel), (2) managerial functions (strategic planning, management control, and operational control), or (3) management support for decision making. The last classification relates the nature of information and managerial levels to three types of decision making: unstructured, semistructured, and structured. This orientation suggests that MIS is a multilevel information system that incorporates transaction processing, decision support, and expert systems.

A major issue of the early 1980s was whether DSS might be just a new name for MIS, a subset of MIS, or a step beyond MIS. In reality, it is not particularly important what we call such a system. What is important is recognizing that there are differences in the types of decisions made at various organizational levels—therefore, information and decision support needs. As we will see in Chapter 12, expert systems are not a panacea for structured or unstructured decisions. They are another tool with applications throughout the decision-making spectrum.

An integrated MIS requires appropriate hardware, software, and professionals to develop the system. MIS coordinators trained in computer technology and managerial decision making are helpful in this process.

By the end of this chapter, you should know:

1. MIS structure classifications
2. The difference between MIS and DSS; DSS and expert systems
3. The implications of MIS structure

Introduction

What does a MIS encompass? What kind of a structure does it have? What are its characteristics and scope? How does it differ from decision support and expert systems? This chapter addresses these questions and expands beyond Chapter 1's focus on the definitional and developmental aspects of MIS. Here we focus on MIS not as an entity apart from other information systems, but as a framework that allows various levels of information systems to function for the organization. (In this text the terms *management information system* and *information system* are used synonymously.)

A MIS structure may be described in terms of:

1. *Physical components*
2. *Managerial levels*

3. *Support* for decision making
4. Degree of *centralization*

After reviewing these classifications, we will discuss the relationships between MIS and concepts representing decision support and expert systems. The chapter also proposes alternative views of DSS, how it is perceived by top management, and the implications of MIS structure.

MIS Structure Classifications

MIS Structure Based on Physical Components

Inquiries about an organization's information system are likely to produce descriptions of a physical system—hardware, software, user or operations manuals, and support staff. These are important *resources* of a MIS. Of course, data are now recognized as one of the most important resources of a business.

The Hardware The **hardware** represents "what you see"—the equipment and devices that play four roles:

1. *Data input and entry.* Data must be accessible to the computer before processing. The role of the data entry staff is to enter data either through a keyboard or electronically via a scanning device, using a mouse, touch, voice, or electronic sensing. Quality and accuracy of data entry are crucial.

2. *Processing.* Processing a transaction means acting on the data (inputting, entering), updating a file, handling inquiries, or producing a report (see Figure 2.1). Systems analysts and programmers play a major role in determining how efficiently the computer processes data.

3. *Output.* The end user's primary objective is to secure information (output) to meet the demands of his or her business. Output may be in the form of a screen display, a hard copy, voice, direct action (e.g., dispensing money at an automated teller machine), and the like.

Predefined reports are the traditional "formatted" reports (e.g., sales reports) that describe historical data, summarize transaction activities, or list performance data. In contrast, *ad hoc reports* have their print format and content specified by the user. Also, screen display makes it convenient for the user to view information, edit it, or react to it as needed. The role of an information system is to be responsive to user inquiries in time for the output to be useful.

4. *Storage.* This includes main computer memory and secondary storage such as disk and tape. The role of storage is to store the programs and data for computer processing. More on storage is found in Chapter 3.

Figure 2.1
Three examples of
processing functions.

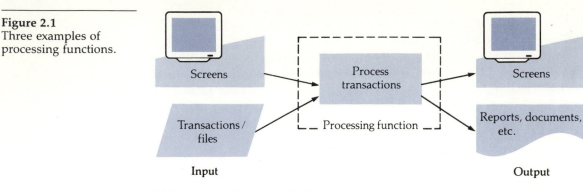

Input   **Output**

(a) **Transaction Processing: Updating patient records**

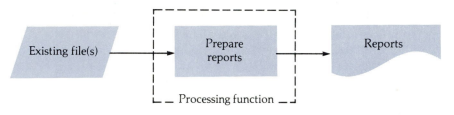

(b) **Producing Reports: Requesting a list of credit card transactions**

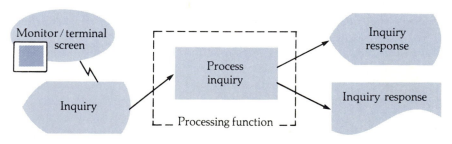

(c) **Handling Inquiries: Using an ATM for balance inquiry**

The Software   Software is a set of instructions to the computer to perform a task. Software is classified as *system* for performing internal computer functions or *applications* for problem solving. An example of system
software for the personal computer is MSDOS (disk operating system),
a group of programs that provides a way to organize and use the information you place on disks. The DOS programs also control the way the
PC uses application programs, how to return or write information that
the programs supply to the user, and similar functions. Finally, DOS
allows the user to make use of devices such as printers and disk drives
with the computer. In contrast, applications software are programs the

user writes. Examples are payroll, student grade processing, accounts payable, and the like.

Under system software we include the database management system (DBMS) that controls the data to be processed by applications software. As discussed in Chapter 1, a DBMS is the software that coordinates files and determines how quickly the user accesses, retrieves, or updates information in the database. A decade ago, DBMS was unique to large corporations with mainframes. Today it is a common MIS component available for virtually every size of computer. More on database concepts and software is found in Chapters 5 and 6.

User and Operations Manuals Manuals document the procedures or the specifications of an information system. A **user manual** accompanies every system and describes how to use the system—loading an application, printing reports, and so on. In contrast, the **operations manual** contains instructions and specifications for maintenance of the system.

Support Staff Computer operators, programmers, analysts, database administrators, technical writers, and managers who develop, operate, and maintain the information system make up the support staff.

1. *Computer operators* do the actual loading and running of the system. This category includes data entry operators and tape librarians who control the use of various applications programs.

2. *Programmers* write step-by-step instructions for the computer to execute. In small organizations programmer/analysts have dual involvement in programming and systems analysis.

3. *Analysts* are methods persons who start with a complex problem, break it down for evaluation, and design a better system.

4. *Database administrators* are specialists whose main tasks are to design, monitor, and manage the database, resolve user conflict, and maintain the system.

5. *Technical writers* write procedures manuals, describe technical specifications, and prepare user manuals. A command of the English language as well as knowledge of the technology is important in this job.

6. *MIS managers* oversee the entire development of systems or applications to ensure that they meet the user's requirements. The goal is to get the correct information to the authorized manager at the right time.

MIS Structure Based on Managerial Levels

Another way of classifying a MIS is in terms of managerial levels. The structure of an information system may be described in terms of three categories of information and three levels of decision making: strategic, managerial, and operational (see Figure 2.2).

Strategic information is future oriented, involving a lot of uncertainty. It deals with long-range policy planning, which is the task of

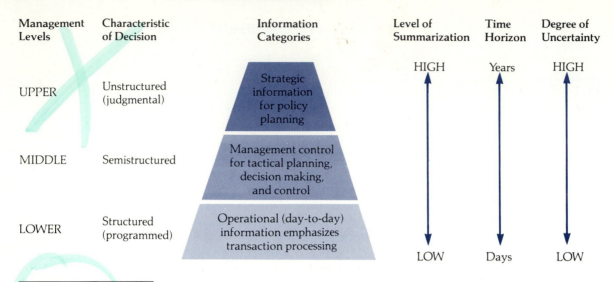

Management Levels	Characteristic of Decision	Information Categories	Level of Summarization	Time Horizon	Degree of Uncertainty
			HIGH	Years	HIGH
UPPER	Unstructured (judgmental)	Strategic information for policy planning			
MIDDLE	Semistructured	Management control for tactical planning, decision making, and control			
LOWER	Structured (programmed)	Operational (day-to-day) information emphasizes transaction processing			
			LOW	Days	LOW

Figure 2.2
Management levels and information categories in a typical organization.

upper management. For example, trends in financial investment, location of a plant, and how technology affects human resources would be the responsibility of senior management, from vice presidents to the president of the firm. The time horizon is measured in months or years, depending on the nature of the decision.

Managerial information is useful to middle management or department heads, who focus on tactical planning and policy implementation. For example, sales analysis, production scheduling, and budget allocation involve a time horizon measured in weeks or months rather than years.

Operational information is the short-term, day-to-day information used in operating the business. It is usually structured and well defined in advance. Examples are employee absence sheets, a decision on a customer's credit rating, and job assignment to an employee.

The nature of the information and managerial levels are also related to three categories of decision making: structured, semistructured, and unstructured. Lower management dealing with operational information generally makes **structured** or routine decisions. For example, completing a sales order is a straightforward procedure not subject to change. In contrast, upper management dealing with strategic information cannot follow a structured approach for policy planning. The nature of the decisions is judgmental and thus **unstructured**, not routine. For example, industry forecasts rely on a combination of experience, foresight, and judgment to determine how possible trends may affect the company's future. There is no formula or procedure that routinely predicts the outcome.

Finally, we can expect a relationship between managerial levels and the level of information detail. Lower management expects detailed operational information for dealing with day-to-day structured decisions. Upper management, for whom long-range objectives are a major concern, require summarized information from a variety of sources. Each managerial level may tap the information provided for lower levels, but the level of summarization increases as we move up the managerial ladder (see Figure 2.2).

MIS is a user-machine system, providing management with a comprehensive picture of specific operations. In reality, MIS is a combination of information systems. In developing MIS, the designer needs to remember the objectives of the organization, determine the type of information needed, at what level it will be used (operational, managerial, or strategic), and how it must be structured.

Experience in MIS installations has shown greater success with systems that provide information for operational and managerial decisions than strategic decisions. Decision support and expert systems are now making strides in filling the gap at the managerial and strategic levels.

Support for Decision Making

The nature of information and managerial levels is related to three types of decision making: unstructured, semistructured, and structured. Strategic planning is subjective and intuitive; the nature of information has more to do with the environment than the organization. Since the decisions do not follow decision rules, we view them as *nonprogrammable*. In contrast, operational control is a routine activity and the nature of information involves the organization rather than the environment. Since operational control is based on definable rules, they are said to be *programmable*. More on this distinction is explained in Chapter 8.

MIS plays an important role in helping managers plan, organize, coordinate, and control their day-to-day business activities. MIS is a source of information for the decisions managers make. A contemporary view of management suggests ten managerial roles that vary with the type of organization and the level of management. Figure 2.3 illustrates the relationships between MIS and managerial roles. They are classified under three sets of roles: interpersonal, information based, and decision related. The *interpersonal roles* focus on information seeking. The simplest role is that of the figurehead, which requires hardly any decision making or information processing. The second interpersonal role belongs to the leader asserting relationships with subordinates. The third role is an exchange relationship with peers and persons outside the organization; the contributions of MIS in this role are procedural (Mintzberg, 1983, 54–99).

The *information-based roles* are those in which the manager may seek or receive a variety of special information or may transmit special information to personnel in the organization or to outsiders about the organization. For example, announcing a new product through a news con-

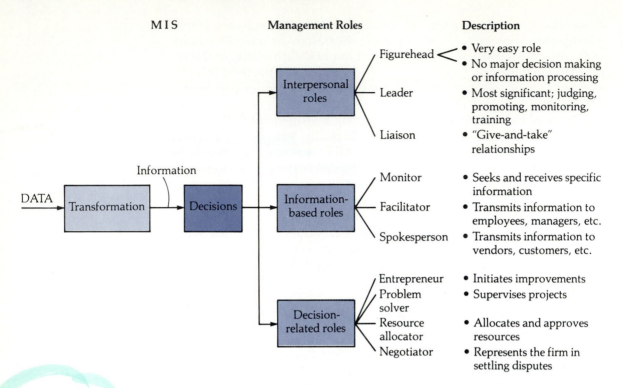

Figure 2.3
MIS and management roles.

ference would be an information-based role. It requires having information about the product and relaying this information to outsiders as a first step in the marketing campaign.

The *decision-related roles* allow a manager to use information for making strategic (long-term) decisions. In the entrepreneurial role, the manager allocates organizational resources; in the negotiator role, the manager uses information to settle a contract.

Together these managerial roles form an integrated whole. Interpersonal roles generate information that in turn results in decisions, creating decision-related roles. This orientation suggests that MIS addresses a multilevel information system: transaction processing, decision support, and expert support systems. Transaction processing is the traditional data processing that serves routine, day-to-day (structured) decisions for operational control. DSS is more amenable to semistructured decisions where the user asks the computer for alternatives and the consequence of each alternative. Expert systems deal with complex problems or those that require expert solution. More on this topic is found in Chapter 12.

Degree of Centralization

MIS structure can also be described in terms of its degree of centralization, decentralization, or distribution. A highly centralized MIS consists of a mainframe that provides and controls information for the entire organization. A decentralized structure consists of components, decisions, and functions that are available in the branches or divisions on the user's premises with no central control. In contrast, a distributed structure has decentralized hardware, personnel, and the like, but under central control (see Figure 2.4).

It is possible to decentralize one source or function while centralizing others. For example, developing an application is a feature that may be distributed at the user's level while the hardware remains centralized. The database may be centralized, decentralized, or distributed depending on the design.

MIS and DSS: What Is the Difference?

A major issue of the early 1980s was whether the decision support system (DSS) was just a new name for MIS, a subset of MIS, or a step beyond MIS. Is MIS solely geared to middle and lower management decision making and DSS to middle and upper management? In any case, what is the difference between MIS and DSS? Where does the so-called expert support system (ESS) fit into the decision-making process? These questions should help us reinforce the definition of MIS as a multilevel information system encompassing these technologies.

Decision Support Systems: An Overview

The term **decision support system** was introduced in the 1970s to describe systems that *support*, not replace, decision-making activities. The pleasant sound of the phrase led virtually any type of information system to become known as DSS: Programmers began referring to their information reporting applications as DSS; vendors touted spreadsheets and information tracking systems as DSS; even the journals used DSS to mean information systems.

DSS is closely related to the decision-making process. As shown in Figure 2.5, decision support depends on information management as well as data processing. The hierarchy suggests a progression from traditional *data processing* to *information management* to *decision support* to **expert support systems** (or **expert systems**). This natural hierarchy is based on the proximity of each system to the decision process.

DSS is an interactive system that helps managers come to a decision. Since it is used for decisions that are only partly structured, some amount of human judgment is needed. DSS also helps in plotting a path to an objective (for example, improved sales) by achieving the best solution

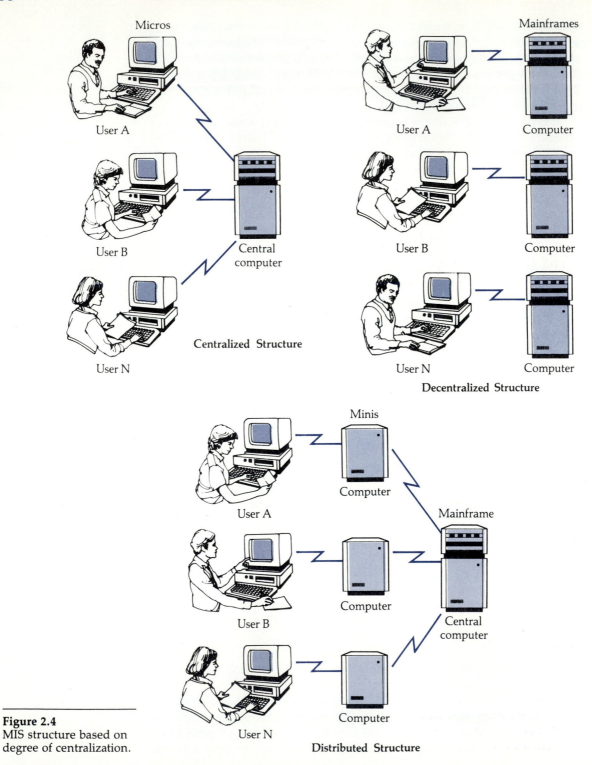

Figure 2.4
MIS structure based on degree of centralization.

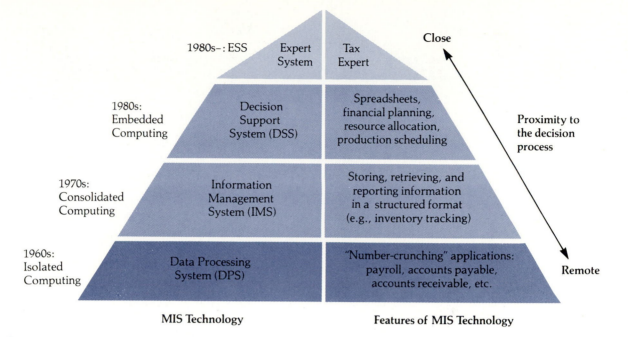

Figure 2.5
The MIS hierarchy.

based on existing constraints. It does not take the next step by saying, "If you are willing to relax salespeople's commissions, you can improve sales." Such a step is taken by an expert support system, which will be explained in Chapter 12.

DP and DSS Within the framework of MIS, data processing (DP) and DSS have several key contrasts. DP reflects *supply economics*, with emphasis on efficiency, cost control, centralized resource allocation, and automation of clerical tasks. In contrast, DSS reflects *demand economics*, with emphasis on service, quick information retrieval, benefits to management, productivity, and value analysis rather than cost justification. The main goal is fast development languages and proficiency with end user tools (see Figure 2.6).

For routine decisions (e.g., computing payroll), a data processing system is ideal. But for financial or production scheduling, the decision process is more complex, requiring a series of "what if" changes before an optimum solution can be reached. These applications are best run using DSS tools.

Definition The literature abounds in views, definitions, and discussions of DSS. Here are the components that comprise a DSS:

1. *Data:* database function
2. *Models*
3. *Information*

Figure 2.6
Data processing and
decision support sys-
tems—a contrast.

MIS	
Data Processing	**Decision Support Systems**
Supply Economics	**Demand Economics**

I. *Preoccupation with:*
- cost controls
- centralized resource allocations
- efficiency
- skills for large-scale projects

II. *DP concerns:*
- hardware considerations
- programmer satisfaction

I. *Emphasis on:*
- service and quick delivery
- benefits to management rather than cost
- fast development languages
- management planning effectiveness
- value analysis rather than cost justification

II. *User concerns:*
- ease of learning
- management satisfaction
- user orientation

4. *"Solvers":* tools to obtain solutions for models with given data
5. *Interfaces:* user interface to all DSS tools—graph output, model and database manipulation

MIS, DSS, and ESS   The main impact of MIS has been on structured tasks in which procedures, decision rules and information flow can be reliably predefined. As in data processing, the payoff has been to improve efficiency through cost reduction, quick turnaround time, and reduction of human resources. The MIS level has relevance for managers' decision making by providing information through reports. From this information, management draws inferences, chooses from the alternatives, and acts accordingly.

An extension of the MIS view is DSS that goes beyond providing information. The additional offering is *inference* drawn from the information. In a DSS environment, "what if" variables are entered and the system provides inferences to assist the manager in a final choice. Inference, then, is embedded in DSS, where it was a manual procedure in MIS (see Figure 2.6).

Within the framework of MIS, the expert support system is emerging as a powerful decision making tool. By combining knowledge of an application area with an inference capability, the expert system makes it possible for the system to "decide" on issues in ways comparable to those used by human experts. Most of today's ESS applications are independent systems that advise users on a specific problem area. As such, they are viewed as intelligent DSS. (For detailed analysis, see Turbin and Watkins, 1986.)

DSS and ESS, then, are not the same. There are three distinct differences:

1. The goal of DSS is helping end users solve a problem. ESS replicates the human expert by giving advice; it essentially makes the decisions itself.
2. The query procedure in DSS begins with the end user interrogating the system. The opposite sequence occurs in ESS.
3. DSS deals with broad problem areas on an ad hoc basis, with no reasoning ability. ESS focuses on a narrower domain through reasoning and is more suited than DSS to give repetitive advice on problems (e.g., diagnosis of bronchitis). DSS does not have such a capability (see Table 2.1).

DSS and ESS are discussed in Chapters 9, 10, and 12.

DSS as Perceived by Top Management

The initial thrust behind DSS was its appeal to managers and the expectation that it would mesh with their skills while extending their decision-making capabilities. Recent software developments have provided new opportunities for enhancing managerial decision making. The question is: How well do managers perceive a real need for DSS?

Several surveys have been conducted on this subject. Among the findings are:

1. DSS cannot yet provide sufficient information. There is a concern about "seat-of-the-pants" decision-making approaches in an environment fraught with uncertainties.
2. Information in the system may not be timely enough to be of use in the decision environment.
3. A possible mismatch may exist between executives' needs and system capabilities. A DSS may require decision-making techniques that conflict with the executive's personal style.

Table 2.1 DSS-ESS Differences

Attribute	DSS	ESS
• Goal	Provide tools for decision making	Replicate a human
• Data manipulation	Numerical	Symbolic
• Decision maker	End user makes decisions	System recommends a decision
• Query sequence	User controlled	System controlled
• Type of problem	Ad hoc	Narrow domain
• Reasoning ability	None	Limited

One conclusion is that DSS is not easy to cost-justify. Many intangibles are involved. Even if they could be measured, the return on investment is not immediate. DSS can be justified only when it becomes obvious to the user that he or she is experiencing improvement in the quality of decisions and the dependability of the software. DSS and MIS technology must still be assembled into systems compatible with the executive's decision environment to be of value. More on DSS design and software is found in Chapters 9 and 10.

Implications for MIS

There are several factors organizations must address to ensure a successful MIS structure. To have an integrated MIS, it is important to have compatible hardware and software. Incompatibility can undermine the entire focus of a management information system (Porter, 1983). This can be alleviated by employing MIS coordinators trained in computer technology and managerial decision making. A coordinator acquires terminals and software to meet the needs of the end user and also ensures that all system components and the network are compatible with the organization's existing system.

Management Issues

Implementation of a MIS brings up a number of management issues as well. One is the impact of the computer on human resources. As computers become more intelligent and take on jobs that were once performed by humans, there is pressure to adjust employment accordingly. For example, General Motors' decision in November 1986 to close eleven plants eliminated 29,000 human jobs in preference for robots.

A related issue is the social responsibility of business. In the General Motors case, the decision had a negative impact on employees and union. Although some employees were retrained and others were placed in different jobs, the bad feelings lingered. The social cost of automation has a long-term effect that, in extreme cases, could cost a business its community support and even its market.

A further managerial issue is use of management time. When DSS improves a manager's effectiveness in decision making, how does he or she use the time saved? Likewise, office automation has been known to save time for the secretary as well as the manager. How well do they use the extra time? There is no doubt that MIS makes life easier, but at the same time it raises the question of making best use of the time saved through automation.

A final issue is strategic planning. As an organization begins to realize its potential through MIS, it should soon develop strategic plans that will coordinate the steps for implementation. Such plans take time, effort, and support. This is perhaps the most challenging issue for management information systems.

Management Support

An important factor in effective MIS installation is management support and user acceptance. For an information system to be successful, top management must be involved in initial design and provide the leadership through its implementation. User acceptance has a lot to do with how well trained employees are in the use of the system. As a matter of strategy, organizations that provide computer training to employees early in their careers stand a good chance of securing support as computer-literate employees move through the management ranks.

The Executive Workstation

An attractive part of an MIS environment is on-line interactive processing, which allows the end user to manipulate decision models and ask ad hoc questions for problem solving. Related to interactive computing are the concepts of office automation and the executive workstation, both of which deal with a human dimension. During the past five years, there has been increased emphasis on networking the company's computing and communication activities. The basic unit is the **workstation**—an area with an "intelligent" terminal and voice transfer devices such as the telephone and video recorders. The transfer is accomplished via memos, Telex messages, written reports, oral briefings, and the electronic mail (see Figure 2.7). It is important for managers to be familiar with these devices. More on networking is covered in Chapter 7.

The personal computer is one of the more controversial components of the executive workstation. Several studies have shown that users in general do not relish the idea of learning to use the personal computer. During training, some executives quickly work at the keyboard; others perceive PCs as staff tools, regarding data entry as a secretarial, not a managerial, function. Learning to work with software packages is time consuming. Operating a computer in general diverts attention from the more critical aspects of management.

These concerns have recently been met by the availability of touch-sensitive terminal screens, voice recognition, on-line "help" by the touch of one key, and English-like programming languages. With incoming computer-literate employees moving up the organization, acceptability of the workstation is expected to be on the increase. The appearance of desktop computers could become as common a tool as the telephone.

Figure 2.7
The ideal executive
workstation. (Source:
Gruber, 1983, 44).

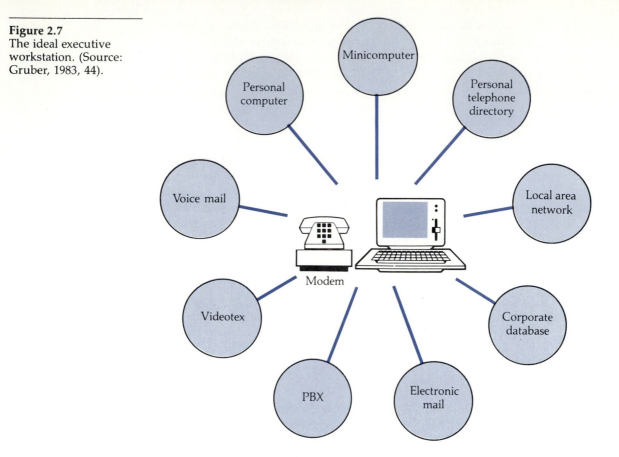

The Economic Factor

In deciding on an MIS installation, management has the responsibility of ensuring a cost-effective system. This means a system capable of producing the right information at an affordable price. But there are exceptions. For example, it is difficult to quantify the contributions of DSS to decision making or profitability to the firm. The intangible costs and benefits are subjectively defined and differ with users. Benefits can be long term, yet users experience immediate improvement in the quality of decision making. To this extent, then, the investment can be justified.

Another issue of affordability is the effect of the new tax laws on the purchase or lease of information systems. Traditionally, a corporation that purchased a computer realized a tax advantage from investment tax credit, depreciation allowance, and the treatment of systems as a corporate asset. Under the new tax laws, which became effective January 1987, investment tax credit is eliminated and depreciation allowance stretches over a longer time period simultaneously with a higher corporate tax base. As a result, the purchase/lease decision has taken on a new dimension. It could determine how quickly corporations replace or upgrade hardware rather than emphasizing improved utilization of existing facilities. More on cost/benefit analysis is found in Chapter 14.

Summary

□ MIS structure may be described in terms of physical components, managerial functions, and support for decision making. The physical system is made up of the hardware, software, user and operations manuals, and MIS staff, which includes analysts, programmers, operators, technical writers, and database administrators. The structure of an information system may also be determined according to three categories of information and three levels of decision making. The information categories are strategic (long-term), managerial (intermediate), and operational (short-term) information. They are used by upper-middle-, and lower-level management, respectively. The nature of information and managerial levels is related to whether decision making is structured or unstructured.

□ MIS is a multilevel information system serving the informational needs of various managerial levels. This conceptualization stresses three systems: Transaction processing, decision support systems addressing semistructured decisions, and expert systems addressing unstructured and semistructured decisions.

□ DSS is a database and report writing function that uses graphics and provides human interface for all decision support tools; it is computer-aided management that aids rather than replaces management with problem-solving tasks. Unlike data processing, which is preoccupied with cost control and efficiency, DSS emphasizes service, quick delivery, and value analysis rather than cost justification.

□ MIS has its main impact on structured tasks. The main payoff has been to improve efficiency through cost reduction and reduction of human resources. In contrast to MIS, DSS extends beyond providing information to inference drawn from the information.

□ DSS provides a limited kind of analysis. The expert system or ESS goes a step further into decision making by doing the choosing. It will not do "what if" analysis but instead confronts the user with questions such as, "What if I tried . . . ?"

□ To ensure an effective MIS structure, organizations must ensure that (1) all system components are compatible with the organization's existing system, (2) top management must support the design and implementation of the system, and (3) the software must facilitate a dialog where the decision maker can use decision models for problem solving. The ultimate goal is to implement a cost-effective information system in the organization.

Key Terms

Decision support system (DSS)	Software
Expert system	Strategic information
Hardware	Structured decision
Managerial information	User manual
Office automation	Unstructured decision
Operations manual	Workstation
Semistructured decision	

Review Questions

1. The structure of MIS may be described in three ways. Explain briefly.

2. What types of information do reports and inquiry responses provide the user? Elaborate.

3. How is software classified? Define each classification.

4. "Experience in MIS installations has shown greater success with systems that provide information for operational and managerial decisions rather than for strategic decisions." Do you agree? Support your answer.

5. What key positions represent the MIS staff? Explain each briefly.

6. Discuss the difference between MIS and DSS. In what way are they similar? Illustrate.

7. In what way is DSS related to decision making? Explain.

8. The text describes a natural hierarchy of MIS progressing from data processing to expert systems. Do you agree? Discuss.

9. Distinguish between:
   a. DSS and ESS
   b. DP and DSS

10. "The objective of information systems is to improve the performance of knowledge workers—not data storage, producing reports, or expediting information access." Do you agree? Elaborate.

11. How is DSS perceived by top management? Should a change in their perception be encouraged? Discuss.

12. How important do you think management support is in MIS development? At what level should such support be emphasized? Why?

13. During the past five years, there has been increased emphasis on ergonomics and integration through internal networking of the organization's computing and communication activities. What units (hardware, departments, etc.) are involved in such integration? What are the benefits of this approach? What implementations are there for management decision making?

Application Problems

1. Review recent journal articles or books and cite one example each on a specific DSS installation and two DSS tools. Explain why each example represents the category you assigned to it.

2. Contact a local MIS department or someone in an organization who has helped develop a specific DSS. Describe the purpose of the DSS, the tools used, and the benefits desired from such an installation.

3. Review the literature since 1985 and write a four-page essay discussing DSS developments—how they differ from those covered in this chapter, the perception of DSS as a subset of MIS, and the directions DSS is taking toward improved decision making.

4. B/G restaurant in Pittsburgh, Pa. recently installed a microcomputer-based information system that will help in improving operations and providing control over the day-to-day operation of the business.

When an order is taken, the waitress enters it directly via one of four terminals located in the dining facility. The order is transmitted to one of four printers for processing—The cold-item printer for salads or sandwiches, the hot-item printer for hot plates or dinners, a beverage printer for ice cream, soda, coffee, or carryout, and a bar printer for liquor or beer.

The printed check lists the items ordered and prices, eliminating the waitress's handwritten order. If a menu item should be sold out, a message is immediately displayed on the screen. The customer is then asked to place another order.

A unique feature of the software is that it breaks down meals by food and labor costs. It also produces daily reports, showing the order rate of each item on the menu. The software was programmed by one of the part-time waitresses who was working on a graduate degree in computer science at a university across the street from the restaurant. In designing the system, she interviewed and worked closely with the nine full-time waitresses and the two chefs. Acceptance of the system was favorable. Customers noticed the clarity of the bill and improvement in service.

QUESTIONS

a. In managing restaurants, what information is necessary for strategic, managerial, and operational decision making? How does this system contribute to each level of decision making? Explain.

b. In what respect is this system a transaction processing system? MIS? What would it need to become a complete MIS?

c. What probable impact will the system have on restaurant servers and management?

Selected References

Bennett, John L. *Building Decision Support Systems.* Reading, Mass.: Addison-Wesley, 1983.

Doll, W. J. and Ahmed, M. "Managing User Expectations." *Journal of Systems Management,* vol. 34, no. 6, June 1983, 6–10.

Gordon, G. B. and Olson, M. *Management Information Systems: Conceptual Foundations, Structure, and Development.* New York: McGraw-Hill, 1984.

Gruder, Rubin. "Raising the Management Workstation to Executive Status." *Computerworld on Communications,* Sept. 17, 1983, 44.

Spiegler, Israel. "MIS and DBMS: Where Does One End and the Other Start?", *Journal of Systems Management,* July 1983, 34–42.

Sprague, Ralph H., Jr. and McNurlin, Barbara C. *Information Systems Management in Practice.* Englewood Cliffs, N.J.: Prentice-Hall, 1986, chapter 14.

Thiel, Carol Tomme. "DSS Means Computer-Aided Management." *Infosystems,* March 19834, 39ff.

White, Kathy B. "Dynamic Decision Support Teams." *Journal of Systems Management,* June 1984, 26–31.

PART II

INFORMATION SYSTEM TECHNOLOGY

How Computers Work

Chapter Contents

Driving by the Glow of a Screen

MORE THAN TWO DECADES have passed since movie-goers first watched James Bond tail a Rolls-Royce to Goldfinger's Alpine retreat by tracking a moving blip across a screen on the dashboard of his Aston Martin. Now advances in computer technology have turned this Hollywood fantasy into automotive reality.

In California, some 2,000 motor vehicles—from Michael Jackson's Mercedes-Benz to Palo Alto garbage trucks—have been equipped with a gadget called the Navigator, which helps drivers get to a destination by displaying their vehicle's location on a glowing green map. And beginning next month, visitors to three hotels and six Budget Rent-a-Car stations in and around San Francisco will have access to counter-top Driver Guide units, which can calculate the shortest route between any two addresses in the Bay area and print out a concise set of directions. Later this year, Driver Guide will also become available in a smaller, dashboard version.

The Navigator, introduced last year by Etak, a Menlo Park, Calif., company, is an electronic road map that calculates position by means of dead reckoning. Data from a solid-state compass installed in the vehicle's roof and from sensors mounted on its wheels are processed by a computer in the trunk and displayed on a dashboard screen. The car's position is represented as a fixed triangle; the map, showing a web of streets and avenues, scrolls down as the car moves forward and rotates sideways when it turns.

Driver Guide, produced by Karlin & Collins, a Sunnyvale, Calif., firm, is the electronic equivalent of rolling down a window and asking for directions. The prototype unit looks like an automated-teller machine, but it issues information rather than cash. By punching buttons and choosing from a variety of screen menus, users specify where they want to go. Twenty seconds later, the machine spits out a printed sheet of driving instructions constructed from a database that contains the location of every intersection and alleyway in the Bay area, including 3,400 turn restrictions and 4,800 traffic lights. Says Barry Karlin, president of K&C: "We save fuel, and we save time."

How the devices will fare in the marketplace remains to be seen. Their current price tags will certainly limit sales: Navigator sells for $1,395, and the Driver Guide is expected to cost about $1,000. Toyota already offers a computerized dashboard map on an expensive model sold only in Japan, but while U.S. automakers are testing the devices, none have plans to offer them as options before the early 1990s.

Etak and K&C remain optimistic and are busy expanding their cartographic data bases. Etak has computerized the maps of 85% of the nation's urban areas, while K&C is programming Los Angeles, Miami and Atlanta. Both companies speak confidently of the day when onboard computers will act as mobile information systems, displaying everything from the latest traffic conditions to the location of the nearest hospital. Predicts Karlin: "Ten years from now, nobody will need to drive with a road map folding and flapping in the steering wheel."

—Excerpted from Philip Elmer-DeWitt, Time, April 20, 1987, 63.

AT A GLANCE

To understand MIS, we need to be familiar with the computer—its structure, capabilities, and operation. All computers do essentially the same thing. Some are easier to program, some are faster, but they all share common capabilities and limitations.

Computers have gone through five generations of technological improvements and growth—from the vacuum tube technology to today's VLSI (very large-scale integration). Computers are classified by size (microcomputers to supercomputers) and by type (digital, analog, hybrid). For MIS purposes, our focus is on business-oriented, general-purpose, digital computers of all sizes.

Data entered into computers are represented in memory using various binary schemes. In today's computer, the byte is usually the smallest addressable unit of memory.

Direct access devices are represented by disk-based and diskette-based systems. The trend in the computer industry favors direct data entry and direct access. For output devices, there are impact and nonimpact printers, terminals, computer-output microfilm, plotters, and interactive graphics readily available. The whole purpose behind the computing process is to help organizations gain a competitive edge.

By the end of this chapter, you should know:

1. The elements making up a computer system
2. How the computer progressed over three decades of technological improvements
3. Various computer classifications
4. How data are represented in memory

Introduction

Computers make it possible for organizations to obtain information that reduces uncertainty in decision making and improves their competitive edge. The ever-increasing dependence on information technology makes it necessary for students of MIS to study computers. If you have had a recent course in computer systems, you should find the following easy reading.

This chapter is an introduction to the fundamentals of the computer—its structure, capabilities, and operations. We will focus on the underlying concepts that have remained stable while hardware and software have developed and changed. Our main objective is to summarize the technology and reflect its impact on business.

A computer is essentially a system of input/output devices and a processor. The computer performs arithmetic and logic operations in a **central processing unit (CPU)**, based on program instructions. The two major capabilities most computers share are:

1. *High-speed processing.* Processing speed of hundreds of million operations per second is now a reality. Most computers process repetitive *high volume* applications such as payroll and handle more than one job at the same time. For example, inventory control and accounts receivable may be handled by the same computer simultaneously. This is called *multiprocessing.* The computer switches control from one job to another so fast that one gets the impression that all jobs are processed at the same time.

2. *Arithmetic and logic.* The computer performs arithmetic. Its logic ability means the computer can compare two numbers and decide whether one number is greater than, less than, or equal to another. Arithmetic and logic ability are two unique attributes that distinguish a computer from a calculator.

The computer has three limitations:

1. *It must be told what to do*—when to start, stop, compute, and make the next move. To do a job, all decision rules must be provided before processing.

2. *Failure to correct the wrong instructions.* The computer will do what you say regardless of what you mean, and it will do the wrong thing a hundred million times per second.

3. *Physical breakdown* can be a problem, especially with no backup.

Computer Generations

The computer industry is the fourth largest industry in the world, with over 3,000 firms. Forty years ago there were no computers. The original first-generation computer (1950–58) was the UNIVAC I (1951) built by Remington Rand. *First-generation computers* were bulky and inflexible, used vacuum tubes for main memory, required air conditioning, and handled one program at a time. Programming was performed in machine language.

Second-generation computers (1959–64) replaced vacuum tubes with transistors, and magnetic core became standard memory. Thus they were more reliable, faster, and more versatile than first-generation computers.

Second-generation computers also used disk storage for some on-line processing and symbolic rather than machine language for programming. (**On line** means having data entry devices directly controlled by the computer's CPU.) This period also marked the development of high-level languages such as COBOL and FORTRAN and the emergence of today's programmers and analysts. IBM 1401 was the most popular computer of this era.

Third-generation computers (1964–70) were characterized by timesharing, multiprocessing, integrated circuits, increased popularity of minicomputers, and improved reliability and speed. The appearance of software houses and the IBM 360 was a response to the exponential growth and demand for computer use.

Fourth-generation computers (1970–80) featured the introduction of very large-scale integration (VLSI) with circuit densities of 100,000 components per chip. The period gave rise to special software for managing databases, known as database management systems (DBMS). This meant more direct and immediate access to records. Increased availability of minicomputers made it possible to decentralize computer power to the user level rather than the traditional computer center.

Fifth-generation computers (1980–90 est.) are represented by the microcomputer, decision support systems, and office automation. These areas are covered in later chapters. A summary of the five generations is given in Table 3.1.

Computer Classifications

Computers are classified in three ways: by *type* (digital, analog, or hybrid); by *capability* (business oriented and scientific); or by *size* (micro, mini, mainframe, or supercomputer). Learning to identify a computer is important for hardware selection.

Analog, Digital, and Hybrid Computers

Analog computers are known for prompt response to data generated by a continuous physical process without the internal conversion required in digital computers. Analog computers are used in electric power plants, chemical plants, and petroleum refineries.

A **digital computer** computes electronically by digits. It maintains accuracy by carrying the solution to as many decimal places as necessary. Most computers today are digital. They are the mainstay of management information systems.

A **hybrid computer** combines the measuring capabilities of the analog computer and the logic and control capabilities of the digital computer.

Table 3.1 Computer Generations: A Summary

Generation	Year	Characteristics
1	1950–58	• vacuum tubes for CPU • machine language • bulky and unreliable
2	1959–64	• transistors for memory • disk for secondary storage • processed one program at a time
3	1964–70	• time-sharing environment • multiprocessing/multiprogramming • improved reliability and speed
4	1970–80	• very large-scale integration circuitry • introduction of DBMS • decentralized computing
5	1980–90	• introduction of the microcomputer • appearance of DSS and office automation

Among the applications for hybrid computers are space vehicle simulations and training of space and airline pilots.

Business-Oriented and Scientific Computers

Business-oriented computers can perform any computation, input, and output functions. They are strong in file-handling capability where there is high volume input and output with elementary arithmetic functions. In contrast, *scientific computers* such as those used for nuclear research and weather forecasting are all highly mathematical. Scientific systems require a computer to perform arithmetic operations at high speed (see Figure 3.1).

Processor Power

Computer power measures the number of instructions that can be processed in a given time period. More powerful supercomputers can process millions of instructions per second, whereas the less powerful microcomputer processes thousands of instructions per second.

There is a direct relationship between power and performance. More powerful computers handle more complex jobs and serve more users at the same time. Let us focus on four levels of computers—microcomputers, minicomputers, mainframes, and supercomputers—and look at their key roles.

Figure 3.1
A special-purpose computer. Spray-painting robots are directed from the control room of this General Motors auto plant.

Microcomputers   The technological breakthroughs that produced the microcomputer have far outstripped every other development in computer hardware. No longer new or novel, microcomputers play a key part in business and government. Today's workplace is dominated by managers and end users who interact with computers through small microcomputers. Microcomputers are becoming standard working tools for executives, doctors, salespeople, secretaries, and personnel in general.

What made the microcomputer or personal computer (PC) so popular in less than ten years? The advantages and limitations of the PC are summarized in Table 3.2. In general, the microcomputer meets a wide range of requirements. What is more, microcomputers are inexpensive and easy to use. The three major capabilities that have made the microcomputer so popular are (1) *correspondence* through word processing, (2) *budgeting* and planning using electronic spreadsheets, and (3) *distributed processing*, providing processing capabilities at the user's level, where the data are created and handled. These details are discussed in Chapter 11.

The Hardware   The configuration of microcomputer hardware depends largely on the needs of the job(s) to be performed. There is a wide range of microcomputer devices to meet virtually every need. For example, an architect wants graphic output using a color monitor and a plotter that

Table 3.2 The Personal Computer: Advantages and Limitations

Advantages	Limitations
1. Portability	1. Different files at different locations often result in multiple, inconsistent data files and data management problems
2. Low marginal cost of computing	
3. Availability of color and graphics display	
4. Low hardware maintenance	2. Size of application programs limited by main memory
5. Computer power available at the convenience of the user	
6. Full control of applications by user	3. End user responsible for backing up file, installing the software, and interpreting error messages
7. Software needs less support because of limited complexity prototype	
	4. PC vendors are newer and have less reliable record than established mainframe vendors

generates line drawings, instead of a printer. By contrast, a secretary might want a basic monochrome (one color) monitor for word processing. System configurations typically include:

1. A keyboard for inputting data or instructions for processing
2. A processing unit for arithmetic and logic operation
3. Disk drives that read from and store data on floppy disks (fixed disk can also be used for permanent storage of data and programs)
4. A monitor for displaying and editing data
5. A printer to produce output or hard copy

The main question about microcomputers is: What features must be taken into account when buying one? As we shall explain in detail in Chapter 16, after reviewing individual needs, the following considerations are most important:

1. *Usability:* How regularly will the PC be used?
2. *Software compatibility:* How well will the machine run all the software that you have or plan to acquire?
3. *Expandability:* How much more memory can be added to the PC for advanced or complex applications?
4. *The monitor:* Should the system incorporate a monochrome or a color monitor?
5. *Disk drives:* What capacity hard disk should be considered?
6. *Training and support:* How easy is it to secure adequate training for the staff?
7. *Service:* How quickly can the machine be serviced in the event of breakdown?
8. *Warranties:* How long is the warranty? What does it cover?

Careful shoppers should review these guidelines before making a final choice. Unfortunately, many users buy first and ask questions later.

The microcomputer is driven by special software to perform a variety of tasks. System software controls the operation of the hardware. There are also *utility programs* that perform functions such as copying data from a disk, printing a report, formatting a disk, and so on.

Overall, word processing and text editing, spreadsheets, database management, inventory control, desktop publishing, general ledger, and sales analysis are common microcomputer applications. There are hundreds of other applications as well. These include production monitoring, forecasting, trend analysis, speech recognition, and electronic mail. As software becomes easier to use and learn, end users will make better use of the microcomputer. Improvements in linking the microcomputer to the mainframe should increase the role of the microcomputer in MIS.

The Next Generation in Personal Computing   The idea behind the PC was one person, one personal computer. As vendors kept improving the computers, user requirements grew even faster. In mid-1987 a new generation of PCs appeared with emphasis on speed, integration of functions, and overall performance. Depending on the model, standard memory now exceeds 1 million (1MB) bytes, expandable to 16 MB. Hard disk storage also runs up to hundreds of MB. A **hard disk** is a nonremovable secondary storage device located inside the PC. More on hard disks is found later in the chapter.

Many of the features that were once options are built into the Personal IBM System/2 computer (see Figure 3.2). They include serial, parallel, and mouse ports, high resolution color/graphics, and memory board expansion. The new system can paint up to 256 colors on the screen at once, drawing from a palette of over 256,000.

The most advanced System/2 (model 80) uses Intel's 80386 microprocessor, which performs jobs about three times faster than the IBM AT. Computers this capable used to fill whole rooms. Priced at $10,995, the System/2 has essentially the same power as an IBM mainframe computer, which cost over $3 million thirteen years ago, or as a MAC II, which costs less than $6,000. The model's key emphasis is on performance, reliability, and **multitasking**—ability to handle more than one task at a time.

Minicomputers and Mainframes   The minicomputer, structured around a CPU (central processing unit) and one or more input/output and storage devices, is used primarily for accounting applications (payroll, accounts receivable, and processing orders for small- and medium-sized businesses. Minicomputers generally support 10 to 100 users simultaneously and are priced anywhere from $10,000 to $1 million.

In the minicomputer field, Digital Equipment Corporation (DEC), Data General, and IBM are the key vendors, with DEC having the largest installed base of minicomputers. Other minicomputer manufacturers include Wang, Hewlett-Packard, and Prime.

Figure 3.2
IBM System 2/Model 50.

For over two decades, the mainframe has been the "number cruncher" of government and business computing. These computers are found in air-conditioned rooms in large organizations such as the airlines, General Motors, and the Internal Revenue Service. Colleges and universities also use mainframes for administrative and academic computing. Most mainframes can service hundreds of terminals; most systems have multiple independent processors to handle multiple communication channels linked to remote terminals and continuous multiprocessing operations. Prices for mainframes range from $500,000 to over $10 million (see Figure 3.3).

Supercomputers A supercomputer is the ultimate number cruncher, processing gigantic amounts of repetitious information. Its distinctive character is vast processing power applied in a narrow range of applications and certain kinds of problems. Fewer than 100 supercomputers have been installed—mostly by government laboratories, defense, and scientific divisions of large corporations. In industry, chemical companies use supercomputers for decoding the molecular structure of complex proteins and designing new drugs.

Figure 3.3
Mainframe computer. IBM announced the Sierra, the most advanced computer in its mainframe line, in 1985. Despite all the talk of the IBM personal computer in the trade press, mainframes remain IBM's most important business by far. Two thousand Sierras (also known as the IBM 3090 series) were ordered in the first week after it was announced, despite the machine's price tag. Depending on the amount of memory, a Sierra costs between $4.6 million and $9.3 million.

The speed of a computer is measured in **millions of instructions per second**, or **MIPS**. The fastest supercomputers, built by CRAY Research and AMDAHL corporations, exceed 250 MIPS in performance. Other supercomputer makers are Control Data Corporation and Hitachi. Purchase price runs over $20 million (see Figure 3.4). A selling price is usually a good indicator of the computing power being acquired.

Technological advances and competition steadily increase performance and lower the price of computers. Technology may change the classification of computers, too, as micros become supermicros and minis become superminis.

It is important to realize that whether the computer in question is a micro or a mainframe, it is designed according to John von Neumann's concept of storing program instructions in the computer's main memory for processing an application. The current trend seems to be not so much to speed up von Neumann's architecture but to design a different kind of computer—a new generation computer that performs faster than today's supercomputers and has "intelligence."

Main Memory and Data Representation

Since the early 1970s, the building block for computer memory has been the silicon chip. A **chip** is a rectangular slice of silicon (called wafer) on which an integrated circuit is etched. Each chip is mounted on a

Figure 3.4
Top: CRAY 2 supercomputer. Bottom:
AMDAHL 1200E
supercomputer.

Figure 3.5
A silicon chip.

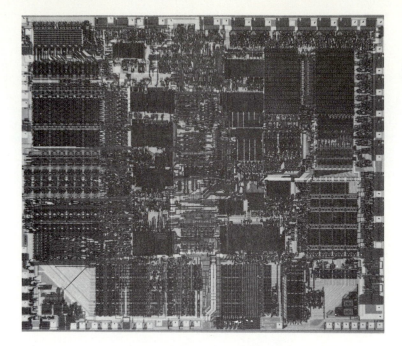

board. The pins of the chip allow it to be plugged into the board (see Figure 3.5).

There are essentially two types of chips: **random-access memory (RAM)** and **read-only memory (ROM)**. ROM has built-in microprograms and stores a set of instructions to be executed by the computer. RAM is the main memory where data and application programs are stored for processing.

Instructing the Computer

Computer operation is controlled by programs. Program instructions are stored in main memory in machine (computer) language before execution. Figure 3.6 shows how an instruction looks in memory and how it is executed. Instruction formats vary with different computers, although instruction elements remain the same.

A computer instruction has two major components:

1. The **operation code** specifies the operation to be performed. For example, "A" represents "add"; "S" represents "subtract," etc.
2. The **operand** has the **addresses** or locations of the values to be worked on. "3000" is the address of the first value (1234) and "5000" is the address of the second value (7987) to be added. Some units also include an operand length indicator.

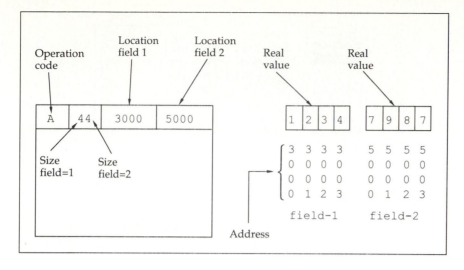

Figure 3.6
Components of a computer instruction.

To execute this instruction, the computer locates address 3000 and finds 1234 stored in locations 3000–3003. Next, it locates address 5000 and finds 7987 stored in 5000–5003. After addition is performed, the sum is stored at locations 3000–3003.

The control unit moves an instruction to main memory and loads it in the instruction register—a temporary storage area. As it is being executed, another instruction is being fetched for execution, and so on until the entire program is executed (see Figure 3.7).

How Are Data Represented in Memory?

Numerical data are represented in the computer's memory in binary code. Binary coding uses only two digits: 0 and 1. Each digit is called a **bit** (short for *binary digit*). To represent in binary a decimal digit greater than 1, the next higher binary number is formed by adding 1 to the number's predecessor; this is known as a **binary-coded decimal (BCD)**. As shown in Figure 3.8, the value of each binary digit is a greater power of 2 (2, 2, 2, etc.).

Today's computers use an eight-bit storage unit called a **byte.** The byte is the smallest addressable unit of main memory in most computers. For example, one keystroke is a byte. Bytes are numbered sequentially. The characters 1 2 A are represented by three bytes, as shown in Figure 3.9. Groups of four bytes are usually wired to form a unit called a *word*. A 32-bit (4 byte) word can hold numeric values in the range ± 2 billion.

Figure 3.7
The function of the
arithmetic/logic unit
(A/LU) and control unit
in executing program
instructions.

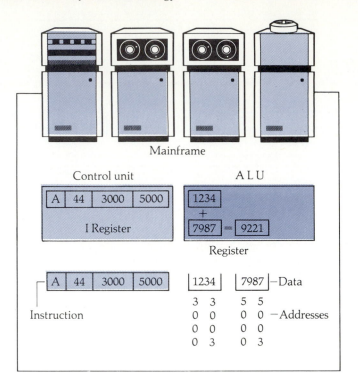

Mainframe

Figure 3.8
Binary representation.

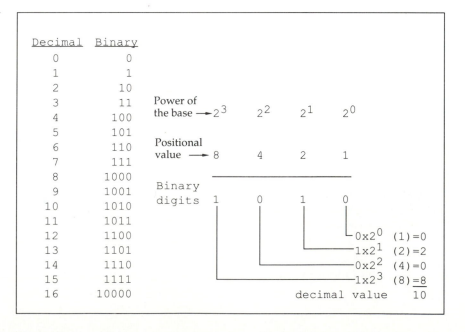

Figure 3.9
Byte representation.

Computer Architecture

If you look inside a computer, you might think you are in a science fiction scene with rows of low buildings and "roads" that link them together. The basic component of this architecture or design is the *semiconductor chip,* which consists of hundreds of thousands of transistors. Individual transistors are combined to store information or do arithmetic or logic operations. Semiconductor chips are used for main memory and the CPU.

In microcomputers, memory chips are mounted on the main circuit board, called a **motherboard**. Figure 3.10 is a picture of a microcomputer architecture. There are slots for other boards that allow the microcomputer to meet special needs. For example, a board can be added on for expanding main memory, another board for a graphic monitor, or a third board for transmitting and receiving data from another computer.

Types of Memory   As mentioned earlier, there are two types of memory: RAM and ROM. RAM represents the microcomputer's main memory. RAM is *volatile* memory, in that loss of electric power means loss of all data stored in memory (see Figure 3.11). ROM is a preprogrammed chip for performing specific jobs such as starting the computer when power is turned on or handling special input or output tasks. The programs in ROM are recorded permanently. They are not lost when electric power is lost. ROM, then, is *nonvolatile.* Its major advantage is protecting valuable information that is permanently stored. On the other hand, ROM is a problem when that information needs to be updated, because the chips have to be removed from the computer.

The latest ROM, called **electrically erasable programmable ROM (EEPROM)**, allows an occasional update of the stored program or data without having to remove the chips from the computer. EEPROM chip technology, for example, may be used in retail stores to update price lists, tax rates, and the like.

Different microcomputer chips use different internal designs and have a different range of instructions and machine cycle speed. For example, the IBM AT uses Intel's 80286 microprocessor chip, while the Apple Macintosh uses Motorola's 68000 chip. The newest microcomputer chip is Intel's 80386, which is available in IBM's System/2 (see Figure 3.12a, b, c). Intel is designing a still faster 80486 chip that would operate at a rate

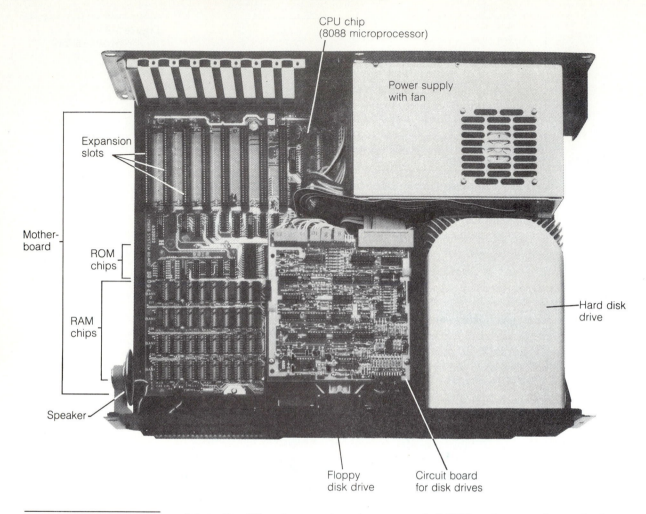

Figure 3.10
Microcomputer motherboard. The innards of the IBM PC XT. This photo shows what you would see if you removed the cover from an IBM PC XT. A typical XT probably has some of the expansion slots filled with a memory board and an internal modem.

of 4 to 5 million instructions per second (MIPS)—the speed at which many mainframes run.

Secondary Storage

No matter how much information the computer holds, there is still a need to store programs and data somewhere when the system is turned off. Such **secondary storage** is also attractive because it is cheap and nonvolatile. Since the early 1980s, floppy and hard disks have been the most common media for mass storage on computers. Magnetic tape is also in use for processing sequential files. We shall briefly explain the function and uses of this technology, since it is the standard form of mass storage on microcomputers.

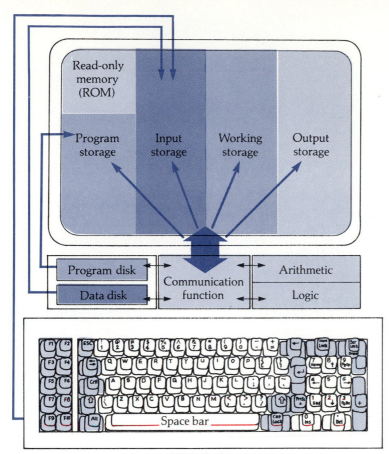

Figure 3.11
General microcomputer
structure.

KEYBOARD

Floppy Disk

The **floppy disk** or diskette is a small magnetic disk made of plastic and coated with an oxide substance. A floppy is a very popular storage medium for microcomputers. It is easy to handle and store and light enough to mail, weighing less than 2 ounces. The diskette is permanently stored in a jacket and comes in two sizes: 8″ and $5\frac{1}{4}″$ (see Figure 3.13).

Note that physical characteristics distinguish floppy from hard disks. Both use a ferrous oxide coating for storing data through magnetic impulse. In both media, reading data from and writing data on disks are made possible by a read/write head that is positioned on top of the requisite track. Disks also require careful handling and a clean environment. They store a great deal of information and are known for storing data as accurately as those data were received. A high-capacity floppy disk stores up to 1.6 million characters of data.

Figure 3.12
Microprocessor develop-
ments. (a) IBM System
12 Model 50 uses the lat-
est 80386 chip. (b) The
key features of Intel
80286, which was intro-
duced for the microcom-
puter in 1984, are con-
trasted with those of
Intel's 80386 chip.
(c) The even more pow-
erful 80486 is expected
to appear in late 1988 or
1989.

(a)

Microprocessor Power Comparison

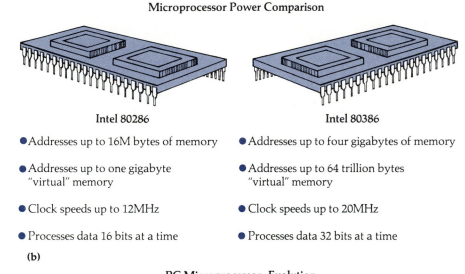

Intel 80286

- Addresses up to 16M bytes of memory
- Addresses up to one gigabyte "virtual" memory
- Clock speeds up to 12MHz
- Processes data 16 bits at a time

Intel 80386

- Addresses up to four gigabytes of memory
- Addresses up to 64 trillion bytes "virtual" memory
- Clock speeds up to 20MHz
- Processes data 32 bits at a time

(b)

PC Microprocessor Evolution

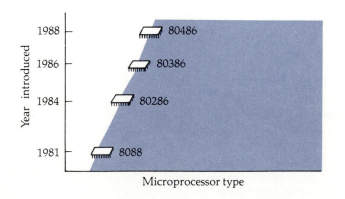

(c)

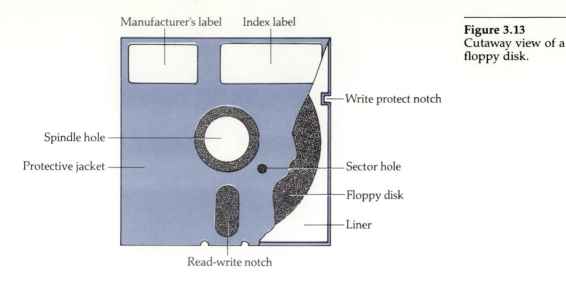

Manufacturer's label   Index label

Write protect notch

Spindle hole

Protective jacket

Sector hole

Floppy disk

Liner

Read-write notch

Figure 3.13
Cutaway view of a
floppy disk.

Since the mid-1980s, some firms have introduced a yet smaller-sized (3.5″) diskette called the **microfloppy**. This medium is a component of microcomputers such as Apple's Macintosh and the new IBM System/2. How popular its use will be is yet to be determined (see Figure 3.14).

Another recent development that increases the storage capacity of floppy and hard disks is **vertical recording**. By aligning magnetic fields vertically into and out of the disk surface, it is possible to store as many as 100,000 characters per inch per track, compared to 15,000 characters per inch for longitudinal recording where magnetic fields are aligned along the track.

Hard Disk: How Does It Work?

A **hard (fixed) disk** is a nonremovable sealed aluminum disk or platter covered with a thin iron oxide coating. It is permanently sealed with its read/write head to protect it from dust and the elements. The read/write head hovers above the disk surface as it rotates at about 3600 revolutions per minute. Data are stored along concentric tracks divided into sectors. There are between 250 and 300 tracks per inch on a disk's surface, with about 10,000 bits per inch stored along each track (see Figure 3.15).

A single-sided hard disk uses one read/write head. A four platter double-sided drive contains eight heads, as shown in Figure 3.16. Each head moves in and out under the control of the disk drive controller. This motion allows the head to read and write data on the disk's tracks. Each track begins at a radius called the *index* position. From this point, the track is divided into sectors. In a reading mode, the read/write head moves to the proper track, detects the index position, and starts reading

Figure 3.14
The $3\frac{1}{2}''$ microfloppy
diskette fits in a shirt-
pocket.

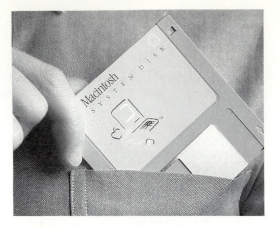

Figure 3.15
Hard disk surface.

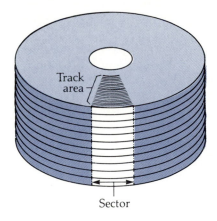

data at the desired sector when it passes under the head. The same
procedure applies to writing data on the disk (see Figure 3.17).

Remember that a hard disk, like a floppy, must be *formatted* before it
can be used. This means creating a number of addresses that identify
the location of the tracks and sectors and storing this information in a
data dictionary on the disk. Formatting also erases any previously stored
information. This formatting information obviously takes up disk space.
Therefore, when a hard disk is rated at, say, 100 megabytes, part of this
capacity is reserved for the formatted information and the remainder for
data storage.

Magnetic Tape

A third secondary storage medium is magnetic tape, a thin plastic tape
coated with magnetic material. The tape passes over a read/write head

Figure 3.16
Fixed disk drive. Note that there are two read/write heads on each access arm. Each arm slips between two disks in the pack. The access arms move simultaneously, but only one read/write head operates at any one time.

that either creates or senses a magnetic set of bits. Similar to the audio cassette or cartridge, tapes can be written over and reused many times. They are compact, portable, and inexpensive, but are vulnerable to dust and extreme temperatures (see Figure 3.18).

The storage capacity of a tape depends on how the records are stored. Records are typically separated from one another by interrecord gaps or IRGs. But an IRG can be up to one-half inch. To minimize wasted tape space, a number of records are *blocked* between interblock gaps or IBGs (see Figure 3.18). This improves the time it takes to access records from tape because a block of records is read into memory in one step.

Magnetic tape is ideal for batch or sequential data processing where each record must be updated. Examples are the weekly payroll or the monthly accounts receivable reports. Since all records in the files are affected, they can be processed in their existing sequence. They can also be sorted in any sequence prior to processing.

The Computer at Work

A computer system environment is made up of hardware, software, and the staff that manages the system. Let us focus on the hardware and use a basic illustration to highlight the main concepts of a computer.

Hardware is what you see—the physical devices that process and produce information. As shown in Figure 3.19, the functional compo-

Figure 3.17
Reading data from a
disk. (Source: Powell,
1984, 118).

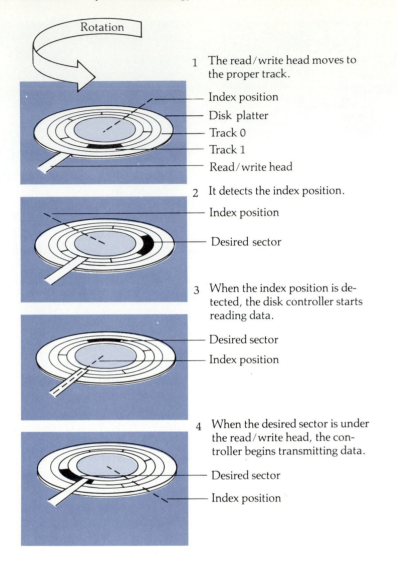

Rotation

1   The read/write head moves to
the proper track.

— Index position
— Disk platter
— Track 0
— Track 1
— Read/write head

2   It detects the index position.

— Index position

— Desired sector

3   When the index position is detected, the disk controller starts
reading data.

— Desired sector

— Index position

4   When the desired sector is under
the read/write head, the controller begins transmitting data.

— Desired sector

— Index position

nents are common to all computers. They are input, processing, and
output devices.

Computer Processing Cycle

Let us take a bank's check processing procedure and show how a computer is used to generate information. The first step is to enter or *load*
specific instructions into main memory. Figure 3.20 illustrates how a
deposit is processed. After the account number, type of transaction, and
amount of deposit are loaded through the terminal (Figure 3.20a), the

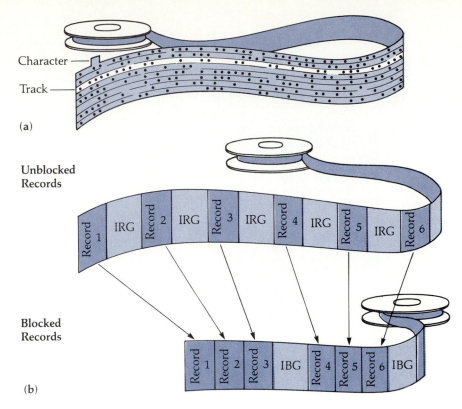

Figure 3.18
(a) Magnetic tape char-
acters recorded on col-
umns of tracks. (b) Rec-
ord layout.

Character

Track

(a)

Unblocked
Records

Blocked
Records

(b)

master record showing a $85 balance is also loaded into main memory (Figure 3.20b).

This loading process is initiated when the CPU acknowledges data from the teller terminal. A part of the control unit is instructed to select the first set of instructions (read a transaction record) into memory. The instruction is executed when the data entered by the teller are read into main memory. The second set of instructions (get master transaction record) is executed by retrieving the customer's record from disk storage into main memory. The third set of instructions updates the record by adding the $85 deposit to the $80 balance, resulting in a new balance of $165. The fourth set of instructions rewrites the new record back to the disk. The final set sends the new balance to the teller terminal, where it is displayed on the screen for verification.

After the instructions have been executed for one customer, the processing cycle is repeated for the next customer, and so on. When devices like terminals are controlled directly by the computer's CPU, they are said to be **on line**. When data transactions are captured and processed as they occur, we say the computer is in **real time**. Finally, when a teller or an end user carries on a dialog with the computer, the exchange is called **interactive processing**. In our example (Figure 3.20), the computer

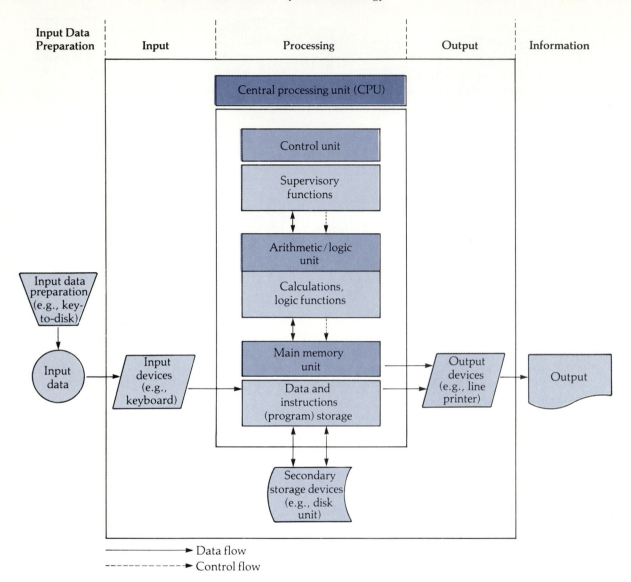

Figure 3.19
Functional units of a
computer system.

asks the teller to enter an account number. The teller enters the number. After the computer verifies the number, it asks whether the entry is a deposit or a withdrawal, and so on until all the necessary information is entered for processing.

Entering Data into the Computer

Every day, organizations face the task of inputting data into the computer for processing. How data are entered depends on the volume of data,

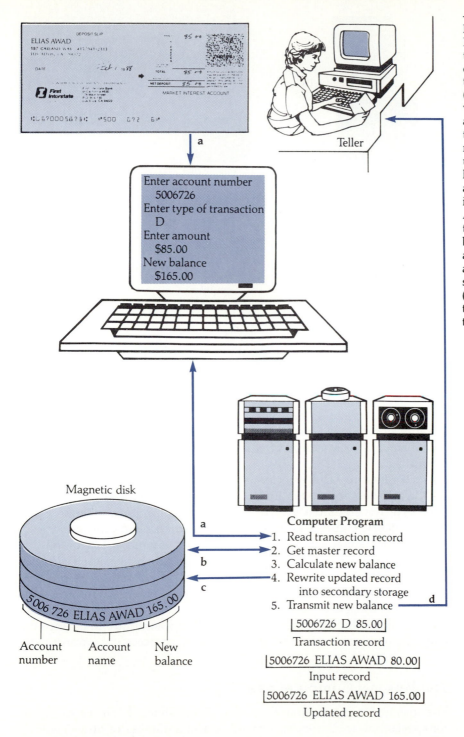

Computer Program

1. Read transaction record
2. Get master record
3. Calculate new balance
4. Rewrite updated record
   into secondary storage
5. Transmit new balance

| 5006726 D 85.00 |

Transaction record

| 5006726 ELIAS AWAD 80.00 |

Input record

| 5006726 ELIAS AWAD 165.00 |

Updated record

Magnetic disk

Account number Account name New balance

Figure 3.20
Processing a checking transaction. (a) Teller enters account number, type of transaction (D = deposit, W = withdrawal), and amount. The data are transmitted to main memory. (b) Computer uses account number to locate record in secondary storage and reads it into main memory. Amount of deposit is then added to present balance. (c) The new balance and rest of record are rewritten back into secondary storage. (d) The new balance is transmitted back to the teller.

Figure 3.21
Checks are sorted and the information is stored on magnetic tape for processing later in the day. Checks are read and the information is transmitted directly to the mainframe as well as to magnetic disk to be stored as a backup. On-line processing is quicker and more efficient than off-line processing, but also more expensive.

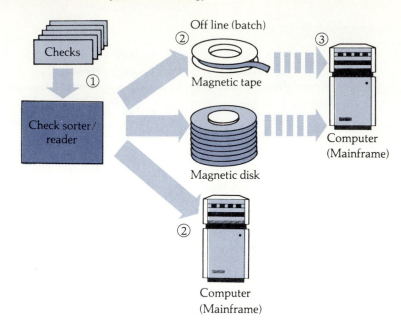

time requirements, and cost. Data are entered either in batches or on line. In **batch processing**, a group of similar transactions is entered for processing at a later time. For example, in our check processing example, all checks drawn on the bank's customers' accounts are normally grouped in batches and later sorted on a sorter-reader. The information is temporarily stored on the bank's computer disk and, later in the evening, it is transmitted to a computer mainframe for final update of checking accounts.

In contrast to batch processing is on-line processing. As in Figure 3.20, a teller enters the amount of deposit (or withdrawal) through the keyboard. The amount is then received by the computer and entered into main memory. Figure 3.21 illustrates batch and on-line processing.

From a managerial point of view, when should batch or on-line processing be selected? In a banking application, where cash changes hands frequently and the account balance must be current and reflect all transactions accurately, each transaction must be processed immediately. In this case, the tellers must be on line. In contrast, for sorting the checks and preparing the resulting information for the computer to balance the bank's accounts once at the end of each day, batch processing is appropriate.

The Personal Computer as a Terminal

The terminal is predominantly a data entry device. It can be designed for specialized applications, data entry, and a number of other general-purpose functions. Terminals are used for on-line data entry, word processing, electronic mail, and so forth. Terminals have been classified as dumb or intelligent. **Dumb terminals** are nonprogrammable; they simply transmit and receive information between the user and the computer. **Intelligent terminals** are user-programmable. They consist of a processor, a main memory, a high-level language such as BASIC, and features such as editing, formatting, blinking, and dual intensity.

In an organization where managers and administrators need special information from the centralized computer, microcomputers are becoming popular as terminals. As we will see in Chapter 7, a microcomputer could be linked to the larger computer via a telephone line. The micro performs all the data entry functions of an intelligent terminal in addition to performing processing tasks independent of the host computer.

Special Input Devices

In choosing a computer, MIS managers must determine how their data will be stored. The three major storage alternatives are tape, disk, or diskettes. There are also applications that require special input devices such as magnetic ink character recognition (MICR), optical character recognition (OCR), point-of-sale (POS), bar code data entry, and electronic funds transfer (EFT). Each device is briefly described below.

Magnetic ink character recognition (MICR) is used in banking for check processing. Data on the face of the check are encoded with special ink that is readable by a reader linked to the computer for processing (see Figure 3.22).

Optical character recognition (OCR) is scanning a form and converting the reflected impulses to electrical signals that represent characters. OCR readers are widely used by electric utilities and petroleum companies with heavy billing requirements. They are used in retailing to code cans, shirts, and other products (see Figure 3.23).

Point-of-sale (POS) allows the retailer to enter data directly to the computer at the time the transaction occurs. POS systems are used in

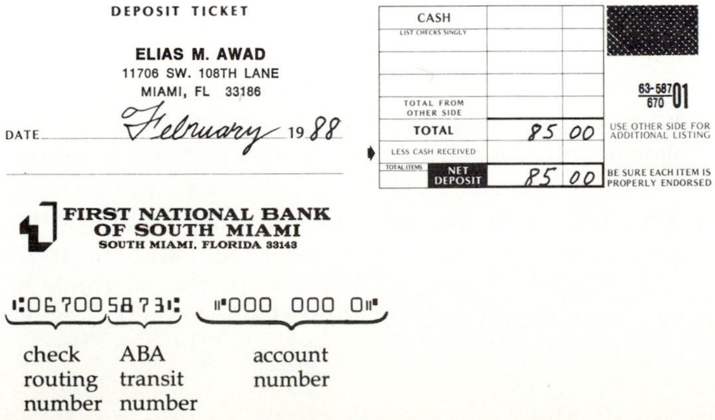

DEPOSIT TICKET

ELIAS M. AWAD
11706 SW. 108TH LANE
MIAMI, FL 33186

DATE _____ *February* 19 88

FIRST NATIONAL BANK OF SOUTH MIAMI
SOUTH MIAMI, FLORIDA 33143

⑆067005873⑆ ⑈000 000 0⑈

check   ABA   account
routing   transit   number
number   number

CASH		
LIST CHECKS SINGLY		
TOTAL FROM OTHER SIDE		
TOTAL	85	00
LESS CASH RECEIVED		
TOTAL ITEMS NET DEPOSIT	85	00

63-587/670 01

USE OTHER SIDE FOR ADDITIONAL LISTING

BE SURE EACH ITEM IS PROPERLY ENDORSED

Figure 3.22
MICR encoding. The teller enters the amount of a check into an encoding machine. The amount is printed in MICR Code that the computer can pick up along with preprinted routing and sorting information.

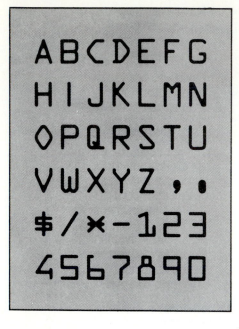

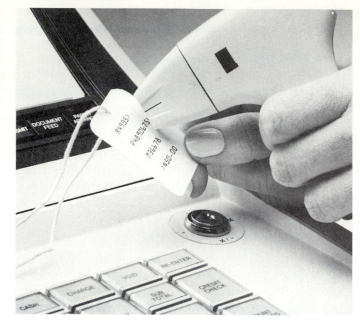

Figure 3.23
Optical-character recognition. *Left:* A standard OCR typeface. *Right:* A wand reader, a hand-held photoelectric scanning device that can read OCR characters.

department stores, cash and carry supermarkets, and fast food stores (see Figure 3.24).

Bar codes are the coded lines that identify products, prices, sizes, and the like. When the code is read by a scanner, the readout is displayed in decimal figures on the cash register screen for customer verification. The store's computer also captures the data for inventory update (see Figure 3.25).

Electronic funds transfer (EFT) enables banks to handle customer transactions around the clock at electronic speed. The technology handles pay by phone, direct payroll, and automated teller machines or ATMs (see Figure 3.26).

Output from the Computer

We have seen that entering data into the computer is a major step in the computer processing cycle. Once the data are processed, some form of output information is expected. Let us return to our banking example. The customer approaches the teller window and wants to make a $80 deposit. The teller counts the cash, inserts the deposit slip in the machine, brings up the customer's account on the screen, and enters the amount of deposit—$80. The computer then credits the customer's checking account and generates one form of output for documentation or reference.

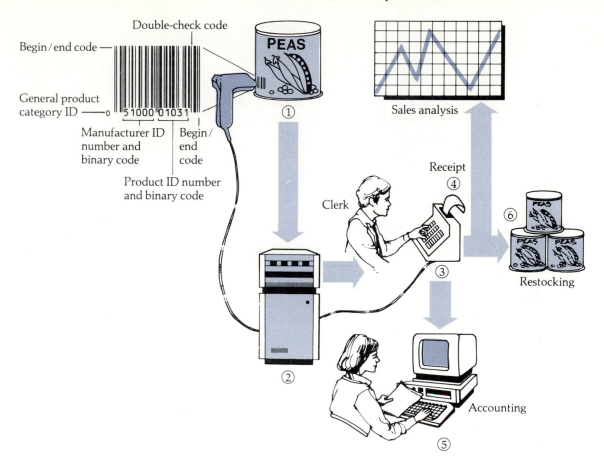

Figure 3.24 Point-of-sale system. *Top left:* A standard POS terminal, used to enter sales data. These terminals are found in many retail stores, such as drug stores. *Bottom left:* Example of bar code—the Universal Product Code used on retail products. *Middle left and above:* What bar code readers do in the supermarket. The supermarket checker moves the grocery product's bar code (1) past the barcode reader, which reads it with a light beam and sensor. The price and description of the item, which is stored in (2) the computer system, is sent to (3) the POS terminal, where it is (4) printed out as a receipt for the customer. The information from the POS terminal is also used by the store, on the one hand, (5) for accounting purposes and, on the other hand, (6) for restocking store inventory and for analyzing which products sell better than others.

What are the forms of output? The first form is the **soft copy**, the screen display of the customer's amount of deposit and the new balance. This provides a temporary record and visual verification of the processing of the transaction. The second form of output is the **hard copy** (data printed on paper), actually two hard copies: a receipt showing the amount of deposit and the new balance and a printout on the teller machine's paper tape for reference (see Figure 3.27).

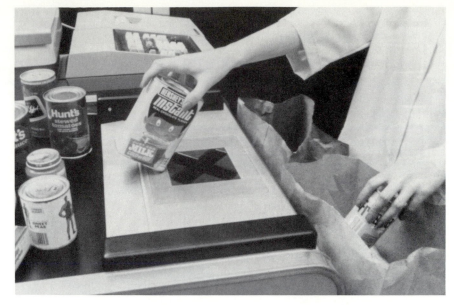

Figure 3.25
Bar codes. This photo-electric bar code scanner, often seen at super-market checkout counters, reads the product's zebra-striped bar code. The code identifies the product to the store's computer, which retrieves price information. The price is then automatically rung up on the point-of-sale terminal. (Reprinted with permission of Unisys Corporation.)

A third form of output is computer **graphics.** In business there is a variety of graphics applications. For example, decision support graphics is management reporting that allows the executive to identify potential problem areas quickly without having to wade through volumes of numerical data. The data are displayed in a form understandable to the user (see Figure 3.28).

Cathode ray tubes (CRTs) are available in single or multiple color. Single-color displays are called **monochrome monitors**. They are used in microcomputer systems to display text information, usually in green or amber on a black background. **Color monitors** display graphics and text in different colors. Screen resolution (crispness or clarity of displayed data) is very important in selecting color monitors. Traditionally, color monitors have had lower resolution than monochrome monitors for displaying text data. A new monitor, called *enhanced color monitor,* combines the text quality of a monochrome monitor and the color of the color monitor.

Print Devices

Our bank example is one illustration of the need for some form of printed output that serves as a record of the transaction. Since users have different requirements for print output quality, a wide choice of printers and options is available. There are several ways to form a character, including fully formed, dot-matrix, or image.

Fully formed, or *letter-quality,* characters are printed as solid images on the page. The electric typewriter produces fully formed characters. Com-

Figure 3.26
Automated teller machine (ATM). *Left:* An ATM mounted on the wall of a bank.
Below: How an ATM works. Customer (1) inserts special ATM card into slot, (2) keys in his or her personal identification number, (3) pushes button identifying transaction, such as cash withdrawal, (4) indicates amount, (5) lifts door and removes money, (6) removes card and paper record of transaction.

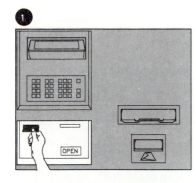

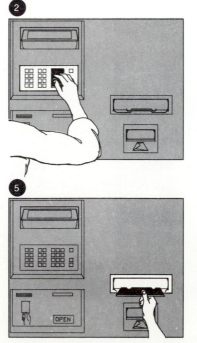

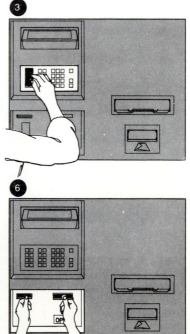

Figure 3.27
Forms of output.

FREE SAFE DEPOSIT BOX
with qualifying deposit
— PROTECT —
Legal Documents•Stock Certificates•Valuables

SuperCheck Deposit Receipt
This deposit is subject to verification, collection and conditions of the rules and regulations of Dominion Federal Savings & Loan Association.

SEP-10-87 23 30005786 61   630.00

PI DD -- -- 6   LC BAL   8,669.72

THE SUPER S&L™
DOMINION FEDERAL
SAVINGS & LOAN ASSOCIATION

LOCAL CHECK HOLD-5 BUSINESS DAYS
OUT OF STATE CHECK HOLD-9 BUSINESS DAYS   *Thank You*

```
ACCOUNT NO.      105006726       REGULAR CHECKING

PREVIOUS BALANCE . . . . .      06-23-87         5,114.23
    2 DEPOSITS AND CREDITS   .                   1,269.15
   18 CHECKS AND DEBITS . . .                    5,853.07
CURRENT BALANCE  . . . . .      07-23-87           530.31

          - - MISCELLANEOUS DEBITS AND CREDITS - -
DATE    CHECK #       AMOUNT       DESCRIPTION
06-25                931.65 CR    CREDIT MEMO
07-22                337.50 CR    DEPOSIT
```

Figure 3.28
Graphics display on the
Hewlett-Packard Vectra.

puter printers generate fully formed characters using a "golf ball," a daisy wheel, or a chain mechanism (see Figure 3.29). These options represent *impact* printing, in that each character is impacted against an inked ribbon to print the character on the form. Most printers are **bidirectional**, printing in both directions.

The *dot matrix* printer forms a character by a pattern of dots. The heavier the density of the dots, the closer the character is to being fully formed (see Figure 3.30).

The third character formation is by image. This is called *nonimpact* printing. Selected dots are "turned on" on a one-line-at-a-time basis. When all the lines are scanned, the resulting image captures the characters in their respective locations. An example of image printing is the laser printer (see Figure 3.31).

Voice Output Devices

Yet another form of output is the speech synthesizer, which serves an important function. You are already familiar with a telephone company's phone message to an old phone number: "The number you have dialed is no longer in service." Dialing the old number activated a prerecorded message that reproduces an actual human voice. A newer version is a computer-generated voice output or a speech synthesizer. A common approach, called the *analysis technique,* stores words in digitized form in memory. When a message arrives, it chooses the appropriate words and links them together to form the voice response. Although the output is

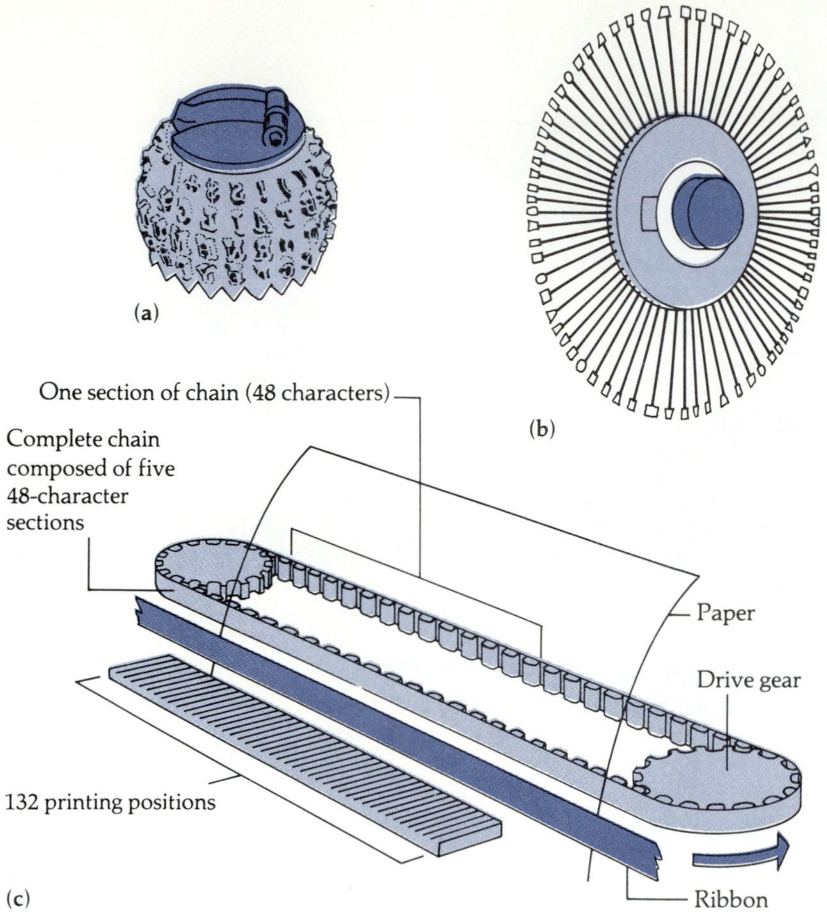

Figure 3.29
Printing options.
(a) Golf ball. (b) Daisy
wheel printer. The daisy
wheel (inset) consists of
a set of spokes, and each
spoke carries a raised
character. A printer can
have several interchange-
able daisy wheels, each
with a different type
font. When inserted in
the printer, the daisy
wheel rotates to the
spoke with the appropri-
ate character. A hammer
strikes that spoke
against the ribbon,
which then strikes the
paper and leaves an
imprint. (c) Chain
printer, which can reach
speeds of up to 3000
lines per minute.

(a)

(b)

One section of chain (48 characters)

Complete chain
composed of five
48-character
sections

Paper

Drive gear

132 printing positions

(c)

Ribbon

good, it sounds somewhat mechanical. The message has none of the
inflections that make it sound natural. An example of computer-
generated voice output is a response to a number that has been
changed, "That number has been changed. The new number is 2
(pause) 6 (pause) . . ."

Despite the limitations, voice synthesis has been used to aid the hand-
icapped and visually impaired persons, to guide travelers to the right
concourse in airport terminals, and so on. The system can also be a useful
tool for professionals in a number of ways. For example, a sales representative could access inventory information instantly during a meeting
with a customer; an investor could get the last quote and other information from the stock brokerage house. More and more of such applications are becoming available to other professionals—doctors, lawyers,
and engineers.

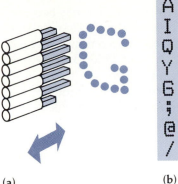

(a)

A	B	C	D	E	F	G	H
I	J	K	L	M	N	O	P
Q	R	S	T	U	V	W	X
Y	Z	&	1	2	3	4	5
6	7	8	9	0			

(b)

Figure 3.30
Forming dot-matrix characters. (a) This art shows the letter G being printed as a 5 × 7 dot-matrix character. The moving matrix head has seven vertical pins, which move back and forth as necessary to form each letter. (b) Letters, numbers, and special characters formed as 5 × 7 dot-matrix characters.

Figure 3.31
A laser printer. Laser printers are expensive but they are fast, quiet, and produce output as high in quality as the electric typewriter.

Implications for MIS

We have seen that computers have already changed our way of looking at things. The advent of the microcomputer and specialized software such as the electronic spreadsheet allows the user to enter numbers into the system and perform the "what-if" function. Integrated packages also offer graphics, word processing, and database management. Today's high-speed computer can create reports quickly, accurately, and in line with the user's requirements. Such software falls under the category of decision support systems (DSS).

These developments and the probable advances in very high-level languages mean that choosing the right computer system has become a more perplexing assignment than ever before, yet the decision between a stand-alone system and a decentralized system is becoming easier with the availability of telecommunication networks. The 1980s provided network capabilities linking the micros to the mainframe. In this way the user can run his or her application on the premises and simultaneously tap the files or programs at the mainframe for processing. File organization and database design are covered in Chapters 5 and 6. Information coming out of the computer is rarely useful unless it can be moved. Telecommunications allow that movement. Telecommunications and networking are discussed in Chapter 7.

Summary

□ A computer consists of an input device, a processor, and an output device. Among its capabilities are high-speed processing and arithmetic and logic. A viable computer system requires hardware, application and system software and (for mainframes) qualified personnel for programming and maintenance.

□ The computer industry has undergone five generations of technological change:
   a. First-generation computers used vacuum tubes, were bulky, and handled one program at a time.
   b. Second-generation computers used magnetic core memory instead of vacuum tubes, were more reliable, faster, and more versatile than first-generation systems.
   c. Third-generation computers introduced multiprocessing/multiprogramming, timesharing, and improved reliability and processing speed. Minicomputers using chip technology became popular.
   d. Fourth-generation systems featured very large-scale integration (VLSI), and database management systems (DBMS).
   e. Fifth-generation systems are represented by the microcomputer, decision support systems, office automation, and ready-to-use software for similar applications.

□ In microcomputer memory, processing chips are mounted on a main circuit board called a motherboard, with slots for expansion or for special boards for graphics, printer control, and so on.

□ The building block of computer memory is the chip. One type, called RAM (random-access memory), is main memory. Another type, called ROM (read-only memory), has microcomputer or system software etched in it.

▫ Data are entered into the computer via tape, disk, or an input/output device. Specialized input devices such as MICR, OCR, POS, and bar code are also used in specialized applications.

▫ Computers may be classified as follows:
   a. By *type*: analog, digital, hybrid.
   b. By *capability*: business-oriented, scientific.
   c. By *size*: Microcomputers, minicomputers, mainframes, supercomputers.

▫ Microcomputers are everywhere. Three primary areas of applications are correspondence, distributed processing, and budgeting and planning. Microcomputers are driven by system software and utilities and offer a choice of options to suit virtually every need.

▫ Computers in general are structured around a CPU (central processing unit), storage, and input/output devices. The mini is used for accounting applications for small- to medium-sized business and in departments and divisions of larger organizations. In contrast, the mainframe is designed for large-volume, large organization computing; universities use the mainframe for administrative and academic computing. The ultimate in computing power is the supercomputer, with processing speeds exceeding 200 million instructions per second.

▫ Secondary storage centers around disk media and devices—floppy and hard disk. Floppy disk comes in 8″ or $5\frac{1}{4}″$, storing up to 1.6 MB of data. A hard disk holds tens to hundreds of times the storage and operates at over twenty times the speed of a floppy disk.

Key Terms

Address
Analog computer
Batch processing
Bar code
Bidirectional
Binary-coded decimal (BCD)
Bit
Byte
Central processing unit (CPU)
Chip
Coding
Color monitor
Digital computer
Dumb terminal
Electrically erasable programmable ROM (EEPROM)

Electronic funds transfer (EFT)
Floppy disk
Hardware
Hard copy
Hard disk
Hybrid computer
Intelligent terminal
Interactive processing
Magnetic ink character recognition (MICR)
Microfloppy
Millions of instructions per second (MIPS)
Monochrome monitor
Motherboard
Multitasking

On line
Operand
Operation code
Optical character recognition
   (OCR)
Point-of-sale (POS)

Random-access memory (RAM)
Read-only memory (ROM)
Real time
Secondary storage
Soft copy
Vertical recording

Review Questions

1. Do computers have limitations? Explain.

2. One capability of a computer is "arithmetic and logic." What does this mean? Give an example.

3. Distinguish between:
   a. Dumb and intelligent terminals
   b. Digital and hybrid computers
   c. Fourth- and fifth-generation computers

4. Briefly describe the key features of the five generations of computers. In your opinion, which generation had the greatest impact on business? Why?

5. In what way do general-purpose and special-purpose computers differ? Illustrate.

6. A microcomputer is structured around ROM and RAM. What do these terms mean? How are they related? Explain.

7. In what way does a personal computer perform as a terminal?

8. In what respect are microcomputers approximating the configuration of the minicomputer?

9. What is the difference between:
   a. Mainframe and supercomputers
   b. RAM and ROM
   c. On-line and real-time

10. How does a distributed processing network function? What advantages does it offer over a centralized computer facility?

11. Illustrate the procedure used in computer instruction execution.

12. Illustrate how data are represented in memory.

13. What is a byte? What coding schemes are used to code alphabetic characters?

14. In how many ways are data entered into the computer? Explain briefly.

15. How does a chain printer differ from a serial printer? An impact from a nonimpact printer?

16. "Intelligent terminals are user-programmable." What does it mean? What do they include?

17. What is the difference between a floppy and a hard disk? Which one would you choose? Why?

18. Write a two-page essay explaining the implications of microcomputers for MIS.

Application Problems

1. Crutsfield Electronics has a large warehouse in Charlottesville, Virginia that sells electronic units (auto radios, tape recorders, walkie-talkies, etc.) to 72 retailers in Virginia, West Virginia, and Maryland. Each day a truck leaves the warehouse on a four-day trip throughout the tristate territory to make deliveries.

The vice president in charge of warehousing wondered if a MIS might minimize inventory problems at the main warehouse and affiliated retailers. At least, the truck wouldn't have to make many trips. Furthermore, the dealers on the end of the four-day route would not have to wait as long for deliveries. Could the firm install a computer system that tied the warehouse directly with its retailers to expedite deliveries? Could there be a computer-based way of processing products by retailers?

Using the material covered in this chapter, write a two-page report showing how a computer can be used to meet a retailer's needs quickly and effectively. How is the system used to cut down on costs and improve the profitability level of the firm? Consider also the role of the microcomputer in this project.

2. Leggett's is a chain of 37 department stores with operations in Virginia and North Carolina. In the firm's three-level information system, the first level is the store's minicomputer, which captures data from the various POS terminals located in each department in the store. The POS terminal is a basic data entry device that clerks use in entering all items sold, amounts received, and other sales information.

The second level represents the two regional computers in Lynchburg, Va., and Charlotte, N.C. Their function is to integrate transactions from designated stores in the region. The third level is the mainframe computer that integrates data from both regions.

Leggett's has its own credit card system. When a customer wishes to charge a purchase, the clerk inserts the card into the terminal for validation and authorization to accept the amount of purchase. The computer checks the credit balance on the account and determines if it is an authorized card. If credit is approved, the sales clerk scans the bar code on the item via a light pen. The price is provided by the store's computer, which means that sale prices no longer have to be marked on individual items. The whole operation is carried out in an on-line, real-time environment.

The credit sale is recorded and processed against the customer's account in the customer's account file. Each sale is also entered in the sales file to update the master sales accounts of that sales department. From the sales person's ID number accompanying each sale, sales commissions are computed and credited to each sales clerk for sales analysis and payments.

The system at the store level monitors sales, returns, and demands for leader items to give management information for reacting to changes and trends. At the end of the day, performance reports are available for the store's managers. Inventory status information is also included.

The computers at the 37 stores communicate with the regional computer via communication lines at a high transmission speed. The bulk of the information transmitted deals with inventory control and reorder. The regional computer's reorder application polls the inventory files of each store's computer after hours. Inventory orders are processed based on predefined formulas stored in computer memory. The regional computer then prepares merchandise order printouts for each store. The next day, inventory personnel fill the orders from the main warehouse or place them by phone with various buyers, jobbers, or wholesalers.

QUESTIONS

a. Evaluate the overall structure of Leggett's computer system. What changes (additions, deletions) would you make to improve the performance of the store's computer?

b. At what level should billing and cash receipts be handled? Why?

c. What are the benefits of having the computer provide the prices of items on sale rather than placing the sale price on each item?

d. For what other purposes does the entry of the clerk's ID serve than computing commission? Explain.

e. Should the system be designed to allow the clerk to void a sale on line if a customer cancels a sale? Why?

Selected References

Archbold, Pamela and Hodges, Parker. "The DATAMATION 100." *Datamation,* June 15, 1986, 43–65.

Athey, Thomas H. and Zmud, Robert W. *Introduction to Computers and Information Systems With Basic.* Glencoe, Ill.: Scott Foresman, 1986.

Elmer-DeWitt, Philip. "Driving By The Glow Of a Screen." *Time,* April 20, 1987, 63.

Grayson, Ashley. "You Thought Laptops Were Only For Loners." *Computerworld,* February 23, 1987, 61–62ff.

Hurst, Rebecca. "Desktop Publishing." *Computerworld*, April 13, 1987, S1–3ff.

Johnson, Randolph. *Microcomputers—Concepts and Applications*. Santa Cruz, Calif.: Mitchell, 1987.

Makrias, Stephanie and Honan, Patrick. "The Complete Guide to IBM Compatibles." *Personal Computing*, April 1987, 141–43ff.

Powell, David. "Speed and Precision Are the Hallmarks of Hard Disk Technology." *Popular Computing*, May 1984, 118.

Senn, James A. *Information Systems in Management*. 3rd ed. Belmont, Calif.: Wadsworth, 1987.

Watt, Dan. "Mass Storage." *Popular Computing*, May 1984, 113–27.

Williamson, Mickey. "Desktop Publishing—Balance of Elements." *Computerworld*, April 13, 1987, S1–3ff.

Computer Software

Chapter Contents

DEVELOPERS PICK BASIC FOR HIGH PRODUCTIVITY

Programming Languages Used

Approximate percentages of BCS members responding to the survey

Language	Percentage
BASIC	80%
FORTRAN	60%
PASCAL	35%
C	33%
ASSEMBLY	30%
LISP	10%
COBOL	5%
PROLOG	5%
FORTH	5%
OTHER	2%

SOURCE: THE BOSTON COMPUTING SOCIETY

DESPITE THE PROLIFERATION OF programming language options, a recent Boston Computing Society survey revealed that 85 to 90 percent of its members choose for at least some development an old workhorse: BASIC.

Many also admitted some shame at passing by trendy challengers such as C and MODULA. But the phenomenon of BASIC's dominance amid scorn and competition from other languages may be based on programmer productivity.

"We're under a lot of pressure to standardize on C," said a programmer who develops in-house applications at a New England high-technology company." "But most of the time it's quicker and more efficient to develop in interpreted BASIC and then compile it. Once it's compiled, the users don't know, or care, what language it's in."

"Like Mark Twain, reports of BASIC's death are greatly exaggerated," said Stewart Chapin,

marketing vice president at True Basic, developer of the TRUE BASIC 2.0 language.

Competition among BASIC vendors has helped keep the language attractive. In the last year, traditional leader Microsoft Corporation overhauled the user interface to the DOS version of its BASIC Compiler, adding windows, productivity-oriented debugging features and structured program control options to the $99.95 Quick BASIC 3.0. One Microsoft insider said 3.0 was driven by the arrival of a significant competitor, TURBO BASIC.

TURBO BASIC, a $99.95 compiler from Borland International, has expanded an already large BASIC market. Borland wrote a TURBO PASCAL-like interface for its BASIC and added math coprocessor support, features now matched by Microsoft's 3.0.

The $99.95 TRUE BASIC, out for two years, answered the changing market with a lower price and update. Developers will be able to connect at link-time separate programs in one program's work space for better debugging and code interaction analysis, Chapin said. Users can share identical source code among MS-DOS, Macintosh, Amiga, and Atari ST machines, and Chapin said the company is writing versions for the Mac II and 80386-based systems.

—Excerpted from Jeff Angus, Infoworld Software, June 22, 1987, 11.

AT A GLANCE

Software plays an important role in system development. It is the "driver" of the hardware. Accessing, modifying, and retrieving data are determined by the software in computer memory. Without software, obviously, there can be no computer processing.

An effective program ensures accuracy, flexibility, and good response to inquiries. Regardless of how it is acquired, a program goes through design, coding, and testing before it is ready for use.

To understand the current focus on end-user computing, we need to emphasize that programming languages have gone from a period of writing in machine language for a specific computer to assembly languages using symbolic code to high-level languages with emphasis on algebraic and English-like syntax, to fourth-level nonprocedural languages that allow the user to simply define the task, leaving the actual procedure to be handled by the computer.

The benefits of nonprocedural languages are encouraging more and more end users to develop applications for their own use. Report and application generators, using query languages, have proven their usefulness in a variety of ways. The role of high-level (conventional) programming, once the backbone of the computer center operations, is giving way to nonprocedural programming suitable for end user and computer professional as well. We can expect this trend to continue for the next decade.

By the end of this chapter, you should know:

1. The features and characteristics of software
2. The programming cycle and place of application programs in system development
3. How fourth-generation languages differ from procedural languages
4. The design features of a programming language
5. The key factors in selecting a programming language

Introduction

As we saw in Chapter 3, much emphasis has been placed on computer speed, storage capacity, and lower cost of processing. But hardware alone is not enough to achieve these goals. The *driver* of the hardware is the **software**—the computer's operating system and application programs that produce the information for the end user.

Software is an important component of an information system for two reasons: First, hardware won't run without software. Software gives the computer the "intelligence" it needs to do the job. This means that accessing, storing, retrieving, and modifying information are all determined by the programs in computer memory. Second, software controls virtually every activity affecting the database. For example, if you were to ask a bank teller for the balance of your checking account, the entries the teller makes through the terminal are interpreted by the software, which goes to the file, looks up the account, retrieves the balance, and displays it on the screen in a matter of seconds. This response is made possible when the teller enters inquiries by following a specific procedure defined and controlled by the software.

Computer software is too encompassing a subject to cover in detail in one chapter. We will focus here on the characteristics and types of software, program development process, programming language features, and the trend in software development without conventional programming. The objective is to review the essentials of software and its role in developing information systems. It is assumed that MIS students have had experience in a basic programming language through an introductory data processing or a programming course.

The Characteristics of Software

An effective program has four characteristics:

1. Accuracy
2. Good documentation
3. Flexibility
4. Performance

Accuracy means that the software must be free of syntax and logic errors. A *syntax error* results from using an improper form of a command or misusing symbols. For example, misspelling the command PRINT would signal a syntax error. Syntax errors are identified by the software. Thus, they are easy to find and relatively easy to correct.

A *logic error* results from improper use of syntactically correct statements. For example, a payroll program that withholds 80 percent rather than 20 percent of gross earnings for federal income tax contains a logic error. A program with logic errors will usually produce some output, but the output will not be correct in all cases. Logic errors can be very difficult to find. In some cases, programs run for years before all the logic errors are detected and corrected.

Software requires *documentation*, which provides directions for using the software. Good documentation describes procedures for operating the software in a clear and concise manner. This includes flowcharts, troubleshooting guidelines, and an index with cross references. More and more software packages include a condensed version of the manual built into the software. "Help" screens, menus, and the like allow the user to operate the software virtually without reference to manuals. These aids describe the major commands and function keys or specify solutions to common problems faced in using the software. In addition, templates that lie over function keys on the keyboards remove any need for having to memorize codes or procedures.

Flexibility in a software system means that the software is capable of handling a large variety of transactions and responds to different situations. For example, the user may wish to display results on a screen, print the results only, or perhaps do both. In the case of display, the user may want to have a summary report on the screen or a detailed report displayed one screen at a time. These options also characterize the software as user friendly, stemming from its flexibility to adapt to various types of inquiries.

The fourth characteristic of software is *performance,* or the efficiency with which the program responds to inquiries from the user. Much of the software's performance level is constrained by the nature of the inquiry and the way the files are organized as well as by the software itself. That is why an organization or business must test the software for performance before committing it to regular use.

How Is Software Acquired?

An organization will acquire computer software from one of three sources: in house, off the shelf, or from a contractor. *In-house* software programs are those developed by the company's programming staff. Programmers go through the entire process of developing programs, a process explained later in the chapter. The decision to adopt in-house software depends on:

1. Staff *caliber.*   Are they well trained? How familiar are they with the user's problem area?

2. Staff *reliability.*   Will the programs be completed within a reasonable time frame? Are programmers available to maintain or upgrade the information system?

3. *Cost-effectiveness.*   Is an outside firm cheaper in the long run? Large firms can well afford to develop many of their programs in house. Programmers are already on payroll, so one more program is not that much of a financial burden. Nevertheless, it may be cheaper, quicker, and easier to acquire certain programs elsewhere. For most small firms, it is not cost effective to hire and retain full-time staff to do part-time programming. Small firms generally either acquire the software readymade or contract for it.

4. *Commonality* of the software.   For example, applications such as payroll are quite similar across firms so that an off-the-shelf package is often the best. By contrast, an application that keeps track of the sales

staff of a company within 50 miles of the sales territory would be best developed in house because it is *unique* to the organization.

Acquiring readymade or *off-the-shelf* software packages is a common alternative to developing software in house. A software package is a set of programs designed to perform a specific job. For example, a payroll software package will calculate gross pay, deductions, and net pay, and will prepare periodic reports. Readymade software is usually cheaper than in-house development because the vendor recoups development costs over hundreds of installations. A broad user group generates feedback that helps the vendor enhance the software.

The third alternative to programming is to freelance or *contract* the job to an outside firm that does this work on a full-time basis. Generally, if a company does not have experience in developing software and the nature of the application cannot be met by off-the-shelf software, contract programming is the best route. It may not be the cheapest alternative. An "in-between" approach is to modify or customize an off-the-shelf package. For example, an organization may want a payroll package to withhold 5 percent of employee gross wages for the pension fund. This feature would require incorporating a basic program to perform such a deduction on a regular basis. More on "purchase versus make" software is found in Chapter 16.

The Application Program in the System Life Cycle

Application programs are written to follow a system design. In system design, output, input, file, and processing specifications are determined. Application programming transforms these design specifications into code. That is, it converts the "what" part of the system design into the "how" end of the operation of the information system.

Software design is analogous to the *blueprint* for a building. The blueprint is a layout of the structure—for example, the dimensions of the offices, the height of each floor, and the number of offices in each level. But the contractor determines how the construction is actually to be executed—how the cement is to be poured, how the electric cables are to be installed, and so on. None of the "how" part of the construction can be executed without the blueprint. Likewise, without the software design specifications document, the blueprint for system development, the application program cannot be written. Programmers can easily get lost going back and forth trying to debug the program.

In developing application programs, programmers work individually on modules that must fit together. This requires direction for coordinating assignments and ensuring a successful test of the software, as application programming is more complex when several programmers work as a group on software development. Project leadership and control is discussed in Chapter 17.

How Are Programs Developed?

With programs as the driver of the hardware, a logical question is: What is involved in program development? The program development cycle represents four steps:

1. *Program design:* specifying the logical steps required to meet an information processing task.
2. *Coding:* converting the program design into a program language.
3. *Testing:* checking the accuracy of the coding and the program design (see Figure 4.1).
4. *Documentation:* a description of the work performed on the program(s).

Most people have the false impression that the programming development is mostly coding. Actually, coding is the most mechanical part of the whole program development cycle. As shown in Figure 4.1, it represents only 20 percent of the total development time. Almost one-third of the time is devoted to program design, while 50 percent is spent in testing and debugging the program. Although these four steps follow a sequence, they are not always straightforward. Programmers often move back and forth to make design changes resulting from testing which, in turn, requires changes in coding, retesting, and so on. This is what makes programming, as a step in the system life cycle, so time consuming and expensive.

Program design involves a clear understanding of the purpose of the program and its relationship to other programs in the information system. The programmer should also understand alternative approaches to design and how to produce a program design that will do the job well. This means a program that is efficient, low cost, and easy to maintain and upgrade. The program design is then checked before coding to ensure that it is accurate. (It is easier to modify poor thoughts than poor coding.)

Figure 4.1
Program development cycle.

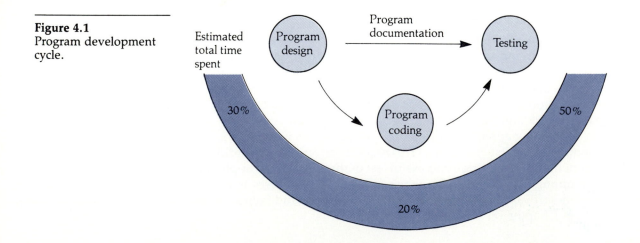

Flowcharting and Pseudocode

There are two methods for developing program design: flowcharting and pseudocode. **Flowcharting** is a graphic approach to the representation of the instructions and their sequence (see Figure 4.2). In contrast, **pseudocode** is a verbal technique representing program steps. Since pseudocode uses simple English, it can be used with ordinary word processors or editors and is easily revised. All logic flow can be expressed by a combination of three structures: sequence, condition (IF/THEN), and iteration/repetition (DO/WHILE). In pseudocode they are represented as follows:

```
1. (Sequence):
                a
                b
                c
2. IF condition THEN
      Sequence
   ELSE (optional)
      Sequence
   ENDIF
3. DO
      Sequence
   UNTIL condition   (or)   WHILE condition
                               Sequence
                             ENDWHILE
```

Steps are listed in the order they are to occur. A sequential step or condition can be any English statement that tells what should happen. These generally described sequential steps can later be expanded into detailed steps. Steps dependent on a condition or to be repeated are indented to show they belong within that set of total steps. A DO step must be carried out at once before the dependent condition can be tested. In contrast, a WHILE tests the condition first, so if the condition is already false, the enclosed sequence will be skipped without ever being carried out at all.

One advantage of pseudocode is that it is easy for the user to discuss the design with the programmer. There is no need to learn special symbols or languages. Figure 4.3 is an example of a program written in pseudocode.

Coding Program Design

Once program design is tested, it is coded using a programming language. **Coding** translates the logic specified by the flowchart or pseudocode into statements in a specific language. To understand the con-

Figure 4.2
Program flowcharting
describing a payroll
procedure.

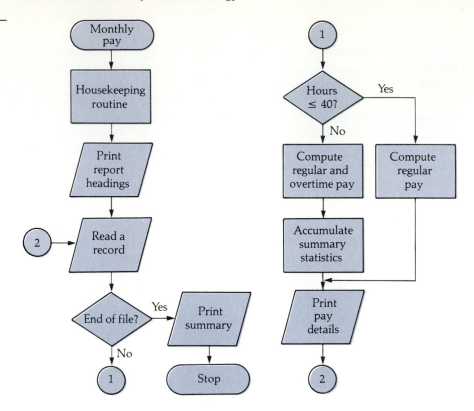

version process, we need to know something about programming
languages. This area is covered in the next section.

Testing Software

Once a code is created, it is tested for syntax and logic errors. Resulting
corrections may require a change in program design or a recoding of one
or more modules of the programs. Testing software is a part of testing
the entire system. A test procedure checks for quick response, how well
the system performs under stress, and how quickly it recovers from
failure. The success of testing depends on a well-thought-out plan that
specifies the steps and procedures for program, systems, and user acceptance testing. More on software and system testing is found in
Chapter 17.

Program Documentation

Finally, the entire program must be properly documented. *Program documentation* is essentially a carbon copy of the work performed on the
program. It improves communication among the people involved in the

```
Read a record

WHILE there is a record
   Print name
IF new charges THEN
     Compute new balance
   ENDIF
   Print balance
   Try to read next record
ENDWHILE
Count is 0
DO
   Print blank line
   Add 1 to count
UNTIL count is 3
Print end
```

Figure 4.3
A pseudocode program
to compute account
balances.

```
Comment
Then the step "Compute new balance" can be specified
separately in a similar way
 +

 +
```

system development process. Ideally, program documentation is produced at each level of the program design cycle, although many programmers wait till the end to write it up. Such a practice has a number of drawbacks. Detailed program design and coding are often forgotten. Programmers also have a tendency to view documentation as a secondary item—and therefore lack the motivation to do a good job, especially when a new project is waiting. In any case, every effort should be made to collect all the facts related to the program for future maintenance or enhancements. Figure 4.4 indicates the levels at which documentation is produced.

At this point it becomes important to incorporate two key points: program review and user participation. When large application programs are written, programmers get together and criticize one another's work. A programmer "walks through" his or her share of the work and makes changes accordingly. This **structured walkthrough** improves the overall program performance and ensures its success. Related to program review is user participation. Since software requirements are "best guess" efforts, user participation verifies these requirements while the program is being developed. User participation is often encouraged by prototyping—a "quick and dirty" replacement of the system being developed. Prototyping is covered later in the chapter. It relies on user feedback for making changes as a part of the final program design. Other approaches to user

Figure 4.4
Areas of program
documentation.

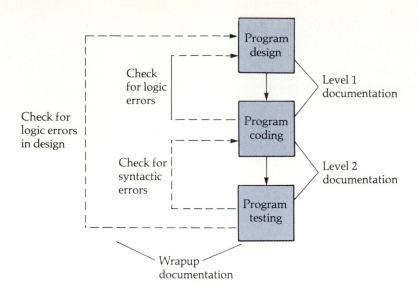

participation such as periodic meetings or questionnaires are also used,
depending on the need and level of cooperation provided by the user
staff. System development is covered in Chapters 14 through 17.

Programming Languages

A program is coded in a specific language. A programming language is
a means by which a programmer communicates the design to the computer. In this section, we review four levels of programming languages:
machine, assembly, high-level, and fourth-generation languages.

Machine Languages

Early computers were initially designed to solve one problem at a time.
In order to do anything else, the computer had to be rewired or switches
had to be physically moved. Then von Neumann pioneered the concept
of storing directions to instruct the computer in memory. The computer
executed one instruction at a time. To make the computer do something
different, a different set of instructions (program) was read into memory.
This *stored program* concept is an essential characteristic of any real computer.

The first generation of computers was coded in machine language
that was specific to each make or model of computer. Machine language
programming was a tedious and boring job. Programmers had to know
the idiosyncracies of the hardware and think like the computer as well.
They had to remember a long list of code numbers or operation codes
and know where instructions were stored in computer memory.

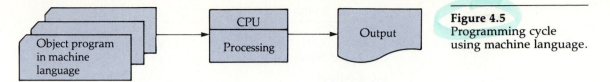

Figure 4.5
Programming cycle using machine language.

A program written in machine language is called an **object program**. It requires no translation to computer language because it already is in machine language (see Figure 4.5). This approach was efficient, because it was all ready to go. But testing the program was a big job. Correcting "bugs" meant going through program instructions from beginning to end.

Assembly Languages

The programming task of machine language was significantly simplified by the creation of assembler or translating programs in the early 1950s. Programs were written in easier-to-remember symbolic codes instead of numerical codes. Memory addresses were also referenced by symbols rather than addresses in machine language. An **assembler** translated assembler language programs into machine code for the computer. Table 4.1 shows examples of symbolic and machine language operation codes.

The program development cycle using **assembly language** is shown in Figure 4.6. Briefly, the cycle consists of the following steps:

1. The program is written in symbolic language. This is called the **source program**.
2. The vendor-provided assembler reads the source program and converts it into **machine language**, or the object program.
3. Any syntax errors detected during assembly are printed for correction.
4. The object program is loaded into computer memory for processing.

Compare Figure 4.7 with Figure 4.5 and note the diagnostic feature in Figure 4.7 that made it easier to detect and correct programming errors. Despite this benefit, assembler language was tedious and time consuming, requiring the programmers to have detailed knowledge of the way computer instructions are handled. Some programs are still written in assembly language when peak efficiency is required.

High-Level or Procedural Languages

Assembly and machine languages were *machine dependent*. A program worked on only one type of machine. The instructions had to be rewritten in a different assembly language to work on another type of computer. In addition, assembly and machine languages are difficult to learn, code,

Table 4.1   Symbolic and Machine Language Codes

Command Name	Symbolic Code	Operation Code
Input-output		
Halt input-output	HIO	9E
Start input-output	SIO	9C
Test input-output	TIO	9D
Data movement and manipulation		
Convert to binary	CVB	4F
Convert to decimal	CVD	4E
Execute	EX	44
Load address	LA	41
Move	MVI	92
Move characters	MVC	D2
Move numerics	MVN	D1
Store	ST	50
Translate	TR	DC
Arithmetic		
Add	A	5A
Divide	D	5D
Multiply	M	5C
Subtract	S	5B
Logic		
Compare	C	59
Transfer of control		
Branch on condition	BC	47
Supervisor call	SVC	0A

update, or maintain. As a result, a variety of machine-independent languages appeared in the 1960s. Known as **high-level** or **procedural languages**, these languages allow the programmer to specify at a higher level of abstraction than assembly languages how the computer is to perform tasks. Procedural languages must of course, like assembly languages, be translated into machine language for computer processing.

High-level languages such as FORTRAN, COBOL, and many others introduced several new language features that were standard in their instructions. That is, the instructions were essentially the same for every computer. A special program for each computer, called a *compiler*, translated the standard instructions into the special machine language for a specific model computer. This meant the same instructions could be translated by different compilers (on different machines) without having to rewrite the original program.

Another development was that the languages were designed for specific classes of applications; FORTRAN was designed for coding scientific

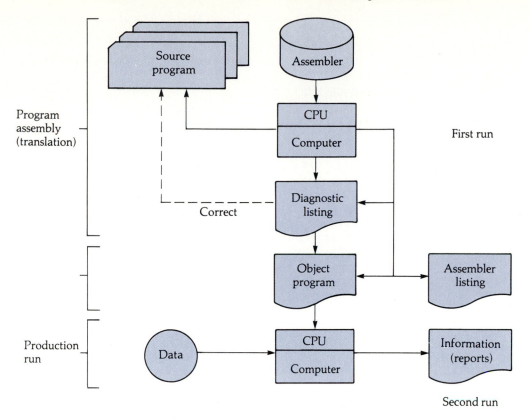

Figure 4.6
Program development
cycle using assembly
language.

problems, while COBOL was designed for business data transaction processing. In addition, these high-level languages were more like human languages. They were easier for people to use than assembly language.

There is a variety of high-level languages in use today. **COBOL** is the premier business language, scientific languages include **FORTRAN**, **ALGOL**, **PASCAL**, and general languages include **BASIC**. Most of today's computer applications are written in high-level languages, although newer fourth-generation languages are also being used for developing today's applications. Figure 4.7 illustrates programs in several high-level languages.

Compared to assembly languages, high-level languages have two distinct advantages:

1. The programming commands are problem oriented rather than machine oriented. This means that the programmer can focus on the problem solving.
2. A programming command is generally translated into a number of machine instructions rather than only one translation in assembly language. This obviously makes developing an application in a procedural language much faster.

Figure 4.7a
BASIC program to calculate a stock turnover rate.

```
 10   REM STOCK-TURNOVER RATE CALCULATION
 20   PRINT "STOCK-TURNOVER RATE CALCULATION"
 30   LET T = 0
 40   READ C$,N/S
 50   FOR I = 1 TO N
 60   READ V
 70   LET T = T + V
 80   NEXT I
 90   LET A = T/N
 95   LET R = S/A
100   PRINT USING 102,C$
101   PRINT
102   :COMPANY 'LLLLLLLLLLLLLL
105   PRINT USING 106,N/S
106   :TOTAL SALES FOR *** PERIODS = $*******.**
108   PRINT USING 109,A
109   :AVERAGE RETAIL STOCK = $*****.**
110   PRINT USING 111,R
111   :RATE OF STOCK TURNOVER RATE = $***.**
120   DATA "XYZ",12,236542.00
121   DATA 1000.0,1200.0,1450.0,2010.5,1340.0,1400.0
122   DATA 1400.0,1350.0,1300.0,1800.0,2000.0,2050.0
200   END

READY
RUN

MARKT          12:00          22-JAN-88
STOCK-TURNOVER RATE CALCULATION
COMPANY XYZ
TOTAL SALES FOR 12 PERIODS = $236542.00
AVERAGE RETAIL STOCK = $ 1525.04
STOCK TURNOVER RATE = $155.11

TIME: 0.14 SECS.
READY
```

Fourth-Generation Languages

A move away from the emphasis on programming languages by professional programmers and toward user-oriented, easy-to-learn languages is what we call **fourth-generation languages (4GL)**. They include a broad range of languages that have common features. These very high-level or **nonprocedural languages** differ from procedural languages in four ways:

1. They are easier to use and learn.

Figure 4.7b
A simplified payroll pro-
gram written in COBOL.

```
//JTESTING JOB (10137.1),'CYNTHIA MA',MSGLEVEL=1,CLASS=A
//  EXEC    COBUCLG
//COB.SYSIN DD *
        IDENTIFICATION DIVISION.
        PROGRAM-ID.
            'PAYROLL'.
        AUTHOR.
            SANDY TREMAINE.
        INSTALLATION.
            ACCOUNTING DEPARTMENT.
        DATE-WRITTEN.
            DECEMBER 11, 1988.
        DATE-COMPILED.
            DECEMBER 18, 1988.
        REMARKS.
            THIS PROGRAM PROCESSES THE PAYROLL OF THE
            STAFF OF THE ACCOUNTING DEPARTMENT. IT IS
            DUE BY THE LAST DAY OF EACH WEEK.
    ********************************************
        ENVIRONMENT DIVISION.
        CONFIGURATION SECTION.
        SOURCE-COMPUTER.
            IBM-370.
        OBJECT-COMPUTER.
            IBM-370.
        INPUT-OUTPUT SECTION.
        FILE-CONTROL.
            SELECT FILE-1
                ASSIGN TO UT-S-SYSIN.
            SELECT FILE-2
                ASSIGN TO UT-S-SYSPRINT.
    ********************************************
        DATA DIVISION.
        FILE SECTION.
        FD  FILE-1
            LABEL RECORDS ARE OMITTED
            DATA RECORD IS EMPLOYEE-CARD-REC.
        01  EMPLOYEE-CARD-REC.
            02 SOC-SEC-NO       PIC X(9).
            02 EMPLOYEE-NAME     PIC A(20).
            02 HOURLY-RATE       PIC 99V99.
            02 FILLER            PIC XX.
            02 HOURS-WORKED      PIC 999V99.
            02 FILLER            PIC X(40).
        FD  FILE-2
            LABEL RECORDS ARE OMITTED
            DATA RECORD IS PRINT-AREA.
```

(continued)

Figure 4.7b
(continued)

```
        01  PRINT-AREA           PIC X(133).
        WORKING-STORAGE SECTION.
        77  WEEKLY-WAGE          PIC S9(4)V99 VALUE ZEROS.
        77  KOUNTER-W            PIC S9(5)V99 VALUE ZEROS.
        01  HEADING-1.
            02 FILLER            PIC X(30) VALUE SPACES.
            02 FILLER            PIC X(21) VALUE 'WEEKLY
PAYROLL REPORT'.
        01  HEADING-A.
            02 FILLER            PIC X(45) VALUE SPACES.
            02 TOTAL-A           PIC X(22).
            02 TOTAL-B           PIC $ZZZZZ.99.
        01  SUB-HEADING.
            02 FILLER            PIC X(4) VALUE SPACES.
            02 FILLER            PIC X(23) VALUE 'SOC-SEC-
NO'.
            02 FILLER            PIC X(15) VALUE 'NAME'.
            02 FILLER            PIC X(12) VALUE 'HOURLY-
RATE'.
            02 FILLER            PIC X(16) VALUE 'HOURS-
WORKED'.
            02 FILLER            PIC X(13) VALUE 'WAGE'.
        01  PRINT-LINE.
            02 FILLER            PIC X(5) VALUE SPACES.
            02 SOC-SEC-NO-P      PIC 9(9).
            02 FILLER            PIC X(5) VALUE SPACES.
            02 EMPLOYEE-NAME-P   PIC X(20).
            02 FILLER            PIC X(5) VALUE SPACES.
            02 HOURLY-RATE-P     PIC $ZZ.99.
            02 FILLER            PIC X(2) VALUE SPACES.
            02 HOURS-WORKED-P    PIC ZZZ.99.
            02 FILLER            PIC X(4) VALUE SPACES.
            02 WEEKLY-WAGE-P     PIC $ZZZZZ.99.
        **********************************************
        PROCEDURE DIVISION.
        PARA-1.
            OPEN INPUT FILE-1, OUTPUT FILE-2.
            MOVE HEADING-1 TO PRINT-AREA.
            WRITE PRINT-AREA BEFORE ADVANCING 1 LINES.
            WRITE PRINT-AREA FROM SUB-HEADING AFTER
ADVANCING 4 LINES.
        PARA-2.
            READ FILE-1 AT END GO TO PARA-4.
            MOVE SOC-SEC-NO TO SOC-SEC-NO-P.
            MOVE EMPLOYEE-NAME TO EMPLOYEE-NAME-P.
            MOVE HOURLY-RATE TO HOURLY-RATE-P.
            MOVE HOURS-WORKED TO HOURS-WORKED-P.
```

```
        PARA-3.
            COMPUTE WEEKLY-WAGE ROUNDED = HOURLY-RATE *
HOURS-WORKED.
            MOVE WEEKLY-WAGE TO WEEKLY-WAGE-P.
            MOVE PRINT-LINE TO PRINT-AREA.
            WRITE PRINT-AREA AFTER ADVANCING 2 LINES.
            ADD WEEKLY-WAGE TO KOUNTER-W.
            GO TO PARA-2.
        PARA-4.
            MOVE 'TOTAL WEEKLY-WAGE' TO TOTAL-A.
            MOVE KOUNTER-W TO TOTAL-B.
            WRITE   PRINT-AREA   FROM   HEADING-A   AFTER
ADVANCING 4 LINES.
        END-JOB.
            CLOSE FILE-1, FILE-2.
            STOP RUN.
/*
//GO.SYSPRINT  DD   SYSOUT=A ⎫  Control Statements
//GO.SYSIN DD *             ⎭
234455678ROBERT ALLAN       0320   04500 ⎫
345566789MARY JOHNS         0650   04000 ⎪
346677890JOHN JOHNSON       0575   03600 ⎬  Data
456678901JOAN KELLY         0850   05000 ⎪
467789542PETER SMITH        1050   02000 ⎪
346678234JAMES WELLS        0650   04000 ⎭
/*
```

Figure 4.7c
A payroll program written in FORTRAN.

```
    XM=100.0
    XMAX=1000000.00
    READ(5,10)PRINC,I
 10 FORMAT(F6.2,I1)
    RESLT=PRINC
    XI=I
    XI=I/XM
    GO TO (20,30,40),I
 20 DO 25 J=1,12
    XINT=RESLT*XI
    RESLT=RESLT+XINT
    IF(MAX-RESLT)100,25,25
```

(continued)

```
25 CONTINUE
   GO TO 50
30 DO 35 K=1,24
   XINT=RESLT*XI
   RESLT=RESLT+XINT
   IF(MAX-RESLT)100,35,35
35 CONTINUE
   GO TO 50
40 DO 45 L=1,36
   XINT=RESLT*XI
   RESLT=RESLT-XINT
   IF(MAX=RESLT)100,45,45
45 CONTINUE
50 WRITE (6,60)
60 FORMAT (1H1,15X,29HCOMPOUND AMOUNT CALCULATION,45X)
   WRITE(6,70)PRINC,I,RESLT
70 FORMAT(1H0,10HPRINCIPAL=,2X,F6. 2,5X,9HINTEREST=,2X,11,5X,7HRESULT
   1,2X,F10.2)
   GO TO 110
100 WRITE(6,80)
80 FORMAT(1H1,57X,5HERROR)
110 STOP
   END
```

Figure 4.7c
(continued)

2. The translation software performs the processing logic. Thus the programmer specifies the task(s) to be performed, not *how* they are to be performed.

3. Screen design features make it easy to show what you want written on a monitor and easy-to-choose features like highlighting, blinking, reverse video, and other accents. Changes are easy to make and the results are seen instantly (see Table 4.2 and Figure 4.8).

4. Fourth-generation languages can do *report writing*. The report is described by the user and the processor figures out how to produce it. For communications and networks, other features allow the user to specify who can access what information. Perhaps most important, fourth-generation language integrates all these features into one program. Figure 4.9 is an example of a fourth-generation language program.

Although fourth-generation languages have features that make it possible to solve problems on computers much more quickly than with the traditional software and its standard high-level languages, some of the disadvantages of previous languages may reappear. For example, often the language is designed to run on software that must be run on one particular type of machine.

```
PROGRAM EXERCISE ONE (INPUT , OUTPUT) ;

    (* THIS PROGRAM READS IN THE AMOUNT OF A LOAN AND PRINTS  *)
    (* THE PAYMENT NUMBER, THE MONTHLY INTEREST, THE INTEREST *)
    (* REPAYMENT, AND THE RESIDUAL BALANCE.                   *)

    CONST ANNUALRATE = 8 ; (* PER CENT *)

VAR NUMBER : 1 ..MAXINT ;
    INTEREST, REPAYMENT, LOAN, PAYMENT,
    RESIDUE, MONTHRATE : REAL ;

BEGIN
    READ(LOAN) ;
    WRITE ( 'AMOUNT BORROWED = ', LOAN:12:2) ;
    PAYMENT := LOAN/100 ;
    WRITELN ('':10, 'MONTHLY REPAYMENT =', PAYMENT:10:2);
    WRITELN ; WRITELN ;
    WRITELN (' NUMBER INTEREST REPAYMENT RESIDUE') ; WRITELN ;
    MONTHRATE :=ANNUALRATE/100/12 ;
    NUMBER := 1;
    RESIDUE :=LOAN ;
    REPEAT
      INTEREST :=MONTHRATE*RESIDUE ;
      REPAYMENT :=PAYMENT-INTEREST ;
      RESIDUE :=RESIDUE-REPAYMENT ;
      WRITELN (NUMBER:7, INTEREST:10:2, REPAYMENT:10:2, RESIDUE:10:2) ;
      NUMBER := NUMBER + 1
    UNTIL RESIDUE+RESIDUE*MONTHRATE <= PAYMENT ;
    WRITELN ; WRITELN ;
    WRITELN ('LAST PAYMENT =', RESIDUE+RESIDUE*MONTHRATE:10:2)
END
```

Figure 4.7d
PASCAL program for calculating the interest and balance of installment losses.

As you can see, the aim of fourth-generation languages is to allow people to program easily, naturally, and more quickly. This is accomplished by having people specify what they want and letting the computer create the instructions it will use in the program. In the same way that changes to high-level languages influenced program design through the introduction of flowcharting and pseudocode, fourth-generation languages have influenced design techniques. The new technique, called **prototyping**, is quickly becoming a part of the programming cycle. It allows the user to see exactly what will be available in the final program and to refine the specifications at an early stage of the program development. This, in turn, can save a lot of time later on.

Table 4.2   A Comparison of Third- and Fourth-Generation Languages

Third-Generation Languages	**Fourth-Generation Languages**
1. Geared for experienced programmers	1. Users as well as programmers may use it
2. Originally developed for a batch environment	2. Ideal for on-line environment
3. Deals with a file-related environment	3. Deals with a database-related environment
4. Must specify how to perform a task (see Figure 4-9)	4. Must specify what results are desired; the information system decides on the "how" end of the process
5. Generally requires many procedural instructions	5. Far fewer instructions are needed
6. Program code is not easy to learn or maintain	6. Commands make the language easy to learn and maintain

Figure 4.8
BASIC versus SQL—
finding average salary
for all senior
programmers.

```
BASIC

Open "SALARY,FIL" AS FILE # 1 MAP(SAL)
MAP(SAL) 10=6, FILL=73, POS=8, FILL=11, PAY=4
LET SUM=0
UNTIL EOF(1)
  GET #1
  IF POS= "SRPROG" THEN SUM=SUM + PAY
     NUMBR=NMBR +1
NEXT
PRINT "AVG. SALARY"; SUM/NMBR

SQL

  SELECT AVG(PAY)
    FROM PERSONNEL
    WHERE POS= "SRPROG"
```

Prototyping uses a fourth-generation language with its speed to create the first version of a program. Sometimes this version is used without further enhancement. Sometimes a faster production version is developed from the prototype using a traditional high-level language. The finished version may have additional parts not included in the prototype. Alternatively, the high-level language may prove faster in the finished version than the fourth-generation language would have been. Or the program may need a traditional language to fit together with previously developed programs.

Figure 4.9
This 4GL program was generated on a microcomputer using Informix–SQL.

```
{"AGREEMENT.PER" agreement information screen}

database
  local_18
screen
{

--------------------------------------------------------------------------------
                          LOCAL 18   IUOE
                          AGREEMENT INFORMATION
--------------------------------------------------------------------------------

Agreement Number   [f000   ]   Agreement Type [a0 ]    Originating District [al]

Agreement Name     [f001                            ]

Effective Date     [f002   ]   Expiration Date     [f003    ]

}
end
  tables
  agreement
attributes
f000 = agreement.cont_no;
  a0 = agreement.kind;
  al = agreement.orig_dist,
       upshift,
       include = (" ", "PB", "A", "B", "C", "D", "E", "RA");
f001 = agreement.cont_name,
       upshift;
f002 = agreement.start_date,
       format = "mm/dd/yy";
f003 = agreement.end_date,
       format = "mm/dd/yy";
instructions
   delimiters "::";
end

database local_18  end

define
        variable age integer
        variable cummage integer
        variable baseage integer
```

(continued)

Figure 4.9
(continued)

```
        variable br1      integer
        variable br2      integer
        variable br3      integer
        variable br4      integer
        variable br5      integer
        variable br6      integer
end

output
        report to printer

        left margin 0
        right margin 78
end

select
        birthdate,
        status
        from members
        where birthdate > 1
                and
            status >= 1
                and
            status <= 8
end

format
first page header
        let baseage = year(today)
        let age = 0
        let cummage = 0
        let br1 = 0
        let br2 = 0
        let br3 = 0
        let br4 = 0
        let br5 = 0
        let br6 = 0
on every row
        let age = baseage - year(birthdate)
        let cummage = cummage + age
        if (age < 20) then let br1 = br1 + 1
        if (age < 30 and age >= 20) then let br2 = br2 + 1
        if (age < 40 and age >= 30) then let br3 = br3 + 1
```

```
        if (age < 50 and age >= 40) then let br4 = br4 + 1
        if (age < 60 and age >= 50) then let br5 = br5 + 1
        if (age >= 60) then let br6 = br6 + 1
        let age = 0
on last row
        print column 36,
              "Local 18"
        print column 31,
              "Analysis of Member Age"
        skip 2 lines
        print "The average age in years is   ",
        cummage/count
        print "The number of members averaged",
        count
        skip 2 lines
        print "Analysis by Age Groups"
        print "----------------------"
        skip 1 line
        print "Age Group",
        column 30,
        "No of Members",
        column 45,
      "Percent of Members"
print "----------------------------------------------------------------"
print "Less than 20",
      column 30,
      br1,
      column 45,
      br1/count * 100
print "20 to 29",
      column 30,
      br2,
      column 45,
      br2/count * 100
print "30 to 39",
      column 30,
      br3,
      column 45,
      br3/count * 100
print "40 to 49",
      column 30,
      br4,
      column 45,
      br4/count * 100
```

(continued)

Figure 4.9
(continued)

```
print "50 to 59",
      column 30,
      br5,
      column 45,
      br5/count * 100
print "60 and over",
      column 30,
      br6,
      column 45,
      br6/count * 100

end
```

What Language Is Best for You?

From the general information presented thus far, we can see that each programming language level offers certain capabilities. Language also became more *people oriented* with each progression (see Figure 4.10). Hundreds of programming languages have been developed at these four levels—some very successful such as COBOL, FORTRAN, and BASIC; others not so widely used. The key question here is: What features must a language have to make it successful? Another question is: How do we know which language to use for solving problems?

The strengths and limitations of a programming language can be evaluated against a number of design features that are well known to programmers. The main features are:

1. Ease of use
2. Flexibility
3. Interactive programming
4. Level of control structure
5. Nonprocedural orientation
6. Portability

Ease-of-use is an attractive feature because the programming language can be learned quickly and more nontrained people can use it. Programs can also be written easily. Normally, an easy-to-use language incorporates English-like commands such as STORE, GET, SORT. High-level and fourth-generation languages provide easy-to-use commands.

The *flexibility* of a language has to do with how well the programming language can be applied and how easily it can be changed. Assembly language can handle virtually all types of processing chores. Yet to pro-

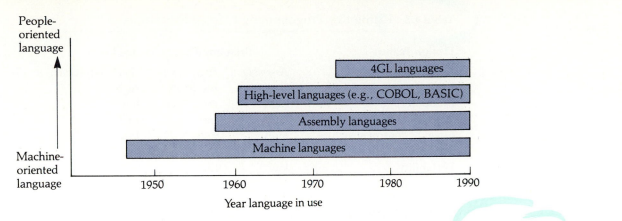

Figure 4.10
Progression toward people-oriented languages.

duce high-quality graphics displays, a graphics-oriented (special-purpose) programming language handles the job more easily and flexibly than high-level language.

Interactive programming allows the programmer to develop the program by entering program instructions directly into the computer. The immediate response helps in locating and correcting programming errors. The main drawback is that interactive languages take more time to execute than compiled languages. Interactive languages also tempt the programmer to speed through program design to get into coding.

An important design feature of a programming language is the level of sophistication of its *control structure*. A program design that has a clearly defined logical structure results in fewer errors and requires less development time to execute. Likewise, a programming language that is built around a logical control structure generates an easy to understand code. High-level languages such as PASCAL provide a sophisticated logic control structure.

An attractive language feature is one where the programmer simply describes the processing to be carried out, leaving the processing procedure to the translation software. Such *nonprocedural* accommodation makes it easier to develop business applications. The fourth-generation programming languages are best known for their nonprocedural commands.

The final design feature of a programming language is portability. *Portability* allows a program to be developed with a standard and used on different computers or on different operating systems. *Standardization* means the syntax rules of a programming language are similar across versions developed for different computers. That is, the source code is similar across different versions and is processed by different computers. When this feature is available, the program is said to be portable across computer systems. Table 4.3 shows the three programming language levels compared against the features we described.

Table 4.3   Rating Key Programming Language Features

Design Feature	Programming Language Level		
	Assembly	High-Level	Fourth-Generation
Ease of use	low	moderate	high
Flexibility	high	moderate	low
Interactive programming	low	moderate	high
Level of control structure	high	high	low
Nonprocedural orientation	low	low	high
Portability	low	high	low

With these features in mind, we go back to our key question: What language is best? As a general guideline, when efficiency is essential, the flexibility and performance of the assembly language is the preferred choice. In fact, most computer software incorporates subroutines in assembly language. In contrast, for day-to-day, high-volume business applications, the portability and power of high-level programs are very attractive. The popularity of assembler and high-level programming languages is illustrated in Figure 4.11. COBOL continues to be the most popular high-level programming language in business.

In selecting a programming language, several factors are considered:

1. *Performance requirements of the application.*   Applications that require quick response time and that run continuously in a multiuser environment cannot operate effectively by the programming language with lower efficiency. For example, an airline reservation system must provide under a 3-second response time to be satisfactory. In contrast, the daily update of a store's inventory has a longer "stretch time" for providing the daily report.

An application's language is invariably related to the performance requirements. To determine how these requirements are met, the programmer needs to know the capability of the language—that is, what can be programmed with the language. Obviously, this requires familiarity with the detailed features of the languages themselves. For example, COBOL is ideal for processing a large volume of data with low computational requirements. It is also easy to use because of its English-like commands. Yet COBOL is less efficient in execution than assembly language. FORTRAN is more efficient to code and it executes numerical data more efficiently than COBOL. COBOL is self-documenting and has powerful operators such as the command SORT. The overall conclusion, then, is for the programmer to determine the performance requirements of the application before deciding on the language for program coding.

2. *Machine-language fit.*   With the efficiency factor in mind, the next consideration is to know how well the programming language can be used by the existing computer system. In the case of a mismatch, the next best choice is another programming language. By the same token,

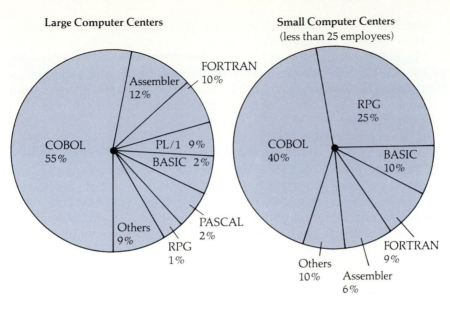

Figure 4.11
Use of key high-level programming languages in large and small computer centers.

there should be a check on how easily the new programming language operates on any new hardware that might be acquired in the future.

   3. *Time, money, and talent.*   A third factor in the selection decision is the time and funds allotted for a programming project and the skill level of the programmers assigned to the project. In situations where programming talent is limited, then easy-to-use programming languages would be a prime choice.

Generic Packages

In addition to assembly and higher-level languages and with the increase in the use of microcomputers, several types of generic packages have appeared. These packages are designed for a broad class of applications but also have a kind of language of their own. One example is LOTUS 1-2-3, which is a spreadsheet whose **macros** (special commands) give it a programming language capability. dBASE III Plus was designed for database management, but in addition to creating, entering, and retrieving data from databases, you can use it for programming. The primary function of these generic packages is highly automated and simplified, but additional capabilities can be obtained by using the special language that comes with the package. Other generic packages are available for word processing, graphics presentations, statistics, desktop publishing, scheduling, and many other general-purpose tasks that can be performed by computers.

   Generic application packages are just one type of software available today. Other types of software are more specific applications: college class registration, banking, doctor's office management, and MIS modeling of decision making and planning.

Probably three of the most important types of software today are database software, operating systems/utility software, and communication software. Database software is discussed in Chapter 6. Operating systems, utility software, and communication software are discussed in the next sections.

Operating System   An **operating system** is a special type of software that controls a large portion of the computer hardware resources when many users share the machine. It also provides an interface between application programs and hardware for many operations, especially input/output. Operating system commands are used to carry out users' requests. To control hardware resources, large general-purpose operating systems service database management, programming development, and even personal computing systems. They provide truly general-purpose services—on line and batch, local and remote, ensuring a balance of efficiency and response time requirements. An example of this kind of large operating system is IBM's Multiple Virtual Storage System (MVS).

In general, an operating system carries out several specific functions:

1. Manages the memory contents of a system.
2. Manages the set of application programs running in the system.
3. Enforces policies about who can use the computer and how long each user should have to wait for a turn.
4. Schedules multiple users on the computer.
5. Allocates memory for each user.
6. Checks user identification and passwords.
7. Imposes locks to protect shared resources.

Some operating system functions are explicitly requested by an application program while it is running. An operating system may be requested to READ, PRINT, GET STORAGE, WAIT, and so on. These are called or requested services that are a part of the overall capabilities of an operating system. Selected examples of operating system commands for the personal computer are shown in Table 4.4.

Table 4.4   Examples of Operating System Commands

Command	Meaning
COPY	Copies information from one file to another
DIR	Displays a list of names of all files
TYPE	Displays (lists) the contents of a file on the screen
RENAME	Changes a file's name
ERASE	Deletes the specified file(s)
DISKCOPY	Copies the data stored on one disk to another disk

The operating system commands are a special language. Each operating system has its own commands, but the functions are usually very similar. Once you know that there is a way to find out what files exist on a disk, you just have to find the command in the manual for the particular operating system. Commands can often specify extra information for the operating system to include when it carries out the task requested. This extra information is called a *command option.*

If command options are not used, the operating system uses standard options or default options. For example, if you ask for information and do not say where you want it to be put, the standard place (or default) is usually your display screen. However, you may have a choice, for example, specifying a printer or a storage file.

Utilities   In order to help microcomputer users who have little computer experience, **utility software** is available for special functions. There is utility software to make better use of the space on storage devices such as disks. Other utilities reorganize data by sorting a file or merging files. There are utilities to keep track of the use of resources on the computer and to analyze this usage. The programs that translate programs from high-level languages to the computer code are also utilities.

Both utilities and application programs must use the operating system to work with the computer hardware. This means they must use the specific commands of the operating system for the computer on which they are to be run. It is important that a software package not created on the system being used be compatible with the operating system.

Communication Software   The third type of software is *communication software.* Today, computers are not isolated machines working by themselves. Instead, they work with other computers using direct connections or transmissions over some distance. There are many kinds of local and wide area networks and modems to connect computers. Virtually all sizes and models of microcomputers, minicomputers, and mainframes may communicate with each other. Since so many kinds of hardware can be involved, software is often used to make the connections understandable from one machine to another.

Communication software must be able to handle sending and receiving the message as well as controlling the medium of transmission. Communication software features include storing and calling numbers, waiting for a transmission and then answering it, and saving the information being sent in addition to displaying it on a terminal.

Probably the most important part of communication software involves putting the message into the proper format (layout) for the medium. When two computers communicate, they have to agree on the format or protocol to be used. A *protocol* is a predefined procedure that specifies how computers communicate with one another. Factors like the speed of the message being sent, error checking, the codes being used, the method to delineate each byte of information and the ability of any one type of equipment to emulate another are all controlled by communication software. More on communication is covered in Chapter 7.

Application Development Without Conventional Programming

The 1980s have promoted the increasingly popular theme that anyone can easily develop applications on the computer without learning a conventional programming language. This opportunity is made possible by nonprocedural languages and techniques. The impetus behind this attitude is the increasing cost of traditional programming. In the United States the average cost of a ready-to-use programming statement is well over $10. The demand for new applications is rising faster than programmers can supply them. One alternative is to give end users a nonprocedural language that they can use to develop applications—therefore the phrase "application development without conventional programming."

The Software

There are several types of application development software suitable for end users:

1. Query languages
2. Report generators
3. Application generators
4. Parameterized application packages

A **query language** allows the user to enter, retrieve, or update data from the database without writing lengthy procedural instructions or defining the data format. The user can query (ask) the computer in an English-like format. For example, a query requesting a list of sales by branch for the months October and December may be:

```
LIST ALL SALES BY BRANCH FOR OCTOBER,DECEMBER
```

The computer produces the results by first sorting the data by month and branch, prepares a total for each branch, and produces a report in a user-acceptable format. These steps are performed directly by the computer. To do the same in a high-level language such as COBOL would require over 100 instructions.

Report generators allow users to extract information from existing files or databases. The report is described in a query language, giving the user control over the format and content of the output (see Figure 4.12). The computer figures out how to produce the report.

```
FILE          DECEMBER-SALES

HEADING...   'SALES PROFILE BY SALESMAN'

SUM SALES_SUMMARY BY SALESMAN,ITEM

LIST SALESMAN,ITEM,SALES_SUMMARY
```

```
              SALES PROFILE BY SALESMAN

SALESMAN       ITEM          SALES SUMMARY

ADAMS       Ribbon            119
            Printer           360
            Hayes modem       617

                            1,096

JONES       PC Plus         2,035
            dBASE             695

                            2,730

    .

    .

    .

JENSTER     Supplies          135
            Disks              85

                              220
```

Figure 4.12
Report generator output.

Both query languages and report generators are output oriented. They simply display or produce reports. In contrast, **application generators** are programs that produce entire programs to generate applications for end users and MIS professionals. For the end user, application generators can produce output in graph or chart form, arrange headings or instructions on a computer screen, and set up a procedure for accepting data entered into memory while simultaneously displaying the keyed data on the screen. For the MIS professional, an application generator can manage and edit data files, maintain processing requests, and protect records from unauthorized modification (see Figure 4.13).

A **parameterized application package** is a preprogrammed software package designed to run a specific application. For example, it is possible

Figure 4.13
How an application gen-
erator is used.

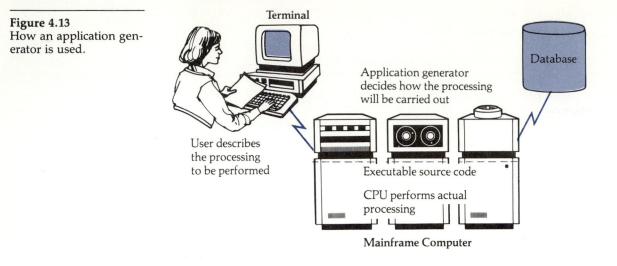

to acquire a package to keep track of the safe deposit boxes in a bank. The overall procedure is common to all commercial banks, yet some tailoring might be required for the user bank to fit the parameters of the organization. One example would be a parameter to debit the customer's checking account automatically by the annual box rental fee.

More and more application packages are marketed directly to end users. Many packages that run on the personal computer require no installation or computer skills.

User-driven computing is gaining popularity in industry. Applications are created with a generator in less time than it takes to write system specifications in traditional application development. The application development time is now measured in days rather than months. Interactive documentation is also created at the same time as the application. In contrast to these benefits are such possible pitfalls as the software firm that owns the packages going out of business, the great expense of modifying the package to meet the parameters, or the difficulty in maintaining the package. This means that a decision to acquire a package should be made only after a thorough evaluation of the benefits, drawbacks, and costs. Software acquisition is discussed further in Chapter 16 and end user computing is covered in Chapter 11.

Implications for MIS

What activities are taking place in software today that will influence programming in the future? The answer centers on ways for computers to solve problems more easily and quickly. More easily means a continuation of the trend of languages becoming simpler for people to use. The emphasis is on defining the problem and letting the computer solve it rather than coding the solution and letting the computer follow the steps. Many people feel this type of language will be increasingly important.

The other important factor is speed. How much faster can computers get? On one hand, some microcomputers are already faster than can be used for most jobs. One advanced feature is using multitasking and multiusers on microcomputers. When the UNIX operating system runs on a microcomputer, several users (multiusers) and/or one user can run several different programs (multitasking) on the same PC in the same way that a mainframe can be shared by many users and jobs. Microcomputers today are easily powerful enough to handle this, even though early microcomputers were not. With so much power, one user doing one task at the keyboard is too slow to keep the computer busy.

There is a general consensus that computers will not show significant increases in speed comparable to the jumps characteristic of earlier generations of computers. Instead, hopes for the future center on **parallel processing**. In parallel processing, several processors work together on part of the problem. They all work simultaneously and in parallel so the total problem is solved more quickly.

An example of a parallel program would be a job estimate. The materials cost and the labor cost could be computed in parallel on two different processors. This would be faster than first computing the materials cost and then the labor cost on one computer. In many ways, this creates situations similar to those seen in earlier stages of language development. For example, the programmer must decide details about matters such as:

- How many processors should be used?
- What part of the problem should be given to each processor?
- Are all processors working to capacity?
- Is one processor waiting for data from another?
- How does one processor know to which other processor to send specific data?

These problems create much more complicated programming tasks than any other programming languages faced. For people to understand what is happening in many processors at once makes programming much more difficult. Once again, then, we need to work on finding an easier way for humans to communicate with the computer. It has been said that parallel languages are still at the machine language stage of development. We have a long way to go to get to the "4GL" of parallel languages.

Summary

□ Effective software has four characteristics: Accuracy, good documentation, flexibility (handling a variety of transactions), and high performance. It may be developed in house, acquired off the shelf, or free-lanced. The in-house alternative requires competent and reliable staff. Cost/benefit analysis is also important.

□ Off-the-shelf packages are usually cheaper than in house ones, although they need to be modified and supported by a reputable software house. Organizations with no prior programming experience requiring customized work resort to contract programming.

□ Application programming transforms software design specifications into real inputs, files, and outputs. The program development cycle involves program design, coding, and testing. Program design is facilitated by flowcharting or pseudocode. Coding is the actual writing of program instructions that are later tested to make sure the program works to standards.

□ There are four levels of programming languages:
   1. *Machine language:* writing programs in codes tied directly to the computer.
   2. *Assembly language:* writing programs in English-like (symbolic) codes rather than machine codes. An assembler, then, translates the symbolic codes into machine codes for processing.
   3. *High-level language:* a procedural or problem-oriented language that performs tasks at a much higher level than assembly language. High-level languages such as COBOL and FORTRAN are compiled (translated) into special machine language for processing.
   4. *Fourth-generation language:* a nonprocedural language that requires fewer lines of code than a high-level language. The programmer needs only to specify the task, not how it is performed. The translation software does the rest that has to do with processing.

□ Three of the most important types of software today are database software, operating system/utility software, and communication software. Database software controls the operation of the database files. Operating system software controls the computer hardware resources. Utilities are programs that perform specialized functions such as reorganizing computer storage or data in storage. Communication software handles communications traffic between computers or between the end user and the host computer.

□ Deciding on the best language has a lot to do with features such as ease of use, flexibility, the interactive nature of the language, the level of sophistication of its control structure, nonprocedural orientation, and portability. Factors such as the requirements of the application, the machine-language fit, time, money, and talent constraints are also considered.

□ Today's emphasis on developing applications without programming in traditional languages is making it possible for end users to develop their own applications. This approach has also reduced the backlog and pressure on the organization's MIS personnel. Nonprocedural software includes:

1. *Query languages:* accessing or updating data by simple, English-like queries or commands.
2. *Report generators:* producing reports by simply specifying the format and content of the output.
3. *Application generators:* producing source code or entire programs to generate output in graph form, arrange headings, or set up a procedure for entering data for processing.
4. *Parameterized application packages:* designed to run specific applications. Changes in the programs are made to fit the parameters set by the organization.

□ User-driven computing is a definite trend for the future. It is easy, quick, and low cost, except when major modifications become necessary. If the software house goes out of business, it could turn the acquisition into a bad experience. Therefore, careful shopping is important.

Key Terms

Application generator
Assembler
Assembly language
BASIC
COBOL
Coding
Flowcharting
FORTRAN
Fourth-generation language (4GL)
High-level language
Machine language
Macro
Nonprocedural language
Object program
Operating system

Parallel processing
Parameterized application
 package
PASCAL
Procedural language
Prototyping
Pseudocode
Query language
Report generator
Software
Source program
Structured walkthrough
Utility software
Walkthrough: See structured
 walkthrough

Review Questions

1. Since the early 1980s, more and more people have been talking about software, software packages, and the like. Why the big fuss about software? In the context of its relationship to hardware, how important is software for application development? Elaborate.

2. If you were considering software for your firm, what characteristics would you look for?

3. How would one decide among in-house, off-the-shelf, and freelanced software? Discuss.

4. Where do application programs fit in the system development life cycle? Explain.

5. Distinguish between:
   a. Program design and coding
   b. Flowcharting and pseudocode
   c. Assembler and high-level languages
   d. Report and application generators

6. Documentation has been known to be a part of various phases of the system development life cycle. Where in program development is documentation required? Explain.

7. What is "structured walkthrough"? How does it relate to prototyping?

8. If high-level languages have to be compiled into machine code before the computer processes an application, why not code directly in machine language? Be specific.

9. What is the difference between an object program and a source program? Is a COBOL program a source or an object program?

10. Elaborate on the key features of fourth-generation languages. In what respect are they nonprocedural? Explain.

11. An operating system is an important piece of software for information processing. What does an operating system contribute to application development? How does it differ from utility software? Communication software?

12. What design features help in evaluating a programming language? How important are they? Explain.

13. If you were asked to select a programming language for a small firm with no MIS experience, what factors would you consider? Elaborate.

14. What is application development without programming? Discuss the features, the software, and your assessment of the future of this nonprocedural technique.

Application Problems

1. Leggett Furniture Company is a large retail chain in Charlottesville, Virginia. It was founded by Jack Leggett in 1951 as a mail order house catering to local residents. Today, Leggett Furniture has seven stores in

the city and two other stores in a neighboring suburb. Total annual sales exceed $40 million.

In June 1988, Mr. Holt, the company's executive vice president, decided to incorporate computer technology into the retail operations. He wants to implement a computer-based system that will perform two essential jobs. The first is a direct order entry system that will allow the salesperson to enter customer orders that include the items ordered, quantity, price, and delivery instructions. With this amount of data, the system should be capable of producing invoices and billing memos.

The second application is related to the first—an inventory control system. As orders are filled, the system must be capable of determining the remaining items on hand and must determine the inventory to be ordered so that there is always enough inventory to meet customer demands.

The company has no prior computer experience. It is considering whether to purchase the software packages off the shelf, since there are a number of such order entry and inventory control packages on the market. Management is also looking into the feasibility of hiring an outside consultant to develop the software and acquire the appropriate hardware to ensure its success.

QUESTIONS

a. Discuss the pros and cons of the two approaches considered by the firm. Which approach would you recommend? Why?
b. What issues are involved in introducing new software or applications to a firm with no prior computer experience?
c. Since Leggett is a business firm, how strongly would you recommend developing the software in COBOL? Why?

2. Organizations are becoming increasingly dependent on software to solve day-to-day problems. Information systems analysts and programmers know that software reliability is a number one issue. Enhancements and various maintenance details must be incorporated into existing software accurately and responsibly. It is also known that over one-third of the programs written fail sooner or later.

Suppose that a software error causes a bank's teller to be short $10,000. Who is responsible for the shortage? Supposing the software house that developed the software corrected the errors, how can the bank be sure that such errors won't recur? Be specific.

3. A third-year MIS student is faced with the decision of which programming languages to learn, if any. There are numerous arguments in favor of and against COBOL, BASIC, PASCAL, fourth-generation languages, and the like. Supposing the student is planning to work in the business sector, preferably in large computer centers, how important are high-level languages? Fourth-generation languages? Discuss in detail.

4. One of the worst-kept secrets about software is the quality of documentation. Most documentation seems to suffer from one of two problems: poor writing style or incomplete coverage. Some software developers are so anxious to reach the total market that they set the reading level at about the eighth grade and load the manual with so-called easy-to-follow charts. On the other extreme, some manuals are so full of technical details that only professionals can navigate them.

Obviously, a great deal is involved in developing a manual. The level of the end user must be identified. Then a balance of terms, procedures, illustrations, and exercises should all be made with the end user in mind. Suppose you were a supervisor of a department and you located a software package that meets your needs, but the documentation is inadequate. Would you acquire the package? What are your choices? If you were making a decision under tight time constraints, what options would you have? Explain.

Selected References

Alsop, Joseph. "4GLs Migrate to Micros." *Computerworld*, April 16, 1986, FOCUS/ 51ff.

Angus, Jeff. "Developers Pick BASIC For High Productivity." *Infoworld*, June 22, 1987, 11.

Barbary, Clifton. "A Database Primer on Natural Language," *Journal of Systems Management*, April 1987, 20–25.

Finkelstein, Richard. "Exploring SQL." *Data Based Advisor*, February 1987, 8ff.

Harrison, William. "Over the Rainbow in a Software Garage Shop." *Computerworld*, April 27, 1987, 63ff.

Jordan, John J. "Waging War Against Formidable Software." *Data Management*, May 1987, 31–36.

Joyce, Ed. "Software Bugs: A Matter of Life and Liability." *Datamation*, May 1987, 88–92.

Kolodziej, Stan. "4GLs Find a Home." *Computerworld*, May 6, 1987, FOCUS 47–48ff.

La Plante, J. "PC Managers Have Unique Set of Software Needs." *Infoworld*, June 22, 1987, 38.

Rosenthal, Morton. "Choosing Nonstandard Software: A Desktop Publishing Example." *Data Management*, May 1987, 30ff.

File Organization and Data Retrieval

Chapter Contents

Hard Disks

Among many microcomputer users, the hunger for disk storage space is never satisfied. Manufacturers are feeling the steady market demand for more and more storage as users push to upgrade their PC systems with add-in internal hard-disk drives.

For some users, the sheer volume of data they need to keep on hand simply compels them toward a hard-disk upgrade. Programs are becoming big storage consumers as they grow larger and more sophisticated, often requiring a hard disk. All the way down to the smallest of laptop computers, hard disks are making inroads as users look for better ways to organize and store their data.

When considering a move to increase storage space with an internal hard disk, buyers need to weigh four major factors. The first is storage capacity. The other considerations are reliability, data-access speed and, of course, price.

With hard drives storing anywhere from 10M bytes to 520M bytes, prospective purchasers must ask themselves how much storage space they will realistically require now and in the future. In general, said industry sources, applications requiring frequent and high-volume input/output operations can benefit most from hard-disk technology.

Analysts point out that speedy data-access times are most important when the disk drives are being used in multiuser environments, where the PC AT is often found. The complexity of hard-disk drives also makes reliability crucial. Because the read/write heads in a hard-disk drive hover above the disk surface by a distance smaller than a hair's thickness, damage to data can occur if the drive unit is moved or jarred while running.

Data-access times are fastest and most accurate in drives that use voice-coil technology, a method of electronically moving the read/write heads across the bands of data on the surface of a disk. The technology has dramatically cut data-access time compared with the older, band-stepping technology.

Market analysts who keep track of developments in the hard-drive field point out that prices have followed a steady downward trend in the past year without a serious drop in equipment quality. What is seen as the biggest issue is that the hard disk is starting to be more of a commodity product line and the prices are going down drastically. In any case, the main point of emphasis is data storage. It is the lifeblood of a company. It is too dangerous to lose.

—*Adapted from Paul Karon,* PC Week, *July 8, 1986, 97–105.*

AT A GLANCE

In a database environment, we need to organize and store data to produce the user's view as defined by the data model. We must also illustrate how data structuring is created through physical storage methods and how physical storage interfaces with DBMS for data storage and retrieval.

A file is organized in one of three types of structure: sequential, indexed sequential, or direct (random). Sequential organization means storing data in contiguous blocks within files on a disk. Indexed sequential organization uses an index to store and locate data. Random storage means placing records at locations determined by mathematical transformation of their keys. Each method has its advantages and limitations, depending on the application and processing requirements.

There are three ways of establishing relationships among records: physical proximity, pointers, and chains. Three data structures are used for ordering record relationships in flat files: sequential lists, chained lists, and inverted lists. In sequential lists, records must be duplicated for each order of record relationships. They are usually kept in sequential order, although they can be stored using any of the three types of file organization. In contrast, chained and inverted lists are used without record duplication. They are stored either in indexed sequential or random file organization.

By the end of this chapter, you should know:

1. How data is stored
2. The various file organization methods
3. How to establish relationships among records
4. The difference between pointers and chains in file organization

Introduction

An important beginning step in the technical structure of MIS is an understanding of the way files are organized and the way data is retrieved. This chapter will illustrate how data structuring is physically represented and describe how data relationships are created through various physical storage methods. The next chapter will explain the objectives of a database and the different ways data are structured. The goal is to design a database that meets the user's requirements.

To illustrate data organization and retrieval, consider an airline's flight system. An airline's main source of revenue is flying passengers to destinations. The primary entities are *passengers, flights,* and *cities.* Figure

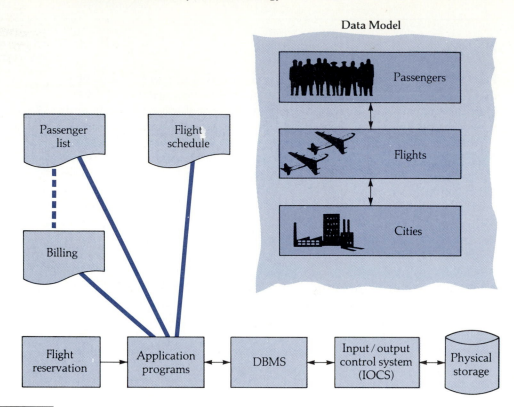

Figure 5.1
Airline flight system based on three entities of a data model: passengers, flights, and cities.

5.1 shows the data model representing these entities. All applications use common physical storage via the DBMS.

How Are Data Stored?

Before we show how data are stored, we need to know some basics about file hierarchy. A business may want to maintain specific data about each employee—name, address, phone, salary, and so on. Individual data items can be grouped into groups. For example, business firms group employees into departments. In this way employees who work in the accounting department are called accounting employees. Similarly, employees who work in the marketing department are treated as a marketing group for identification purposes. Therefore, through grouping, we can retrieve the entire set of employees at one time.

To fully understand data hierarchy in a file, we need to start with the lowest levels of data, called *data items* or *fields*. A group of related fields is called a *record*—for example, an employee record. A group of related records makes up a *file*. Data structured to meet a variety of information

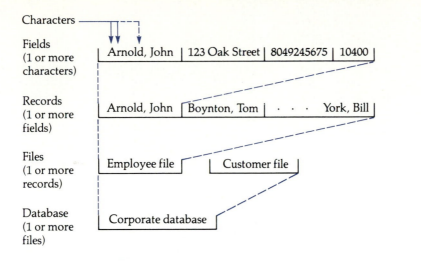

Figure 5.2
Data hierarchy within
the database.

requirements that can be integrated into a single file make up a *database* (see Figure 5.2).

Data Entities

The *data item* is a fact about some **entity** (a person, event, place, or thing) of potential interest or use. For example, in Figure 5.3 a salesperson is an entity about whom we may want to gather or store data. It is described by **attributes** (data items) such as salesperson number, name, sex, age, and height. An attribute takes on a value. The number "210-30-6800" is a value of the attribute "salesperson number"; "Neil Snyder" is a value of the attribute "name," and so on. An attribute takes on a single value at one point in time for a specific **instance** or occurrence of an entity.

The data item itself has characteristics such as name, size, and type. The *size* of each data item name specifies the number of characters or

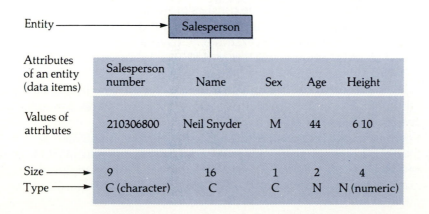

Figure 5.3
Attributes of an entity.
Note that although the
value of the attribute
"name" occupies 11
characters, the maxi-
mum allowable number
of characters is 16.

Figure 5.4
Record SALESPERSON:
an example.

Data item	Size	Type
Name	25	C (character)
ID number	4	N (numeric)
Title	8	C
Department code	2	C
Salary	5	N

numbers provided for stating its value. The *type* specifies whether the data item is alphabetic, numeric, or a special character. For example, in Figure 5.3 the size of the Name field is 16 characters and the type is C for "character." This means it can be alphabetic, numeric, or a combination of both. We can see a relationship between the five data items and the data entity "salesperson." Size and type describe the data items. Data entities and data items are used later in the next chapter.

Records and Files

A *record* is the next higher level in the hierarchy of data. It is a collection of related data items or associated attributes about an entity. Each record is assigned a descriptive name for identification purposes. For example, in Figure 5.4 a record about the entity "salesperson" contains name, ID number, title, department code, and salary. Size and type specifications are also identified. An instance of a record is one that has values associated with the data items, as shown in Figure 5.5. Figure 5.6 shows three record instances.

In contrast to a record, a file consists of a collection of logical records. Each record contains the same data items with different instances of the same data item values. For example, a payroll file must contain only payroll records, although each record is about a specific employee with a different name, ID number, title, and so on.

Files are stored on disk in some format. As we saw in Chapter 3, a disk is divided into a number of sectors. A sector stores a number of contiguous records (see Figure 5.7).

When an application program requests a record, the DBMS searches a buffer (an area in main memory) to determine if it is available from a previous inquiry. If found, the record is released to the application program. Otherwise, the record is fetched from disk storage. The infor-

Data item	Size	Type	Value
Name	25	C	J O H N E L A M . . . . .
ID number	4	N	0 7 2 1
Title	8	C	A U D I T O R
Department code	2	C	A 6
Salary	5	N	1 9 5 4 3

Figure 5.5
Record SALESPERSON:
a 44-character record.

mation, then, is transferred to main memory where it is processed by an application program.

To illustrate the data retrieval routine, suppose an airline agent requests access to flight 147. The DBMS effects the transfer of the first block to main memory. This means any other flights in the block (Denver, Fresno, etc.) are also available for access (see Figure 5.8).

File Organization Methods

A file is organized around three traditional types of structure: sequential, indexed sequential, and direct or random access. These types of file organization have various acronyms. For example, SAM stands for *Sequential Access Method*, ISAM (pronounced I-SAM) represents *Indexed Sequential Access Method*.

Sequential File Organization **Sequential organization** allows data to be stored in physically contiguous blocks of storage on a disk. Records are also in sequence within each block (see Figure 5.8).

The sequential nature of record storage means that records can only be added to the end of the file, which might then be sorted and stored

Salesperson Name	ID Num	Title	Dept. Code	Salary
John Elam	721	Auditor	A6	19543
Bruce Arnold	416	Analyst	M4	32110
Arthur Tremaine	190	Clerk	10	14001

Figure 5.6
Three record instances:
an example.

Figure 5.7
Disk storage layout.

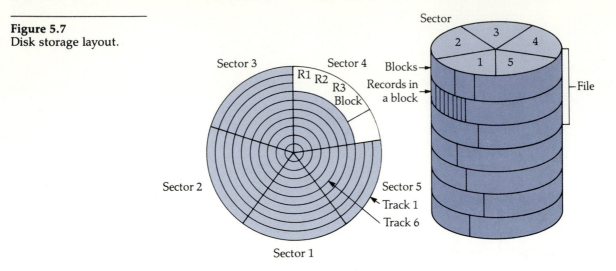

back to the disk in the correct order. This can be a very long process and is to be avoided whenever possible.

Sequential processing is ideal in situations when the entire file or a major portion of it must be processed at the same time. Take the example of generating labels for magazine mailing. The subscribers' file would probably be ordered by zip code. During a label print run, new subscribers would be added and the expired ones would be deleted. As shown in Figure 5.9, the processing cycle has three inputs: the original master file, the additions to the file, and the deletions from the file. The two outputs are the updated master file and the labels.

During processing, records are read from the three files. If the record read from the master file is not to be deleted and if the record to be added does not go before this one, the record is printed and then written to the new master file. Then another record is read from the master file. If the record is to be deleted, it is removed from the file, then another record is read from the master file. The next record is also read from the list of those to be deleted. When there is a record to be added to the file, it is stored in its correct position in the new master file by examining the keys of the master file and then writing the new record to the new master file at the time its key follows the one just written to the new master file.

Binary Search   If we need to access a record in a sequential file other than by key, the file has to be read until the record is found. But if the record in storage will be identified by record key, the process can be speeded up considerably by using the *binary search*. The basic concept to be examined is discarding one-half the file after each read.

To illustrate, suppose we have a file, shown in Figure 5.10. We wish to retrieve the record with key 340971. In the first probe, we look at the

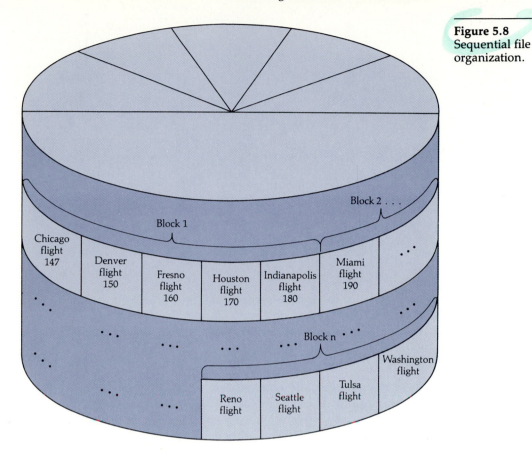

Figure 5.8
Sequential file
organization.

middle record in the file—key 370871. We know then that the record we seek is somewhere between the first and the middle record. In the second probe, we examine the record that is halfway between the first and the middle—the key is 330165. Our record (340971) is now between 330165 and the midpoint of the file. In the third probe, we read records sequentially until we locate the record with key 340971.

Using the binary search, we have found our record by reading three records—not half the file. The minimum number of records to be examined would be one if the target record were exactly the middle record in the file. The maximum number of records to be examined is:

```
NO PROBES = LOG₂ᴺ
N = FILE SIZE
```

Figure 5.9
Basic data processing cycle. At the end of the cycle, the updated master file becomes the "old master file." These data are used along with additions and deletions from separate tapes to update the master file and produce new reports.

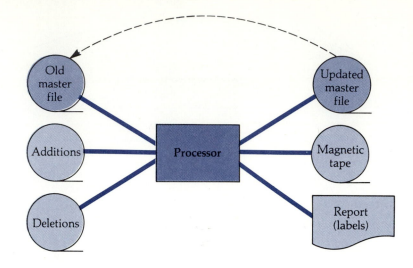

This maximum value occurs at four places in the file. If the desired record is either the first or last or lies on either side of the middle record, then the maximum number of probes will be required. In Figure 5.10, these would be record numbers 1, 100, 49, and 51.

Indexed Sequential File Organization   Like sequential organization, the **indexed sequential access method (ISAM)** initially stores the records in a file sequentially. (This scheme has been extended to VSAM, or virtual sequential access method, a process too complicated to explain within the scope of this text.) The difference lies in the use of an index to locate records. Both the physical storage of the records and the index entries are manipulated as records are added or deleted from the file.

There are three major components to an indexed sequential file. These are:

1. The **prime area**: a set of cylinders on disk reserved for storing the sequential file.
2. The **overflow area**: a reserved storage space on each cylinder to be used for records that logically belong to the sequential file but for which there is no space in the prime data area.
3. Index tables: used to find where records are or where they should be placed.

Figure 5.11 illustrates the three basic parts of an ISAM file. Assuming that the disk pack is made up of five platters, there are ten tracks per cylinder. One track on each cylinder has been reserved for the track index, while two tracks are to be used for overflow, leaving seven tracks for the prime data area. Space has been allocated for a cylinder index on another cylinder. Finally, a cylinder has been reserved for overflow.

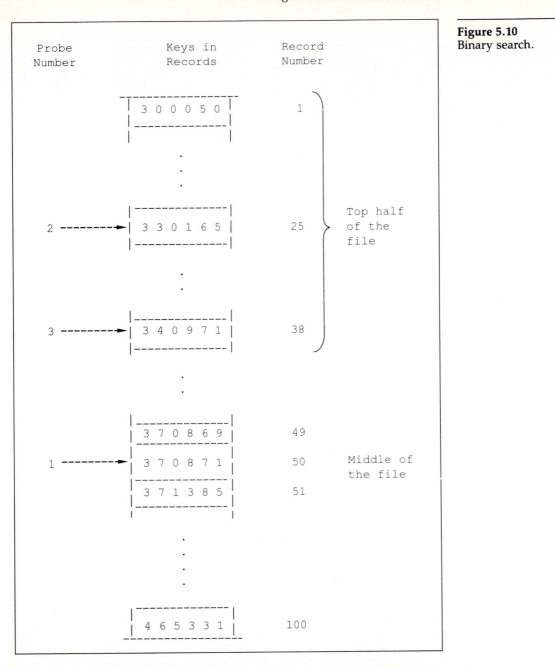

Figure 5.10
Binary search.

Initially, the file is loaded into the prime data area as would a sequential file. That is, each record is placed in key order one after the other. Figure 5.12 shows a portion of the loaded file. First, note the cylinder index. It is made up of two parts: The first indicates the highest key on the cylinder and the second is the address of the cylinder. Key 3610 is

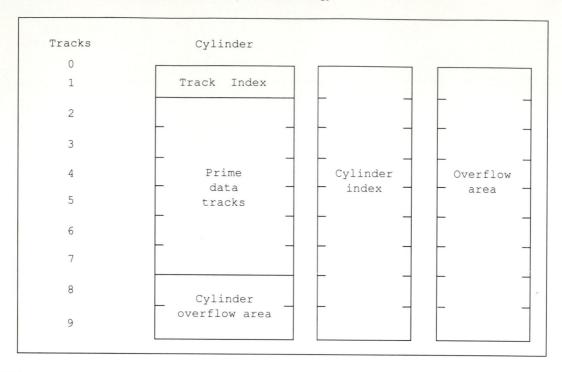

Figure 5.11
The major file areas of
an ISAM file.

the highest value in cylinder 0, the record whose key is 4500 is the last
record on cylinder 1, and 5975 is the highest key on cylinder 2. Examining
the track index for cylinder number 0, we see that each track has two
indexes: The first is for the normal track and the second is for any overflow. In this case, since the file has just been loaded, there is nothing in
overflow, so the track indexes are the same. For track 1 the highest key
is 3014, while for track 7 the highest key is 3610, as indicated in the
cylinder index.

   To find a record in the ISAM file, it is necessary to go through two
levels of indexes. To illustrate, suppose we want to find record 3003. First
we examine the cylinder index and find that 3003 is less than 3610 (the
highest key) on the first cylinder—cylinder 0. Therefore, our record would
be on cylinder 0. Note that had we been looking for record 4106, we
would have observed that it was higher than the highest key for cylinder
0, but lower than 4500, which is the highest key for cylinder 1. Record
4106, then, would be on the second cylinder.

   Returning to record 3003, the next step is to examine the track index.
We observe that this record is less than the highest key related to track
1. Therefore, the record is on track 1. This was easy, because there are
no records in the overflow areas.

   As the file is processed, records are added and deleted. Suppose we
add record 3010 to our file. By examining the cylinder index, we note

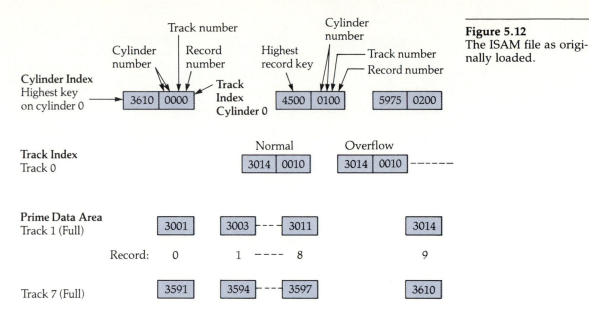

Figure 5.12
The ISAM file as origi-
nally loaded.

that it belongs on cylinder 0, because it is less than the highest key associated with that cylinder—3610. We then examine the track indexes for cylinder 0 and determine that the record should go on track 1 because it is less than the highest key associated with the track—3014. However, track 1 is full as a result of the initial loading of the file. Since we want the new record to be in sequential order, we move record 3014 to the overflow track (no. 8) and insert 3010 in its place on track 1. The records on track 1 are now in order, but one record (3014) is in overflow. As the indexes now stand, there is no way of accessing that record. To eliminate this problem, the indexes must be changed. The normal index for track 1 is changed to show that the highest record physically on the track is 3011. The address portion of the overflow index is changed to point to track 8, record 0. These changes are shown in Figure 5.13.

Now let us add record 3013 to the file. The cylinder index has not changed. As before, the record is to be on cylinder 0. When we examine the track index, we note that record 3013 is higher than the highest record on the physical track, 3011—therefore it will not go on the prime data track. However, it is lower than the highest record (i.e., 3014) in the overflow index for track 1. Therefore it goes into the next available space in the overflow area—in this case, record slot 2 on track 8. A pointer is added to record 3013 in overflow to point to record 3014. The address of the first record in overflow logically associated with track 1 is changed so that it is track 8, record 2. These changes are seen in Figure 5.14.

As the overflow chain associated with any track gets longer and longer, the time needed to process a record in that chain increases. The way to correct this is to reload the file so that all records are in the prime area

Figure 5.13
The ISAM file after addition of record 3010.

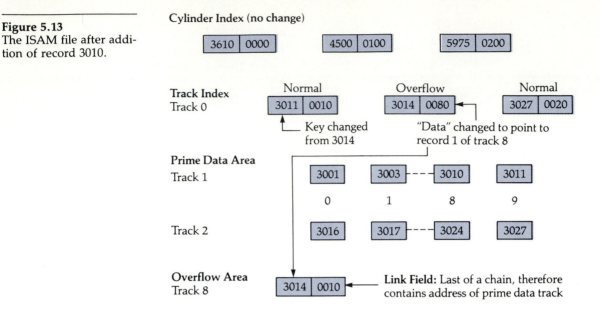

and none in the overflow areas. This is done by reading the records in logical order and writing them out to a new prime area in physical order.

The simplest approach to a deletion from the file is to merely put a flag in a field of the record that can be examined during processing. The record is ignored if the flag is present. The next time the file is reloaded, records with such flags are ignored and are not written out to the new file. An alternative approach is to reorganize the track each time a deletion takes place. If there is a record in an overflow area, it is moved back to the prime track and the indexes are updated.

Direct File Organization   Sometimes the primary use of a data file is rapid retrieval of existing records and addition of new records. In this case, the **direct access method (DAM)**, or **random file organization**, can be used. In this method the key of the record is converted to an address and the record is stored at that address. The records can be easily retrieved by merely applying the conversion formula and then going to that address to retrieve the record. There are three problems associated with this method:

1. Selecting a conversion formula that minimizes secondary problems
2. The strategy for dealing with multiple records mapping to the same address
3. The efficient utilization of memory

Key Transformation   The concept of converting a key to an address appears to be simple at first glance (see Figure 5.15). The trick is to find a way that has a minimum of synonyms for converting the key. A **synonym**, or

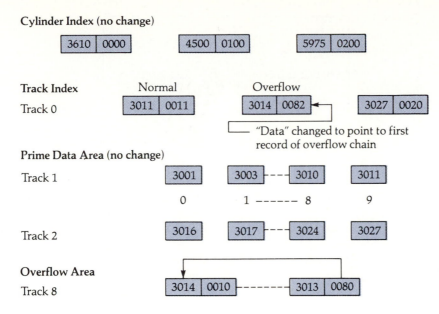

Cylinder Index (no change)

| 3610 | 0000 | | 4500 | 0100 | | 5975 | 0200 |

Track Index   Normal   Overflow

Track 0 | 3011 | 0011 | | 3014 | 0082 | ◄ | 3027 | 0020 |

└── "Data" changed to point to first record of overflow chain

Prime Data Area (no change)

Track 1 | 3001 | | 3003 |----| 3010 | | 3011 |

           0   1 ------ 8   9

Track 2 | 3016 | | 3017 |----| 3024 | | 3027 |

Overflow Area

Track 8 | 3014 | 0010 |-------| 3013 | 0080 |

Figure 5.14
The ISAM file after addition of record 3013.

collision, is said to take place when two or more records convert to the same physical address. We want our key conversion procedure to produce as few collisions as possible.

A large number of key conversion techniques have been developed. They range from very simple, such as folding, to extremely complex, such as radix conversion (which we will not discuss in detail). *Folding* is selecting some columns from the key and bringing them together in a different order to produce the address. In Figure 5.16, the key 18JW1735 produces the key 311835. Note that the letters have been converted to numbers by substituting their ordinal value in the alphabet: J = 10 and W = 23. This procedure is quite satisfactory in some cases. Perhaps the most important disadvantage of folding is that the address produced can be anywhere in memory. This means that other data can be overwritten unless a large area is reserved for these records, such as a disk pack.

One of the more commonly used conversion techniques is *prime number division*. In this procedure, an area in secondary memory is set aside for the file in question. Then the key is divided by the area size to produce an address guaranteed to be in that area by virtue of the division process. Making the area size a prime number is highly recommended, as it tends to reduce the number of collisions.

Let us assume that we have a file containing 1100 records to be stored as a direct file. We will allocate 2501 storage spaces and place one record

Figure 5.15
File organization: key transformation.

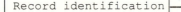

| Record identification | → | Key transformation | → | Record location |

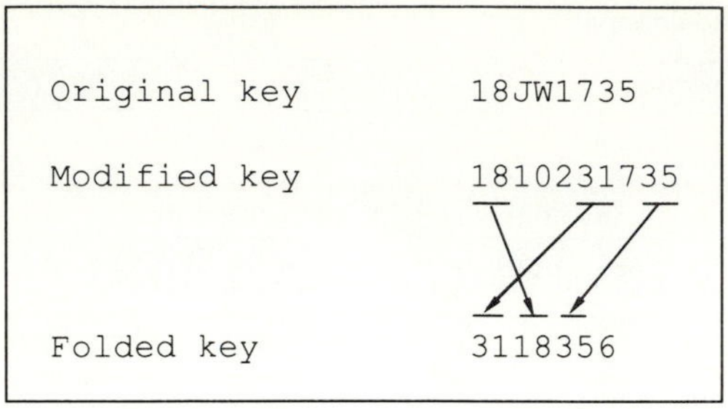

Figure 5.16
Key conversion by
folding.

```
Original key          18JW1735

Modified key          1810231735

Folded key            3118356
```

in each. By dividing each record key by 2501 and discarding the quotient, the remainder will be our address. The remainder will be a number between 0 and 2500. By adding 1 to this number, we have the range of addresses we want—1 to 2501.

To illustrate, if the first key is 3986432, we divide it by 2501, resulting in a remainder of 2339 + 1 = 2340 (see Figure 5.17). The record whose key is 3986432 will therefore be put in location 2400. Each key, in turn, will be transformed to a physical address in the same way. If a query is received for some data from the record whose key is 3986432, the query software will make the same transformation. Then it goes to location 2400 to find the record, assuming no synonyms exist at that address.

Synonyms   We mentioned earlier that a synonym or collision exists when two or more records have the same physical address. Let us assume that a record whose key is 6487432 is to be added to the file illustrated in Figure 5.18. You see that both records 3686432 and 6487432 have the same address—2400. We want to place the new record 6487432 at address 2400. But record 3686432 is already there. We have a collision or synonym.

Finding this synonym is not an unusual event. Lots of record keys will result in the same physical location. In fact, we can predict the number under certain conditions. Figure 5.19 shows the number of synonyms

Figure 5.17
Prime number division:
an example.

```
                         1593
            2501  /  3986432
                     3984093
                     ───────
                        2339


        Quotient   =   1593
        Remainder  =   2339
        Address    =   2339 + 1 = 2400
```

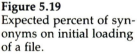

$$
\begin{array}{r}
2593 \\
2501 \overline{\smash{\big)}\, 6487432} \\
6485093 \\
\hline
2339
\end{array}
$$

```
Quotient  =  2593
Remainder =  2339
Address   =  2339 + 1 = 2400
```

Figure 5.18
Prime number division.

to be expected on the initial loading of a direct file for various load factors. The load factor is the designed percent utilization of the storage space. In our illustration, it is 1000 divided by 2500, or 40 percent utilization. From Figure 5.19, we can expect about 19 percent, or 190 synonyms, on the initial loading of this file.

There are two basic methods of dealing with synonyms: chaining and contiguous placement. *Chaining* means adding another field to each record. If a synonym occurs, we search sequentially for the next open space and place the new record there. The record address is placed in its normal home address. Let us see how this would be applied to our previously discussed pair of records with the same storage address. Assume that after location 2400 was found occupied when the second record arrived, a sequential search through the file area showed the first unused space

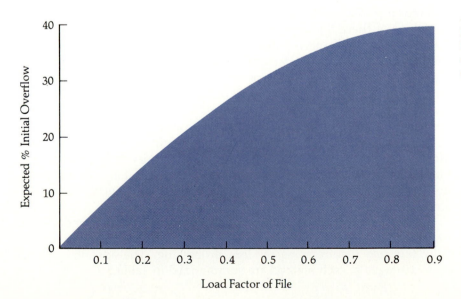

Figure 5.19
Expected percent of synonyms on initial loading of a file.

Figure 5.20
Record storage using
pointers.

Location	Record	Link
2400	6487432	2478
.	.	.
.	.	.
.	.	.
2478	3686432	*

was at 2478. Without the use of pointers, the record would go into the same spot. The procedure without pointers is, if the home address of the record is occupied, to look forward until the first unoccupied slot is found. The record is then stored there (see Figure 5.20).

Space Utilization   A direct file must be lightly loaded to achieve good performance. This means we are trading off space economies with time economies. The question facing the database system designer is the user's requirement for quick response against the low utilization of the secondary storage system. But if a direct access file is to be used, then low storage utilization invariably follows or performance will suffer.

Which Method Is Best?

There is no one best method for file organization. Each of the three basic methods just discussed serves a purpose. There are literally hundreds of variations of these file organization methods and even combinations of them. The systems analyst must decide which method best serves the needs of the system being designed. Many applications can well use the sequential methods. Systems such as payroll and subscription fulfillment require every record to be processed extracting information or printing. There is no need for random processing in such applications. In fact, random processing would seriously slow down the application.

For some systems, sequential processing would be a very poor choice. Most on-line interactive systems fall into this category. When the system must quickly react to a request such as verifying credit data, selling airline tickets, updating financial data, or checking bank balances, the direct access method is very frequently selected.

Finally, indexed sequential falls between sequential and random file organization—that is, systems that require a file to be processed sequentially but also require some random processing. The advantages and disadvantages of each method are summarized in Table 5.1.

Table 5.1 Advantages and Disadvantages of File Organizations

File Organization Method	Advantages	Disadvantages
Sequential	· simple to design · easy to program · variable length and blocked records available	· records cannot be added to or updated in the middle of the file
Indexed sequential	· records can be inserted or updated in middle of file · processing may be carried out sequentially or randomly	· processing is occasionally slow · periodic reorganization of file required
Random	· very fast access to a record · records can be inserted or updated in middle of file · better control over record allocation	· calculating address required for processing · variable-length records nearly impossible to process · sequential processing a bit messy

Establishing Relationships

Traditional file organization methods are inadequate for database processing. A DBMS must go beyond these methods by creating and maintaining specialized data structures for ordering record relationships. Before we discuss these structures, we need to demonstrate briefly how record relationships are formed in physical storage. There are three ways of establishing relationships: by physical proximity, pointers, and chains.

Physical Proximity

In physical proximity, records are stored sequentially and sorted on common keys to imply the relationship. Recall the overall data model in Figure 5.1, depicting *passengers* and *flights*. There is a many-to-many (M:N) relationship, which suggests that many passengers can have reservations on many flights. We could implement the relationship between passengers and flights by physical proximity with a file laid out as shown in Figure 5.21.

To use the file, we look up passenger number (key) and then read the flight record(s) until a new passenger number is detected. The problem with relationships via proximity is its *unidirectionality*. In our example, it is easy to find the flights reserved for a passenger, but searching for passengers on a given flight could be time consuming because of the sequential arrangement of the file.

Passenger 1	Passenger 1 Flight 147	Passenger 2	Passenger 2 Flight 147	Passenger 3	Passenger 3 Flight 147 . . .

Figure 5.21
Record relationship by
physical proximity.

Pointers

Some entities are reached through other entities via **pointers**. Suppose
in our passenger/flight model (see Figure 5.22), we decided to add the
"stops" a flight will make. The entity "Stops" has no direct access point.
It is accessed only via the "Flight" entity. To implement the relationship,
Flight-to-Stops, we add a direct pointer from the "Flight" entity to the
"Stops" entity. In Figure 5.23, we could have the Houston flight that
makes two stops: Waco and Austin.

Chains

A **chain** is created when records are connected by means of pointers.
Several approaches to chaining are beyond the scope of this discussion.
In a simple chain, for example, records are ordered in logical order by
key. The records can be arranged in any physical order; the logical order
is maintained by pointers, as shown in Figure 5.24.

Supporting Data Structures in Ordering Records

We use three supporting data structures in representing record relationships: sequential lists, chained lists, and inverted lists.

Figure 5.22
Adding stops to flight
model.

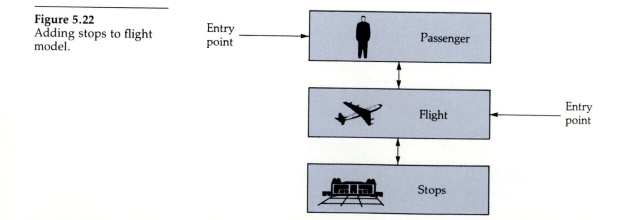

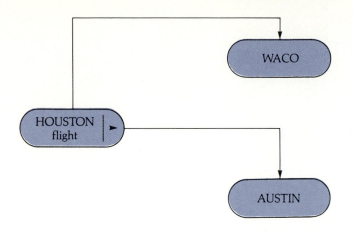

Figure 5.23
Use of pointers.

Ordering Records with Sequential Lists   Data listed in sequential order uses a sequential file organization format and a **sequential list** structure. Figure 5.25a illustrates a file that can be stored using sequential, indexed sequential, or random file organizations. To produce a passenger list, we process the records in passenger-number sequence, as shown in Figure 5.25b. Likewise, to produce a flight schedule, we process the records by flight-number sequence (see Figure 5.25c).

This procedure requires two sort runs, which is time consuming. To have all possible schedules, we can store a sorted file by as many schedules as there are variables. But storing multiple copies by different fields is a waste of storage space and creates data integrity problems. The alternatives are to use either *chained lists* or *inverted lists*.

Ordering Records with Chained Lists   The main purpose of **chained lists** is to associate parent-child records—for example, to relate Flight to Passenger. To create a chained list, a field is added to each record to hold the address of the next record in sequence. In Figure 5.26, our file has a passenger chain field that links record 2 (first sequential passenger number) to record 4 (second sequential passenger number); record 4 to record 1, and so on, until the entire file is linked sequentially by passenger

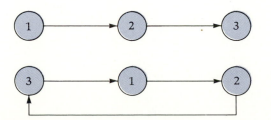

(a) **Simple Chain**

(b) **Simple Chain Where Physical Order Differs from Logical Order**

Figure 5.24
Simple chain.

FLIGHT-Record

Passenger-Number	Flight-Number	Departure-Time
110	147	8
014	150	10
206	160	8
107	180	10
610	170	11
230	190	11

(a) File

Passenger-Number	Flight-Number	Departure-Time
014	150	10
107	170	10
110	147	8
206	160	8
230	190	11
610	180	11

(b) File Sorted by Passenger Number

Passenger-Number	Flight-Number	Departure-Time
110	147	8
014	150	10
206	160	8
610	170	11
107	180	10
230	190	11

(c) File Sorted by Flight Number

Figure 5.25
FLIGHT data stored in
sequential lists.

Record-number	Passenger-number	Flight-number	Department-number	Passenger chain record number
1	110	147	8	3
2	014	150	10	4
3	206	160	8	6
4	107	180	10	1
5	610	170	11	0
6	230	190	11	5

Beginning of passenger list = 2

Figure 5.26
Sorting a flat file by passenger name using chained lists.

Record-number	Passenger-number	Flight-number	Department-number	Passenger chain	Flight number chain
1	110	147	8	3	2
2	014	150	10	4	3
3	206	160	8	6	5
4	107	180	10	1	6
5	610	170	11	0	4
6	230	190	11	5	0

Beginning of passenger list = 2
Beginning of flight list = 1

Figure 5.27
Sorting records using two-chained lists.

number. Note that the last passenger number (record 610) has no chain; therefore, it is 0.

This procedure essentially substitutes for a sort run that otherwise is required to produce a specific list. Using our example in Figure 5.25b,c, the two-sort FLIGHT file may be ordered with two chained lists; one list maintains the passenger number sequence. Maintaining the chain, however, is very expensive (see Figure 5.27).

Ordering Records with Inverted Lists   An **inverted list** is just an *index* on a given field. It is a copy of the list that has been inverted into a given sequence and in which duplicated data have been replaced by chains (pointers) to the original list (see Figure 5.28). To process the records sequentially, we process the index sequentially, which reads the records in the Flight file as indicated by the pointers.

In summary, we have seen three supporting data structures for ordering record relationships in files: sequential lists, chained lists, and inverted lists. Sequential lists can be used on condition that records be duplicated for each order of record relationships. They can be stored using any of

Record- number	Passenger- number	Flight- number	Department- time
1	110	147	8
2	014	150	10
3	206	160	8
4	107	180	10
5	610	170	11
6	230	190	11

(a) Flight Record

Passenger- number	Flight- number	Department- time
014	150	10
107	180	10
110	147	8
206	160	8
230	190	11
610	170	11

**(b) Flight Records Inverted
on Passenger Number**

Passenger- number	Record- number
014	2
107	4
110	1
206	3
230	6
610	5

Figure 5.28
Inverted list: an
example.

**(c) Inverted List (pointers refer duplicated
data to the original file)**

Figure 5.29
Supporting data struc-
tures and file organiza-
tion for flat files.

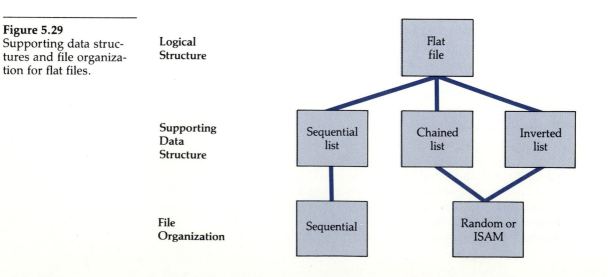

Logical
Structure

Supporting
Data
Structure

File
Organization

the three types of file organization (sequential, indexed sequential, or random), although they are commonly kept in sequential files. In contrast, chained and inverted lists are used without record duplication. They may be stored either in indexed sequential or random file organization, although they are always stored on random organization files (see Figure 5.29).

Implications for MIS

File design and management is a complex task. It determines how well data are accessed and the flexibility expected by the end user. Management information systems often suffer from inadequacies stemming from poor file organization and design. Inferior file design results from poor planning, inattention to alternatives, and tradeoffs such as storage versus speed that have to be considered. The design process requires managerial judgment as much as technical skills. Therefore, both the MIS manager and the end user should be familiar with basic file organization and processing methods to ensure the development of efficient and effective management information systems.

There are several important file management issues to consider. File security, file recovery, and file administration are examples. Standards and procedures must be set to ensure that files can be recovered quickly and accurately after a disaster. Since the objective of a MIS is to create a system that is both technically balanced and behaviorally acceptable, it is important to secure management cooperation and support at all levels. Related to file design is database design, which takes on a more involved technical framework and can affect the organization as a whole. Management and technical considerations of a database system are covered in the next chapter.

Summary

□ The hierarchy of data begins with the data item—the lowest level of data. Data items are grouped together to form a record that, in turn, is grouped to form a file. Interrelated files represent a database.

□ Data is stored on disks for on-line, real-time environments. A disk is divided into sectors, which, in turn, are divided into blocks. Each block stores data records.

□ A file is organized around three types of structures: sequential, indexed sequential, and direct or random.

   a. *Sequential* organization means storing data in physically contiguous blocks within files on a disk. To access a record, previous records within the block are scanned. Sequential file organization is used by DBMS for producing journal files.

b. *Indexed sequential* organization uses an index to locate records. Indexes are arranged in key sequence in a multilevel format. One index points to the next level index until the lowest level index points directly to the data in the prime area.

c. *Random (direct) file organization* consists of records stored randomly throughout the file. They are accessed via addresses that specify record locations on the disk.

▫ There are three ways of establishing relationships in physical storage: by physical proximity, pointers, and chains.

a. *Physical proximity.* In this format, records are stored on common keys to imply the relationship. The main problem with this design is its unidirectionality.

b. *Pointers.* Direct pointers are used in cases where entities with no direct access point are reached.

c. *Chains.* A chain is created when a series of records are connected by means of pointers. A simple chain arranges records in logical order by key. The logical order is maintained by pointers.

▫ There are three supporting data structures for flat files:

a. *Sequential lists.* Data listed in sequential order uses a sequential file organization format and a sequential list structure.

b. *Chained lists.* Chained lists keep records in logical order. To create a chained list, a field is added to each record to hold the address of the next record in sequence. Chained links demonstrate a definite advantage over sequential lists when adding or deleting records.

c. *Inverted lists.* An inverted list is just an index on a given field. It is a copy of the list that has been inverted into a given sequence and in which duplicated data have been replaced by chains to the original list.

Key Terms

Attribute	Inverted list
Chain	Overflow area
Chained list	Pointer
Collision: See synonym	Prime area
Direct access method (DAM): See random file organization	Random file organization
	SAM
Entity	Sequential list
Indexed sequential access method (ISAM)	Sequential organization
	Synonym
Instance	

Review Questions

1. How are data stored on a disk? Illustrate.

2. There are three methods of organizing files. Explain each method and give an example.

3. Explain the main features and differences between indexed sequential and direct file organization. Which method is ideal for answering inquiries? Why?

4. What is the function of the prime area in disk storage? The index area?

5. According to the text, indexed sequential storage arranges indexes in key sequence in a multilevel format. Illustrate this procedure using an example of your own.

6. Distinguish between:
   a. Chain and pointer
   b. Chained list and inverted list

7. What alternative approaches are used in addressing records?

8. Contrast and compare three major means of establishing relationships.

9. How do pointers differ from chains? Give an example.

10. How are records ordered with sequential lists? Give an example to illustrate.

11. According to the text, chained links demonstrate a great advantage over sequential lists when adding or deleting records. Explain in detail.

12. What is an inverted list? How are records ordered with inverted lists? Explain.

Application Problems

1. The following is a list of six U.S. presidents presented in random order:
Dwight Eisenhower
Richard Nixon
Herbert Hoover
Lyndon Johnson
Ronald Reagan
George Washington

QUESTIONS

a. Organize the presidents using a linked list.
b. Using the linked list, show how the pointers are rearranged when we logically delete Herbert Hoover.
c. Create a circular linked list.

2. In August 1985, the National Bank of Elgin decided to launch a comprehensive review of its MIS operations. A team of four vice presidents and an outside consultant spent five weeks reviewing processing procedures, end user activities, the existing information systems, and MIS personnel.

The outcome of the assessment was a report detailing the status of the MIS and a set of recommendations to provide an integrated database environment for the four major departments of the bank: installment loan, commercial loan, operations, and trust. The proposal was well received and was accepted as a statement of direction to lead the bank through the 1980s.

It was apparent to top management that they had developed applications with no regard to possible usage by other end users. There was no database environment. For example, when an installment loan officer processed a loan application, he needed information about the customer's checking account, past loan experience (and payments) with the bank, whether or not he/she had a savings account, and so on. Getting such information meant calling separate departments that would retrieve information through individual applications. Consequently, the bank was highly labor intensive and loan decisions took as long as five working days.

With this in mind, there was considerable pressure to go the database route. A database committee was formed. Selection criteria were quickly agreed upon and a request for proposal was drafted and mailed to three DBMS vendors for a response.

QUESTIONS

a. What can we say about the makeup of the initial team? Elaborate.
b. Evaluate the approach taken by the bank in selecting a DBMS.
c. Are you satisfied with limiting the choice of vendors to three? What criteria should be used in selecting vendors? Be specific.
d. Processing checking and savings accounts is usually sequential, although the setup of the files is invariably random for quick data retrieval. What characteristics do you expect a proposed DBMS to provide? Explain.

Selected References

Athey, Thomas H. and Zmud, Robert W. *Introduction to Computers and Information Systems With Basic.* Glencoe, Ill.: Scott Foresman, 1986, 199–214.

Awad, E. M. "File Organization and Design Methods." Working paper, University of Virginia, 1987.

Senn, James A. *Information Systems in Management* (3rd ed.). Belmont, Calif.: Wadsworth, 1987, 286–328.

Database Management

Chapter Contents

Designing a Database Application

Frequently, people inadvertently buy a database that isn't capable of providing the functions they seek. They wind up being unhappy with the product and blame the database manager. In one application, for example, a database manager was asked to keep a customer file on a PC. Computer memory was large enough to hold the file which could reside on one floppy disk. It was assumed that there would be no problem. And there wasn't—until it was time to print mailing labels for a promotional mailing to the customer list.

The program wouldn't print labels three in a row as required by the company. A new database manager was subsequently purchased, one that could handle this capability. This program worked . . . and worked . . . and worked. Because the printer was so slow, it took all day to print the customer list. That wasn't the program's fault, but it got the blame.

The first problem involved a product that wasn't designed to do the task that was required. The second problem was more basic. It turned out that this PC/printer combination shouldn't have been used for this application at all. It could do the job, but at a terrific cost in wasted time.

The first step in designing a database application is selecting a program that meets the needs of the application. Determining how the system will operate is the second step. Take the case of John Mangano, assistant director of the corporate research division of the Traveller's Insurance Corporation. He has developed a PC AT-based database and application program that predicts the insurance exposure the company faces in the event of natural disasters, like hurricanes or earthquakes. When Hurricane Gloria steamed up the East Coast last fall, the system was fairly accurate in predicting the amount of claims to expect.

In operation, the program develops a model of a hurricane, using factors such as wind speed and area of effect, from parameters that operators enter into the computer. These parameters are modified to take account of local conditions. For example, the winds will be less in a city than in open country, for a given storm. Then the adjusted hurricane is mapped onto the likely locations of a storm landfall, with the locations pulled from the place-names database, and the program develops a report of the structures that will suffer damage given the statistical probability of damage at a given wind speed. This number, multiplied by the number of policies in that region, is the estimated number of claims.

Designing and implementing a database application involves several people in a department or even all over the company. It is a long and complex task, but it will yield the proper results, if the correct steps are followed.

—*Adapted from David Gabel*, PC Week, *April 29, 1986, 9–13.*

AT A GLANCE

A database is a necessity for virtually every MIS installation in business. The primary objectives of a database are accuracy and integrity, clarity and ease of use, controlled redundancy, data independence, fast recovery from failure, powerful end user languages, and privacy and security.

In a database environment, a database management system (DBMS) is the software that manages and controls data, determines data sharing, and protects data from unauthorized access. In addition, it enforces procedures for data integrity, controls concurrent processing, and provides utility services for database maintenance.

Data are structured according to a data model. Relationships between entities make up a data structure. The data model represents data structures that are described to the DBMS in data definition language. Relationships between entities may be one to one, one to many, or many to many. Data structuring in a DBMS determines whether the system can create 1:1, 1:M (many), or M:N relationships between entities.

In database design, two major ways of conceptualizing data are considered: the logical view and the physical view. The logical view is what the user perceives. The physical view is the way data are actually stored. Database design involves normalization, which simplifies relationships and establishes logical linkages between files without losing information.

By the end of this chapter, you should know:

1. The objectives of the database and the role of DBMS
2. How data are structured
3. The differences among hierarchical, network, and relational structures
4. The process of normalization

Introduction

A decade ago, database processing was an exotic term, of interest only to large corporations with the largest computers. As database software became available on smaller computers, MIS managers and end users quickly saw it as a tool for decision making. Although not all MISs require this technology, database processing has become a necessity for virtually every MIS installation in business.

Databases favor people at the expense of computers. End users are able to access and update information more effectively through a database than through a conventional file system. With the continued rise in the cost of labor and decline in the cost of computers, the database approach is attractive because it trades people resources for machine resources.

The outcome is a significant increase in the number of database applications. Since the early 1980s, the availability of database packages for the microcomputer (some under $300) places database applications within the reach of every user.

What Is a Database?

Suppose you were the president of a large mail order house and the following activities were taking place:

- Customers order merchandise for shipment.
- Merchandise is shipped to customers.
- Customers are billed for merchandise ordered.
- Sales trends are observed.

Coordinating these activities requires different areas within the company to share information. Historically, each department has been responsible for its "own" information. There are two problems with this practice:

1. *Problem of duplication.* The sales department, for example, might have its own billing application and the purchasing department its own computer-based inventory system. Each department commits resources to a system that accomplishes many of the same objectives—data storage, retrieval, and so on. The potential for duplication can be enormous.

2. *Problem of coordination.* If the sales department acknowledges a customer's order, its records show certain merchandise has been ordered. If the billing department does not have information about the order, the order could easily go unnoticed. Something must be wrong.

We can see, then, that when data are stored in separate files for each application, managing information becomes difficult. As shown in Figure 6.1, a system without a database requires a sort/merge method that combines selected data items from several files to produce the required information. There are many files that contain many of the same data items.

It can be seen, then, that in data processing environments where each department has its own files, the computer is of little value addressing questions such as personnel implications of a change in a marketing strategy or labor costs associated with a surge in sales. By contrast, in a database environment, a database system is like a superclerk who rushes from one department's books to another searching and matching data. The structure of data is defined in advance so that interdepartmental access is possible.

The idea that information is a corporate resource to be controlled and allocated just like financial resources is gaining in acceptance. The general theme behind a database is to make it possible for an organization to handle its information as an integrated whole. This means no more

Figure 6.1
A system without a database: redundancy and inflexibility. Imagine 1000 such files. (Source: James Martin, *Principles of Data-Base Management*, © 1976, p. 37. Reprinted by permission of Prentice-Hall, Inc. Englewood Cliffs, N.J.)

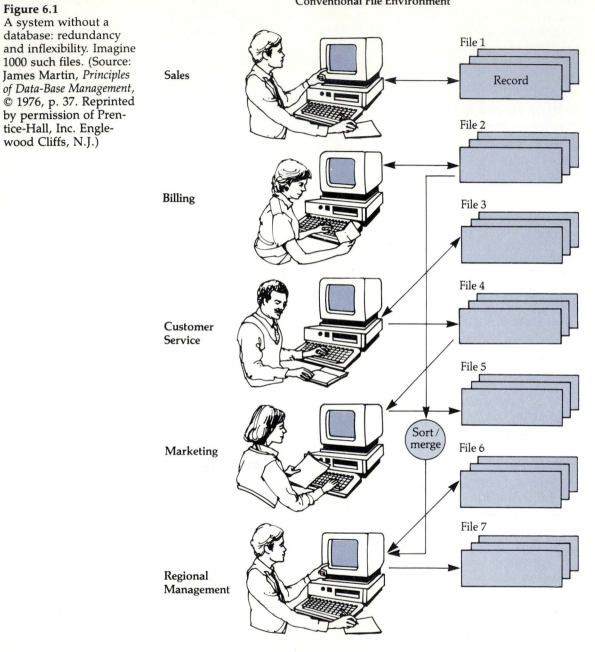

Conventional File Environment

independent files for separate applications. This pool of interrelated data can now be accessed by multiple users using a procedure that controls for accuracy and integrity.

Objectives

Ideally, a database system makes information access and retrieval easier, cheaper, quicker, and more flexible for the user. As a repository of information, stored data must be accurate, current, and protected from unauthorized use.

In organizing a database, there are objectives to consider:

1. *Accuracy and integrity.* In a database system, accuracy controls assure that the system does not have conflicting versions of the same data items that may be in various stages of updating. Integrity means reliability. Uncontrolled file redundancy and multiple updates often lead to integrity problems.

2. *Clarity and ease of use.* A feature of a "user-friendly" database is that users understand and know what data are available to them. They also have access to the data in an easy, straightforward fashion. Related to this is the further requirement that the database structure can be updated without having to change the procedure for accessing the data.

3. *Controlled redundancy.* **Redundant** or repetitious data waste storage space and allow inconsistency. When different versions of the data are in different phases of update, the system often gives conflicting information. Typically, data are stored only once except in situations where for technical reasons there can be no redundant storage.

4. *Data independence.* An important objective of a database is to be able to change physical or logical storage representation without having to rewrite application programs; this is known as **data independence**. The ability of the DBMS to migrate data without impact on programs is certainly a good measure of the degree of data independence.

5. *Quick recovery from failure.* An integrated database is usually accessed by many users simultaneously and is usually available at all times. With so much dependence on the database, it is important that quick recovery after system failure is assured without loss of transactions. This objective helps maintain data accuracy and integrity and promotes system performance.

6. *More information at low cost.* One major objective of a database is providing more information at a low cost. The cost factor of using, storing, and modifying data is important. Although the cost of storage is steadily decreasing, the cost of programming and software is not. This means that application programming should be kept simple and easy to update. The logical structure of the data is designed with this objective.

7. *Performance.* The data requested by the user have to be available when needed. The response time depends on the user. For example, an

inquiry about flight seat availability that takes more than 5 seconds can be annoying. In contrast, an inquiry about the total bank deposits available for loans that takes several minutes should be quite adequate. Even in peak periods, most databases should offer response time of under 3 seconds to a single record.

8. *Powerful end user languages.*   A major objective of a database and a DBMS is to make it possible for a novice user to query, search, or modify data without having to write a program. The ease with which users retrieve information makes a database application quite attractive.

9. *Security.*   Data should be protected as a matter of policy. For data to be protected from unauthorized access, security measures are taken as a part of the DBMS and the design of the database. An effective database security ensures that the data are protected from destruction and unauthorized alteration and access.

Pros and Cons

In evaluating the pros and cons of a database, the advantages generally outweigh the disadvantages. The major advantages include minimum data redundancy, program data independence, and greater availability of information through integration of files. There are several disadvantages:

1. Overall *cost.*   Database design can be expensive. In addition, the DBMS itself can cost over $200,000. The initial costs also include additional memory, specialized training, conversion, day-to-day operating costs, and maintenance.

2. *Recovery* from failure may be difficult.   In an MIS facility centered around an integrated database serving many users, maintaining a viable database requires highly specialized personnel who are not easy to find.

3. Centralization of information *resources* through integration tends to make the organization *vulnerable.*   If one database component fails, it could stop the entire system. Securing uninterrupted availability means improved backup and a full complement of specialized staff—both adding to the cost.

Key Terms

Assume that we have an application called *sales status system.* Its purpose is to collect sales data by salesperson and provide periodic reports on sales activities. In Figure 6.2, we emphasize four major terms: user's view, processing, data model, and data file.

The **user's view** is how the user sees the data. In the example, the user sees a report showing the sales activities of salespersons during a

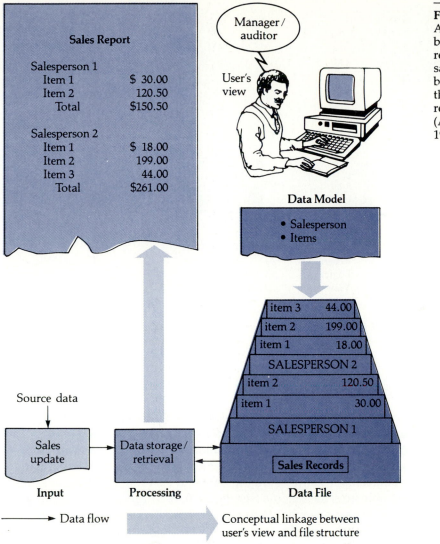

Figure 6.2
A data file system that
begins with the user's
request for a report. The
sales data is retrieved
based on a data model
that represents the
report content.
(Adapted from Awad,
1985, 234.)

time period. The purpose of a database is to capture end user views and
synthesize them into a database structure.

Processing is a routine that changes the data file to the user's view.
To produce the sales report, sales records are processed. The sales report
is the user's view.

The **data model** is an image of the way the data are represented. This
is the overall database.

The **data file** is the physical representation in the data model. In our
example, data are organized by salesperson and items.

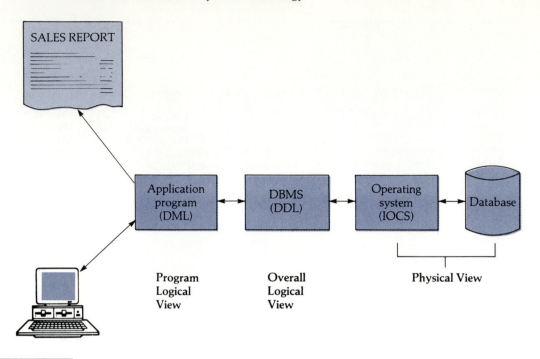

Figure 6.3
Three views of data.

Logical and Physical Views of Data

In database design, there are three ways of looking at data: the overall logical view, the program logical view, and the physical view (see Figure 6.3). The overall **logical view** defined by the database or **schema** is the logical structure of the complete database. The database administrator is responsible for defining the schema and assuring that the subschema is derivable from the schema (see Figure 6.4). The *program logical view,* called the **subschema,** is what the program actually sees in order to produce a specific user's view. In Figure 6.4, user A views the database as being data items 8, 13, and 14. User B is using data items 1, 2, and 10. Each user has interest only in the data that mean something to him or her.

In addition to the overall and program logical views, is the **physical view**. It is the way data are positioned on disk or in physical storage. Specifically, it relates to:

1. How data are stored (disk, tape, etc.)
2. How data are accessed (sequential, direct, indexed sequential, or chained)
3. How data are related to other data in storage (via pointers, indexes, etc.) and what the physical format of the data looks like (see Figure 6.5); (these details have been explained in Chapter 5)

Schema

Subschemas

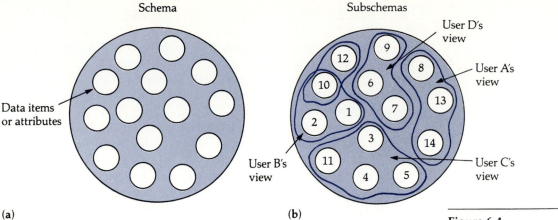

Data items
or attributes

User D's
view

User A's
view

User B's
view

User C's
view

(a)   (b)

Figure 6.4
Schema and subsche-
mas. (a) The schema is
the logical structure of
the entire database.
(b) Each subschema rep-
resents a user's view. For
example, user view B
has special interest in
data items 1, 2, and 10.
A subschema, then, is
only a "piece" of the
schema.

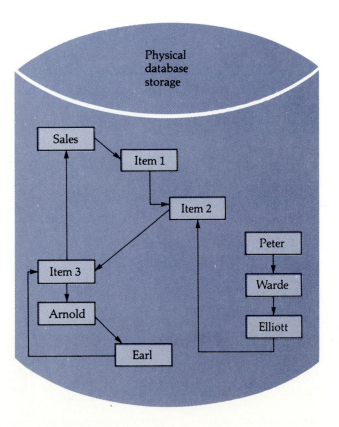

Physical
database
storage

Sales

Item 1

Item 2

Item 3

Arnold

Earl

Peter

Warde

Elliott

Figure 6.5
The physical view. In a
database, items are
linked to salespersons,
users, and so on based
on predefined sets of
relationships.

The Database Management System (DBMS)

Every organization has an information resource, called a **database**—papers stored in a file cabinet, a box of ledger cards, or records stored on computer tape or disk. A database refers to integrated computer files that are managed by a set of integrated software called a **database management system** or **DBMS** (see Figure 6.6).

Before the database concept was developed, users had application programs that handled only their own data. In this conventional file environment with no data integration, sharing data across applications was a complex process. With a database, data became available to programs of different users. The result was storage savings and a significant reduction of redundant data and improved integrity.

A DBMS concentrates on the management and control of a shared data resource. Applications now retrieve and store data via the DBMS, Application program requests are handled by the DBMS that determines data sharing and protects data from unauthorized access (see Figure 6-7).

The inquiry cycle is straightforward. A request by the application program is sent via the DBMS in a special language called the **data manipulation language (DML)**. To produce the user's view, the data model describes the view in a language called the **data definition language (DDL)**. It specifies for the DBMS how the data must be structured. In Figure 6.8, a salesperson is related to sales items. This means that the user's report should be organized by salespersons and their respective items sold during the period. The DBMS then uses the database to retrieve the information that will produce the user's view.

Figure 6.6
Information resources.

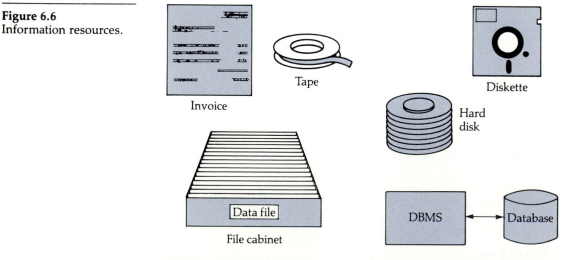

Invoice

Tape

Diskette

Hard disk

Data file

File cabinet

DBMS ←→ Database

(a) Manual Information System   **(b) Computer-Based Information System**

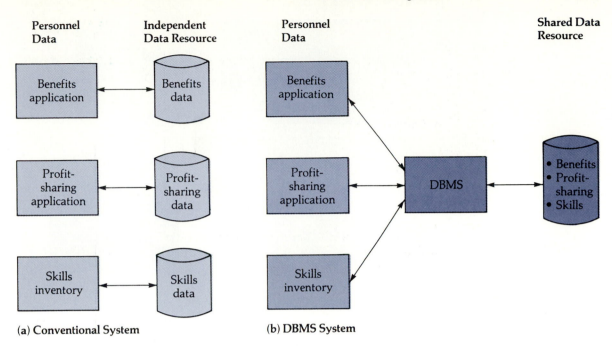

| Personnel Data | Independent Data Resource | Personnel Data | Shared Data Resource |

(a) Conventional System   (b) DBMS System

Figure 6.7
Conventional and DBMS environments. Note the improved efficiency of a database over the conventional file system.

The processing phase of the database system is essentially the same as that of the conventional system (see Figure 6.7). The main difference is that the application program passes input/output requests to the DBMS and uses the DBMS to store and access data. The DBMS is the "manager" of data in the database. It determines the most efficient way of storing data.

The DBMS approach can be more easily understood by comparing it to the activities of a library with closed stacks. Suppose that a student requests a book by its library number (e.g., ard942.125). The number or code uniquely identifies the book. The student, in this case, is the application program. The language (DML), understandable to the DBMS, is the librarian. The DBMS accepts the DML request and responds to it by using DDL language that describes to an assistant (operating system) where the book is located in the stacks (physical database). The clerk retrieves the book to the student through the librarian (see Figure 6.9).

We may conclude, then, that:

- DDL describes *how* the data are structured.
- DML *manipulates* data. It tells the system *what* is required.
- DBMS *manages* and coordinates data according to DDL descriptions and DML specifications.

A DBMS has other functions as well. It:

1. Controls concurrent processing.
2. Maintains procedures that ensure data integrity.

Figure 6.8
A database system. The application program uses DDL to interface with the DBMS. The user's view focuses on a data model that defines for the DBMS the nature and layout of the sales report.

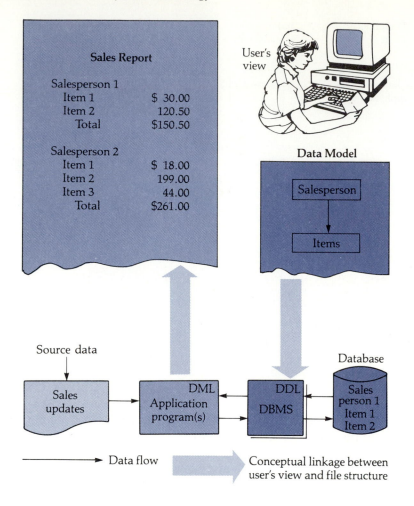

3. Provides security facilities that identify the user and authorize requests.
4. Provides recovery from machine failures, disk crashes, user errors, and the like.

A system that does not provide these functions is not truly a DBMS. How a DBMS performs these functions can be used as decision criteria in selecting a system.

Data Structure

Data are structured according to the data model. In our example (see Figure 6.2), sales items are linked to their respective salesperson. In database design, the salesperson and items are entities. Relationships

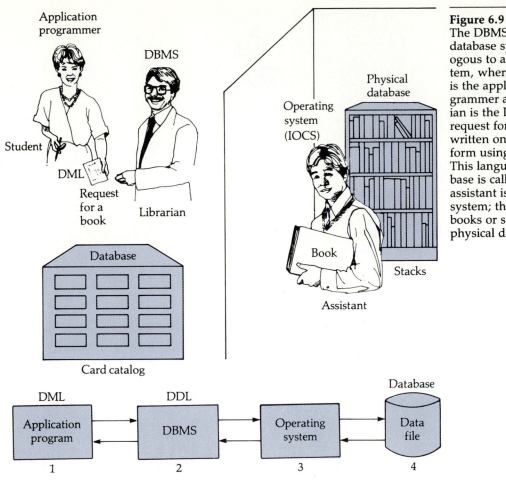

Figure 6.9
The DBMS approach. A database system is analogous to a library system, where the student is the application programmer and the librarian is the DBMS. The request for a book is written on a special form using a book code. This language in database is called DML. The assistant is the operating system; the library of books or stacks is the physical database.

between entities make up a **data structure**. The **data model** represents the data structure (see Figure 6.10).

Types of Data Relationships

Three basic types of relationships can exist between entities: one-to-one, one-to-many, and many-to-many relationships.

A *one-to-one* (1:1) relationship is an association between two entities. For example, in our culture, a husband has one wife; an employee has one social security number, and so on (see Figure 6.11).

A *one-to-many* (1:M) relationship describes an entity that may have two or more entities related to it. For example, a supervisor may have many employees; a student many grades; an employee many skills, and so on (see Figure 6.12).

Figure 6.10
Data structure. Note the
association among the
entities, salesperson,
and user: one-to-many.
This means that a sales-
person may sell many
items.

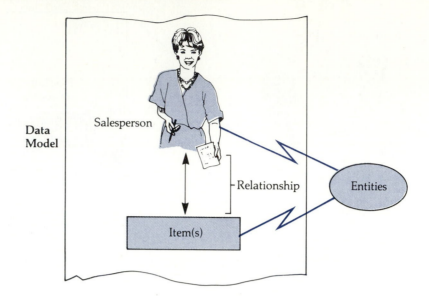

A *many-to-many* (M:N) relationship relates to entities that have many relationships in both directions. For example, students may carry many courses and courses may have many students (see Figure 6.13).

Types of Data Structures

Data structuring represents 1:1, 1:M, or M:N relationships between entities. Database management systems differ in the way they structure data. There are three primary types of data structure: tree, network, and relational structures.

Tree   A **tree** (also called **hierarchical**) **structure** has data elements arranged in treelike formation. The rule is that an entity can have only one owning entity. The owning entity is called the **parent**; the owned entity, the **child**. A parent with no owners is the **root**. There is only one root in a tree structure, but there are any number of root occurrences. Nodes that have the same parent are called **siblings**.

In Figure 6.14, P is the root. As a parent, it has child types (**nodes**) A and B. So a parent can have many children (1:M), whereas a child can have only one parent. As parents, A has three children or siblings (C,D,E) and B has three children (F,G,H). An example of how a tree structure is represented using a linked list is shown in Figure 6.15. A vendor may send various invoices and payments, each having different items and payments, respectively.

The tree structure is easy to design when the information structure is inherently hierarchical. Unfortunately, few real information structures

Figure 6.11
Example of a 1:1
relationship.

conform to a hierarchy. For example, in Figure 6.16, if two persons open a joint account, we are representing a nontree structure, which makes the DBMS description quite complex. The alternative is often resolved by using a network structure.

Network A **network structure** is a representation of M:N relationships between entities. Figure 6.17 is an illustration of a network structure. Consider the automakers and the auto parts store they deal with. If an automaker sells spare parts only to a new car dealer in a given territory, there is a 1:1 relationship in that territory. If the automaker supplies many other car dealers, then there is a 1:M relationship. The 1:1 and 1:M relationships can be represented by a tree structure, but when several auto parts dealers stock spare parts from many automakers, we have a M:N relationship, which is a network structure.

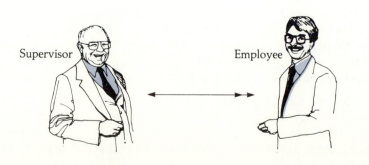

Figure 6.12
1:M relationship.

Figure 6.13
M:N relationship.

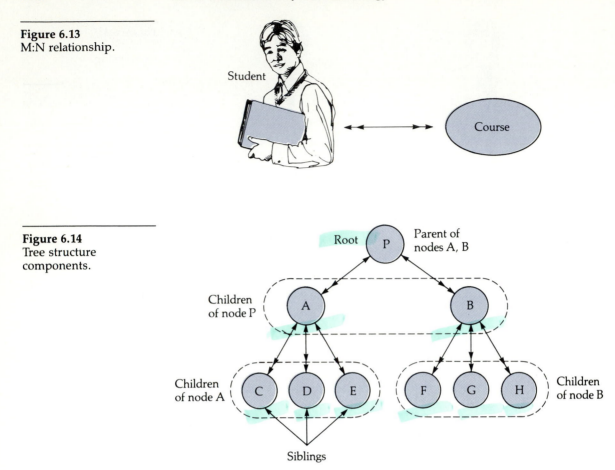

Figure 6.14
Tree structure
components.

A network structure can be a challenge to design. One solution is to break down the network into a number of trees with duplicates. This results in relationships no higher than 1:M (see Figure 6.18).

Relational A **relational structure** has data and relationships represented in a two-dimensional (rows and columns) table called a **relation**. A relation is another name for a file or a table of records. Each row represents a record. A row is also called a **tuple** (rhymes with couple). Figure 6.19 is a relation describing the entity EMPLOYEE by four attributes: ID, name, years with firm, and salary. The relation is an 8-tuple (row) file.

The basic rules of a relation are:

1. Entries in a table are single valued.
2. Entries in any column are all of the same kind. For example, the age column shows only numbers representing age.
3. Each column has a unique name. The order of the columns is immaterial.

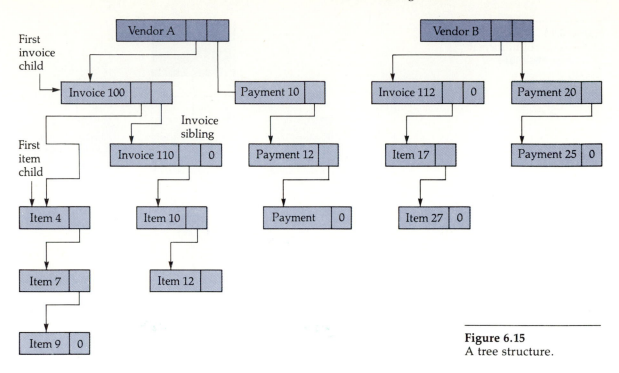

Figure 6.15
A tree structure.

4. No two rows in the table can be identical. The order of the rows is immaterial.

To illustrate, suppose a relational structure consists of two relations: the EMPLOYEE relation (Figure 6.19) and the EMPLOYEE EDUCATION (EMPED) relation (Figure 6.20). A query requesting the employee(s) with three or more years with the firm and a BS would result in the following routine:

1. A temporary table of employees with three or more years is generated from the EMPLOYEE RELATION and placed in the file. This file is deleted once the query has been answered.

2. The information in the temporary table and the EMPED relation are used to answer the query. This results in a second temporary table with the answer Davis. The two temporary tables are shown in Figure 6.21.

Compared to the tree or network structure, a relational database offers three key advantages:

1. Data independence—perhaps the most important advantage of a relational database. Data independence means isolating the user's *logical view* of a database from the hardware's physical storage requirements.
2. Ease of use with relational tables. It is ideal for novice users. Much of this depends on the user query language.
3. Ease to modify the structure and implement the system.

Figure 6.16
Checking account format
using tree structure
model.

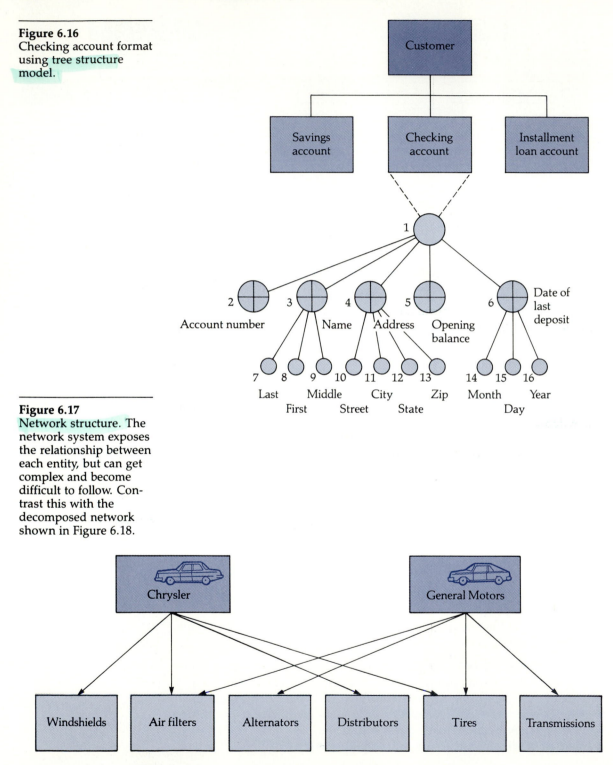

Figure 6.17
Network structure. The
network system exposes
the relationship between
each entity, but can get
complex and become
difficult to follow. Con-
trast this with the
decomposed network
shown in Figure 6.18.

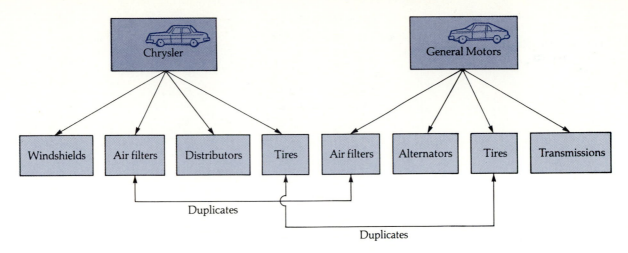

Figure 6.18
Decomposed networking. The advantage of a decomposed network is clarity of organization. It does, however, introduce redundancy of subordinate entities.

Primary and Concatenated Keys   An important aspect of the relational model is the concept of **key**. A **primary key** is an attribute or attributes that uniquely identifies a record. No two records may have the same key. In our example, employee ID could be chosen as a primary key. It uniquely identifies an employee.

The nice feature about relational systems is that access may be by any attributes—not just keys. In situations requiring the linking of more than one attribute together for query response, we have what is called a **concatenated key**. For example, to provide information about seat availability on a flight, a ticket agent must enter the date and the time of the flight. Date and time, two keys taken together, make up a concatenated key.

Figure 6.19
A relation for EMPLOYEE.

```
                Employee(EMP) Relation

                                 Years with
    Attributes   ID    Name        firm        Salary

        (4)    ⎡ 124   Arnold        2          18500
               ⎢ 241   Davis        14          26500
               ⎢ 362   Elam          7          22000
    Tuples     ⎢ 180   Mandelbaum    6          21200
     (8)       ⎨ 820   Sibly         1          16000
               ⎢ 762   Travis        3          19000
               ⎢ 215   Unger         5          20010
               ⎣ 500   Ziegler       9          23145

    Values of NAME attribute
```

Figure 6.20
A relational structure.

```
Employee  Education  (EMPED)  Relation

    ID        Name          Degree
    124       Arnold        B.S.
    241       Davis         B.S.
    362       Elam          Ph.D.
    180       Mandelbaum    MBA
    820       Sibly         B.S.
    762       Travis        MA
```

DML for the Relational Model   There are a variety of relational DMLs. A DML must perform four major functions:

```
INSERT     new data
DELETE     old data
UPDATE     old data
RETRIEVE   stored data
```

The first three operations are usually performed by an application program. RETRIEVE is a query operation that can be performed by novice users. For example, to retrieve a list of employees under 30 years of age, the query in dBASE III Plus (a database language) is:

```
LIST ALL FOR NAME='EMPLOYEE'.AND. AGE < 30
```

In the relational model, there are three approaches to DML languages: relational algebra, structured English, and graphical language.

Relational algebra is a set of operations that acts on relations to produce new relations. Some of the frequently used relational operations are:

Figure 6.21
Temporary relations for
query response.

```
JOIN, PROJECT, and SELECTION
```

```
Temporary Employee Relation           Query Response Relation

    ID      Name                           ID      Name
    241     Davis                          241     Davis
    362     Elam
    180     Mandelbaum
    215     Unger
    500     Ziegler
```

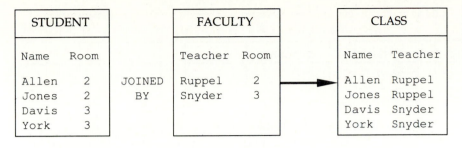

Figure 6.22
JOIN of STUDENT and FACULTY relations.

The **JOIN operation** is the most complex. The format (JOIN relation-1 attribute-1 comparator attribute-2) produces a new relation that has all the combinations of rows from relation 1 and relation 2 that meet a specified condition(s). Figure 6.22 illustrates joining the file Student to the file Faculty to form a new relation "class." The question is "list the names of students and their teachers." The JOIN command in dBASE III Plus is:

```
JOIN STUDENT WITH FACULTY TO CLASS FOR;ROOM=FACULTY->ROOM FIELDS NAME,TEACHER
```

Projection selects specified attributes from a relation to produce a new relation with the "new" attributes. The format (PROJECT relation-1 attribute-1 . . . attribute-n) produces a new relation for relation-1 by deleting from each tuple the attribute(s) specified in the query. For example, in dBASE III Plus, the commands:

- USE INVENTORY
- LIST BRAND, COST, PRICE

will go to the inventory file (records) and list the information under the attribute specified in the second command.

Selection takes horizontal rows in a relation or identifies the tuples to be included in a new relation. The procedure is to specify the relation name, followed by a key word WHERE and a condition involving attributes. For example, the query

```
SELECT JUNIOR WHERE MAJOR='MATH'
```

will pull all tuples with the attribute *major-math*.

Structured English produces queries that are usually quite readable. To illustrate, using our example in Figure 6.22, the following English query can be used based on the *Select-From-Where* construct of IBM's query language SEQUEL:

```
SELECT NAME,TEACHER FROM STUDENT,FACULTY
  WHERE FACULTY.ROOM=STUDENT.ROOM
```

Class   Faculty   Student

NAME	TEACHER
!	SNYDER

TEACHER	ROOM

STUDENT	ROOM

Figure 6.23
Graphics template.

The *graphics* approach displays templates of each relation involved. It provides the user with a picture of the structure of a relation. The user fills in an example of what he/she wants. The system responds with the actual data in the format. In our student-faculty-class example, the display is shown in Figure 6.23. The user then prints special marks in the field that has the desired data or labels the attributes for connections between relations. Examples of marks in IBM's Query-by-Example (QBE) notation are printed in the CLASS template to mean:

! = print the attribute NAME SNYDER. The teacher's name must be SNYDER.

Normalization

One of the steps necessary for effective database design is called **normalization**. It is a way of creating relations that have minimal redundancy and a small chance of inconsistency. Normalizing a file involves three steps that will be illustrated with an example. An unnormalized file is shown in Figure 6.24.

Figure 6.24
Unnormalized file.

SALESPERSON DATA   SALES DATA

ID	Name	Branch	Dept.	City	Item No.	Description	Price	Qty.
201	Jack Holt	Main	Hardware	Orlando	SA10	Saw	19.00	1
					PT65	Drill	21.00	1
					AB165	Lawnmower	245.00	1
301	Ann Trent	Dade	Appliance	Miami	TT14	Humidifier	114.00	1
					DS104	Dishwasher	261.00	1
419	Harry Bell	Cutler	Auto Parts	Miami	MC164	Snow tire	85.00	4
					AC1462	Alternator	65.00	1
					BB1000	Battery	49.50	1
612	Tom Hays	Barracks	Men's	Tampa	HS101	3-Pc. suit	215.00	1

★ ID	Name	Branch	Department	City
201	Jack Holt	Main	Hardware	Orlando
301	Ann Trent	Dade	Appliance	Miami
419	Harry Bell	Cutler	Auto parts	Miami
612	Tom Hays	Barracks	Men's	Tampa

★ ID	★ Item No.	Qty.	Description	Price
201	SA10	1	Saw	19.00
201	PT65	1	Drill	21.00
201	AB165	2	Lawnmower	245.00
301	TT14	1	Humidifier	114.00
301	DS104	1	Dishwasher	262.00
419	MC164	4	Snow tire	85.00
419	AC1462	1	Alternator	65.00
419	BB1000	1	Battery	49.50
612	HS101	1	3-pc. Suit	215.00

Figure 6.25
First normal form.

1. An examination of the file in Figure 6.24 reveals that it would be difficult to process in its current form. There are repeating fields containing the sales data in each row, resulting from the fact that some salespeople sold more than one product. Since it is normal for a salesperson to make more than one sale, these repeating groups of sales data should be separated from the data about the salespeople.

As a result of separating the repeating fields containing the sales data from the data concerning the salesperson, there are now two relations, as in Figure 6.25. This is called the first **normal form**. The first relation—salesperson data—contains the information about the salesperson and its key is the salesperson's ID number. The second relation—salesperson-item—contains the data about the sale. Its key is a concatenated key made up of the salesperson's ID and the item number. Note that it was necessary to add the code for the salesperson to the sales relation so that each sale could be associated with a particular salesperson.

2. The first normal form for this database contains some processing problems. One problem is that the salesperson-item relation is accessed by a concatenated key made up of the salesperson's identification code and the item number. But the item's description and price are not related to the salesperson, only the item number. The concatenated key is necessary, however, to perform statistical analysis of sales by salesperson. Another problem is that an item can be recorded only when a sale occurs.

The solution to the problem in the salesperson-item relation is to divide it into two relations: an item relation in which the item number, its price, and its description are stored, and a salesperson item relation in which the sales for each salesperson are recorded. By separating the

Figure 6.26
Second normal form.

* ID	Name	Branch	Department	City
201	Jack Holt	Main	Hardware	Orlando
301	Ann Trent	Dade	Appliance	Miami
419	Harry Bell	Cutler	Auto parts	Miami
612	Tom Hays	Barracks	Men's	Tampa

* ID	* Item No.	Qty.	Item No.	Description	Price
201	SA10	1	SA10	Saw	19.00
201	PT65	1	PT65	Drill	21.00
201	AB165	2	AB165	Lawnmower	245.00
301	TT14	1	TT14	Humidifier	114.00
301	DS104	1	DS104	Dishwasher	262.00
419	MC164	4	MC164	Snow tire	85.00
419	AC1462	1	AC1462	Alternator	65.00
419	BB1000	1	BB1000	Battery	49.50
612	HS101	1	HS101	3-pc. Suit	215.00

Figure 6.27
Third normal form.

* ID	Name	Branch	Department
201	Jack Holt	Main	Hardware
301	Ann Trent	Dade	Appliance
419	Harry Bell	Cutler	Auto parts
612	Tom Hays	Barracks	Men's

* Branch	City
Main	Orlando
Dadeland	Miami
Cutler	Miami
Barracks	Tampa

* ID	Item No.	Qty.
201	SA10	1
201	PT65	1
201	AB165	2
301	TT14	1
301	DS104	1
419	MC164	4
419	AC1462	1
419	BB1000	1
612	HS101	1

* Item No.	Description	Price
SA10	Saw	19.00
PT65	Drill	21.00
AB165	Lawnmower	245.00
TT14	Humidifier	114.00
DS104	Dishwasher	262.00
MC164	Snow tire	85.00
AC1462	Alternator	65.00
BB1000	Battery	49.50
HS101	3-pc. Suit	215.00

information about each item from the sales data, each may be processed independent of the other. This set of three relations is called the *second normal form* (see Figure 6.26).

3. If we now examine the three relations in Figure 6.27, we see that there is no problem with the salesperson-item relation. The quantity sold is determined by the salesperson's ID number and the item number (assuming the data are for a specified date). In technical terms, all nonkey attributes—quantity in this relation—are dependent on the entire key, ID number and item number. If we now turn our attention to the salesperson data relation, we see that there is a problem. The branch to which a salesperson is assigned is dependent on the salespeople, but the location of the store is not dependent on the salesperson. Instead it is dependent on the store identification. This is called a transitive relation.

The solution to the problem of a relation containing a transitive relationship is to divide the relation in two. One relation containing salesperson data and the other containing store data. This is shown in Figure 6.27. The relations are now all in the *third normal form*, and can now be processed with a minimum of problems.

Implications for MIS

The database concept is both powerful and simple, yet it can be oversold or misunderstood. Not all of an organization's data is kept in the database, nor is a database the MIS panacea for constructing a reservoir in which a diversity of users can access information. In fact, the reservoir notion—that a database stores all the organization's data—can lead to management *misinformation* systems. A data-oriented rather than decision-making emphasis can emerge in which too much of the wrong data is a part of the database.

Although the notion of a corporate database capable of meeting all needs is an illusion and a dangerous notion, the database concept has many attractive features and uses as long as the problems it raises are overcome at the outset. For example, the assumption of a database that data relationships do not respect departmental boundaries means there must also be management policies and security controls to protect the data resources from abuse. Management has the responsibility to direct database development, participate in the design process, and ensure qualified database administration.

Adopting a DBMS is a matter of tradeoff between the benefits of greater access to more accurate and timely corporate data and the higher cost of database management software, more highly skilled staff, and the impact of temporary failures of the DBMS on the organization. The trend is for organizations to use DBMS as the center for meeting their data needs. This trend should continue as vendors improve the reliability of database recovery and security procedures.

Corporations with daily needs for sharing large volumes of corporate data should consider the large-size DBMS. Since the early 1980s, however, more and more microcomputer DBMSs priced under $1,000 have been attractive to small organizations or departments that need to share a limited amount of data. Present research focuses on linking the mainframe DBMS to the personal computer. Such PC-mainframe connectivity allows the end user to query the DBMS or use the information as input for forecasting and decision making. Communication technology and networks are discussed in the next chapter.

Summary

- The idea behind a database is to make an organization able to handle its information as an integrated whole. The data are designed to be independent of the programs that operate on the data. Several database objectives are:
  a. Accuracy and integrity
  b. Clarity and ease of use
  c. Controlled redundancy
  d. Data independence
  e. Fast recovery from failure
  f. More information at low cost
  g. Performance
  h. Powerful end user languages
  i. Privacy and security

- A database management system (DBMS) is a set of integrated software for managing and controlling data in a database. It handles requests from the application program that are issued in a special language called data manipulation language (DML). To produce the user's view, the data model describes the view in a language called data definition language (DDL). It tells the DBMS how the data must be structured. Therefore, DML manipulates data, DDL describes the data structure, while DBMS manages and coordinates data according to DML requests and DDL descriptions.

- A data model represents entities related to one another in some way. An entity is something of interest about which to collect or store data. Each entity has attributes, which in turn represent values. A key identifies an entity for processing.

- Relationships between entities make up a data structure. There are three types of relationships: one-to-one, one-to-many, and many-to-many. There are also three types of data structure: tree or hierarchical, network, and relational.

a. The *tree* or *hierarchical* structure has data elements arranged in tree-like formation. An entity can have no more than one owning entity. It is easy to design and understand.

b. The *network* structure allows 1:1, 1:M, or M:N relationships between entities. It reflects the real world, although it can become complex.

c. The *relational* structure has data and relationships represented in a flat, two-dimensional table called a relation. A relation is equivalent to a file.

□ A relational DBMS allows the user to update records, provides an inquiry capability against a given label, and can merge two or more tables to form one relation based on the user's request. It develops new relations on user command.

□ In the relational model, three approaches to query languages are emphasized: relational algebra, structured English, and graphics.

a. *Relational algebra* is a set of operations that act on relations to produce new relations. Some of the relational operations are UNION, INTERSECT, JOIN, PROJECTION, and SELECTION.

b. *Structured English* produces queries using simple English words.

c. The *graphics* approach displays templates of each relation involved. It provides the user a picture of the structure of a relation.

□ In database design, four views are considered:

a. The *user's view* is what the user actually sees.

b. The *program logical view* (subschema) is what the program sees to produce the user's logical view.

c. The *overall logical view* (schema) is a chart of the types of data that are used. It is the view that the DBMS must have for deciding on the data in the database to be available in memory when requested by the application program.

d. The *physical view* is the way data exist in physical storage.

□ The data model is refined through a process called normalization. The goal is to simplify relationships and establish logical linkages between files without losing information. The linkages are established by maintaining common attributes between files.

□ A normal form is the criterion for designing relations. Normalizing a file involves three steps:

a. Repeating groups are isolated from an entity. Each attribute is assigned its own name and repeating group elements become individual tuples.

b. The relation is simplified further to remove anomalies. This produces the second normal form.

c. Further problems encountered in the second normal form results in further normalization or the third normal form.

□ One inherent problem in normalization is data redundancy and the consequent processing inefficiency it generates.

Key Terms

Child	Normalization
Concatenated key	Parent
Database	Physical view
Database management system (DBMS)	Primary key
	Processing
Data definition language (DDL)	Program logical view: See subschema
Data file	
Data independence	Projection
Data manipulation language (DML)	Redundancy
	Relation
Data migration	Relational algebra
Data model	Relational structure
Data structure	Root
Hierarchical structure: See tree structure	Schema
	Selection
JOIN operation	Sibling
Key	Structured English
Logical view	Subschema
Network structure	Tree structure
Node	Tuple
Normal form	User's view

Review Questions

1. What is a database? How does it aid the user in decision making? Explain.

2. Elaborate on the objectives and drawbacks of a database. Which objective do you consider the most important? Why?

3. Distinguish between:
   a. Entities and attributes
   b. Schema and subschema
   c. One-to-many and many-to-many relationships

4. Explain in detail the functions of, reasons for, and procedure followed by the DBMS to provide the user's view.

5. What is the difference between DML and DDL? How does each language contribute to providing the user's view?

6. Give an example to illustrate three entities and their respective attributes and values of attributes.

7. How does a data structure differ from a data model?

8. If a one-to-one relationship is an association between two entities, what is a one-to-many relationship?

9. Compare and contrast the three types of data structures. Which type is the closest to a user orientation? How?

10. Distinguish between:
    a. Root and parent
    b. Parent and child
    c. Root and nodes
    d. Nodes and siblings

11. Describe briefly the rules of a relation.

12. How does a concatenated key differ from a primary key? Give an example.

13. A DML must perform four major functions. Give an example of each function.

14. What is relational algebra? Describe and illustrate three relational operations.

15. Distinguish between:
    a. Join and projection
    b. Projection and selection

16. How is a schema different from a subschema? Illustrate.

17. Explain briefly the three logical views of data. Which view is the schema?

18. Elaborate on the function and steps used in normalization.

Application Problems

1. a. What is wrong with the following table?

```
Book-No.   Title        Author

146        MIS          Arnold
201        Database     Newcomb, Johnson
146        MIS          Arnold
```

b. What is the name of the relation?

c. What are the attribute types?

d. Is Database an attribute type or an attribute value?

2. The following Customer-Part table shows the quantities of parts ordered by four customers:

Customer number	Customer name	Part no.	Part description	Qty.
12	Arnold	21A	Brake shoes	4
12	Arnold	16Q	Battery	3
14	Arnold	16Q	Battery	2
19	Crunk	19M	Battery	4

a. Which of the following are examples of redundant duplication of data values? Why?
(1) The two occurrences of cust. no. value 12
(2) The two occurrences of Arnold in rows 1 and 2
(3) The two occurrences of battery in rows 1 and 3

3. The following table represents the degree held by six employees, each with a unique employee number.

Employee no.	Employee name	Degree
114	Snyder	BS
114	Snyder	BA
114	Snyder	MBA
116	Ruppel	PhD
118	Ruppel	PhD
118	Ruppel	MD

a. How many Snyders are there?
b. How many Ruppels are there?

4. The following table shows the skills of each employee and the dates when they qualified in their skills:

Employee no.	Employee name	Skill name	Date acquired

a. What is the normalized table type?

5. A course is taught by only one instructor, but a lecturer may teach many courses. A course may have many students and a student may enroll in many courses. Devise an entity-relationship structure containing only two binary relationships.

6. Consider the entities House, Buyer, Owner, Title, and Inspection for a real estate agency. Develop a hierarchical, simple network and a relational model for this setup.

Selected References

Ashton-Tate, Inc. *dBASE III Plus Manual*, 1986, 4–60A.

Awad, E. M. *Systems Analysis and Design.* 2nd ed. Homewood, Ill.: Irwin, 1985.

Date, C. J. *Introduction to Database Systems*, vol. 1, Reading, Mass.: Addison-Wesley, 1986.

Davis, Richard K. "New Tools and Techniques to Make Data Base Professionals More Productive." *Journal of Systems Management*, June 1984, 20–25.

Egyhazy, Csaba J. "Microcomputers and Relational Data Base Management Systems: A New Strategy For Decentralizing Databases." *Data Base*, Fall 1984, 15–20.

Everest, Gordon C. *Database Management-Objectives, System Foundations and Administration.* New York: McGraw-Hill, 1986.

Gallagher, Leonard J. "Database Conversions Demand Common Standards For Data Structure." *Data Management*, January 1985, 22–28.

Holsapple, C. W. "A Perspective on Data Models." *PC Tech Journal*, July 1984, 113–16ff.

Inman, W. H. "What Price Relational?" *Computerworld*, Nov. 28, 1983, ID 33ff.

———— and Bird, Thomas J., Jr. *The Dynamics of Database.* Englewood Cliffs, N.J.: Prentice-Hall, 1986.

Martin, James. *Principles of Database Management*, 1976.

Millsap, Ed; Sloan, Ken; and Gerrard, Steve. "Relational DBMS." *Computerworld*, Mar. 4, 1985, ID 1–6ff.

Shah, I. "Data Administration: It's Crucial." *Datamation*, January 1984, 187–88ff.

Sweet, Frank. "What, If Anything, Is a Relational Data Base?" *Datamation*, July 15, 1984, 118–20ff.

Data Communication and Networking

Chapter Contents

Send It By Satellite

RECENT ADVANCES IN SATELLITE technology and the wide range of satellite-based communication services now available have made satellite networking a sensible option for many companies. A growing number of firms, especially in the U.S., have decided that satellites are the fastest and most efficient medium for sending data.

But on a global scale the use of satellites as part of corporate networks is still patchy. So far only a handful of companies in Europe and Asia have chosen the satellite option because of the galaxy of regulatory, economic, and technical problems.

One of the first companies in Britain to switch from cable to satellites for an international data link was the U.K. offshoot of American engineering company Bechtel, which took to the skies in 1981. The company's West London offices are connected to five U.S. sites, including Bechtel's head office in San Francisco, via a 56000 bits per second link provided by British Telecom. "We opted for a satellite link for plain economic reasons," says Paul Dickinson, Bechtel's development and support manager. "If we were to try to establish conventional 9600 bits per second lines it would be much more expensive."

Bechtel's daily traffic, which includes data, voice, telex, facsimile, and electronic mail, is piped by land line to British Telecom's earth station at Ealing, West London, and then via an Intelsat satellite to New York Teleport on Staten Island. The final leg to San Francisco and U.S. destinations is again made by land line. Traffic consists of financial information, which accounts for the bulk of data movements, and engineering design applications, which are light on communications needs but heavy on processing.

"We have had no major operating problems as far as our applications are concerned," says Dickinson. "Our link has gone down, but usually it is the land lines that are to blame." Bechtel plays safe with its applications. Before anything goes live over the communications link it is tested at Bechtel's data center in San Francisco on a satellite simulation system. The simulator is able to duplicate the behavior of transmissions on single hops, double hops, and with varying blocks of data.

At present, there is no receiving station for transatlantic traffic in San Francisco. Moves are afoot by British Telecom International and FTCC (the firm that organizes U.S. reception for Bechtel) to set up a station there. When that happens the cost savings to the firm will be tremendous. Removing the land line link will cut costs by as much as a half.

What of the future? In many ways, satellite links are a technology in search of applications. One needs to be processing a lot of data to justify these high speeds. We are just beginning to think of how we might use them.

—*Adapted from staff report*, Datamation, *May 1, 1986, 55ff.*

AT A GLANCE

In today's knowledge-based society, telecommunications are becoming increasingly important for providing effective user-machine interface. In MIS, networking brings information to the end user and makes telecommunication a necessary element in system design.

Telecommunication is used in a wide range of computer processing activities, especially in information inquiry and source data entry. The main elements are the modem, a front end processor, the main computer, terminals, and a telecommunication line to carry data from source to destination. A new dimension is teleconferencing for problem solving, task coordination, or information exchange.

Teletransmission employs simplex, half-duplex, or full-duplex channels. Data may be carried asynchronously or synchronously. In either case, cost and user requirements for information availability are key considerations for the choice.

The local area network or LAN is distinguished from other networks by the area it covers, speed of transmission, and how quickly new devices are added. The end user can choose from a wealth of information through the network. LAN networks have three common configurations: star, ring, and bus. Each network has advantages and limitations, although all are governed by protocol.

In evaluating a network, one needs to be familiar with the common carriers and their services. The oldest carrier is Western Union. Common carriers, in general, offer switched or leased (private) services, although a class of service, called the value-added network (VAN) is also available. In any case, we can see that telecommunication is an attractive delivery system for MIS operation. Such long-haul transmission is here to stay.

By the end of this chapter, you should know:

1. The elements of a telecommunication system
2. How satellites make data transmission possible
3. The types of channels and mode of transmission
4. The common carriers and the services they offer

Introduction

In the previous chapter, we discussed the importance of a corporate database to serve the many needs of the user for decision making. To make this interface possible, we need a telecommunication system that will facilitate the flow of information to the intended user when needed.

Therefore, a basic understanding of this technology is important, since it is a critical element in the planning of information and office systems.

Nowhere else in information technology is the merger of separate technologies so significant. Telephone networks now allow computers to "talk" to one another, computers handle telephone messages, and new networks allow office machines to handle computer messages. This merger means that managers must be familiar with the basics of telecommunication technology. For the organization, telecommunication is becoming the "highway" for funneling information within and between organizations.

As a technology, telecommunication is in a period of revolutionary change. New developments include: fiber optics, electronic mail, videotex, electronic funds transfer, teleconferencing, satellite transmission, and local area network (LAN). The more we read about this topic, the greater we are struck by its impact on the MIS and the end user.

Today's businesses have a growing need to exchange information between remote locations. This exchange is made possible through telecommunications, a technology that permeates virtually every aspect of our society. Business, finance, education, the retailing of merchandise— all are embedded in the concept of telecommunication. The current trend of expanding businesses makes it important to provide information between branches and headquarters or among departments within the firm. The dependence of computers on telecommunication is obvious. Telecommunication links the computer to branches in remote locations. Computers process the data through communication channels regardless of distance or location.

The saga of telecommunication began on May 24, 1844 when Samuel Morse, a New England portrait painter, transmitted the world's first telegram 40 miles over an iron wire linking the chambers of the U.S. Supreme Court in Washington, D.C. with the Baltimore and Ohio Railroad station. The decoded message read, "What hath God wrought." It marked the beginning of a communication network that would revolutionize the world's business structure.

Thirty-two years later, Alexander Graham Bell's famous message to his assistant—"Mr. Watson, come here, I want you"—illustrated the capability of the telegraph to transmit "the timbre of a sound." Bell's telephone was here to stay. In 1897, Marconi sent the first wireless telegraph signal across the English Channel, using a standard Morse code. From Bell and Marconi came the enterprises we know today as Western Union, AT&T, and many others.

The next pivotal step was taken in 1950 by George Stibitz of Dartmouth College when he transmitted a coded message intended for a data processing device over a network. After that, developmental steps in communications came in such rapid succession that they could hardly be singled out. Today the ease with which we transmit and receive data

Table 7.1   Key Developments in Telecommunications

Date	Development	Impact
1844*	Morse code	Beginning of a communication network
1876*	Telephone patent (Bell)	Basic concept
1878	Telephone exchange	Interconnection of telephones
1897*	Marconi's wireless telegraph	Beginning of Western Union
1899	Loading coils	Made long distance transmission possible
1914*	Vacuum triode	Amplification of signals
1915	Electronic wave filters	Allowed many signals on same wire
1918	Carrier telephony	Practical use of one pair for many signals
1936	Coaxial cable transmission	Increased transmission capacity and lowered cost
1947	Microwave relay	Reduced cost and increased transmission capacity
1948*	Transistor	Miniaturization, reliability
1950	George Stibitz's data transmission	Beginning of data transmission network
1951	Customer direct long distance dialing	Improved service
1956	Transatlantic cable	Reliable overseas telephony
1960	Integrated circuits	Extreme miniaturization, reliability
1965*	Satellites	Reduced cost and improved service
1970*	Fiber optics	First practical application of optical communications

*Technological breakthroughs.

is a critical aspect of the computer industry. Relying on fiber optics and satellites for information transfer means quick and timely information for the enduser. Key telecommunication developments are summarized in Table 7.1.

Definition

Telecommunication (also called data communication) means moving information by electrical transmission among multiple sites. Telecommunication users work with networks of thousands of miles of transmission lines, hundreds of data sets or modems using terminals, workstations, and computers.

Telecommunication networks serve three purposes. They:

1. Provide access to databases for inquiry and update.
2. Reduce the operation costs by making information immediately available for decision making.
3. Support management control of the business.

Application Categories

Telecommunication is used in a wide range of data processing activities. The key application categories are information inquiry/retrieval and source data entry.

Information Inquiry and Retrieval

This type of interface provides extensive interaction between the user and the computer. In inquiry processing, remote terminals are linked to the central files for realtime access.

Information retrieval is a terminal-computer network that makes it possible for MIS to supply information on a question in a relatively short time (see Figure 7.1). For example, an airline reservation system provides a travel agent information about flight schedules and seat availability. The agent can cancel or reserve a seat but cannot make changes in flight schedules.

Source Data Entry

A data entry system is one-way transmission of source data from a remote terminal to the computer. The data are first displayed and edited on the screen before transmission. In an on-line batch environment, the data are stored directly (on line) on the computer's disk or diskette for processing in batches at a later time. For real-time applications, the computer acts on inquiries as they are received (see Figure 7.2).

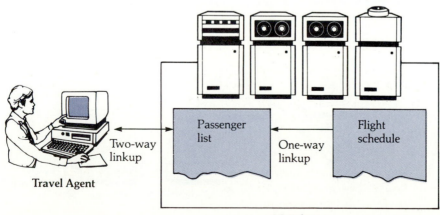

Travel Agent

Two-way linkup

Passenger list

One-way linkup

Flight schedule

Mainframe

Figure 7.1
Information retrieval. The travel agent may retrieve information from both databases but can change records only in the database called "Passenger List."

Figure 7.2
One-way transmission.

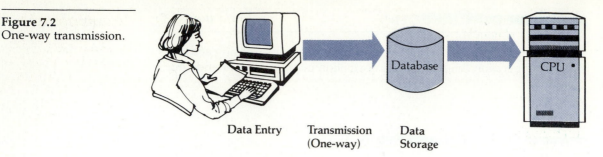

Data Entry   Transmission   Data
               (One-way)   Storage

Terminals offer a remote user the convenience of direct access to the computer. The main benefit is quick data handling and data availability. As terminals become more user friendly, less training should be necessary to access files or download information when needed.

Elements of a Telecommunication System

A telecommunication system may be designed in various ways. A basic configuration is shown in Figure 7.3. The key steps are:

1. The user enters an inquiry through a terminal.
2. A *modem* converts the data from digital to analog (or vice versa).
3. A telecommunication *line* (telephone line, cable, fiber optics, satellite, etc.) carries the uncoded inquiry to its destination.
4. At the receiving end, a *modem* converts the inquiry from analog to digital for processing.
5. A *front end processor*—a message manager—checks the inquiry for communication errors before processing.
6. The *computer* acts upon the inquiry. Transmitting back a response is

Figure 7.3
Basic data telecommunication network. System components: Data originated from (1) a sending device is (2) converted by a modem to data that can be carried over (3) a link and (4) reconverted by a modem at the receiving end before (5) being processed by a front-end processor and (6) sent to the computer. (Adapted and reprinted with permission of Unisys Corporation.)

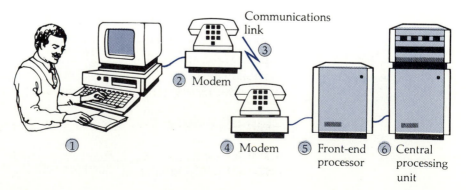

Communications
link

② Modem

① ④ Modem   ⑤ Front-end   ⑥ Central
                processor   processing
                               unit

the same routine in reverse. In a real-time environment, the whole process is handled in seconds.

A telecommunication network consists of three components: Terminals, modems, and telecommunication channels. Let us briefly explain each.

Terminals

A telecommunication network may employ dumb or intelligent terminals. A **dumb terminal** displays or prints data as it receives it. It uses no communication protocol. By **protocol**, we mean a prearranged way of handling transactions. In a protocol-less configuration, the computer cannot control the terminals. This means they must be on separate lines (see Figure 7.4). **Intelligent terminals**, on the other hand, are often standalone computers in the network. They handle applications and interface with the host computer (see Figure 7.5).

Modems

A **modem** is an abbreviation of *mo*dulator/*dem*odulator. It performs one major role—converting a digital message to analog signals before transmission. This is called *modulation*. On the receiving end, analog signals are decoded to digital data for computer processing. This is called *demodulation*. The same sequence occurs when information is transmitted back to the user.

Telecommunication Channels

A telecommunication **channel** carries data between transmission points. The line may be leased from a common carrier. The carrier is a company

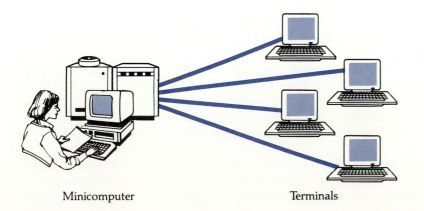

Minicomputer   Terminals

Figure 7.4
A typical "protocol-less" configuration using dumb terminals.

Figure 7.5
Intelligent terminal.

licensed by the Federal Communication Commission (FCC) or a state agency to provide telecommunication service to subscriber organizations. Several telecommunication channels are available:

Telephone Line   The voice-grade telephone line is a standard transmission medium, using the existing telephone network available throughout the world. The wire carries voice as well as data across the network.

Coaxial Cable   This is a high-quality, high-frequency communication line that handles up to 18,740 telephone calls at a time. It is also used heavily in data transmission (see Figure 7.6).

Microwave (line of sight) Transmission   **Microwave** or **line of sight transmission** has higher speed than telephone transmission. Special towers spaced approximately 30 miles apart are built for "line of sight" transmission. Each tower picks up, amplifies, and transmits the signal to the next tower, and so on, until transmission is completed.

Satellite Transmission   Another vehicle for handling high volume traffic is the communication satellite. A geostationary orbit, 22,250 miles above the equator, takes on the appearance of a great parking lot where satellites

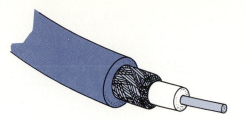

Figure 7.6
A coaxial cable. This cable is designed for use with video display terminals.

are stationed. Examples are Westar, Comstar, and Satcom (see Table 7.2). They scan the entire country with a microwave pulse in a hundredth of a second, relay 6.3 billion bits of data per second or 12,000 telephone conversations simultaneously. The *Encyclopedia Britannica* can be transmitted in under five minutes (see Figure 7.7).

The Network Concept   The satellite is a sophisticated device used for transmitting data between two points. A microwave radio signal is relayed from an "earth station" (say, point A) to the satellite. The satellite changes its frequency and transmits the signal back to earth (point B). The "distance insensitive" network means that it costs no more to send a message from New York to Los Angeles than from New York to Boston (see Figure 7.8). The satellite can also relay signals over long distances not practical in a single terrestrial chain because of the curvature of the earth and atmospheric conditions. Interceptions of communication via satellite are illustrated in Figure 7.9.

Figure 7.7
The satellite dish is becoming a common sight as organizations and even individuals expand their communications horizons.

Table 7.2 North American and Domestic Satellites

Satellites in Operation	Orbital Location	Satellites Being Planned
Satcom V	143°	
	139°	Satcom I-R
Satcom I	136°	
	135°	Galaxy I
Satcom III-R	131°	
Comstar 4	127°	
Westar II	123°	Westar V
	122°	ASC* USSSI*
Satcom II	119°	Spacenet I
	116°	Anik C-2
Anik A-2/3	114°	Anik D-2
	112.5°	Anik C-I
Anik B-I	109°	Anik C-3
	106°	GSTAR
Anik A-I	104°	Anik D-I
	103°	GSTAR
SBS-I	100°	
Westar IV	99°	
SBS-II	97°	
Comstar I/2	95°	Telstar I
	94°	SBS-III
Westar III	91°	Advanced Westar
	88°	ASC* USSSI*
Comstar 3	87°	Telstar II
Satcom IV	83°	
	79°	Advanced Westar
	74°	Galaxy II
	70°	Spacenet II
	66°	Satcom II-R

While space itself is limitless, only a limited area is usable for communication satellites. This area is an imaginary ring around the earth. The satellite orbits the earth every 24 hours, which makes it appear to be "parked" in one spot over the equator. It operates like a high antenna, reaching 43 percent of the earth's surface with a single radio signal. Since international agreement requires a minimum of 1,800 mile distance between satellites, there are fewer and fewer slots available in the communication ring.

Illustration In 1882, when Charles Dow and Edward Jones began reporting financial news, the latest technology that helped the then-young Dow Jones rush the news to its customers was the human hand. A group of

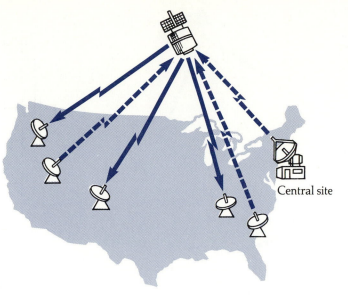

(a)

Figure 7.8
Network concept. (a) An earth station transmits a microwave signal to the satellite, which in turn changes its frequency and transmits the signal back to an intended receiving station on earth. (b) Examples of satellite use.

Central site

Selected Financial Applications

- Account inquiry
- Automatic teller
- Bad check lists
- Credit verification
- Electronic funds transfer
- Inventory control
- Point-of-sale

Selected General Applications

- Inquiry/response
  Computer time-sharing
  Database access
- Remote data collection
  Environmental status
  Security alarm monitoring

(b)

scribes used tissue-and-carbon paper sandwiches to produce 24 handwritten bulletins at a time. Through the years, new technology had to be found to get the news in time for it to be of use. Today, the *Wall Street Journal* bounces pages of news off communication satellites to more than 6 million readers daily. Since 1974, Dow Jones and the Communication Satellite Corporation have been transmitting journal pages in a communication satellite system. In 1981, the *Asian Wall Street Journal* began printing in Singapore by satellite transmission from Hong Kong.

Satellite-based Teleconferencing According to one study, 20 million meetings are held in the U.S. every day. Eighty percent of all meetings last less than 30 minutes. Sixty percent could be handled by voice communications; 35 percent are for information exchange only. With executive time at a premium, many corporations are looking into alternative ways to get executives together.

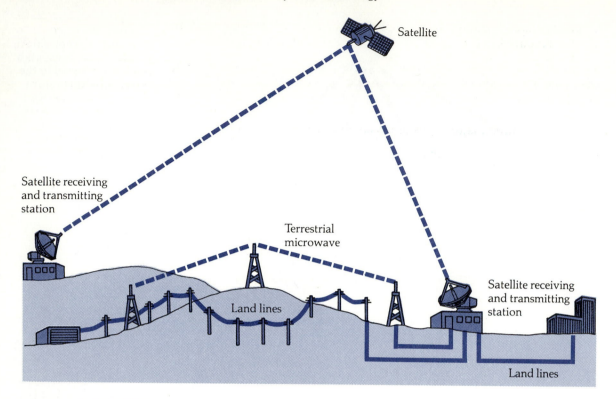

Figure 7.9
Satellite communication reception and rebroadcasting. Satellite and terrestrial microwave signals are broadcast at different frequencies to avoid interference; both require line-of-sight transmission. Once picked up from a satellite, the signal will be converted to another frequency and rebroadcast using land-based stations. The signal may also be transmitted through conducted media.

During the 1980s, business has experienced a new dimension in communications—the **teleconference**. This is an interactive software system that provides group communication between two or more sites through a computer-based network. Most organizations have used teleconferencing for three functions:

1. *Information exchange* such as sales data, policy forecast, budget estimates, etc.
2. *Task coordination* among geographically dispersed personnel
3. *Problem solving,* especially through group decision making or brainstorming

There are several advantages of teleconferencing. It:

1. Reduces unnecessary travel and saves time and expense; no waiting at airports.
2. No time restrictions; no one is ever late for a meeting.
3. No special skills are required.
4. The system is always there—no geographical restrictions.
5. Improves the quality of decision making by allowing issues to be dealt with when they come up.

6. Because time is limited by technological constraints, participants come well prepared and tend to be considerate of one another.

A major drawback of teleconferencing is transmission and installation cost. One hour of transmission between Los Angeles and New York costs over $2,000 over AT&T's Picturephone Meeting Service (PMS), including facilities.

There are three major types of teleconferencing:

1. *Video conferencing* simulates face-to-face meetings with two-way full motion video along with two-way audio. Participants can view one another during long-distance conferences (see Figure 7.10).

Figure 7.10
Typical satellite-based teleconference network. Both audio and visual media can be transmitted by satellite. Transmittal work and reception are limited only by the availability of transmitting and receiving satellite stations.

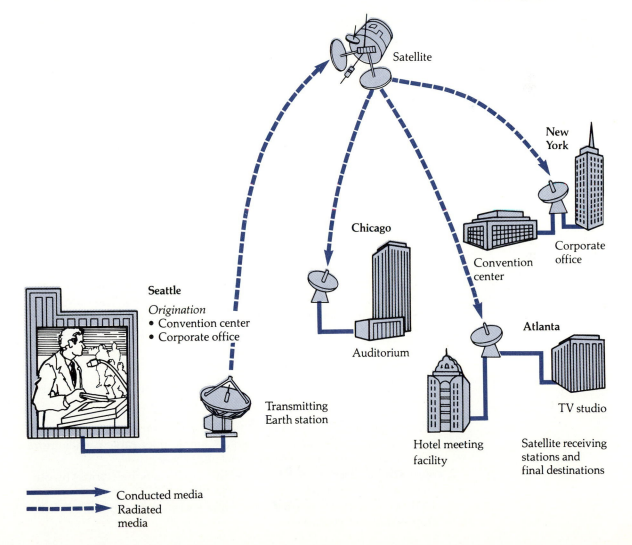

2. *Video seminars* combine one-way video with two-way audio. This type is ideal for announcing new products or addressing a large audience. The audience gathers in large groups in various cities and watches on TV monitors. A two-way phone link allows attendees to ask questions that are heard by those in all locations.

3. *Audio conferencing* is basically a telephone call conference involving telephone conversation of three or more persons in geographically dispersed locations. Participants sit in conference rooms specifically equipped with microphone-activated telephones to conduct the meeting.

Unlike conferencing that can be used on an ad hoc basis, video conferencing and video seminars require special facilities and planning for scheduling participants' time and use of the facilities. Video conferencing is the only form of teleconferencing that meets the need for full interaction. Participants see reactions to their ideas and reactions can be very important. Audio conferencing seems more natural than video conferencing because it appears to be a simple extension of the telephone call.

Organizations considering a teleconferencing environment should first assess their need for any form of electronic meetings. They should also consider geographical distance, number and frequency of meetings, and type of organization structure. Large formal meetings are ideal for video seminars, with remote questions and answers providing interaction. For ad hoc conferences where two or more individuals want a meeting right away, audio conferencing is appropriate. For project teams and groups that require visual feedback and a sense of interaction with remote participants, video conferencing is the best choice.

Fiber Optics   A new telecommunication technology, the optical fiber or **fiber optics**, transmits information using a hair-thin glass (silica) in the form of light waves. The fibers are made of three layers. The outer layer is a plastic coating to protect against dirt. The second layer, called **cladding**, reflects the light waves into the third layer, the core (see Figure 7.11).

Why Fiber Optics?   Compared to traditional communications forms, fiber optics offers several advantages:

1. Higher-capacity transmission that allows the user to expand the system without additional cable costs. A single-fiber cable carries more than 30,000 telephone messages simultaneously.

2. No electrical interference, because fiber optics is nonelectric. The outcome is data reliability.

3. High transmission security. Fiber optics cannot be tapped by direct connection to the wire.

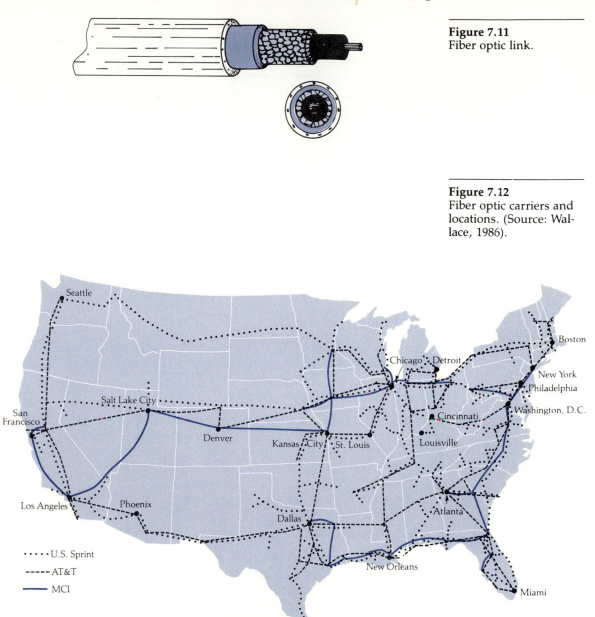

Figure 7.11
Fiber optic link.

Figure 7.12
Fiber optic carriers and locations. (Source: Wallace, 1986).

4. Virtually nonexistent downtime. Projected downtime is less than 30 seconds per year. Existing and planned fiber optics carriers and locations are shown in Figure 7.12.

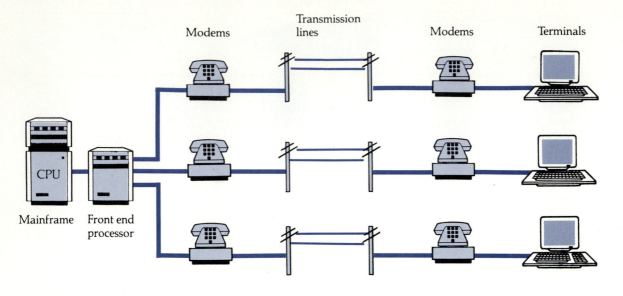

Figure 7.13
Front end processor.

Front End Processors

A sophisticated control unit used in telecommunication networks is the **front end processor**. It is a computer that controls transmission between the main computer and remote terminals (see Figure 7.13). The front end processor performs several functions:

1. Assigns ID to messages and checks their accuracy.
2. Logs incoming and outgoing messages and edits their form and content.
3. Handles message priority.
4. Polls terminals to determine if they are ready.
5. Decides on alternative paths for transmission.

Telecommunication Computers

The final element in a telecommunication network is the main computer. It is the center of all operations. The stored program controls the network and the interface between the user and the computer within the network. The configuration of the computer depends on the number of users, the volume of data traffic, complexity of application, and access time. These factors are evaluated in planning a telecommunication network.

Transmission Speed and Data Traffic

Data are transmitted by a frequency that is affected by the bandwidth of the transmission medium. Bandwidth determines how fast data can be transmitted, measured in bits per second or **baud**. There are three classes of bandwidth:

1. **Narrow band** (low speed): up to 300 baud, depending on the service.
2. **Voice band** (medium speed): used for communicating by human voice over public or leased lines. Maximum speed is between 4,800 and 9,600 baud, depending on the modem.
3. **Wide band** (high speed): transmits in excess of 9,600 baud and up to 50,000 baud over private-line channels. High-speed lines require microwave, fiber optics, or satellite communication. They are used normally in a computer-to-computer data communication environment.

Types of Channels

Three types of channels are used in teletransmission: simplex, half-duplex, and full-duplex.

The **simplex transmission** channel transmits in one direction only. There is no interchange between the user and the computer (see Figure 7.14). A simple example is the telegraph system, which transmits information one way from a remote location.

The **half-duplex transmission** channel transmits in either direction, but in one direction at a time. This mode is typical in data processing systems, where the operator enters the data and then receives a response from the computer (see Figure 7.14).

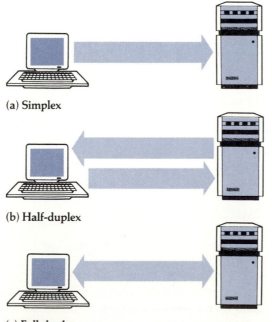

(a) Simplex

(b) Half-duplex

(c) Full-duplex

Figure 7.14
Types of channels. Transmission directions: (a) The seldom-used simplex transmission sends data in one direction only. (b) Half-duplex transmission can send data in either direction, but only one way at a time. (c) Full-duplex transmission can send data in both directions at once.

Figure 7.15
Asynchronous and synchronous transmission. (a) Asynchronous transmission uses start/stop signals surrounding each character. (b) Synchronous transmission uses a continuous stream of characters.

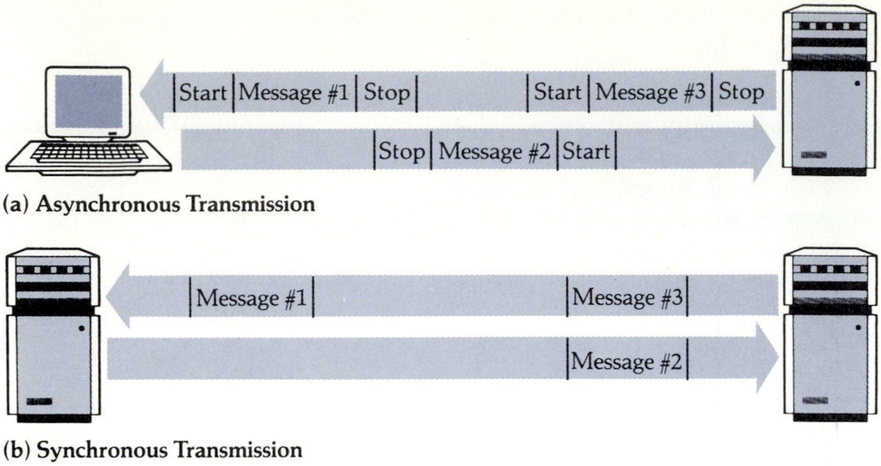

| Start | Message #1 | Stop | | Start | Message #3 | Stop |

| Stop | Message #2 | Start |

(a) Asynchronous Transmission

| Message #1 | | Message #3 |

| Message #2 |

(b) Synchronous Transmission

The **full-duplex transmission** channel transmits in both directions simultaneously. It is the same as two simplex lines or one half-duplex line in opposite directions. This arrangement is ideal for high-speed transmission between two computers (see Figure 7.14).

Mode of Transmission

Telecommunication lines carry data asynchronously or synchronously. In **asynchronous transmission**, data are transmitted one character at a time, each with its own start and stop bits. The procedure is repeated, character by character, until the entire message has been transmitted. In contrast, **synchronous transmission** sends a continuous stream of data at a time. When the start bit is sensed, the sending equipment begins transmission in a continuous stream without the intervening start and stop bits (see Figure 7.15).

Asynchronous transmission is used for low-volume, low-speed data transmission. Synchronous transmission is used for high-volume, high-speed transmission.

Line Configurations

Regardless of the channel, mode, or transmission speed, we need to know how to connect computers and terminals in conjunction with communication lines. There are two line configurations: point-to-point or multidrop lines. A **point-to-point** (or single drop) **network** is a direct line between a terminal and a computer. Each terminal uses a separate line with the remote computer (see Figure 7.16). This choice is cost effective

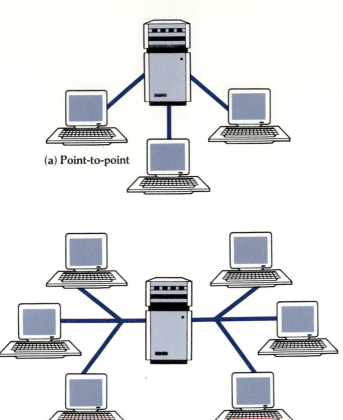

(a) Point-to-point

(b) Multidrop

Figure 7.16
Point-to-point and multi-drop lines. (a) In point-to-point lines each terminal is connected directly to the central computer. (b) In multidrop lines several terminals share a single line, although only one terminal can transmit at a time.

when a single location transmits a large volume of data regularly with little waste of time. This arrangement also ensures fast response time.

Transmission costs can be reduced by linking multiple terminals to a single line, referred to as a **multidrop network**. The advantage is that all points on the line are capable of receiving the data at one time. The drawback, though, is that only one terminal can transmit at a time; other terminal users wait in a queue. This line configuration is used mostly when the connecting sites are many miles apart (see Figure 7.16).

Common Carriers and Services

In evaluating a network, we need to know about the common carriers and their services. A **common carrier** is a government-regulated organization that offers public telecommunication facilities such as telephone service. It is under the jurisdiction of the Federal Communications Commission (FCC) when dealing with interstate traffic and each state's public utilities commission when dealing with intrastate traffic. These agencies set standards, rules, and tariffs that regulate the carriers' offerings and charges. The oldest common carrier is Western Union Telegraph Co., a subsidiary of Western Union Corporation. Among its services are Telex and Twx, data terminal services, and a wide variety of dedicated network facilities.

Services

Common carriers offer switched and leased lines. A **switched service** connects the sender and the receiver only for the duration of the call. A **leased service** may be point-to-point or multidrop. It provides a fixed path between the user and the receiver. Since it is a fixed circuit, no alternative routing is available in case of line failure.

The Value-Added Network (VAN)

Value-added networks (VANs) are a unique class of common carrier that offer high-speed packet-switched networks based on the Advance Research Projects Agency Common Communications Network (ARPANET) of the U.S. Department of Defense. Through the packet switching technique, a value-added carrier allows many users to share its communication facility. "Value" is added by managing the sharing of costs among the users.

In value-added networks, the procedure divides a message into one or more packets. Each packet is funneled through a different path, depending on network traffic conditions. The message is reassembled into its original form before it becomes available to the user.

The Local Area Network (LAN)

If each knowledge worker has a workstation or a microcomputer system and every clerk has a word processing system for typing, editing, filing, and so on, it becomes useful to communicate among systems. An efficient approach to this kind of networking is the local area network or LAN.

LAN is distinguished from other networks by the area it covers, its transmission speed, and the ease of adding new devices. LAN is an electronic communication linkage in which all sources and recipients are located in one office, a single building, or a single work site, typically less than one mile in radius. A major objective is to improve human productivity and provide resource sharing. The end user is free to choose from a wealth of information and technology available through the network. This includes making voice links within and outside the building, receiving as many as fifty documents daily, and processing information without having to line up behind others for a single computer resource.

Consider a manufacturing environment in which various phases of the production process must be monitored. A single computer can do the job, but it may not be able to handle more than one or two users at a time. LAN uses a number of microcomputers on the user's location to communicate with the central computer on command. Data and records may also be accessed from several points within the production complex (see Figure 7.17).

LAN is described by several characteristics:

1. It is contained entirely within a small geographic area.
2. It transmits information, usually in digital form; that is, there is no conversion to analog.
3. It is easy to interconnect among terminals on the network.
4. Each terminal can communicate with every other terminal.

LAN is also described by the typology of the network, transmission techniques, and the protocol performed.

Typologies of the Network

LAN design should connect a large number of terminals, handle a large volume of data, be fast enough for workers to function at their pace, and flexible enough to allow easy physical connection. In many large office buildings, wiring terminal links can cost as much as the terminal itself. As a rule, one connection point is installed for every workplace. This eliminates the problem of sharing terminals.

In selecting a LAN, cable layout is an important consideration. There are three common cable layouts or typologies (Burch, 1985, 34, 37ff): star, ring, and bus.

Star Network   The *star* design is the simplest configuration for the smaller microcomputer LAN. Each terminal is linked by a separate line to a host computer. The computer routes data and instructions among the "nodes" or computer stations. It runs the network by polling the "slave" stations for data transmission. This network design is economical, because it requires only one host computer linked to terminals by a common telephone and a modem. However, the whole system will fail if the host goes down (see Figure 7.18).

Ring Network   Another typology is the ring network. Several processors or microcomputers are linked together to form the equivalent of a ring (see Figure 7.19). Data lines connect each unit to adjacent ones only. This typology is often the least costly way to design a LAN. The design significantly reduces the amount of cable, although the installation can

Figure 7.17
LAN in a manufacturing
environment.

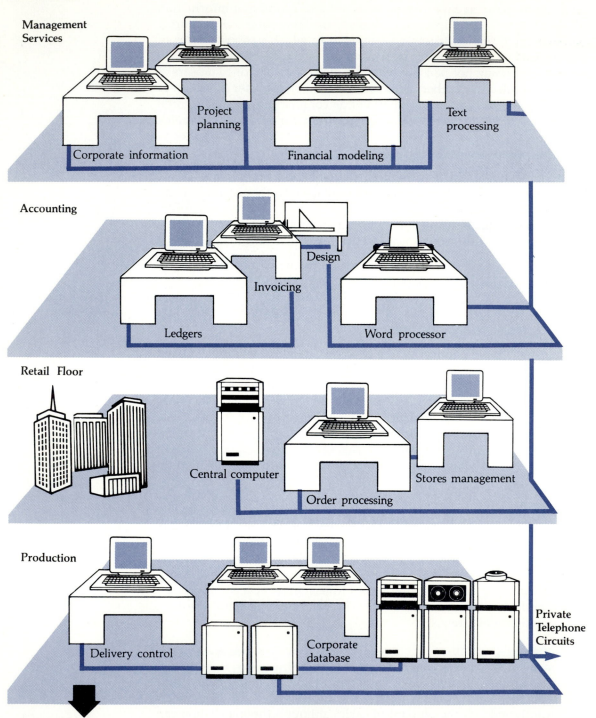

Management
Services

Project
planning

Text
processing

Corporate information

Financial modeling

Accounting

Design

Invoicing

Ledgers

Word processor

Retail Floor

Central computer

Stores management

Order processing

Production

Delivery control

Corporate
database

Private
Telephone
Circuits

be intricate since the ring must be continuous. Also, if one node fails so that it cannot pass on data, the whole system will be idle.

Bus Network This form of cable layout requires a length of coaxial cable, called bus cable. It is more like an electrical "highway" that carries communication signals. All functional devices connect to the *bus*. An electrical signal uses the bus that decides the connecting path to its destination.

Xerox Corporation has promoted the bus typology as a standard for LAN. ETHERNET, as the standard is called, has been adopted by computer vendors such as Apple and the Digital Equipment Corporation (DEC) (see Figure 7.20). A summary of LAN typologies is given in Table 7.3.

Transmission Techniques

LANs are divided into two main transmission networks: broadband and baseband.

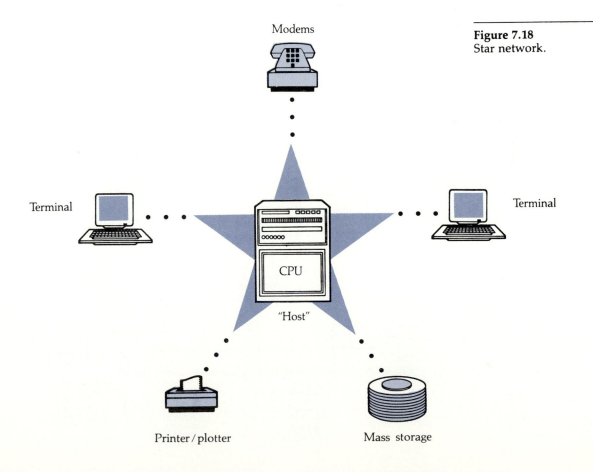

Figure 7.18
Star network.

Modems

Terminal

Terminal

CPU

"Host"

Printer/plotter

Mass storage

Figure 7.19
Ring network.

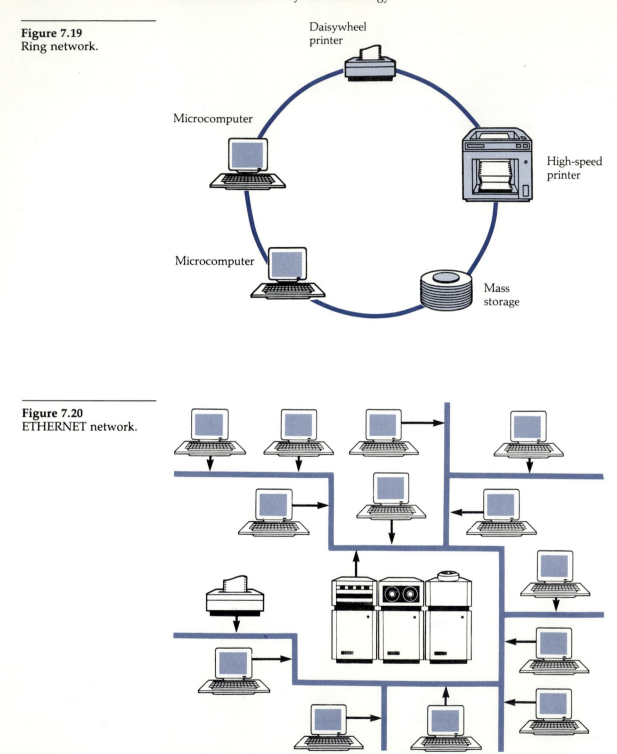

Figure 7.20
ETHERNET network.

Table 7.3 LAN Cable Layout Typology

Net Type	Connection	Interface	Error Impact	Common Method
Star	Single central node (computer). All other terminals are rapidly connected off it	Data switched between each station via central control mode	None; if a station is idle, it is not switched	Switching
Ring	Station (terminal) physically connected to two adjacent stations in closed loop	Transmission carried out from left to right	All stations must be operational; if one fails, it must be bypassed	Token passing
Bus	Stations connected to common "roadway"	Each station can hear everything	No impact, even if station is idle	Token passing

	Advantages	Disadvantages
Star	· Ideal for many-to-one configurations · Suited for dumb terminals	· Laying cables can be expensive · Vulnerable to central computer failure; if disabled, the entire network goes down · Network reliability depends on the whole loop
Ring	· No dependence on a central device; single break in network won't cause failure · Routing is simple · Easy transmission error check · Low error rate	· Difficult to add new terminals without reconfiguring the loop · Cable installations can be tricky
Bus	· Best suited to broadband method, since transmissions are modulated analog signals	· Each station can hear everything

Adapted from International Data Corp., "Networking Microcomputers and Office Systems (NMOS)." Framingham, Mass., 1984.

Broadband Network   A **broadband network** is a large-capacity cable that can be partitioned into several channels, each channel representing a separate line. The network can carry very high data rates over long distances. The technology has been used for many years in the analog world of cable TV. Because of high data rates, it can also support voice and video signals.

Baseband Network   LANs unique to telecommunications are called **baseband networks**. This is a newer development, introduced with multiple digital terminals in mind. The transmission mode is entirely digital, which means very low error rates. It can also be used for one-way stored voice messages as required by office automation terminals.

The vast majority of LANs are baseband systems. Because they are founded in digital technology, they are more cost effective than broadband. The cost factor is important when we consider the hundreds of terminals connected to one LAN. Yet where video traffic is necessary, broadband technology with its 50 million bits per second is a better solution. There is actually no problem linking broadband and baseband networks. The baseband can be used for its data-handling capacity, while the broadband network is essentially for video traffic.

Protocol

In LANs, data "collision" occurs when two or more terminals transmit at the same time. To avoid this problem, protocol, or a set of control rules, is required. Such rules determine how a terminal is addressed and how a line contention is handled. Many esoteric terms illustrate how protocol is achieved. **Polling** is a request to each available terminal to accept or transmit a message (Bryant, 1984, 116). **Contention** is a method of network control that lets the computer sense a bid from the terminal and authorizes it to begin transmission.

A common method of gaining access to a ring or bus network is token passing. **Token passing** is a procedure that allows a terminal to transmit only while it holds a logical "token" that is passed from one terminal to another in a sequence. The token passes every terminal at a designated time interval, much like a boxcar on a railroad line. If a terminal wishes to send information, it waits for an empty token to arrive, fills it with data and sends it on the way. The data is later unloaded at its destination. When empty, it continues on its route. The major problem is possible "loss" of the token. When this happens, no terminal can access the network (see Figure 7.21). A summary of LAN types and their protocols is shown in Table 7.4.

PCnet: An Illustration

One of the first LANs available for the personal computer (PC) was PCnet, by Orchid Technology. PCnet provides relatively simple, low-cost resource sharing and intercommunications among IBM PCs, using the IBM disk operating system (DOS). The PCnet hardware has an adaptor card that plugs into the expansion slot on each PC in the network. The card comes with the software that integrates the network into PC DOS.

A feature of PCnet allows each PC to share hard disk drives installed in another PC. For example, if a user PC has one disk drive (say, A) and

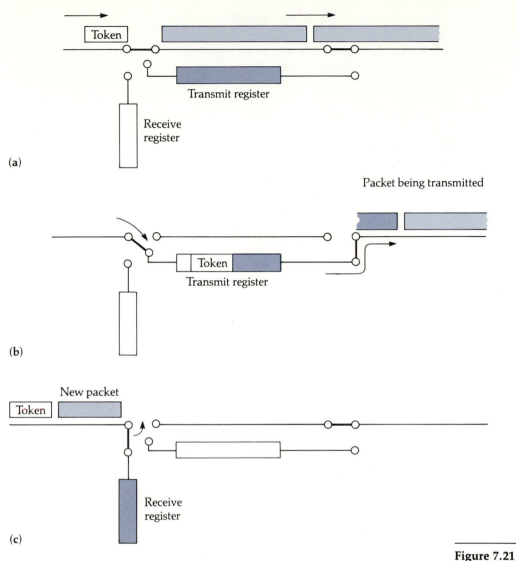

(a)

Token

Transmit register

Receive
register

Packet being transmitted

(b)

Token

Transmit register

New packet

Token

(c)

Receive
register

Figure 7.21
Token-passing ring.
(a) Waiting for token.
(b) Transmitting packet.
(c) Removing packet.
(Source: Gee, 1983, 67.)

shares a hard disk via the network, the user can use drive A (local) and the shared hard disk instead of another drive (B,C,D) (see Figure 7.22). Future reference to them is B:filespec, C:filespec, or D:filespec saving, loading. The hard disk is tapped as though it were a part of the user PC.

What to Consider in LAN Selection

MIS managers who are implementing a LAN must first identify the specific computing requirements of its end users and the appropriate equip-

Table 7.4   A Comparison Between Baseband and Broadband Networks

LAN Type	Characteristics	Transmission	Protocol	Support
Baseband	Pattern of digital data transmission; very low error	Single channel (one way)	Token passing	Voice-data-voice must be digitized
Broadband	Modulating data pattern, CATV compatible	Multiple channels, each reporting a separate line; carries very high data rates over long distances	Token passing, simultaneous different channels CATV	Supports data, video over same link

	Advantages	Disadvantages
Baseband	· Medium totally passive · Easy to attach and install new terminals	· Anyone with the right equipment can listen without detection · Messages sometimes collide
Broadband	· Suited to continuous high-speed traffic · Can mix data, voice, video, etc on one cable · Easy to install cable	· Modems are costly

Adapted from Gee, 1983, 3.

ment that will meet these requirements. The network system required by end user applications may be evaluated by two criteria:

1. How time-sensitive the processing requirements of the applications are.
2. Whether the applications require a host computer (hierarchical) or can manage alone with users (peer to peer).

Figure 7.22
A typical PCnet configuration.

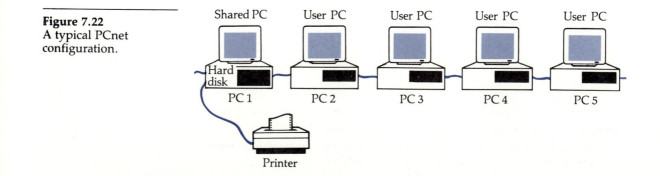

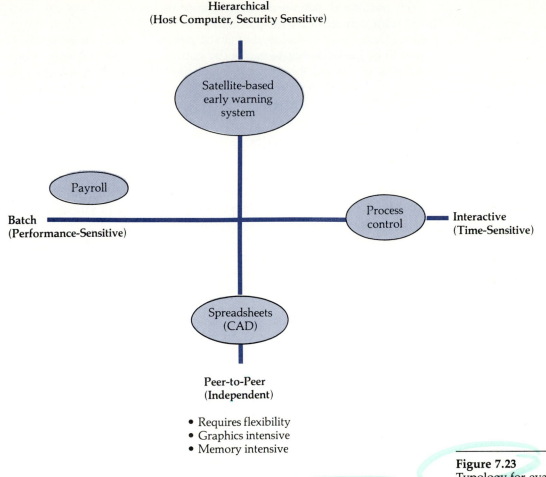

Hierarchical
(Host Computer, Security Sensitive)

Satellite-based early warning system

Payroll

Batch
(Performance-Sensitive)

Process control

Interactive
(Time-Sensitive)

Spreadsheets (CAD)

Peer-to-Peer
(Independent)

- Requires flexibility
- Graphics intensive
- Memory intensive

Figure 7.23
Typology for evaluating LAN solutions. The X axis suggests that an application becomes more time sensitive the more interactive it is—for example, as in process control. For the Y axis, applications requiring a host computer tend to be more security sensitive than peer-to-peer applications are. (Source: Graham and Scott, 1987, F68.)

Figure 7.23 is a typology that helps MIS managers in evaluating LAN applications and services.

The top ellipse in figure 7.27 represents a hierarchical network in which requests for application services are routed through a mainframe. This model works well for extremely sophisticated applications requiring a high level of security, predictability or coordination among many contributing data stations. For example, a satellite-based early warning system uses several strategically placed satellite units that feed data continuously into a host computer, which organizes it into information useful to the military. The system must be consistent and failsafe.

A *peer-to-peer* network operates at the opposite extreme. Like a round table conference, users may exchange information and work independent of a computer center, with applications that require flexibility and a broad range of capabilities from their equipment. Typical applications are spreadsheets and computer-aided design (CAD).

The horizontal axis measures whether an application must be executed with dispatch or with precision. For example, a payroll requires great accuracy, but is processed over the period of a week or a month; it is said to be performance-sensitive. By contrast, a factory's process control demands immediate computer response to the random activities of the plant—a week's response time will be useless. This type of application is said to be time-sensitive.

Implications for MIS

Telecommunication is a delivery system for MIS. In today's business world, managers or clerks no longer have to be near a computer to deal with information. Sales clerks enter data through terminals. Production workers enter job completion and material utilization from floor shop terminals linked directly to the host computer. Branch managers can query a database and a status report is transmitted electronically.

The role of telecommunications has improved the availability of information to management for decision making. This was long-haul (external) communication. The introduction of the microcomputer, user-friendly languages, word processing, electronic mail, and the executive workstation has encouraged end user computing and transmitting data inside a building. This is represented by LAN—short-haul (internal) transmission. It is obvious that decision making depends on the availability of information. The two go together for successful management. The decision-making process is discussed in detail in the next chapter.

Summary

- The history of telecommunication dates back to Morse's first telegram in 1844. Bell's telephone followed in 1876. Today's use of fiber optics and satellite transmission makes information processing available for quick and timely decision making.

- Telecommunication is the movement of information by electronic transmission among multiple sites. Telecommunication networks are used in a variety of applications, especially in information inquiry/retrieval and source data entry.

- The key elements of a telecommunication system are terminals, modems, acoustic couplers, and telecommunication channels. Terminals transmit, display, and/or receive information, depending on whether they are intelligent or dumb. The main feature of an intelligent terminal is user programmability.

- The primary function of a modem is to convert a message from digital to analog for transmission and back to digital for delivery. Telecommunication channels carry the information from source to destination. They may be a telephone line, coaxial cable, or microwave (line of sight) channel.

□ The communications satellite is a distance-insensitive network, carrying messages quickly regardless of distance. It operates like a high antenna, reaching 43 percent of the earth's surface with a single radio signal. Because of this unique feature, teleconferencing became an acceptable and cost-effective approach to information exchange and problem solving in many firms. It reduces unnecessary travel and improved decision making. Because of the high transmission cost, however, organizations considering investment in a teleconferencing environment must first determine their need and how well it can be supported by management.

□ Fiber optics transmits information along a hair-thin glass in the form of light waves. It offers unique features such as immunity from electrical interference, high-capacity bandwidth, high transmission security, and virtually nonexistent downtime.

□ There are three types of channels: simplex (one-way transmission), half-duplex (two-way) transmission, but one way at a time, and full-duplex (two-way simultaneous) transmission. Telecommunication lines carry data asynchronously (one character at a time) or synchronously (sending a stream of data at the same time). Obviously, the latter form of transmission is more efficient for high-volume, high-speed requirements, but it is more costly than asynchronous transmission. LAN is distinguished from other networks by the area it covers, speed of transmission, and ease of adding devices. LAN is an important part of strategic plans for office automation, with the objective of providing resource sharing to multiple users. It is contained within a specific geographic area, transmits information in digital form, and provides easy interconnection between the terminals on the network.

□ LAN is described by the typology of the network (star, ring, or bus layout), transmission techniques (broadband or baseband network), and the protocol performed by the network.

□ In the star network, each terminal is linked separately to the host computer which routes messages among the network nodes. In the ring network, several microcomputers are linked together to form the equivalent of a ring. Data lines connect each unit to adjacent units only. The bus network is more like an electrical "highway" that carries data to its destination. Each network has advantages and limitations.

□ The telecommunication network is classified as switched or nonswitched. A switched service funnels data into a switching center to complete the transmission. A leased service may be point-to-point (direct line) or multidrop. In the latter design, terminals transmit or receive in a line-up mode. Each terminal waits for its own address for action.

▫ The two primary services provided by common carriers are switched and leased services. In a switched service, a line is available for the duration of the call. In contrast, a leased service provides a permanent path between user and receiver.

Key Terms

Asynchronous transmission
Baseband network
Baud
Broadband network
Channel
Cladding
Common carrier
Contention
Dumb terminal
Fiber optics
Front end processor
Full-duplex transmission
Half-duplex transmission
Intelligent terminal
Leased service
Microwave transmission
Modem

Multidrop network
Multipoint network: See multi-
   drop network
Narrow band
Peer-to-peer network
Point-to-point network
Polling
Simplex transmission
Switched service
Synchronous transmission
Telecommunication
Teleconference
Token passing
Value-added network (VAN)
Voice band
Wide band

Review Questions

1. Elaborate on the key developments in telecommunications.

2. Define the following:
   a. Telecommunication
   b. Full duplex
   c. VAN
   d. Cladding

3. What application categories are handled by telecommunication? Explain briefly.

4. Illustrate the elements of a telecommunication system. What element is considered the most critical? Why?

5. Why is protocol important in telecommunication transmission?

6. What is the difference between:
   a. Dumb and intelligent terminals
   b. Simplex and half-duplex
   c. Point-to-point and multidrop networks
   d. Front end processor and a computer

7. How does a modem work?

8. What channels are available for data transmission? Explain briefly.

9. Why is microwave referred to as "line of sight" transmission?

10. What is so unique about satellite transmission? How does the communication satellite concept work? Illustrate.

11. Describe the concept and functions of teleconferencing. What are its advantages and limitations?

12. Briefly distinguish among the three major types of teleconferencing. How does an organization determine which type is best for its needs?

13. What features does fiber optics offer over other forms of communications? Explain.

14. Distinguish among the three classes of bandwidth. Which class offers the highest speed?

15. Telecommunication lines carry data synchronously or asynchronously. How do the two modes of transmission differ? Illustrate.

16. Distinguish between a switched and nonswitched network. What features does each offer? Explain.

Application Problems

1. While banks around Miami strain against strong competition and tightening budgets to contain costs, the First National Bank of South Miami is delivering more services to customers at lower cost. According to senior vice president Lester Mandelbaum, a recent switch to distributed data processing is making a big difference.

   The bank has a solid customer base of 23,000 checking accounts, 11,000 savings accounts, and a number of installment and commercial loans. Until 1986, a central computer handled the processing of checks and produced daily reports to management. With computer utilization of 28 percent, personnel turnover, and high maintenance costs, the bank decided to make a switch and went distributed. The central computer was replaced with a new minicomputer that linked to a mainframe in Atlanta.

   Each of the bank's seventeen branches has a terminal linked directly to the mainframe. Branch tellers can now access account balances and do all account updates instantly. The minicomputer captures the daily transactions, processes the checks on the premises, and transmits balances to the mainframe for final processing and reconciliation of the bank's business for the day. Early next morning, the mainframe transmits the reports to the minicomputer's printer. The reports represent the previous day's bank activities.

Converting from a centralized to a distributed system made it possible for the bank to place computer power where it is used the most—on the teller line. At the same time, it significantly reduced the load on the bank's data processing staff. In fact, since the conversion the total staff was reduced by 60 percent. The result was expanded service to tellers and officers. In early 1988, four ATMs were installed in shopping plazas. They will be linked directly to the mainframe, which will process the transactions and provide daily reports to management through the minicomputer's printer.

The outcome of this conversion is significant savings in costs, improved service, and a more reliable system, since the mainframe has a backup on the hardware and electric power round the clock.

QUESTIONS

a. What applications other than checking and savings could such a system serve?
b. Evaluate the cost saving area. To what would you attribute it? Why?
c. Discuss the pros and cons of centralized versus distributed processing in a banking environment. Is networking a solution for all organizations? Why?

2. Assume the following activities of an order processing system:
   a. Sales clerk enters customer and order information into terminal.
   b. System displays order form on screen.
   c. System determines expected shipping date.
   d. System computes total price of order.
   e. Terminal displays completed order form.
   f. System routes instructions to hardware terminal in the sales department for authorizing order.
   g. System looks up customer credit rating at corporate mainframe.
   h. System conveys information to terminal.

QUESTIONS

a. Which activities are data processing?
b. Which activities are data transmission?
c. Which activities are communication interface?

3. A cluster of fifteen terminals operating 30 characters per second (cps) is installed in Miami, Florida. All terminals need to interface (point-to-

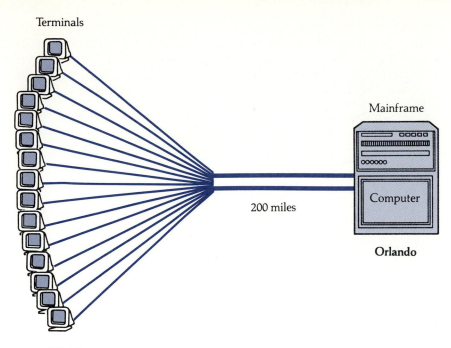

Terminals

Mainframe

200 miles

Computer

Orlando

Miami

point) with a mainframe located in Orlando, 200 miles away. Assume full usage of each terminal in such a way that it must be connected to the network on a continuous basis.

The cost of a single narrowband line that operates at 30 cps is as follows:

- First 100 miles: $1.75/mile/month
- Second 50 miles: 1.45/mile/month
- Last 50 miles: .90/mile/month

Since a theoretical maximum of 450 characters per second (15×30) can be transmitted to the mainframe, we can secure a wider-band line capable of handling this traffic (450 cps) over the Miami-Orlando link with the appropriate multiplexing devices to provide the same level of service (see page 230).

The cost of the wider-band is as follows:

- First 50 miles: $3.45/mile/month
- Second 100 miles: 1.60/mile/month
- Last 50 miles: .98/mile/month

QUESTIONS
a. What is the monthly line cost of the point-to-point configuration?
b. What is the monthly line cost under the wider-band configuration?

Terminals

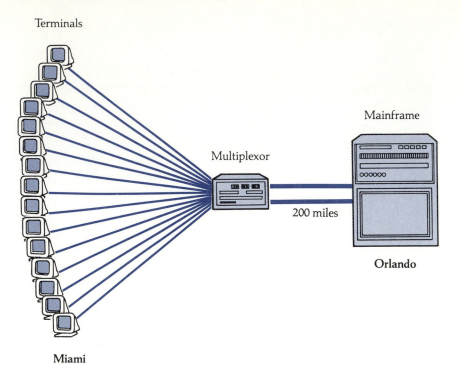

Miami

Selected References

Adrian, Merv. "The Work Connection." *Computerworld*, February 16, 1987, S1–2.

Bryant, Susan F. "LANs Versus Multiuser Systems: Which Is Best for Team Computing?" *Computer Decisions*, October 1984.

Burch, John B. "Network Typologies: The Ties that Bind Information Systems." *Data Management*, December 1985, 34–37ff.

Chester, Michael. "Business Forms and the X-400 Protocol Help Drive E-Mail." *Systems & Software*, March 1985, 61–63.

Cullum, Ronald L. "Iterative Development." *Datamation*, February 15, 1985, 92–94ff.

Davis, Dwight B. "Managing Computer Communications." *High Technology*, March 1987, 24–27.

Gee, K. C. E. *Introduction to Local Area Network.* New York: John Wiley & Sons, 1983.

Graham, Gig and Scott, Tom. "Don't Miss the Mark in Network Selection." *Computerworld*, April 1, 1987, Focus 67–69.

Grantz, Paul C. "Mainframe Programs Talk to One Another." *Systems & Software*, February 1985, 95ff.

Hillhouse, Joseph. "The New World of Telecommunication." *Computer Decisions*, September 15, 1985, 95ff.

"The Rewiring of America," special report, *Business Week*, September 15, 1986, 188–190ff.

Sprague, Ralph H. and McNurlin, Barbara. *Information Systems Management in Practice*. Englewood Cliffs, N.J.: Prentice-Hall, 1986, 138–171.

Stix, Gary. "MIS Bets on Smart Nets." *Computer Decisions*, December 2, 1986, 36–38.

Tucker, Michael. "Connectivity." *Computerworld*, April 1, 1987, Focus/47ff.

Wallace, Bob. "Who's Got the Fiber?" *Network World*, March 31, 1986.

Wlosinski, Larry G. "A Fundamental Approach to the Basics of Networking." *Data Management*, September 1986, 13–19.

8

The Decision-Making Process

Chapter Contents

Litton Resources Solution: Cullinet

LITTON RESOURCES SYSTEMS, a division of Litton Industries, Inc., hired Wayne Johnson in 1982 to help the organization choose and implement a manufacturing system. The biggest problem was materials movement. The biggest question in management's mind was how Litton had been able to manage manually for all that time. The answer was that the company was relying on a few key people who had been with the company for many years and had much of the critical business information in their heads.

"We looked at this and said, 'One of these days we're not going to have all these people, and [when that day comes,] there go all of our systems.' We had islands of information. One person would be knowledgeable but everything was in his head, not on paper or in a system. Therefore, he couldn't transfer that information to new people who came on board or quickly communicate to other people throughout the company's functional organization," Johnson explained.

The company had multiple IBM and Amdahl Corporation mainframes in its many data centers, but most were handling scientific processing. None of the materials management or manufacturing applications resided on the big machines.

The hardware choice was made pretty quickly. Once selected, the study committee came up with some criteria for the software. It studied 18 products initially, quickly weeding that number down to five vendors. Eventually, the study team chose Cullinet's IDMS, and there is reportedly not a regret in the bunch.

At the end of 1984, Litton installed the information database, all the manufacturing application software for purchasing, bill of materials, inventory, shop floor control, order entry, accounts payable, master production schedules and a cost control module.

The technology has helped the firm weather an economic storm. They had to do the job with fewer people, and at the same time, a lot of the key people decided to take retirement. It is a whole different world today, and the firm more than justified the cost of the system. Hindsight tells management it was a good decision.

—*Excerpted from Lee White,* Computerworld, *July 9, 1986, Focus/19–21.*

AT A GLANCE

An important MIS area consists of tools and procedures for problem solving and decision making. Problem-solving activity is seeking courses of action that will solve a problem. Choosing among alternatives is decision making.

The decision-making process may be viewed in terms of normative or descriptive models. At the center of these approaches is the concept of rationality—making a choice based on a known set of alternatives with corresponding outcomes, a set of relations that orders the alternatives, and maximizing something definitive such as cost, profit, and so on.

Knowledge of outcomes considers three cases: certainty, risk, and uncertainty. Decision making under *certainty* is a situation in which the probability of an event occurring is 1 and in which all other events have a probability of 0. Decision making under *risk* is a situation in which the states of nature can be assigned a probability value. Decision making under *uncertainty* is a situation in which no probability value can be established for the states of nature. For such problems maximin or maximax criteria can be used, depending on the assumptions.

This approach is tabular in that the decision making information is organized in tables. An alternative is the graphic approach, such as the decision tree. There are also other computer-based decision-making techniques and management science models to improve the quality of final decisions. Management science is a decided contribution to organizational performance, allowing managers to make effective decisions using computer-based models.

By the end of this chapter, you should know:

1. The components of decisions and the process managers go through to make effective decisions
2. How organizational and cultural factors affect decision making
3. The various models of decision making
4. The criteria for decision making
5. How management science and behavioral models contribute to management decision making

Introduction

In the previous chapters, we have talked about information system technology—computer fundamentals, databases, and data communications to produce information for decision making. Successful management depends on people and technology. We need to know how managers make decisions and how decisions and information are related. This is the theme of this chapter.

What good are concepts and theories? In developing a technology-based environment, especially in MIS, we prescribe procedures based on testable concepts and experience. The field of MIS is still embryonic. The transition from theory to practice will certainly grow stronger with hands-on experience and additional research.

Users have a better feel for what an information system must provide the clearer they understand the need for information, how decisions are made, and how decisions depend on information. The same applies to analysts and database designers. Their role is to translate the user's decisions into a successful MIS installation.

In this chapter we will review problem solving, various approaches to decision making, and how decision-making concepts relate to information system design. Many authors confuse problem solving with decision making. A problem arises when the end user is bothered by a poor procedure, inefficient report, and the like. The **problem-solving** activity is the seeking of solutions or alternative action. The choice among these solutions is decision making. A number of approaches are used in making decisions throughout the problem-solving process.

Problem Solving

Managers spend much of their time solving problems. Some problems are more complex than others, but all problems need a certain level of attention. In an organizational context, there are various types of problems. For example:

1. Company performance does not meet standards.
2. Present sales record indicates that the competition is taking the lead.
3. New management is making changes that will result in consolidation of functions.

A problem is the deviation between what is and what ought to be. Problems occur as a result of *change* in the corporate environment, managers' objectives, the functioning of the business, and the roles personalities play in running a business. The MIS function may signal a possible problem area by reports that document declining performance. A good MIS will detect and identify problems and their impact on the organization on a regular basis.

Corollary to the nature of the problem is its structure. A problem can vary from well structured to ill structured. In well-structured problems, the methods for solving, the data, and the anticipated solution(s) are all known. In contrast, ill-structured problems present a situation in which only a general problem-solving approach is available, data are normally incomplete and unreliable, and the nature of the solution is ambiguous.

Regardless of structure, the problem solver must define the problem and its relationship to the total system. To illustrate, let us consider an organization that has been a leader in the microcomputer market for its unique portable computer. Sales have suddenly started to decline as more companies offer cheaper systems with similar performance. The problem could be formulated as follows:

Elements

1. The organization's overall objectives.
2. The organization's product features and costs.
3. Level of the technology used in manufacturing the product.
4. The competing product's features and costs.
5. Advertising and pricing policies of the company and its competitors.
6. Projected demand for the current portable computer.
7. The caliber of the participants in the problem-solving process.

Present state

1. The firm has experienced tremendous growth for the portable computer until six months ago.
2. Sales have dropped 20 percent in the last six months.
3. Research and development have not produced an advanced product for over a year.
4. A giant mainframe computer manufacturer announced entry into the portable computer market.

Desired state

1. To market a portable computer to small business that requires minimal training.
2. To return to the number one spot in sales.
3. To have a clear identification of market potential.

Constraints

1. Research and development is limited to 10 percent of sales.
2. Problem solution must be implemented in less than three months.
3. Present dealers and marketing outlets must be maintained under present contracts.
4. Management is determined to stick it out rather than sell out.

Criteria for solution

1. Minimum reshuffling of corporate staff required.
2. Projected market share must be over 30 percent.
3. Image of a highly reliable portable computer must be maintained.

In practice, a real problem situation is more detailed and can be more complex than our scenario. The important point here is that the more detailed the facts, the clearer (and potentially easier) will be the resulting problem formulation. In solving the problem, the elements of the problem may be structured through models and a database that becomes a part of MIS. Except for the "present state" elements, all other factors can be altered through simulation to figure out the net effect on the solutions.

The Decision-Making Process

No matter from what perspective we view management, it essentially involves **decision making**. This process helps us evaluate, select, and implement a course of action for problem solving. Of the managerial functions of planning, organizing, directing, and controlling, we place great emphasis on planning and controlling decisions. **Planning** means that a manager must evaluate and select an alternative course of action to achieve objectives as they are integrated within organizational plans. Similarly, **controlling** decisions keeps the firm's activities in step with plans.

Definition

The "decision-making school" of management was given impetus by Herbert Simon (1960), who views decision making as synonymous with managing. During the same period, Peter Drucker's (1961) decision theory predicted that managerial emphasis would be understanding decision making. The prediction became in part a reality with integrating quantitative decision making models within the MIS framework. The implication for this trend is that today's manager can no longer work alone, evaluating all possible factors for making a good decision. The computer assists the manager in solving statistically oriented problems in a matter of minutes instead of the days it once took with the manual method.

A definition of decision making is widely associated with making a choice among alternatives. According to H. Ofstad, "To make a decision means to make a judgment regarding what one ought to do in a certain situation after having deliberated on some alternative courses of action" (1961, 15). Churchman also offers a clear definition of decision making: "The manager is the man who decides among alternative choices. He must decide which choice he believes will lead to a certain desired objective or a set of objectives" (1968, 17).

Herbert Simon viewed decision making as a three-phase continuous process model beginning with intelligence, followed by design and choice (see Figure 8.1). The process is invoked by the recognition of a problem. The resulting decision is then directed at solving the problem.

The **intelligence** phase of decision making is the result of dissatisfaction with the current state. It aims at an awareness of a problem and a

Figure 8.1
Simon's decision-making
process.

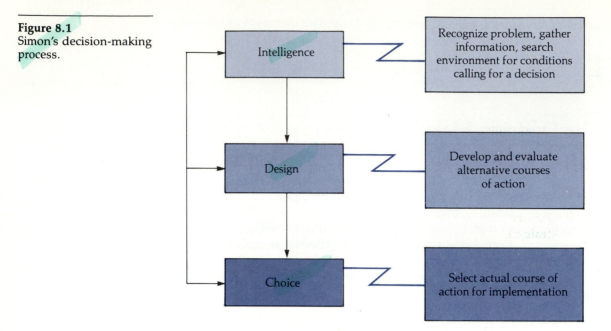

thorough evaluation of variables and their relationships. An important
consideration in this phase is distinguishing between symptoms of a
problem and the real problem. For example, a symptom of a problem is
the high rate of auto accidents; the actual problem might be the state's
discontinued auto inspection, low minimum drinking age, inadequate
police force to enforce speed limits, or a combination of all these factors.
Once the data are collected, it calls for a decision. In chapter 10, we will
see how decision support systems play a major role in providing intelligence through information retrieval and statistical software.

The **design** phase focuses on evaluating decision alternatives and
various computer-based models. Decision support systems play a role
in decision design under uncertainty. The output of the model(s) is the
basis for the **choice** phase of decision making.

In evaluating Simon's model, note the flow of activities from intelligence to design to choice, and a return to any phase as needed. For
example, the decision maker may reject one or more alternative courses
of action and return to the design to generate additional ones.

Criteria for Decision Making

The decision-making process may be viewed in terms of normative (prescriptive) or descriptive models. The *normative* decision-making model
tells how a consistent decision maker should act to make rational decisions. Normative models (e.g., linear programming and game theory)

are developed by management scientists. They describe the "best" answer to a problem. They also provide recommended courses of action. In contrast, *descriptive* decision-making models describe how decisions are actually made. For example, the block diagram of a program is a descriptive model. It does not predict or recommend.

The Concept of Rationality   At the center of these approaches is the concept of **rationality**. A rational person makes a choice based on a known set of alternatives with corresponding outcomes, a set of relations that orders the alternatives, and maximizing something definitive such as cost, profit, or some utility (Thierauf, 1984, 80).

A decision situation revolves around four elements:

1. The *objective* to be met in making a decision
2. The **strategies** or possible alternatives available
3. The **states of nature** or possible conditions occurring such as economic conditions, threat of a union strike, and so on
4. The outcomes or **payoff**, assuming a certain strategy and a state of nature

Table 8.1 illustrates a typical decision matrix showing the possible outcomes for a combined strategy (S_n) and a state of nature (N_m). Obviously, the value developed for payoff as perceived by the decision maker prompts a decision in a specific direction. If the payoff is highly profitable, for instance, the decision maker would be motivated to move in that direction and vice versa. More on the decision matrix is found later in the chapter.

In the normative model, decisions are influenced by the decision maker's time constraint, personal values, importance of the decision, and the certainty of the outcome. In the descriptive model, the decision maker goes through three basic stages:

1. Sets out an ideal level of accomplishment translated into one or more action goals that can be attained.
2. Searches for and defines various alternatives and respective outcomes.
3. Chooses a satisfactory alternative that is in line with the action goal(s).

Table 8.1   Decision-Making Matrix

		States of Nature		
Strategies	N_1	N_2	. . .	N_m
S_1	O_{11}	O_{12}	. . .	O_{1m}
S_2	O_{21}	O_{22}	. . .	O_{2m}
.	.	.	. . .	.
.	.	.	. . .	.
.	.	.	. . .	.
S_n	O_{n1}	O_{n2}	. . .	O_{nm}

Knowledge of Outcomes An **outcome** specifies what will happen if a given alternative is chosen. Knowledge of outcomes can be extremely important when a number of alternatives face the decision maker. We will consider three states of outcome in this chapter:

1. **Certainty:** the availability of complete, factual knowledge of the outcome of each alternative; each alternative has one outcome.
2. **Risk:** possibility of a number of outcomes of each alternative; a probability of occurrence is attached to each outcome
3. **Uncertainty:** same as risk, except that no knowledge of the probability of occurrence can be attached to each outcome

The criterion for a choice among alternatives in the normative model is maximization or optimization of a utility or expected value. If the outcomes are known and the values of the outcomes are known with certainty, then the decision maker would compute the optimal outcome. For example, a traveler is considering two different airlines that fly to the same destination, but one airline's fare is 30 percent less than the other. All factors considered (such as parity of equipment, service, and so on), the traveler will fly with the cheaper airline. The optimizing criterion in this model is least cost that is maximum utility.

The criterion of decision making under risk, when only the probabilities of the outcomes are known, is to maximize **expected value**. For example, a shopper is considering two cars. Car A with a thirty percent probability will go 50,000 miles without major repairs. Car B with seventy percent probability will go 100,000 miles. The very likely choice is B, because it has a higher expected value in terms of miles driven before failure. The formula is:

Probability × outcome = expected value

In our example,

	Probability	× outcome	= expected value
Car A	.30	× 50,000	= 15,000
Car B	.70	× 100,000	= 70,000

For decision making under uncertainty, we need to supply the unknown probabilities in order to treat the problem on decision making under risk. A convenient way is to assign equal probabilities for all the outcomes. We can also minimize the regret or use the maximin or maximax criteria. These will be discussed later in the chapter.

The Decision-Making System

Decisions are rarely made in a vacuum. They are a part of a system consisting of the decision maker, the information system, and the decision environment. Models depicting a decision-making system provide the conceptual framework for examining MIS performance. Let us briefly define each component.

The *decision maker* (user) has attributes that affect the way a decision is made. For example, cognitive style, attitude, and intelligence play an important part in decision making. The *decision environment* also is an active part of the decision making system. A dynamic environment differs from a stable environment and has different information requirements. Departments within a business (accounting, purchasing, and so on) also have their own information needs. Level of organization is a factor in the decision environment. For example, upper-level management operates under different kinds of pressure, makes different decisions, and requires different types of information than lower levels. The decision environment, then, is a function of the individual situation.

Information systems vary in makeup. Some are on line, others are batch; some offer graphics, others offer interactive features. The decision performance, then, is the combined interaction of the information system, the decision maker, and the decision environment.

Conceptual Models

A number of decision-making system models have been proposed within the context of MIS. They vary in purpose and detail. Early models described the components that address decision making. More recent models emphasize the context and the processes of using an information system.

The Jenkins Model A. M. Jenkins (1982) proposed a decision-making model in which the *user* relies on an *information system* in a *decision environment* to improve *performance*. As shown in Figure 8.2, the elements are interrelated. Let us briefly explain the model.

The Decision Maker The decision maker or the user is an important part of the decision-making process. A person's decision-making style affects the final decision. Personal style is based on demographic background, psychological state, managerial style, motor skills, and motivation. Cognitive style also can be an important part of and affects the decision making system. Users can also make decisions using problem-sensing, information-gathering, or information-using styles. A manager senses a problem and decides either to avoid it by ignoring information or to work toward a solution. In problem solving, the manager gathers information that meets certain criteria before deciding on the action (see also McLeod, 1986, 139–140).

In addition to problem sensing and information gathering, the third style is the way managers go about using information. Some users follow a systematic (prescribed) procedure; others go by intuition. Figure 8.3

Figure 8.2
Jenkins' decision-mak-
ing system.

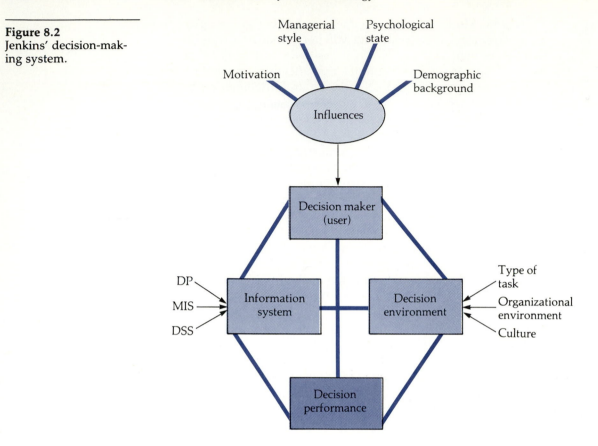

illustrates the three dimensions. There are a maximum of eight combinations of styles (2 × 2 × 2 = 8) that can be derived from the cube.

These differences in managers mean that decision situations are viewed and handled differently, although the solutions often are the same. The overall conclusion is that end users are an important element in MIS decision making. They use MIS information in different ways and for different reasons. This makes it critical that the database be designed to accommodate the decision-making needs of all levels of management.

The Decision Environment   In addition to the personal factors in decision making, there are environmental considerations as well. These include the types of tasks, the organizational environment, and the cultural environment.

The type of task that a manager performs is proposed in a model by Gorry and Morton (1971). They referred to Simon's programmable tasks as structured tasks (decision types) and nonprogrammable tasks as unstructured tasks. They also proposed a middle category called semi-structured tasks that can be only partly represented. In Table 8.2, we

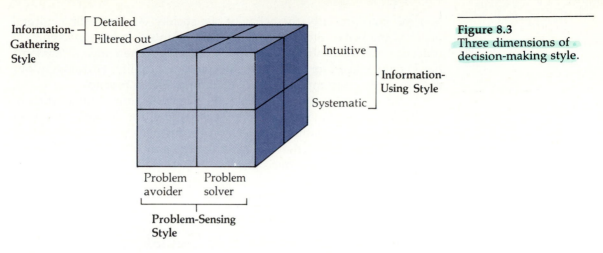

Information-Gathering Style
- Detailed
- Filtered out

Intuitive — Information-Using Style — Systematic

Problem avoider   Problem solver

Problem-Sensing Style

Figure 8.3
Three dimensions of decision-making style.

find that running an accounts receivable application is a structured activity involving lower-level managers. In contrast, planning a new product is a highly unstructured strategic management activity. Strategic planning is discussed in Chapter 13.

Among the organizational factors that affect decisions are level of centralization, importance of the decisions, and amount of information available. In a *highly centralized* organization, managers at the top make most of the important decisions. *Decentralized* firms allow more and more decisions to be made at lower levels. This design brings the decision maker closer to the problem area that requires a decision. The importance of the decision is often determined by how badly the organization needs to act based on the decision. More timely decisions are also effective because of the availability of the information.

Culture is an important consideration in decision making. **Culture** is the set of values, attitudes, and norms passed down from generation to

Table 8.2   The Gorry and Morton Framework

	Management Activity		
Decision Type	*Operational Control*	*Management Control*	*Strategic Planning*
Structured	Accounts receivable	Budget analysis— engineering costs	Warehouse and factory location
Semistructured	Production scheduling	Budget preparation	Mergers and acquisitions
Unstructured	PERT/cost systems	Sales and production	New product planning

generation to prescribe the behavior of a society. An interesting cultural factor is the bribe. Stories are told about countries where government officials approve contracts only after kickbacks. When such a "custom" has been practiced for so long, it becomes a way of life. Fortunately, our culture neither accommodates nor condones such a practice.

At the subcultural level, we may observe the conservative dress of the banker or the blue suit of the IBM executive, for example. All these symbols, values, or attitudes represent the formalization of the way the business is structured; they are a part of the subculture that influences the way managers make decisions.

Information Systems and Decision Performance

The last two components of Jenkins' decision-making system are the information system and the decision aids that improve the quality of decision making. For example, the use of graphics (textual and graphic output) is becoming popular among managers, especially at the personal computer level.

Information systems are categorized as data processing systems (DP), management information systems (MIS), or decision support systems (DSS). Each type provides information to management for decision making, but for different types of tasks and management activities. DSS is covered in Chapters 9 and 10.

Why Jenkins' model? This conceptual model serves to illustrate that there is more to decision making than the information system per se. Users are influenced by the environment in which problems occur and adopt a decision style to evaluate problem solutions through information systems. In this way, an information system is merely a tool that serves a purpose in a context. It also processes decision models to solve special problems and remove uncertainties. Model-building concepts are covered next.

Models in Decision Making

Management Science Models

For over three decades there have been increasing demands on managers to use management science models. The obvious impact of the computer has placed special importance on model building and implementation.

Management science is the application of scientific methodology to management decisions. The main steps in management science are:

1. *Identify the problem:* For example, declining market demand for product X.
2. *Formulate a model in mathematical or symbolic form:* For example, a break-even analysis model measures the relationship between revenues and costs. The equation is net profit = sales revenue − total costs. Symbolically, it may be $n = pv - cv - f$. The graphic model is shown in Figure 8.4.
3. *Evaluate the model using a variety of analytical tools:* In our break-even example, we draw a vertical dotted line at the point where the revenue line intersects the total cost line to identify the specific sales volume necessary to break even.
4. *Apply a solution to the actual problem:* Frequently, this means a computer program. A computer program for our breakeven problem could determine break-even volume, the sales volume to ensure a user-defined net profit, etc.

Criteria for Decision Making   A management science decision model consists of the objective, the decision alternative, states of nature, and the outcome. We choose a final alternative based on decision criteria set in advance. A **decision criterion** is a rule for choosing an alternative that will best meet the objective. The choice depends on the certainty of predicting the state of nature facing the decision maker. The best way to illustrate these concepts is by an example.

The Problem and Objective   Winchester Technologies manufactures fixed disk drives for the personal computer. The unique features of the product created back orders that prompted management to consider expanding the production facility. The problem in this case is unfilled orders. The solution is increasing capacity under one of three alternatives. The decision objective is maximizing profits.

The Alternatives and States of Nature   Top management has three alternatives to address the problem: Expand present facility, build a new plant in a geographically attractive location, or do nothing. Before making a final choice, management is divided about the long-term demand for fixed disks. Some managers feel that future demand will steadily surpass current demand; others look into the late 1980s as a period of accelerated growth in fixed disk systems and even more so through the 1990s. A third group of managers view the surge in demand as temporary and likely to level off to previous levels. These demand levels are the states of nature that will determine the outcome or the payoff from each decision alternative.

Computing Decision Outcomes   A decision outcome is the alternative that will realize the most profit. The first step is to determine the cost of expansion. Let us assume that it will cost $75,000 to expand the present facility and $150,000 to build a new one. The present facility now yields $250,000 profit each year and will be sustainable for future demand levels.

Expanding the existing facility is expected to yield at current demand level an additional profit of $100,000, or a total profit of $350,000. If the demand level drops to previous demand levels, no additional profits can be earned beyond $250,000.

Building a new plant is expected to yield additional profit of $180,000 based on higher demand level, or a total of $430,000. If the demand remains at the current demand level, the new plant will earn the same profit as that of expanding the facility ($100,000), or a total of $350,000. If the demand drops to previous demand levels, no additional profit can be earned over $250,000.

First, we compute the outcome for each demand level and expansion alternative by subtracting expansion costs from net profit. In Table 8.3, the outcome for no expansion is $250,000 for all demand levels, because current product capacity is limited to earning $250,000 only.

Expanding the current facility gives a different outcome. If the demand returns to its previous level, it results in a net profit of $175,000 ($250,000

Table 8.3   Decision Alternatives, States of Nature, and Outcomes for Winchester Technologies

	States of Nature		
Decision Alternatives	*Previous Level Demand*	*Current Level Demand*	*Higher Level Demand*
Expand current facility	175*	275	275
Build new facility	100	200	280
No expansion	250	250	250

*In $1000s.

profit less $75,000 expansion cost). If current or higher demand levels are maintained, the net profit is $275,000 ($350,000 profit less $75,000 expansion cost).

Building a new plant also results in a different outcome, depending on the demand level. At current demand levels, profit will be $200,000 ($250,000 + $100,000 less $150,000). At higher demand levels, profit will be $280,000 ($250,000 + $180,000 less $150,000).

Choosing a Decision Criterion   The final choice depends on the *probability* set for each of the states of nature. Choosing a criterion also depends on how the decision maker looks at the outcomes and the risk attached to each outcome. The three criteria are making a decision based on 100 percent certainty, deciding with a risk factor, or deciding with complete uncertainty.

Decision making under certainty is a situation where the outcome is known. In our example, if one buyer (e.g., IBM) agrees to purchase all the disk drives of Winchester Technologies at a price based on present demand levels, then the future demand state would be known with 100 percent certainty. Looking at Table 8.3, the best decision alternative under the current level of demand is to expand the current facility and realize $275,000 in profits. This is higher than building a new plant ($200,000 profit) or no expansion ($250,000 profit). In real-life decision making, though, absolute certainty is not realistic.

The second decision criterion is to assume that a certain risk factor is associated with the choice. In this case, we assign each state of nature a realistic probability value. In our example, each event has a probability p_j of occurring.

The criterion used for solving problems under risk is called the expected value criterion. We compute a weighted average outcome for each alternative. This gives us the expected value of choosing a decision alternative. The best choice is the alternative with the highest weighted average. In our example, we assign probability values of .05, .40, and .55 for three demand levels. We compute the expected value of each alternative by totaling the products of the probability by the weighted average profit for each alternative. In our example, the expected value "expand current facility" is:

$$(.05)(175) + (.40)(275) + (.55)(275) = 270$$

This shows that the highest profit (expected value) of $270,000 would be obtained from expanding the current facility.

A third decision criterion is a situation where we can identify the states of nature but have no clear idea on how likely they are to occur. A new product decision is an example of decision making under uncertainty. There are several rules for making decisions under uncertainty. One rule is to *minimax* the regret. (A regret is the difference between the

Table 8.4 The Regret Criterion

| | States of Nature | | | |
Decision Alternatives	Previous Level of Demand	Current Level of Demand	Higher Level of Demand	Maximum Regret
Expand current facility	75	0	5	75
Build new facility	150	75	0	150
No expansion	0	25	30	30

actual outcome received and the outcome, had the best strategy been chosen.) We compute a regret table by subtracting each column entry from the column's highest value. Then we select the action that minimizes the maximum regret. In our example (see Table 8.4), the maximum regret for each decision alternative is shown in the right margin. The action that minimizes the maximum regret here is to do no expansion. This is equivalent to selecting the best of the worst.

There is subjectivity in decision making. The goal of information systems is to help the user make decisions, using realistic choices. The final decision varies with the level of certainty set by the decision maker. Regardless of the figures produced by the information system, the user has a final say on the choice.

Using Decision Trees   An alternative to the tabular approach to decision making is the graphic approach. An example is the **decision tree**, a pictorial way of organizing a decision situation. It is called a tree because the decision alternatives form branches from an initial decision point.

The decision tree for the Winchester Technologies example (Table 8.4) is illustrated graphically in Figure 8.4. The procedure is simple:

1. We list each decision alternative and its states of nature, with probabilities and outcome values.
2. Working backwards, we calculate the expected value for each decision alternative by multiplying event outcomes by their respective probabilities and summing the products.

Since the objective is to maximize profit, we choose "Expand current facility." The maximum expected profit is $270,000.

The Role of the Computer   We have seen that the quality of the decisions made will determine the organization's ultimate success. In today's technology, more computer-based applications deal with complex problems and structured situations in which the decision alternatives and states of nature are known. One such decision-making technique, called the *exponential comparison method (ECM)*, is designed to find the best alternative for the user's final decision. To illustrate, suppose the user is

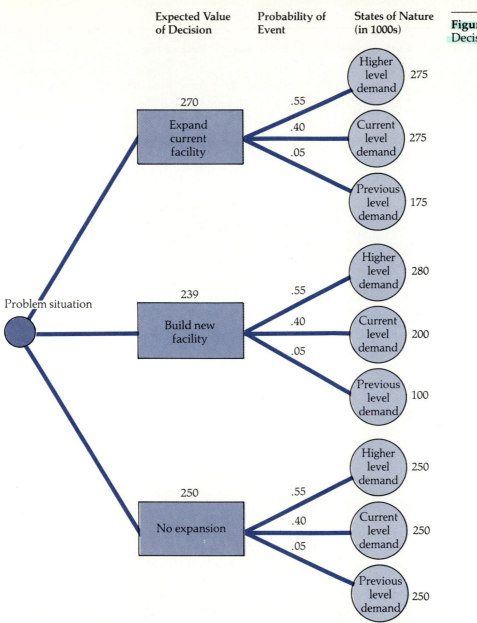

Figure 8.4
Decision tree.

interested in acquiring a microcomputer. The ECM application performs the following steps:

1. Lists the alternative micros such as Apple McIntosh, IBM PC, Compaq, and so on.
2. Specifies the evaluation criteria for each microcomputer: cost, ease of use, service, price, reliability, and so on.

Table 8.5   Decision Matrix

Computer Alternative	Cost	Service	Expansion	Ease of Use	Delivery	Rank
A	5	3	4	2	1	3
B	3	2	5	3	4	5
C	4	3	3	4	5	3
D	5	4	5	4	3	1
E	5	3	3	5	4	2
Importance of criteria	5	3	3	5	4	

3. Rates the criteria on a scale of 1 (unimportant) to 5 (very important). Combining steps 2 and 3, we have the following:

Criterion	Rating
Cost	5
Delivery	4
Ease of use	5
Expandability	3
Service	3

4. Rates the alternatives for the criteria, using 1 for the alternative that rates low on a criterion and 5 for the alternative that rates high on that criterion (see Table 8.5).
5. Computes a score for each alternative and then ranks the choices. Then, it writes a computer program to do the work.

Table 8.5 is a completed decision matrix. When the analysis is completed, the computer ranks the alternatives as shown in Table 8.6.

Behavioral Models

The management science approach to decision making is known to improve the quality of final decisions, reduce costs, improve service and net profits, and so on. In contrast, there are behavioral models that influence perceptions which, in turn, improve decision making. A contrast between the behavioral and the management science approach can be illustrated by the case of a bank's customer who complained about the long wait to pull up to the drive-in teller window. The president hired a consultant who saw the problem as one of slow tellers using old equipment. New equipment was installed and tellers underwent more training. But the president was unhappy because customers continued to complain. A psychologist later diagnosed the problem and determined that all along it was customer boredom, not slow tellers or outdated equipment. He recommended dog biscuits for customers' pets and balloons for the kids. The problem was solved. Complaints dropped sharply.

Table 8.6 ECM-Generated Ratings and Score

Ranking	Score	Computer Alternative
1	7200	D
2	6600	E
3	6200	C
4	6000	B
5	4600	A

Ratings for each alternative
  (value = Rating × 200)

Computer D ***********************72
Computer E ******************66
Computer C **************62
Computer B **********60
Computer A *****46

One can see that objectivity and technical skills can be the "right" solution to the "wrong" problem. The analyst must be familiar with behavioral considerations and be capable of a behavioral approach to problem solving in line with the needs of the user and the organization as a whole.

A behavioral approach to decision making helps the designer understand the constraints imposed on an end user. The designer may be focusing on rationality when the decision maker may be worried about how the installation is going to affect the employee. Behavioral models formalize a procedure that reaches users from their own perception of the problem situation.

Information Overload and Decision Making Humans are information processors. They pick up signals through the eyes, ears, etc and transmit them to the processing unit (brain). The results are responses or decisions. Human capacity to accept input and provide output, however, has its limitations. Beyond this capacity, the decision maker experiences information overload. The question is: How does a manager deal with this problem? According to Miller (1978), there are several ways of managing information overload. For example, a manager may do one of the following:

1. *Omit* certain parts of a message to suit a given situation. For example, a user may tailor the picture of the problem he or she presents to the system designer to suit the constraints of the user's position in the department.

2. *Filter* information by prioritizing messages. You have heard of the executive who comes back from a vacation and finds a stack of telephone

messages on the desk. He selects the most important messages, responds to them, and leaves the rest to a later time.

3. *Transmit* messages over multiple channels at the same time. For example, a project manager might assign several programmers to work simultaneously on a program to meet a deadline.

4. *Escape* from the task. This is common in situations where the estimated costs of a project are so out of line that the end user lets the proposal sit on the desk for weeks before he mails his response.

These are important considerations for systems designers and users. In implementing information systems, it is important to plan the details of the design and the procedure for user training at the pace of the user and staff. Otherwise, if an installation is introduced prematurely, the user may simply delay the installation date or even sabotage the new operation.

An obvious conclusion is never to overload the user with unnecessary or conflicting information. There are several ways of removing information uncertainty. One way is to use graphs and charts to highlight summaries and trends or to analyze relationships. Another way is to present summary information where appropriate. Finally, information per se can be presented in stages so that the user is not overwhelmed with information that has no immediate use. Perhaps a combination of these approaches might be appropriate for certain users.

The business world abounds with information. Unfortunately, we get more information than we are able to use. Decision making identifies the relevant data and screens out data judged irrelevant to the decision situation. When decisions have to be made under a stringent time frame, the resulting stress intensifies the screening process. For example, during a period when the company's computer system is down, the MIS director will concentrate on bringing up the facility, ignoring all other less important inquiries.

The speed of change in today's business and the resulting information overload that managers face are serious problems. Managers are constantly required to operate in a crisis state, resulting in more stress and reduced performance. Although managers plead for more relevant information for decision making, the real problem seems to be overabundance of unnecessary information. System design must be capable of summarizing or otherwise reducing the amount of information in line with the needs of the decision maker.

The Value of Information

We have seen how decisions are made under certainty, risk, and uncertainty. In making decisions under certainty, the decision maker assumes perfect information about outcomes; decision making under risk assumes

Table 8.7   Computer-Aided Decision Making

Decision Alternative	Previous Demand Level	
a. Expand present facility	275*	275
b. Build new facility	200	400
c. No expansion	250	250

*In $1000s.

information about the probability of each outcome occurring. Decision making under uncertainty assumes no information about probabilities but knowledge of possible outcomes. We have also shown how to compute a value of information for each decision-making approach.

Since a decision maker decides based on the information at hand, new information causes a different set of decisions to be made. The *value* of the new information is the difference between the outcome of the new decision and that of the old, less the cost of obtaining the new information. To illustrate, let us assume that a decision maker faces three decision choices and one state of nature. Based on past experience, the outcome is shown in Table 8.7, line A. If new information from a $10,000 market survey assures with certainty that building a new plant will increase sales by 100 percent, then the manager will decide on alternative B. The value of information in this case is $200,000 (400,000 − 200,000) − 10,000, or $190,000.

No decisions are realistically made with perfect information, because getting it means controlling future events, which is difficult if not impossible. The concept of the value of perfect information, however, is useful because it illustrates how information has value in the way it affects decisions. The example also illustrates the reason for assigning market surveys a value. The quantitative approach in decision making emphasizes the value of seeking information, although decisions are made with imperfect information for obvious reasons—lack of knowledge that certain information exists, getting information is too costly, and similar considerations.

Implications for MIS

We have seen how quantitative and behavioral decision-making approaches can be effective in moving an organization to a competitive position. To effect such a change, managers are expected to possess technical and managerial backgrounds. *Technical* background means familiarity with quantitative models and understanding their capabilities and limitations.

Managerial background means ability to translate the technology into a procedure that the user can learn and support.

No doubt, MIS performs key decision-making functions. Managers can make effective decisions through computer-based models. The quality of the outcome is a function of tradeoffs between costs, benefits, and objectives.

The complexity of organizational life and human limitations makes it necessary to limit the decision maker's considerations of alternatives. True rationality or the gathering of complete information and the evaluation of all possible alternatives can be realized in practice when the decision maker selects a few alternatives and uses the most effective computer-based means for evaluation. Insight, intuition, and plain business judgment based on experience continue to have a place in successful decision making.

Finally, we can see how systems in general affect decision making in the organization. George Huber of the University of Texas has evaluated the changes that will occur as a society moves from an industrial to an information orientation. His main conclusion is that business decision making will be more frequent, will be made much more quickly, and will be more complex because of the increasing changes and complexities of the environment in which business operates.

To meet decision-making needs, two technologies are required: high-speed computers and telecommunication networks, and decision-making groups. According to Huber, more people will be involved in decision making on an ad hoc, informal basis via high-speed computers and telecommunication in the form of computer message systems, teleconferencing, and the like. Also, there will be continuing pressure for more meetings by decision groups through computer conferencing without having physically to gather in a meeting.

All this acts as an impetus to management to use computer technology and the information it generates to improve the quality of decision making for rapid response to changes in the competitive environment. With the availability of the personal computer, its linkage to the mainframe, and the ease with which decision support packages are being used for ad hoc decision making, more and more organizations are expected to adopt information systems as the requisite tool for making day-to-day decisions. Decision support tools and software are covered in the next two chapters.

Summary

□ Managers spend much of their time solving problems. Problems occur as a result of change in the corporate environment and other related reasons. A good MIS will detect and identify problems and their impact on the organization as a whole.

- The decision-making process involves evaluating, selecting, and implementing a course of action for problem solving. Decision making is widely defined as making a choice among alternatives. Simon viewed decision making as a process model beginning with intelligence and moving toward design and choice. The whole decision-making process is initiated by the recognition of a problem, with the resulting decision directed at solving the problem.

- The decision-making process may be viewed in terms of normative (prescriptive) or descriptive models. The normative model defines how a decision maker should act to make rational decisions. Descriptive decision-making models describe how decisions are actually made. At the center of these approaches is the concept of rationality.

- A typical decision situation requires consideration of strategies, states of nature, and outcomes. An outcome is what will happen if a given alternative is chosen. There are three states of outcome: certainty, risk, and uncertainty.
  a. Decision making under *certainty*: If the outcomes are known and the values of the outcomes are known with certainty, the decision maker computes the optimal alternative or outcome.
  b. Decision making under *risk*: When only the probabilities of the outcomes are known, the decision maker maximizes expected value.
  c. Decision making under *uncertainty*: The decision maker assigns the unknown probabilities to treat the problem in decision making under risk. One way is to assign equal probabilities for all the outcomes. The decision maker can also minimize the regret, or use the maximin or maximax criteria.

- Various decision-making models have been proposed within the context of MIS. Early models such as Mason and Mitroff's described the components of decision making. They recognized the personal dimension as an important part of the information system. In the early 1980s, the Jenkins model emphasized a decision-making system designed around four key variables: the decision maker, the decision environment, the information system, and decision performance.
  a. The *decision maker*. As a decision maker, the user is known to have a unique decision-making style that determines the final decision. Behind these differences are psychological factors. This means that decision situations are handled differently, although the solutions often are the same. This makes it critical for the database to be designed to accommodate all managerial levels for problem solving.
  b. The *decision environment*. The decision environment is examined from three perspectives: the type of tasks (programmable or nonprogrammable), the organizational environment (centralized or decentralized), and the cultural environment.

c. The *information system* and *decision performance*. Information systems are classified as data processing, MIS, or DSS; each type is geared to different tasks and management activities.

□ Scientific methodology is a process for developing models that explain and predict real-world behavior. The key aspects of management science process and their relationships are problem identification, model formulation, analysis and solutions of the model, and implementation of the solution to the actual problem.

□ A decision model consists of the objective, decision alternatives, states of nature, and the outcome or payoff. Decision outcomes are computed in terms of the decision objectives. A final decision depends on the degree of information known about the likelihood of the various states of nature. The choice of criterion depends on the decision maker's evaluation of the outcomes and risks involved. The criteria are decision making under certainty, under risk, and under uncertainty.

□ Decision making under certainty is a situation where the probability of an event occurring is 1, where all other events have a probability of 0. Decision making under risk is a category that is considered when the states of nature can be assigned a realistic probability value. The criterion for solving problems under risk is called the expected value criterion. Decision making under uncertainty is chosen when states of nature can be identified but no probabilities can be established for them. Various criteria are suggested for problem solving of this type, depending on the decision maker's own level of pessimism and psychological state.

□ An alternative to using the tabular approach to organize a decision-making problem is the graphic approach, such as the decision tree—called a tree because the different decision alternatives branch from an initial decision point.

□ In addition to management science models, there are behavioral models that influence perception which, in turn, contributes to effective decision making. In essence, such models alert the designer to the organizational constraints on a decision maker.

Key Terms

Certainty	Decision tree
Choice	Design
Control	Expected value
Culture	Intelligence
Decision criterion	Management science
Decision making	Outcome: See payoff

Payoff   Risk
Planning   State of nature
Problem solving   Strategy
Rationality   Uncertainty

Review Questions

1. "A problem is the deviation between 'what is' and 'what ought to be." Do you agree? Explain.

2. What does the decision-making process involve? Elaborate.

3. Contrast Simon's and Drucker's views on decision making.

4. In what way do Ofstad and Churchman differ in their definition of a decision?

5. Elaborate on Simon's three-phase decision making process.

6. Distinguish between:
   a. Intelligence and design
   b. Strategies and states of nature

7. Illustrate the use of items representing a typical decision situation.

8. What is an outcome? What states of outcome are considered in a decision-making situation? Define each.

9. How does the criterion of decision making under risk differ from the criterion of decision making under uncertainty? Give an example.

10. According to the text, models depicting a decision-making system provide the conceptual framework for examining MIS effectiveness. What components make up such a system? Discuss.

11. The Jenkins model has been proposed as a decision-making system model within the framework of MIS. What are the unique features of the model? Explain.

Application Problems

1. Arnold & Cook, Inc. is an electronics corporation with annual sales of $600 million. In the late 1980s, the president is confronted with a critical decision. A company employee has developed a new electronic scale and has obtained a U.S. patent on the unit. Since the device was developed on her own time, she wants to sell the patent rights for $100,000 or $50,000 plus a 3 percent royalty on total sales.

From the experience of the firm's sales staff, the demand for the electronic scale will be one of three levels:

a. The scale will find no measurable acceptance by the consumer. It means the total investment in the patent is lost, plus $155,000 needed to develop and market the unit.

b. A demand level of 30,000 units. The selling price of the scale will be $30.00 and the variable cost (excluding patent and development cost) approximately $18.00.

c. A demand level of 185,000 units.

Now that the parameters have been defined, what decision would you make? Illustrate the payoff matrix and the approach you used in reaching the decision.

2. Your brother Bruce is graduating from high school this year. He has two decisions to make: What college to attend and what field of study to major in. He is free to choose which college to attend. After much soul searching, he has narrowed his selection to two schools, both of which have accepted him: a major state university (Virginia) and a local private college (Mary Baldwin). Now he has to decide between computer science and MIS for a major. Because of the nature of the two schools, Bruce has a different probability of graduating, depending on the school and major.

a. If he attends Virginia and takes up MIS, his probability of success is .65. If he chooses computer science, his probability of success is .75.

b. If he attends Mary Baldwin and chooses MIS, his probability of success is .90. But if he chooses computer science, his probability of success is .96.

c. A Virginia MIS graduate averages $36,500 per year for the first five years of employment. Most graduates work for the Big Eight accounting firms. Computer science graduates, however, average $32,000 per year for the first five years of employment.

d. A Mary Baldwin MIS graduate averages $27,000 per year for the first five years of employment. A computer science graduate averages $29,500 per year for the first five years of employment.

e. If Bruce fails to graduate, he will average $15,000 per year for the first five years of employment.

No matter what school or major Bruce chooses, he will either graduate or flunk out. Let:

1. S_1 = Graduate from Virginia's MIS program
2. S_2 = Fail from Virginia's MIS program
3. S_3 = Graduate from Virginia's computer science program
4. S_4 = Fail to graduate from Virginia's computer science program
5. S_5 = Graduate from Mary Baldwin's MIS program
6. S_6 = Fail from Mary Baldwin's MIS program
7. S_7 = Graduate from Mary Baldwin's computer science program
8. S_8 = Fail from Mary Baldwin's computer science program

d_1 = Choose to go to Virginia
d_2 = Choose to go to Mary Baldwin
d_3 = Choose to major in MIS
d_4 = Choose to major in computer science

QUESTIONS

a. In approaching Bruce's problem, assume that his sole criterion for making a decision is to maximize average expected income over the first five years. What decisions must Bruce make?

b. Draft a decision tree, presenting Bruce's problem.

3. The president of a large electronics firm must decide how to invest $9 million of the firm's excess profits. He could invest the total amount in supercomputer research or he could invest it to research an advanced version of computer memory chip. His only other choice is to split the money even between the two areas of research. There is an estimated 800 percent return on investment if supercomputer research is successful and a 400 percent return on investment if the memory chip is successful.

QUESTIONS

a. Develop a payoff table for this problem.

b. Based on the minimax regret criterion, what decision must the president make?

c. Based on the maximin criterion, what decision must the president make?

d. Based on the maximax criterion, what decision must the president make?

In answering the question, assume:

S_1 = Neither supercomputer nor memory chip research is successful.

S_2 = Memory chip is successful; supercomputer research is unsuccessful.

S_3 = Supercomputer research is successful; memory chip research is unsuccessful.

S_4 = Both supercomputer and memory chip research are successful.

d_1 = Invest in supercomputer research only.

d_2 = Invest in memory chip research only.

d_3 = Invest 50 percent in each type of research.

Selected References

Anthony, R. N. *Planning and Control Systems: A Framework for Analysis.* Cambridge, Mass.: MIT Press, 1965.

Behling, O., Grifford, W. and Tollivar, J. M. "Effects of Grouping Information on Decision Making Under Risk." *Decision Science*, April 1980, 272–283.

Churchman, C. West. *Challenge to Reason.* New York: McGraw-Hill, 1968.

Dannenbring, David G. and Starr, Martin K. *Management Science: Introduction.* New York: McGraw-Hill, 1981.

Dickson, G. W., Senn, J. A. and Chervany, N. L. "Research in Management Information Systems: The Minnesota Experiments." *Management Science,* May 1977, 913–923.

Drucker, Peter F. *The Age of Discontinuity.* New York: Harper & Row, 1961.

Gorry, G. A. and Morton, M. S. Scott. "A Framework for Management Information Systems." *Sloan Management Review,* 13, 1 (Fall 1971), 55–70.

Hackathorn, R. D. and Keen, P. G. W. "Organization Strategies for Personal Computing in Decision Support Systems." *MIS Quarterly,* September 1981, 21–27.

Henderson, J. C. and Nutt, P. C. "The Influence of Decision Style on Decision Making Behavior." *Management Science,* April 1980, 371–386.

Huber, George P. "The Nature and Design of Post-Industrial Organizations." Working paper, Dept. of Management, University of Texas.

Jenkins, A. M. "A Program of Research for Investigating Management Information Systems (PRIMIS)." Working paper, 1982.

McFarlan, F. W. and McKenney, J. L. *Corporate Information Systems Management: The Issues Facing Senior Executives.* Homewood, Ill.: Irwin, 1983.

McLeod, Raymond. *Management Information Systems* (3rd ed.). Chicago, Ill.: SRA, 1986.

Miller, James G. *Living Systems.* New York, N.Y.: McGraw-Hill, 1978.

Ofstad, H. *An Inquiry into the Freedom of Decisions.* London: Allen & Co., 1961.

Peters, T. J. "The Mythology of Innovation." *The Stanford Magazine* (Stanford Alumni Assn., Bowman Alumni House, Stanford, CA. 94305) Pt. 1, Summer 1983, Pt. 2, Fall 1983.

Robey, D. and Taggart, W. "Human Information Processing in Information and Decision Support Systems." *MIS Quarterly,* June 1982, 61–73.

Senn, James A. *Management Information Systems.* Belmont, Calif.: Wadsworth, 1987.

Simon, Herbert A. *The New Science of Management Decisions.* New York: Harper & Row, 1960.

Thierauff, Robert J. *Effective Management Information Systems.* Columbus, Ohio: Charles Merrill, 1984.

Decision Support Systems (DSS)

Chapter Contents

Planning and Building a DSS

SO YOUR BOSS FINALLY wants to get into computing, in person. Not that he or she hasn't always been aware of computing, but until recently, people at the top had no direct experience with data processing in their organizations, other than a monthly review of payroll and accounting reports. Micros have brought computing to everyone, and now the more highly placed managers think it is time to get a system they can use. This trend has been enhanced by the emergence of decision support systems (DSS) and the attendant confusion between their fancy accessories and their underlying purpose—namely, to help key people make important decisions.

I recently helped develop a highly ambitious DSS for the Environmental Protection Agency. The agency decided to take a new approach in which all of its information resources would be brought to bear on individual geographic locations. Traditionally, the EPA has dealt separately with each type of pollution problem in a given location. Now, with the aid of a DSS, it has begun to consider all problems at once for a specific area.

The EPA wanted to be able to identify and measure pollutants, trace them through the entire ecological chain, determine the total human and environmental exposure and consequent risks, and identify where and how these pollutants could be controlled. We came up with PIPQUIC (for Program Integration Project Queries Using Interactive Commands, a name based on an early conception of the system), a system that enables officials for the first time to look at a geographical area for pollutants across all media (air, water, and land) and then to subject them to a variety of analyses. Questions like "To what extent will stiffer lead emission standards reduce the rate of risk to the local population?" or "What percentage of the emissions of pollutant X in a given area are from general sources (like cars and dry cleaners) as opposed to big industrial plants?" are now posed on PIPQUIC.

A DSS does not replace or compete with other systems; instead, it extracts from other systems the information that is essential to the process of decision-making. You wouldn't want to develop an entire national environmental policy solely around PIPQUIC outputs because its information base is too small. But it's quick on its feet and can be very helpful in making people think about the problems that a broader policy might eventually address. It also helps you narrow your choice of solutions to pursue, thereby saving time and money that would otherwise have been spent on trials and errors.

—*Adapted from David J. Alexander,* Datamation, *March 15, 1986, 115–116.*

AT A GLANCE

A decision support system is a high-tech tool that helps decision makers evaluate problems, pose ad hoc questions, and test assumptions with corporate data. A good DSS focuses on decisions, can be used by all levels of management for semistructured problems, and is user friendly.

DSS consists of a database, a DBMS, DSS tools and languages, and an application building environment. An effective DSS must manage large volumes of data, provide powerful modeling and analytic capabilities for achieving objectives, and support varying managerial styles, skills, and knowledge.

Traditional data processing and DSS support different activities. Data processing uses programming to automate an application with no user involvement. DSS supports rather than automates the decision structure for a variety of unstructured and semistructured problems. This includes extensive participation by the end user in developing DSS.

With the availability of various technologies, managers and technicians play three roles: user, builder, and toolsmith. The user is concerned with how specific DSS can assist him/her in problem solving and decision making. The DSS builder (designer) draws on computer-based tools and methodology to provide the decision support required by the user. The toolsmith, like a programmer, is concerned with developing technology components, a new language to be used for the DSS, and how they can be integrated to form a DSS generator with the requisite capabilities.

An important question in building DSS is: What motivates DSS acquisition? The overall thrust behind DSS development is improving the quality of decision making. Introducing this technology requires management support for success.

By the end of this chapter, you should know:

1. The characteristics of DSS
2. DSS components and requirements for effective DSS
3. The key roles in DSS development and use
4. Management's role in DSS design and implementation

Introduction

In Chapter 8, we saw how important information decisions and decision making are to the organization. The right decision can build a corporation's fortune; the wrong one can destroy it. Increasingly, decision makers are arming themselves with high-tech tools—ones that let them create their own business models, pose ad hoc questions, and test their assumptions with corporate data. Why the rush to such decision support systems (DSS) and information technologies? The trend is obvious— organizations are redefining their roles in the marketplace. As they evaluate problems, managers have an intensive need for information and insight with DSS. They can scan data directly from all areas of the business and access information from external sources as well.

DSS provides a limited kind of analysis. It plots a path to an objective (e.g., increased profit margin) by posing alternative approaches within stated constraints. For example, a DSS helps a manager determine: "This is the best I can do, given what I have." It does not take the next step by saying, "If you double advertising, you could quadruple sales." The latter answer is provided by an expert system, which is covered in Chapter 12.

In this chapter, we will define the characteristics and functions of DSS and the role it plays in decision making. In Chapter 10, we discuss the software available for DSS and the approaches used in developing DSS.

Characteristics of DSS

As we mentioned in Chapter 2, a *decision support system* (DSS) is a collection of tools, data, and techniques to help managers make ad hoc decisions. The term **ad hoc** means that the need for specific information results from interaction with the decision support system and could not have been predicted in advance.

To illustrate ad hoc decisions, suppose a plant manager needs to know how long it would take to deliver a rush order to a major customer. If he does not meet the request, he might lose the account. There are weekly reports on the status of inventory and a daily report on all customer orders. Each report gives information about the level of operation of the plant. How much of this information is useful to fill the rush order?

In order to handle the rush order, the plant manager must pull together data on inventory level, production rate of the plant, and order priorities before he can decide how quickly he can fill the order. Decision support systems provide this type of ad hoc inquiry. The plant manager describes the needed data and the processing operations to be carried out. The DSS then retrieves the data from the database, performs the processing operations, and produces the results. The manager might not like the results. So he enters a different set of requirements or levels of priorities. The DSS, in turn, goes through the same cycle and produces another set of results, and so on until the manager decides on the combination that ensures the delivery of the rush order (see Figure 9.1).

Compared to data processing or MIS, DSS has unique characteristics:

1. A focus on *decisions* and use of the computer to *support* judgment.

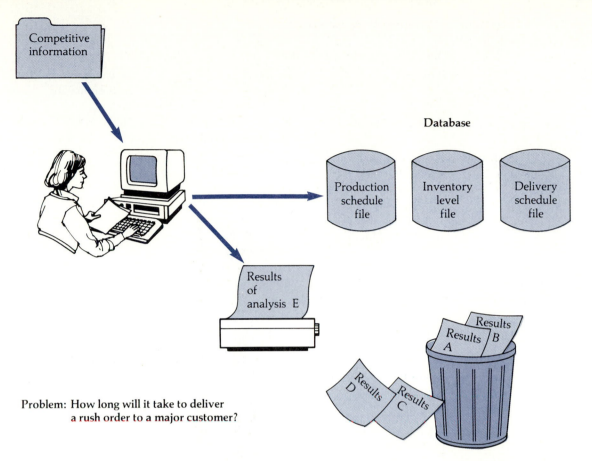

Problem: How long will it take to deliver a rush order to a major customer?

Figure 9.1
Problem-oriented decision support information.

2. Applicability to all levels of management for solving *semistructured* problems or ones where part of the information is computer based, but where the manager's judgment is needed to provide a solution.
3. An individualized, manager-oriented, user-friendly, and iterative environment that makes it possible to explore a problem situation using a combination of the computer's analytic model and the manager's judgment. The DSS must be easy to create, easy to understand, and easy to use (see Table 9.1).

Components of DSS

DSS may be viewed as consisting of four components: data/database, DBMS, DSS tools, and an application-building environment. Figure 9.2 illustrates the layout of a DSS framework.

Table 9.1 System Characteristics: A Summary

	EDP	MIS	DSS
Focus	· Data	· Information	· Decisions—supports decision making
Target group	· Operational level	· Mostly middle and upper management	· All levels
System strategy	· Designed from technical perspective · Application oriented · Synthesis of manual and ADP methods	· Designed from organization's perspective · Business function oriented · Synthesis of EDP and information dissemination methods	· Designed fron manager's perspective · Individual manager-oriented perspective · Synthesis of MIS and MS methods
Operations	· Centralized processing · Emphasizes transaction processing · Computer hardware optimization · Rigidly structured procedures · File-driven system	· Diffused processing · Emphasizes structured information flow · Inquiry and report generation optimization · Semistructured procedures · Integrated files and database driven system	· Localized processing · Emphasizes user-friendliness, ease of use, flexibility, and adaptability · User initiation and control, optimization · Unstructured procedures · Personal managerial decision methodology–driven system
Output	· Declarative reporting · Summary reports	· Interrogative reporting · Standardized reporting	· Interactive-iterative reporting · Unstructured reports
Impetus	· Expediency · Excess volume genesis	· Efficiency · Information fragmentation genesis	· Effectiveness · Complex variable interaction genesis

Adapted from Raho and Belohlov, 1982, 19.

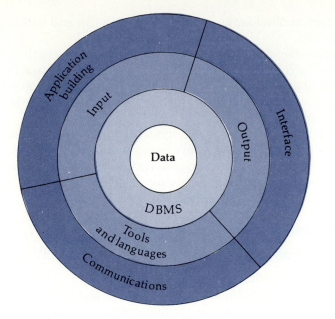

Figure 9.2
Layout of a DSS framework.

1. *Data/database*. The heart of a DSS is data and the importance of data acquisition and data sharing. A centralized DSS database is derived from a broad base of internal and external sources, made available to authorized users. Consistency, currency, and reliability are important issues in DSS architecture.

2. *DBMS*. Once the database is installed, a DBMS must be available to manage the data. It must provide access to a large number of end users while maintaining data security, integrity, and auditability.

3. *DSS tools and languages*. The third ring in the DSS framework makes it possible for users to enter, retrieve, and report information from the database. To do so, the DSS must include screen-based data entry, query languages, modeling and simulation tools, graphics reporting, and formatting.

Languages may be procedural and nonprocedural. A **procedural language** (e.g., COBOL, BASIC, PASCAL) requires the user to provide the logical steps or procedures to the computer for problem solving. Most of today's end users do not use procedural languages, although they are employed in solving certain problems that the nonprocedural language cannot address.

A **nonprocedural language** requires that the user only specify the characteristics of a problem or what is to be solved, leaving the logical "how" steps to the DSS. An example of a nonprocedural command is:

```
"LIST ALL FOR SALES GREATER THAN 400000
FOR ALL DOWNTOWN STORES"
```

Such nonprocedural language is both English-like and user friendly for easy learning.

4. *Application-building environment.*   The outer ring of the DSS framework has the function of collecting data from the database through the DBMS. It also makes available a wide variety of application-building management science models such as regression analysis and goal programming.

The building of a descriptive model is the central purpose of most DSSs. It is invariably in the form of a two-dimensional table such as the electronic spreadsheet. The spreadsheet allows the user to store data in a two or more dimensional matrix form. Any cell in the matrix can be made a function of any other cell.

Requirements for an Effective DSS

An effective decision support system must provide the following features:

1. Manage large volumes of heterogeneous data.
2. Provide modeling and analytic capabilities and options for maximizing or minimizing objectives within given constraints.
3. Provide a flexible array of reporting and display of alternatives. Examples are user-defined reporting, plotting, and color graphics.
4. Support a range of managerial skills and knowledge. It does not enforce a particular pattern.
5. Be modular in design, providing the user easy-to-switch interface from one module to another.

In terms of modularity, the key DSS modules are:

1. *Dialog:* a set of easy-to-use commands, known as **dialog**, to allow communication between user and system. The simplest interface is through rows and columns of a spreadsheet as we shall see in the next chapter. Simple-word commands across the top of the screen displaying the information offer the user the processing options.
2. *Database:* integrated files for storage and retrieval.
3. *Data creation:* creation of data according to user specification.
4. *Analysis:* statistical evaluation of modeling assumptions and availability of capabilities such as sensitivity and risk analyses. In marketing, for example, the "Analyze" function might be used to examine sales data over the past years to determine product trends for use in planning activities.
5. *Optimization:* a move from "what if" to "what's best."
6. *Color graphics:* interactive, multicolor graphics for presentation of results (see Figure 9.3).

In addition to these features, several areas must be addressed for DSS performance:

1. Management must address the right problems and determine to what

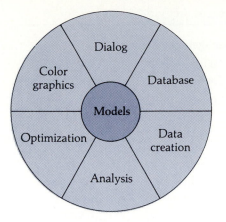

Figure 9.3
Modules of a decision
support system.

extent DSS should support multiple processes. As mentioned in Chapter 2, a DSS must be *demand driven*, not supply driven.

2. DSS developers must arrange for proper use support and produce a system that meets user requirements. Otherwise, management may decide DSS is not useful after all.

3. DSS software must have the features specified earlier or users may reject the installation.

Many human factors influence the success of a DSS installation, including decision makers' inherent resistance to change. Individuals who control certain information may not want to relinquish that control for a new system for fear of loss of their job. Cost-justifying a DSS for all managerial levels is not easy because of the subjectivity of determining the resulting benefit from DSS. In addition, users and DSS provide good results when there is a congenial relationship among members of the support staff. A cooperative environment and supportive top management help swing such innovation into place.

DSS and Decision Making

DSS can be used for a variety of decisions, but it applies better to some decisions than to others. As we have discussed in Chapter 8, Gorry and Morton refer to programmable tasks as *structured* tasks and nonprogrammable tasks as *unstructured*, so as not to confuse the type of task with whether it has been "programmed" on a computer. They also added a third category—*semistructured* tasks. A semistructured task has certain subtasks that are programmable and others that are nonprogrammable.

P. G. W. Keen and Scott Morton combined Anthony's and Simon's frameworks, using the type of managerial activity (Anthony's operational

Table 9.2   Decision Types by Management Activity*

Types of Decision	Operational Control	Management Control	Strategic Planning	Support Needed
		Management Activity		
Structured	Inventory reordering	Linear programming method	Plant location problems	EDP or management science models
Semistructured	Bond trading; production scheduling	Setting market budget for consumer products	Capital acquisition analysis; mergers	DSS
Unstructured	Selecting a cover for LIFE	Hiring managers	R&D portfolio development	Human intuition

*Based on Gorry and Morton's framework. See Table 8.2.

control, management control, and strategic planning) and the types of decision tasks (structured, semistructured, and unstructured) as dimensions for the three task categories (1978, Chap. 4; see also Davis and Olson, 1984, 369–371). The result is a matrix that suggests the types of activities that fit within the cells. See Table 9.2.

It can be seen that DSS is directed toward middle and upper management, although low level (operational control) managers can also benefit from it. DSS is meant to operate in a more flexible manner than MIS, providing support for unstructured and semistructured decision making tasks. Unlike traditional EDP, which programs as much of the decision as possible, DSS supports rather than automates the decision structure for a variety of unstructured and semistructured decision processes. This means:

1. Extensive user participation in DSS development.
2. Use of technology that is unique to flexible access. Microcomputer or intelligent terminals and local area networks play a critical role in DSS design.
3. Greater emphasis on small, easily understood and updated models. For example, a single product planning model that can be updated via ad hoc analyses would be more effective for the user than a static, large-scale, integrated model.
4. In addition to technical skills, DSS designers must have experience in the end user's business. This improves the effectiveness of the decision support system.

Examples of Decision Support Systems

The following examples illustrate how different organizations use DSS and how they were valuable:

Oldsmobile, a division of General Motors, found itself with an application backlog in its MIS center in Lansing, Michigan. The operating staff used DSS to prepare budgets, forecasting analysis and reporting the company's financial information. The firm's senior accountant discussed the benefits of DSS:

> Every company needs to generate financial data and they have a couple of choices. If they don't use a decision support system they have to have the information center programmers code the system. That type of system does not lend itself to the needs of business, because if needs change overnight, I can't go to the programmer and have him change my application so that it does something different in a very short time. A decision support system allows you to merely change the model entirely in a very short time. (Snyders, 1984, 52–54.)

Firestone Tire and Rubber Company in Akron, Ohio uses a DSS for unstructured problems such as R&D budgeting and merger acquisition analysis with many alternatives. The firm sees two major benefits to installing a DSS:

1. It offers an advantage over the traditional transaction processing systems. Firestone's DSS has a database that includes 200 competitive tires. This allows analysts to look for relationships between financial and external variables, including microeconomic theories such as total car production and gross national product (GNP). Additional information is included on construction, tread volume, and other competitive data.

2. The use of a "base case set of logic." Several variables in the decision-making process have been tied together by a model. All operating groups and support staff have agreed to the model so that making decisions and setting budgets are understood by everyone.

At Florida Power and Light Co., the DSS showed that the existing inventory distribution system would result in inefficiencies. Result: the Miami-based utility saved $13.5 million in one year in inventory carrying costs.

The interactive feature of DSS must be reinforced by responsiveness for making effective decisions. According to Davis and Olson (1984), **responsiveness** is a combination of:

1. *Power:* the degree to which the system can answer the most important questions.
2. *Accessibility:* the degree to which the system can provide answers in a timely and consistent manner.
3. *Flexibility:* the degree to which the system can adapt to changing needs and situations.

For many decision situations, the best responsiveness for the price is hiring people to do analyses apart from the company's computer system. For other situations, strong reliance on computer technology is a better choice. For a third group, there are no truly satisfactory choices, because the most important questions (e.g., what really will happen next year?) defy any formal or systematic combination of human intelligence and computer technology.

Evaluating DSS

One difficulty in evaluating a DSS is that its impact is not always self-evident. When the literature discusses the benefits of a DSS, it specifies intangibles such as improving communication and managing more effectively. Qualitative benefits are difficult to translate into monetary terms.

Another difficulty in evaluating a DSS is that systems are evolutionary in nature and may take years to be fully in place. A third difficulty is making evaluation *post facto*, or after the fact. An approach should be established to begin evaluation before a system is designed. As the system is being implemented, evaluation should continue until the termination stage is reached.

Justifying the costs and benefits of a DSS should be an ongoing process throughout the development life cycle (see Table 9.3). Such an approach cannot be made too rigid, since the central aim is to ensure that the elusive "soft" issues are well handled.

The Evolving Roles of DSS

In building a DSS, some technologies are useful for the various roles that managers and users will play. Three levels of technology and three corresponding role holders are involved in developing and using a DSS. As shown in Figure 9.4, the three levels are specific DSS, DSS generators, and DSS tools.

Specific DSS allows the user to deal with a specific set of related problems. For example, a sales force allocation system allows a salesperson to display a map of the firm's marketing territory, showing sales volume by area, product type, and size of staff. The interactive capability of the system enables the sales manager to alter product location and try out a variety of strategies quickly and easily.

The nature of a specific DSS depends on the problem, how the user approaches the problem, and the organizational environment. The major value is to accommodate change, to persuade managers to use DSS, and to come to a decision that might have to be made on a recurring or a one-time basis. Specific DSS is the most widely used form of computerized decision support.

Table 9.3 A Process for Justifying DSS Use

Development Stage	Procedure/Description
Entry	Define the aims of the system priorities, tradeoffs, resources, and responsibilities. For example, it may be desirable to: 1. Save hard dollars 2. Change the way decisions are made 3. Improve communication or information flows 4. Have responsive and easy to use system It is essential to define each item and agree on what key indicators will be used to evaluate the success of each aim.
Design	The design must contribute to each of the aims, as reflected in the priorities.
Action	As the system is brought on stream, track how each aim is being met, via the key indicators.
Evaluation	In order to determine how complete the system is, several questions must be considered: 1. Have the predefined aims been met? 2. Do the key indicators show that the system is generating the changes and benefits expected? 3. What are the costs (in dollars and time) required to reach "success"? Are they worth paying? If the system evaluation shows it is incomplete, it may be necessary to cycle back through Design and Action.
Termination	The project is ready for the consultant to disengage when one of two conditions applies: 1. Evaluation shows the system is self-sustaining, and training and new procedures are satisfactorily completed. 2. Evaluation shows it is incomplete, but there is consensus among the interested parties that the marginal costs of the extra effort needed are not justified.

Adapted from Keen, 1975, 28.

A **DSS generator** is a hardware/software package that builds a number of specific DSS within a class of decision support applications. It enables nonprogrammers to develop a customized DSS for specific applications. For example, the sales force allocation may be built using a relational database system. By incorporating various memos, display formats, and command strings, the software can develop a specific DSS to support the sales force.

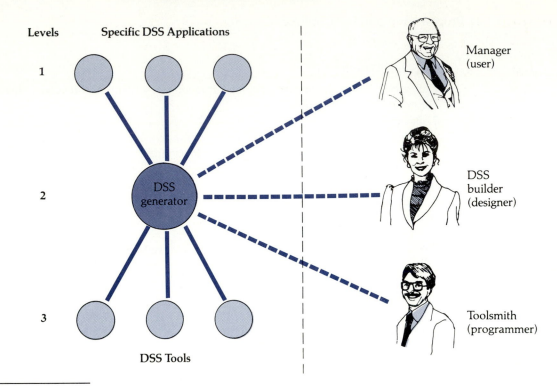

Figure 9.4
Levels of DSS technology and associated roles for managers and technicians. (Sprague/Carlson, *Building Effective Decision Support Systems*, © 1982, p. 14. Adapted by permission of Prentice-Hall, Inc., Englewood Cliffs, N.J.)

The third level of technology are **DSS tools** that develop a specific DSS or a DSS generator. For example, a high-level language such as FORTRAN becomes a tool for building subroutine packages. This is the same approach used in developing traditional applications with general-purpose languages as a tool.

Key Roles

Given these levels of technology, three key roles evolved that managers and technicians will play: The user, the builder, and the toolsmith.

The User   Users are concerned with what the specific DSS (level 1) can do for them. Here problem solving and decision making tasks are important. Users will tap the DSS for assistance. From the user's view, DSS must provide capabilities for decision making. It should:

1. Be easy to use and learn.
2. Provide support for the types of decisions that have virtually no support from data processing or MIS.
3. Provide support for users at all managerial levels, since each user faces problems within the context of their respective environment.
4. Support all phases of the decision-making process.

The Builder The DSS **builder** or designer assembles the necessary capabilities from the DSS generator (level 2) for configuring the specific DSS that will meet user needs. The builder draws on computer-based tools and methodology to provide the decision support required by the user. The main concern is determining how the generator's capabilities can be assembled to create the specific DSS.

A promising aspect of DSS is its capability to integrate decision models. One major problem has been that DSS builders were often preoccupied with the structure of the model. Models tended to suffer because of the difficulty of developing integrated models to handle a realistic set of interrelated decisions. Communications between models were left to the user as a manual process.

With this background, a DSS model must have two major capabilities:

1. Create and maintain a variety of models to support all levels of management.
2. Have interrelated models with proper linkages through the residing database. The availability of these features reflects positively in the effectiveness of the specific DSS in meeting the user's needs.

The Toolsmith The DSS **toolsmith** is similar to a systems programmer. He/she is concerned with developing a new language and technology and how they can be used to form a DSS generator with the predefined capabilities.

The two areas that concern the toolsmith are data and model management. Modeling languages make it possible to link relationships among variables so that the user can simulate or develop "what-if" models. The model management area has also a potential for incorporating expert systems to bear on DSS. As we will see in Chapter 12, recent work uses semantic networks for model representation. This unique approach elevates DSS to a higher level of contribution than ever before.

Note that the three roles we have discussed do not necessarily align with persons on a one-to-one basis. For example, one individual may be partly a builder and partly a user. The appropriate role assignment depends on the nature of the problem and the person's technical background.

Overall, the DSS should support all phases of the decision-making process. As an adaptive system, it consists of all three levels of technology and operates with the roles (participants), and the technology adapting to changes over time. The specific DSS allows the user the capabilities to *search* the environment for conditions calling for decisions. Over time, changes occur in the user's expectations or the organization. This means that the specific DSS *learns* to handle these changes through the DSS generator with the aid of the DSS builder. Over the longer time period, new tools evolve that provide the technology for upgrading the DSS generator, out of which the special DSS is constructed with the help of the toolsmith.

The notion of adaptive design for DSS has also been discussed by Keen. He argues that the final DSS can be developed only through an adaptive process of learning and evaluation. A key aspect of adaptive design is the *builder-user link*. Based on the assumption that users do not always know what they need, the builder develops an initial system to which users can respond and then clarify what they want. This *middle-out* approach is a means by which the builder learns from the user. It also ensures that the user drives the design process.

The Expanding Role of Graphics

For over two decades, computer graphics systems have been promoted for use in business management. Since the mid-1980s, this has been a high demand area. Using graphics workstations and desktop publishing systems, managers are already putting their budget allocations into pie charts, studying trend data in line graphics, and comparing sales figures on bar charts. Graphics are especially helpful in decision making because they allow the manager to visualize relationships and data summaries. A wide variety of graphic forms can be generated on the computer, especially on the microcomputer. Some of the graphics are:

1. *Bar* and *pie charts* are used to display values by the size of the bar or pie and breakdowns such as sources of revenues by product (see Figure 9.5).
2. *Time series charts* are commonly used for showing the value of one or more variables against time (see Figure 9.6).
3. *Hierarchy charts* such as organization charts and structure charts are also widely used in business. An organization chart, for example, shows relationships between departments, chain of command, and authority relationships (see Figure 9.7).
4. *Sequence charts* lay out the sequence of activities or events. Examples are data flow diagrams and program flowcharts (see Figure 9.8).
5. *Text graphics* have the capability to create captions, highlight words of importance and produce banners (see Figure 9.9).
6. *Scatter charts* are two-dimensional formats that show point locations where coordinates represent the values located on the X and Y axes (see Figure 9.10).

As you can see, graphics speak louder than words. They are widely used for *reports,* for *presentations* in meetings and conferences, for *supporting* management decisions, and in *production drawings* such as computer-aided design (CAD) and computer-aided manufacturing (CAM). Graphics are also used in teleconferencing and videotex activities.

Graphics are best used when the tasks involve comparing pattern changes over time or analyzing the relationships among variables. In

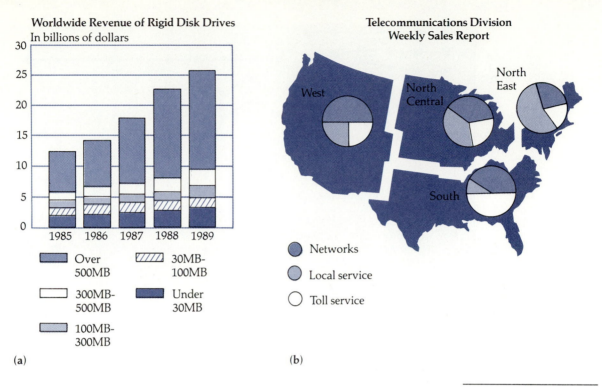

Figure 9.5
(a) Bar chart. (b) Pie chart. Adapted from Datamation, May 1, 1987, p. 64.

contrast, tabular data representation is best used in situations where the manager needs to record specific data values or determine percentage changes between two numbers. According to a University of Minnesota study, the primary user is the middle manager. It is expected, though, that this function will move to lower managers with easier-to-use software and standardization on the user interface.

A major study justifying the use of business graphics was conducted by Wharton Business School at the University of Pennsylvania in 1981. The study assessed the use of overhead transparencies in business meetings. The highlights of the findings were:

1. More executives acted on the recommendations of the presenter who used transparencies than on the recommendations of presenters who did not (see Figure 9.11).
2. Presenters who used graphics were perceived to be better prepared, more persuasive, and more interesting.
3. Length of meetings was shorter and individuals made decisions earlier when overhead transparencies were used.

Compared to manual graphics, computer graphics are less expensive and can be changed more quickly to reflect last-minute changes in data or events. The low cost and speed make answering "what-if" questions

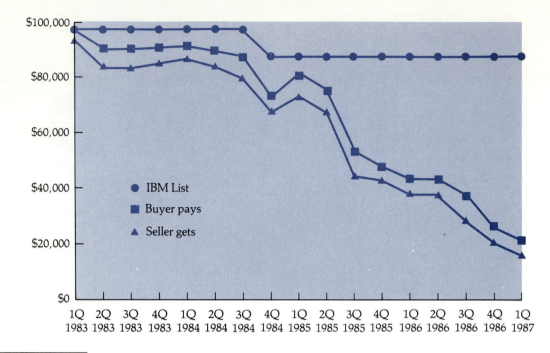

Figure 9.6
Time series chart.

Figure 9.7
Organization structure.

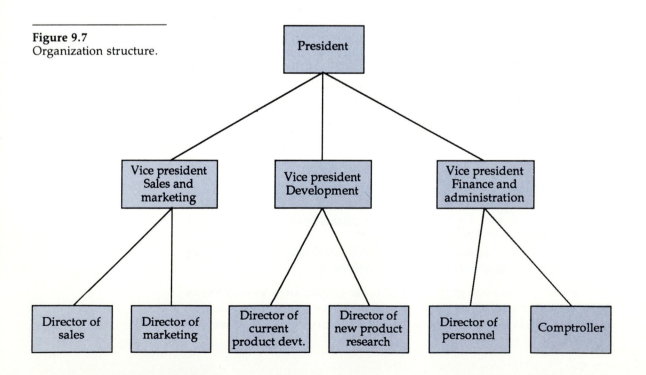

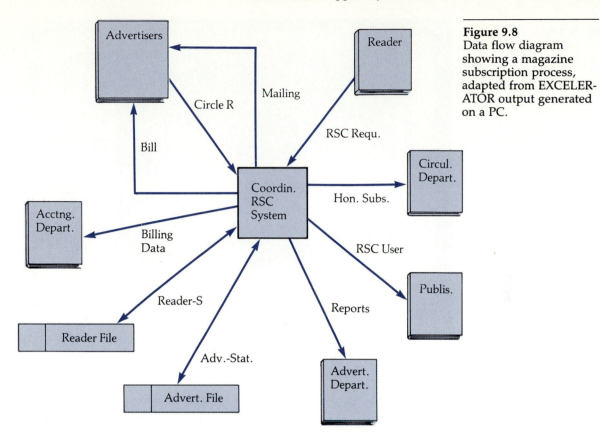

Figure 9.8
Data flow diagram
showing a magazine
subscription process,
adapted from EXCELER-
ATOR output generated
on a PC.

practical. For example, a manager may ask, "What would be our personnel size this year if our sales . . .?" These questions can be asked on the
spot and the resulting graphs can be generated and displayed very quickly.

One problem with graphics is that few people know how to use them
effectively. Deceptive graphics design is not uncommon. One study found
that more than 40 percent of corporations' annual reports have at least
one misleading graph. Another study by the University of Minnesota
found charts and graphs with inconsistent scaling. Understanding the
message, for example, is not enough in an application in which the format is as important as the content.

With today's increasing emphasis on graphics and a wide range of
colors, the user needs to know what to do with color. What is the average
user going to do with 100 colors? One solution is to embed an "expert
system" software for graphics. In one such software, the user inputs
information and the software applies graphic design rules to it. Typically,
it has been shown to give about 80 percent of the presentation. Then the
user can review the results and override the system to finalize the 20
percent of the presentation.

Figure 9.9
Computer-aided decision making: IBM's TopView and Microsoft's Windows. These IBM PC operating environments can run several programs concurrently and let users follow their progress on a screen divided into windows. Both TopView and Windows offer easy-to-use menu systems, the ability to transfer data among different types of files as well as user-friendly access to the operating system. (a) TopView uses overlapping windows, but (b) Windows uses an approach called tilting, which arranges windows to fit the screen completely to make the best use of the screen display area.

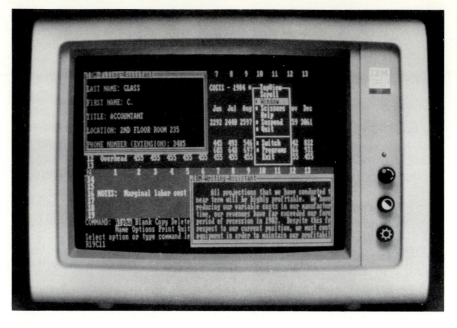

(a)

(b)

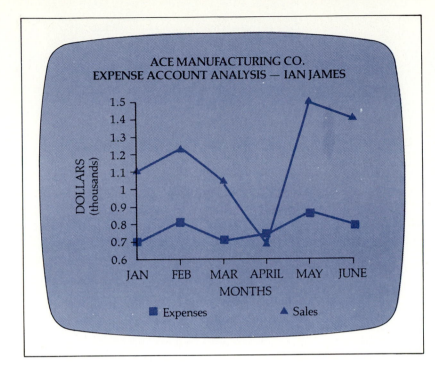

Figure 9.10
Scatter chart. LOTUS
1-2-3 presents a line
graph of sales and
expense figures.

Graphics design quality is closely related to decision-making quality. The user needs training and experience before benefiting regularly from graphics.

The Role of the Microcomputer

The concepts and procedures of DSS provide an attractive framework for integrating microcomputer capabilities and the mainframe. Since the personal computer appeared in the late 1970s, we have seen the introduction of Visicorp's VISICALC electronic spreadsheet as a DSS tool. Price and performance have changed so quickly that the LOTUS 1-2-3 surged instantly over VISICALC. The trend is toward integration and making use of the power of microcomputers such as IBM's AT and System/2 and Compaq's fixed disk system.

In characterizing the role of the mainframe and PC in business graphics, mainframes are ideal for satisfying production demands for charts. Yet they are impractical in situations requiring graphic editing, because they cannot compare with the interactive features of personal computers, which offer easy editing and high-level interface with the user. The trend is a joint mainframe–PC environment for business graphics software.

The true payoff of DSS is becoming more and more dependent on effective integration of a variety of information resources. This means

Figure 9.11
Use of graphics and
decision making.

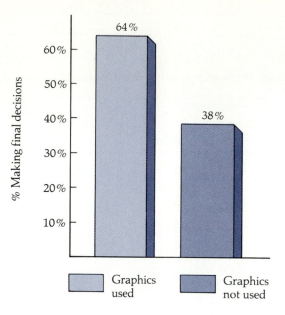

more than mere integration of functions at a workstation. In a distributed DSS environment, for example, we would expect significant complexity of hardware, software, and networking along with competent end users and top management. For a micro-mainframe design, users can access corporate data in computer-accessible form, which includes spreadsheet analysis on the microcomputer.

This approach provides support design for decision making. When implemented, highly paid managers no longer need to enter data into a micro spreadsheet graphics package from newspapers or company reports. The cost and inaccuracy of data entry made it attractive for the DSS user to secure direct access to the mainframe database.

In determining a micro-mainframe environment, we need to make sure of the availability of a DSS that provides personal and organizational support. Personal support has to do with the user's individual use within the department. For example, departmental budgeting provides the manager with ways to enter, access, and update budget figures and values. Decisions calling for organizational support require interdependence between a user's department and other departments in the organization. For example, organizational support for budgeting should be capable of storing budget data at the departmental level and integrating these figures by department and for the organization as a whole. Organization and control of data, models, and procedures are important for system success.

Levels of Micro-Based DSS   In today's DSS-dominated environment, there are DSS packages for different levels of applications and user

Table 9.4   Key DSS Packages and Levels of Applications

Level	DSS Product	Application
1	Spreadsheet model	Written by or for the user with no special user interface
2	Specialized DSS model (e.g., statistical analysis, risk analysis)	Greater complexity of design than level 1
3	Integrated model (e.g., Symphony)	Ties together several related models, requiring extensive control and data cross-communication requirements
4	Versions of levels 1, 2, 3 with automatic interface	Incorporate full-screen menus, prompting an automatic dispatching of commands; such "models" can then be run by end users with no training
5	Third party creation of vertical market software	Developed in DSS languages versus standard programming languages to reduce development and maintenance costs and ensure transportability across microcomputers

Adapted from Earle, 1984, 18–19.

sophistication. A summary of the key DSS packages and the applications they address are listed in Table 9.4. New users develop applications at level 1. As they gain experience and begin to adopt more complex problems, developing users move progressively to higher levels.

The Role of Management

DSS has become an important computer-based tool for supporting user decisions. Since the mid-1970s, the worth of the DSS concept has been demonstrated by the large number of successful DSS installations. The abundance of these systems now allows full-fledged research into the managerial and organizational aspects of DSS development. The technology has already reached a maturation level and has proven its worth. At this point it is relevant to examine the support DSS has been getting as a basis for adoption.

A key question in building DSS is: What motivates DSS acquisition? Several authors suggest that the thrust behind a DSS installation is improving decision-making effectiveness. According to Hogue and Watson (1983, 16), however, the most commonly suggested factor is the strong support of users who expect to benefit from the proposed DSS. The eventual user, viewed as a middle- or upper-level manager, is also the one who initiates the idea of developing a DSS.

DSS development generally begins with a specific manager's need. Consequently, managers must play an active role in supporting and controlling DSS projects. Since DSS installations invariably require change in the user's environment, management's review of the DSS is expected to be heavy throughout the development cycle.

Hogue and Watson conducted an intensive investigation of eighteen DSSs to determine how they were approved and administered. The study produced interesting findings:

1. The most frequently cited factor for developing a DSS is a need for accurate and timely information.
2. The eventual users of the DSS are those who most actively support its development. Those pushing for the creation of DSS were the end users.
3. The decision to adopt a DSS was based more on an intuitive feeling about the potential impact of DSS on decision making rather than on cost/benefit or value analyses.
4. Most of the organizations studied made no formal attempt to measure the financial impact of the DSS after it became operational. Likewise, planning for the development of DSSs is more an ad hoc than an integrated process. DSS was developed with little thought given to developing additional DSS.

The message of this study is that introducing technology requires management support for success. In the case of DSS, it is very likely that administration is controlled almost exclusively by middle and upper management at the department level because DSS utilization tends to be limited to those within a single department.

Implications for MIS

A DSS helps in planning an uncertain future. A smaller business where information requirements are not so great may survive without a DSS. Large corporations, however, will benefit with a computer-aided system to help structure ill-defined problems and opportunities. Cost/benefit analysis makes a difference, depending on the decision-making environment. Because of the variety of decision-making processes, a DSS is more likely to be cost-effective if it supports multiple processes. If a specific DSS is designed for only one type of decision, any changes in the decision require a change in the DSS to accommodate changes in the information processing requirements. However, since a DSS may be difficult to cost-justify, there is at least a need to address the goals of the organization as defined by top management.

While it is true that DSS will not transform bad decision makers into good ones, it can work to improve those qualities in a decision maker for successful decisions. Decision makers should be meticulous about facts and should be intuitive. They should also have a good comprehension of the company's overall operations. Good decision makers can distinguish between genuine merit and unreasonable bias.

Summary

▫ DSS is a collection of tools, data, and techniques to help users make ad hoc decision requests. The unique characteristics of DSS are:
  a. Focus on decisions and the use of computers to support the user's judgment.
  b. Available to all managers for semistructured problems.
  c. Provides an easy-to-use, user-friendly, iterative environment for problem solving.

▫ DSS has several components:
  a. DSS *database* made available to authorized users.
  b. *DBMS* to provide access to a large number of end users while maintaining data security, integrity, and auditability.
  c. DSS *tools* and *languages* to enter, retrieve, and report information from the database.
  d. *Application-building environment* to make available a wide variety of application building management science models.

▫ An effective DSS must have the following features:
  a. Manage large volumes of heterogeneous data.
  b. Provide powerful modeling capabilities.
  c. Provide a flexible array of reporting and display alternatives.
  d. Support varying managerial styles, skills, and knowledge.
  e. Modular design, providing easy-to-switch interface from one module to another.

▫ In addition to these DSS features, management must address the right problems for their organization. DSS developers must also arrange for proper user support in DSS development and representative DSS software.

▫ Keen and Morton use Anthony's and Simon's frameworks to develop a matrix of decision types by management activity. Their work showed that DSS is meant to provide support for unstructured and semistructured decision making tasks. DSS also supports rather than automates the decision making structure.

▫ One difficulty with DSS is that its impact is not always self-evident. Another difficulty is that DSS is evolutionary in nature and may take years to be fully in place. A third difficulty is that evaluation is generally done post facto. Therefore, justifying costs and benefits of a DSS should be on an ongoing basis.

▫ In building a DSS, some technologies are corresponding to various management roles. According to Sprague, there are three levels of technology and three corresponding role holders:

a. The *specific DSS* is the system that provides tools to amplify a user's judgment.

b. The *DSS generator* with the capability to build a specific DSS is for the DSS builder or designer.

c. *DSS tools* help develop a DSS generator or a specific DSS.

▫ The concepts and procedures of DSS provide an attractive framework for integrating microcomputer capabilities and the mainframe. The true payoff of DSS is becoming more and more dependent on effective integration of a variety of information resources.

▫ A variety of DSS packages are aimed at different levels of applications and user sophistication. For example, a level 1 package such as a spreadsheet model is written by or for the user with no special user interface. In contrast, an integrated model such as Symphony, ties together several related models, requiring extensive control and data-cross communication requirements.

▫ A key question in building DSS is: What motivates DSS acquisition? In many cases, it is the strong support of users who expect to benefit from the proposed DSS. According to Hogue and Watson, the most frequently cited factor is a need for accurate and timely information. Most of the organizations they studied made no attempt to measure the financial impact of the DSS after it became operational.

Key Terms

Ad hoc	Nonprocedural language
Builder	Procedural language
Dialog	Responsiveness
DSS tools	Specific DSS
DSS generator	Toolsmith

Review Questions

1. Define DSS. What characteristics distinguish it from DP or MIS? Elaborate.

2. What components make up a DSS? How do they relate to one another? Illustrate.

3. Distinguish between:
   a. Procedural and nonprocedural language

b. DSS builder and toolsmith
c. Design and choice

4. Discuss the features a DSS must provide. What feature do you consider the most critical? Why?

5. Explain briefly the key DSS modules.

6. Illustrate and describe Keen's and Morton's matrix. What aspects of the matrix are Simon's?

7. In what way are structured and unstructured decisions related to management activity?

8. Why is DSS difficult to evaluate? Discuss.

9. Elaborate on the process of justifying use of a DSS.

10. Sprague proposed a framework that considers three levels of technology and three corresponding role holders in developing and using a DSS. Illustrate these levels and their relationships to the respective role holder.

11. In what way is the DSS toolsmith similar to a systems programmer? How does the toolsmith differ from the DSS builder? Be specific.

12. What is the role of the microcomputer in DSS? Explain in detail.

13. Specify the levels of applications addressed by key DSS packages. What level does the new user function at?

14. Write a short essay on the role of management in DSS development.

Application Problems

1. Arnold Hammer, Inc., is a large import/export company based in Washington, D.C., with four divisions and outlets all over the globe. The MIS center has three key functions:
a. Coordinates the overall processing activities of the DP centers of the divisions.
b. Provides information processing for headquarters.
c. Develops one-time applications for smaller divisions on request.

The organization chart of the MIS center is shown in Figure 9.A1.
After attending a conference on DSS, the vice president of MIS sensed that he has cleared three projects that might be labeled specific DSS:
(1) A subscription to a time-sharing service that offers a variety of statistical and financial analysis packages to assist executives in preparing requests for capital expenditure authorizations.
(2) A request from the executive vice president to compare the pro-

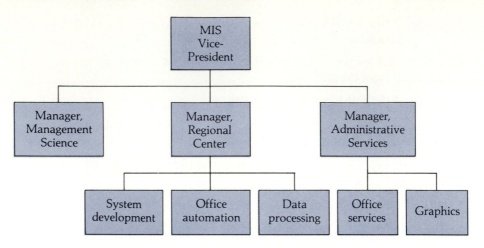

Figure 9.A1
Organization chart of an
MIS center.

ductivity of each division with selected companies of similar characteristics.

(3) A subscription to a service that provides trends computation, analysis, and tracking of financial and economic data.

Evaluate each project and determine to what extent it can be viewed as specific DSS.

2. One author suggested that we do not understand enough about how managers make decisions to develop DSS. Therefore, we need to know what their needs are to assist them in decision making. Then we are in a better position to develop the information technology to suit the needs. Do you agree? Explain.

Selected References

Alter, Steven L. *Decision Support Systems: Current Practice and Continuing Challenges.* Reading, Mass.: Addison-Wesley, 1980.

Anthony, R. N. *Planning and Control Systems: A Framework for Analysis.* Cambridge, Mass.: MIT Press, 1965.

Brigham, Ivan-Carol. "Graphics' Best Use Decision Support." *Computerworld,* December 8, 1986, 83.

Davis, G. B. and Olson, M. *Management Information Systems: Conceptual Foundations, Structure, and Development.* New York: McGraw-Hill, 1984.

Desmond, John. "Window to MIS: Graphics Focuses Business Pictures." *Software News,* April 1986, 44ff.

Dickson, Gary and Lehman, John A. "Quality Graphics Design Supports Quality Decisions." *Computerworld,* March 16, 1987, 57–58.

Earle, Robert J. "DSS Comes on Down to Micro Markets." *Data Management,* January 1984, 18–19.

Hogue, Jack T. and Watson, Hugh J. "Management's Role in the Approval and Administration of Decision Support Systems." *MIS Quarterly*, June 1983, 16.

Huber, George P. "Cognitive Style as a Basis for MIS and DSS Designs: Much Ado About Nothing?" *Management Science*, May 1983, 567–579.

Keen, P. G. W. "Computer-Aided Decision Aids: The Evaluation Problem." *Sloan Management Review*, Spring 1975, 28.

_____. "Adaptive Design for Decision Support Systems." *Data Base*, Fall 1980, 19.

Melymuka, Kathleen. "Presentation Graphics." *PC Week*, August 19, 1986, S/3–5ff.

Orr, Jack. "The Promise of Pictures." *Computerworld*, March 16, 1987, S1–2.

Puzzarghera, Paul. "Get an Inside Look at the 'True' DSS." *Software News*, December 1984, 34.

Raho, Louis E. and Belohlov, James A. "Discriminating Characteristics of EDP, MIS, and DSS Information Interface." *Data Management*, December 1982, 19.

Simon, Herbert A. *The New Science of Management Decisions*. New York: Harper & Row, 1960.

Snyders, J. "Decision-Making Made Easier." *Infosystems*, August 1984, 52–54.

Sprague, R. H. and Carlson, Eric. *Building Decision Support Systems*. Englewood Cliffs, N.J.: Prentice-Hall, 1982.

_____and McNurlin, Barbara C. *Information Systems Management in Practice*. Englewood Cliffs, N. J.: Prentice-Hall, 1982.

PART III

DECISION SUPPORT AND END USER COMPUTING

DSS Software and Tools

Chapter Contents

DSS at Phillips Gushes Strategic Information

GIVING A NEW TWIST to "user friendly," Phillips Petroleum Co., Bartlesville, Oklahoma, has implemented an extensive program of software acquisition, training and support to make executives "user responsible" for decision support system (DSS) applications.

It is possible through DSS to weave together the functions of the operating groups of Phillips, which include: minerals; exploration and production; gas and gas liquids; corporate; petroleum products; and chemicals. They can work autonomously or interchangeably through DSS.

Phillips had formerly handled DSS in more traditional ways. Data processing groups generated decision support reports based on criteria given by management or operating teams. This was a time-consuming process. However, new software packages that are no longer programming-oriented but user-oriented "fourth generation" languages enable the decision makers to generate these reports themselves, as needed.

"DSS gets us out of the software development business and puts the user into it, without having to sacrifice the power to develop complex applications," explains R. C. Burness, operations research analyst at Phillips.

In some cases the user can be taught in only one day to create an application program, with a user friendly interface developed by a programmer-analyst, offering full-screen scrolling and system-edited reports with color graphics.

This DSS support and education architecture is a means for Phillips to achieve its ultimate goal of shifting total DSS responsibility into the end user community. A significant part of the program revolves around the operating groups' developing and maintaining their own models.

"We're very far along, but only by continued efforts to broaden employee awareness of DSS, data processing in general and Phillips business will we completely integrate user and computer," explains Burness.

—Adapted from Data Management, *February 1986, 20–21.*

AT A GLANCE

The heart of DSS is its software, which provides a quick and easy way for setting up a mathematical model, entering the information into it, and reporting the results. DSS software is arbitrarily classified into spreadsheet software and integrated systems. The spreadsheet is limited to manipulating data and graphics. Integrated systems perform additional functions such as word processing and database management.

The increasing demand for DSS software stems from demand for information, increasing computer literacy, and need for integration of user needs in a single system. User-oriented criteria for DSS software derive from general, technical, vendor, and cost considerations. Overall, these requirements emphasize user friendliness, functionality, reliability, data display, and reporting capabilities.

The spreadsheet processor is most widely used for simple model building. Built on a framework of data and formulas, it is given form by the formats, explanatory text, and labels the user chooses. The spreadsheet processor simplifies the procedure for finding solutions to many problems: when one figure is changed, all the affected entries are recalculated.

In evaluating DSS software, six criteria are used: ability to generate statistics, ease of use, spreadsheet design, printing options, data entry, and documentation. Users have a variety of packages to choose from in a market that has responded well to various levels of user sophistication.

By the end of this chapter, you should know:

1. The trends in DSS software
2. Software selection criteria
3. Spreadsheet basics
4. What to consider in developing DSS

Introduction

In the previous chapter, we saw that DSS is a new way of thinking about managerial uses of computers. DSS improves the productivity of managers facing poorly structured decision situations. It also provides computational aids where managers need to integrate information, judgment, and experience. DSS also provides management the equivalent of the pilot's flight simulator for pretesting different solutions before adopting them in the real world.

The heart of any DSS is its software. The software provides a quick and easy way for setting up a mathematical model, entering the information into it, and reporting the results. It can be used to prepare budgets, analyze sales, calculate cash flow and commissions, and evaluate stock purchase in a record (row) and a field (column) format.

DSS software is arbitrarily classified under two major categories: spreadsheets and integrated systems. **Spreadsheet software** is normally limited to manipulation of spreadsheet data and graphics. **Integrated systems** perform additional functions such as word processing and database management. Both categories operate like a multicolumnar accounting worksheet with built-in math and financial formulas, variable column widths, and provision for making as many changes as necessary before the final draft is ready. A third category emphasizes statistical and other modeling packages for mainframes and micros linked to the mainframe. In this chapter we will discuss DSS software with an emphasis on selection criteria.

Trends in DSS Software

DSS software has undergone extensive change to reach users at all levels. Since the early 1970s, when managers began to look to computers for assistance in decision making, they found partial solutions—individual, stand-alone packages for statistical analysis and financial modeling, and others for database management. No software package could be used with another.

In the early 1980s, users began to demand software that integrated the major applications needed for analysis. This need led to the development of the first integrated DSS. The personal computer created significant demand for DSS software and introduced managers to the value of DSS applications (Bergstrom, 1984, 35).

To understand DSS software trends, we need to consider three industry forces:

1. Demand for information
2. Increasing computer literacy
3. Need for integration

Demand for Information   Traditionally, end users have been concerned with three types of information: private, corporate, and public. Of particular importance is access to the corporate database. As a valuable resource, such information can no longer be locked away in COBOL programs. Software must provide either direct access to data residing in various systems or interface database management packages as a gateway to information resources. As we will see later in the chapter, various packages are available with a wide variety of offerings for the user.

Increasing Computer Literacy   The surge in computer literacy and computer acceptance has been on the rise since the early 1980s. More and more business schools, for example, are requiring students to purchase personal computers before admission. This means that decision makers of the future will have a strong understanding of computer technology and the applications it handles. Accepting a computer as a tool means a potential for increasing the user's own productivity and improving the effectiveness of the overall organization.

Need for Integration   One of the most pressing of user concerns is integration. In the hardware area, a number of DSS centers face the problem of interfacing micros and mainframe software, a process that often involves diverse operating systems and vendors. Such a flexibility in delivery systems is important for large organizations with multiple DSS center offerings.

To satisfy DSS user requirements, two alternatives are available. One is to integrate everything the user needs in a single system. This way, when the user accesses the system, everything is ready for use. The other is to integrate selected activities such as graphics, risk analysis, DBMS, statistical analysis, and the like. On the surface it seems that the presentation of integrated solutions is more a marketing concept than a practical reality. Users must evaluate the pros and cons of each alternative.

Software Selection Criteria

No clear definition exists for determining what is or is not a DSS software package. There are over 100 different DSS products ranging from LOTUS 1-2-3, of which over 2,000,000 copies have been sold for $200–$500, to EXPRESS, of which about 300 copies have been sold for more than $200,000 each. The LOTUS 1-2-3 runs on the personal computer, whereas EXPRESS usually requires a mainframe. A microcomputer version of EXPRESS has recently become available at a price competitive with LOTUS. With price a consideration, we need to focus on features that support the user's needs, level of expertise, and the types of decision situations that require a DSS environment.

The user has two choices in selecting DSS software: locating software that will operate on existing hardware or finding the right DSS software first and then acquiring compatible hardware. The choice depends mostly on the performance requirements of the software, cost considerations, and the intended use of the software.

In many respects, the selection process for DSS software is similar to that of any software. Yet there are differences, stemming from end user requirements and reflected in the makeup of the selection team and the selection criteria (Reimann and Warren, 1985, 166–179). User-oriented selection criteria for DSS software are arbitrarily categorized under general, technical, vendor, and cost considerations (Meador and Mezger, 1983, 27–29).

General Considerations

Several general factors are considered in selecting DSS software: compatibility, functionality and ease of use, reliability, and integration of functions.

Compatibility   The DSS must fit in with an existing hardware/software environment; i.e., it must possess **compatibility**. In a network environment, the software should be capable of communicating with the mainframe and accessing central files.

Functionality and Ease of Use   By **functionality** we mean that the DSS software must meet the functional purpose at hand and be easy for nontechnical people to use. It must perform complex tasks through English-like menu selection or single-function key operation.

Ease of use is related to how much knowledge is required to use the software effectively. Some software consists of a simple two-dimensional spreadsheet calculator with notations that refer to the rows and columns of the model. Other software has comprehensive database management and other functions for addressing data.

User Friendliness   Most of today's DSS software vendors claim **user-friendly** packages. According to a study by H. Ledgard and colleagues (1984), however, they differ significantly in their degree of friendliness. A command language based on common, natural English phrases and use of syntax significantly increase the productivity of novice users as well as experienced programmers. Ideally, a novice user should be able to operate the system without documentation such as users' manuals or tutorials. The availability of HELP or error messages built into the system, full screen entry, and editing of data with appropriate menu formats reduces the need for documentation.

Another user-friendly feature is the ability to enter and edit data when needed. Full-screen entry and edit simplify the job for the end user (see Figure 10.1). Related to this feature is **nonprocedurality**, which allows the user complete freedom in the order of entering equations.

Reliability   This factor emphasizes the importance of the software's capability for performing without failure. Related to reliability is the maintenance factor—the amount of effort required to keep the system up and running.

Figure 10.1
LOTUS screen showing matrix and data. The cursor is over cell F20, the final total, which was computed by adding the contents of cells F17 and F18.

```
F20: (C2) (F17+F18)                                              READY

      A      B              C              D        E          F
 1  Item   Part                                  Unit       Total
 2  No.    No.          Description     Quantity  Cost       Cost
 3  ------------------------------------------------------------------
 4    1    150174   CPU System Unit (256K)   20  $1,933.00  $38,660.00
 5
 6    2    151001   Monochrome Display       20  $345.00    $6,900.00
 7
 8    3    504900   Display & Printer Board  20  $300.00    $6,000.00
 9
10    4    152002   Graphics Printer         20  $500.00    $10,000.00
11
12    5    525612   Printer Cable            20  $55.00     $1,100.00
13
14    6    124061   Disk Operating System    20  $60.00     $1,200.00
15                                                ---------------------
16                                          Subtotal        $63,860.00
17                                  Discounted Price        $44,702.00
18                                         State Tax        $3,531.46
19
20                                          TOTAL =         $48,233.46
```

Integration of Functions   The software should all work together using commonly developed information. The user should not have to switch from word processing to a spreadsheet to a graphics package, and so on. More and more of today's DSS software is moving in this direction.

Technical Considerations

The major technical considerations for DSS selection are interface design, modeling, data display, reporting, and data security and integrity.

Interface Design   DSS software should support novice as well as experienced users. This is not a straightforward consideration, since each user may have different expectations and format requirements. The DSS interface may be as simple as the rows and columns of a spreadsheet or a rigorous command structure in which commands and instructions describe the model and specify the processing. For system outputs, interface capabilities include graphics in full color to enhance information presentation to the user.

Modeling   Much of today's DSS software involves two-dimensional analyses: the monthly balance sheet, for example. Three-dimensional **models** are useful in situations such as evaluating a new product line by geographic area and time period. Examples of a simple three-dimensional model consisting of several locations, a product line, and customer types are: "What will be the effect on net profit of a 20 percent increase in sales of product X to customer type Y?" "What must advertising costs be for product X in location C to achieve a 5 percent increase in net profit?" Multidimensional data management that also incorporates external data from other databases makes it possible to perform the necessary analysis.

One obvious purpose of a DSS package is to expedite development, testing, and modification of some descriptive model. The modeling capabilities of DSS software reveal its ability to simulate business situations. This is the characteristic that most clearly distinguishes DSS from MIS.

The model, then, is the heart of the DSS application. It uses a set of mathematical functions or formulas to represent an organizational activity or situation. It also allows the user to study the alternative courses of action available and their respective outcomes. The commonly known "what-if" approach evaluates the effects of changes in various parameters.

In contrast to "what-if" is goal seeking, or the **backward iteration** approach, that calculates backward the parameters of the problem, given the parameters of the results. For example, in an income and expense statement, a "what-if" question might be: "What would be the gross income if I cut payroll by 15 percent?" A goal-seeking or backward iteration question might be: "What changes can I make in my expenses to realize $150,000 in net income?"

A logical extension of "what-if" and iteration functions is **risk analysis**, which is the systematic display of risk using the function of *Monte Carlo simulation* of uncertainty. Named after the famous casino, this model draws a random sample from a probability distribution of key unknowns, then repetitively computes and displays the relative frequency of a predefined measure.

For example, suppose that the expected sales growth of a computer vendor could be described by a probability distribution centered at 20 percent, with a minimum of 5 percent and a maximum of 40 percent. Assume further that the cost of goods sold is described around .65 and ranges from .55 to .75. A risk analysis model samples functions from a probability distribution and computes the several hundred resulting values for measures such as earnings per share (EPS) or return on investment (ROI).

Data Display Display of modeling activities is essential in examining outcomes. Presentation-quality reports should be produced with proper formatting. Graphics output, whether they are bar charts, line charts, pie charts, or scatter plots, must also be properly displayed.

Reporting Related to the display feature is the reporting function, which includes standard and custom report formats. Although less vital to management decision making than modeling, good reporting facilitates a manager's tasks by making sense of results and making them available to others. An important consideration is how easily users can produce, view, and modify report formats to suit their needs. This function makes reports more attractive and readily usable for decision making (see Table 10.1).

Table 10.1   A Typical Report Layout

Titles are automatically centered, but can be right or left justified.

Built in functions for dates, time, page numbering.

Column widths are automatically adjusted.

Decimal precision, $ and % signs may all be specified.

Row titles can be as large as 128 characters.

XYZ Products Corporation
5 Year Forecast
Apr. 22, 1986

Page 1

Figures in (000's)

	1985	1986	1987	1988	1989	Total
01 Total market	$169,102	$180,962	$194,611	$210,487	$229,183	$984,346
02 Market Share %	4.0%	8.0%	10.6%	12.4%	11.2%	9.5%
03 Gross sales	$ 6,764	$ 14,477	$ 20,629	$ 26,100	$ 25,783	$ 93,753
04 Cost of goods sold	2,841	6,080	7,633	9,657	9,540	35,751
05 Gross profit	3,923	8,397	12,996	16,443	16,243	58,003
06 Profit margin %	58.0%	58.0%	63.0%	63.0%	63.0%	61.9%
07 Market growth rate	5.3%	7.0%	7.5%	8.2%	8.9%	36.9%
Expenses						
08 Promotion	4,800	3,200	2,400	2,400	2,000	14,800
09 Marketing	1,218	2,606	3,713	4,698	4,641	16,876
10 G & A	169	362	516	653	645	2,344
11 R & D	284	608	866	1,096	1,083	3,938
12 Depreciation	1,500	1,275	1,159	985	999	5,918
13 Total expense	7,971	8,051	8,654	9,832	9,368	43,875
14 Expense as % of sales	117.8%	55.6%	42.0%	37.7%	36.3%	46.8%

Table 10.1   (*continued*)

XYZ Products Corporation
5 Year Forecast
Apr. 22, 1986

Figures in (000's)

	1985	1986	1987	1988	1989	Total	
15 Before tax income	(4,048)	346	4,342	6,612	6,876	14,128	**Commas in numbers are automatic, but can easily be removed.**
16 Income taxes	–	173	2,171	3,306	3,438	9,088	
17 After tax income	(4,048)	173	2,171	3,306	3,438	5,040	
18 ATI as % of sales	(59.8%)	1.2%	10.5%	12.7%	13.3%	5.4%	**Subtitles may be placed anywhere on a page.**

Cash Flow Summary

	1985	1986	1987	1988	1989	Total	
19 Income after tax	(4,048)	173	2,171	3,306	3,438	5,040	**You can print both numeric and alphabetic data.**
20 Depreciation	1,500	1,275	1,159	985	999	5,918	**Zeros can be represented as dashes, zeros, or blanks.**
21 (CHG working capital)	1,353	1,543	1,230	1,094	(63)	5,157	
22 Operating cash	(3,900)	(95)	2,099	3,196	4,501	5,801	**Parentheses indicating negative values are standard, but can easily be changed.**
23 (Investments)	10,000	–	500	–	500	11,000	
24 Residule value	N/A	N/A	N/A	N/A	18,002	18,002	
25 Net cashflow	(13,900)	(95)	1,599	3,196	22,003	12,803	**Discounted cash flow and internal rate of return are built in functions.**
26 DCF	(13,900)	(80)	1,129	1,895	10,957	0	
27 ROI	17.4% ********						

Table 10.2   User-Oriented Evaluation Criteria for DSS Software

Evaluation Criterion	Features
Analysis	· Goal seeking · Optimization · Sensitivity · What-if
Cost factors	· Conversion costs · Documentation · Initial license fee · Maintenance · Resource utilization
Data management	· Automatic audit trail · Common database manager · Data dictionary · Security · Simultaneous access
Forecasting and statistics	· Basic statistical functions · Curve fitting · Multiple regression · Multivariate statistics
Graphics	· Basic plots and graphs · Complex charts · Format and layout control · Multiple graphs per page · Multicolor support

Vendor Considerations

The software vendor and vendor support play an extremely critical role for the end user. Areas of concern are the availability of a "hot line" for help, training provisions, research and development, financial stability, continuing enhancements, and customer-base growth (see Table 10.2).

Cost Considerations

A most important consideration in DSS software selection involves the initial and ongoing costs. We must carefully determine what goes into

Table 10.2   *(continued)*

Evaluation Criterion	Features
Modeling	· Mathematical and financial functions · Multidimensionality · Nonprocedurality (ability to write equations and statements in any order desired) · User-defined functions
Reporting	· Custom report format(s) · Edit and test for report formats · Standard report format(s)
User friendliness	· Command abbreviation · Consistent, natural language commands · Data entry and editing, full screening mode · Documentation · Menus and prompts · Novice and expert modes · Spreadsheet display of data and results · User-defined commands
Vendor support	· Active R&D · Continuing enhancements · Financial stability · Growth of customer base · Hot line · Local branch offices · Organized user group · Quality of staff · Technical support personnel · Training

Adapted from Reimann and Warren, 1985, 168.

the license fee. Vendor support, user training, development costs, and maintenance may or may not be included in the acquisition price, depending on the terms of the contract. More on costs and contract negotiations is found in Chapter 17.

With these considerations, we should note that the categories are not mutually exclusive. Many features might appear in other categories and those categories are listed only in alphabetic order in Table 10.2. In the final analysis, the user's application determines the categories relative importance. For example, some users may require graphics, but others may not.

Table 10.3   Selected DSS Packages

Decision Support Package	Manufacturer	System Configuration	Market Orientation and Functionality	Comments
20/2D	Access Technology, Inc.	· 2 disk drives or hard disk · 192K bytes memory · Graphic board	· A portable and integrated spreadsheet package for micros and mainframes; primarily a spreadsheet, but with graphics, database management capability, and product scheduling facility	Mainframe versions communicate with microcomputer software such as LOTUS and MultiPlan
EIS Micro-Workstation	Boeing Computer Services	IBM PC hardware	· An integrated decision support including graphics, report writing, forecasting, statistics, modeling, and database management	PC can tap into Boeing's mainframe database in a timesharing environment
ENCORE	Ferox Microsystems, Inc.	· 2 disk drives or hard disk · 256K bytes memory · Graphic card	· Has financial modeling capabilities such as budgetary planning and control, cash flow and financial statement forecasts, and investment analysis; also has graphics and text editor	Designed especially for the IBM PC

From "Can Decision-Support Systems Solve Your Problem?" by David Callopy. *Business Computing*, Pennwell Publishing Co., Littleton, MA.

Developing a Decision Support System

Installing a DSS requires a decision on whether the problem situation justifies the investment. In many cases, a manual approach to decision support is adequate. To what extent a computer-based DSS is cost effective depends on the complexity of data manipulation, iteration requirements, and user needs for reanalysis. In any case, the need to ask "what-if" questions and expect a quick response is one of the most important

Table 10.3   *(continued)*

Decision Support Package	Manufacturer	System Configuration	Market Orientation and Functionality	Comments
IFPS/Personal	Execucom Systems Corp.	· 2 disk drives or hard disk · 256K bytes memory	· A modeling language for analysis; includes color graphics, report writing, spreadsheet, and text editor	Performs various specialized applications via mainframe communication
MICROFORESIGHT	Information Systems of America, Inc.	· Hard disk · 512K bytes memory	· Fully functional modeling system includes report generator, risk and sensitivity analysis, statistical forecasting, and goal seeking	Any text editor can be linked to the program to manipulate data files
XSIM	Chase Econometrics/ Interactive Data Corp.	· 2 disk drives or hard disk · 256K bytes memory	· Connects to popular spreadsheet programs · Has the capability of downloading data from mainframe to perform analysis on the IBM PC	Mainframe becomes a depository of data and the PC a workstation to manipulate user's design

benefits of a DSS package. Once the package is installed, the cost of iterations is relatively small.

The Model Generator

Developing a DSS model requires a model generator or a spreadsheet processor. The **model generator** is a comprehensive DSS software that defines models, performs statistical analysis, links the model to a database, and provides a user-machine dialog. The objective is to allow the development of a variety of models and interactive system designs. This means the generator should have dual capability: to create easy-to-use models for the novice user and to possess the analysis capability to support a variety of users and problems.

Many types of model generator packages are available. A summary description of modeling packages for the microcomputer is presented in Table 10.3. One of the better known packages is EXPRESS, by Manage-

```
DCL ACTUALMOD DATABASE EQBANK  LINEITEM DIVISION   EQBASED LINEITEM
LD ACTUAL MODEL BY LINEITEM AND DIVISION
EQBANK
SALES = IN
COGS = IN
GROSS = SALES - COGS
SALARIES = LAG(SALARIES, 1 YEAR) * COLA
TRAVEL = IN
COMMISS = IN
ADVERT = IN
PROMO = IN
SELLING = SALARIES + TRAVEL + COMMISS + ADVERT + PROMO
OTHOPEXP = CORP.OH/12 * SALES/TOTAL(PRODSALES MONTH)
NIBT = GROSS - SELLING - OTHOPEXP
TAXES = .46 * NIBT
NIAT = NIBT - TAXES
"

"
"
"

LIMIT DIVISION TO DEFENSE
COGS = .62 * SALES
LIMIT DIVISION TO COMMCN
COGS = .59 * SALES
END
```
a.

Figure 10.2
Modeling (EXPRESS).
(Adapted from Reimann
and Warren, 1985, 170.)

ment Decisions Systems, Inc. This generator supports analysis and modeling requirements, integrates ad hoc and formal reporting, preprogrammed financial procedures, color graphics, and financial modeling capabilities. Figure 10.2 illustrates various modeling equations for different divisions of the firm. The cost of goods sold is calculated differently for the defense, construction, and communications divisions. It is only necessary to specify the equations that are different; the model remains the same across divisions. Figure 10.2b shows the equations for a forecast model. Different equations can easily be maintained for the same list of items.

The Spreadsheet

A real issue in defining decision support tools is not so much their range of functionality as how (and by whom) that functionality can be used. Decision support has to do with how a program is used. For example, the electronic spreadsheet is a generalized program that allows the user

```
    DCL FORECASTMOD DATABASE EQBANK    LINEITEM    EQBASED LINEITEM
    LD FORECASTMOD BY LINEITEM
    EQBANK
    SALES = 4.065 + .0132 * CONSUMPTION .81 - 2.876 * RELATIVE
          PRICE + 34.21 * RELATIVE ADVERT
    COGS = SALES * (.361 * AVG.WAGE + 3.617 * COST.CAPITAL +
          14.388 * PROD.PRICE.INDEX)
    GROSS = SALES - COGS
    SALARIES = LAG(SALARIES, 1 YEAR) * COLA
    TRAVEL = LAG(TRAVEL, 1 YEAR) * INFLATION
    COMMISS = .098 * SALES
    ADVERT = .045 * SALES
    PROMO = .85 * ADVERT
    SELLING = SALARIES + TRAVEL + COMMIS + ADVERT + PROMO
    OTHOPEXP = CORP.OH/12 * SALES/TOTAL(PRODSALES MONTH)
    NIBT = GROSS - SELLING - OTHOPEXP
    TAXES = .46 * NIBT
    NIAT = NIBT - TAXES
    END
b.
```

Figure 10.2
(continued)

to create models for handling a variety of problems. It can also be used for automating a business function. When it aids in decision making, it is a DSS tool; when it is used simply for automation, it is a data processing tool.

The spreadsheet processor is the most widely used and available model building software. Built on a framework of data and formulas, a spreadsheet is given form by the formats, explanatory text, and labels the user chooses. The attractive feature is that it simplifies the process of finding solutions to mundane problems (Miller, 1985, 55). It is easy and elegant in design: The user simply enters the numbers, develops formulas, gets the results, and moves on to the next model. The formulas draw upon relationships among data and specify new information as they extend the reach of the user's work. To make changes, only one figure needs to be altered for all the affected entries to be recalculated automatically. The approach used in developing a spreadsheet is thinking *backward,* as follows:

1. Picture what the final report is going to look like. How will it be set up? What will it include?
2. Plan the layout of the spreadsheet. What area or section will be used for formulas? Where will the various level calculations be located? A **formula** is an instruction that describes the calculations to be performed on the data (see Figure 10.3).
3. Think about data and the explanatory text that gives meaning to the spreadsheet.

Preceding Plus Sign (+)
If the first character of an entry is a letter, the spreadsheet assumes that you are entering a label, but you may actually be typing a cell address for a formula—for example, E7. To let the spreadsheet know that the entry is a formula to be evaluated, rather than a label to be displayed, place a value indicator such as a plus sign before the first character.

Multiplication sign (*)
The asterisk indicates multiplication.

@Sum (argument-list)
The @SUM function calculates the sum of all the cells included in the list.

Division Sign (/)
The slash indicates division.

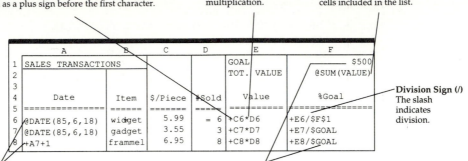

	A	B	C	D	E	F
1	SALES TRANSACTIONS				GOAL	$500
2					TOT. VALUE	@SUM(VALUE)
3						
4	Date	Item	$/Piece	#Sold	Value	%Goal
5	==============	=====	=======	=====	===========	===========
6	@DATE(85,6,18)	widget	5.99	= 6	+C6*D6	+E6/F1
7	@DATE(85,6,18)	gadget	3.55	3	+C7*D7	+E7/$GOAL
8	+A7+1	frammel	6.95	8	+C8*D8	+E8/$GOAL

Date Arithmetic
The @DATE (year, month, day) function returns a number representing the number of days that have elapsed since December 31, 1899. Thus, January 1, 1988—@DATE (0,1,1)—returns the serial number 1. Like any other value, a date number can be used in formulas. If you add 1 to a date number, you get the serial number for the following day. The difference between two date numbers is the number of intervening days. *Symphony* and *Jazz* include fractional numbers that are used to calculate time within each day.

Range Names and Named Ranges
The Range Name Create command gives a "name" to any rectangular group of cells. You can use a range name instead of a cell address in any formula, @function, or command. Once a range is named, subsequent movement of that range does not affect the validity of the name. Formulas that reference the range by name remain accurate. The named ranges in this spreadsheet are *value*, which refers to cells E6..E8, and *goal*, which refers to cell F1.

Figure 10.3
Formulas in a spreadsheet format. The @ functions (e.g., @SUM) are formulas that simplify complex calculations. (Adapted from Miller, 1985, 57.)

4. Decide on the labels and their locations. A **label** (also called a string) is a nonnumeric or alphabetical character that is preceded by a label prefix (see Figure 10.4).

Software   Spreadsheets are available for virtually every computer. In this section, we focus on the spreadsheets that are available for major personal computers and the evaluation criteria. Table 10.4 sums up the software for the Apple and IBM PC. Six evaluation criteria are used:

1. *Statistics* includes math functions for formulas, sorting alphabetically, numerically, or by column (highest to lowest values), linking to other spreadsheets, and communicating with other programs such as database and word processing.
2. *Ease of use,* especially in terms of error handling, naming cells rather than formulas, and similar functions.
3. *Data entry* and moving around from one row/column to the next, from beginning to end of the spreadsheet, and replicating portions of rows/columns or other sections of the sheet.
4. *Spreadsheet design* specifying individual column width, moving rows/columns, and defining column cells to contain $ symbols, percent, and so on.
5. *Printing options* such as printing a cell formula instead of its value, numbering pages, and separating rows/columns by lines.

Long Labels
Labels too long to fit in one cell spill over into adjacent empty cells to the right.

Using Value Indicators or Numbers in Labels
Preceding a number or number symbol ($) with a label prefix (^) turns it into a nonnumeric label.

Label Prefixes
The alignment, or justification, of a label in a cell is determined by the first character, called a label prefix. Label prefixes are neither displayed nor printed, and they do not affect the result of string formulas.

Left-Aligned Entries
If the first typed character of an entry is a letter, a preceding apostrophe (') is automatically inserted as the label prefix. This default label prefix, which you can change, will left-align the label.

Repeating Labels
Typing a backslash (\) as the first character of an entry creates a label that repeats across the width of the cell.

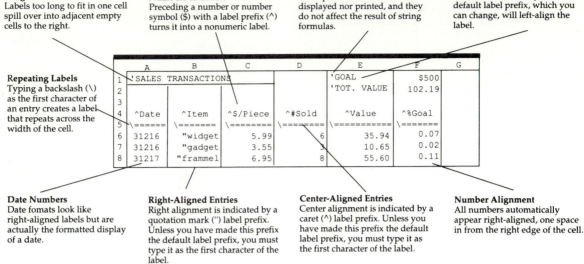

	A	B	C	D	E	F	G
1	'SALES TRANSACTIONS				'GOAL	$500	
2					'TOT. VALUE	102.19	
3							
4	^Date	^Item	^$/Piece	^#Sold	^Value	^%Goal	
5	\======	\=======	\========	\=======	\===========	\=======	
6	31216	"widget	5.99	6	35.94	0.07	
7	31216	"gadget	3.55	3	10.65	0.02	
8	31217	"frammel	6.95	8	55.60	0.11	

Date Numbers
Date fomats look like right-aligned labels but are actually the formatted display of a date.

Right-Aligned Entries
Right alignment is indicated by a quotation mark (") label prefix. Unless you have made this prefix the default label prefix, you must type it as the first character of the label.

Center-Aligned Entries
Center alignment is indicated by a caret (^) label prefix. Unless you have made this prefix the default label prefix, you must type it as the first character of the label.

Number Alignment
All numbers automatically appear right-aligned, one space in from the right edge of the cell.

Figure 10.4
Use of labels.

6. *Documentation,* or the availability and quality of such items as the user's manual, a **tutorial** (step-by-step guide for creating a spreadsheet), and an index.

Uses   In the remaining part of the chapter, we will describe a procedure for developing the electronic spreadsheet. The uses of the spreadsheet are almost innumerable. For the purpose of illustration, consider the following scenario:

> Bob Williams had a car accident caused by his vehicle's faulty brake system. He sued the automaker, based on similar lawsuits filed by other owners of the same model car. His willingness to settle out of court for $3 million presented the manufacturer with a dilemma: Should it settle with Williams or take its chances in court, hoping to settle for much less? (Jones, 1985, 64)

This common legal question falls under litigation risk analysis, which assesses the implications of various legal strategies for damage awards. Risk analysis may be attempted manually, but it requires many calculations every time a single value in the decision tree is changed. The electronic spreadsheet's ability to adapt to a changing set of numbers makes it an ideal tool for risk analysis.

Figure 10.5 is an illustration of litigation risk analysis using LOTUS 1-2-3. Visual inspection shows that the manufacturer can lose $5.5 million

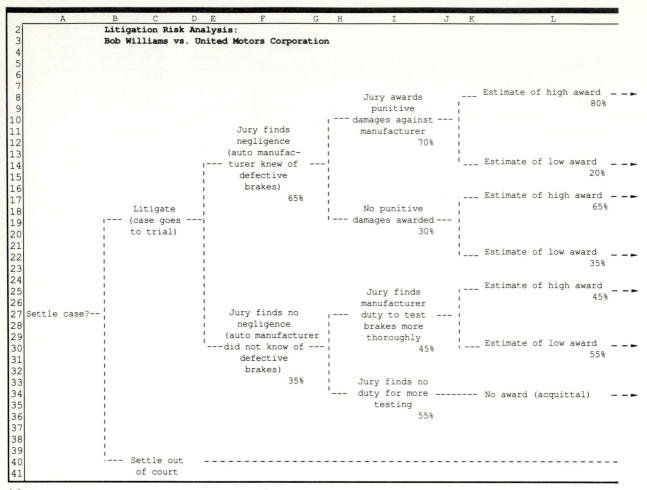

(a)

Figure 10.5
Litigation risk analysis. LOTUS 1-2-3 is used to decide if this auto company should risk litigation or settle out of court. (a) A decision tree showing the alternatives and probability of each alternative.

if the case is allowed to go to trial. The $3 million out-of-court settlement in this case is more attractive.

Setting up the model requires several steps:

1. Do a decision tree, plotting on paper the various paths a legal settlement may take.
2. Set up a spreadsheet model based on the decision tree.
3. Assign a percentage value indicative of the relative probability of occurrence to each path.
4. Multiply the percentage values along each path to quantify the overall

	M	N	O	P
2				
3			Probability	Formulas
4			of this	for
5			scenario	column O
6	Punitive amount:	$2,500,000.00		
7	Compensatory amount:	$3,000,000.00		
8	======================			
9	Total amount:	$5,500,000.00	36%	+F17*I13*L9
10				
11				
12	Punitive amount:	$1,000,000.00		
13	Compensatory amount:	$1,500,000.00		
14	======================			
15	Total amount:	$2,500,000.00	9%	$F17*I13*L15
16				
17				
18	Total amount:	$3,000,000.00	13%	+F17*I21*L18
19				
20				
21				
22				
23	Total amount:	$1,500,000.00	7%	+F17*I21*L23
24				
25				
26	Total amount:	$2,500,000.00	7%	+F33*I30*L26
27				
28				
29				
30				
31	Total amount:	$500,000.00	9%	+F33*I30*L31
32				
33				
34	Total amount:	$0.00	19%	+F33*I36
35			============	=============
36			100%	@SUM(O9..O34)
37				
38				
39				
40	Settlement amount:	$3,000,000.00		
41				

(b)

probability of that course of events. The total of the path's probability must not exceed 100. Column P shows the formulas used in column O.

This illustration is greatly simplified. Most risk analysis worksheets take into consideration factors such as present value of the dollar over the years the case may be carried. The benefits of the process are clearly worth the effort. Spreadsheet risk analysis helps the attorney decide what to do tactically. It also shows when it is best to stay out of the courtroom altogether. A summary of major spreadsheet software for microcomputer applications is shown in Table 10.4.

Figure 10.5
(continued)
(b) A chart showing the probable dollar value of each alternative. A settlement offer of $3,000,000 is their most attractive choice. (Adapted from Jones, 1985, 66–67.)

Table 10.4   Major Spreadsheet Software for Microcomputers

Major Spreadsheet Software	Manufacturer	Price ($)	Memory Requirements	Maximum Rows/ Column
APPLE				
APPLEWORKS	Apple Computer	250	64K	999/127
MULTIPLAN (MacIntosh)	Microsoft	195	128K	255/63
VISICALC	Software Arts	179	64K	254/63
SUPERCALC	Software Arts	395	128K	9999/127
IBM PC				
CREATIVE CALC	Creative Software	59	128K	255/63
FLASH CALC	Paladin Software	129	64K	254/63
HOME ANALYST	Peach Tree	99	128K	254/63
LOTUS 1-2-3	Lotus Development Corp.	495	120K	2048/256
MULTIPLAN	Microsoft	195	128K	255/63
MY CALC	Computer Easy	19	128K	255/62
PERFECT CALC	Thorn EM1	199	128K	255/52
PFS: PLAN	Software Publishing	140	128K	48/20
SUPERCALC 3	Sorcim Corp.	395	96K	254/63
VISICALC	Software Arts	179	192K	254/63

Implications for MIS

Decision support systems represent the fastest-growing segment of the information system environment, aided by a burgeoning supply of mainframe and inexpensive microcomputer packages. For DSS software to serve the long-term needs of the end user, strategies and plans must be carefully laid out. Unfortunately, in the world of management information systems few managers devote much effort to DSS planning. Planning for DSS is not a top priority for most organizations because it represents a fraction of current information systems expenditures.

The advent of graphics is having a significant impact on decision support in the organization. Communicating effectively through graphics means reducing ambiguities, crystallizing thought, and promoting consensus in decision making. MIS managers who do not act quickly

Table 10.4 *(continued)*

File Handling	Error Handling	HELP Features	Overall Performance	Comments
Excellent	Excellent	Excellent	Excellent	Easy to use and learn
Good	Excellent	Excellent	Excellent	Feature-laden: makes good use of mouse
Good	Good	No	Average	All the essentials
Excellent	Excellent	Excellent	Excellent	For the more serious user
Average	Good	No	Good	A no-frills comprehensive package
Excellent	Poor	Good	Good	Spruced-up Visicalc
Excellent	Good	Good	Good	Includes helpful templates; good for beginners
Good	Excellent	Excellent	Excellent	Doubles as a powerful database
Excellent	Good	Good	Good	Complex but comprehensive
Poor	Good	Good	Excellent	Probably best buy
Good	Good	Excellent	Excellent	Interfaces with database and word processor
Average	Good	Excellent	Good	Interfaces with database and word processor
Excellent	Excellent	Excellent	Excellent	For the more serious user
Average	Poor	Good	Average	Junior version now on market

can expect problems because MIS should assume the responsibility for training in graphics and other decision support tools as well.

With the surge in DSS software and improvements in low-cost, user-friendly, menu-driven DSS tools, it is not difficult to see the day when DSS activity and end user computing represent a clear majority of information systems budgets and usage. End user computing is covered in the next chapter. The next step forward for MIS will be expert systems, which are slowly being introduced for complex decision-making situations, and using natural languages, to be discussed in Chapter 12.

Summary

▫ DSS software provides a quick and easy way for setting up a mathematical model, entering the information into it, and reporting the results.

It is broken down into *spreadsheet* software for manipulating data and graphics and *integrated systems,* which perform additional functions such as word processing and database management.

▫ Three industry forces contribute to changes in DSS software:

1. *Demand for information.* Today's user demands software that provides access to data residing in various systems or interface database management packages as a gateway to information resources.
2. *Increasing computer literacy.* Increasing computer literacy means accepting the computer as a tool and expecting more effective DSS packages to deliver the quality information needed for decision making.
3. *Need for integration.* Users' demand for accessing information in one step or with one system has resulted in designs that integrate everything the user needs in a single system or that integrate specific activities such as graphics packages, risk analysis, and so on.

User-oriented criteria for DSS software are categorized under general, technical, vendor, and cost considerations.

1. *General considerations* include:
   a. Mainframe and operating system compatibility
   b. User friendliness
   c. Reliability of software
   d. Integration of functions
2. *Technical considerations* include:
   a. Interface design to support novice and experienced users.
   b. Two- and three-dimensional modeling to evaluate a new product line and simulate business situations.
   c. Data display of modeling activities for examination of outcomes.
   d. Reporting function, which includes custom report formats, standard report formats, and edit and test for report formats.
3. *Vendor considerations* focus on:
   a. Financial stability
   b. Hot line
   c. Continuing enhancements
   d. Active R&D
   e. Growth of customer base
   f. Quality staff
   g. Technical support personnel
   h. Adequate training facilities
4. *Cost considerations* that determine software selection include the initial and ongoing costs, costs of user training, development costs, and maintenance.

▫ Developing a decision support system takes into consideration the programming *language*(s) used in programming the model, the model *generator* for performing statistical analysis, linking the model to a database, and so on, as well as the use of an electronic spreadsheet for model building.

□ The spreadsheet is built on a framework of data and formulas. It is given form by the formats, explanatory text, and labels the user chooses. The spreadsheet simplifies finding solutions to mundane problems. The user simply enters the numbers, develops the formulas, gets the results, and moves on to the next model.

□ Six evaluation criteria are used in evaluating spreadsheets:
1. Statistics and various mathematical functions.
2. Ease of use.
3. Data entry and moving around the spreadsheet.
4. Spreadsheet design in terms of specifying individual column widths, moving rows/columns, defining column cells, and so on.
5. Printing options such as printing a cell formula rather than its value, numbering pages, and so on.
6. Documentation: user's manual, tutorial, and index.

Key Terms

Backward iteration	Model
Compatibility	Model generator
Formula	Nonprocedurality
Functionality	Risk analysis
Goal seeking: See backward iteration	Spreadsheet software
	Tutorial
Integrated system	User friendliness
Label	

Review Questions

1. There are two categories of software. Define briefly each category. How do they differ?

2. "DSS software has undergone extensive change with the objective of making DSS usable to users at all managerial levels." Discuss.

3. Why is the need for integrating DSS software becoming so important? Elaborate.

4. What choices does a user have in selecting DSS software?

5. In what way is the selection process for DSS software similar to that for acquiring any software? Explain.

6. Expound on the general and technical considerations in selecting DSS software.

7. What is functionality of use? How does it differ from ease of use? Be specific.

8. What is nonprocedurality? Reliability? Modeling?

9. Distinguish between "what-if" and backward iteration. Give an example to illustrate.

10. Explain the primary function(s) of a model generator. How does it help the novice user?

11. If you were to explain to a novice user the basics of a spreadsheet, what would you say? Elaborate.

12. According to the text, the approach used in developing a spreadsheet is "thinking backward." Do you agree? Explain.

13. Elaborate on the spreadsheet evaluation criteria. Which one do you consider the most critical? Why?

Application Problems

1. Suppose you were a member of a corporate planning committee of a large organization. You have heard of a popular software package, LOTUS 1-2-3. How strongly do you recommend it for:
a. Risk analysis of a merger
b. Projection of cash flow
c. Calculations for potential acquisitions
d. Comparison of company to industry sales

2. Allied Corporation—a firm specializing in the moving business—is considering the use of LOTUS or a financial planning language to answer a number of "what-if" questions it faces in its current allocation of trucks to different territories. The MIS director found to her surprise a variety of software packages, each package purporting to answer her questions.

   What six key criteria should she adopt for the final selection? What makes these criteria so important? Explain.

3. Russ Aldrich, manager of advanced product planning at Apple Computer, Inc., measures his productivity with computing tools. MacIntosh's integrated software concept handles a variety of administrative tasks. It features a copying program that allows users to operate together bud-

geting, writing reports, and programming lists, graphs, and so on, so users can move from one operation to another without switching floppies. They can even move data from one document or spreadsheet to another in a "Cut, paste, and print" operation.

MacIntosh's simplified interface has unique features: Its on-screen format features a single "palette" of icons, drawn electronically, that represent such items of the real-world office environment as waste paper baskets (for dumping files, file folders, sales reports, and so on). The user can use a mouse to select a blank stationery scratch pad from the screen, tear off a sheet and title it.

Using MacIntosh's CALC, the user can develop a budget for quarterly employee hiring, entering data in a columnar and row format showing salaries, expenses, totals, and budgeted amounts, plus the number of employees added on. The user can alter the assumptions and reduce the raises or benefits versus percentage of salary to balance the budget.

In graphics, MacIntosh GRAPH develops a pie chart, integrating some text into the document to explain selected details. From these, the user can obtain a menu of shapes that flash onscreen. For example, a tabular shape may be used to create a flowchart of the organization. After all that, the user can select "writing paper" from MacIntosh's WRITE to create an interoffice memo. When the system is printing the memo, the cursor turns into the hourglass icon to show that the computer is tied up. (Adapted from *Personal Computing*, December 1983, 107.)

QUESTIONS

a. In what respect can this software be viewed as DSS? As integrated DSS software?

b. What else should a package such as MacIntosh's offer? Elaborate.

c. How strong a trend is this type of software? What are its advantages? Drawbacks?

Selected References

Bergstrom, Leonard. "Decision Support Systems." *Software News*, December 1984, 35.

DeSanctis, Geraldine and Gallupe, Brent. "Group Decision Support Systems: A New Frontier." *Data Base*, Winter 1985, 3–10.

Desmond, John. "Windows to MIS: Graphics Posing a Challenge To Mainframe Market Leaders." *Software News*, April 1987, 44ff.

Jenkins, A. Milton. "Surveying the Software Generator Market." *Datamation*, September 1, 1985, 105–107ff.

Jones, Edward. "Risk Analysis with LOTUS 1-2-3." *Lotus*, July 1985, 64.

Ledgard, H., Whiteside, J. A., Singer, A., and Seymour, W. "The Natural Language of Interactive Systems." *Communications of the ACM*, February 1984, 126–133.

McGrath, Brian. "Corporate Graphics: Take a Look at the Big Picture." *Computerworld*, December 8, 1986, 81–84ff.

Meador, C. Lawrence and Mezger, Richard A. "Decision Support Systems for Minis and Micros." *Small Systems World*, March 1983, 27–29.

Miller, Steven E. "The Anatomy of a Spreadsheet." *LOTUS*, July 1985, 55.

Needle, Davis. "Deciding about Decision Support." *Personal Computing*, June 1985, 85–89.

Reimann, Bernard C. and Warren, Allan D. "User-Oriented Criteria for the Selection of DSS Software." *Communications of the ACM*, February 1985, 166–179.

Spencer, Cheryl. "Financial Modeling." *Personal Computing*, April 1987, 69–71ff.

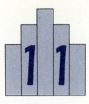

Office Automation and End User Computing

Chapter Contents

Computer-Based Training Tutors
Ensure Quality Education

COMPUTER-BASED TRAINING AND end user volunteer tutors are two of the unique ways that Mutual of Omaha's information center Customer Education Section leverages its training staff.

"Leveraging our instructors is an important concept for us," explains Mark Eibes, project leader, Customer Education Section. "We can make our customers more productive—and help them realize those productivity benefits faster—by providing up-front education."

The number of end users has grown rapidly in the six years since the information center (IC) began in 1980 with only five staff members. At that point, the center served only 50 timesharing customers. Now, the IC must keep up with the needs of 1,500 end users on both micros and mainframes. The IC has 34 people on its staff and is divided into three areas.

Customer Service takes care of the administrative foundations, conducts needs analysis and also includes the customer education center. Customer Support provides a timesharing and microcomputer consultation service on both hardware and software. Research tests and recommends new products. The Customer Education Section was created to provide formalized education programs for microcomputer users. Eibes and his four-member staff handle all the training. Currently, there are 300 micros in use within departments, with three to five users per machine.

Computer-based training (CBT) currently forms the core of the micro training program at the company. It is heavily augmented with live instructors in a formal classroom equipped with ten micros. The mainframe CBT courses are prefaced by an instructor-led overview which lasts about an hour. "This gives the student the appropriate mind set for learning the product. We feel that an hour's worth of instructor time at that point is extremely beneficial." After the overview, the student is given a manual that guides him or her in and out of the CBT course. Specific Mutual of Omaha case studies also are included.

Computer-based training will play a role in the company's future training plans. Eibes plans to explore a more automated curriculum for micro users. There also is a growing demand among managers for systems education. "People learn in various styles; classroom situations are really not appropriate for everybody," says Eibes.

Whatever tools the Mutual of Omaha information center staff chooses, improving the quality of education and training always will be one of the foremost goals.

—*Adapted from staff report,* Data Management, *May 1986, 31–32.*

AT A GLANCE

The local area network (LAN) integrates office automation, end user computing, and intelligent workstations and user-friendly languages for executives and workers alike. The key component of office automation is the workstation, an interface device that places the end user at the logical center of information resources. The single most sought-after application for the executive workstation is the electronic spreadsheet. In addition to mundane tasks, the workstation also provides personal computing, administrative support functions, electronic messaging, and database management. It functions best when connected to a system that provides it with information to manipulate.

There are several ways to classify end users: as nonprogramming, command level, end user programmers, functional support personnel, or DP programmers on one hand—or, in another categorization, as developers or nondevelopers, novices or experts, occasional or frequent, and primary or secondary users. In any case, the emerging user environment favors ease of use and user-friendly tools, menus, windows, and the like.

By the end of this chapter, you should know:

1. The role of office automation in business
2. The importance of end user computing
3. The characteristics of fourth-level languages

Introduction

Communication technology is today's cornerstone of MIS and corporate success. Any business must communicate its information and decisions quickly and efficiently for it to be of use. In Chapter 7, we focused on telecommunications as a "long-haul" network system linking the organization with its branches and the outside world. We also discussed the local area network (LAN) as a "short-haul" network for improving the productivity of the knowledge worker. In this chapter we will review office automation and end user computing. The latter includes the intelligent workstation, document processing, user-friendly languages, and facilities for improving human performance.

Office automation (OA) is the integration of computer and communication technology with human patterns of office work. It all began with the Penny Post in England. A packet of information was transmitted within the city limits of London with guaranteed same-day delivery. The service soon led to information exchanges such as Reuters (1849), which provided a commodity market and political news service. By the turn of the century, communications within buildings used pneumatic tubes that shuttled messages from one office to another. Today, LANs, single user workstations, user-friendly languages, and electronic messaging represent the trend for end user productivity.

There are several arguments in favor of office automation that involve different aspects of productivity. Increasing clerical salaries, decreasing work ethics, and the continuing shift toward an information-based economy are all factors that make it necessary for the decreased number of competent office workers to be more productive and for managers to handle more activities on their own. There was a time when a manager dictated a letter and gave it to a secretary, who typed and checked all errors. Now it is common for the manager to correct the secretary's spelling. In response to these problems, several office automation technologies are now available:

1. *Word processors* allow improvement in report preparation.
2. *Workstations* linked to the mainframe ease the workload of the central computer.
3. *Voice messaging* combines the convenience of the telephone with the flexibility of the scribbled note.
4. *Fourth-generation languages* allow the end user to code his/her own queries.
5. *Relational databases* provide access files in user-specified formats and quick response to complex searches.

All these topics will be covered in this chapter.

The Knowledge Worker and Office Automation

"Knowledge worker" is a buzzword that has been getting a lot of attention. In contrast to manual work that involves physical effort, knowledge work focuses on thinking, using information for processing, and recommending. The primary activities of knowledge work are diagnosis, decision making, monitoring, and scheduling (Davis and Olson, 1984, 409).

A **knowledge worker** may be defined as a manager, a supervisor, or a clerk who is actively involved in thinking, processing information, analyzing, or recommending procedures based on the use of information. The information comes variously from the organization, the environment, or the knowledge worker's experience.

The use of this term does not describe a new position but rather those aspects of tasks across jobs that involve knowledge work. For example, a stockroom clerk's job may be highly structured; therefore it provides limited knowledge work. In contrast, a bank's head teller's job entails a significant amount of knowledge work, including:

1. *Diagnosing* the amount of cash available in the teller's drawer before the lunch break.
2. *Deciding* on the procedure to use in handling irate customers.
3. *Monitoring* cash over-and-short of drive-in tellers on Friday when employees of a local plant cash their paychecks.
4. *Scheduling* lunch breaks of available tellers during the flu season.

Most persons have a native ability for problem solving. But routine activities often make it difficult to concentrate on the creative phase of problem solving. This situation can be improved in an office automation environment that provides:

1. An information collection/retrieval system that generates information quickly
2. Interactive functions to derive feasible solutions
3. Functions to communicate a knowledge worker's activities to the appropriate persons at the appropriate time

The ultimate goal of office automation systems, then, is to create a working environment that provides these conditions. There are various types of equipment to configure office automation systems. The equipment that is basic to such systems is classified into three categories: Workstations, LANs, and office processors. The LAN has been covered in Chapter 7 (see Figure 11.1).

The Intelligent Workstation

The key component of office automation is the **workstation**. It automates repetitive, tedious tasks, freeing the knowledge worker's time for more creative work. Through the keyboard, the end user performs a host of functions, ranging from customer tracking to illustrated reports and from calendaring to database management. The single most used application for the executive workstation, however, is the electronic spreadsheet.

The capabilities of today's workstation fall in line with linear thinking—processes that are carried out step by step in a specific sequence. The organization still depends on the knowledge worker to synthesize the information and develop conclusions. In addition to the mundane tasks, an executive workstation should perform the following functions:

1. *Administrative support* functions such as maintaining tickler files, scheduling meetings, and electronic telephone directories. With the position of private secretary on the wane, professionals are taking on a number of support tasks.

Figure 11.1
Workstation functions.

Local Area Network (LAN)

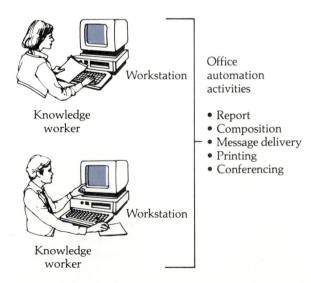

Workstation

Knowledge
worker

Workstation

Knowledge
worker

Office
automation
activities

• Report
• Composition
• Message delivery
• Printing
• Conferencing

2. *Personal computing,* including spreadsheets and business graphics that have brought fame to the personal computer.
3. *Electronic messaging* that includes text (electronic mail) and voice. They can reduce the frustrations of telephone tag and delays in response to inquiries.
4. *Database management* with report-writing capability. A user-oriented database allows managers to create and maintain information on an ad hoc basis.

It is important to know that the workstation functions best when connected to a mainframe where data can be downloaded to workstations for administrative functions. This is where the LAN becomes essential.

Today's intelligent workstation has a high-resolution screen with graphics display capability. It also handles database activity, file transfers, word processing, and voice and message switching.

The Word Processing Function   One of the early applications of office automation was *word processing,* computer-assisted preparation of user documents and reports. The hardware unique to word processing is the single workstation or a multiple workstation sharing a secondary storage device. The procedure is simple. The display feature allows for moving sentences or paragraphs, adjusting margins, highlighting words, and various other functions before final printing.

Most of today's software packages provide text editors that capture text data and help format the final report—all performed on the computer. Traditional text editors are a subset of a word processor. In a database environment, for example, end users manipulate the database and generate their own reports through the built-in text editor. Other database packages provide compatible interface with word processing packages. Once information is stored in the database, a basic command instructs the word processing package to download the text from the database.

Desktop Publishing   A new image processing capability in book publishing is **desktop publishing**. It is a new way to use the personal computer and laser printer to generate near-typesetting-quality publications quickly and cheaply. Desktop publishing also integrates graphics, design, photographs, and typography on the same page and takes hardly any operator training. Even a casual user can learn to produce a two-column, multifont page in less than two hours. Simplicity, accessibility, and the ability to see the results of a script on the screen make this new software technology an attractive addition to office automation (see Figure 11.2).

Desktop publishing is ideal for certain applications, but not for others. Based on the current state of the art, desktop publishing is not suited for very long documents (more than 100 pages), very large volumes, or color output. The printers are intended for the small-volume run. The

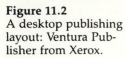

Figure 11.2
A desktop publishing layout: Ventura Publisher from Xerox.

average life cycle is typically 100,000–150,000 copies between overhauls. On the other hand, desktop publishing is ideal for newsletters, instructional materials, and personnel documents. In these applications, the user benefits from the integration of data and graphics, halftones, nice fonts, type sizes, and the like.

Regardless of the application, the intention behind desktop publishing is to improve output quality and keep the work close to its originator. It is obvious that aesthetic judgment—an integral part of professional printing—is left out. Perhaps such ability will be incorporated some day into artificial systems, permitting the creation of printing experts.

The Role of Ergonomics   With hours spent in front of the PC or workstation screen each day, end user productivity and comfort are closely interrelated. No matter how sophisticated the electronic support, an end user cannot achieve full productivity without proper design of the work environment. Ergonomics is a key issue here. As discussed in Chapter 1, ergonomics involves "comfort, fatigue, safety, understanding, ease of use, and any other areas that affect welfare, satisfaction, and performance of people working with user-machine systems (*Data Management*, 1985, 12–13).

The list of factors that affect the ergonomics of knowledge workers and clerks falls into three categories:

1. *Environmental* issues that include proper lighting, layout, and temperature. Indirect lighting, covering windows near the workstation with blinds or curtains to reduce the glare, and positioning terminals at right angles to windows—all contribute to work productivity.
2. *Hardware* issues that focus on furniture, comfortable seating, and well-designed workstations. An ergonomically acceptable chair should be

adjustable and supportive. Proper lumbar (lower back) support eases back strain over extended hours of work. The workstation itself might have a built-in swivel to tilt to the angle of the user (see Figure 11.3).

3. *User-system interface* that addresses software, user training, and easy-to-follow documentation.

The user-system interface emphasizes several features:

1. *Minimum worker effort and memory.* This means that data should be entered only once and nonproductive work eliminated. Documentation should also be available on line in the form of a HELP routine. User manuals should be clear, complete, and easy to follow.
2. *Best use of human patterns.* Workstations should consistently place similar information on screens in the same position, by familiar screen formats, and so on. The knowledge worker should use a consistent approach and terminology for all functions. Performing these functions should require minimum training.
3. *Prompt problem notification.* The knowledge worker should be alerted to changes taking place that might adversely affect problem solution. For example, if a file is approaching capacity (say, 90%), a message should be displayed to indicate the status of the file.
4. *Maximum task support.* Task documentation should be complete and readily available so that the knowledge worker is not required to use other resources for task performance.

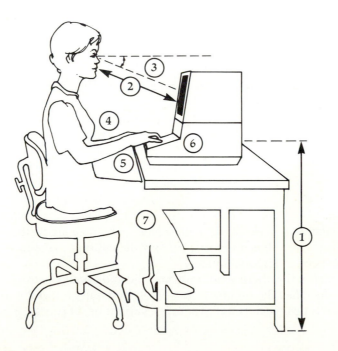

Figure 11.3
Ergonomic environment and features. (Adapted from Wright, 1982, 37.)

Demand for systems with good ergonomic designs continues to increase, pointing to the growing importance of the human factor. The benefits that ergonomics contribute to productivity are not readily quantifiable, partly because it is not easy to measure productivity.

Message and Document Communication

We have seen in Chapter 7 how computers and communication elements provide "short-haul," in-house support for knowledge work. The workstation and the applications it supports in a LAN environment signal a new trend in decision making. The LAN can also be utilized for transmission of documents and messages between locations. This can minimize paper flow, memos, and telephone calls. Two key developments are worth discussing: the electronic message system and voice mail.

Electronic Message Systems (EMS)

The roles of the secretary and the file clerk are rapidly being challenged by electronic messaging and the electronic mailbox. Historically, electronic messages began with the telegraph in 1837. Since then, facsimile, Telex, and satellite data transmission have been successively introduced. Computerized message switching services are the latest developments in electronic message systems (EMS).

The EMS concept is built around peer-to-peer networks or electronic mail and voice. The **peer-to-peer network** uses a personal computer to transmit or receive "mail" or electronic calls through an outside vendor. Using an electronic or E-mail service, users dial up the mail service through a public telephone network and read messages that are deposited in their electronic mailboxes.

Electronic messaging is message transmission and movement of information between two points. It may be communication between companies or individuals and other individuals as far as a continent apart via microcomputer, terminal keyboard, or hybrid systems such as the mailgram. To illustrate electronic mail service, Figure 11.4 shows a typical sales reporting system in which forms are filled out interactively by a terminal user. A branch administrator enters sales data from each sales representative into electronic mail "forms." The data are further processed on the network. Sales reports are sent to various managerial levels in their respective regional offices.

Conceptually, there is nothing complicated about electronic mail. The sender specifies the name of the person he wants to send a message to and then types the message. There are variations, of course. For example,

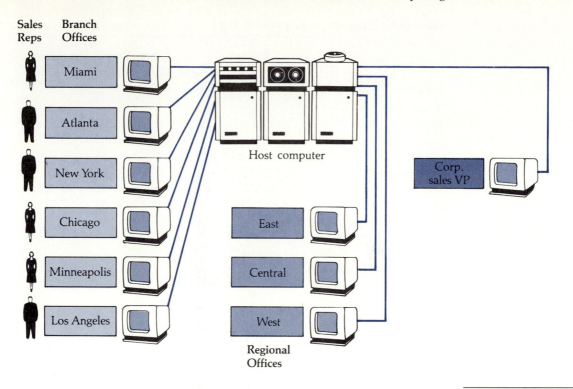

Sales Reps | Branch Offices

Miami

Atlanta

New York

Chicago

Minneapolis

Los Angeles

Host computer

Corp. sales VP

East

Central

West

Regional Offices

Figure 11.4
Electronic mail.
(Adapted from *Systems & Software*, 1985, 62.)

some E-mail systems allow mailing a message to multiple destinations. Other systems have a "return receipt requested" feature that identifies the time when the receiver got the message. Though simple in concept, electronic mail is different than the telephone. It is a "cold" medium that does not carry facial expressions or moods. It is straightforward and highly productive.

Electronic messaging offers several benefits:

1. *Reduction of "shadow functions"* such as leaving messages with the intended recipient's secretary. Since only 28 percent of phone calls make connection with the called party, EMS makes messages directly and readily available to the recipient when he or she wishes to read it.
2. *Elimination of interruptions.* Most phone calls are delivered during a recipient's prime time, causing interruptions. A cuing system that delivers messages at the appropriate times is translated into labor savings.
3. *No more "telephone tag,"* because the message is stored by the computer until the recipient is ready for it. In a telephone tag, one manager repeatedly tries to reach another by phone and the other makes unsuccessful attempts to return the calls. The average cost of a tele-

Table 11.1   The Cost of Telephone Tag

Outcome	Percent of Calls (%)	Length (min.)	Labor Costs ($)	Phone Costs ($)	Total Cost /100 Calls ($)
No answer	5	1	.27	—	1.35
Answer machine	2	1.5	.40	.65	2.10
"Out of office"	20	2	.51	.65	23.20
"Out to lunch"	18	1.5	.40	.65	18.90
"In a meeting"	20	2	.51	.65	23.20
"On the phone"	15	2.5	.62	.91	22.95
"Not available"	7	1.5	.40	.65	7.35
"Please hold" but reach party	3	12.5	2.82	2.92	17.22
Reach party	10	10	2.27	2.37	46.40
Real cost of each successful call				$12.82	$162.67

Adapted from Coudal, 1982, 18.

phone tag to a vice president of a large firm has been estimated at well over $10 (see Table 11.1).

4. *Low preparation costs and quick message distribution.* Unlike the telephone that allows one phone call (message) at a time, electronic messaging means simultaneous distribution of messages to their respective destinations. A person can also keep in touch from any location where a terminal is available.

Voice Mail   Great advances have taken place to make the telephone more accessible and easier to use, yet this device has changed little since its invention over 100 years ago. Telephone use requires two parties to be on the line. Only one-third of phone calls to managers are completed the first time, and one party is almost always interrupted.

An alternative to interruptions, missed connections, and unproductive social exchange is **voice mail**. A computer-based system is capable of storing voice messages digitally. Voice mail continues to allow the use of the telephone but eliminates simultaneous exchange. It is ideal for one-way information transfer and an excellent supplement to telephone communications.

The voice mail format is simple. The caller uses the standard telephone to record a message, listens to it before it is transmitted, or changes it if necessary. When convenient, the recipient checks his or her voice mailbox, scans to see who sent the incoming messages, and chooses to listen to some now and others later. After hearing the message, the recipient can draft a response, save the message, or forward it to a third party.

Voice mail offers four major advantages over traditional telephone use:

1. *Lack of simultaneity:* sender and receiver need not be on the line at the same time.
2. *Time and geography:* no need to know time-zone differences to catch the other party in the office.
3. *Zero redundancy:* eliminates the need to place a number of calls when many individuals should get the same message.
4. *Performance:* sender can talk six times faster by phone than by entering data. Emotional cues are more easily communicated by voice.

A voice mail system includes a minicomputer, a disk drive, communication ports that recognize touch tone signals, a digitizer to convert voice to digital bit streams, and a device to convert the bit stream to analog for playback. An important resource is the disk for storing a good-quality reproduction of the human voice. The number and size of messages are the major factors that determine the size of the disk drive.

Selecting a voice mail system depends on the communication profile of the organization, the number of people it will serve, and the communication problems it will solve. In any case, voice is a concept that is gaining acceptance. When integrated with the telephone, voice mail should be as common as indoor plumbing for everyday use in organizations.

End User Computing

We have seen how an intelligent workstation allows the end user to operate user-specific software or access software in the network. This raises several questions: "Who is the end user?" "What tools are available?" "What about support facilities?" In this section, we will explore these questions and highlight the trend in end user computing.

Who Is the End User?

The simplest categorization of end users is provided by the Codasyl End-User Facilities Committee (1979):

1. *Indirect end users* use computers through others; for example, a passenger making reservations through a travel agent.
2. *Intermediate end users* call for specific information that they later receive; for example, sales personnel.
3. *Direct end users* actually use terminals. Within the "direct" end user category, Martin (1982, 102–106) breaks them down further:
   a. *Nondata processing* trained end users who know nothing about programming but use code written by others to perform their tasks.

b. *Data processing amateurs* who write code for their own use.

c. *Data processing professionals* who write code for others.

Rockart and Flannery (1983) did an extensive study involving 200 end users and fifty information system support staff. They classified end users into six types, each of them needing different education and support:

1. *Nonprogramming end users* access computer-based data through software provided by others. Access is usually through a limited menu-driven format.
2. *Command level end users* perform simple inquiries, generate reports for their own use, and are able to specify the information they want through report generators such as FOCUS and EXPRESS software. They are willing to learn just enough to do their work.
3. *End user programmers* develop their own software which is often used by others.
4. *Functional support personnel* are proficient programmers supporting other end users in specific functional areas. They view themselves more as market researchers or financial analysts rather than as programmers per se.
5. *End user computing support personnel* are in a formal computer facility such as an information resource center. They are knowledgeable in end user languages and develop applications and "support" software.
6. *DP programmers* program in end user languages.

The study also found over half the end users supported complex data analysis such as financial analysis. The bulk of the systems they used have been developed by "functional support" personnel. The majority of the applications are also used as needed rather than on a regular basis.

Finally, Davis and Olson (1984, 503–533) suggest four categorizations of users:

1. *Developers and nondevelopers:* A system developer is someone who builds an information system to be used by others (nondevelopers).
2. *Novices versus experts:* In this chapter, the distinction is by the experience level of the user.
3. *Frequent versus occasional users:* A frequent user becomes more expert than an occasional user and will use the system for routine tasks. The occasional user, much like a novice, probably uses the system on an ad hoc basis.
4. *Primary versus secondary users:* A novice who is a primary user sends memos or notices through an electronic messaging system. In contrast, an expert who is a primary user might use the computer for financial analysis or simulation. Secondary users (e.g., data entry operators) typically enter data into the computer as a major part of their job.

The Emerging End User Environment

Today's end user systems are distinguished from traditional data processing systems by the decision support functions users perform. The user's environment provides user friendliness through fourth generation tools, alternative input devices, and training through the organization's information resource center.

With the end users' varying levels of expertise, it is difficult to determine how easy a system is to use. Most easy user interfaces are simple for the novice but time consuming and even irritating for the expert. For example, a totally menu-driven system is easy for the novice; all the user has to do is to select an option. For the experienced end user, however, a menu limits the way commands can be entered. This does not mean that menu interfaces are undesirable. On the contrary, without the simple menu interface, the end user might not have been attracted to the system in the first place. The point is that a successful interface must adapt to the end user as needs and experience dictate. A software package, in addition to being easy to use and learn, should incorporate more advanced tools for the experienced user.

User-Friendly Tools   These are tools and features designed to break down barriers between the end user and the computer. A survey of corporate managers revealed that most managers are reluctant to use a personal computer or a workstation, simply because they can't type. So they delegate office computing to others.

If the user is unfamiliar with the keyboard, a computer may seem a formidable machine. Consequently, the introduction of user-friendly interactive dialogs has opened the door to a whole new class of end users. Their main benefits are ease of moving about the screen and information display. Interactive dialogs include:

1. Menus
2. Forms
3. Windows
4. Mouse
5. Icons
6. Touch pads
7. HELP facility
8. Function keys

Menus   A **menu** provides a list of options. The user chooses an option by positioning a cursor next to it or by entering the option number on the screen. Menus are easy to learn and require minimal training to use. Most current software packages have *submenus*, where the option from the main menu leads to a detailed submenu to use for specifying the

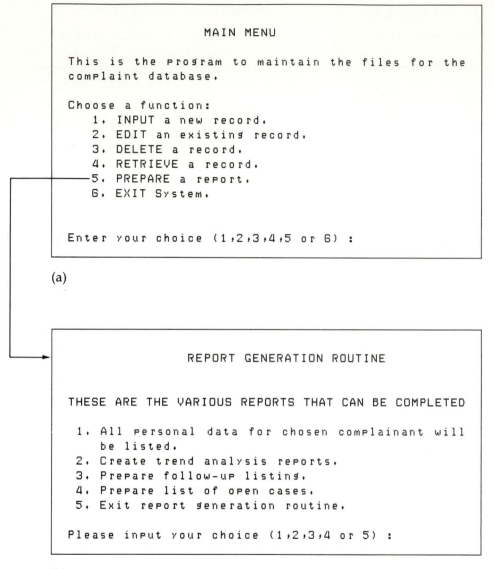

(a)

(b)

Figure 11.5
(a) Main menu. (b) Sub-
menu for option 5.

operation. For example, an integrated office automation package has a
main menu, shown in Figure 11.5(a). Choosing option 2 leads to the display of the submenu that offers a more specific set of options to choose
from (see Figure 11.5[b]). The submenu simplifies a complex set of operations for processing.

Menu selection is more attractive to novice than expert users, who
prefer commands to access the files.

```
PERSONAL INFORMATION

Last Name  ▓                    First Name              Middle Initial

Address                                      Zip Code

Telephone               Date of Birth    /   /     Sex
                                    mm/dd/yy        m/f

Marital Status: S-Single, M-Married, D-Divorced, W-Widowed
                    Status:

First Name of Spouse or Former Spouse

Is Spouse a Member?
                y/n
Educational field of study

Occupation              Business Phone

Place of Employment
```

Figure 11.6
A computer form.

Forms   Filling in a **form** is a simple procedure. After completing a field, the cursor is automatically positioned in the next field for entry, and so on, until the entire form is filled out (see Figure 11.6). Often color or highlighting differentiates form layout from user-entered information on the screen.

The main difference between a form and a menu is that a menu invariably presents a clear choice; a form layout presents blanks to be filled out. Blank fields are usually less intimidating for the novice user than a blank screen or a blinking cursor. Once used, forms can be a convenient user-machine interface.

Windows   Whereas human end users are excellent multiprocessors, most computers are serial in nature—they can accomplish only one task at a time. Since 1981, computers have introduced the **window** feature, which divides the screen into a number of rectangular areas (see Figure 11.7).

Windows can be selected portions of a balance sheet or from different applications. For example, an end user can edit a document with a word processor in one window while retrieving data from a database in another window. Output from one window can be directed to another window. Various processes can also be interconnected to perform special user functions. The windowing concept increases user productivity compared to the traditional serial approach.

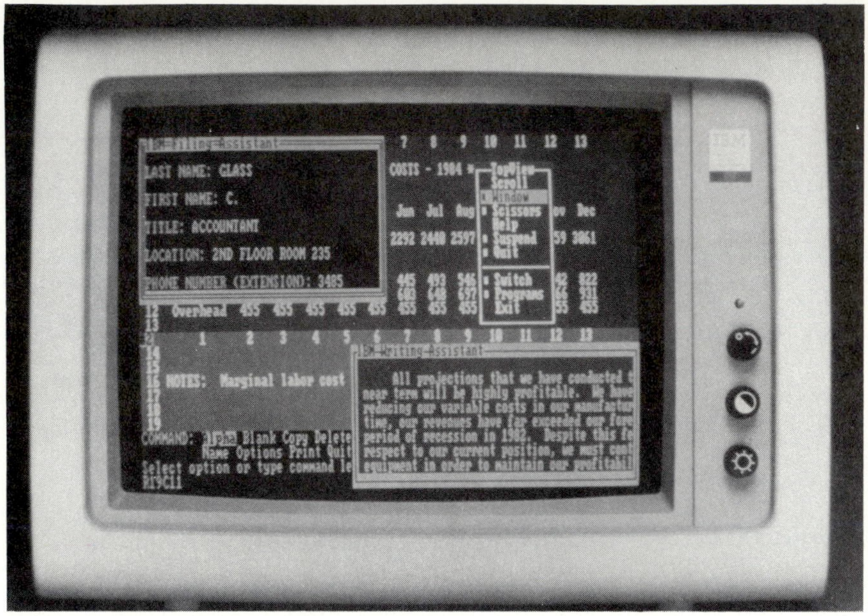

Figure 11.7
Five different software
programs can be seen at
once on this screen,
thanks to special soft-
ware that creates "win-
dows" on the screen.

Mice and Icons   The **mouse** is an interface tool introduced initially on the Apple Macintosh personal computer. It is commonly used with icons that symbolically display objects. An **icon** is a picture of a function. For example, a waste basket may represent a delete function (see Figure 11.8).

Many users find it easier to use the mouse than the arrow keys on a keyboard to locate data about a screen. With the mouse, the user can select a task, change the size and shape of graphs, and move them around on the screen. A user editing a letter or a manuscript points at the beginning of a block, holds down the button, and drags the mouse across the screen, highlighting all the words in between. One drawback of the mouse is that it is ill suited for freehand drawing.

Touch Pads   Touch pads and touch screens make it possible to choose options on menus or in applications that require only limited interaction with the computer. The *touch pad* gives a miniature screen with a menu of commands. Instead of typing the command through a keyboard, the user simply touches the pad (see Figure 11.9).

With *touch screens,* instead of memorizing a series of instructions, the user simply touches the appropriate screen item to initiate the instructions. If a block of words is to be deleted from a letter, for example, the user marks the beginning and end by pointing them to the menu item DELETE.

Touch screens can also be used in environments where the user may need one hand for some other function and only has to select from a menu—in order-entry systems, for example.

(a)

Figure 11.8
Mouse and icons.
(a) The original Macintosh was so dedicated to using the mouse as an input device that it had no cursor control keys on its keyboard. (The Mac Plus does have cursor control keys.) The rolling mouse moves the cursor to select an option from a list of choices by pressing the button on the mouse.
(b) Icons on a screen.

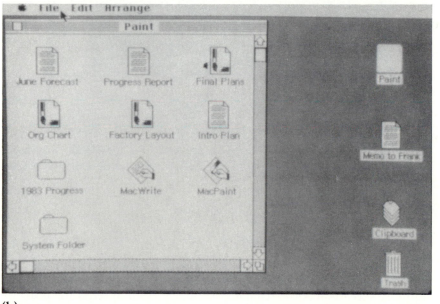

(b)

HELP Facility   A useful tool for accommodating a diverse group of users is the **HELP facility**. Like a user's manual, it provides additional information at any point during the interaction. In some software applications, HELP is assured via a function key. For example, in dBASE III Plus, pressing function key F1 prompts the system to load the HELP menu on the screen. The user then selects the desired option (see Figure 11.10).

Figure 11.9
Touch screen. Light beams from the screen edge detect a pointing finger and note the location of the beams intersecting at the touch point.

Function Keys   A **function key** is dedicated to special functions such as HELP, ESC (escape out of an application) and END (end the program). Function keys are valuable features for both novice and expert users (see Figure 11.11).

Fourth-Generation Languages

The end user typically looks for tools that require a short learning curve. The tools are expected to allow for the definition of ad hoc reports and inquiries, spreadsheets, and database updates without requiring the professional training necessary to use programming languages such as COBOL. The end user is more interested in achieving a desired result quickly and easily than becoming a computer expert. Simple fourth-generation languages seem to fit the nonprofessional end user's level.

A *fourth-generation* (4GL) *language* is predominantly nonprocedural. It tells the computer what to do without specifying how it should be done. Most 4GLs, however, require some degree of explicit order to the operation. By this definition, most microcomputer spreadsheet packages qualify as fourth generation.

```
— maximum help —
                              dBASE III Main Menu
                              ====================
                              1 — Getting Started
                              2 — What Is a ...
                              3 — How Do I ...
                              4 — Creating a Database
                              5 — Using   an   Existing
Database

                              6 — Commands and Functions
```

Figure 11.10
A HELP menu for
dBASE III.

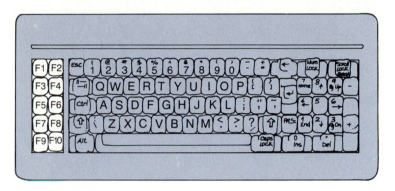

Figure 11.11
Function keys.

A fourth-generation language has several features:

1. *Result-oriented programming:* The end-user gets information without having to write program instructions. For example, to generate a report, all the user needs to do is specify the format, page breaks, and labeling information. The fourth-generation language translates the request into a procedure that produces the report.
2. *User-machine independence:* The user of a fourth-generation language need not be knowledgeable about any hardware or software used in conjunction with the language.
3. *User database capability:* The way the user wants to view information is not tied to the way it is stored in the database. Stored data can be rearranged to fit the format specified by the user.
4. *User help:* The fourth-generation language provides on-line HELP facility to assist the end user in the use of various functions.
5. *Adaptability to user level:* A fourth-generation language responds to the user's own level of knowledge, but a language suited to the naive user is hardly adequate for the professional, and vice versa.

An important aspect of 4GLs is the level of analysis they offer the user. For example, users of an electronic spreadsheet such as LOTUS 1-2-3 find the package appealing primarily because it provides a set of primitive functions at an appropriate level of analysis for a broad set of business problems. Of course, ease of use and ease of learning are additional factors.

The Managerial Role

Because the microcomputer plays a vital role in end user computing, it must be well managed. One approach to managing microcomputers in the workplace is for the organization to adopt a policy that preserves end user autonomy and central integration. A policy should be designed to encourage cost-effective applications of microcomputers and provide the necessary hardware, software, and training to ensure their success. A sound management policy will:

1. *Appoint a coordinator for each department.* The coordinator should be experienced in microcomputer acquisition and use. He or she will identify a number of hardware configurations, proven and reliable software that is easy to use and learn, and establish procedures for acquiring microcomputers. The coordinator must be familiar with software and be prepared to answer users' questions about it.

2. *Require users who wish to acquire software and hardware to work through the coordinator* and in cooperation with the manager of the user department. Users are urged to select their preference from the recommended list. The coordinator will provide training material and installation support for these.

3. *Identify user responsibilities for the microcomputer and software in use.* Users must comply with all legal and vendor license requirements, follow a procedure for system security and data integrity and, most importantly, enforce a standard of ethics against illegal copying of copyrighted software.

The requirement that users be responsible for system security, data integrity, and ethics places obvious bounds on user freedom. This is an issue for user management. The issue of accountability for results rests directly with the user, where it belongs.

Support Facilities

The move toward workstations draws much of its impetus from two developments: an increase in computer knowledge among middle management and acceptance of the information center for end user training and technical service. The personal computer supports end user activities through software that facilitates interactive involvement.

Information Resource Center (IC) The term **information center** (IC) was coined by IBM to describe a facility for helping users interact with computer center facilities. The IC is a physical site providing hardware, software, and consulting support to allow quick information retrieval. The impetus for such a center stems from end users' desire to control their own computing. This means:

1. Better information for decision making
2. Timely information retrieval by executives on their own terms
3. Cost reduction and cost avoidance
4. Increase in office productivity

ICs offer several important services. Figure 11.12 lists the most common services reported in a study by Brancheau and colleagues (1985). The majority of the end users reported troubleshooting, consulting, and training as the most important IC services. Word processing support was reported as the least important. Overall, the consensus of the users participating in the study reinforced the importance of the IC for support of end user computing.

There are benefits and drawbacks to the IC concept. Among the benefits are:

1. Fewer software development backlog problems at the organization's computer center.

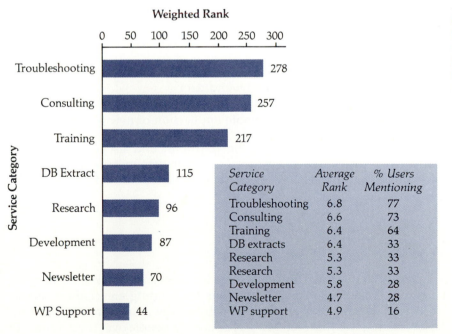

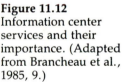

Service Category	Average Rank	% Users Mentioning
Troubleshooting	6.8	77
Consulting	6.6	73
Training	6.4	64
DB extracts	6.4	33
Research	5.3	33
Research	5.3	33
Development	5.8	28
Newsletter	4.7	28
WP support	4.9	16

Figure 11.12
Information center services and their importance. (Adapted from Brancheau et al., 1985, 9.)

2. End users become more aware of what can and cannot be done at the computer center.

The major drawback of an information center is possible lack of regular use. This is a question of efficiency. A survey of 70 major corporations showed that only 10 percent of the users actually use the personal computer. Management attitude is partly to blame. Other drawbacks include:

1. Operating cost of the center
2. Reduction in central control
3. Development of incompatible systems
4. Replication of data
5. Poor documentation
6. Failure to develop systems with organizationwide relevance

Typical Components   The major components of an IC include:

1. *DSSs* that normally reside in the host computer and are accessed through terminals at the IC. Many DSS tools are in the workstation.
2. *Color graphics* capable of providing easy-to-interpret pictures.
3. *Personal computers* networked to the host computer.
4. *Software application* packages that address the problem areas of the end user.

No matter how up-to-date the hardware or how powerful the software package, the IC must be supported by qualified staff to help the user get started. User training must have several characteristics. It must:

1. Be targeted to meet specific end user needs
2. Use actual cases familiar to the end user
3. Be tied to the organization's way of doing business
4. Use peers as trainers to promote application of new technology

If management believes in the payoff in end user computing by enhancing individual performance, it must demonstrate a supportive attitude. The truly successful IC must be marketed throughout the organization on a regular basis.

The Role of End User Training

Most office automation systems have been installed with little thought given to the intended user. Provisions for training are made on an ad hoc basis, leaving little preparation time for the trainer or end user. End user training was first seen as a way of getting people over their computer phobia. Hordes of people were ushered into training rooms for "computer literacy" courses. The orientation of these sessions usually followed one of two scenarios:

1. *"Touch it and it won't break."* Classes focused on getting people to use computers in any shape or form, using examples that were trivial or had little to do with business applications.

2. *"More is better."* Within five hours or so of training, commands and functions were thrown at the end users in rapid succession. This approach attempted to make the end user fully knowledgeable about every capability of a system.

Each approach produces its own set of problems. In the "touch it and it won't break" approach, presentations usually deal with trivial applications, unrelated to users' problems. Transference of skill across domains is not easily achieved. The "more is less" approach runs the risk that trainees will forget most of what they were taught. Commands need to be presented a few at a time within a meaningful context.

In order to see an increase in productivity from an office automation system, greater attention must be placed on training from the outset. Objectives should include planning, training for the life of a system, and reinforcement. With this approach, training becomes an integral part of the development and maintenance of an office automation system. End user involvement will highlight the importance of OA and increase the chances of its acceptance.

The first step in planning an office automation system is to determine what type of training is best suited for employees. Soliciting information and opinions from employees can identify the perceived level of existing office automation knowledge and training needs. Staff's participation in the startup of the system will rally support and enthusiasm. This involvement will make them more receptive to the idea of converting to an automated process.

Aspects to be considered in the preparation of a training session are location, duration, and class makeup. Although on-site training has the advantage of convenience, training away from the office eliminates interruptions and allows participants to learn at their own pace. If time permits, training should be cut to two-hour segments with one main topic presented during each segment. These segments can be presented over several consecutive days or at weekly intervals.

Classes should be conducted with homogeneous work groups. People's background and potential use of the system should be considered in their class placement. Unfortunately, individual talents don't emerge until after a system has been installed. Employee feedback through a questionnaire can often provide insight for a manager about the level of training required.

What about course material? How should it be presented? Material should be presented in the context of business problems closely related to those the end users are likely to encounter. Concepts rather than key strokes are the focus of any good presentation. However, working these concepts into applications at an appropriate level is probably the most difficult aspect of course development. On one hand, the application must be transparently clear. Examples should make total sense with no possibility of the student's misunderstanding. This approach, however, runs the risk of oversimplification. Demonstrations should reflect actual applications as closely as possible. Ultimately, the goal of a trainer is to present complex concepts in the clearest context possible.

Next to training, course documentation is vital in initiating a system. Readability and ease of use are key factors in the success of documentation. Optimally, end users should be able to open the documentation two months after class, quickly find a description of a process, read it, and understand it.

After planning and training, the third phase of training is skills reinforcement. This phase starts from the time the first end user completes the training course. Unfortunately, although most managers seem willing to allow time for training, very few provide time for practice and applying the new skills. End users should be assigned a first project within a week of training. The project should present variations of the examples presented in class. Subsequent projects should build upon basic concepts, each one presenting a greater complexity of problem solving. This approach allows the immediate application of skills learned and increases knowledge of system functions.

As demand for shared corporate bases increases, end users will become more accountable for their data. Eventually, data will be accessed by any workstation in the company. Preparing end users for this "totally automated office" is not a trivial task. Issues such as standardization techniques, documentation standards, data verification, and overall system controls need to be addressed for the office of tomorrow.

Implications for MIS

The information center can be instrumental in promoting the user-machine interface. Office technology is altering the way people work. Knowledge workers are provided productivity improvements as the technology makes it possible for them to shift from execution to planning, from direction to coordination, and from delegation to participation.

It is easy to predict that the next wave of offerings in office systems will be user-integrated applications. The goal is for the user to develop application programs without programmers. The MIS manager has already begun to serve a new class of end users who won't be content with long lead times for delivery or clumsy interfaces. The office system has already shown how the end user can survive the "trauma" of dealing with machine intelligence. The end user is also beginning to recognize the satisfaction derived from user-friendly software as an approach to problem solving.

Related to the use of the personal computer are the varied roles of the MIS manager, which include controller, specifier, coordinator, and informal advisor. The extreme roles of controlling personal computer use in the organization or merely advising when asked are ineffective. The controller role is too rigid for most end users and the informal advisor role is too passive. The middle roles of specifier or coordinator of hardware and software acquisition and use are appropriate for most MIS organizations. The role of coordinator is one of the most likely to result in a successful meshing of end user and organizational needs while accommodating rapidly changing technology.

Finally, advanced office systems help organizations shift responsibility downward so that the organization structure is flattened, forcing the merger of many professional positions. At the same time, effectiveness in decision making through technology provides a basis for employing more and more professionals. The conclusion is that high technology creates rather than eliminates jobs for business.

Summary

□ Office automation (OA) is the integration of computers and communication technology with human patterns of human work. It dates back to the early 1800s when packets of information were sent within the city for quick delivery. Today, the local area network (LAN) combines workstations, easy-to-use languages, and electronic messaging to do the same work in fractions of a second.

□ The ultimate goal of OA is to create an office working environment that provides interactive functions to derive feasible solutions along with functions to communicate a knowledge worker's activities to the right person at the right time. The key hardware in this effort consists of workstations, LAN, and office processors.

□ The workstation is an interface device that takes over repetitive, tedious tasks, freeing the knowledge worker's time for creative work. The single most sought-after application is the electronic spreadsheet. In addition to repetitive tasks, a workstation also performs administrative support functions, personal computing, electronic messaging, and database management.

□ An early OA application is word processing—computer-assisted preparation of user documents and reports. The hardware centers around a workstation sharing a secondary storage device. Most current word processing packages provide text editors that help format the final report.

□ An end user can achieve full productivity in a properly designed work environment. OA ergonomics focuses on environmental issues (lighting, temperature), hardware (furniture, seating design), and user-system interface that emphasizes user comfort and productivity.

□ The two major implications of OA for MIS are the electronic mail (EM) and executive workstations. EM's main function is movement of information rather than paper. Electronic messaging reduces shadow functions, eliminates interruptions and "telephone tag." The executive workstation is a support unit for improving the end user's productivity.

□ End users may be direct (actually use terminals), indirect (use terminals through an assistant), or intermediate (call for specific information they later receive). Direct end users may be non-DP, DP amateurs, or DP professionals.

□ End users may also be characterized as developers or nondevelopers, novices or experts, occasional or frequent users, and primary versus secondary users. Regardless of the classification, however, today's end user environment is user friendly, with tools that are easy to use and learn, attractive input devices, and access to training when needed.

□ General interactive user dialogs are available to promote user-friendly computing: menus, forms, windows, icons, touch pads, help facility, and function keys. Almost all these features are a product of the microcomputer and the early 1980s.

□ In addition to these features, fourth-generation, nonprocedural languages allow the end user to tell the computer what to do without specifying how it should be done. Several features are associated with such languages: workstation environment, result-oriented programming, user-machine independence, user database capability, user help, and adaptability to user level.

□ The notion of an information resource center for end user training had its impetus from end users' desires to control their own computing. ICs provide timely information retrieval, cost reduction and cost avoidance, increase in office productivity, and improved executive image. The major drawback of such centers is lack of regular use.

Key Terms

Desktop publishing	Menu
Electronic messaging	Mouse
Form	Office automation (OA)
Function key	Peer-to-peer network
HELP facility	User-friendly
Icon	Voice mail
Information center (IC)	Window
Knowledge worker	Workstation

Review Questions

1. What background events led up to current office automation?

2. Select four technologies that deal with "short-haul" communication. How do they improve user productivity?

3. Who is the knowledge worker? Does a secretary's job provide knowledge work? Explain.

4. What makes a workstation intelligent? Discuss its features, functions, and advantages.

5. Elaborate on the categories that represent office automation systems.

6. Define the following:
   a. Text editor
   b. Workstation

7. In what respect is ergonomics a key issue in office automation? What factors affect the ergonomics of the knowledge worker? Elaborate.

8. Briefly discuss the major points that characterize the user-system interface.

9. Explain the functions and uses of the electronic mail in the business environment.

10. What format and configuration are used in voice mail? What advantages does this technology offer over traditional telephone use? Explain.

11. In how many ways can end users be categorized? Elaborate on each category. Which do you think is representative of the end users in your school? Why?

12. Discuss the emerging end user environment. How much of it is applicable to academic computing?

13. What is the difference (or relationship) between ease of use and user friendliness? What interactive dialogs are available for the end user?

14. Distinguish between:
    a. Menus and forms
    b. Windows and icons
    c. Help facility and function keys
    d. Trained and expert user

15. What is a fourth-generation language? What makes it nonprocedural? Explain.

16. According to the text, the user of a fourth-generation language need not be aware of any hardware or software being used in conjunction with the language. What does that mean?

17. The concept of the information center has appeared in the literature since the microcomputer gained momentum in the early 1980s. Review the benefits and drawbacks of such a concept. What components are required for an IC installation?

Application Problems

1. The board of directors of a large, Chicago-based bank authorized an independent consultant to look into ways of improving office work and transactions carried out among the officers and employees throughout the thirty-nine branches. Several board members had heard workstations and other high-tech features touted during a national computer conference that was in progress during the board meeting.

The first step the consultant took was to ask each officer to keep a diary of the times he/she spent in meetings, supervisory activities, on the telephone, preparing reports, travel, and a few miscellaneous activities. Seventeen senior officers, fourteen junior officers and assistant cashiers, and five office managers participated in the study. The survey showed the following breakdown:

Meetings	38%
Telephone calls	22
Supervisory activities	21
Preparing reports	7
Travel	4
Misc. activities	8

The consultant recommended an integrated office information system to include:

- Electronic mail
- Word processing
- Telephone directories
- Calendaring
- Personal computing

The system was user friendly. It featured a user's general menu and "soft" messages in case the user failed to follow directions. The initial findings showed that officers in general were realizing savings of about one hour a day. Instead of walking down the hall or telephoning other officers, they found that the electronic mail curtailed their meetings and cut down on their use of the telephone. Messages were now captured on the workstation, ready to scan at will; no more missed telephone calls. Likewise, the electronic calendar cut down on use of the telephone and mundane memos for arranging meetings.

A followup questionnaire showed that assistant vice presidents and vice presidents were utilizing the electronic mail 58 percent of the time the system was in operation. Personal computing also improved, accounting for 15 percent of the total time. Word processing was not a popular item with senior officers, since most of them had secretaries who took over the task with no difficulty. The overall effectiveness record has increased by 18 percent.

QUESTIONS
a. Can you foresee the usefulness of office automation for company presidents and executive vice presidents? How? Discuss.
b. How would you evaluate the worth of such a system in terms of the amount of time saved?
c. How do you cost-justify this system? Explain.

2. A production manager arrives at his office and reviews his mail; a financial analyst reviews budgetary data; a professional produces several bar charts for a board presentation; a regional sales executive leaves a telephone message for a sales rep in Colorado. Although these are activities people routinely perform in the office, they are specific and different from each other. Each function was performed electronically on an executive workstation.

QUESTIONS
a. What is so important about the ability to carry out office functions electronically?
b. Is office automation a solution to all end users or organizations? How would one know where the ideal installation should be recommended?

3. A large international freight forwarder is using a terminal network as a strategic tool to serve its customers' needs. According to the firm's MIS director, an on-line freight inventory system tracks shipments and paperwork for its clients. Three hundred terminals and printers in seventy of the firm's U.S. offices communicate over private leased lines with an interactive database that runs on a 16M byte IBM 4341 at headquarters.

Nine of the firm's major clients have terminals in their own offices connected over leased lines to the freight inventory system. Smaller clients rely on the shipper's branch offices to provide them with information from the inventory system. Clients can reserve space for shipment on planes or ships and can confirm their reservations instantly. The database enables the firm to provide its larger customers with analyses of shipping routes and orders to help them identify profitable routes and monitor expenses.

QUESTIONS
a. Based on the information provided, what are the key features or characteristics of the terminals used?

b. Do you find a relationship between on-line terminals and telecommunication technology? Discuss.

Selected References

Allen, Leilani. "Who Are End Users?" *Computerworld*, November 19, 1984, 19–20ff.

Brancheau, J. C., Vogel, D. R., and Wetherbe, J. C. "An Investigation of the Information Center from the User's Perspective." *Data Base*, Fall 1985, 4–17.

Clark, Andrew. "Supporting Peer to Peer Connectivity." *Computerworld*, November 12, 1986, F45–47.

Coudal, Edgar. "Electronic Mail." *Small Systems World*, February 1982, 18.

Davis, G. B. and Olson, M. *Management Information Systems: Conceptual Foundations, Structure, and Development*. New York: McGraw-Hill, 1984, 409, 503–33.

"Electronic Mail." *Systems & Software*, March 1985.

"Ergonomics Increase End-User Productivity, Efficiency." *Data Management*, February 1985, 12–13.

"The Evolution of End Users." *Datamation*, October 15, 1984, 203–204.

Hurst, Rebecca. "Desktop Publishing." *Computerworld*, March 4, 1987, F23–28.

Martin, James. *Application Development Without Programmers*. Englewood Cliffs, N.J.: Prentice-Hall, 1982, 102–106.

Olson, Margarethe H. and Turner, Jon A. "Rethinking Office Automation." *Data Base*, Summer 1986, 20–28.

Rockart, John F. and Flannery, Laura S. "The Management of End-User Computing." *Communications of the ACM*, October 1983, 776–84.

Winkler, Connie. "Desktop Publishing." *Datamation*, December 1, 1986, 92–95.

Wohl, Amy. "Classifying Desktop Publishing." *Computerworld*, November 12, 1986, F27ff.

Wright, David. "Designing Terminals for the Human Factor." *Canadian Data Systems*, April 1982.

Expert Systems

Chapter Contents

Purdue System Aids Farmers

AMERICAN FARMERS ARE, as a group, in deep economic trouble these days. Foreclosures are up, farm prices are down, and it is becoming increasingly difficult for farmers to stay afloat. Anything that can help them reduce expenses or get a better price for their crops is a welcome sight.

Researchers at Purdue University have produced just such a tool—the Grain Marketing Advisor, an expert system to help farmers select the best way to market their grain. The system, produced with the Texas Instruments Personal Consultant expert system development tool, is being field tested, and could be available to many farmers soon.

"Selecting grain marketing alternatives relies on a lot of different factors," says Ronald R. Thieme, knowledge engineer for the system and a graduate instructor in research in the Agricultural Engineering Department. "Economic factors, personal preferences, personal outlook—only an expert system could bring all of these together. Problems in agriculture are well-suited to this approach because they rely heavily on human expertise."

Although Thieme was the knowledge engineer, he says this was his first hands-on experience with expert systems. He and other team members began developing the system in the spring of 1985. A prototype was completed in about three months, and a complete 180-rule system was ready for field testing early this year.

Farmers have several options for marketing their grain. The options include when to sell, when to deliver, and when to set a price. They can do all three at harvest time, store the grain for later sale in hopes that increased market prices will offset storage costs, deliver grain for a price to be set at a later date, agree on a price before delivery, and so on.

Selecting from among the available alternatives requires an intimate knowledge of the marketplace, storage costs, finance charges, and many other factors. Making a selection also involves personal preferences—"rules of thumb" developed by each farmer over time.

The Purdue expert system takes all of these factors into account. It looks at current and historical price and basic data as well as information about the farmer's physical set-up (availability of storage and drying facilities), the farmer's personal preferences about delivery location, his familiarity with the futures market, and many other types of information.

Thieme believes farmers are ready for expert system technology. "We have an annual computer conference at Purdue, and at the most recent one, our department demonstrated some expert systems," he says. "The general reaction was that this was the first new thing for farmers people had seen in several years. This is something that can help them make decisions, and they like that."

—AI Applications, *Texas Instruments, Inc.,* *Spring 1986,* 2–3.

AT A GLANCE

An important motivation for natural language and expert systems is the way the conceptual structure of English can match the user's conceptualization of the problem. Expert systems represent a key MIS development, advancing user/machine interface and problem solving. They use the computer's capabilities to manipulate natural language to retrieve answers to questions as well as providing the line of reasoning for the answers.

An expert system has several characteristics: expertise, reasoning by symbol manipulation, exhibiting intelligent behavior, conversion to expert rules, and reasoning abilities. Expert systems builders are called knowledge engineers. They build systems by interviewing recognized authorities in a given field and capturing their knowledge in computer programming. Knowledge engineers combine cognitive psychological and symbolic programming to develop expert systems.

The architecture of an expert system centers around a knowledge base and an inference engine. The knowledge base contains facts and inference rules for determining new facts. How facts are related in a knowledge base is determined "on the fly" as needed to solve a problem. The inference engine contains the inference strategies and the controls for manipulating facts and rules.

The best known dialect in logic programming is PROLOG. A prolog system responds to a question by searching for facts that match the question. There will be a match if the predicate and the arguments are the same.

By the end of this chapter, you should know:

1. The arguments for and against computer "intelligence"
2. Knowledge engineering and knowledge representation basics
3. How an expert system draws inference
4. The key expert system tools and applications

Introduction

From the information we have on database and DSS, we soon find the technology to be restricted and restrictive. Most of the "intelligence" has to be supplied by the user. One obstacle in database systems is the mismatch between end users' needs and their ability to communicate these needs to the computer. A decision support system also has severe restrictions. Formal inquiry languages have been a barrier to nontechnical users (von Limbach and Taylor, 1984), although interfaces (e.g., spreadsheets

```
In COBOL

PUT SKIP LIST('1987 OCT ACT SALES', '1987 OCT EST SALES',
   'DIFFERENCE', '% CHANGE')'
DO WHILE('1'B);
   READ FILE (EMPLOYEE_FILE INTO EMPLOYEE_RECORD)
      .
      .      (missing statements)
      .
   PUT SKIP LIST(Y1987_OCT_ACT_SALES,Y1987_OCT-EST-SALES,
      DIFFERENCE,CHANGE);
    END;
   END;
WRAP_UP

In Query

   PRINT 1987-OCT-ACT-SALES,1987-OCT-EST-SALES,
      .
      .      (missing statements)
      .
   (100**1987-OCT-ACT-SALES-1987-OCT-EST-SALES
    /1987-OCT-ACT-SALES)
   WHERE(DEPT='MEN' OR DEPT='WOMEN');

In Natural Language

   FOR THE MENS OR WOMENS DEPTS, COMPARE
   ACTUAL AND FORECASTED SALES FOR LAST MONTH.
```

Figure 12.1
Comparison of COBOL, QUERY, and natural language. (Adapted from Rauzino, 1983, 47.)

and menu-driven systems) have improved the interface for many semi-repetitive tasks (Bates and Bobrow, 1983). In contrast, a natural language interface makes it possible to manipulate a database without possessing a technical understanding of its functions (see Figure 12.1). Natural language can also be used to specify the input to a DSS and pose questions using plain English. These features make it appropriate to explore how artificial intelligence that relies on natural language is used for improving database usage and MIS performance.

One advantage of natural language is that it avoids conscious translation (programming) of user requests from English-like language to computer language. Natural language is ideal in situations where the user knows what the computer must do and can express this in English but not in computer language.

An important motivation for understanding natural language is the way the conceptual structure of English matches the user's conceptualization of the problem. A natural language interface eliminates the need for learning computer syntax. An effective communication system for user-machine interface in complex decision-making tasks, then, is facilitated by a procedure using a natural language (Woods, 1984; also Li, 1984).

More and more corporations are exploring ways to apply AI to tasks ranging from robotics to production management. Some success has been achieved by **expert systems** that use represented knowledge and inference procedures to solve problems that otherwise require significant human expertise (Duda, 1983). The key to problem solving is more in knowing the right information than constructing a solution from logical principles. In this chapter, we will discuss the concepts and structure of expert systems as a branch of artificial intelligence (AI) and the basics of PROLOG for problem solving.

What Is Artificial Intelligence?

Managers make decisions often based on incomplete data or knowledge. Until recently, decision making relied heavily on the information produced by the computer. But such information is historical and "perishable." Since the early 1980s, artificial intelligence (AI) has been touted as a powerful way to solve complex problems in business.

AI promotes a change in computer design. Most books label the four generations of computers (vacuum tube, transistorized, integrated circuit, and very large integrated, or VLSI) as the *von Neumann design*— after the computer pioneer John von Neumann. The computer has a central processor, memory, an arithmetic unit, and input/output devices. According to Edward Feigenbaum and Pamela McCorduck (1983), the **fifth-generation computer** that supports AI will provide new memory organizations, programming languages, and architecture to handle symbols—not just numbers. This will signal a shift from mere data processing by today's computer to an intelligent *processing of knowledge*.

AI suggests supplanting rather than supplementing or depriving rather than extending human efforts to arrive at solutions. A collection of techniques and procedures called *knowledge-based expert systems*, is playing an important role in problem solving and decision making in business. Expert systems assist managers with complex planning and task scheduling. They are changing the way organizations behave by promoting a different way of looking at problem solving.

Most expert systems have demonstrated that a computer is capable of behavior similar to that of a physician making a diagnosis or a sales executive allocating new territories for a new product. These systems combine textbook knowledge with rules of thumb or **heuristics** to make informed guesses about a specific problem. Such expertise is often referred to as "intuition, inspiration, and professionalism" (Feigenbaum and

McCorduck, 1983). When a machine exhibits similar behavior, there is a good reason for calling it intelligence, too.

Definition

The word *intelligence* originates from the latin *legere,* which means to gather, to assemble; hence, to choose and form an opinion. Intelligence implies a choice among—understanding and knowing. Thinking machines have always intrigued us. During the machine age, an obsession with artifacts that had "intelligence" had developed, culminating in the early nineteenth-century novel *Frankenstein*—the nameless monster that represented science that ran amok. At about the same time, Charles Babbage, a British mathematician, built the "Analytical Engine," a machine that was perceived to be a thinking machine. Babbage conceived it to do away with the "drudgery of thinking."

What promoted AI as a science in the present computer age was the notion that computers are capable of handling not only numbers, but all sorts of symbols. Computers can be used to tackle logical as well as numerical problems (Aleksander, 1984). Eventually, certain strategies of intelligent behavior have been supported. These include:

1. Searching for a solution using the "rules of guessing"
2. Generating and testing solutions (keep trying for an acceptable solution)
3. Reasoning backward from a specified goal

When represented in the form of computer programs, such strategies became necessary steps for intelligent behavior.

With these elements in mind, a representative definition of artificial intelligence is "doing on computers that which, if done by humans, would be called intelligent" (Aleksander, 1984). This includes learning from experience, understanding and speaking natural language rather than traditional computer commands, assessing information, and drawing conclusions.

Arguments Regarding Computer "Intelligence"

The ultimate aim of AI as a science is to produce computers in which intelligence is measured more by how well it meets human needs than how well it outsmarts the human user. Two major arguments have been made against machine intelligence:

1. Thinking requires originality, creativity, and consciousness of having done things. Consciousness is a major part of intelligence. There is no machine to date that meets these criteria.
2. Machines can never think and have no emotions. These are human properties.

Other differences between human and artificial intelligence include the following:

1. Human intelligence is *creative*; artificial intelligence is *uninspired*.
2. Human intelligence is *adaptive*; artificial intelligence *needs to be told*.
3. Human intelligence has a *broad focus*; artificial intelligence has a *narrow focus*.
4. Human intelligence is *perishable*; artificial intelligence is *long lasting*.
5. Human intelligence is *difficult to transfer*; artificial intelligence is *easy to transfer*.
6. Human intelligence is *unpredictable*; artificial intelligence is *consistent*.
7. Human intelligence is *expensive*; artificial intelligence is *affordable*.

So, there are problems in asking whether a computer can "think." To date, human intelligence far outsmarts the most intelligent machine and is likely to continue making the decisions.

Historical Developments

The growth of computers as numerical processors generated interest in learning how well they manipulate non-numerical symbols. Concerned with human problem solving, computer scientists and psychologists began to develop programs that would simulate human behavior (Harmon and King, 1985). Over the years, these two branches of science have formed the interdisciplinary subfield of computer science called **artificial intelligence**—developing systems that produce results associated with human intelligence.

AI may be divided into three independent categories:

1. Natural language
2. Robotics
3. Expert systems

The development of **natural language** for computers requires programs capable of reading, speaking, or understanding human language. Understanding natural language systems is important in decision making. A manager, for example, should be able to interact with an information system as easily as with humans and in a language that matches his/her own cognitive abilities. The preferred medium is natural English for entering instructions at different levels of detail. English makes it easier for the user to match his/her conceptualization of the problem.

Another category of AI is *robotics*, the development of smart robots to perform human chores in industry and chores that can move and relate to objects as humans (Horwitt, 1985). AI also includes expert systems, programs that use symbolic reasoning to mimic the decision making and problem solving of human experts. A summary of these areas is presented in Figure 12.2.

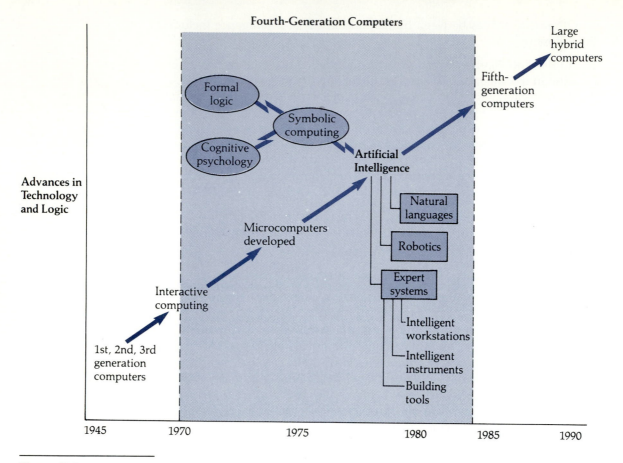

Figure 12.2
Major categories of artificial intelligence in the historical context. (Adapted from Harmon and King, 1985, 3.)

Expert Systems

Expert systems are programs for solving difficult problems requiring expertise. They simulate human reasoning using logical deductions or facts and rules of thumb used by experts. Edward Feigenbaum, a leading researcher in this field, defines an expert system as an:

> intelligent program that uses knowledge and inference procedures to solve problems that are difficult enough to require significant human expertise for their solution. The knowledge of an expert system consists of facts and heuristics. The "facts" constitute a body of information that is widely shared, publicly available, and generally agreed upon by experts in a field. The "heuristics" are mostly private, little discussed rules of good judgment (rules of plausible reasoning, rules of good guessing) that characterize expert-level decision making in the field. The performance level of an expert system is primarily a function of the size and the quality of a knowledge base it possesses. (in Harmon, 1985, 5)

This definition of expert systems includes:

1. Expertise
2. Reasoning by symbol manipulation
3. Exhibiting generally intelligent behavior
4. Conversion to expert rules
5. Reasoning abilities about its own processes

Expertise here consists of using high-level rules and high quality performance by high-level inference patterns (hunches) that come from years of experience at a task. The measure of an expert is that no matter how fast a task is performed, hardly anyone would be satisfied unless the result is accurate judgment. How quickly a decision is made is also an important factor. In a medical expert system, for instance, even the most accurate of diagnoses slowly arrived at would be useless if the patient dies.

Reasoning by symbol manipulation refers to the fact that human experts solve problems by choosing symbols to represent the problem situation and applying specific approaches to manipulate these situations. An expert system employs knowledge symbolically, with symbols representing problem situations. A **symbol** in expert systems means a group of characters that stands for a real-life situation. Examples of symbols are:

```
WOMEN
MOTHER
```

We can combine these symbols to represent relationships between them. Examples of symbols structures are:

```
(WOMEN mothers)
(MOTHER Ann)
```

We may interpret these structures to mean:

Mothers are women
Ann is a mother

An expert system can use these two facts to perform deductive reasoning from the two structures as follows:

All mothers are women. Ann is a mother. Therefore, Ann is a woman.

The choice and interpretation of symbols used can be very important for fast, efficient responses to inquiries. In this simple example, we refer to knowledge as *representational*.

Exhibiting a generally intelligent behavior is a product of the principles the system knows and the level of detail at which it knows them. The quality of reasoning depends on how well the facts and principles are available and how efficiently the inference procedure is implemented.

Conversion to expert rules is a changeover in which expert knowledge is expressed in the form of expert rules. This is referred to as the *reformulation* dimension of expertise.

Reasoning abilities about its own processes means that an expert system must be able to reconstruct the inference paths it has taken to arrive at a given conclusion. How a conclusion was derived requires an ability to link the inference steps with basic expert rules as justifications.

In summary, an expert system uses expert rules, performs at a high level, reasons by manipulating symbols, displays on request its line of reasoning in plain English language, is in command of fundamental domain principles, and has reasoning abilities about its own processes. It deals with complex problems and takes a problem description in simple terms and converts it into representation for processing using its expert rules (Brachman et al., 1983).

Knowledge Engineering

Expert systems builders are called **knowledge engineers**, a term coined by Edward Feigenbaum of Stanford. Expert systems are built by interviewing a human authority in a given field and capturing his/her knowledge. This *expert* is someone who is widely recognized for solving a particular type of problem that most other people are unable to solve as well. Such a person also has a large amount of domain-specific knowledge. The knowledge engineer attempts to replicate the behavior of the expert in solving a narrowly defined problem. This involves:

1. Identifying the specific knowledge that an expert uses in solving a problem.
2. Determining the facts and heuristics (rules of thumb) that the expert uses.
3. Specifying the inference strategy that the expert employs in an actual problem situation.
4. Developing a system that employs similar knowledge and inference strategies to simulate the behavior of the human expert, a feature known as *transparency* (Webster and Miner, 1982).

It can be seen that expert systems are knowledge-intensive programs that use heuristics to focus on a specific problem. They do not reason broadly over a field of expertise. They are limited to using the specific facts and heuristics that they were "taught" by a human expert. In this respect, expert systems lack common sense and cannot reason by analogy. For example, they assist a personnel manager in analyzing a specific type of labor turnover but would not be able to analyze a potential patent infringement. On the other hand, expert systems display unbiased judgment, do not jump to conclusions without confirming evidence, and consistently attend to details on a regular basis.

Symbolic Programming Emphases Expert systems use **symbolic programming**, which is quite different than conventional programming. Conventional programs follow algorithmic (step-by-step) routines that lead to certain conclusions. Knowledge engineering combines theorem-proving techniques with symbolic programming to develop expert systems. Symbolic programming is highly interactive and relies on heuristic search for its structure. A user can interrupt processing and ask how a conclusion is reached. In contrast, the code and procedure in a conventional program are best known to the programmer.

Other contrasts between an expert system and a conventional program are:

1. Conventional programming is algorithmic; the solution steps are explicit. Expert system programming is heuristic search; solution steps are implicit.
2. Conventional programs can be quite complex, requiring experienced programmers. The knowledge base of an expert system is easy to read and modify.
3. Conventional programmers work apart from the expert to write a program. Knowledge engineers use interactive techniques to develop expert systems. They meet frequently with an expert, produce a first-cut at the problem, ask the expert more questions and generate a second version of the proposed system, and so on, developing the expert system in a series of approximations.
4. In conventional programming, the best possible solution is usually sought. In expert system programming, satisfactory answers are usually acceptable.

Knowledge Representation

The architecture of an expert system consists of two parts (see Figure 12.3):

1. The knowledge base
2. The inference engine

A key aspect of building expert systems is analyzing an expert's knowledge and formalizing it in the knowledge base. The **knowledge base** includes facts and inference rules for determining new facts. The knowledge is represented in symbolic form that can be used by the inference engine. A most common representation is the **object**. As we will see later, an object is associated with other objects by symbolic references, using links in the memory. A typical associative taxonomy for stating facts is the one known as "is-a" hierarchy. For example, "The parrot *is a* kind of bird" and "The bird *is a* kind of animal that can fly." The knowledge base software can deduce, then, that parrots can fly. The rule, on

Figure 12.3
The architecture of an expert system. The inference engine stands between the user and the knowledge base. It examines facts and rules and provides the user with advice and explanations. (Adapted from Frenkel, *Communications of* 1985, 580.)

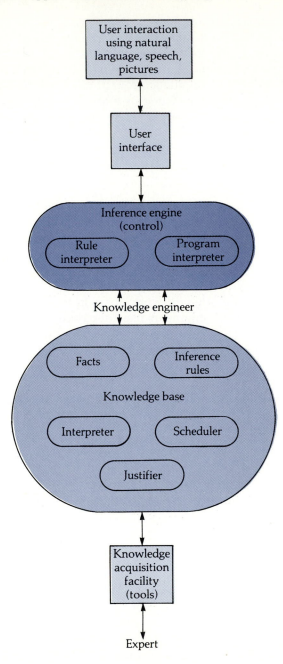

the other hand, is a collection of "if-then" statements that help in machine decision making.

The **inference engine** stands between the user and the knowledge base (see Figure 12.3). It contains the inference strategies and controls for manipulating the facts and rules. It also decides the order of making

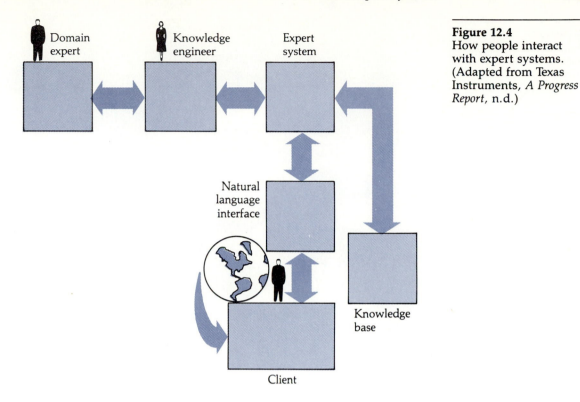

Figure 12.4
How people interact
with expert systems.
(Adapted from Texas
Instruments, *A Progress
Report*, n.d.)

inferences. The inference engine draws logical conclusions based on the data in the database and general knowledge of the subject domain (Harris, 1983).

The Knowledge Base   The first step in building an expert system is to obtain and analyze some knowledge. The pattern of interaction between people and expert systems is shown in Figure 12.4. The knowledge engineer interviews an expert on a specific subject. The following is a summary of data an expert (Jim Harding) gathered about a flight instructor (Fred Olesek) for a personnel knowledge base relating to specialists in pilot testing:

> It is a fact that Fred Olesek has been a flight instructor for PAN AM for seven years. The insignia on his shirt sleeve identifies him as a flight instructor. His license certifies him as a specialist in air rescue and emergency landing procedures. (By Jim Harding, PAN AM Personnel Division)

The knowledge of the expert (in our example, Jim Harding) is expressed in basic elements rather than complex statements. To create a personnel knowledge base, we need to include elements such as Olesek's license, a list of the characteristics of each element, and a way to link things together. For example, we need to record the fact that the insignia on Olesek's shirt sleeve signifies a flight instructor.

Figure 12.5
Personnel knowledge
base.

Inheritance

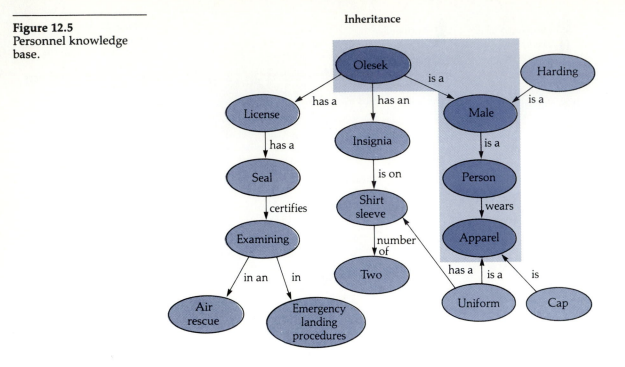

We can see how a knowledge base is an important part of an expert system. It contains the *facts* and the problem-solving *rules*. It also uses an *interpreter* that applies the rules, a *scheduler* that coordinates the processing of the rules, and a *justifier* that explains how the expert system arrives at the solution (see Figure 12.3).

Representing Knowledge   There are a number of ways to encode facts and relationships that represent knowledge. Popular representation schemes include semantic networks, rules, frames, and logic.

Semantic Knowledge   This is a semantic network or a collection of nodes linked together to form a *net*. Figure 12.5 illustrates the key nodes that represent Jim Harding's knowledge. The key elements are the following:

1. A **node** may be a physical *object* (e.g., shirt sleeve, insignia) or a conceptual entity—an event (e.g., "2", PAN AM). It may also be a **descriptor** that provides additional information (e.g., insignia).
2. A **link** connects nodes and descriptors. Links include:
   a. *"Is-a"* represents the class/instance relationship. In our example, Olesek *is-a* male. He is an instance of the large class, male. A male, in turn, is an instance of the larger class, person.
   b. *"Has-a"* identifies a node that is a property of another node. For example, a uniform *has-a* shirt sleeve. It shows part, subpart relationship.

```
Rule:

a.                  ┌ If      the site of the clouds is black and
   Premise          ┤         the force of the wind is over 35 mph and
  (situation)       └         the height of the waves is over 18 feet,

   Conclusion  ┌ Then    it is likely(.8) that the classification
    (action)   └              of the storm is a hurricane


b.                             Attribute      Object     Value
                    ┌ If       site           clouds     black
   Premise          ┤          force          wind       over 35 mph
                    └          height         waves      over 18 ft

   Conclusion { Then    classification   storm      hurricane
```

Figure 12.6
(a) Structure of a rule.
(b) Its elements.

c. *"Wear"* is a definitional link. In our example, the wear link between person and apparel is a definitional link.
d. Some links represent heuristic knowledge. For example, "License *certifies* examining . . ." (see Figure 12.5).

A major advantage of semantic net is what Harmon and King (1985) refer to as **inheritance**. This means that instances of one class are assumed to have all the properties of more general classes of which they are members. To illustrate this concept, let us take a simple hypothetical example. From our personnel knowledge base, the question, "Does Olesek wear a uniform?" is answerable by determining that Olesek is a male, males are persons, and persons wear apparel.

Rules   **Rules** are conditional statements that specify an action to be taken, if a certain condition is true. In expert systems vocabulary, they are called *premise-conclusion* or *situation-action* rules. Expert systems rules differ from the traditional "if-then" programming statements. They are relatively independent of one another and are based on heuristics (experiential reasoning) rather than algorithms.

Figure 12.6(a) specifies a rule consisting of a premise and a conclusion. The premise has three expressions or clauses, each having an attribute, an object, and a value. The conclusion has one expression or a clause with an attribute, an object, or value as shown in Figure 12.6(b).

Frames   A **frame**, like a rule, carries knowledge. It associates an object with facts, rules, or values. Each fact or value is stored in a **slot** that is related to a specific object. So a set of slots and their associated entries represent a frame. Figure 12.7 illustrates a frame of our personnel knowl-

```
Object: Letter

    Slot                                     Entry

Instructor                                   Olesek

Verification                                 Letter

Unique feature of verification               Seal

Teaching certification                       Air rescue
Teaching certification                       Emergency landing procedures
```

Figure 12.7
A frame representing
Olesek's letter.

edge base. Olesek's letter is the object. The slots represent the properties of the object.

Logic **Logic** is a system that prescribes rules for manipulating symbols. A widely studied formal language for symbol structures is predicate calculus. A *predicate* is a statement about an object. An object is an elementary unit in predicate calculus. For example, "is-instructor (Olesek)" is an assertion that Olesek is an instructor. This assertion is either true or false. A predicate can address more than one object, however. For example, "instructor-at(Olesek, PAN AM)" illustrates a two-place predicate. The statement asserts that Olesek is an instructor at PAN AM.

Connectives or operator symbols can be used to link predicates into large expressions. They include "$\wedge$" [and] "$\vee$" [or], and "$\Rightarrow$" [implies]. In Figure 12.8, A, B, C, D, E, PERSON, BOAT, BOAT-MOTOR are **terms** used for the names of things. IS-A, PART-OF, and ON are predicate names that represent relations between things. The formula *Person D is on Boat A and Person E is on Boat A* is represented by the connectives as:

```
ON [DA] ^ ON [EA]
```

Remember that when we assert a fact in predicate calculus, its value must be either true or false.

Figure 12.8
Predicate calculus representation for information on a boat with two persons on it.

Predicate Name

(IS-A E PERSON)
(IS-A D PERSON)
(IS-A A BOAT)
(IS-A C MOTOR-BOAT)
(IS-A B BOAT-BOW)

(PART-OF B A)
(PART-OF C A)
(ON D A)
(ON E A)

Table 12.1   Rules About Getting to School on Time

Rule	Premise (IF)		Conclusion (THEN)
1	Distance > 2 miles	→	Mode is "drive"
2	Distance > 1 mile and time < 30 minutes	→	Mode is "drive"
3	Distance > 1 mile and time > 30 minutes	→	Mode is "bus"
4	Mode is "drive" and location is "North Campus"	→	Action is "ride a bike"
5	Mode is "drive" and location is not "North Campus"	→	Action is "drive your car"
6	Mode is "bus" and weather is rain	→	Action is "take a coat and ride the bus"
7	Mode is "bus" and weather is "clear"	→	Action is "bus"

Drawing Inferences

In order for a system to reason, it must be capable of inferring new facts from what it has already been told. This means creating new symbol structures from the old ones. After we select a method for representing knowledge in the knowledge base, the next step is to draw **inferences** (logical conclusions) based on the data. To illustrate, Table 12.1 is a knowledge base that represents facts and rules about getting to school on time. Rule 1 is, "If school is more than two miles away, then, you should drive." Rule 2 is, "If distance is more than one mile and you have less than 30 minutes to get to school, then you should still drive." Rule 4 is, "If school is North Campus and getting to school is by driving, then the action is to ride a bike." The conclusion that we "ride a bike" if the premise of rule 4 is true results from deriving new facts from existing rules and known facts. It is a rule of inference used in proof procedures and an intuitive way of conducting reasoning.

Expert Languages

Knowledge engineering means forming and assembling knowledge and the tools that make this possible. Whatever programming language is chosen, an expert system requires two components: an inference engine and a body of rules. The preferred strategy is to consider the rules first and express them in an appropriate language. Each rule must then satisfy a set of conditions to be usable.

There are several layers of software between the computer hardware and the human problem domain. The first task in building an expert system is to decide on a software package that will assist or replace the expert in a domain. Figure 12.9 illustrates the levels of software spanning the hardware-problem domain range. The most primitive software level is machine language. Most of today's programming is written in high-level languages.

PROLOG (PROgramming Language for LOGic)

The best known dialect in logic programming is **PROLOG**. The popularity of logic programming has been motivated by a Japanese fifth-generation project that uses PROLOG and relational data management. PROLOG was initially developed in 1972 by A. Colmerauer and P. Roussel of the University of Marseilles (France). This language is suitable as an implementation language for expert systems.

Programming in PROLOG involves three steps:

1. Specify *facts* about objects and their relationships.
2. Specify the *rules* about objects and their relationships.
3. *Ask questions* about objects and their relationships.

The database contains the facts and rules relevant to a problem. To solve the problem, the user asks questions as to whether certain relationships are true. The characters

```
?-
```

are displayed on the screen to mean, "I am ready to answer your questions."

To illustrate PROLOG, let us say that Dave likes Ann. We have two objects (Dave and Ann) and a relationship with a particular order: Dave likes Ann, but not necessarily Ann likes Dave. The statement "Dave likes Ann" is written in PROLOG as a fact:

```
likes(dave,ann).
```

The following remarks are noteworthy:

1. The relationship (likes) is written first; the objects are written inside parentheses and separated by a comma. A lowercase letter begins each object or relationship.
2. Each fact ends with a period.
3. The sequence of the objects must be written the same everywhere in the PROLOG program. In our example, *dave* is the owner object and *ann* is second. They should be in that sequence.

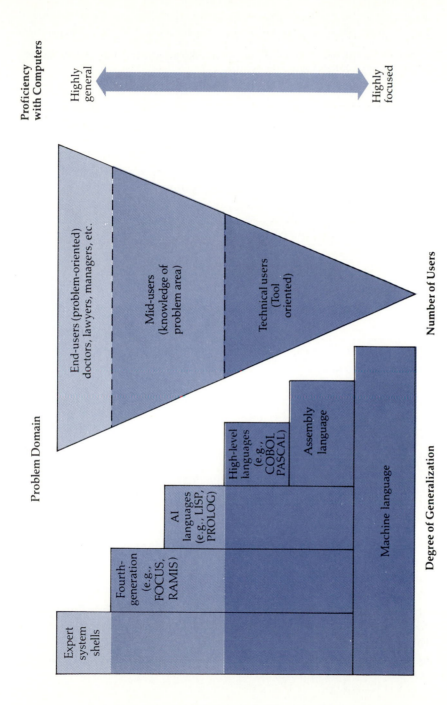

Figure 12.9
Software levels between the computer hardware/language and the user's problem domain.

4. The objects inside the parentheses (dave, ann) are called the **arguments** and the name of the relationship (likes) is called a **predicate**. In our example of a fact, we have one predicate and two arguments.

Once the facts are collected, we can ask questions. For example, we enter "Does Dave like Ann?" as follows:

?- | `likes(dave,ann).` |

PROLOG searches in the database for facts that match the question. There will be a match if the predicate and the arguments are the same. In our example, the answer is *yes*. If the arguments are reversed; that is,

?- | `likes(ann,dave).` | , the answer will be *NO*. This means

there is no fact in the database where Ann likes Dave.

We can use variables to represent objects that could not be named at the time the PROLOG program was written. For example, we may ask:

?- | `likes(dave,X).` |

meaning "What is it that Dave likes?"

In the database, one fact matches the question. It is:

`likes(dave,ann)`

So PROLOG would print:

| `X=ann.` |

When the fact *X is ann* is found, the variable X is said to be **instantiated** to Ann. This means that X has an instance—Ann. Consequently, any occurrence of X in the question is substituted by Ann.

Rules   Facts are often expressed in the form of rules. In our illustration, it would be easier to store a rule about what Dave likes rather than listing all those whom he likes. Suppose we wish to store a rule that Dave likes X on condition that X likes mangos. This is actually a two-part rule separated by : | `:-` | as follows:

| `likes(dave,X) :- likes(X,mangos).` |

The meaning is:

Dave likes X if X likes mangos.

Let us take another example: We have X and Y. X is the classmate of Y provided X is male and X and Y are in the same course. The definition is written as a PROLOG rule as follows:

```
classmate(X,Y) :-course(X,Z), course(Y,Z),
```

Facts pertaining to this rule might be as follows:

```
course(dave,science),
course(ann,science),
course(john,database),
```

The single rule along with these three facts allows us to ask questions about certain relationships about a certain classmate. For example,

1. ?- `classmate(dave,ann),`

   yes

   (It is a fact that Dave is a classmate of Ann. They take a science course.)

2. ?- `classmate(X,Y),`

   X = dave, Y = ann

Tools and Applications

Early Systems

Once expert languages began to be applied, various tools and applications appeared. Expert tools are arbitrarily divided into early pre-1980 systems that were primarily medical tools and those appearing since 1980. Table 12.2 summarizes key early systems. The first large expert system to perform at the level of a human expert was MYCIN. It is a medical diagnosis application that provides advice comparable to that of a physician who specializes in bacteremia and meningitis infections.

Commercial Systems

Expert systems for business have emerged since the early 1980s. Some products run on personal computers and have less than 400 rules. Larger systems contain between 500 and several thousand rules. A representative sample of commercial products is summarized in Table 12.3. Recent

Table 12.2 Early Expert Systems

	DENDRAL	MACSYMA	HEARSAY III	MYCIN	PROSPECTOR	PUFF
Developer/data introduced	Stanford 1965	MIT 1969	Carnegie-Mellon 1978	Stanford 1975	Stanford Research Institute 1978	Stanford 1979
Features/purpose	Used by chemists to determine probable molecular structures (organic chemistry)	Mathematical problem-solver for algebra, calculus, differential equations, etc.	Demonstrates possibility of a speech understanding system	Medical diagnosis for bacteremia (infections that involve bacteria in the blood) and meningitis infections	The electronic geologist; geological site evaluation system	Small-scale decision aid; diagnosis of obstructive airway diseases
Input data needed	Histogram giving mass number of intensity pairs	Formulas or commands (interactive)	Speech wave	Interview questions to physicians to make diagnoses and therapy recommendations	Geological survey data	Instruments
Output produced	Description of the structure of the compound	Solutions to complex symbolic problems	List of hypotheses of what was said	A set of diagnoses and therapy recommendations	Maps and site evaluations	Printout to physicians to review and followup

Table 12.3 Selected Expert Systems Products

Name of System	Features/Tasks	Developer
· ACUMEN	Evaluate psychological characteristics in terms of management theory	Human Factors Advanced Technology Group
· AIRLINE SEAT ADVISOR	Allots discount fares to flights	Sperry (Intellicorp)
· COCOMO 1	Assists in planning and scheduling software development projects	Level Five Research
· DRILLING ADVISOR	Advises oil drilling crew about problems	Tecknowledge, Inc.
· EXPERT/EASE	Small knowledge decision-making spreadsheet	Expert Software International (Scotland)
· FINANCIAL ADVISOR	Help managers in analyzing capital investment proposals	Palladian Software
· MATERIAL HANDLING	Material handling and scheduling discount manufacturing areas	EXON
· MORE	Identifies potential buyers from mailing list	Persoft, Inc.
· PERFORMANCE MENTOR	Guides managers in shaping the performance of subordinates	AI Mentor, Inc.
· PLANT SAFETY ADVISOR	Advises managers on appropriate safety procedures	Stone & Webster Engineering
· THE REQUIREMENTS ANALYST	Helps accounts choose software for their specific needs	Computer Training Services
· WAREHOUSE PLANNER	Helps in automated warehousing	Hitachi

systems focus on commercial applications and are more efficient than earlier systems. Large-scale proprietory systems such as Drilling Advisor are a growing area in many corporations. A rapidly expanding market for small expert systems (50–200 rules) that run on the personal computer is also a definite trend.

Implications for MIS

What implications do expert systems have for the manager? Expert systems are a carryover of previous efforts to extend the manager's ability to understand the business and control its processes. In fact, they extend the thinking range of managers. With expert systems, managers can begin to use facts and rules to structure complex human problems, extending the realm of the possible.

Table 12.4   MIS Dimensions and Their Characteristics

	MIS Dimensions		
Role	*Data Processing Systems*	*Decision Support Systems*	*Expert Systems*
Purpose	Doing things right	Doing things well	Doing the right thing
Machine role	Automate, compute	Organize, simplify	Enhancing the reasoning power of the human mind
User role	Operate machine	Work faster and more efficiently	Work more intelligently and wisely
Designer	Electronics engineer	Systems analyst/ programmer	Knowledge engineer
Knowledge/ discipline	Electronic engineering; computer science	Languages, system science, ergonomics	Information science, AI
Software	Machine languages	Command languages	Natural (human) language
Memory	Magnetic tape, disk	Databases, computer programs	Heuristic knowledge, expert experience
Input	Electrical signals	Data (unprocessed information)	Information
Output	Electrical signals	Information	Solve problems, provide new knowledge

Horton, 1984, ID7–11.

Expert systems are earning a reputation for expanding the scope of information systems to add new applications and leverage old ones. In many contexts, a small amount of embedded knowledge may drastically relieve the amount of processing for an answer. This means that managers can begin to tackle badly structured problems for solutions that improve the competitive edge for the firm.

Managers are also beginning to recognize that certain problems that once depended heavily on human intelligence cannot be reliably supported forever. People retire, transfer, or simply leave the organization for other opportunities. Artificial intelligence is more permanent, easy to transfer, consistent, and affordable. Therefore, the challenge for managers is to select the critical problems that are candidates for expert systems and determine their solution through this technology.

In the changing MIS environment, future users will not want updated information. They will want knowledge. The days of wading through reams of reports and statistics are now being replaced by viewing windows on a screen showing the critical components of the problem and the consequences for each alternative. Table 12.4 summarizes the shift from data processing to DSS to expert systems and their respective characteristics.

We may foresee potential uses of combining database management systems and expert systems for modern business applications. The large body of facts usually required for large applications can be made available to an expert system through existing DBMSs. The DBMS as a part of MIS can also be used more intelligently if it is coupled with expert system features. A higher level of semantic knowledge and deductive capabilities built into the database would make an MIS more user friendly, user supportive, and more efficient in operating a business than a conventional database environment.

Summary

- Natural language interfaces provide users a wide range of capabilities. End users need not be familiar with the technical characteristics of the DBMS to query databases. Natural language interfaces eliminate the need for syntax learning.

- The entire research effort, including robotics and decision-making systems, has proved instrumental in solving problems and making decisions in business. Artificial intelligence (AI) has the capability of tackling logical as well as numerical problems. This includes searching for a solution, generating and testing solutions, and reasoning backward from a specified goal, and the like.

- Artificial intelligence is taking on jobs that humans consider intelligent. These include the capability to learn from experience, understanding and speaking natural language rather than traditional computer commands, and assessing information and drawing a new conclusion.

- A major development in AI has been the *expert system*. It uses the computer's capabilities to manipulate natural language that communicates with a human expert in some field and asks questions. The computer builds the data obtained during the questioning into memory that is later used by a lesser expert. The computer can retrieve the answers as well as providing the line of reasoning that led to its answers.

- AI may be divided into three categories:
  1. *Natural language:* computer programs capable of reading, speaking, or understanding human language.
  2. *Robotics:* smart robots that can do human chores in industry and ones that can move and relate to objects as humans.
  3. *Expert systems:* programs that use symbolic knowledge to mimic the decision-making and problem-solving thought processes of human

experts. They are problem-solving programs designed to solve difficult problems requiring expertise.

▫ Expert systems embody several fundamental qualities:
1. *Expertise:* using high-level rules and high quality performance in minimal time.
2. *Reasoning by symbol manipulation:* representation of knowledge in its domain of concern.
3. *Exhibit a generally intelligent behavior:* a product of the principles the system knows and the level of detail at which it knows them.
4. *Conversion to expert rules:* changing over from a description in layman's terms to a form appropriate for processing by expert rules.
5. *Reasoning abilities about its own processes:* reconstructs the inference paths the expert system must have taken to arrive at its conclusion.

▫ Those who build expert systems are called knowledge engineers. Expert systems are built by interviewing a known expert and capturing his/her knowledge—hence, expert systems. The knowledge engineer replicates the behavior of an expert in solving a narrowly defined problem.

▫ Expert systems adopt symbolic programming—quite different than conventional programming. Conventional programming uses a numerically addressed database, maintained by programmers. Symbolic programming uses a symbolically structured knowledge base, maintained by knowledge engineers and experts.

▫ The architecture of an expert system consists of the knowledge base and the inference engine. The *knowledge base* has the unstructured set of facts and the inference rules for determining new facts. The object is a common representation that is associated with other objects, using links in the memory. The *inference engine* stands between the user and the knowledge base. It contains inference strategies and controls for manipulating the facts and rules.

▫ A popular way to represent knowledge is by a semantic network or nodes linked together to form a net. A major advantage of a net is inheritance, or instances of one class having properties of more general classes of which they are members.

▫ In addition to semantic knowledge, rules, frames, logic, and connectives are used for representing relationships. A *rule* is a conditional statement that specifies an action to be taken. A *frame,* like a rule, helps describe the syntax of the knowledge base. *Logic* is a system that prescribes rules for manipulating symbols. A *connective* links predicates into large expressions.

▫ A widely used AI tool is PROLOG, which employs a simplified version of predicate calculus and is the closest to a true logical language. Programming in PROLOG involves three steps: specifying facts about objects and their relationships, specifying the rules about objects and their relationships, and asking questions about objects and their relationships. To solve a problem, the user asks questions about whether certain relationships are true. PROLOG searches the database for facts that match the question.

□ The first large expert system was MYCIN—a medical diagnosis application. Recent (post-1980) systems focus on commercial applications using PROLOG to a large scale.

Key Terms

Argument	Link
Artificial intelligence (AI)	Logic
Connective	Natural language
Descriptor	Node
Expert system	Object
Fifth-generation computer	Predicate
Frame	Premise
Heuristics	PROLOG
Inference	Rule
Inference engine	Slot
Inheritance	Symbol
Instantiate	Symbolic programming
Knowledge base	Term
Knowledge engineer	

Review Questions

1. In what way is natural language a step ahead of DBMS and DSS? Explain.

2. What is artificial intelligence? Elaborate on its scope, function, and categories.

3. Distinguish between:
   a. Intelligence and expertise
   b. Conventional and symbolic programming
   c. Knowledge base and database
   d. Knowledge base and inference engine

4. There are arguments for and against computer "intelligence." Discuss.

5. Summarize briefly the historical developments in AI.

6. Explain the major categories of AI. How do they contribute to problem solving?

7. Elaborate on the basic qualities of expert systems.

8. How does a knowledge engineer attempt to replicate an expert's behavior in problem solving?

9. "Expert systems are knowledge-intensive computer programs that use heuristics to focus on key aspects of a specific problem." Do you agree? Explain.

10. Review the major differences between expert systems and conventional programming.

11. The architecture of an expert system consists of the knowledge base and the inference engine. How do these components work together to solve problems?

12. Distinguish between:
    a. Object and link
    b. Physical object and conceptual entity
    c. Rule and frame

13. In your own words, explain how knowledge is represented.

14. What forms a semantic network? Illustrate.

15. How does a link relate to nodes and descriptors? Illustrate.

16. In what respect is predicate calculus important in expert system development?

17. A connective is used to link predicates into large expressions. Illustrate.

18. Elaborate on the role of the inference engine for drawing inferences.

19. Explain fully the basic principle behind PROLOG. What features does it offer? How well is it gaining ground for business problem solving?

20. In your own words, elaborate on the role of expert systems in business and their potential for MIS development.

Application Problems

1. The Japanese are quite confident they will build a fifth-generation computer by 1991. Some forty computer engineers at Tokyo's Institute for New Generation Computer Technology (ICOT) have already developed an algorithm for the natural recognition of the syntax. Other engineers have already developed a logic programming language, "VERSION 0," and are close to building a sequential inference machine, a

large computer that crunches logic (instead of numbers) at a rate of 20,000 logic inferences per second (lips).

ICOT has received government funds of over $60 million since 1982. One of the project's goals is to achieve a system capable of making inferences, like an artificial brain. So far, ICOT has developed an advanced logic programming language, called FGKL (Fifth Generation Kernel Language) for parallel inferences. The advanced version of FGKL should be developed by late 1988, combining parallel inferences with the knowledge base. For knowledge-base development, ICOT will develop a relational database management system capable of accepting questions, searching the database, and producing an answer. A prototype system is being built (Inaba, 1983).

QUESTIONS

a. What aspects of ICOT's work are characteristic of artificial intelligence? Explain.
b. Search the literature and assess the research carried out by universities and firms in the U.S. that compete with ICOT's research.
c. How do you foresee this type of research affecting U.S. business? Elaborate.

2. TAXADVISOR, developed in 1982, performs a consultant's role. It uses rules of thumb to decide on a planning alternative such as purchase of a gas shelter for a client. The system's main purpose is to arrange a client's financial affairs in a way that will minimize income and death taxes, but not at the expense of adequate insurance or sound investment. Actions such as life insurance, retirement planning, and tax shelters and others are considered.

The system interacts with a human tax consultant (not a client) as follows:

a. A heading is displayed to inform the consultant of the questions, contexts.
b. The system asks questions about the client in need of tax advice. The consultant types in the responses—yes or no.
c. When the system acquires enough information, it displays a recommendation on the terminal screen. When the consultation is completed, a summary list of recommendations is produced.

The questions and recommendations are generated by "if-then" rules. TAXADVISOR contains 275 rules. It decides by proceeding in a deductive manner, as do human decision makers, starting with the system's general goal and moving down the tree in search of recommendations for the client.

QUESTIONS

a. Is TAXADVISOR an expert system?
b. If the system asks too many questions, does it suggest anything negative about its performance? Elaborate.

Selected References

Aleksander, Igor. *Designing Intelligent Systems: An Introduction.* New York: UNI-PUB 1984.

Bates, Madeleine and Bobrow, Robert. "Natural Language Interfaces: What's Here, What's Coming, and Who Needs It." In *Artificial Intelligence Applications for Business,* Proceedings of the NYU Symposium, Walter Reitman, ed., May 1983, 180.

Brachman, R. J., Amarel, Saul, Engelman, Carl, Engelmore, Robert S., Feigenbaum, Edward A., and Wilkins, David. "What Are Expert Systems?" In Hayes-Roth, Frederick, D. A., Waterman, and D. B. Lenat, eds., *Building Expert Systems.* Reading, Mass.: Addison-Wesley, 1983, 47.

Buchanan, B. G. "New Research on Expert Systems." In J. E. Hayes, D. Michie, and J. H. Pao, eds., *Machine Intelligence,* vol. 10. Edinburgh Univ. Press, 269–299.

Clancey, W. J. "Knowledge Acquisition for Classification of Expert Systems." *Proceedings of the ACM 1984 Conference,* October, 1984, 11–14.

Clocksin, W. F. and Mellish, C. S. *Programming in PROLOG.* New York: Springer Verlag, 1984.

Cowart, Robert and Robyns, Ann. "Artificial Intelligence Enriches Programmers' Languages." *PC World,* August 27, 1985, 45–64.

Duda, R. O. and Shortleiffe, E. H. "Expert Systems Research." *Science* 1983.

Elmer-Dewitt, Philip. "How to Clone an Expert." *Time,* September 2, 1985, 44–45.

Feigenbaum, Edward A. and McCorduck, Pamela. *The Fifth Generation.* Reading, Mass.: Addison-Wesley, 1983.

Fersko-Weiss, Henry. "The Intelligent Computer." *Personnel Computing,* October 1985, 62–63ff.

Frenkel, Karen A. "Toward Automating the Software-Development Cycle." *Communications of the ACM,* June 1985, 580.

Harris, Larry R. "Fifth Generation Foundations." *Datamation,* July 1983, 148–150ff.

Harmon, Paul and King, David, *Artificial Intelligence in Business.* New York: John Wiley & Sons, 1985.

Hayes-Roth, Frederick, "The Industrialization of Knowledge Engineering." Proceedings of the NYU Symposium, May 1983, 2.

Hayes-Roth, Frederick, Waterman, Donald A. and Lenat, Douglas. "An Overview of Expert Systems." In Hayes-Roth, Frederick, Waterman, Donald A. and Lenat, Douglas B. *Building Expert Systems,* New York: Addison-Wesley, 1983, 3–29.

Horton, Forest Woody Jr. "Software's New Dimension." *Computerworld,* June 25, 1984

Horwitt, Elizabeth. "Exploring Expert Systems." *Business Computer Systems,* March 1985, 48–49ff.

Inaba, Minoru. "Japan: We'll Have Fifth-Generation CPU by 1991." *MIS Week,* November 30, 1983.

Kinnucan, Paul. "Computers that Think Like Experts." *High Technology,* January 1984, 30–71.

Lee, Ronald M. "Information System Semantics: A Logic-Based Approach." *Journal of Management Information Systems*, July 1986, 7–10.

O'Shea, Tim and Eisenstadt, Marc. *Artificial Intelligence: Tools, Techniques, and Applications.* Philadelphia: Harper & Row, 1984, 22–62.

Rauch-Hindin, Wendy. *Artificial Intelligence in Business, Science, and Industry.* Vol. 1, *Fundamentals.* Englewood Cliffs, N.J.: Prentice-Hall, 1986.

Tomeski, Edward A. and Klahr, Michael. "How Artificial Intelligence Has Developed." *Journal of Systems Management*, May 1986, 6–10.

Von Limbach, Geoffrey and Taylor, Michael B. "Expert System Rules Read Natural Languages." *Systems & Software*, August 1984, 119–125.

Waterman, James A. *A Guide to Expert Systems.* Reading, Mass.: Addison-Wesley, 1986.

Webster, Robin and Miner, Leslie. "Expert Systems: Programming Problem Solving." *Technology,* January/February 1982, 62–72.

Williamson, Michey. *Artificial Intelligence for Microcomputers: The Guide for Business Decision Makers.* Philadelphia: Brady, 1985.

Woods, W. A. "Natural Communication with Machines: An Ongoing Goal." In Walter Reitman, *Artificial Intelligence Applications for Business.* Norwood, N.J.: Ablex, 1984.

PART IV

APPLICATION PLANNING AND SYSTEM DEVELOPMENT

MIS Planning

Chapter Contents

Planning Amid Change

THE SPEED OF CHANGE at Pfizer has been so rapid that systems management decided to focus on the planning process and the ability to manage change instead of writing a static long-range plan. To begin with, the senior systems managers went off site for three days in order to initiate a program for systems planning. They established certain guidelines for the planning process: identify users, define objectives, identify the issues to be managed by systems planning, group them into the strategies required, and implement a program of managed change.

The commitment of senior systems managers to the planning process came in response to their need to articulate an almost-formed vision. The managers' focus on this vision transformed the whole process from reaction to proaction. Their proactive approach transformed the role of systems management from satisfying the aggregate need of all end users to one of leading the organization in the adaptation of technology to its greatest advantage.

The planning process was initiated to correct the inability to communicate the proactive vision of senior systems management. The first day was devoted to brainstorming the issues. How could documents be transferred between Wang word processors and IBM personal computers? Was electronic mail here to stay? Who was going to call the shots on what cables to install in the office buildings? Ultimately, conversation halted with, "Look, we've got to define who the audience is, or we'll never be able to write anything down."

And so the group systematically identified the various audiences the plan would serve.

The next stage in the process was to develop an action plan for each domain. Planners developed these plans over several weeks, using a draft document to record their decisions. Drafting the plan not only identified myriad issues but also explicitly identified just whose cooperation and support was needed, which in turn led to a plan to secure that cooperation.

Initially, the systems staff, the next group of users to be involved, were not uniformly persuaded of the plan's benefits. Indeed, it was not until management presented the first formal annual update, coupled with a review of progress to date, that the plan gained the systems staff's enthusiastic support. The plan concluded with a review of existing and anticipated projects. For each project there was a discussion of the objectives, benefits, implementation plan, and resources to be applied. The strategies developed in the remainder of the plan provided the infrastructure for the whole set of projects.

With so much resolved in one year, systems managers are now able to appreciate new opportunities and new strategies. They believe they have defined a way of translating and combining a mixture of theoretical underpinnings, technological opportunities and a hazy vision into the process of managing change.

—*Excerpted from Vita Cassese, William Gruber, and Max Huges,* Computerworld, *December 9, 1985, 71ff.*

AT A GLANCE

Today's emerging technology dictates that the MIS manager must plan to deal with a crisis-oriented environment. As the MIS function assumes a more central role within organizations, strategic MIS planning becomes more vital to ensure that the role played by MIS is in line with that of the business organization.

In planning information systems, we need to specify the organization's mission, its goals, strategies, and policies. These elements must be seriously considered before the MIS function can set clear objectives and determine policies and decisions.

At the MIS level, planning has undergone four stages of development: initiation, expansion, control, and integration. MIS planning is carried out within the organization's overall plan. Broad corporate strategic objectives should be the basis for system development objectives that determine the operating goals of the system.

MIS planning emphasizes a three-stage model consisting of strategic planning, organizational information requirements analysis, and resource allocation planning. Each stage has its own methodologies.

By the end of this chapter, you should know:

1. The makeup of organizational planning
2. The nature and dimensions of planning
3. How corporate and MIS plans are linked together
4. The importance of the three-stage planning model
5. Commonly used methodologies in MIS planning

Introduction

The complexity of today's information technology requires planning for success. Planning makes it possible to identify objectives, goals, and strategic options. **Planning** may be defined as an ongoing organizational function that provides the framework for activities at all levels. A plan is a basis for action. In order to imbed information systems into organizations, planning must be an integral part of system development (Kotteman and Konsynski, 1985, 46).

In Chapter 14 we will find that launching a systems project requires an MIS master plan backed by management. Such a plan must also cut across the entire system development life cycle. Therefore, understanding the MIS planning function and how it relates to organizational planning ensures proper fit for system performance.

Too often, MIS managers have been forced to deal with routine, day-to-day activities. As a result, planning has taken a back seat to managing a crisis-oriented environment. With today's emerging technology, how-ever—office automation, personal computers, and so forth—the days of "firefighting" are gone. As the MIS function assumes a more central function in organizations, planning becomes increasingly vital. This chapter discusses the nature and role of MIS planning and its relationship to overall organizational planning.

The Components of Organizational Planning

Planning is a formal approach to deciding in advance what action to take for achieving a goal. A formal plan guides activities and offers several advantages. It:

1. Encourages an organization to act rather than react.
2. Helps top management take advantage of opportunities.
3. Provides a basis for measuring performance.
4. Provides early indication of various needs.
5. Trains management to think for the future.

The process of planning and managing information systems involves a number of components: mission, goals, strategies, policies, and deci-sions. Taken together, they make up strategic planning (see Figure 13.1).

Mission

Every organization exists to accomplish something in the larger environ-ment. A mission is future oriented—a long-run vision of what the orga-nization is trying to become. A planner asks, "What activities should the organization carry out to attain its goal(s)?" The **mission** of an organi-zation thus consists of the well-defined directions in which it elects to concentrate its efforts. For example, the mission of a university may be to provide a high-quality education or, more specifically, to develop the best-trained graduates in arts and sciences in the nation.

An organization deciding to change its mission to adapt to changes in the environment can have a fundamental impact on its future activities or growth. For example, the OPEC (Organization of Petroleum Exporting Countries) action in 1973 caused many oil firms to consider a change in their mission from the production and marketing of oil products to the supply of energy through coal, solar energy, and the like. The impact of such a change on the image, behavior, and operation of the organization as a whole is easily observable. Therefore, with a clear understanding of the mission (scope of activities it will engage in) and the goals (where the organization is heading), planners can select the strategies (routes) to take for making decisions (see Figure 13.1).

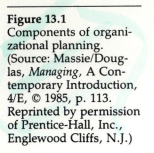

Figure 13.1
Components of organi-
zational planning.
(Source: Massie/Doug-
las, *Managing*, A Con-
temporary Introduction,
4/E, © 1985, p. 113.
Reprinted by permission
of Prentice-Hall, Inc.,
Englewood Cliffs, N.J.)

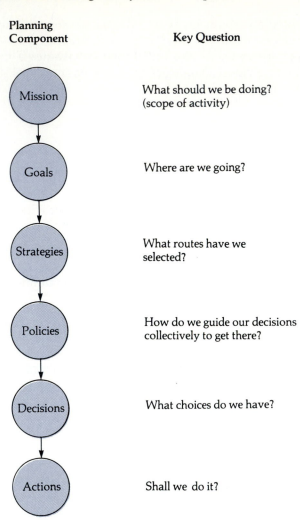

Planning Component	Key Question
Mission	What should we be doing? (scope of activity)
Goals	Where are we going?
Strategies	What routes have we selected?
Policies	How do we guide our decisions collectively to get there?
Decisions	What choices do we have?
Actions	Shall we do it?

Goals

A **goal** is an ultimate end toward which effort is aimed. A retail store may decide on profit as a goal. It may also have multiple goals—one goal, to provide instant information to customers; another, to reduce response to customer inquiries without increasing the number of personnel. These two goals are actually subgoals that jointly serve to improve the profitability of the store.

An organization chooses goals based on the needs of the environment (in our example, from customers). The goal of installing an information system must then be set within the overall goal of serving the needs of the environment. Once goals are identified, planning can be developed to control performance.

Goals and objectives are closely related. An **objective** is management's *intention* to accomplish its mission, while a goal is a *statement* of specifics that quantify the objective. For example, one objective might be to "maximize return on investment"; the goal would be to "achieve 15 percent return by 1988 (currently 8%)." Objectives, then, may be viewed as general statements of what is to be done, whereas goals are the quantification of objectives (e.g., how much, by whom, etc.)

Strategies

When an organization has formulated its mission and specified its goals, it should know where it wants to go. The next planning task is to develop a strategy or a "grand design" to get there. A **strategy** identifies the general approach that directs how goals are achieved. In contrast, **tactics** are specific guidelines used to implement strategies. For example, a bank's market penetration strategy is to get depositors to use the new automated teller machines (ATMs). A tactical approach is to install ATMs in shopping plazas on a 24-hour-a-day basis.

The choice of a strategy depends on the organization's mission and its distinctive abilities. In our example, the bank's mission is service to customers; the strategy of getting depositors to use ATMs is designed to provide the ultimate service—24 hours per day.

Policies Plans are implemented primarily through policies. Unlike strategies, which deal with the activities of the organization and its environment, **policies** are guidelines to make decisions within the organization. They are longstanding decisions that specify how the organization should accomplish its mission. For example, an organization may adopt a policy of "maintaining a healthy work environment." This policy is implemented through rules. For example, rules that prohibit employees from smoking on the premises uphold the healthy work environment policy.

In summary, planning consists of determining the mission of the organization and identifying its goals, strategies, and policies for decision making. Once specified, MIS planning may be carried out within the framework of the organization's strategic plan.

Bases for MIS Planning

Starting with a plan is a practical way to develop information systems. As early as 1916, planning was a natural and intrinsic part of managing business. The pattern of this functional element of management was first set by the French industrialist Henri Fayol (1949), who referred to planning as one of the five key functions of management along with organizing, command, coordination, and control.

The importance of MIS planning has become apparent in recent years for other reasons:

1. There has been a growing realization among managers that MIS is an emerging tool for competitive advantage. This new awareness has motivated organizations to include planning for information systems to achieve competitive dominance (Benjamin et al., 1984).

2. The investment level in MIS has increased significantly because of the proliferation of products and support based on the new generation of computers and telecommunication technology. Organizations will continue investing not only in efficiency-based products and services (e.g., word processing, data processing, etc.), but also in effectiveness-oriented products and services such as artificial intelligence for sharpening their competitive edge. Such a commitment requires systematic planning (Venkatraman, 1985–86, 67).

3. Decisions affecting the MIS function have organization-wide impact. For example, MIS installations influence personnel recruitment, turnover, and motivation. For this reason MIS planning must be coordinated with personnel planning.

4. Information systems that are complex, require a long time to build, use common databases, or have a greater competitive edge require formal, long-range planning (McLean and Soden, 1977, 6).

In developing formal planning, it is important to consider the planners, the planning process, and the plan itself. As we will find later in the chapter, planning involves process, people, and technology. To be successful, MIS planning must be carried out within the larger framework of corporate planning.

Evolutionary Stages in Planning

Managers have always shied away from the rigors of planning. Planning is hard work, not readily rewarding, detracts from operating the business, and does not quite fall within the mindset of Type A managers. Type A managers are known to be aggressive, action oriented, impatient with procedures that do not have immediate payoff, and self-serving—always in a rush. Therefore, they show an expected block toward the planning function (Warrick et al., 1985, 88ff).

The 1960s were characterized by a negative organizational environment for planning. The 1970s saw the emergence of an improved (although still largely indifferent) attitude toward planning. The early 1980s initiated what Kanter (1982) calls **action planning** that addresses the firm's key business directions. Whatever the cause, it has become evident that a manager's job is now dependent on the dual responsibility of meeting immediate goals and planning to meet future ones.

At the MIS level, planning has undergone four stages of growth:

1. Initiation
2. Expansion (contagion)
3. Control
4. Integration

The *initiation* phase is characterized by the emergence of **project planning**. It was a response to user dissatisfaction with early installations and the poor match between user requirements and system performance. Systems were almost never completed on schedule and cost more than the initial estimates. It was soon learned that setting delivery schedules, identifying milestones, and periodic project review produced better results than before.

The *expansion* or **contagion** phase represented heavy demand for computer use and a period of processing application backlogs. The concept of **capacity planning** was introduced to project future volume requirements based on current workload.

The *control* phase was a response to sharply increasing costs of data processing, prompting **resource planning**. This meant looking a year or so ahead and deciding on the hardware, software, and personnel needs to handle the growing number of computer applications.

The *integration* phase has focused on short-range planning and integration of applications. During the control stage, applications lacked the integration of databases, which made it difficult to coordinate information for decision making. This prompted long-range planning of three years or longer. Long-range planning is unique to the late 1970s and the 1980s in most firms.

The four development stages are based on Nolan's growth curve model, shown in Figure 13.2, which he subsequently expanded to six stages with the addition of data administration and maturity. On balance, it is a useful conceptual model that provides a framework for dealing with change and a guideline for MIS planning.

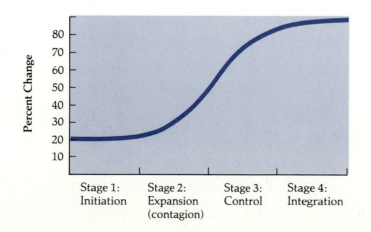

Figure 13.2
The initial Nolan four-stage model. (Adapted from Nolan, 1979).

Dimensions of MIS Planning

As we mentioned earlier, MIS planning must be done within the organization's overall MIS plan. The planning effort may be viewed from two dimensions:

1. The *time* dimension that specifies whether the plan is short term (under one year), medium term (one to three years), or long term (over three years)
2. The *focus* dimension that identifies the plan focus as strategic, managerial, or operational

Strategic Planning

Forward-looking executives recognize the importance of strategic planning to manage their organizations in a changing environment. Experience has shown that organizations that do an effective job of strategic planning fare best in a changing environment. **Strategic planning** is a formal approach that identifies the long-range objectives of the organization and the policies that govern how to achieve them. It is "a process that identifies the policies that can change the character or direction of the organization" (Anthony, 1965, 4).

Steiner defines strategic planning as: "an orderly process which, to oversimplify, sets forth basic objectives, and tactical plans to make sure that strategies are properly implemented" (1983, 12–17).

Figure 13.3 is a conceptual model of the structure and process of strategic planning. It illustrates how the process of comprehensive corporate planning can be carried out. In a subsequent "report card," Steiner

Figure 13.3
Structure and process of business planning. (Source: Steiner, McLean and Soden, 1977, 34.)

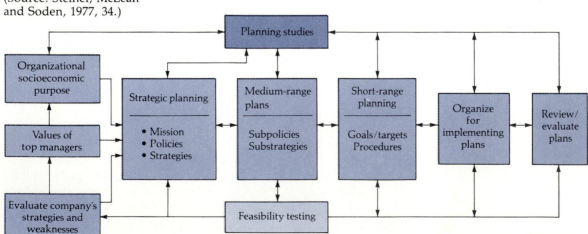

Table 13.1   Hallmarks of a Good Planning System

Criterion	Score
1. Strategic planning throughout entire management process	8
2. Top executive's personal commitment and responsibility	8
3. Clear identification of purposes of strategic planning; well-designed system	5
4. Balance among intuition, judgments, values, and analytical processes	8
5. Congenial planning climate	6/7
6. Manager's conceptual skills; understanding and use of analytical tools	
(a) Strategic thinking	5/6
(b) Creative process	5
(c) Understanding of analytical tools	7
(d) Use of sophisticated quantitative models	8
7. Realistic appraisal of uncertainties	9
8. Line managers' acceptance and involvement	
(a) Top managers	8/9
(b) Middle managers	5
9. Focus on strategy formulation; but attention to current operations	8
10. Attention to effective implementation of strategies	7
11. Linkage of capital allocation to strategic planning	5
12. Appropriate management reward system	4
13. Organizational level and influence of staff planning director	7/8
14. Simple, flexible system of planning	7/8

From Steiner, 1983, 14.

assesses the strategic planning performance of the larger U.S. firms against a list of fourteen essential characteristics (criteria) for a first-rate strategic planning system. Each criterion is assigned a numerical grade on a scale of 1–10, where 1 is the lowest and 10 the highest grade possible. The results of the evaluation are shown in Table 13.1. Strategic planning, top management support, appraisal of uncertainties, and use of quantitative models were among the most important planning criteria.

We can see so far that strategic planning is a logical and systematic process that allows top management to reach an accord on the strategic issues of the firm. The planning process should encourage creativity, communicate plans throughout the organization, integrate planning and decision making, and build senior management support. The outcome is a strategic plan that helps the organization address major issues and capitalize on its strengths and potential. Other benefits include:

1. Integrating policies and functions throughout the organization.

2. Providing a *process* that identifies in advance what is to be done, when it should be done, and how to do it.
3. Documenting the expected impact of today's decisions.

Strategic Planning and Competitive Advantage   There is no point in having a strategy unless it provides a competitive edge. Information technology represents three major strategic views:

1. Developing efficient and effective organizational processes and achieving goals.
2. Creating competitive advantage by giving top management new ways to outperform the rivals.
3. Generating new business or choosing the industry to compete in, referred to as *business portfolio strategy* (Porter and Millar, 1985).

The three strategies are closely related to one another. For example, a commercial bank may install automated ATMs in plazas and branches. This network can improve the efficiency of customer service—an aspect of internal strategy. This makes it more difficult for customers to switch to other banks with fewer services, contributing to the competitive strategy of the bank. ATMs have also been known to capture deposits during off hours that could affect the bank portfolio strategy.

A number of authorities have emphasized the application of information technology to create competitive advantage. For example, Porter and Millar (1985) have discussed the strategic significance of information, using a value chain concept. This concept divides an organization's activities into separate value activities. A value activity is the most that a buyer is willing to pay for a product. As shown in Figure 13.4, Porter's value chain examines costs in all parts of the organization, from the support activities across the top half of the diagram to the primary functions in the vertical columns of the lower half. The value chain concept should help the firm quantify, in terms of value and margin (total value cost of performing value activities), whether it is doing well compared to its rivals. Once a company has determined where the costs are, it should choose a strategy to exploit its competitive advantage.

Initially, organizations used information technology for accounting and clerical functions and inventory control. Today, information technology permeates the value chain of operations, performs marketing, sales, service, and other value activities. It performs clerical as well as judgmental functions. It affects the competitive scope and reshapes the way products meet the consumer's needs. For example, a large appliance service shop in Miami uses a database containing the accumulated experience of the factory engineers to respond instantly to customer inquiries. Effects such as these help explain why information technology has acquired such a strategic significance.

It can be seen, then, that strategic MIS planning is crucial to helping the organization maintain a competitive advantage in the marketplace.

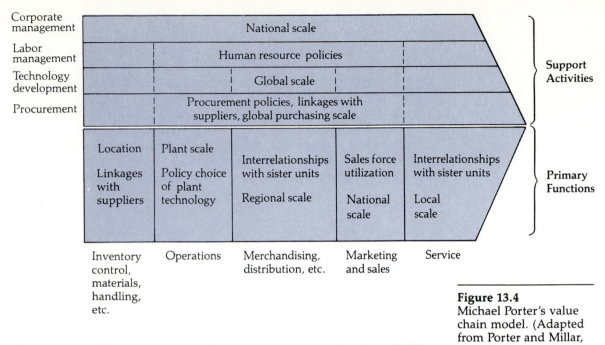

Corporate management	National scale			
Labor management	Human resource policies			
Technology development	Global scale			
Procurement	Procurement policies, linkages with suppliers, global purchasing scale			

| Location

Linkages with suppliers | Plant scale

Policy choice of plant technology | Interrelationships with sister units

Regional scale | Sales force utilization

National scale | Interrelationships with sister units

Local scale |
|---|---|---|---|---|
| Inventory control, materials, handling, etc. | Operations | Merchandising, distribution, etc. | Marketing and sales | Service |

Support Activities

Primary Functions

Figure 13.4
Michael Porter's value chain model. (Adapted from Porter and Millar, 1985, 151.)

MIS executives are also compelled to become more *proactive* than reactive to the organization's information needs.

Strategic and Long-Range Planning   There is an important difference between strategic and long-range MIS planning. Following Anthony's definition of strategic planning, *strategic MIS planning* is a process of deciding on both the objectives for the MIS division and the policies that govern the acquisition, use, and disposition of vital resources. In contrast, *long-range MIS planning* is concerned with the future MIS needs of the organization with a time horizon of three years or more.* It is not a focus on specific projects, but a plan for the future needs of the MIS organization. Related to long-term MIS planning is the *medium-range MIS planning* that deals with the organization's present MIS needs between two to three years in the future. The lowest level of planning is *short-range MIS planning* that handles budgets, schedules, and timetables for under one year.

There are several benefits of good long-range planning:

1. *Efficient allocation of corporate resources.* By determining in advance the priorities for MIS projects, resources can be allocated over a longer timeframe with greater success.

---

*The length of the planning horizon varies among industries. For example, utilities have a long-term planning of ten to twenty years, since they are capital intensive and take a long time to change plant size. In contrast, retailers are able to change image and store location every three to five years. The MIS long-range planning horizon usually is affected by the industry it operates.

2. *Improved user-analyst relations.* MIS installations that respond poorly to user inquiries create negative feelings that could affect future installations in the organization. Long-term planning encourages cooperation between users and designers in the planning process.

3. *Performance and profitability.* An MIS long-range plan facilitates coordination of future MIS activities, better utilization of personnel and resources, and improves the flow of information throughout the firm.

4. *A basis for control.* Because certain performance standards are specified in advance, the manager of the MIS project must know what must be done, who is to do it, and when it must be completed. Control of deadlines can be extremely critical.

Managerial and Operational Planning

Managerial planning is a process in which predefined functional plans show how strategies are implemented to achieve long-range plans. The next step is short-range or **operational planning** that specifies the day-to-day activities of the system. For example, the corporate strategic plan to eliminate labor-intensive activities is executed by having an operating expense and human resource budgets for each system proposal before building the system. The budgets are essentially short-range plans implementing the organization's master plan.

Linking Corporate and MIS Planning

In MIS planning, we identify three levels of analysis:

1. Planning at the application level, such as inventory control and check processing. Emphasis is on *information efficiency* for an individual system.
2. Individual systems to serve decision-making needs at all levels of the organization. Emphasis is on *information effectiveness* for an integrated system.
3. The *relationship* between the MIS plan and the organization's overall strategic plan. Emphasis is on the role of MIS and how it can be used for competitive advantage.

The third level of analysis is the most crucial for MIS development. Since a major purpose of information systems is to evaluate new opportunities for competitive advantage, it is essential to link MIS planning to corporate planning.

There are several issues to consider in MIS planning: First, we must ensure that system planning identifies the applications that fit the organizations priorities. Second, long-range MIS plans must also respond to

Stages of
Development

Personnel
Involved

Figure 13.5
The relationship be-
tween corporate strategic
planning and MIS
activities.

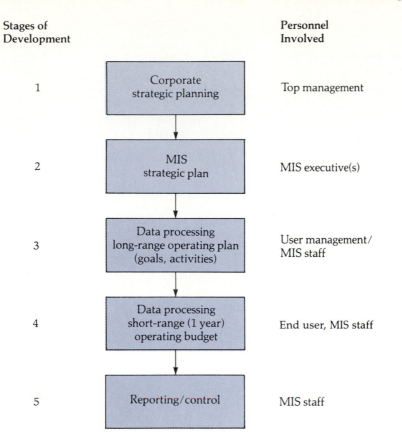

Stage	Box	Personnel
1	Corporate strategic planning	Top management
2	MIS strategic plan	MIS executive(s)
3	Data processing long-range operating plan (goals, activities)	User management/ MIS staff
4	Data processing short-range (1 year) operating budget	End user, MIS staff
5	Reporting/control	MIS staff

short-range applications. Finally, competing methodologies should be carefully selected for allocating system and operations resources in advance.

In a nutshell, corporate strategic objectives should be the basis for system development objectives which, in turn, determine the action plans. Figure 13.5 illustrates the relationship between a corporation's strategic plan and its MIS activities.

A Three-Stage MIS Planning Model

An MIS operational plan requires the heaviest day-to-day user involvement for defining system requirements. The important link between the organization's strategic plan and system development has been described in a three-stage planning model proposed by Bowman, Davis, and Wetherbe (1981). The MIS planning activities are: strategic MIS planning, organization information requirements analysis, and resource allocation.

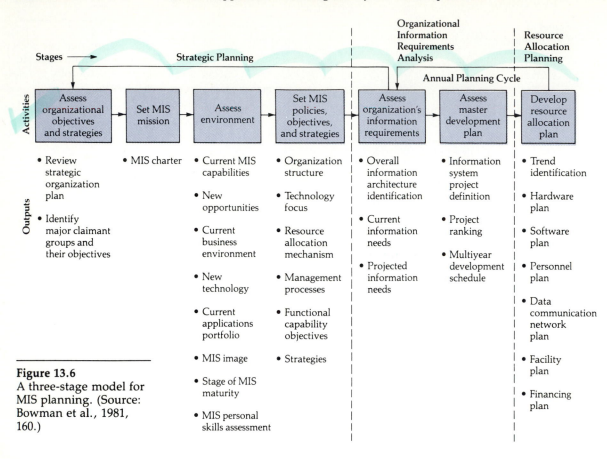

Figure 13.6
A three-stage model for MIS planning. (Source: Bowman et al., 1981, 160.)

Bowman, Davis, and Wetherbe identify the planning activities, their sequence, and the methodology used in their implementation (see Figure 13.6).

Strategic Planning

In MIS strategic planning, we create MIS goals and strategies that are in line with those of the organization. The outcome is an MIS charter for developing MIS projects.

Analysis of Organizational Information Requirements

Once goals and strategies have been specified, the next stage is to evaluate the organization's information requirements and the applications and databases to design for meeting the requirements. Related to this plan is a decision on the system project, a priority ranking of projects, and a development schedule or a timetable.

Resource Allocation Planning

The third planning stage of the model identifies the hardware, software, data communications, facilities, personnel, and financial resources for executing the development plan. The output is a resource allocation plan that includes hardware, software, communication network, personnel, and financial plans. Obviously, once a comprehensive planning model of this kind is implemented, it is unnecessary to execute it in all its phases for each planning cycle. Much depends on how quickly the organization's strategic plan is changing and how such changes impact information systems requirements.

MIS Planning Methodologies

The three-stage model is a useful conceptual framework for clarifying the requirements for MIS planning. Next, the plan is executed, using an appropriate methodology. Three of the most widely used methodologies are:

1. Strategic planning methodology
2. Corporate information requirements analysis methodologies
3. Resource allocation planning

Strategic Planning Methodology

The most difficult part of MIS planning is the procedure of deriving it from overall corporate strategic planning. There are specific methodologies that ensure proper transformation. One such methodology is King's (1978) "strategy set transformation." The process produces goals and strategies for the information system through four stages:

1. Identify the corporate strategy set. The starting point is the organization's strategic plan. If such a plan does not exist, then a strategy-set construction process identifies claimants (owners, managers, employees, competitors, etc.); defines goals, organizational purposes and strategies for each claimant group; and reviews the derived strategy set with top managers.
2. Transform the corporate strategy set into an MIS strategy set.
3. Construct alternative structures subject to MIS strategies and constraints.
4. Present alternatives to management.

To illustrate, a corporation's strategy to maintain profitability may be an improvement in customer merchandise delivery. An information system objective, then, is improving the speed of order taking. This can be translated into system design strategies such as "dry runs" for on-line order taking.

This methodology addresses the strategic planning phase of the three-stage model. Information analysts play a critical role by carefully enumerating the strategy-set elements and developing the chosen design for the overall architecture.

Corporate Information Requirements Analysis Methodologies

Several methodologies have been recently proposed for identifying corporate information requirements. Two of the most widely used are IBM's business systems planning or BSP (IBM, 1981; Zachman, 1982) and critical success factors or CSF (Rockart, 1979).

Business Systems Planning (BSP)   Business systems planning (BSP) is a systematic way of analyzing an organization in terms of its data classes, data elements, business processes and functions, and relating them to the information needs of the organization. The process translates business strategy into MIS. It also supports the goals and objectives of the business, addresses the needs of all levels of management, and provides consistency of information throughout the organization. The basic philosophy of BSP rests on three principles:

1. Top-down planning with bottom-up implementation
2. Management of data as a corporate resource
3. Oriented to business processes

The top-down principle presumes that information systems are an integral part of business, are critical to its overall effectiveness, and represent major investment of human and financial resources. Therefore, it is essential that they support the organization's true business needs and help in achieving its objectives. This concept is shown in Figure 13.7. The concept of managing data as a corporate resource is founded on the premise that data are of considerable overall value to an organization and should be managed accordingly. Data should be potentially available to and shared by the total organization on a consistent basis, not controlled by a limited number of end users.

A BSP study is oriented to business processes rather than the information needs of a specific department or other corporate entity. A *business process* represents a basic activity and decision area regardless of the reporting hierarchy. It is assumed that a logical set of these processes can be defined for any type of business and will undergo minimum change as long as the firm's product or service area remains essentially the same.

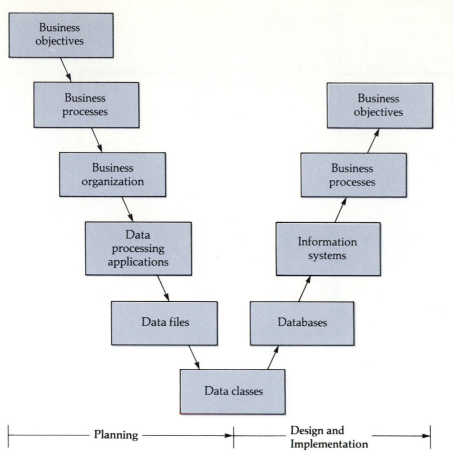

Figure 13.7
Top-down analysis with
bottom-up implemen-
tation. (Source: IBM,
1981, 9.)

In its general form, the BSP methodology is described as a four-step
process:

Step	Purpose
1. Define the business objectives	Ensure that all executive levels agree on where the business is going.
2. Define the business processes	Establish the prime long-term basis for MIS support in the organization.
3. Define the data classes	Identify the data to be managed as a resource across the business unit. A *data class* is a category of data that supports one or more business processes—for example, customer information.

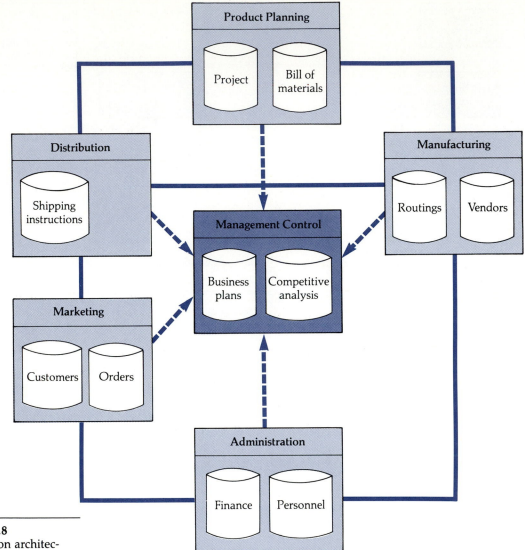

Figure 13.8
Information architecture, showing the relationship among various business processes. (Source: IBM, 1981, 10.)

4. Define the information architecture

Identify the MIS modules to be built according to the priorities of an MIS plan. Each module becomes associated with one or more data class. An example of information architecture is shown in Figure 13.8.

The major activities of a BSP study may be summarized as follows:

1. *Gain commitment:* A BSP study begins only after a top executive sponsor agrees to participate in it.

2. *Prepare for the study:* Executive participants and the BSP team need to know what will be done and what is expected of them. A control room is established and a study control book is prepared containing a work plan, interview schedules, a checkpoint review schedule, the business facts, and an outline of the final report.
3. *Start the study:* Begin with a meeting of all participants. In the meeting, the executive sponsor, the team leader, and the information system director present BSP objectives, the business facts, the decision process, the major problems, and so on.
4. *Define business processes:* The major output of this step is a list of all the processes, a description of ends, and identification of the key persons in the organization.
5. *Define data classes:* This entails grouping data into logically related categories and relating them to business processes for defining the information architecture.
6. *Analyze current systems support:* Current business processes, applications, and data files are analyzed for redundancies and understanding of the business process.
7. *Determine the executive perspective:* This activity validates the work done by the study team, determines the objectives, problems, and information needs and their value, and gains executive rapport and involvement.
8. *Define findings and conclusions:* Identified problems are divided into categories, and findings and conclusions are drawn from them. The results lead to setting priorities among the subsystems of the information architecture.
9. *Define information architecture:* In this step, the structure of information systems is sketched out. Once structured, it allows for step-by-step migration from today's applications to tomorrow's information system.
10. *Determine architecture priorities:* Set priorities by listing the subsystems contained in the information architecture, establishing criteria, and rating prospective applications projects against the criteria.
11. *Review information resource management (IRM):* Establish a controlled environment in which the information architecture can be developed and implemented efficiently.
12. *Develop recommendations and action plan:* The action plan assists management in deciding on the recommended projects. It also identifies specific resources, schedules, and interactions of the projects.
13. *Report the results:* The final report and executive presentation serve to obtain management commitment for implementing recommendations from the BSP study.

The BSP methodology is a comprehensive and thorough process, involving a large number of individuals. By seeking to identify the major data classes and business processes within an organization, it generates a clear picture of the organization's information structure. The data orientation allows a close link to a database development approach. The business processes emphasize the prospective business, not technical needs. The information architecture produced by a BSP is reasonably stable in the face of the organization's changing information needs. BSP has the widest use of any information systems planning tool. Well over 1,000 U.S. firms have used BSP in information systems planning.

The disadvantages of BSP are that it is an expensive and a time-consuming process, requiring considerable organization resources. The danger is that BSP can become an end in itself rather than a starting point for subsequent information systems development activity. In spite of its dual top-down and bottom-up orientation, in practice BSP is primarily bottom-up. It describes *what is*—not what is important. Having constructed an information architecture, it provides no specific indicator that identifies what to do next.

Critical Success Factors (CSF)   The second methodology for identifying corporate information requirements is **critical success factors (CSF)**. CSF is a technique for eliciting information requirements of managerial users. It is based on the concept of "success factors" first discussed in the management literature in 1961 by Ronald Daniel. John Rockart (1982) has written extensively about this concept. The objective of CSF is to help MIS directors understand the factors important to senior end users and then develop an information system to achieve these factors. Rockart defines CSF as the new key areas where "things must go right" for the business to flourish. If the results are inadequate, the organization's efforts for the period will be less than desired.

As the name implies, the pivotal characteristic of CSF is the set of factors the manager considers critical for the success of the firm. Once identified, these factors are stated as objectives. The information required to monitor the performance of these objectives is then identified (Kotteman and Konsynski, 1985).

The CSFs for any business or business function are the limited number of areas (usually four to six) in which satisfactory results will ensure the firm's successful overall performance. These are the activities that have a major impact on short-term effectiveness as well as long-term growth. Although CSFs vary widely by industry and across firms, they are generally derived from the same sources. Through a succession of applications of the CSF methodology in several consulting organizations, six major sources of CSFs are identified:

1. *Industry-based factors:* determined by the characteristics of the industry itself. For example, in the automobile industry a CSF is product quality.
2. *Competitive strategy and industry position:* an individual firm's situation determined by its history, competitive position, and strategy. For example, a CSF for a company in financial difficulties could be cash flow.
3. *Environmental factors:* areas over which an organization has little

control—for example, governmental regulations such as energy standards for automobiles or emission controls for steel mills.

4. *Temporal factors:* an activity or activities within the firm that become critical for a time period, because an unusual event has occurred. These factors may be "problems" or "opportunities"—for example, inventory management.

5. *Managerial role:* each functional managerial position has a generic set of CSFs associated with it. For example, production managers are concerned with cost control, productivity, quality, and so on.

6. *Managerial "world view":* the perspective brought to their job by managers. Perceived CSFs differ significantly from manager to manager—for example, carrying out the role of caretaker versus the role of change agent.

The CSF approach is a series of individual interviews with a firm's executives to determine their own CSFs as they perceive them in their current roles (Jenster, 1986–87). The interviews (usually involving five to twenty executives) are conducted in two or three sessions. The results are then analyzed to determine the organization's CSFs. If the top two or three levels of executives are interviewed, the CSFs will usually reveal a hierarchical structure, and the CSFs for the organization as a whole can be extracted from the lists of individual CSFs.

Since it was devised, the CSF methodology has been most frequently utilized in three ways: clarifying managerial focus, developing top management information needs, and setting information system priorities.

Clarifying Managerial Focus   The use of CSFs can help reconcile diverging individual views of the organization even if there exists a clearly defined corporate mission and explicitly stated objectives. The process of "securing managerial agreement" is essential, because it is necessary to define what is critical for different functional areas before an information system can be built to assist the managers of those areas.

Developing Top Management Information Needs   CSFs are interpreted so that we can identify the information databases or decision support systems needed by top management.

Setting Information System Priorities   In this case, the CSFs are analyzed to determine the relative priorities among the systems to be developed. Since CSFs provide strong evidence of areas that management considers important to the success of the organization, it follows that systems supporting these areas should receive priority.

A schematic representation of the three uses of CSF concepts in information systems planning is shown in Figure 13.9.

The strength of the CSF process is that it focuses on an organization's most important information needs by identifying the key factors essential to its survival and success. Compared to BSP, CSF analysis is relatively

Figure 13.9
Information systems
planning applications of
the critical success fac-
tors (CSF) concept.
(Source: Rockart, 1982,
20.)

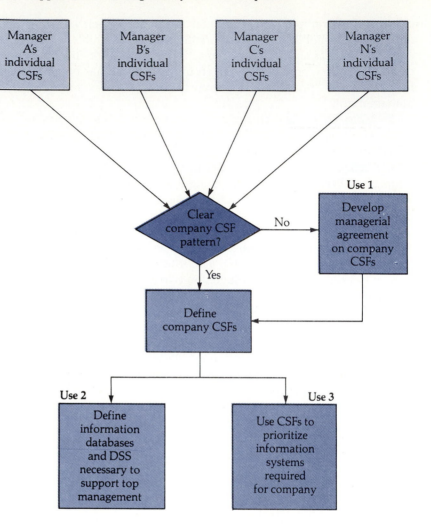

inexpensive and can be accomplished in a reasonably short time period. Similar to BSP, it is almost exclusively top-down in perspective, with focus on the few critical needs rather than a comprehensive view of the organization. Management users of the CSF process have reported an improved insight and understanding of what is important in their organizations.

To some extent, CSF analysis is the mirror image of BSP. CSF is not a comprehensive approach to identifying organization-wide information requirements. The transaction processing and operations management information systems are not addressed. The analysis is focused on factors that are *currently* important to the organization. These factors may not be so important in the future. CSF is not as stable or personality independent as BSP. As with any planning process, it is easy to get caught up in the process and overlook the product—an action plan for building needed information systems. Finally, for CSF to be successful, it requires skillful analysts. In this respect, BSP is a more structured process, and thus easier for a beginner to learn.

Regardless of the methodology used in determining organization information requirements, the process must result in a master development plan that clearly defines specific system projects, a priority ranking of such projects, and a proposed development schedule or timetable.

Resource Allocation Planning

As previously indicated, the third stage of the three-stage model of MIS planning requires the specification of a set of highly interrelated resource allocation decisions to determine which applications must be implemented and in what order. Where large sums of money or substantial human and physical resources are involved, MIS projects often compete with other resource allocation decisions within the firm. It is essential, then, that each MIS project be identified and prioritized in terms of costs and benefits as follows:

1. All costs related to hardware, software, personnel, communications, and facilities must be carefully estimated for each project in the master development plan.
2. All benefits should be listed for each project. They include:
   a. *Financial benefits* such as payback, return on investment, cost avoidance, and so on.
   b. *Intangible benefits* such as improved decision support, better and faster presentation of information.
   c. *Technical benefits* such as sequencing projects to accommodate staff capabilities.

Most organizations have in place a well-defined planning and budgeting system. The issue here is the linking of MIS planning and resource requirements with overall planning and budgeting so that they mesh together in the annual planning cycle of the organization. The preparation of the resource requirements plan for MIS is usually accomplished by MIS personnel.

Role of the Steering Committee   In some organizations, the total resources for implementing the prioritized MIS development plan are provided in a central annual allocation, expended in accordance with the plan. A steering committee of executives from key functional areas in the organization is established to oversee the process. The goal is to arrive at an optimal allocation of resources throughout the organization. In some organizations, projects are funded by charging the principal user's area budget as the project is developed. This chargeback approach has the advantage of holding users responsible for the resources used in developing and maintaining their information systems. In this capacity, MIS functions as a service unit and its costs are "recovered" from the users.

Implications for MIS

Considering the various MIS planning methodologies, it is evident that strategic planning is crucial for successful system development. Although each planning approach has unique features, there is no one "right" approach to system planning for all business organizations. Each planning approach helps explain one, but not all, planning dimensions.

To illustrate, BSP produces a comprehensive application development plan but fails to link directly to the organization's strategic business plan. Likewise, CSF is a method of choice for top management. It fails to define effectively information requirements at the middle and operational managerial levels (Schultz, 1986). Of all the planning techniques, King's strategy-set transformation is preferred, since it depends directly on the organization's formal strategic business plan (Dickson and Wetherbe, 1985).

A critical question in strategic MIS planning is: "What information does the business need to maintain a competitive edge and what information system should be built to achieve the objectives?" MIS executives will be under increasing pressure to anticipate the organization's need for information. An effective MIS plan, then, should consider the strategic direction of the organization and adjust the services delivery to meet the user requirements. Planning strategies should also consider the organization's existing information technology and the economic feasibility of alternative information systems.

Summary

- Planning is determining in advance what action must be taken to achieve a goal. In planning and managing information systems, several factors are considered:
  1. *Mission* of the organization should be long term.
  2. *Goals* of the organization are derived from the needs of the environment. The goals of MIS must be within the organization's goals.
  3. *Strategies* provide the general approach that provides direction for achieving goals. The choice of a strategy lies in the organization's mission.
  4. *Policies* provide guidelines to carry out actions.

- There are four elements to the planning process: recognizing a problem with potential payoff, inventing alternatives, reducing uncertainties about the outcome of each alternative, and deciding on an alternative for action. Planning involves a process, people, and technology. MIS planning must be carried out within the organization's plan.

▫ At the MIS level, planning has undergone four stages of growth:
   1. *Initiation:* a response to user dissatisfaction. It precipitates the emergence of project planning.
   2. *Expansion:* a period of high demand for processing application backlogs.
   3. *Control:* a response to sharply increasing processing costs, prompting resource planning.
   4. *Integration:* emphasis on short-range planning and integration of applications.

▫ Planning for information systems must be done within the organization's overall MIS plan. The planning effort focuses on strategic, managerial, or operational levels. *Strategic* planning is long-range planning. It provides efficient allocation of corporate resources, improved user/ analyst relations, and contributes to performance. *Managerial* planning is a set of functional plans for implementing strategies. *Operational* planning focuses on the day-to-day activities of the system.

▫ System development must support the organization's strategic plan. This important link has been described in a three-stage model consisting of:
   1. *Strategic MIS planning:* creating goals and strategies that align with those of the organization. It also involves setting an MIS mission, assessing the environment, and setting MIS policies, objectives, and strategies.
   2. *Organizational information requirements analysis:* assessing the information requirements of the organization. This results in a master development plan with a development schedule or a timetable.
   3. *Resource allocation planning:* identifying trends, planning hardware and software, and personnel planning.

▫ With the three-stage model, various methodologies are employed:
   1. *Strategic planning methodology.* King's strategy-set transformation produces goals and strategies through four stages: identifying the organizational strategy set, transforming the strategy set into an MIS strategy, constructing alternative structures for the overall architecture, and presenting alternatives to management.
   2. *Organizational information requirements analysis.* The two most widely used methodologies are business system planning (BSP) and critical success factors (CSF).
   3. *Resource allocation planning.* Each MIS project is prioritized in terms of costs and benefits.

▫ BSP is a process that translates business strategy into MIS. The basic philosophy rests on top-down planning with bottom-up implementation and orientation toward business processes rather than the information needs of a specific department or manager. The basic methodology involves a definition of the business objectives, the business processes, the data classes, and the information architecture. In this way, BSP generates a complete picture of the information structure of the organization. The main disadvantage, though, is the time it takes to produce a BSP. Also, BSP describes what is, not what is important.

▫ The CSF method helps MIS directors understand what factors are important to executive MIS users so that they may then develop an information system to achieve these factors. The pivotal characteristic is the set of factors that the manager considers critical for the success of the firm. The CSF approach involves a series of individual interviews with the executives to determine their own CSFs as they perceive them in their current roles. The data are then analyzed to determine the organization's CSFs.

▫ To some extent, CSF is the mirror image of BSP. The analysis focuses on current, not future, factors that are important to the organization. CSF is not as personality-independent as BSP. It also requires skillful analysts.

Key Terms

Action planning
Business systems planning (BSP)
Capacity planning
Contagion
Critical success factors (CSF)
Goal
Information resource management (IRM)
Managerial planning

Mission
Objective
Operational planning
Planning
Policy
Project planning
Resource planning
Strategic planning
Strategy

Review Questions

1. Define planning. How does it differ from control? In what respect are they related?

2. Distinguish between:
   a. Mission and goal
   b. Strategy and tactic
   c. Action planning and project planning

3. Discuss the relationships among the key components of organi-

zational planning. Which component do you consider the most critical? Why?

4. According to the text, the choice of a strategy lies in the organization's mission and its distinctive competencies. Do you agree? Give an example to illustrate.

5. For what reasons has MIS planning become visible in recent years? Explain.

6. What causes managers in general to shy away from planning? Explain.

7. Explain the key stages of growth in MIS planning.

8. In your own words, what is strategic planning? How does it differ from long-range planning? Explain.

9. Discuss Steiner's structure and process of business planning.

10. Good long-range planning has several benefits. What are they? Are there drawbacks? Explain.

11. How is managerial planning different from strategic planning? Discuss.

12. Why is it important to link corporate and MIS planning? Are there situations where such a linkage is not important? Explain.

13. Discuss in detail Bowman and colleagues' three-stage MIS planning model. What features and advantages does it offer?

14. King proposes a strategic planning methodology. Illustrate its stages and features.

15. What is BSP? What phase of the three-stage model does it address? How does it translate business strategy into MIS?

16. "One basic philosophy of BSP is top-down analysis with bottom-up implementation." Do you agree? Discuss.

17. The BSP methodology has been described as a four-step process. Explain the steps and their relationships.

18. Explain briefly the major activities of a BSP study.

19. Summarize the advantages and disadvantages of the BSP methodology.

20. What is CSF? How does it differ from BSP methodology?

21. Identify and explain briefly the major sources of CSF.

22. In what ways has the CSF methodology been most frequently utilized? Elaborate.

23. According to the text, CSF analysis is the mirror image of BSP. Do you agree? Why?

Application Problems

1. You have been discussing with a friend the effect of social changes on the management of his information system division. After you have expressed disagreement with a number of his ideas, he has asked you to write down your proposals for policies that he should adopt. He has given you the following policy issues on which you and he differ:
a. Hiring minorities in the systems analysis area.
b. Hiring women.
c. Offering priorities to special managers.

   Write a statement of policy for each issue as a guide for his department in making decisions.

2. You are skilled in software development and want to organize a specialty firm in a large-sized town for developing applications for end users. You find that two other software houses have been successful by developing systems in their shops. Several smaller software firms have specialized in developing software for banks. In a short study of the needs of the business community, you have found that none of the present shops specializes in microcomputer software for the churches—membership analysis, pledges, contributions, and so on.

QUESTIONS
a. What mission should you select? Provide software development with existing software houses? Specialize in the area not already occupied?
b. State your recommended strategy or strategies and explain the reasons for your selection.

3. The Legis Corporation produces a variety of small electrical appliances in three divisions. Since it was founded in 1934, it has maintained a conservative old-line approach—old markets, old equipment, and manual data processing—well into the early 1980s. The accounting vice president soon introduced a used minicomputer for accounting data capture. He learned to program and load basic accounting applications by reading the machine manual.

   The president was quite impressed with the speed of processing and the availability of information for analysis. He encouraged other departments to use the system and make best use of machine idle time. The system became available to the three divisions that began to load applications as they saw fit.

   After five months, it became apparent that the accounting and cost analysis reports were not being made available on time. The system was so overworked that either the reports were late or errors made them virtually useless for decision making. Most of the software developed to date was constantly being debugged.

Use this case to give an example for each of the following items:

a. Lack of planning for hardware/software
b. Key information not available to management
c. Evidence of the lack of corporate planning
d. Failure to adopt project planning
e. Failure to use a strategic MIS plan

Selected References

Anthony, R. N. *Planning and Control Systems: A Framework for Analysis.* Boston, Mass.: Harvard University Graduate School of Business Administration, 1965.

Bakos, J. Yannis and Teacy, Michael E. "Information Technology and Corporate Strategy: A Research Perspective." *MIS Quarterly,* June 1986, 107–119.

Benjamin, R. I., Rockart, J. E., Scott, Morton, M., and Wyman, S. J. "Information Technology: A Strategic Opportunity." *Sloan Management Review* 25, 3(1984), 3–10.

Bowman, B., Davis, G. and Wetherbe, J. "Modeling for MIS." *Datamation,* July 1981, 155–164.

Camillus, J. C. and Venkatraman, N. "Dimensions of Strategic Choice." *Planning Review,* 12(1984), 26–31.

Dickson, Gary W. and Wetherbe, James C. *The Management of Information Systems.* Minneapolis, Minn.: West, 1985.

Doll, W. J. and Ahmed, M. U. "Objectives for Systems Planning." *Journal of Systems Management,* December 1984, 26–31.

Fayol, Henri. *General and Industrial Management.* London: Sir Isaac Pitman & Sons, 1949, chap. 5.

Gibson, C. F. and Nolan, R. L. "Managing the Four Stages of EDP Growth." *Harvard Business Review,* January–February 1974, 76–88.

IBM Corporation. *Business Systems Planning—Information Systems Planning Guide,* Publication No. GE20-0527-3, July 1981.

Jenster, Per V. "Firm Performance and Monitoring of Critical Success Factors in Different Strategic Contexts." *Journal of Management Information Systems,* 3, 3 (Winter 1986–87), 17–33.

Johnson, James R. "Enterprise Analysis." *Datamation,* December 15, 1985, 97–99ff.

Kanter, Jerome. "MIS Long Range Planning." *Infosystems,* June 1982, 66.

King, W. R. "Strategic Planning for Management Information Systems." *MIS Quarterly,* March 1978, 22–37.

Kotteman, Jeffrey E. and Konsynski, Benn R. "Information Systems Planning and Development: Strategic Postures and Methodologies." *Journal of Management Information Systems,* Fall 1985, 46.

Long, Larry. "Long-Range MIS Planning." *Computerworld,* July 26, 1982, 27–32ff.

Massie, J. and Douglas, J. *Managing: A Contemporary Introduction* (4th ed.). Englewood Cliffs, N.J.: Prentice-Hall, 1985.

McFarlan, F. W. "Information Technology Changes the Way You Compete." *Harvard Business Review* 62, 3(1984), 98–103.

McKenney, J. L. and McFarlan, F. W. "The Information Archipelago—Maps and Bridges." *Harvard Business Review,* September/October 1982, 109–119.

McLean, Ephraim and Soden, John. *Strategic Planning for MIS.* New York: John Wiley & Sons, 1977.

Nolan, Richard L. "Managing the Crisis in Data Processing." *Harvard Business Review,* April 1979, 115–26.

Porter, Michael E. *Competitive Advantage: Creating and Sustaining Superior Performance.* New York: Free Press, 1985.

———— and Millar, Victor E. "How Information Gives You Competitive Advantage." *Harvard Business Review,* July–August 1985, 150–156.

Rockart, J. F. "Current Uses of the Critical Success Factors Process." *Proceedings of the Fourteenth Annual Conference of the Society for Information Management,* September 1982, 17–21.

Schultz, David I. "Strategic Information Systems Planning Sharpens Competitive Edge." *Data Management,* June 1986, 20–24ff.

Steiner, George A. "Formal Strategic Planning in the United States Today." *Long-Range Planning,* 16, 3, (1983), 12–17.

Thistlethwaite, Glenn E. "Strategic Planning Requires Dynamic, Ongoing Process." *Data Management,* August 1985, 34–35.

Vanecek, Michael. "Computer System Acquisition Planning." *Journal of Systems Management,* May 1984, 8–13.

Venkatraman, N. "Research On MIS Planning: Some Guidelines From Strategic Planning Research." *Journal of Management Information Systems,* Winter 1985–86, 67.

Warrick, D. D., Gardner, Donald G., Couger, J. Daniel and Zawacki, Robert A. "Stress." *Datamation,* April 15, 1985, 88ff.

Determining Information System Requirements

Chapter Contents

The Orderly Ways of Analysts

STRONG ANALYSTS SEE THEMSELVES as factual, down-to-earth people, and in a sense they are. They see the world as logical, rational, ordered (or orderly), and predictable. The analyst prefers rationality, stability, and predictability; he or she prefers to concentrate on objective data, procedure, and the "best" method. Analysts want to be sure of things, to know what's going to happen next. They take pride in their competence, in their ability to understand all the facets of any situation.

The initial impression made by analysts can pose a problem. They appear to be cool, studious, perhaps distant, and hard to read. Conversing with them can be difficult, especially if you happen to be trying to convince them of something. They are easy to identify in casual conversations, often prefacing their remarks with "It stands to reason," "If you look at it logically," and, of course, "If we just go about it scientifically . . ."

Let's look at how an analyst conducts a meeting with high-level people in a forklift-manufacturing company.

Eleanor: All right, we're in agreement. The big push will be on the new narrow-aisle machine.

Lou: Right. And we have agreed that the primary target will be medium-sized distributors.

Jack: Yes. We'll get the advertising people right onto it.

Eleanor: It's a heck of a market. I have visions of terrific sales. What's your opinion, Sam?

Sam (analyst): Well—I have a couple of factors I'd like to think about. Don't misunderstand me, I think the new machine is a great product. But I'm not sure about the timing.

Eleanor: What do you mean?

Sam: Let's assume the ads really work, and suddenly we have all sorts of inquiries and orders. Can we meet the demand?

Lou: Production says we can.

Sam: In my opinion, their estimates are fuzzy and overly optimistic. I'd like more data from them before we rush ahead.

Eleanor: Well, for heaven's sake, why didn't you say so earlier, before we got this far down the road?

Sam: I've been sort of listening and thinking about it. Sometimes it takes a while, you know.

There is a doubt that Sam's analytic abilities are an asset to the group. The difficulty for analysts in such a situation is that, instead of being an appropriate brake, their strategy can look like a damper to others. When everyone is keyed up and ready to move, who wants to hear some wet blanket say, "Wait a minute, do we really know enough about what we're doing?" Analysts need to be more assertive in their requests that others pay attention to details and constraints. They can sound like voices crying in the wilderness, and they need to be listened to.

When the analyst approach goes wrong, it is obviously wrong. That is because of the nature of analyst strategies: clear-cut, visible, and logical. On the other hand, when they work, one hardly notices. That is because, in the appropriate situation, analyst strategies are so logical and right.

—One-page excerpt Styles of Thinking: Strategies for Asking Questions, Making Decisions, and Solving Problems by Robert M. Bramson and Allen F. Harrison, Copyright © 1982 by Allen F. Harrison and Robert M. Bramson. Reprinted with permission of Bantam, Doubleday, Dell Publishing Group, Inc.

AT A GLANCE

In an MIS environment, system development goes through a cycle that begins with a problem definition and ends in a running installation. Building systems and helping users run a profitable business is the basis for a successful MIS organization.

Systems analysts work with users to identify problems and build systems to solve them. The key part of the initial investigation is gathering information about the present system. The proper use of tools for gathering information is the key to successful analysis. Tools help analysts assess the present system and provide the groundwork for recommending a candidate system. Traditional tools such as interviews and questionnaires have benefits and drawbacks. Structured tools such as data flow diagrams, data dictionary, and Structured English provide alternative ways of designing a system. In real-life applications, a combination of traditional and structured tools is used.

The outcome of the initial investigation is determining whether an alternative system is worth doing. A feasibility study is carried out to select the best system that meets performance requirements. This involves identification, description, and evaluation of candidate systems, and selection of the best system for the job.

The role of the analyst requires skills, experience, and common sense. The fact that a system is designed for a specific user means that the analyst should have interpersonal skills. Users must understand how the analyst relates to them and how the interface should be maintained.

By the end of this chapter, you should know:

1. The stages of development in a system project
2. What it takes to do systems work
3. The uses of various tools and the steps in the initial investigation
4. How a feasibility study is conducted
5. The procedure for cost/benefit determination

Introduction

A management information system should meet end user requirements. *Systems analysts* work with users to identify problems and build systems to solve them. Developing a system is a process that begins with the recognition of user needs, followed by a feasibility study and detailed design, testing, and implementation of the new system. The entire cycle is carried out within the framework of an MIS plan, as discussed in Chapter 13.

This chapter focuses on the analysis of an information system. In the system development life cycle, *analysis* begins with the initial investigation, using specialized tools. The next step is determining feasibility, culminating in a proposal to be approved for design. Analysis is a *prerequisite* to design. Systems design is covered in Chapter 15.

The System Development Life Cycle

An information system (also called a **candidate system**) has a life cycle, just like a living system. Developing MIS is keyed to the **system development life cycle (SDLC)**, a structured sequence of phases for implementing an information system. As shown in Table 14.1, the major stages of SDLC are:

1. Recognition of need
2. Feasibility study

Table 14.1   The System Development Life Cycle: A Summary

Stage	Key Question	Outcome
Recognition of need (initial investigation)	What is the problem?	· Statement of objectives · Performance criteria
Feasibility study · Data collection · Evaluation of present system · Analysis of alternative systems · Cost analysis	What are the facts? What are the user's requirements? Is the problem worth solving? What must be done to solve the problem?	· Cost/benefit analysis · Statement of new objectives
Design · General and detailed specifications of output, input, files, and procedures · Coding and testing	How must the problem be solved?	· Design of candidate systems · Test plan · Hardware/software implementation details · Security, audit, and operating procedures
Implementation · File/system conversion · User training	What is the actual operation? Are user manuals ready?	· User-friendly documentation · Training program
Postimplementation · Maintenance · Enhancements	Should the system be modified?	· User requirements met · Satisfied user

3. Design
4. Implementation
5. Postimplementation and maintenance

Recognition of Need   The basis for a new system is satisfying a need for improving an information system. This leads to a preliminary investigation to determine if an alternative system can solve the problem. For example, suppose a labor-intensive accounting department using a manual procedure for maintaining the general ledger fails to produce reports on time. If the problem is serious enough, the initial investigation is expanded to a more detailed feasibility study. Otherwise, minor changes are recommended or a decision is made to simply make no changes. We shall find later that problem definition is a very important step. Mistakes made at this phase tend to show up at the implementation phase when the user tests the system.

Feasibility Study   The feasibility study is a procedure that identifies, describes, and evaluates candidate systems and selects the best system that meets performance criteria. The result of the study is a proposal that summarizes what is known and what is going to be done. Once approved by management, the proposal paves the way for system design.

Analysis   Systems analysis is a major aspect of a feasibility study. It is a detailed evaluation of the operations performed by a system and the relationships within the user's area of operations. Emphasis is on *what* must be done to solve the end user's problem. Later in the chapter we will discuss how information is gathered and what tools are used in analyzing a system.

Design   Once analysis is completed, the next step is to decide how the problem might be solved. Design is the most creative phase of the SDLC. It addresses the technical details that will be applied in operationalizing a new system. This includes program coding and testing and developing various operating procedures. The key question in design is: *How* should the problem be solved?

Implementation   The implementation phase is concerned with file conversion, user training, and site preparation. When the new system includes remote terminals, the telecommunication network is also covered under implementation. Conversion takes place at about the same time as user training.

Postimplementation   After the system becomes operational, either the user's requirements change or the system ages with prolonged use. In the former case, *enhancements* are incorporated to bring the system in line with the requirements. Otherwise, the changes fall under *maintenance*. This means keeping the system in tune with the established (not new) user requirements.

A project may be terminated at any time before final implementation. This occurs if the existing design cannot meet changing user objectives, if the benefits do not justify the costs, or if the project greatly exceeds the time schedule. In contrast to project termination, an information system often fails to meet user requirements for several reasons:

1. Poorly defined user requirements
2. Lack of user participation
3. Inexperienced analysts or programmers
4. Inadequate user training
5. Uncooperative user staff
6. Deficient hardware or software, or both

Of these systems, user participation is most critical. When users actually participate to improve the work environment, they become *proactive* rather than *reactive* (Moran, 1981), or less resistant to change. User participation also fosters an attitude of shared responsibility for the success of the project. Finally, it has been known for some time that the longer it takes to build a system, the further away the system will be from meeting user requirements (Welke and Konsynski, 1982), unless the user actually participates in the entire process (see Figure 14.1).

Formal SDLC Methodologies: An Example

Several consulting firms have developed formal SDLC methodologies for managing and developing systems projects. One popular methodology is Arthur Andersen's Method/1. Method/1 is a structured design methodology aimed at implementing information systems efficiently and on time. The package is illustrated in Figure 14.1.

Method/1 is a practical approach to system development. The major phases are planning, design, implementation, and support. The products of each phase are summarized in Table 14.2. As a practical methodology, Method/1 strikes a balance between user and management involvement by utilizing responsibility matrices. Keyed to each phase and task in the methodology are the needed skills for performing and supporting each task (see Table 14.3).

An important contribution of such methodology is involving the users throughout the SDLC by having end users participate in designing the human-computer interface, testing the final system, and approving the system before final conversion. Such an involvement has been known to cement a lasting relationship between the systems designer and the user, as well as securing the necessary support for system installation and use.

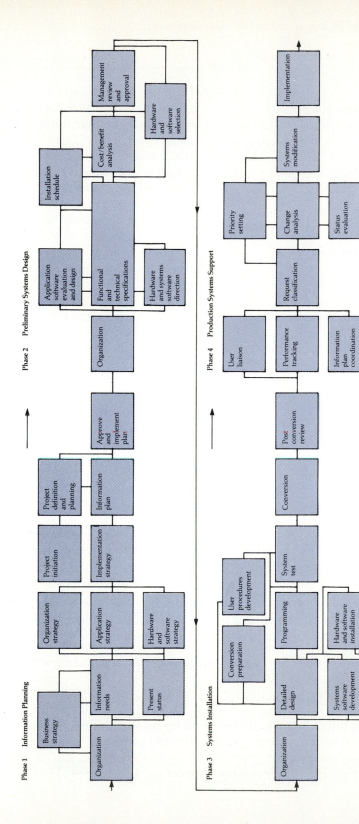

Phase 1   Information Planning

Business strategy

Organization

Information needs

Present status

Project initiation

Organization strategy

Application strategy

Hardware and software strategy

Project definition and planning

Implementation strategy

Approve and implement plan

Information plan

Phase 2   Preliminary Systems Design

Organization

Application software evaluation and design

Functional and technical specifications

Hardware and systems software direction

Installation schedule

Cost/benefit analysis

Hardware and software selection

Management review and approval

Phase 3   Systems Installation

Organization

Detailed design

Systems software development

Conversion preparation

User procedures development

Programming

Hardware and software installation

System test

Conversion

Post conversion review

Phase 4   Production Systems Support

User liaison

Performance tracking

Information plan coordination

Request classification

Priority setting

Change analysis

Status evaluation

Systems modification

Implementation

Figure 14.1
Method/1 by Arthur
Andersen & Co.

421

Table 14.2   Method/1: Information System Methodology

Phase	Product	Content
Information planning	Information plan	· Statement of information requirements related to the strategic plan of the organization · Evaluation of the present system and the organization · Strategies for hardware, software, and organizational MIS
	Project definition	· Description of scope of project · Overall project data model · Work plan · Summary of costs and benefits
Preliminary system design	Functional specifications report	· Input/output descriptions · Procedural flows
	Technical specifications report	· Technical architecture design · Logical and physical database design · Programs and modules · Testing and conversion procedures · Resource requirements
	Management summary report	· Functional and technical design overview · Summary of resources and benefits

The Initial Investigation

The initial investigation has the objective of determining how seriously a user's request should be taken and whether a feasibility study should be made. The user's request identifies the need for change that authorizes the initial investigation.

Determining the User's Information Requirements

One of the most difficult tasks in system development is determining user requirements. Several reasons account for the problem:

1. Except for experienced users, articulating requirements is a challenge.
2. Creating user motivation to participate is a job in itself.

Table 14.2   Method/1: Information System Methodology (*continued*)

Phase	Product	Content
System implementation	Programming specifications	· Summary installation plan · Recommended course of action · Structure charts · Module narratives · Input forms layouts · Report and screen layouts
	User procedures and trained personnel	· Procedure manuals · Ongoing user training
	System and program documentation	· Program documentation · System operation documentation
System support	Periodic status report	· Actual performance versus estimates for implementing change · Actual performance versus planned performance and operating cost · Overall evaluation of the production system
	Updated system and program documentation	· Updated programming specifications · Users trained in the revised procedures

3. User-analyst interaction is not simple except in situations where there has been shared experience on past projects.
4. Most users think that "all systems are created equal." This attitude is influenced by the transaction processing orientation that limits innovations in new system installations.

Users and analysts invariably have contrasting views on problem identification. Therefore, we can expect users to be on the defensive, using strategies to define their information requirements. Such strategies include overstating needs and requesting several system features when only one or two are needed. The extra requests are used as bargaining chips.

Humans in general have problems specifying information requirements. According to Davis (1982), humans are biased in the selection and use of data and have a limited capacity for rational thinking. Simon

Table 14.3   Skills Needed to Perform a Task: Review Present Status

Task 352: Review Present Status

Step	Manager	Project Manager	User Management	User	Analyst
		Responsibility			
1	Determine areas to be reviewed	Perform	Perform		
2	Prepare interview schedule	Perform	Review		
3	Prepare for interviews				Perform
4	Request advanced information				Perform
5	Conduct interviews			Perform	Perform
6	Summarize the current system	Review	Review	Assist	Perform
7	Determine current costs			Perform	
8	Analyze the system for strengths and weaknesses	Review	Approve	Assist	Perform

described the latter constraint as the concept of **bounded rationality**. It means that rationality for determining information requirements is constrained by limited training and user attitudes that may obscure the real situation (Newell and Simon, 1972).

Strategies for Defining Information Requirements   Defining user needs is the primary task of the analyst. It is the analyst's responsibility to sort out the user's needs from wants and provide a system that emphasizes the former.

There are three strategies for gaining information about the user's requirements:

1. *Asking* users about their requirements, by **brainstorming** sessions, in which participants are asked to define ideal solutions and then select the most feasible ones, a good technique for eliciting nonconventional solutions to problems, or by **group consensus**. In the latter approach, participants are asked for their expectations about specific variables. For example, in a **Delphi inquiry** (a debate by questionnaire), participants fill out the forms and the results are handed to them with a followup questionnaire. The results are again summarized and fed back to participants until their responses have converged sufficiently.

2. *Data analysis*, which asks the user about information currently received and information required. Missing information is filled in through interviewing. This method requires users to articulate their needs.

3. *Prototyping*. Regardless of how effective the analyst-user interface is, problems apparently remain in designing systems that meet the user's exacting requirements. One reason is the user's inability to describe what is needed; another reason is the complex nature of the system and the months it takes before the system becomes operational.

One answer to this difficulty is **prototyping**, or constructing a physical model or a sample end product that the user can see, modify, and use. The prototype is tentative and its purpose is to capture the essentials of a later system. It is refined and tested and the process is repeated until the user is satisfied with the results. Figure 14.2 illustrates the role of prototyping within the broader system development life cycle of MIS.

Prototyping is a discipline that benefits from tight schedules. For example, if a month passes without end users seeing tangible results that they can relate to, they tend to assume that the project is having problems. Prototyping fulfills that need; it is also results oriented rather than project oriented. Emphasis is on developing the new system for users in a form they can recognize, use, and support. By immediately proving the workability of the design, prototyping demonstrates the extent to which the investment to date has matched the user's requirements. At the same time, the user is made more tangibly aware of the time and money that go into the development of a system.

The initial prototyping period of the new system's life cycle builds sample logical and physical files. Next, the order of processing is checked against specifications. The third step is testing the file(s) with user-defined data. The initial investment is kept low to avoid justifying why so much money and effort were spent on a seemingly basic phase of development.

The walkthrough can be extremely useful in prototyping. A **walkthrough** is a peer group meeting in which the system development documentation is reviewed. The objective is to gain the end user's participation in building the system from that point on so that the designer is not the sole determiner of the project's success or failure. There are various ways to conduct a walkthrough, but the most effective is to have the end user operate the prototype while the designer takes note of possible changes. This also gives the designer and user an opportunity to form strategies for the rest of the project.

Since we are dealing with a prototype rather than a finished system, changes and modification can be made conveniently. For example, fields can be added to or deleted from a file; source codes can also be changed. Each change is prototyped before the final model is made: The designer makes the change, produces the file, and then tests the prototype. Each change is further tested independently to ensure integrity before it is integrated into the working prototype and retested.

Figure 14.2
The system development life cycle with prototyping.

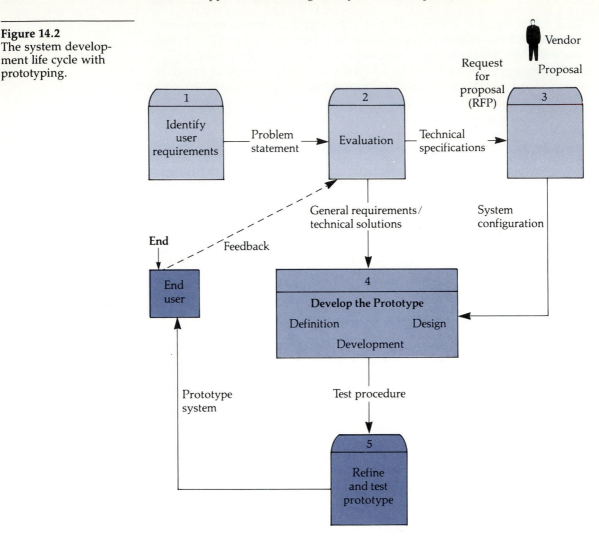

Prototyping offers several advantages. First, it promotes user enthusiasm and cooperation. User involvement also means a better chance for a successful installation and support. These advantages are realized at the relatively low cost of most prototypes when compared to the alternative—the risk of having to overhaul the entire project.

Among the limitations of prototyping are budget overruns and difficulty maintaining user cooperation. Most prototypes require qualified staff who cannot very well produce solutions as quickly as the user expects from a prototype. Recent graph and report generators, along with very high-level languages, are making it possible, however, to provide fast response to user needs throughout the prototyping process.

Fact Finding

After problem definition, the next step in the initial investigation is to examine the present system, the people who run it, the reporting relationships, the procedures reports use, and the quality of documentation. After this background analysis, the system's outputs, inputs, and costs are identified. Traditional and structured tools are used in this information gathering. The traditional tools are existing documents, on-site observations, interviews, and questionnaires (see Figure 14.3). The structured tools are the data flow diagram, data dictionary, decision tree, and Structured English. The latter tools are also used in system design.

Traditional Tools   There are a number of traditional ways in which information about a system can be gathered.

Existing Documents   Procedure manuals illustrate the format and functions of various aspects of the existing system. Well-written manuals are invaluable for analysis because they save hours of data-gathering time. Printed forms also capture information that explains the nature of data flow, its source, and destination. They provide information about the users of the forms and their job status, the departments that get them, their readability and ease of use.

On-Site Observations   This information-gathering approach gets as close as possible to the "real" system under study, in that people and events are recognized and noted in their natural work environment. The analyst needs to know what kind of a system it is, who runs it, the history behind

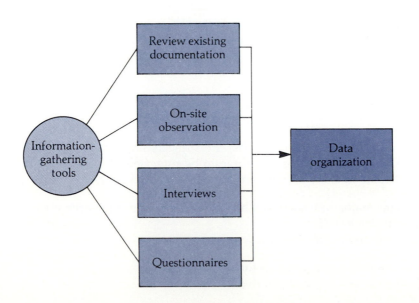

Figure 14.3
Information-gathering
methods.

it, how it got to its present state, and how it relates to other systems in the organization.

There are eight on-site observation methods:

1. **Natural** or **contrived** (such as a laboratory)
2. **Obtrusive** (seen) or **unobtrusive** (behind a one-way mirror)
3. **Direct** or **indirect** (using cameras, videotapes, etc.)
4. **Structured** (looking for specific activities) or **unstructured** (observing the overall system)

Any combination of these methods may be used. Natural, direct, obtrusive, and unstructured observations are recommended for obtaining an overview of an operation. The degree of structure increases when observations have a specific purpose—as, for example, in following the route of a stock order through a brokerage house. Contrived situations are used to test a candidate in training programs to evaluate the progress of trainees.

On-site observation is not without its drawbacks:

1. Subjective selection of what to observe often results in misinterpretation or alters work patterns during observation.
2. Perceptions and attitudes cannot be easily observed—only the behavior that results from them.
3. It is time-consuming and often results in adverse reactions from the user's staff.

To be properly conducted, on-site observations must be well planned. The analyst is expected to be well trained in observation methods and protocol.

Interviews and Questionnaires   The *interview* is a face-to-face interpersonal exchange in which one person (interviewer) asks another person (interviewee) questions about a problem situation. It is the oldest and most frequently used tool for information gathering. The main advantages of the interview are:

1. Flexibility in rephrasing questions to get to the main points or get to the real issue(s).
2. Opportunity to observe what the subjects say and how they say it.
3. The readiness of many people to be interviewed. They usually participate in a situation where all they have to do is talk.

The major drawback of the interview is the long preparation and administration time.

Interviewing is an art. It requires:

1. Experience in arranging the interview
2. Setting the stage to put the subject at ease

Table 14.4 Structured and Unstructured Interviewing

Type	Advantages	Disadvantages
Structured	· Easy to administer and train new staff · Easy to evaluate because of standardization of items	· Reduces spontaneity · Impractical in all situations · High initial preparation costs
Unstructured	· Allows clearer awareness of subject's feelings · Certain information can only be gathered this way	· Time-consuming and costly · Requires experienced trainers and good listeners

3. Establishing rapport to instill trust and openness
4. Asking questions clearly
5. Avoiding arguments about issues
6. Interpreting the outcome of the interview

The *questionnaire* is a self-administered tool that asks questions to which individuals respond. By its nature, the questionnaire has several advantages:

1. Makes an ideal instrument for asking a large-size group to answer questions. In contrast, the interview questions one subject at a time.
2. Provides greater anonymity than the interview because the respondent can answer questions privately.
3. Creates less pressure for immediate response to questions than in an interview.
4. Requires less skill and is more cost effective than the interview.

The key limitation, however, is low return. Many people also have difficulty putting their thoughts down in writing. People in general even dislike writing.

Interviews and questionnaires vary in form and structure. They may be structured or unstructured. The **unstructured interview**, for example, is nondirective. It allows subjects to answer questions in their own words. The responses are usually spontaneous, personal, and self-revealing. In the **structured interview**, each question is asked using the same words and in the same sequence. A summary of the pros and cons of structured and unstructured interviews is presented in Table 14.4.

Similarly, **structured questions** may be open-ended or closed. An **open-ended question** does not require a specific response. For example, the question, "If you were to design the system over, how would you do it?" would be subject to various responses. In contrast, a **closed question** specifies the response as a set of alternatives. There are several varieties of closed questions:

1. **Dichotomous:** answerable by yes or no, or offers a two-answer choice. For example:

> "Have you ever experienced a disk crash?"
>
> ___ Yes ___ No

2. *Fill in the blank:* answerable by filling in the blanks. For example:

> "What is the title of your immediate supervisor?"
>
> _____

3. *Multiple-choice:* answerable by selecting an alternative answer. For example:

> "What is the salary of your systems analyst?"
>
> ___ under $20,000
> ___ $20,000-24,999
> ___ $25,000-29,999
> ___ $30,000 or over

4. **Rating scales:** an extension of the multiple choice design, answerable by choosing a response from a range of responses along a single scale. For example:

"How satisfied are you with the following aspects of your job?" (circle one for each item)

	Very dissatisfied	Dissatisfied	Indifferent	Satisfied	Very satisfied
1. Opportunity to do creative work	1	2	3	4	5
2. Leadership of the department	1	2	3	4	5
3. Compensation for good work	1	2	3	4	5

5. **Ranking scales:** answerable by ranking preferences in a list of items. For example:

```
Please rank the following statements on the
basis of how well they describe the workers in
your area. On a scale of 1-5, write "1" by the
statement that best describes the job and
continue ranking all five statements, using
"5" for a statement that least describes the
job.

Analysts on this job ...

____ find meaning in their work
____ are paid well in comparison with analysts
     in other firms
____ have an opportunity for doing creative
     work
____ are busy all the time
```

Obviously, each type of question has advantages and drawbacks. Open-ended questions are useful in settings where limited information is available, but subjective interpretation (or misinterpretation) of the response could be a severe drawback. In contrast, closed questions are ideal for gathering factual information, although they are costly to prepare. In most interviews or questionnaires, both types of questions are incorporated into the information-gathering instrument.

In constructing questionnaires, the analyst must decide on:

1. The nature of data to be collected
2. Whether the questions should be open ended or closed
3. Proper phrasing of the questions
4. Editing and pretesting (trying out) the questions to ensure their **validity** (determining to what extent the question asked is so worded as to elicit the information sought)

An important point to consider in conducting a questionnaire is the validity (and reliability) of the questions. By **reliability** we mean how dependably the resulting information can be used to make successful decisions. Therefore, the analyst must concentrate on question wording, content, and format. For question content, we need to determine:

1. How necessary the question is and whether the respondent has proper information to answer it.
2. How likely is it that the question will elicit a false response?

For question wording, we need to ask:

1. How easily can the question be misinterpreted?
2. How clear is the wording? Is it pitched toward a particular answer?

For question format, we should determine:

1. Question design: dichotomous, multiple choice, etc.
2. How much the answer to a question biases the answers to the next set of questions.

Structured Tools   Traditional tools have serious drawbacks:

1. English is inherently awkward to use where accuracy of specifications is required. The narrative description often fails to help the user visualize the totality of the system.
2. When we describe a current system, we often focus on the physical rather than the logical requirements. Traditional tools make it difficult to distinguish between *what* happens and *how* it happens in the system.
3. The analyst is quickly overwhelmed with technical information about the system but does not have the tools to structure the details.
4. A change in user requirements forces changes in various aspects of the documents representing the system.

Because of these drawbacks, alternative tools are used that emphasize *functions* rather than physical routines. Such tools are used in **structured analysis**—a technique that makes it possible to develop a new kind of specifications for a proposed system. Graphics replace narrative where possible to improve the user's understanding of the system. Structured analysis also emphasizes the logical rather than the physical aspects of a system. The outcome is a document called **system specifications** that is required for design. The SDLC with structured analysis is shown in Figure 14.4. Using the illustration, structured analysis involves the following processes:

2.1 Study of the present system results in a physical data flow diagram, or DFD (see Figure 14.5a).
2.2 Replace the physical checkpoints with a logical equivalent, leading to the logical DFD (see Figure 14.5b).
2.3 Model the new logical system.
2.4 Consider the hardware necessary to establish user/machine interface.
2.5 Cost-justify the hardware. This results in a cost/benefit summary.
2.6 Select the hardware.
2.7 Develop structured specifications based on the logical DFD and the resulting data dictionary, which lists and defines terms for all the data items of the candidate system.

The *structured specification*, then, consists of:

1. The DFD that graphically shows system functions and their relationships.
2. Documentation of DFD representations through Structured English or decision trees, as we shall explain later.

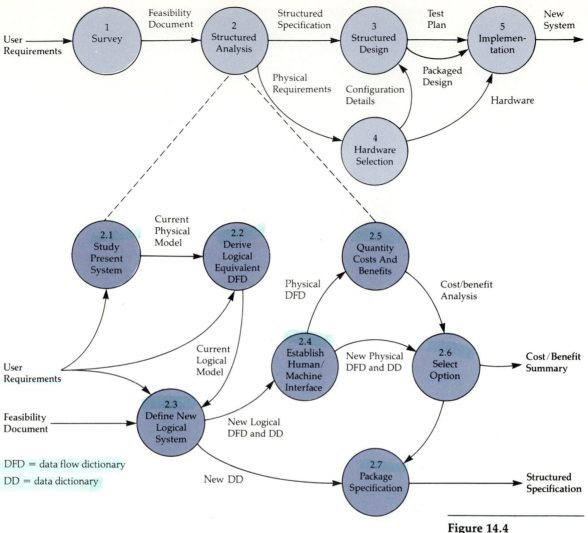

Figure 14.4
Structured analysis within the SDLC (Tom DeMarco, *Structured Analysis and System Specification*, © 1979, p. 26 (A Yourdon Book). Adapted by permission of Prentice-Hall, Inc., Englewood Cliffs, N.J.)

3. The data dictionary that documents data flows, processes, and files as specified in the DFD.

Data Flow Diagram (DFD)   A **data flow diagram (DFD)** breaks down system specifications to the lowest level of detail. It also identifies transformations that will culminate in programs for system design. The DFD is a series of bubbles joined by lines that describe *what* data flows (logical) rather than *how* they are processed. The four symbols are shown in Figure 14.6. They are:

1. *Square:* a source or destination (e.g., customer, vendor, warehouse, etc.)

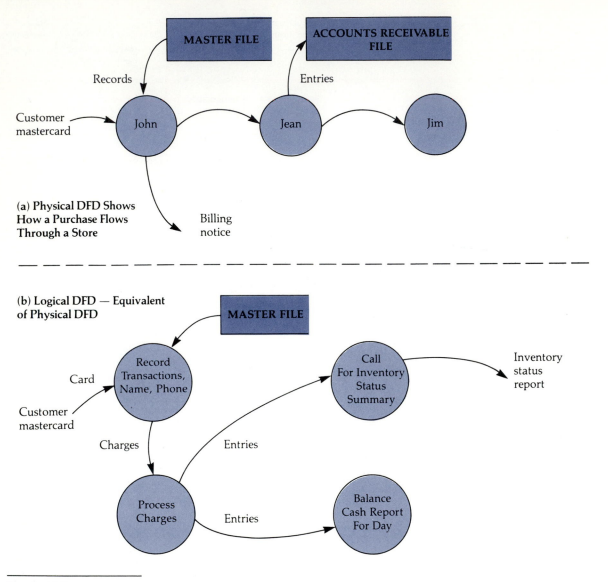

Figure 14.5
(a) Physical data flow diagram and (b) its logical equivalent.

2. *Arrow:* data flow (data in motion)
3. *Circle* (bubble): a process that transforms incoming data flow to outgoing data flow
4. *Open rectangle* (data store): a temporary repository of data

The example verifies a car order, the customer's credit rating, and car availability. When the order is approved, it is processed through the storage lot, where the car is verified before delivery.

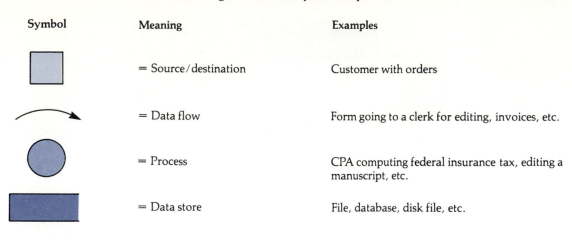

(a) DFD Symbols and Meanings

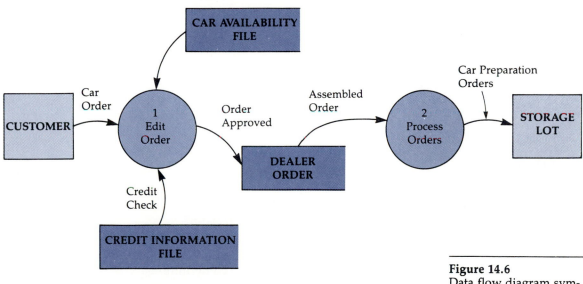

(b) Order Verification and Credit Check

Figure 14.6
Data flow diagram symbols and example.

A DFD may be expanded into lower level details involving each processing step in the general model. Figure 14.7 illustrates how the EDIT-ORDER step is expanded to elaborate on the details of the procedure (Martin and McClure, 1985).

Data Dictionary   A **data dictionary** is a repository of data about data. It contains documentation and definitions of data elements, terms, and procedures. It also provides cross-referencing of data and programs and

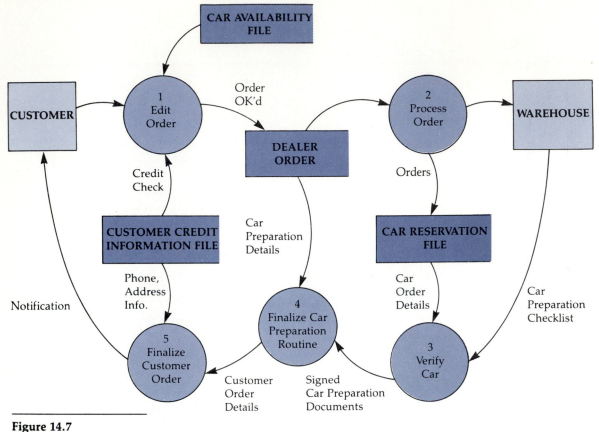

Figure 14.7
A data flow diagram.

keeps track of synonyms. In constructing a data dictionary, several points must be considered:

1. Each data flow in the DFD has one data dictionary entry.
2. Definitions must be accurately written and accessible by name.
3. No redundancy is allowed in data definitions.

Data definition follows a logical hierarchy based on three classes of items: data element, data structure, and data flow/data store. A **data element** (also called a **primitive**) is the smallest unit of data where no further breakdown is provided. For example, the data item CUSTOMER-NAME consists of first, middle, last, and alias (synonym), if any. No further breakdown is possible.

Data structure is a group of data elements treated as a unit. In our earlier example, CUSTOMER-NAME is one of several data elements making up a CAR-ORDER. Other data elements are CAR-BRAND, CAR-MAKE, CAR-COLOR, etc. Therefore, we specify a data structure by defining the data elements it represents. Our CAR-ORDER example and its elements are:

```
┌────────────────────┬──────────────────────┐
│ Data structure     │ CAR ORDER            │
│                    │                      │
│ Data elements      │ CUSTOMER-NAME        │
│                    │ CAR-MAKE             │
│                    │ CAR-MODEL            │
│                    │ CAR-COLOR            │
└────────────────────┴──────────────────────┘
```

A **data flow** is described by the name(s) of the data structure(s) that pass through it. We may also specify the source, volume, and destination of the data flow. Using our CAR-ORDER example, data flows are described as follows:

```
┌──────────────────────────────────────────────────────────┐
│ Data flows          Comments                             │
│                                                          │
│ CAR-DETAILS         From Ron Fisher Auto, Inc. (source)  │
│                                                          │
│ CUSTOMER-NAME       John W. Adams                        │
│                                                          │
│ CAR-MAKE            Cadillac                             │
│                                                          │
│ CAR-MODEL           Sedan de Ville                       │
│                                                          │
│ CAR-YEAR            1987                                 │
└──────────────────────────────────────────────────────────┘
```

A **data store** is described by the data structure and data flows that it relates to. In our example, the data store CAR-ORDER is described as follows:

```
┌──────────────────────────────────────────────────────────┐
│ Data store          Comments                             │
│ ORDER                                                    │
│    ORDER-NO.        Data flow/data structure feeding     │
│                        the data store                    │
│    CUSTOMER-DETAILS Available in the data store          │
│    CAR-DETAILS      Leaving data store by data flow      │
└──────────────────────────────────────────────────────────┘
```

It can be seen that a data dictionary is a critical part of the system specification. Without it, the DFD would have no meaning and without DFD, the data dictionary is of little use. Thus both are necessary for system design.

Once the data elements are defined in the data dictionary, we then look at the processes or the logical description. For example, in Figure 14.6, we need to know what goes into EDIT ORDER. In Figure 14.7, EDIT-ORDER (process 1) can be described as shown in Table 14.5.

Table 14.5   Description of a Process

Name of Process: EDIT-ORDER
**Description: Determine whether customer credit is satisfactory for selling
          a car on credit or whether it must be for cash**

Inputs	Logic	Output
ORDER	Look up customer payment record	Credit approved, no balance due
Customer payment file	If previous customer and car price $15,000, authorize 90% financing. Otherwise, refer to a bank.	
	If new customer, require 40% down payment.	
Balance on order	If under two years, approve order. Otherwise, require 10% down payment.	

Decision Trees and Structured English   The logic of a process may be illustrated by a tool called a **decision tree**. It is a graphic representation of conditions and outcomes resembling the branches of a tree. A decision tree is easy to construct, read, and modify. The logic summarized in Table 14.5 is represented in a decision tree, shown in Table 14.6.

The alternative to a decision tree is **Structured English**. The syntax uses simple declarative sentences, closed-end decision construct, or closed-end repetition construct to carry out instructions. Decisions are formed through IF, THEN, ELSE, and SO statements. They are English statements using indentation to emphasize the logical hierarchy. Our auto

Table 14.6   Decision Tree

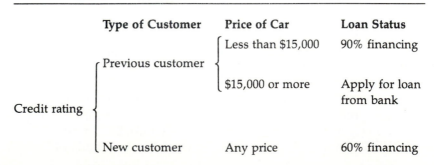

	Type of Customer	Price of Car	Loan Status
Credit rating	Previous customer	Less than $15,000	90% financing
		$15,000 or more	Apply for loan from bank
	New customer	Any price	60% financing

```
        CREDIT-RATING
IF   order is from previous customer
        THEN-IF   order is less than $15,000 per car
            THEN financing is 90 %
            ELSE:  Customer must apply for a loan
                    from a bank
                    no financing is approved
ELSE(customer is new)
            order is for any price
            financing is 60 %
```

Figure 14.8
Structured English for
auto financing.

financing may be represented in Structured English as shown in Figure 14.8. Note the resemblance between Structured English and a decision tree.

In reviewing the pros and cons of each tool, we can draw the following conclusions:

1. The DFD is strongest in representing data flows and quality documentation, but shows poor input and output detail.
2. The data dictionary makes it easier to represent the system's data requirements, although users in general have difficulty understanding it.
3. The decision tree is ideal for logic in problems that have few basic decisions.
4. Structured English is best used in situations where the process can be described in terms of a series of actions and resulting decisions.

Determination of Feasibility

So far we have discussed the initial investigation—determining the user's information requirements and fact finding by means of various tools. The initial investigation culminates in a proposal that recommends whether an alternative system is worth pursuing. When approved by management, the proposal initiates a **feasibility study** that evaluates alternative systems and recommends the system that meets performance requirements.

Three considerations are involved in a feasibility study: economic, technical, and behavioral. *Economic* feasibility, better known as cost/benefit analysis, determines to what extent a new system is cost effective. *Technical* feasibility is determined by evaluating the hardware and supportive software. *Behavioral* feasibility includes the training the user staff must have on a candidate system. All these factors must be viewed collectively for a successful installation.

Steps in Feasibility Analysis

A feasibility analysis can be broken down into the following tasks.

1. *Form a project team.* The first step in a feasibility study is to form a project team of experienced analysts and user staff. In complex studies, an outside consultant and an information analyst are added to the team for the duration of the project.

2. *Prepare system flowcharts.* A **system flowchart** is a physical representation of a system. It specifies what activities must be carried out to convert from a physical to a logical model (see Figure 14.9). System flowcharts represent system activities. They must be prepared prior to final logic design.

3. *Identify the characteristics of alternative systems.* This step considers the hardware that meets the total system requirements. Technical knowledge of hardware and software is crucial at this point.

4. *Evaluate cost/performance of each alternative system.* Whatever the criteria, there must be a close match between system requirements and system performance. Performance criteria are evaluated against cost to determine the most cost-effective system. Obviously, the more tangible the costs, the easier it will be to measure the benefits.

5. *Quantify system criteria and costs.* One procedure for quantifying alternative system criteria is as follows:

    a. Determine a weight factor for each criterion based on its perceived impact on the system.

    b. Assign a relative rating to each criterion. For example, on a scale of 1–5, 1 is rated poor and 5 is rated excellent.

    c. Multiply the weight factor by the relative rating and sum the score for each alternative system. Table 14.7 is an example of a weighted candidate evaluation matrix of three microcomputers.

6. *Select the best system.* Assuming the weight and rating factors are accurate, the system with the highest score is judged the best system. Additional supportive information would be helpful in reinforcing the choice.

The Feasibility Report

The outcome of the feasibility study—in fact, of the initial investigation—is the feasibility report, a formal presentation to management. The content must be brief enough to show how the new system was recommended, but contain enough details to be used later in system design. The report is generally organized as follows:

1. *Cover letter* formally presents the report.
2. *Table of contents* lists parts, exhibits, and their respective locations in the report.

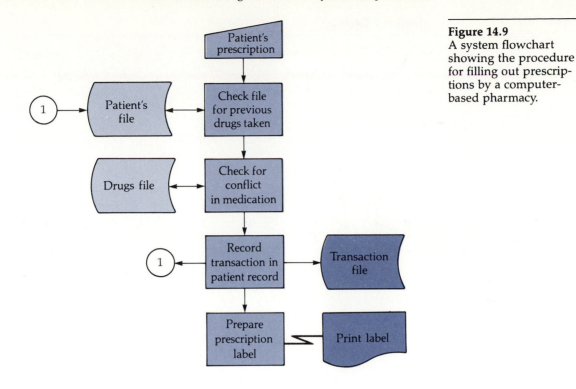

Figure 14.9
A system flowchart
showing the procedure
for filling out prescrip-
tions by a computer-
based pharmacy.

3. *Statement of the problem* describes the current and proposed systems and shows how the proposed system will solve the problem.
4. *Cost/benefit analysis* lists benefits and savings in dollars, presents savings versus costs, and summarizes new hardware/software costs and charges.
5. *Implementation schedule* includes an implementation plan, human resources requirements, and a PERT chart detailing the time factor and duration of the installation.
6. *Hardware configurations* specify computer configuration terminals and the telecommunication network (if any).
7. *Appendix* includes exhibits, correspondence, and supportive documentation.

Unfortunately, written reports have been abused as a tool to communicate with the user. There is a tendency to generate a lengthy document in line with the scope of the study. Complete and well documented reports are certainly justifiable, but reports exceeding 100 pages look unwieldy and discourage the most ambitious managers from reading them. As a rule, top management and boards of directors do not mind reading a two-page report; middle management, between three- and ten-page reports; and lower management, up to fifty-page reports. Any reports exceeding this length are most likely to be skimmed.

Table 14.7   Weighted Evaluation Matrix

		System A		System B		System C	
Evaluation Criteria	Weight	Rating	Score	Rating	Score	Rating	Score
Performance							
Accuracy	4	5	20	5	20	5	20
Enhancement potential	3	4	12	4	12	3	9
Response time	2	4	8	5	10	5	10
User-friendliness	2	4	8	3	6	4	8
Costs							
Payback	2	3	6	4	8	5	10
System development	4	4	16	3	12	4	16
System operation	3	4	12	3	9	4	12
User training	4	5	20	3	12	3	12
Totals			102		89		97

Occasionally a large report may be split into modules, with each module going to managers at different levels and a summary going to top management. In any case, it is important to remember that a report, in addition to its content, must sell the new system, minimize criticism or controversy, clarify facts, address concerns, and inject optimism. Each paragraph ideally represents a single idea. The sentence should be short and simple and the level of writing should be pitched at the user's level. Elimination of jargon and abbreviations such as DFD, DBMS, and the like is important.

In addition to the written report, the analyst or project leader is expected to give an oral presentation to sell the system to management. It is important that the analyst possesses communication skills, knowledge about the new system, and ability to clarify issues in a language understandable to management. The analyst's success record also plays a role in the final decision to adopt the system.

Cost/Benefit Analysis

Analysis of the costs and benefits of alternative systems guides the final selection process. Therefore, a knowledge of cost and benefit categories is important. In determining cost estimates, we focus on hardware, human resources, physical facilities, and operating costs. In addition, each system's benefits must be identified and a monetary value assigned.

Procedure for Cost/Benefit Determination   Cost/benefit analysis provides a statement of the costs, benefits, and constraints associated with

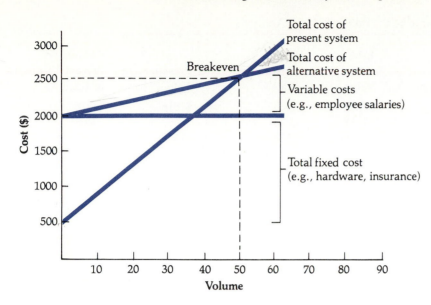

Figure 14.10
Breakeven chart.

each alternative system. A common procedure involves the following steps:

1. *Identify the costs and benefits* relevant to the system. Costs and benefits may be direct or indirect, tangible or intangible, fixed or variable. Figure 14.10 illustrates fixed and variable costs. Most basic accounting texts cover this area well.

2. *Select a method for evaluation.* The primary evaluation methods are:
    a. **Breakeven analysis** is the point at which the costs of the present and the alternative systems are equal (see Figure 14.10).
    b. **Payback analysis** is determining how long it will take a system to produce enough savings to pay for developmental costs.
    c. **Present value** is another term for the current value of money. It is computed by discounting future monetary values backward in time to the present. For example, if we invest $4000 in a microcomputer and the average annual benefit is $2000 for the three-year life cycle, we consider the time value of the money to be invested. This is illustrated in Table 14.8.
    d. **Net present value** means discounted benefits minus discounted costs. The $4000 microcomputer investment (Table 14.8) yields a cumulative benefit of $4970 or a net present gain of $970. This value represents the time value of money. The net present value is expressed as a percentage of the investment— in our example, the $970 gain is 970/4000 = .24 percent. The procedure, advantages, and disadvantages of each evaluation method are summarized in Table 14.9.

3. *Interpret the results and make a final decision.* The results of the evaluation are compared to a standard set in advance. The final decision to

Table 14.8   Present Value Analysis

Year	Est. Future Value		Discounted Rate		Present Value	Cumulative Present Value of Benefits
1	$2,000	×	.908	=	$1816	$1816
2	2,000	×	.826	=	1652	3468
3	2,000	×	.751	=	1502	4970

Interest rate $i = 10\%$

a. Discount factor $= 1/[(1+i)^n]$

b. Present value $= P = F/[(1+i)^n]$

F = future value of an investment $= P + (1 + i)^n$

n = year

Table 14.9   Alternative Evaluation Methods

Method	Procedure	Advantages	Disadvantages
Breakeven	Plots the costs of two systems	Easy to learn and compute	No allowance for time factor and depreciation value of money
Payback	Total investment divided by annual savings	Easy to compute Easy to interpret the choice between alternative systems	Does not compare impact of multiple investment alternatives No allowance for time value of money
Present value	$P = F/[(1 + i)^n]$, where: n = number of years i = interest rate F = future value of an investment $F = P(1 + i)^n$	Allows for time value of money Easy to compute Equates alternative investment opportunities with various costs, benefits, and discount rate	A relative (not absolute) measurement of return on investment
Net present value	Discounted benefits minus discounted costs	Easy to compute Accounts for time value of money	A relative (not absolute) measurement of return on investment

Adapted from Awad, 1985, 249.

adopt a system can be subjective, depending on the reliability of the data and complexity of the system.

We can see that cost/benefit analysis is a tool for evaluating systems, not a substitute for the user's final judgment. Like any tool, it has drawbacks. For example, intangible costs and benefits are not easy to determine. Favoritism can also distort the results of the analysis. One viable system is often ignored in favor of another. This is where ethics and integrity play a decisive role in the evaluation process.

Value of Information in Analysis

How much should information-gathering or analysis be performed before making a commitment to a course of action? Deciding on the value of information helps us confront the decision issue, perform the necessary analysis, and communicate the decision rationale to management. One decision guideline is to ensure that the required cost and schedule of the analysis do not overly curtail its net value. It makes no sense to obtain results that cost more than what they attempt to save.

Another decision guideline is to consider a feasibility study on the basis of its value in training, analyst-user relations, design validation, or improved decision making. There is much subjectivity in determining information value, depending on the nature of the organization and the availability of proper tools for value measurement.

The Role of the Systems Analyst

What Does It Take to Do Systems Work?

The analyst is the key link between user and system implementation. Success in systems analysis requires two types of skills: interpersonal and technical. *Interpersonal* skills are useful in dealing with the end user, establishing trust, resolving conflict, and communicating information. Interpersonal skills instrumental in systems work include:

1. *Communicating:* essentially speaking the language of the user, mediating, working with management at all levels, and political sensitivity.
2. *Teaching and selling:* educating the user on technology, selling and promoting change through information systems. The analyst must also make the user want to "buy" change.
3. *Understanding:* identifying problem areas and determining their impact, grasping user requirements, and being sensitive to the impact of the system on people.

The key *technical* skills are:

1. *Broad knowledge of business practice* in general and ability to translate technical information at the user's level.
2. *Dynamic interface,* making effective use of technical and nontechnical elements in system design.
3. *Knowledge of computers*, software, and technology in general; knowing how information works and how to acquire, design, and install information systems.
4. *Project management,* scheduling people and technology, coordinating teams, meeting deadlines, and absorbing stress.

In real life, we expect greater emphasis on interpersonal skills during the feasibility study. Technical skills are critical during design, when limited interaction is expected with the end user. The two skills, however, converge during the implementation phase, when the technical aspects debug the software, while the interpersonal skills are needed in training the user on the candidate system.

In addition to these skills, a career in systems analysis requires academic preparation and personal qualities. These include:

1. A college degree in business administration, computer science, or MIS.
2. A background in the workings of the business enterprise.
3. Familiarity with the area for which the system is being designed—for example, knowledge of banking operations is useful in installing an asset-liability management system.

The personal qualities that support systems analysis include an outgoing personality, ability to delegate and specify job assignments, creative ability, and communication skills.

The Multiple Role of the Analyst

A systems analyst performs a variety of roles. Various studies have suggested five major roles:

1. *Agent of change:* requiring a style to sell the change. The style ranges from that of persuader to imposer of change, depending on the user's level in the organization and the leverage of the analyst.
2. *Investigator:* identifying the real problem(s) of a system and mapping out procedures for alternative solutions.
3. *"Linking pin":* performing the role of a liaison between the end user's abstract design requirements and the detailed physical design.
4. *Listener:* reaching people, interpreting their thoughts, and drawing conclusions from interactions can be improved significantly by careful and sympathetic listening. This is the other face of effective communication.

5. *Politician:* solving a problem by not creating another—an art in itself. A successful analyst knows whom to contact, what to say, and how to use the information for system design. Diplomacy and finesse in dealing with users can also improve the acceptance of a new system.

Behavioral Issues

Much research has been conducted to understand the user-analyst interface. There are three behavioral issues relevant to system success:

1. *Narrowing user-analyst differences.* Ignoring user suggestions and producing analyst-oriented systems has been known to be a major cause of system failure. At the root of the analyst-user interface problem is the fundamental difference in the way analysts and users process information. Variations in cognitive style play an important role in determining the extent to which a system meets the user requirements. There is a need for mutual understanding between analyst and user. Many of the differences can be alleviated through the user's regular involvement in the project and the analyst's acceptance and encouragement of this involvement.

2. *Establishing user motivation.* The value that the user places on the rewards perceived from a new system determines his or her motivation to use the system. Ensuring a proper fit between system capabilities and user requirements means a technically sound design and user participation throughout the SDLC. A willing user is crucial to system acceptance and implementation.

3. *Neutralizing political factors.* Acquiring an information system is often viewed as a way of acquiring power or improving leverage in the organization. To neutralize political implications, the analyst must understand the motives behind the approval of a new system before initiating design.

Place in the MIS Organization

The systems analyst is a key member of the MIS organization. An MIS facility consists of:

1. *Administration,* which interfaces with the user and has responsibility for long-range planning, budget planning, and control.
2. *Analysis and design,* which deals with the development of applications and information systems in general.
3. *Programming,* which is organized to handle system application programming and maintenance.
4. *Operations,* which deals with the day-to-day scheduling of job runs and the management of supplies.

Of these functions, analysis and design are extremely crucial for system development. The role carries considerable responsibility, high status, and attractive pay. Since the early 1980s, new semiprofessional positions have been developed in performing general support work, such as drafting programs, writing manuals, and updating data dictionaries. Another new job is that of the technical writer. The main function is producing the quality documentation every new system requires.

Summary

□ An information system undergoes a development life cycle consisting of the following steps:
1. *Recognition of need*, leading to problem definition.
2. *Feasibility study*, which entails evaluation of the present system, analysis of alternative systems, and determination of costs and benefits. Analysis involves data gathering and assessing of the present system to determine what must be done to solve the problem.
3. *Design*, which specifies how the problem must be solved. This includes general and detail specifications of output, input, files, and procedures. Coding and testing is also covered under design.
4. *Implementation*, which essentially focuses on file and system conversion and user training.
5. *Postimplementation*, which determines the extent of modification in the system for continued operation.

□ The main objective of an initial investigation is to determine how serious a user request is and whether there should be a feasibility study. Determining user needs is the primary task of the analyst. There are three strategies for gaining information about the user's requirements:
1. *Asking users questions* to specify their requirements.
2. *Data analysis*, which involves an understanding of the information received compared to the information required.
3. *Prototyping*, a model that uses a set of information requirements to build a system that meets user specifications.

□ The traditional tools used in analysis include existing documents, on-site observations, interviews, and questionnaires. The interview is the most popular by far, although it is often abused. Interviews may be structured or unstructured. Questions are open or closed. Open questions may be classified as dichotomous, fill-in-the-blank, multiple-choice, rating scales, or ranking scales.

□ Structured tools are used as an alternative to traditional tools. The structured approach uses graphics rather than narrative to improve communications with the user. It also distinguishes between logical and physical systems. The outcome is the system specification that is a prerequisite for design.

▫ The data flow diagram (DFD) is an important tool in structured analysis. It uses four symbols: square (source or destination), arrow (data flow), circle (process), and open rectangle (data store). Another tool is the data dictionary—a repository of data about data. Data definition follows a hierarchy based on data element, data structure, and data flow/data store. Other tools include the decision tree and Structured English.

▫ Several steps make up feasibility analysis:
1. Form a project team.
2. Prepare system flowcharts.
3. Identify the characteristics of alternative systems.
4. Evaluate cost/performance of each alternative system.
5. Quantify system criteria and costs.
6. Select the best system.

▫ The analysis of the costs and benefits of each candidate system guides the final selection process. In developing cost estimates, we consider hardware, human resources, physical facilities, and operating costs.

▫ Cost/benefit analysis follows the following procedure:
1. Identify the costs and benefits.
2. Select a method of evaluation (breakeven analysis, payback analysis, present value, and net present value).
3. Interpret the results and make a final decision.

▫ Success in systems work requires interpersonal and technical skills, academic preparation, and personal qualities. The interpersonal skills include communication and selling abilities and understanding of problems. Technical skills include knowledge of computers, broad knowledge of business practice, and project management. We expect a greater need for interpersonal skills during analysis but greater technical skills during design.

▫ Three issues are relevant to system success:
1. Narrowing user/analyst differences through deeper user participation.
2. Establishing user motivation for system acceptance.
3. Neutralizing political factors.

▫ An MIS facility consists of administration, systems analysis, programming, and operations. Of these functions, systems analysis is extremely crucial for system development. The job carries considerable responsibility, high status, and attractive pay.

Key Terms

Bounded rationality	Breakeven analysis
Brainstorming	Candidate system

Closed question
Contrived observation
Data dictionary
Data element
Data flow
Data flow diagram (DFD)
Data store
Data structure
Decision tree
Delphi inquiry
Dichotomous question
Direct cost
Direct observation
Feasibility study
Group consensus
Indirect cost
Indirect observation
Natural observation
Net present value

Open-ended question
Payback analysis
Present value
Primitive: See data element
Prototyping
Ranking scales question
Rating scales question
Reliability
Structured analysis
Structured English
Structured interview
Structured question
System development life cycle
   (SDLC)
System flowchart
System specifications
Unobtrusive observation
Unstructured interview
Validity

Review Questions

1. The system development life cycle entails several steps for system implementation. Explain each step and its relationship to the final installation.

2. What is a feasibility study? How does it relate to analysis?

3. Distinguish between:
   a. Analysis and design
   b. Initial investigation and feasibility study
   c. Rating and ranking scales
   d. Maintenance and enhancement

4. Why do systems fail? What reason(s) do you consider the most critical? Discuss.

5. What does it take to be a successful analyst? Elaborate.

6. The systems analyst assumes a variety of roles. What major roles are relevant to analysis? What role would be most important in situations involving experienced users at the upper managerial level? Why?

7. Explain the behavioral issues that are relevant to system success.

8. According to the text, determining user requirements is one of the most difficult tasks in system development. Do you agree? Discuss.

9. Discuss the key strategies for determining information requirements.

10. In what way does brainstorming differ from the Delphi inquiry?

11. An important strategy for determining user information requirements is called prototyping. What is it? How does it work with the SDLC?

12. There are various traditional tools used in data gathering. Summarize the major tools and give examples to illustrate their use.

13. Compare and contrast the pros and cons of interviewing and questionnaires.

14. Under what circumstances is on-site observation best used? Explain.

15. When is it best to use the interview rather than the questionnaire in systems work? Be specific.

16. Explain the difference between structured and unstructured questionnaires. When is one type preferable to the other? Elaborate.

17. Define the following:
    a. Dichotomous questions
    b. Ranking scales
    c. Bounded rationality
    d. Decision tree

18. Compare structured tools to traditional tools in general. What drawbacks do traditional tools have? Structured tools?

19. Explain the basis for and makeup of the structured specification. Why is it important for system design?

20. Explain and illustrate the symbols used in structuring a data flow diagram.

21. What is the relationship between data element and data structure? Data flow diagram and data dictionary?

22. In what way does the structured approach encourage user involvement and improve user-designer communication?

23. What considerations are involved in feasibility analysis? Discuss.

24. Explain carefully the steps taken in feasibility analysis. What role does cost/benefit analysis play in the feasibility study?

25. Explain the procedure for cost/benefit determination.

26. Illustrate the difference between present value and net present value.

Application Problems

1. The steering committee of a large commercial bank is considering a request from the vice president of the mortgage loan department to install the 9200 loan files on line, making mortgage loan information available at the forty-one branches. The bank's central computer operates at 43 percent of capacity and can easily accommodate the additional loan.

To install the application, the bank must acquire a $14,000 software package and install on-line terminals in the branches. Each terminal costs $1050 plus 15 percent for installation and hookup. The existing voice-grade telecommunication network can be used to link the terminals to the mainframe.

Mortgage loan processing is presently carried out in a batch environment. No information about today's activities is available before noon the next day. If a customer requests information, a branch teller phones in or mails an inquiry to the MIS center 18 miles away. The response usually takes one and a half days. With an on-line, real-time environment, the mortgage loan department would have instant inquiry/response and update capabilities.

The bank has been known as a leader in the banking community for introducing labor-saving technology and providing full customer service on a regular basis. In the proposal, the vice president of the mortgage loan department reasoned that with an on-line system, tellers can answer inquiries about mortgage loans in seconds. This would encourage more customers to use the branches rather than the main office for such information. It also means savings in human resources and a more balanced distribution of the workload among the branches. In contrast, the MIS director feels that the nature and frequency of inquiries historically have not been coming by leaps and bounds. None of the information is urgent enough to warrant on-line service.

QUESTIONS

a. Based on the information provided, how feasible is the proposal? Would you recommend that it be pursued? Why? Explain.
b. What information must be gathered before a final decision can be made? How would you secure the information? Be specific.

2. Develop an overall data flow diagram for the following applications:
a. A travel agent making round-trip reservations for a customer from Miami to New York.
b. Making auto loans.

3. In 1985, the safe deposit department of a savings and loan bank housed 5000 boxes of various sizes. Later in the year, projected demand for safe deposit boxes prompted top management to install 5000 additional boxes, bringing the total to 10,000. The addition also increased the number of full-time attendants from three to five.

The rental procedure is simple. A customer fills out a form for a specific box and pays an annual charge in advance. He/she is issued a key that, along with the attendant's key, must be inserted in the box before it is open.

Each rental generates a billing transaction. Bills are processed manually on a six-cycle basis: every five days, beginning with the first of each month. A customer receives a renewal notice one month before expiration date.

For the safe deposit case, Figure 14.A1 is a data flow diagram to install a customer account:

QUESTIONS
a. Are there flaws in the data flow diagram? List the corrections.
b. Develop an expanded data flow diagram for bubble 2.
c. Using the information in the case, develop a data flow diagram to close the customer's account (box).

4. Irv Cox, president and owner of a successful mail-order house of microcomputer supplies, offers discounts to qualified customers based on order size. Discounts are computed as follows:
- If Invoice-Total is $1000 or over, discount is 30%
- If Invoice-Total is $500–999, discount is 20%
- If Invoice-Total is $300–499, discount is 10%

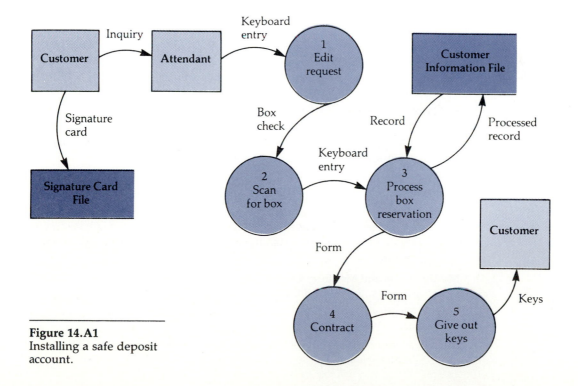

Figure 14.A1
Installing a safe deposit
account.

• If Invoice-Total is under $300, no discount allowed

Shipping and handling charges depend on whether supplies are handled by regular or air mail. If the customer authorizes regular mail, the charges are as follows:

• If weight is under 20 lbs, shipping/handling rate is $20
• If weight is 21–30 lbs, shipping/handling rate is $25
• If weight is over 30 lbs, shipping/handling rate is $25 + (excess weight over 30 lbs × $2).

Air mail charges are computed by multiplying shipping weight by $1.50.

QUESTIONS

a. Construct a decision tree.
b. Write the information in Structured English.

Selected References

Alloway, Robert M. and Quillard, Judith A. "User Manager's Systems Needs." *MIS Quarterly,* June 1983, 22–41.

Awad, Elias M. *Systems Analysis and Design* (2nd ed.). Homewood, Ill.: Irwin, 1985.

———. "Vocational Needs, Reinforcers, and Job Satisfaction of Analysts and Programmers in a Banking Environment." Tenth Australian Computer Conference, Melbourne, Australia, September 1983.

Bramson, Robert M. and Harrison, Allen F. "The Orderly Ways of Analysts." *Computer Decisions,* November 1983, 112.

Davis, G. B. "Strategies for Information Requirements Determination." *IBM Systems Journal,* 21, (1982), 5.

DeMarco, Tom. *Structured Analysis and Systems Specifications.* New York: Yourdon Press, 1979.

Harrison, Ralph. "Prototyping and the Systems Development Life Cycle." *Journal of Systems Management,* August 1985, 22–25.

Hoffman, Thomas R. and Harris, James N. "Para-Professionals in System Development." *Journal of Systems Management,* November 1983, 25–29.

Kauber, Peter G. "Prototyping: Not a Method But a Philosophy." *Journal of Systems Management,* September 1985, 28–33.

Knauer, Gene. "The Rise of the Technical Writer." *Computerworld,* January 9, 1984, ID1–2ff.

Martin, James and McClure, Carma. *Diagramming Techniques for Analysts and Programmers.* Englewood Cliffs, N.J.: Prentice-Hall, 1985, 93–108.

Moran, Thomas P. "An Applied Psychology of The User." *Computing Surveys,* March 1981, 1–11.

Newell, A. and Simon, Herbert. *Human Problem Solving.* Englewood Cliffs, N.J.: Prentice-Hall, 1972.

Pitzgorsky, George. "Analyzing, Defining Systems Needs." *MIS Week*, August 24, 1983, 30.

Rush, Gary. "A Fast Way to Define System Requirements." *Computerworld*, October 7, 1985, ID11–16.

Walsh, Robert J. "Try Talking Before Automating." *Computerworld*, September 17, 1984, ID9–10ff.

Welke, R. J. and Konsynski, B. P. "Technology, Methodology, and Information Systems: A Tripartite View." *Data Base*, Fall 1982, 41–58.

Whieldon, David. "Prototyping: Shortcut to Applications." *Computer Decisions*, June 1984, 138–140ff.

Young, T. R. "Superior Prototypes." *Datamation*, May 15, 1984, 152–155ff.

System Design

Chapter Contents

Accelerated Design Speeds the Application Development Cycle

DURING THE LAST FEW years, many application development aids have been introduced in the MIS environment as part of the search for ways to unlock the application development log jam. Now, a new productivity tool that focuses on the initial stage of the application development life cycle is rapidly gaining popularity with Fortune 500 firms and other large organizations. The tool is called "accelerated design."

Accelerated design is a proven method for helping DP professionals reduce the inevitable inconsistencies that are uncovered during the interview and information-gathering phase of system design. Several accelerated design methodologies are currently in use under such names as Performance Resources' The METHOD, IBM's Joint Application Design (JAD), and Boeing Computer Services' Consensus. While the approaches differ slightly, all are designed to do the same thing: produce high-quality business system specifications faster and more accurately than the traditional approach of conducting a series of interviews with users.

Accelerated design has been used by companies such as AT&T, Mobil, Chase Manhattan Bank, Ford Motor Co., and American Airlines. It is a positive alternative for system professionals who find the traditional approach ill equipped to deal with today's complex, multiuser environment.

The heart of the accelerated design process is a highly structured workshop that is attended by a representative selection of application users and systems professionals who together hammer out a consensus on systems requirements. The final output of the workshop is a user requirement document that includes specific information management requirements, a data dictionary with data definitions and characteristics, input, outputs, and interface definitions and layouts.

By bringing end users together to identify, prioritize, and reach consensus on package features, accelerated design ensures that the package chosen will be the best possible.

The prospects for accelerated design look bright. Based on the success major companies have had in cutting design costs and streamlining the systems design process, it seems safe to say that the use of accelerated design will increase during the coming years.

—*Adapted from Naomi S. Leventhal,* Data Management, *July 1986, 10–13.*

AT A GLANCE

System design is a "how-to" approach to creating a system. This phase provides the mechanics to implement the system recommended in the feasibility study. Design goes through two stages of development: logical and physical design. In logical design, the analyst prepares input and output specifications and maps out test and implementation plans. In physical design, the analyst determines the physical aspects of the system, devises a test procedure, and identifies the hardware and software.

The first step in system design is deciding on output and input formats. In output design, the analyst produces a hard copy in a user-acceptable format. In input design, the analyst develops a computer-based format from user-generated input data. Speed of capture and entry into the system are important considerations. Input design may be in the form of a menu, a form, and a prompt. Other design considerations are file and processing design.

By the end of this chapter, you should know:

1. The process of system design
2. Top-down design and functional decomposition
3. The major development activities in structured design
4. Various approaches to entering data into the computer
5. How forms are designed

Introduction

In the previous chapter, we discussed analysis—studying a system for pinpointing a problem area and deciding whether a solution is feasible. Once completed, management approves systems design—the next phase in SDLC. **Design** is a solution, a "how-to" approach, and a detailed implementation of the system recommended in the feasibility study. It translates system requirements into the means for operationalizing them. Focus is on a new system to take over the old one.

After you understand the requirements of a new system and how they are fulfilled (in terms of the analysis phase), the next question is how a system is designed. In this chapter, we review the process and stages of system design. **System design** includes logical and physical design, design methodologies, input/output and forms design, and file design. Implementing the system design is covered in the next chapter.

The Design Process

The design phase entails a conversion from a user-oriented to a pro-grammer-oriented document. It is a detailed specification of a solution that was selected in systems analysis. Design specifications are forwarded to the programmer for coding, testing, and installation.

Designing a system is a two-phase process involving logical and physical design. **Logical design** depicts the logical flow of the system and provides the system specifications. As we saw in Chapter 14, a data flow diagram (DFD) shows the logical flow of a system. Using the four major symbols, it specifies the inputs (source), outputs (destination), procedures (data flows), and files (data stores). A detailed logical design lays out system specifications at a level with no further breakdown. From such a layout, a data dictionary and Structured English are prepared for system implementation.

In logical design, we specify what the software should do—that is, how will the system meet the requirements identified during systems analysis? We produce four types of specifications documents:

1. *Output specifications:* format, content, and frequency of reports.
2. *Input specifications:* format, content, and flow of document from the input data source to the actual input location.
3. *File design specifications:* record format and sequence.
4. *Processing specifications:* with focus on report layouts (see Figure 15.1).

Logical design leads to **physical design**, which develops program software—the working system. The programmer uses the logical design specifications to write the programs. Starting with a system specification document, a system flowchart and DFD are produced. Next, they are broken down into modules. Each module is converted into program specifications. Modules are then tested independently and later integrated according to the structure chart and tested as a whole program.

Now that we know what is to be done, let us illustrate how a structure chart and Warnier/Orr diagram can be used as modular tools for designing computer programs.

Tools for Structured Design

Large projects are more easily managed if they are broken into smaller modules. Since the early 1970s, a structured or modular set of tools has been introduced for designing computer programs. These tools improve programmer productivity, cut down on cost overruns, upgrade documentation quality and communication between users, analysts and programmers, and standardize the approach to program design.

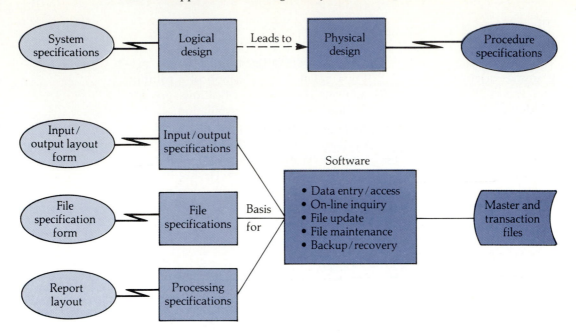

Figure 15.1
Logical and physical
design.

The Structure Chart   A **structure chart** is a treelike diagram that organizes systems design documentation into computer program specifications for each computer program. It is partitioned into a top-down hierarchy of independent modules. A **module** is a set of instructions that has a single entry point and a single exit point. Some modules exist to perform a single function—for example, PRINT A RECORD, CALCULATE NET PAY. Other modules exist to drive the function module. A module should be of reasonable length or consist of a limited number of executable instructions. It should not exceed fifty lines. This means that a program that requires at least fifty lines should be broken down into modules.

An illustration of a structure chart is shown in Figure 15.2. It consists of three elements:

1. Module
2. Connection
3. Couple

A module is represented by a rectangle with a name. The top module is UPDATE CUSTOMER FILE. It is the controlling module within the program. The name is the function of the whole program. It is called a **boss module**, because it calls other modules to do its work. The second level has four modules. They are submodules or **worker modules**. The third level is three submodules that show how to execute the GET NEW TRANSACTION module.

The second element in a structure chart is a **connection**—a vector linking two modules. It means one module has called another module.

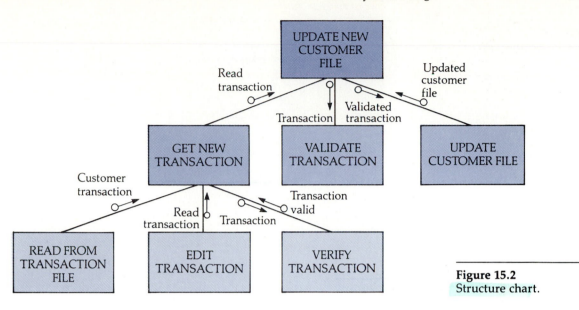

Figure 15.2
Structure chart.

In our example, the UPDATE NEW CUSTOMER FILE module is the *calling* module. It calls the GET VALID CUSTOMER FILE module, GET NEW TRANSACTION, VALIDATE TRANSACTION, and UPDATE CUSTOMER FILE. These four modules are the *called* modules.

The third element in a structure chart is the couple. A **couple** is an arrow with a circular tail. It refers to the dependence one module has on another. It also represents transactions moved from one module to another. In Figure 15.2, there are ten couples. The module UPDATE NEW CUSTOMER FILE calls GET VALID CUSTOMER FILE, passing Valid Master File downward and receiving Valid Customer File back.

In structured design, it is important for the program to be partitioned into independent modules so that each module is easily modifiable. The length of a module is important. Each module must perform only one task that makes it cohesive with the calling and called modules. A structure chart is an effective program design if it meets the two criteria of cohesion and coupling.

The Warnier/Orr Diagram   Another common tool for the modular design of a program is the **Warnier/Orr diagram**, which is simply a hierarchy chart lying on its side. Brackets decompose modules into submodules. Execution is read from top to bottom and left to right. Figure 15.3 is a Warnier/Orr diagram of the structure chart in Figure 15.2.

Specifying Modules   Once we have a structure chart, we then describe the function of each module and specify what it must do when it is executed. Module specification may be procedural or nonprocedural.

Figure 15.3
Warnier/Orr diagram.

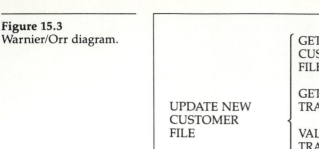

Nonprocedural specifications state the module's function but do not specify how to write the program instructions. **Procedural specifications** are explicit about how the module should be implemented.

A nonprocedural module specification technique includes the following:

1. A description of input and output coupling. For example:

```
Module name: READ FROM TRANSACTION FILE (see
Figure 15.2)
Input couple: None
Output couple
  CUSTOMER
    TRANSACTION:  If successfully read, it
                  contains next record;
                  otherwise file contents
                  unchanged
```

2. *Disk record layout.* This technique is appropriate for modules (usually at the lower end of a structure chart) that perform input/output functions. It specifies the physical details of a file.
3. *Printed report and CRT display layouts.* This technique is appropriate for modules that format printed reports or CRT displays. It uses a two-dimensional grid to show the location of all the information. These layout specifications are explained later in the chapter.
4. *Decision trees.* A decision tree is a specification tool for describing modules that handle compound conditions. Decision trees have been discussed in Chapter 14.

Procedural specifications emphasize module implementation rather than function. The two major techniques are the flowcharts and Structured English. As we have seen in Chapter 14, when we use either tool we describe the sequence required for writing the module's instructions. In this way, it is easy for the programmer to follow. Module logic can also be reviewed prior to writing the code. Controlling modules, then, should be specified procedurally as they often represent complex decisions.

Automated Design Tools: The Excelerator

Since the early 1980s, we have seen a number of software packages designed for the professional systems analyst. One such package is EXCELERA-TOR—a totally integrated system with capabilities for designing and documenting almost any software project. The software runs on the IBM PS/2 and compatibles.

The operation procedure is simple. After the user enters the user ID, password, and name of project, EXCELERATOR displays the main menu, containing seven major facilities: Graphics, data dictionary, screens and reports, analysis, dictionary interface, system specification documentation, and housekeeping (see Figure 15.4).

The *graphics* facility is of particular importance in system design. In this facility, the analyst can draw six different types of diagrams and charts the system design:

1. Dataflow diagrams
2. Structure charts
3. Logical data model diagrams
4. Structure diagrams
5. Presentation graphs

Using a mouse, we simply point to the type of graph wanted and the action we wish to perform. For example, to update a DFD, we point to the dataflow diagram and click the mouse (see Figure 15.5). When we choose MODIFY, it asks us to select the graph. If we do not remember the name, we double click the mouse and it will list names for us. To select the graph, we point to its name and click the mouse. A drawing screen for DFD is shown in Figure 15.6.

To connect two objects, select the CONNECT command and simply point to the objects to be connected. The connecting lines can include arrows to indicate directional flow.

Similar to DFDs, a structure chart is created by drawing function boxes that explode to modules to represent a hierarchical sequence of jobs. Connection between function boxes is explained with couples that indicate the transfer of control between modules. Figure 15.7 illustrates an EXCELERATOR-generated structure chart. EXCELERATOR is becoming a popular tool in many business programs (see *Student Guide* for a tutorial on EXCELERATOR).

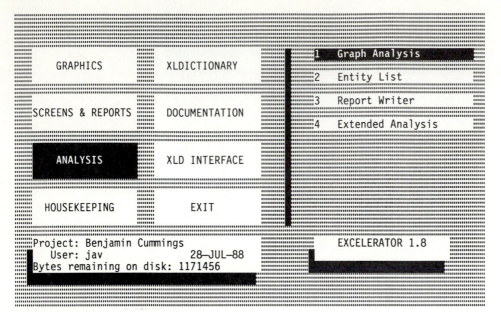

(a) Main menu with analysis selected

GRAPHICS

F Data Flow Diagram
S Structure Chart
M Data Model Diagram
R Entity-Relationship Diagram
D Structure Diagram
P Presentation Graph

Modify   Add   Delete

Copy   Rename   List

Exit   Name

(b) Action menu with modify selected

Figure 15.4
The major facilities of
EXCELERATOR.

Figure 15.5
Using a mouse.

Design Activities

There are four major activities in system design: output design, input design, file design, and software design. While software design is under-way, we develop plans to schedule testing and user training. Software testing is followed by system testing and user training. Software testing is followed by system testing—a bottom-up procedure. All test data and test results become a part of the design specifications to be used later for implementation. User manuals should also be prepared. The manual describes how to use the system and how to enter data and generate reports. Testing and implementation follow system design and are covered in Chapter 16.

In system design, we need to consider the role of audit controls. Accuracy and consistency standards should be incorporated into the soft-ware to minimize errors and check for potential fraud. Error control points should also be evaluated on the basis of error frequency and cost to the user. An *audit trail* that allows the analyst, user, or auditor to verify a process in the new system is a requirement for most applications. We need to incorporate audit routines early in system development so that changes can be made in time.

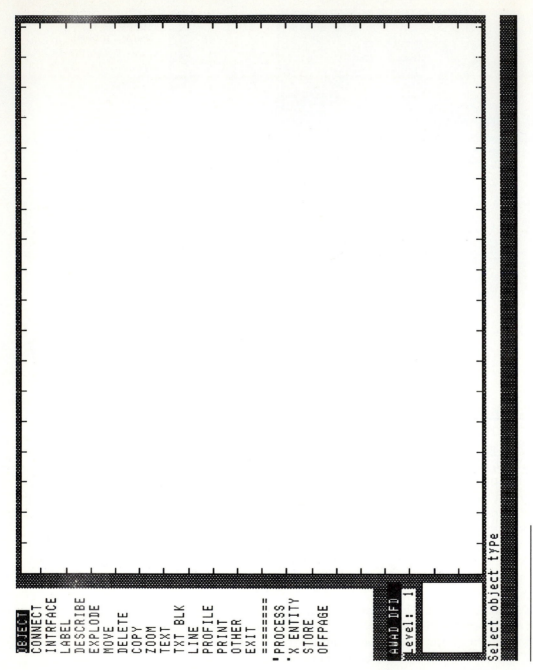

Figure 15.6
Drawing screen for data flow diagram: EXCEL-ERATOR graphics screen.

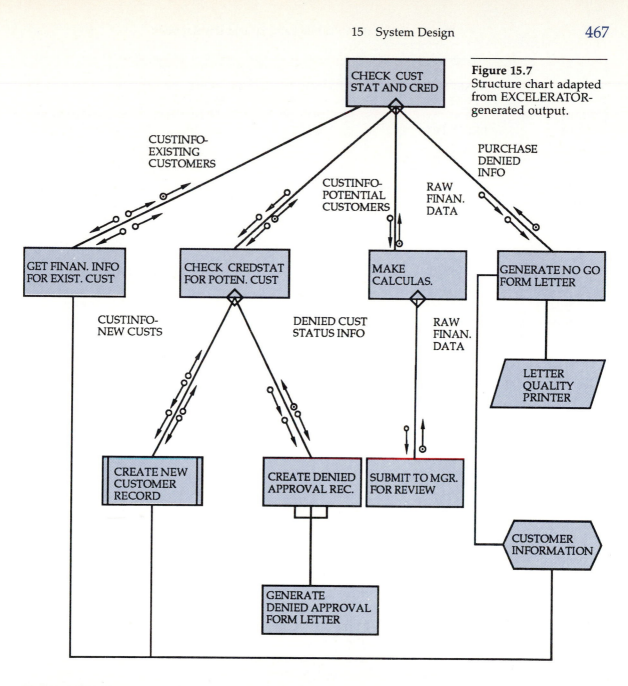

Figure 15.7
Structure chart adapted from EXCELERATOR-generated output.

Output Design

Well-organized, intelligible output improves the system's interface with the user. There are two types of output: business documents and management reports. Business documents such as purchase orders may be hard copy or transmitted electronically from one computer to another. This reduces paperwork and expedites the processing of orders. Another

```
          ASSETS AS OF AUG 31, 1987    40 00 0641 30 2
          FIRST NATL BK OF SO MIA ARNOLD & SONS PENS TR
SHARES/PAR                 UNIT MKT.       TOTAL MKT      INVESTMENT
VALUE     DESCRIPTION      PRICE           VALUE          COST BASIS


          M I S C   C A S H   E Q U I V - T X B L

42,446    FED SHORT TERM PRINC             42,466.00      42,466.00
          TOTAL  MISC CASH EQUIV-TXBL      42,466.00      42,466.00

          C O M M O N    STOCK

   400    CITICORP         62.750          25,100.00      19,872.60
   500    COCA COLA CO     50.625          25,312.50      23,850.60
   300    IBM             168.375          50,512.50      43,601.40
   300    KRAFT INC        59.000          17,700.00      12,964.80
   500    MARRIOTT CORP    41.125          20,562.50     120,244.00

          TOTAL COMMON STOCK              139,187.50     120,244.00

          GRAND TOTAL                     181,654.50     162,710.00
```

Figure 15.8
Turnaround document.

type of business document as output is the *turnaround* document. If you stop by your bank's customer service desk and ask for an activity statement on your checking account, the matrix printer attached to the CRT will produce a turnaround document of the deposits, checks paid, balance to date, and so on (see Figure 15.8).

Several activities take place in output design. First, we decide on the content of the output and how easy it is to read and understand. For example, a report should not look cluttered and, if it is for top management, should be concise and to the point. The layout of the output information should be so designed as to make it easy to follow. A common form layout is the *Z format*: The data are clustered into zones beginning in the upper left corner of the form. It records the same way we read or write in English—top to bottom and left to right (see Figure 15.9).

We also lay out a form using rules and captions. A *rule* is a vertical line that separates columns and a *caption* is a column heading. Whenever possible, we also provide "eyecatcher" areas for special information such as date, finance charges, amount due, and the like (see Figure 15.10).

The second output design consideration is to identify the hardware and software and determine how they will meet the output quality

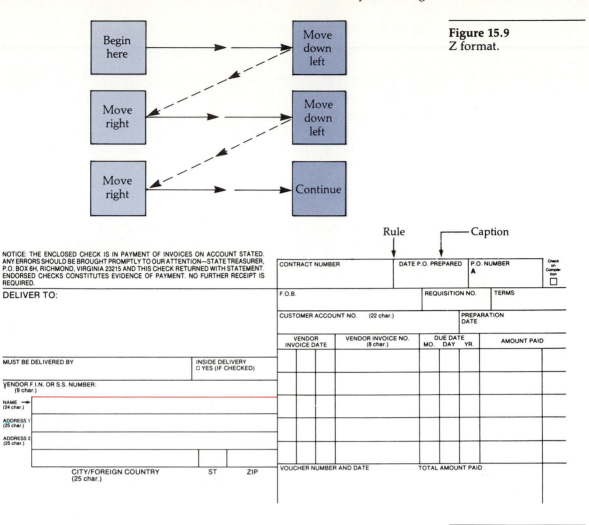

Figure 15.9
Z format.

Figure 15.10
Rules and captions.

requirements. The choice of a printer, for example, depends on the print quality requirement and the turnaround time for producing the report.

In evaluating the overall output design, it is important to have a checklist that verifies that all the necessary information is complete and produced in a timely manner. All reports and documents should also be examined to determine if they could be made more presentable. The use of graphs and charts should also be considered as a part of the output design effort. Finally, the accessibility of output reports to the user should be checked. Questions such as, "Is hard copy required or will the user be satisfied with the same information displayed on a CRT screen?" or "Might users wish to access detailed information on a screen right after reviewing a summary report?" have an important theme—addressing people issues in output design.

Input Design

In input design, we convert user-generated inputs to a computer-compatible format. The purpose of designing input is to make data entry into the computer as easy and as accurate as possible. The data entry operator should understand how fields are allocated, how each field is sequenced, and the format for entering the data.

The first step in the design process is to organize the source document and then decide on the media that will accommodate data entry into the system. A *source document* is an original user-generated form such as a time card, sales invoice, or customer order form. Source data may be captured on tape, disk, diskettes, or hard disk. They can also be read directly from an input device or entered manually through a keyboard. A source document should be logically organized and easy to understand. The areas in the form should be in proper sequence and clearly identified. For example, the date of birth field should be designed in the following sequence:

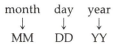

Since the early 1980s, there has been increasing emphasis on interactive computing between the user and the information system. This interaction takes place so that the user can select specific information from the database or enter data for processing. There are four approaches to data entry:

1. Command
2. Menu
3. Formatted form
4. Prompt

In the *command* approach, the user enters a special word or a phrase to trigger a response from the system. For example, in a database system the user may enter the command LIST to list the records of a file, DELETE to erase a record from a file, or COPY to copy information from a file to a temporary location in storage. A list of dBASE III Plus commands and their meanings is shown in Table 15.1.

Commands provide the user utmost flexibility, because it allows direct and immediate action tables on the data or the file in storage. Many users, however, have difficulty remembering commands. Some users purchase a template that fits around the keyboard. The template lists the major commands and matches them to special function keys (see Figure 15.11). Still, many users resist this approach.

An alternative data entry is the menu. A **menu** is a list of options. The user simply enters an option to perform an operation. Figure 15.12

Table 15.1 Selected Commands and Their Meanings

Command	Meaning
ACCEPT	Allows input of character data into a memory variable
COPY	Copies a database file to a new file
EJECT	Ejects a page on the printer
INSERT	Allows insertion of data in a database file
MODIFY STRUCTURE	Modifies a database structure
REPORT	Displays data in report form
SORT	Generates a sort version of a database file in use
WAIT	Suspends program processing until user enters a key

illustrates a menu for adding a record, deleting a record, or exiting to the operating system. A cursor blinks in the space provided for ( ) CHOOSE ONE. It asks the user to type the digit that represents the operation. Inasmuch as a menu limits a user's choice, it guides the user's thinking about how to get answers.

The **formatted form** is a fill-in-the-blank data entry design. A preformatted blank form is painted on the screen. The cursor blinks at the first field to be entered on the form. After entering the data, it moves automatically to the next blank. To skip a field, one simply presses the ENTER key. If the form is more than one screen, most software brings up the next and succeeding screens until the form is completely filled out. After all fields are entered, a function key is pressed to release the data to the computer program (see Figure 15.13).

The **prompt** is a conversational approach to data entry. The system displays one question or instruction at a time and waits for a response. For example, in Figure 15.14 the system requests the user's password, whether it is a deposit or a withdrawal transaction, and the amount of withdrawal.

Software packages verify the ID before responding to requests. The ID is checked against a list of IDs stored in computer memory. If the number does not check out, it displays a message such as, "ID invalid. Try again." After a specific number of tries, it may "kick" the user out of the program. In a bank's ATM, the machine can be designed to retain the user card, to be retrieved later by a bank officer.

Screen Design   We can design the input record (batch) or input screen (on line). The format of an input is an important design step and must be handled accurately by the programmer.

A CRT screen is typically 24 rows of 80 characters each. To design a display, we block out special areas on the screen for data entry/display.

Figure 15.11
WORDPERFECT
template.

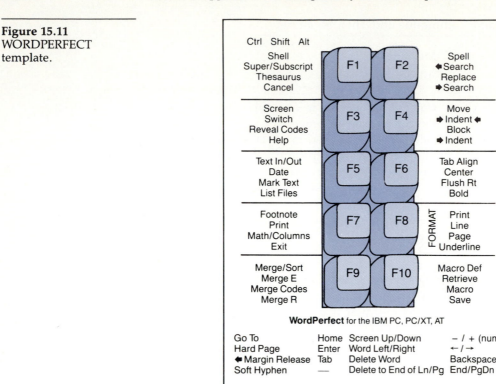

Figure 15.12
A menu.

```
                  FIRST PRESBYTERIAN CHURCH

                     Membership System

                        Main Menu

The church membership system allows the manipulation
of membership data according to the function you
wish to perform.

The function choices are:

      1. ENTER NEW MEMBER INFORMATION
      2. EDIT EXISTING INFORMATION
      3. GENERATE A REPORT
      4. EXIT

PLEASE MAKE A SELECTION (1,2,3,4), AND HIT RETURN KEY
```

```
PERSONAL  INFORMATION

Last  Name▓                    First  Name           Middle  Initial

Address                                              Zip  Code

Telephone                 Date  of  Birth                      Sex
                              mm/dd/yy                         m/f

Marital  Status:  S-Single,  M-Married,  D-Divorced,  W-Widowed
                  Status:

First  Name  of  Spouse  or  Former  Spouse

Is  Spouse  a  Member?
                  y/n
Educational  Field  of  Study

Occupation                Business  Phone

Place  of  Employment
```

Figure 15.13
Formatted personnel
form.

The main point is to specify through programming what information we want to display and where on the screen we want it displayed. To illustrate, we use dBASE III Plus commands in Figure 15.15 to display a menu on the screen. The first option on the menu "Edit an existing membership file" is generated by the first command in the program which says, "At the intersection of row 10 and column 10, display (SAY) the statement between quotes." The instruction WAIT TO A keeps the menu on the screen until the option is entered through the keyboard.

The Integrity Issue   An important aspect of data entry design is data integrity, or the degree to which the data in storage are accurate and secure. To ensure data integrity, we must either rely on the operator to ensure accurate data entry or on the software to detect and prevent errors. For example, review the dialog in Figure 15.16. The software will not allow invalid data to be entered. The operator has to reenter the correct data before data entry continues.

File Design

Business documents and reports are generated from the stored data via computer programs. File and software design are two major activities

```
System:   ENTER ID

   User   :   4569(invisible on the screen for security)

   System:   DO YOU WISH TO DEPOSIT OR WITHDRAW CASH?
             1=Deposit
             2=Withdraw
             ENTER 1 or 2

   User   :   2

   System:   ENTER AMOUNT

   User   :   100.00
```

Figure 15.14
The prompt approach to
data entry.

that transform data into outputs. In file design, we focus on several activities:

1. *Grouping the data items* to be stored, determining the number of data items, their format, and the potential volume of the file. Modifying the layout of fields in data files late in the implementation phase can be both costly and disruptive. The problems are minimal, however, if the data files changes are made through a database management system.

To illustrate, suppose we have two data files: inventory and vendor files. Since the data are already available, we need only list the data files and the data items that would be accessed from each file (see Table 15.2). On the other hand, if there are new data files, we need to lay out the record format and create a data dictionary that defines each field in the record. Table 15.3 shows the file layout of a new file—Accounts Receivable—and a data dictionary describing each data item in the file.

2. *Determining how the files will be processed:* batch versus on-line processing. In batch processing, transactions are accumulated in batches and processed at one point in time to update the file. In on-line processing, transactions are entered into the system as quickly as they occur. In this way the files are immediately updated.

The tradeoff between batch and on-line design is processing cost versus timeliness of information. Obviously, it is less costly to process in a batch mode. This procedure is satisfactory in high-volume transactions where information is not updated between batch processing cycles. The closer the user wants to get to the data in the files, the more attractive on-line processing becomes. In many cases, certain files are on line while other files are updated in a batch mode. In other cases, batch processing is carried out in short cycles to improve the up-to-date status of the files.

Besides file processing methods, the access method—sequential, indexed sequential, or random—must also be considered. A major fac-

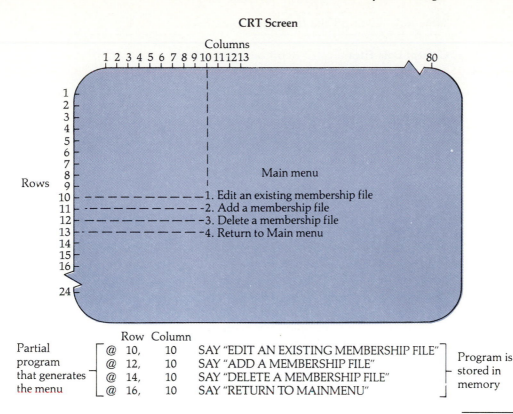

CRT Screen

Columns

1 2 3 4 5 6 7 8 9 10 11 12 13 80

Rows

Main menu

10 — — — — — — — — —1. Edit an existing membership file
11 - — — — — — — — -2. Add a membership file
12 — — — — — — — — -3. Delete a membership file
13 - — — — — — — — -4. Return to Main menu

	Row	Column	
Partial	@	10, 10	SAY "EDIT AN EXISTING MEMBERSHIP FILE"
program	@	12, 10	SAY "ADD A MEMBERSHIP FILE"
that generates	@	14, 10	SAY "DELETE A MEMBERSHIP FILE"
the menu	@	16, 10	SAY "RETURN TO MAINMENU"

Program is stored in memory

Figure 15.15
CRT screen design: the main menu for PFS WRITE.

tor is file activity and file volatility. *File activity* refers to the percentage of actual records processed in a single run. If a small percentage of records is accessed at a given time, the file should be organized on disk for direct access. On the other hand, if a fair percentage of records is affected on a regular basis, then storing files on tape would be more efficient and economical.

File volatility refers to the properties of record changes. File records with substantial changes are highly volatile, which means that disk design would be preferable over tape. Think of the airline reservation system with its high volatility through reservations, cancellations, and special fare arrangements, compared to the payroll application, which is rela-

Figure 15.16
User-machine dialog.

```
SYSTEM DISPLAY:    DATE OF BIRTH(mm/dd/yy)
USER RESPONSE :    12/33/87
SYSTEM RESPONSE:   DAY EXCEEDS 31   TRY AGAIN
SYSTEM DISPLAY:    DATE OF BIRTH(mm/dd/yy)
```

Table 15.2 Listing Data Items and Data Files

Current Data Files	Retrievable Data Items
Inventory	Item NUM
	Present INVENTORY count
	Reorder point = quantity
Vendor	Vendor NUM
	Vendor Name
	Vendor Phone
	Discount Rate

tively dormant. The higher the volatility, the more attractive the use of disks rather than tape.

3. *Designing the checks and internal controls* for accessing the files to ensure integrity and security of the data. Controls should provide assurance that the correct files are being accessed by authorized users and the data are not changed without proper authorization. Moreover, the programs that access the files must be executed based on authorization.

Passwords have traditionally been used to control access to the data files, the database, or the programs stored in memory. But passwords have been shown to be difficult to manage, easy to bypass, and sometimes shared between users. Other more sophisticated controls to file access have been introduced. For example, a computer can verify an authorized user by a "smart" card, programmed electronic key or by fingerprints, voice scans, curvature of the eye, and the like. The important objective of any approach remains data integrity and security of the corporate database from tampering.

Special Design Considerations   File design goes far beyond the simple layout of records. Files are a shared resource. This means that we need to analyze how each program will access the data and then design the file for efficiency of access and update. A significant trend is the use of integrated databases rather than files. With an integrated database, we can control for integrity by controlling data redundancy. Ideally, no data field should be included in more than one logical record. Redundant data wastes storage. When an update comes up, the data must be updated in more than one place to maintain a consistent value. If we do not do so, we will face a data integrity problem.

Yet most systems store redundant data. Why? There are natural relationships between files that serve as cross references. We have seen in Chapter 6, for example, that to normalize a file, we add a field in one relation that serves as a bridge linking it to another relation. Redundancy, per se, is not a big problem. Uncontrolled redundancy is a big problem. That is the reason for restricting redundancy to primary key fields in

Table 15.3   File Record Layout and Data Dictionary Entries

File Layout		Data Dictionary
Position	*Data Item*	
1– 4	Cus NUM	Customer number = 4-digit code
5–25	Cus. name	identifying customer. Code begins at
26–45	Address	"1001" beginning each fiscal year.
46–56	Phone	Customer name = 20 alphabetic characters
57–63	Date	identifying customer full name.
64–71	Prev. balance	.
72–80	Payment	.
81–89	Bal. outstanding	.
		Date = the date of invoice.
		Stored as MM-DD-YY.
		Balance outstanding is 8-digit code
		showing the amount owed by customer.

different records to cross reference files. For example, CUSTOMER NAME is stable, but ITEM PRICE is subject to change.

Data redundancy and integrity are complex issues that are often handled by database specialists. Various internal controls are built into files to control for integrity. For example, files may be accessed only by a password. Some end users may be authorized only to retrieve but not to update files; others have access to both. In a multiuser environment, backup procedures are employed to safeguard the files against accidental or willful destruction. Recovery procedures also relate to backup by specifying how files are restored if they are stolen or destroyed.

Software Design

This important aspect of system design involves the preparation of programs, procedures, and documentation to handle the processing activities. The objective of software design is to ensure that all the required reports and other output information are produced to the user's satisfaction. The structured design tools explained earlier in the chapter can be useful in achieving the software design objective.

After the programs have been coded, the systems analyst or programmer goes through a *structured walkthrough*—a methodical review of the procedure and steps taken in designing the program(s) under review. Usually such a walkthrough involves a project team that is handling the project. All errors or enhancements are discussed and changes agreed upon before the software is approved for final testing and implementation. These steps are covered in Chapter 16.

After the output, input, file, and software are designed, the overall design phases are reviewed with appropriate users, management, and the technical staff. This will provide an opportunity to question the project's feasibility and approve the technical specifications to make sure that nothing has been overlooked.

Analyst-User Differences and System Design

The success (and failure) of system design has much to do with how closely the views of users and designers match. The MIS literature has often pointed to a communication gap between users and analysts that affects system design. Traditionally, users have a broader organizational view than designers and have difficulty spelling out their information requirements. Designers approach problem solving with computer mechanics in mind. The different ways users and designers conceptualize situations have been the cause of many system failures.

Structured design tools have been suggested as the single largest benefit to improving user-analyst communication because they provide a shared logical model of the system. Also, including the user in structured walkthroughs has done a lot to bridge the communication gap.

Kaiser and Bostrom (1982) investigated personality characteristics that might explain analyst-user differences and how these differences affect system design. Using data received from a hundred MIS directors of large private firms, they found users to be "systems oriented" in ways similar to their systems counterparts, the designers. This circumstance made it easier to design systems in these organizations.

One obvious implication is that users need to become computer literate. In this way the communication gap that was once a hurdle to system design success can be narrowed significantly. The late 1980s should find more knowledge workers and better trained analysts for future system installations. System implementation is covered in Chapter 16.

The Role of the Auditor

The presence of an internal auditor in system development can be extremely beneficial to a sound installation. Auditor participation ensures internal system controls and improved system security design.

The way an auditor fits into a project's life cycle relates to his or her role and responsibility. In most cases, an auditor is considered a consultant to the project team. He or she must maintain independence from the user group and steer away from an adversary relationship with other members of the team. As a part-time resource, the auditor's responsibilities must be carefully defined to identify the nature and limits of involvement in the project.

   In system design, the auditor's role is to review the data flow diagrams and the daily operating procedures manual, and to attend walk-throughs on security and control. After design is completed, we will find that auditors are also needed in testing and training. They review the test and training paths, evaluate the test results, and even make recommendations on later enhancements. These are important contributions to system success. System testing is covered in Chapter 16.

Summary

□ System design is a transition phase from a user-oriented document to a document oriented to programming or a database environment. This involves logical and physical design.

□ Logical design shows the logical flow of a system by means of the data flow diagram. It produces system specifications that incorporate output, input, file, and processing specifications. System specifications determine procedure specifications that represent physical design which, in turn, produces the working system.

□ Structured design identifies the inputs and outputs and describes the functional aspects of the system. It partitions a program into a hierarchy of modules organized in a top-down manner with the details at the bottom.

□ The documentation tool is the structure chart. It includes three elements: module, connection, and couple. It is important for the program to be partitioned into independent modules so that each module is small enough to be manageable. Each module must perform only one task that makes it cohesive with the calling and called modules.

□ Various development activities are carried out during system design. They include database and program design, system and program test requirements definition, leading to design specification and system implementation. A well-designed system should also have controls to ensure successful auditing.

□ A first step in system design is preparing input and output formats in line with user requirements. In input data design, we first design the source document and then decide on the medium.

□ A growing number of applications now rely on on-line data entry. For example, the ATM in banking and the POS in retailing have already become a standard for on-line data processing.

□ Three modern approaches for data entry are worth noting: the menu, the formatted (fill-in-the-blank) form, and the prompt. The menu requests the user to choose one option for a specific operation. In the formatted form, the user enters the data in the appropriate location. The prompt is a conversational approach to on-line data entry.

▫ A key aspect of output design is the design of the forms. Forms are classified as action, memory, or report forms. Each form must have a title, provide for maximum readability, reflect a logical sequence, and be easily stored and filed. Computer output uses continuous-strip forms in virtually all applications.

▫ A form is designed with a combination of rules and captions. Whenever possible, it is designed using the box style rule with the caption placed in the upper left-hand corner.

▫ Structured design tools have been suggested as the largest single benefit to improving user-analyst communication and this has a bearing on the success of the design process. As users gain exposure to the computer technology, the communication gap that was once a major hurdle to system design success can be narrowed significantly.

Key Terms

Boss module
Connection
Couple
Design
Formatted form
Logical design
Menu
Module

Nonprocedural specifications
Physical design
Procedural specifications
Prompt
Structure chart
System design
Warnier/Orr diagram
Worker module

Review Questions

1. In your own words, describe the process of system design.

2. Distinguish between:
   a. Logical and physical design
   b. DFD and structure chart
   c. Connection and couple
   d. Couple and cohesion

3. "Structured design provides the best partitioning of a program into small, independent modules organized in a top-down manner." Do you agree? Discuss.

4. Explain and give an example of the makeup of a structure chart.

5. According to the text, a module may be specified procedurally or nonprocedurally. Elaborate.

6. What development activities are carried out during system design? Explain in detail.

7. What is the goal of input and output design? Be specific.

8. If you were to recommend a method for tagging merchandise in a supermarket, what input medium would you choose? Why?

9. What is so unique about on-line data entry? Explain how the CRT plays a major role for input and output.

10. Summarize briefly the key input/output media and devices and their uses in business applications.

11. Elaborate on three on-line approaches for entering data into the computer. How do they differ? What unique features do they have? What applications are they best used for?

12. Discuss the major requirements of forms design. Why are they important?

13. How much instruction does a form need? Are written instructions required on a printed form? Explain.

14. What layout considerations are involved in forms design? Illustrate.

15. If you were asked to develop a forms control program for a firm, how would you proceed? How would you control for unauthorized forms? Be specific.

16. The text suggests perception and other differences between users and analysts. How could these differences be bridged? How do structured design tools reduce the communication between users and analysts? Elaborate.

Application Problems

1. a. Construct a structure chart and show the required couples for the following:

   Calling (boss) module: ENTER GRADES
   Called module: GET RECORD
                           GET PAST GRADES
                           ADD NEW GRADES
                           REPORT DISCREPANCIES
                           CHECK FOR PROBATION
                           CHECK FOR DEAN'S LIST

   b. In the structure chart, show as a calling module and add a called module COMPUTE GPA. Include the appropriate couples.

Figure 15A.1
Structure chart for
updating a customer
master file.

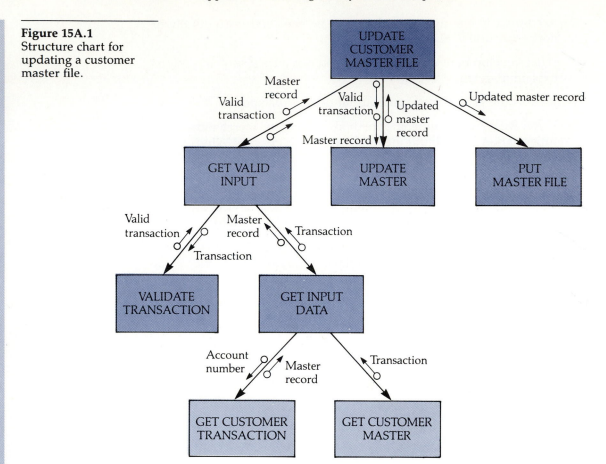

2. Rewrite the structure chart in Figure 15.A1.
   a. How many modules and couples are there? What do they mean?
   b. List the called module(s); the calling module(s).
   c. How many couples are passed to the calling module?

Selected References

Aktas, A. Ziya. *Structured Analysis and Design of Information Systems.* Englewood
   Cliffs, N.J.: Prentice-Hall, 1987, 78–117.

Bostrom, R. P. and Nault, P. "A Comparison of Structured Design Methodologies
   for Logical System Design." *National AIDS Proceedings*, 1980, 210–212.

Dolan, Kathleen. *Business Computer Systems Design.* Santa Clara, Calif.: Mitchell,
   1984, 35.

Edwards, Philip. "The Designing Mind." *Datamation*, September 15, 1985, 105–106.

Kaiser, Kate M. and Bostrom, R. P. "Personality Characteristics of MIS Project Teams: An Empirical Study and Action-Research Design." *MIS Quarterly,* December 1982, 43–60.

Konsynski, Benn R. "Advances in Information System Design." *Journal of Management Information Systems,* Winter 1984–85, 5–32.

Martin, Jason. "From Analysis to Design." *Datamation,* September 15, 1985, 129–130ff.

Myers, Gibbs and Mathies, Leslie M. "Self Instruction on Forms." *Journal of Systems Management,* September 1984, 40–41.

Readers' Forum. "The Art of Structure." *Datamation,* September 15, 1985.

Senn, James A. *Information Systems in Management.* Belmont, Calif.: Wadsworth, 1987, 695–707.

Zahniser, Richard A. "What Do You Mean Structured?" *Small Systems World,* June 1985, 28–32.

Hardware/Software Acquisition

Chapter Contents

Who's Responsible for the Bugs?

ON APRIL 11, 1986, the software industry trade group, ADAPSO, issued guidelines to its members recommending changes in the so-called "as-is warranty agreement" commonly used in the industry. (An as-is warranty assigns all risks to the buyer.) The guidelines call for software manufacturers to offer "warranties of sufficient duration . . . to allow for the discovery of significant errors." These errors should be corrected within a reasonable time or the company should refund the purchase price, according to the guidelines.

Gloria Molina, a California assemblywoman whose proposed legislation catalyzed the warranty debate, has stated that she will drop her efforts to pass the bill if major software manufacturers comply. The bill, which would impose a mandatory six-month warranty and hold manufacturers and dealers accountable for advertising claims and verbal representations, is scheduled to come up for vote in the California state senate in July. Similar legislation in other states may also be forestalled. New York Assemblyman Peter Sullivan plans to reintroduce a consumer-protection measure that was rejected earlier this year by the assembly rules committee.

The Molina and ADAPSO actions concern only warranty issues, and the most serious loss a manufacturer usually suffers in a breach of warranty case is a requirement to return the purchaser's money. Looming beneath the surface is a problem of far greater dimensions. What will happen when a software bug causes serious property damage, loss of revenue or even loss of life?

It is not so farfetched. As microcomputers are increasingly used in process control applications, it is easy to imagine calamitous industrial accidents. An error in an accounting package can play havoc with a small company's accounts receivable. A wrong conclusion from a doctor's expert system program could lead to faulty medical treatment.

LOTUS Development Corporation released its latest version of Symphony with an error that caused the loss of data in certain circumstances. However, since the company quickly acknowledged the problem and acted to resolve it, it would have had a strong defense in a liability case.

Because the best a plaintiff can usually win is the purchase price of the software, a winning suit involving microcomputer programs is almost certainly a losing proposition. Also, few users have suffered serious setbacks because of software bugs. Usually they are able to recover their data from backup files.

—*Daniel Ruby and Shan Chan*, PC Week, *May 27, 1986, 51ff.*

AT A GLANCE

A key aspect of system development is hardware/software acquisition. Familiarity with vendors, where and how hardware/software is acquired, whether to purchase or lease, and how contracts are negotiated are all important decisions for a successful system installation.

Hardware/software selection begins with requirements analysis, followed by a request for proposal, evaluation of the bids, and the final selection of the vendor. Each phase is critical, in that deficiencies in the content of one phase have a direct bearing on succeeding steps. For example, reliable bids usually result from the clarity and thoroughness of the request for proposal. A qualified consultant can be effective in the final selection stage.

A major question raised in system acquisition is whether to purchase or lease. Each option has pros and cons. For example, purchase allows the user to modify the system at will and provide cash savings from depreciation tax credits. In contrast, a lease shifts the risk of obsolescence onto the lessor rather than onto the user, as in a purchase option.

Once a decision is made on a system or a software package, the contract is negotiated to ensure that all commitments and services will be met by the vendor. During the contract negotiation session, care is taken to eliminate any possibility of misrepresentation and hidden clauses. To do a good job, the user can employ various strategies such as negotiating on one's own turf, use tradeoffs, and assume a leadership role throughout the sessions.

By the end of this chapter, you should know:

1. The characteristics of hardware, software, and service vendors
2. How hardware and software are selected
3. The factors to consider in evaluating hardware/software
4. The pros and cons of purchase/lease options
5. How computer contracts are negotiated

Introduction

In the previous two chapters, we have shown how systems and applications are developed. The next step in the system development life cycle is the acquisition of hardware and software, if necessary. This phase falls between system design and the final implementation of the information system. Acquisition is concerned with investment decisions—hardware acquisition (if needed) and the software package(s) that will fit the physical design. Making such decisions requires familiarity with the vendor industry, how hardware or software is acquired, whether to purchase or lease, and how to negotiate the computer contract.

Hardware/software acquisition begins with requirements analysis, followed by a request for proposal (RFP) that invites the vendors to submit bids based on the RFP. The bids are then evaluated and the final vendor is chosen. Contract negotiations include agreement on price, delivery, service, support for the user, and protecting the user's interest in the proposed system. In this chapter, we discuss the procedure for selecting hardware and software, how vendors are evaluated, financial considerations, and the basics of computer contract negotiations.

We need to emphasize at this point that the procedures for system acquisition are typically applicable to mainframe systems. The usual procedures for microcomputer acquisition are more ad hoc because of the high cost of the formal request-for-proposal (RFP) process. Clearly, large system acquisition and software development justify considerable formal evaluation.

The Hardware/Software Industry

The computer industry represents over 3500 hardware and software suppliers who provide a wide variety of hardware and support. A brief understanding of the industry is important for computer selection.

Hardware Vendors

A major source of hardware and supportive software are the mainframe manufacturers. IBM, which reluctantly entered the computer field in the mid 1950s, now has over 50 percent of the total computer market. In 1986, Burroughs and Sperry corporations merged to form the second largest mainframe corporation in the industry, UNISYS. Fierce competition forced companies like RCA, General Electric, and Xerox to bow out of the mainframe business.

Other leading U.S. mainframe makers include Amdahl, Control Data Corporation (CDC), UNISYS, Cray Research, Honeywell, and Digital Equipment Corporation (DEC). Amdahl and Cray Research specialize in very large computers that have military, scientific, or space applications. UNISYS has been traditionally known for its computerized banking applications. DEC has been a specialist in engineering/scientific, mini-computer/microcomputer, interactive usage. Since the mid-1970s, they have established a reputation in the distributed data processing area. IBM is the sole mainframe manufacturer that has demonstrated a strong presence in the microcomputer area. The IBM-PC now represents over 30 percent of the total microcomputer market. Other microcomputer manufacturers include Apple, Tandy, Compaq, Zenith, AT&T, and a host of smaller vendors.

Hardware vendors include mainframe manufacturers, peripheral and media outlets, computer leasing firms, and new and used computer dealers. *Peripheral vendors* supply secondary devices such as disk and diskette drives, line printers, and the like. *Media vendors* specialize in recording media such as diskettes, disk packs, and printer forms.

Computer leasing firms install used or new systems on a lease basis. Used computer dealers purchase computers directly from the users and sell them at reduced prices from retail. Some dealers even install and warrant the installation for a nominal fee. Unless you know what you are looking for, there is a risk in acquiring a used computer. The original manufacturer generally does not extend the warranty once it is sold to a third party.

Software Vendors

Since IBM's **unbundling** in early 1970 (a process that allowed its system and peripherals to be purchased separately rather than in a package as previously), a new market of independents began to offer users a variety of software and services that are compatible with existing hardware. If we were to include the microcomputer, today's market has over 14,000 firms offering more than 8000 systems and ready-to-use applications.

Software is now an industry in itself. The software industry—which includes timesharing, package software products, and contract programming—has been steadily on the increase. There are two major reasons for software growth: (1) Programmer shortages prompted the development of "canned" software packages such as database management systems. (2) Software is becoming highly price effective and does not have the vendor-specific restrictions it once did. The trend is toward **open architecture** that makes it possible for software packages to run on different vendor hardware with minor modifications.

Service Vendors

A variety of computer services is available to users at all levels. The typical user is a small firm or a first-time user. Service vendors include:

1. Service bureaus
2. Facilities management
3. Timesharing vendors

A *service bureau* is a company that provides batch and on-line processing operations. Charges are levied on an hourly, monthly, or per application basis. The main benefit is lower overall cost for users with no previous computer experience or where the volume cannot justify a computer installation. For organizations that own computers, a service bureau may serve as a backup. The primary drawbacks are possible data security and data integrity problems. Users also do not control the processing schedule of most applications.

Facilities management (FM) vendors furnish their own personnel to manage and operate a user-owned installation. Users decide how the FM vendor must operate the system. This approach is attractive to first-time users with little or no computer management experience. An FM vendor such as Electronic Data Systems (EDS) provides and ensures smooth operation without the worry of personnel turnover. The main drawbacks, however, are loss of direct control over the day-to-day operation, high managerial fees, and possible security leaks.

Timesharing vendors provide on-line access to a mainframe computer through remote terminals. User programs are stored in the mainframe. The user starts an application by entering commands via the terminal. Turnaround is virtually instant because the main computer operates in a multiuser, multiprogramming mode. Each user has the impression of having the computer's undivided attention. This is similar to an in-house facility, but with timesharing the user pays a fixed rate for actual computer time (usually in minutes) and for storage space utilization.

A timesharing facility offers each user direct and uninterrupted access to his/her programs and files, which are protected from unauthorized access by passwords or a protocol that requires a unique ID number or a word. Users can have their own private programs or access public programs by the timesharing facility.

One advantage of timesharing over service bureaus is that it makes small jobs feasible and affordable. Timesharing for the casual user is inexpensive, compared to alternative processing methods. Among the drawbacks, however, are potential loss of data, possible unauthorized access, and overall higher charges than those of service bureaus.

Today's maturing market means a wide selection for the user. Searching for the best product, whether it is hardware, software, or service, requires specialized knowledge and experience. The seasoned analyst working through a steering committee supported by management can make a significant contribution to a successful computer installation.

Procedure for Hardware/Software Selection

Gone are the days when a user calls IBM to order the latest computer. Today's selection process requires a choice among a variety of systems. A structured approach to selection has replaced the informal, subjective ways of acquiring computers.

In preparing for acquisition, it is important to consider whether the process should be handled by an organization-wide committee or by the department that requested the computer. The decentralized approach has the advantage of allowing the users who are closest to the application to deal with the acquisition issues. It also motivates local vendors to work closely with the users on an installation. The decentralized approach, however, has drawbacks:

1. It duplicates the lessons learned in past acquisitions by other managers.
2. All too often the hardware or software chosen is not compatible with other systems in the organization.
3. If the inexperienced user acquires a system or a software product, he or she often enters into contracts that do not protect the organization's interests.

Most of these problems can be checked by company policy, standard contracts, and corporate-level review of computer proposals. It is these reasons, though, that suggest basing the selection process on a policy that requires joint participation of analysts, consultants, an EDP auditor, and legal units of the firm.

Prior to selection, several factors are considered:

1. *Identify what the user is interested in.* Is it cost reduction? Improved performance? Improved profit?
2. *Determine the magnitude of the requirements.* That is, is selection a simple replacement of a few peripherals or a decision to install a mainframe?
3. *Evaluate the competence level of the available staff.* Lack of in-house expertise means securing outside help for conversion or even questioning whether the company would be better off with a service bureau.
4. *Develop a timeframe for the selection process.* This helps keep the project under control.

In any case, the selection committee should consider hardware and software as a unit for compatibility. Actually, software selection should precede hardware decisions. Remember that software (not hardware) is the *problem solver.*

Selection is a four-phase process:

1. Requirements analysis
2. A request for a proposal (RFP)
3. Evaluation and validation
4. Vendor selection

Requirements Analysis

The selection process begins with clarification of the user's requirements. This includes a description of how information flows in the department, the major processes, inputs, outputs, and master files. System specifications spell out the user's requirements and the applications to be processed by the proposed system. Each aspect of the system should be clearly and completely specified.

Request for Proposal (RFP)

The **request for proposal (RFP)** document is a communication tool between the user and the vendor. It is a user-prepared bid invitation informing vendors of the requirements their system must meet for selection. At a minimum, the RFP should cover the following:

1. General company information—its objectives, present MIS, etc.
2. Detailed statement of the system specifications as reflected in the current and proposed applications, programming languages, procedures for handling data, files to be maintained, and required output.
3. Reliability backup and vendor service requirements that focus on vendor's responsibilities for conversion, training, system maintenance, and support.
4. Request for financial statement of the vendor. This verifies the vendor's performance record and viability status.
5. Criteria for evaluating proposals. (On what basis will proposals be evaluated?)
6. Warranties and terms of license limitations.
7. Deadline for submitting proposals.

When the RFP is mailed to the vendors, ample time should be given to prepare the proposals. The time frame is normally thirty to sixty days, although large systems may take longer.

Evaluation and Validation

The evaluation phase assesses the attributes of the vendor's system. It is a two-step procedure. In the first step, the vendors are invited to demonstrate their systems. This verifies the features of their proposals and enables the user's staff to compare features across systems.

The second step is to evaluate each system, using performance measure techniques such as benchmark programs, simulation workload models, and monitors. These tools are explained later in the chapter.

Selection Criteria   Hardware or software is formally evaluated based on criteria defined and agreed upon in advance. As we mentioned earlier, the selection process starts with the **systems software**, the problem solver, followed by the hardware. First we will elaborate on the software criteria.

The trend in today's software is toward ready-to-use generalized software packages. Purchasing a software package represents roughly 10 percent of the cost of developing the same in house. A reliable software package offers a number of advantages:

1. *Short implementation time.* Installation of a software package is completed in a matter of days rather than the months necessary for "homegrown" packages. It also contains fewer errors and is of higher overall quality than most in-house software.
2. *Reduced need for resources.* In-house software can be costly and completion dates are hard to predict. Incomplete software projects are not uncommon because of turnover among programming staff.
3. *Lower development cost.* A package can take years to build, great expense to complete, and even more time to maintain. Users do not have the expertise to cost-justify developing such packages.
4. *Greater flexibility.* Users are not "saddled" with a software package as they would be with in-house programs. If the package fails the test, there is no obligation to purchase.

Software packages, on the other hand, are not without drawbacks:

1. *Short track record.* Many of the software houses have been in business less than five years. It is difficult to predict how long they will continue.
2. *Application incompatibility.* For a sophisticated user, extensive modification of a package can be costly. If the user modifies the software, the vendor may no longer be responsible for any errors that arise.
3. *Lack of competition.* Selecting a package is often not straightforward. In some cases, a software package is "one-of-a-kind." In other cases, it is the only available software for the problem.

Software Selection Criteria   Users must decide on their own selection criteria. The criteria depend on the specific applications and the importance placed on various aspects of processing. The following components are generally agreed to be crucial (see Table 16.1):

1. Reliability
2. Modularity and expandability
3. Usability and portability
4. Serviceability
5. Performance
6. Ownership

Reliability has to do with how long software (or hardware) will operate without a failure. It also relates to how accurate and dependable the results are. Software does not fail. It does not even wear out. Invariably, reliability problems are the result of errors overlooked during the development process. In contrast, hardware fails because of "wear and tear" with continued use or inadequate maintenance.

Market pressure to produce software has had an adverse impact on the reliability of software in general. To make things worse, first-time

Table 16.1   Software Criteria: A Summary

Criterion	Meaning
Reliability	Accurate and dependable results
Modularity and expandability	Ease of changing and enhancing a package
Usability and portability	User friendliness and ability to run on different hardware
Serviceability	Well-written documentation and vendor support
Performance	Capacity to meet user requirements
Ownership	Right to make changes or modify a package

users do not know much about software testing. A demonstration by a sales representative is often all it takes to purchase the package. For this reason alone, inquiring about vendor support is crucial.

Modularity refers to the ease of modifying the software across product lines. Software with high modularity operates in computers across product lines. It should be noted that packages such as DBMS, spreadsheets, and word processing are seldom modified by the user. End applications such as order entry, inventory, and the like often require modification.

In contrast to modularity, **expandability** has to do with how well the software can be modified to meet a user's changing requirements. Some expandability questions are:

1. How easily can record formats be changed or relocated?
2. Will the system be unusable if a part of it failed?
3. What are the recovery features of the software?

Related to expandability are capacity and flexibility. *Capacity* refers to the software's capability for file size, volume of transactions, and additional reports. *Flexibility* is the ease of modifying or extending a software package to address changing requirements.

The *usability* factor ensures user-friendly software. For example, the popularity of dBASE II in the early 1980s was attributed to the fact that a novice user could create and maintain a database file in less than four training hours. In this respect, it was highly usable.

Portability is a measure of how well the software will run on different computers. For example, IBM's DB2, which runs on an IBM mainframe, will not run on most other vendors' computers. Therefore, it is not very portable. Most of today's software is designed to run on a specific computer line or an operating system, and so portability becomes a problem. A software package rated high on portability would also be high on usability.

Serviceability emphasizes the importance of vendor services and support. An effective package must be well documented for maintenance and future enhancements. This includes a description of the system logic, data flow diagrams, input/output file descriptions and layouts, and a readable user manual. Vendor support means technical support, software maintenance, and update. On-site training and conversion support are a part of most commercial installations.

Performance is one of the most critical criteria of selection. It is a measure of the software's capacity to meet user requirements and perform under peak loads. The programming language of the software may be a performance factor. For example, a package written in assembler language usually outperforms substantially a similar package written in BASIC. Yet it is cheaper and easier to modify a package written in BASIC than in assembler language. This is where the user can solicit competent advice from an expert before making a final decision.

Acquiring a software package brings up the important question of *ownership*. Most license agreements lease (not sell) the software for an indefinite time period. To protect proprietary rights, the vendor does not provide the source code. Yet the availability of the source code becomes crucial when dealing with a software house that could fold without notice. The questions to consider on ownership are:

1. What is the user paying for?
2. What restrictions are there to copying the software for company branches or other departments within the firm?
3. Who modifies the software? What are the charges? How are modifications made if the vendor goes out of business?

Hardware Selection Criteria   In hardware selection, we consider a range of performance criteria:

1. *Compatibility:* How well matched is the hardware with existing applications?
2. *Support:* How reliable is the vendor in supporting the hardware? What maintenance schedule is available?
3. *System availability:* When will the system be available? How well does it meet the user's delivery date?
4. *User friendliness:* How easy is it to program, modify, and operate the system?
5. *Uptime:* How long does the system continue operating before failure?
6. *Cost:* What are the purchase or lease costs of the system? What about maintenance costs?

Vendor Selection Criteria   In addition to hardware and software evaluation, the vendor's services are also evaluated in terms of conversion, backup, and maintenance. Vendor-assisted *conversion* provides programming support, file conversion, and user training. *Backup* ensures alternative sites for processing applications in an emergency. *Maintenance* ensures against unexpected system failure.

Sources for Evaluation   The user has two primary sources of information for hardware/software evaluation: traditional and structured. In traditional evaluation, current users are asked how satisfied they are with the proposed system, and vendors are willing to provide a list of these satisfied users. Unfortunately, dissatisfied users are not as easy to locate. The problem with this approach is reliability. Even an unbiased recommendation may be based on no more than a few weeks of user experience, which could be followed by months of problems.

In some cases, testimonials can be useful, depending on the user's experience with the system, the similarity of the hardware/software to be acquired, and the relationship between user and vendor (friends, business associates, and the like).

Product reference manuals are another traditional source of information. The search for these manuals can be laborious and their information sometimes dated. Alternatives are trade magazines and published reviews. The vendor should be questioned about any unfavorable information contained in the reviews. Improvements in the product may have been made in the interim.

Structured evaluation uses tools such as benchmarks, monitors, and simulation. A **benchmark** program uses a representative user application to evaluate a system. In the context of software selection, benchmarking may include an acceptance test as specified in the RFP. It might also test for response time to inquiries from remote terminals. The evaluation team records the run times of each application and uses the comparative times and resultant costs for determining a vendor.

Related to benchmarks are *monitors* that supervise the operation of a computer and compile data on idle CPU time, job execution time, and the like. Hardware monitors range from special small computers to more simple metering devices to keep track of channel usage, disk movement, and so on. Software monitors are programs for checking other programs as they are executed. Because software monitors measure a broad variety of conditions concurrently, they are often preferred over hardware monitors.

Simulation is a useful structured evaluation tool that represents the computer hardware, software, and application system in a program model in order to test the system performance on a variety of computer configurations. All major vendors have a simulation program to demonstrate the speed and cost effectiveness of the equipment. Simulation is time consuming and more costly than any other technique. It requires the user to do considerable analysis in defining the test applications.

Evaluation of Proposals   Vendor proposals are reviewed to ensure that they contain complete information and meet RFP requirements. Propos-

Table 16.2   Sample Scoring Method

Selection Criteria	Proposal Scores		
CPU	*A*	*B*	*C*
Computational ability	4	2	3
Communication capability	10	15	23
On-site preparation requirements	5	4	1
Main memory capacity	6	12	16
Multiprogramming/multiprocessing capability	2	3	9
Word size	14	19	16
Subtotal	41	55	68
Vendor evaluation			
Contract flexibility	7	9	8
Installation assistance	8	9	9
Maintenance support	14	18	20
Training quality	15	14	12
Vendor reputation	6	11	9
Subtotal	50	61	58
Benchmark test			
Backup procedures	6	6	7
Ease of use	16	12	21
Functionality	15	20	19
Subtotal	37	38	47
Total (performance score)	128	154	173

als that fail the review are rejected or returned to the vendor for corrections. Time and cost estimates should be a part of the reply. Personality capsules of vendors who will work on the system are also important.

After all proposals have been validated, final selection is determined by a number of approaches: One approach is ad hoc, or a subjective inclination to favor one vendor over others and weight unfairly such a "halo" in the final decision. Vendors are quite sensitive to the risks associated with the ad hoc approach. The organization's record with prior decisions is often the key factor that signals to the vendor whether or not to bid on a proposal.

An alternative to the ad hoc approach is the *scoring* method. Each proposal is rated according to attributes that are given point ratings. In Table 16.2, three proposals are rated using a uniform set of selection criteria. Proposal C earned the highest score and the user's first choice. The chosen system goes through contract negotiation before implementation.

The Role of the Consultant   Evaluation of a vendor proposal is confusing even for experienced users. A qualified consultant can make the difference between a successful system and disaster. The higher status the decision occupies, the more important it is to bring in a consultant.

Payoffs from using consultants can be dramatic, although fees for successful consultants are high. In 1987, experienced computer consultants charged between $800–3,500 per day plus out-of-pocket expenses. The fee depends, in part, on the consultant's overhead and size of staff support. As a rule of thumb, the fee averages up to 15 percent of the net savings.

To illustrate, a user was presented a proposal of $685,000 for a distributed data processing system to handle the company's billing application. A consultant was brought in to evaluate the system. Various hardware/software changes were recommended. After a two-day negotiation with the vendor, the system was successfully installed for $476,000—a saving of $209,000. The consultant's fee was $18,550—95 hours at $150 per hour, plus expenses. It was under 10 percent of net savings.

Organizations selecting their first consultant may consider the following guidelines:

1. Define in advance what it is that a consultant must accomplish, the types of skills required, and when and for how long the consulting service will be needed.
2. Contact a number of consulting firms and review the record of the consultants available. Contact firms that have used them before and get their reactions.
3. Request resumes and interview the consultants. A resume (format, content, level of detail, etc.) reveals a great deal about the success record of the candidate. Successful consultants are not readily available. Therefore, planning is important.

The past decade has seen the growth of in-house consultants in large organizations. The key factor favoring internal consultants is their personal, in-depth knowledge of the user's business. Outside consultants eventually acquire such knowledge, although a bit too late into the project. Table 16.3 summarizes cases when an external or internal consultant is preferable.

Table 16.3   Using Consultants: Internal vs. External

Internal Consultants	External Consultants
1. Outside consultant fees too high	1. Full-time internal consultant a luxury to many organizations
2. Provide quick turnaround	2. Ideal for short-term, one-time projects
3. Understand company structure and politics	3. Expertise based on having done the work elsewhere
4. Inside opinion a necessary counterweight to outside opinion	4. Provide objective opinion detached from internal politics

The Purchase-Lease Decision

A major question in system acquisition is whether to purchase or lease. Each option has its benefits and drawbacks.

The Purchase Option

When purchasing a system, users assume the risks of ownership—maintenance, insurance, obsolescence, etc. Compared to leasing, purchasing has strong benefits:

1. Modifying the system as the situation warrants.
2. Cash savings from depreciation.
3. Lower cash outlay if the system is kept five years or longer.

The major drawbacks, however, are initial high investment costs and the risk associated with computer technology. Maintenance, insurance, and upkeep are also borne by the user. Finally, because of the new tax law, no investment tax credit is allowed.

The Lease Option

A lease is a long-term commitment to a system through a third party or directly from the vendor. Lease periods normally range from three to five years, with an option to purchase the system for a fixed price. Long-term leases have lower charges, although termination charges before the lease expires can be high.

There are three advantages to a lease option:

1. Lease charges are tax deductible.
2. The risk of obsolescence is assumed by the vendor (lessor).
3. A lease can be written to show higher payments in early years to reflect a decline in the value of the system.

The primary limitations of leasing are:

1. In the absence of a purchase option, the lessee (user) loses residual rights to the system.
2. Termination of a lease carries a stiff penalty.
3. In the absence of an upgrade clause, the user could be "saddled" with an obsolete system.

Evaluating Lease Versus Purchase

A basic quantitative method in making the lease versus purchase decision is expressed by a formula called the **net advantage to leasing formula**:

$$NAL = C - L$$

where C is the present value of after-tax cost of ownership and L is the present value of after-tax cost of leasing. The *value of C* is computed as follows:

1. Determine the price of the equipment.
2. Compute the discounted present value of the depreciation tax shields over the period you are going to use the equipment.
3. Discount to present value the salvage value of the equipment, if any.
4. Subtract (2) and (3) from (1) to get C.

The *value of L* is computed as follows:

1. Simply discount back the after-tax cost of the lease payments over the same period to arrive at a present value estimate.
2. In evaluating the leases, you should take note of the lease payment, the length of lease, the salvage value of the asset, and depreciation.

If NAL is greater than 0, the situation implies that leasing is more attractive. If NAL is less than 0, purchasing is more attractive than leasing.

A quick formula that the lessee might use is expressed as: $N = P/L$, where P is the purchase cost, L is the monthly lease cost, and N is the number of months needed to break even. Thus, if the equipment cost is $10,000 and the monthly cost is $250, the breakeven point is 40 months. This means if you are going to use the equipment for more than 40 months, you would be better off purchasing it. The only defect with this formula is it does not recognize the time value of money and the equipment maintenance cost.

We must conclude that the decision to lease or buy a computer system or software is not a clear-cut process. Many factors must be considered before a suitable scheme is chosen. One such consideration is the tax laws. When the Tax Reform of 1986 was passed by the Senate on September 27, 1986, it radically changed the outlook on purchasing or leasing computer systems. The most significant alteration was the repeal of investment tax credit (ITC). Under the previous tax laws, the federal government underwrote 10 percent of the purchase price of new equipment through ITC. Loss of this credit certainly hurts the purchase option.

In other respects, tax reform could tip the balance in favor of purchasing. Why? Since the purchaser cannot benefit from the ITC and the lessee will also not benefit from the ITC credit passed on to them by the lessor, both will suffer a higher cost of purchase price and lease price, respectively. The new tax law, however, lowers the corporate tax rate from a high of 46 percent to 34 percent. This substantial savings may actually motivate companies to purchase more equipment because they have now more money retained for purchase decisions.

Negotiating the Computer Contract

The computer has done a great deal of good—yet also some harm, where performance fails to meet standards. In most of these cases, users signed a vendor-prepared contract that they later regretted. The early 1980s have witnessed an enormous increase in litigation arising from computer software contracts. Failure to exercise aggressive negotiating practices puts the user on the defensive. The user should enter negotiations, clearly define hardware/software needs, and ensure vendor commitment without resorting to litigation.

Vendor-User Relationships: The Duty of Honesty

Morality imposes a certain obligation on the vendor to be honest, not to coerce. Selling is a morally acceptable activity as long as the vendor gives the user accurate information in deciding on a system. The issue is: How much information should the vendor offer? Often this means alerting the user to the limitations of the system or software.

Misrepresentation aside, there are laws that protect the consumer in a purchase even though the agreement is not in writing. The implied warranty, for example, provides two principles as grounds for litigation: **fitness** and **merchantability**. If the vendor knows in advance the user's intended purpose for acquiring a computer and sells the system knowing it won't do the job (i.e., the system is unfit), the user has legal recourse. Merchantability warrants that a system or a piece of software functions for the ordinary purpose for which it is used. The warranty is breached when the system repeatedly fails normal use.

Both principles are related to morality and honesty in the sense that the computer vendor is required to provide a system or software that the user expects. Holding the vendor liable for unfit products is a just practice.

Related to the warranty issue is the **disclaimer.** Most software products come with a disclaimer stating that the vendor makes no promise about the quality of the software. The vendor specifies liability as actual replacement of the software or a mere refund of the purchase price only. The courts usually support the validity of such a clause except in cases where it is shown to be unconscionable.

Learn to Negotiate

With so much at stake, the user must be well represented in a computer contract. *Negotiation* is the process of arriving at an agreement by conference or discussion. It is an art that involves sizing up the other party, devising a strategy for negotiation, and introducing changes that ensure equity and fairness in the contract.

The one mistake many users make when approaching a computer vendor is appearing anxious to get the system. In the absence of competitive bids, the vendor does not have to negotiate anything. Several strategies have been known to work in negotiating computer contracts:

1. Home turf advantage
2. The leader role
3. The good guy/bad guy strategy
4. Use of tradeoffs

The Home Turf Advantage   Psychologically, it is to the user's advantage to negotiate on his or her own turf. Staff support and documentation are readily available during the negotiation process. Certain courtesies are also exchanged when the vendor is a guest on the user's premises.

The Leader Role   If a firm is the first to install a vendor's system and the vendor feels that the installation will encourage other firms to do the same, the vendor will be willing to talk price. On one occasion, this author represented a bank while other banks in the area were waiting to see what system the client bank would adopt and how well it would operate. The vendor knew of the standing of the bank. Negotiations resulted in a 30 percent discount and no-charge maintenance on the equipment for one year. Under a test site arrangement, the vendor was allowed to bring prospective users to view the system within the first year of the installation.

The Good Guy/Bad Guy Strategy   Experienced consultants can easily earn their fees during contract negotiation. The consultant is usually viewed by the vendor as the shrewd negotiator—the bad guy—whereas the user is perceived as the compromiser. Such a strategy means that the consultant can test the waters and make all kinds of offers and counteroffers, subject to the user's approval. The advantage is that the user is under no obligation to comply. In contrast, vendor offers are usually binding, although a sales representative may hedge by saying something like, "I'll have to get headquarters approval on this." In any case, it is to the user's advantage to have someone else do the dirty work.

Using Tradeoffs   Face saving is crucial in contract negotiation. Suppose the vendor stands firm on certain points. What should be done? The strategy is to use tradeoffs that secure commitments while at the same time giving the vendor enough cause for going ahead with the installation. Many times, in dealing with a number of users, the vendor prefers to state the concession by letter rather than in the contract. This is an acceptable alternative, since it helps the vendor save face. Most vendors do not want to make changes in a standard contract, but are willing to give in on certain issues "off the record."

Early in the negotiation, it is customary to bring up the less important items, leaving the tough ones toward the end. If the first proposals were tough ones to negotiate, the vendor might decide that it is going to be an uphill battle (therefore, not worth the effort) and will walk out. It is also a good idea to negotiate over two or more short sessions than one long drawn-out meeting.

Remedies and Responsibilities

A computer contract should specify the user's legal recourse in the event the vendor fails to perform. The remedy process begins with an agreement on the items that make up the system and the services to be provided by the vendor. The remedies are arbitrarily classified under specific remedies, damages, and specific performance.

Specific remedies are practical ones spelled out in the agreement. For example, if the vendor fails to respond to a service request within four hours, the user may opt to cancel the maintenance agreement.

Specific remedies are generally supported by strict damage remedies included to compensate the user for damages resulting from vendor negligence. This serves to warn the vendor of the importance of living up to the spirit of the contract.

What to Look for in a Computer Contract

A hardware contract should stipulate the results to be achieved with the hardware. System performance criteria must be clearly defined. These criteria provide a basis for the user acceptance test when the system is installed.

The major risks inherent in a software package are failure to meet specifications, cost of enhancement, and bankruptcy of the software house. One remedy is to provide for termination of the contract or assistance "at no charge" to make the necessary changes within a specified time period. In the event of vendor bankruptcy, the source code must be provided to the user, usually through a third party.

What about personnel training? User training can be used as a "sweetener" because it saves users time and money not to have to oversee their own training. Training also varies depending on whether it is conducted on the user's premises or at vendor headquarters. In microcomputer-based installations, user-friendly software has virtually eliminated the need for vendor training.

Vendor failure to deliver on schedule can be irritating and costly to the user. A contract should specify a delivery date, how the system is to be delivered, and the remedies in the event of late delivery. In terms of system acceptance, a clause should specify the test(s) that the system must pass for user acceptance. A period of normal use should also be provided to ensure that the new system meets standards.

Related to system acceptance are guarantees of reliability and response to failure. For example, how long must the system run continuously without a shutdown? What is the mean time between failure? In the event of a failure, how long a wait before the vendor provides repairs? Service and support depends on the vendor's experience, location, and reputation. For example, if a terminal is acquired through a mail order house and fails within the warranty, the user may have to ship it back to the outlet at the user's expense. This can be inconvenient and costly. The same applies to off-the-shelf software.

The IBM Contract: A Case Illustration

The IBM contract is typical of those drafted by many vendor and software suppliers. Although it is one sided, this contract protects the user from fraud or misrepresentation in the event of program failure based on vendor promise or promotional literature. It begins by specifying the agreement between the vendor and the user. In the case of software acquisition, the content of the software is specified in the licensed programming specifications. Supplements to the general agreement are clauses that define the meaning of terms and the various aspects of the contract.

A major portion of the contract outlines the license provisions, installation and restrictions, license transfers, and the designated equipment to be used. Other items specify acceptance tests, billing and shipping terms, maintenance agreement, types of programming services provided, and permission to modify program code.

The Express Warranty   According to the contract, the IBM warranty specifies that the software will conform to the licensed program specifications if used on the designated IBM machine. It does not warrant, however, that the software will meet user requirements or will be error free.

The Disclaimer   The express warranty explicitly states the extent of the vendor's responsibility. Under the disclaimer, the vendor cannot warrant anything else.

Contract Remedies   IBM will correct program defects, although it is not liable for damages arising from performance or nonperformance. Damages are limited to a maximum of $25,000 or credit of one year's rent, whichever is greater.

As can be seen, the IBM contract is all-encompassing. It protects the user and IBM from the promises of prior salespersons and damages incurred due to software failure. It is one of the few contracts that are not easy to modify.

Conclusions

Contract negotiations have become increasingly important during the 1980s. Growing competition in an expanding vendor market means that the user has a choice, which improves negotiation leverage. Computer literacy among users has also enabled them to specify exactly what they want, paying close attention to quality and reliability.

Computer contracts are drafted with the vendor in mind. If signed as written, the user is likely to be on the losing end. In today's computerized society, where competition is the backbone of industry, virtually every item is negotiable. If the negotiation is carried out properly, the user can secure a fair contract and cement a relationship based on trust and mutual cooperation between the user and the vendor. Such a relationship cannot be compromised.

Implications for MIS

Acquiring an information system has one important goal—to create, capture, and use information for competitive advantage. The acquisition phase implies a commitment on the part of management to implement an information system based on design criteria. This means capital investment and support of an environment amenable to information technology. To capitalize on an investment in information technology, several actions are worth considering:

1. Senior management must recognize the potential of the information system and take an active role in supporting its installation. This is especially important in first-time installations.

2. Since the real impact of an information system comes in implementation, system acquisition means preparation for a smooth transition of procedures and human resources that will be receptive to the change. This transition is best accomplished through effective user training as soon as the hardware and software become operational.

3. During the process of acquiring equipment or software, it is important for management to review corporate strategy and verify the extent to which the information system links to this strategy. Implicit in this step is providing an atmosphere in which the end user and the technical staff work closely to remove differences and ensure a successful system implementation.

4. In the case of software acquisition, management must decide whether sensitive applications must be developed by outsiders or by staff within the organization. Program change control is an important issue for sensitive applications. Verification procedures, then, are clearly needed prior to actual implementation. The tension over control can be managed by establishing policies defining user domain and senior management's role.

Overall, management should ensure that compatible hardware and software be ready for implementation and that system testing, user training, and conversion activities be carried out successfully within a range of acceptability standards. Implementing information systems is covered in the next chapter.

Summary

- The hardware/software industry is made up of hardware, software, and service vendors. Hardware vendors include mainframe manufacturers, microcomputer vendors, peripherals and supplies outlets. The software sector includes timesharing, package software products, and contract programming. This area has experienced strong growth in response to program shortages and decreasing software costs. Service vendors are service bureaus, facility managers, and timesharing contractors.

- A structured approach to selection has replaced the old, subjective ways of installing computers. A major consideration in acquisition is whether the decision is to be made on a centralized or a decentralized basis. In either case, decisions should be based on organization policies determined in advance.

- In selection, an important point to remember is considering hardware and software as a unit for compatibility. The selection process is represented by four phases:
  1. *Requirements analysis:* spells out user requirements and delineates the actual applications to be handled by the system.
  2. *Request for proposal (RFP):* a user-prepared bid invitation to interested vendors, informing them of the requirements their system must meet for selection.
  3. *Evaluation and validation:* invites vendors to demonstrate their systems and verify the major features of their proposals. The user also uses performance measure techniques such as benchmark programs to evaluate each proposal.
  4. *Vendor selection:* as the outcome of the preceding steps, the selection of the vendor who best meets user requirements.

- A good software package offers short implementation time, lower development costs, and better flexibility than in-house programs. The main drawback is extensive modification of many software packages before they meet the user's requirements.

- For software selection, various elements are considered: reliability, modularity for ease of modification, user friendliness, and ability to perform to standards. Performance is perhaps the most critical element in selection.

◻ Software ownership raises questions regarding what the user is paying for, restrictions to copying software, and the changes in software that can be made without vendor approval. This is a critical issue now being debated in the industry.

◻ Hardware selection requires an evaluation of several performance criteria. They include system compatibility, vendor support, user friendliness, uptime record, and purchase/lease costs. These factors are seriously considered before final selection.

◻ There are two major methods of acquisition: purchase or lease. The purchase option offers cash savings because of depreciation and investment tax credit. But it also offers a lower total cash outflow if the system is kept five years or longer. In contrast, the lease option requires no financing. The risk of obsolescence is also shifted to the lessor.

◻ Contract negotiations require strategies and much preparation. In conducting a negotiation session, representatives must be ready with alternatives and tradeoffs and keep an open mind about handling certain items for final agreement. A contract should clarify a number of issues:
1. The vendor's responsibilities and the recourse available to the user in the event of failure to perform.
2. The penalties for failure of the system to meet user requirements.
3. Warranties and their implications.
4. Assurances of critical elements such as response time to maintenance.

Key Terms

Benchmark	Open architecture
Disclaimer	Portability
Expandability	Request for proposal (RFP)
Facilities management (FM)	Serviceability
Fitness	System software
Merchantability	Timesharing
Modularity	Unbundling
Net advantage to leasing formula	

Review Questions

1. The hardware/software industry consists of various vendors and suppliers. Outline the major vendors, their functions, and the products that they offer.

2. Define the following terms:
   a. Unbundling

b. Benchmarks
c. Reliability

3. Software growth has been attributed to a number of events. Cite two major reasons for such growth. In your opinion, what reasons contributed the most to the growth of the software market? Elaborate.

4. Distinguish between:
   a. Timesharing and facilities management
   b. Modularity and expandability
   c. Fitness and merchantibility

5. Explain in detail the procedure used in hardware/software selection.

6. What factors are considered prior to system selection? Explain.

7. The selection process consists of four phases. Outline each phase and explain how the selection process applies to microcomputer acquisition.

8. According to the text, the RFP is a communication tool between the user and the vendor. Do you agree? Elaborate on the makeup, content, and contributions of the RFP to the final selection phase.

9. What advantages does a good software package offer? Be specific.

10. Summarize the factors to be considered in software selection.

11. What factors are evaluated in hardware selection? How do they differ from those considered in question 10? Explain.

12. Elaborate on the various information sources for hardware/software evaluation.

13. How are vendor proposals evaluated? What method would you recommend for vendors bidding on microcomputer systems? Why?

14. How important is the consultant in system evaluation? Why? How would you select a consultant? Discuss.

15. Explain the features, drawbacks, and circumstances under which computers are purchased versus leased.

16. There are various strategies and tactics in computer contract negotiations. If you were the party representing the user, how would you carry out negotiations? Elaborate.

Application Problems

1. The success story in Richmond is Cavalier Insurance Company's growth. In less than eight years, the company has grown through acquisitions and sheer aggressive marketing. Its MIS activity kept pace with growth

in every way. The mainframe has handled applications for all kinds of insurance. New hardware has been added to match increasing requirements for instant information. The company has added 40 percent each year to the MIS division's budget for the past three years.

Decisions on hardware installations, however, caught the company with three computer makes and five vendors. Software was also acquired through six software houses, and the company's databases were on different media using two database management systems.

The chief executive officer was concerned about the heterogeneity of the hardware. Customers soon began to complain about service. New customers waited at least seven weeks before they received their policy. Likewise, premium billing took weeks to process. In three out of ten cases, customers disagreed on the amount of the premium that they agreed to pay.

A consultant was brought in to review the MIS operation and make recommendations to correct the situation. As can be imagined, the consultant called for sweeping changes in the way the MIS function was managed. The MIS was found lacking in control tools or procedures, and he recommended a method of prioritizing application selection and development. He also pointed to the importance of an integrated database to handle all applications. Finally, he called for the development of a long-range plan and formation of an executive steering committee to direct and coordinate the MIS function on a regular basis.

The president mulled over the recommendations and, considering the fast-paced nature of the business, could not be sure how much of it to approve and how to implement it into Cavalier's way of doing business. He was afraid that abrupt change could backfire unnecessarily. A way had to be found both to correct the wrong manner in which MIS was handling information and simultaneously to keep the traffic going.

QUESTIONS

a. What do you think of the president's way of proceeding?
b. How practical is the consultant's approach to the problem? Can all this be corrected? What are the costs?
c. How would you handle the problem? Be specific.

2. Fisher Auto Parts is the largest auto parts dealer in the states of Virginia and Maryland. The firm's headquarters is in Richmond. It operates stores in seventeen cities in Virginia and eleven in Maryland. Total annual sales are over $35 million. Net income, however, has been decreasing during the past two years, because of the surge in new car sales and the high cost of used car repairs.

The firm's management team is composed of conservative, old-line managers who were once clerks in various stores. They are not impressed with fancy procedures or high-technology gimmicks for operating the business. Recently, an auto parts chain began to open stores in various locations, and management decided to fight this new competition by cutting unnecessary costs. All advertising must now be justified and discounts on parts to independent mechanics were dropped to 20 percent from the traditional 30 percent accorded to established garages.

The MIS organization is run by Al Rubenstein, vice president, who reports directly to Joe Fisher, the president and owner of the chain. Rubenstein has complete MIS responsibility and makes almost all decisions, except those involving major hardware acquisition. The two senior managers are Neil Snyder and Jack Holt. Snyder manages the applications development area, while Holt is in charge of operations. All MIS work is centralized. Information going to or coming from various stores is transmitted via remote batch mode.

Clerks have been receiving complaints about lack of immediate information on parts availability. For example, when a part is not in the store's stockroom, the clerk sends an inquiry via the terminal. Since it is a remote batch environment, it takes two hours to determine whether the desired part is available in the firm's main warehouse. It also takes another two hours for the part to be delivered to the store for final sale.

QUESTIONS
a. What are the pros and cons of this MIS system?
b. Specifically, what problems do you see in the present system?
c. What actions must be taken to bring the operations up to standards?
d. Is cost-cutting an effective way to deal with competition? Why?
e. Are there organizational issues that might relate to the problems raised in question b? Explain.

Selected References

Christoff, Kurt A. "Building a Fourth-Generation Environment." *Datamation*, September 15, 1985, 118ff.

Gabel, David. "Maintenance Contracts." *PC Week*, September 24, 1985, 75–76.

Harris, Edison. "Negotiating Software Contracts." *Datamation*, July 15, 1985, 53–54ff.

Hoffman, W. and Willis, Eugene. *1985 Annual Edition West's Federal Taxation*. St. Paul, Minn.: West, 1985.

Houston, Velina. "Internal Consultants Have Inside Track." *Management Information System Week*, April 27, 1983, 3.

Rosenthal, Morton. "Careful Software Evaluation Increases End User Acceptance." *Data Management*, September 1985, 30–32.

Snyders, Jan. "How to Buy Packages." *Computer Decisions*, July 1978, 52.

Yates, John C. and Jones III, Henry W. "Computer Acquisition: The Role of Due Diligence." *Computer Negotiation Report*, May 1985, 1.

Implementing Information Systems

Chapter Contents

Holiday Fire Puts Firm's Disaster Plan to the Test

IT WAS THANKSGIVING DAY 1982 that Norwest Corp., a Minneapolis financial services business, tested the full scope of its disaster recovery plan.

A fire, set in an adjacent building undergoing demolition, ravaged the firm's seventeen-story headquarters. The office building was almost empty, and there were no injuries. And despite extensive damage to its administrative facilities, the firm, which is the holding company for Norwest bank—an institution with some $5 billion in assets—was able to return to operation by the Tuesday of the following week.

Norwest's disaster recovery plan, completed only six months before the devastating fire, was the firm's savior, according to John Nugent, senior consultant with Norwest's Financial Institutions Group. Nugent said, "Without it, we never would have survived."

Although Norwest lost a number of data and word processing systems, affecting its instant cash and internal controls operations, the 3-in.-thick recovery plan document speeded its return to business. The firm survived, even though its plan "was drafted on the supposition that one or two departments were out of service, not the entire organization," Nugent reveals.

Unfortunately, most organizations need a near disaster to spur them into action. Many corporations have to strive hard to overcome the ingrained mentality that "It can't happen here,"

Nugent says. Questions such as the cost of not operating, legal culpability and financial penalties usually provide the impetus to get upper management moving, he notes.

To that end, corporate executives must ask the hard question: What is the maximum time to belly-up if a data center goes down? "I've spoken with insurance companies who said they could operate without a data center for 30 days or longer," Nugent says. "That's hard to imagine."

In fact, a recent University of Minnesota study indicated that after a data center is down for more than four and a half days, most organizations have a hard time surviving. For financial institutions, a firm is in jeopardy of not surviving after only 38 hours, he adds.

A disaster recovery plan alone does not guarantee survival. A study conducted by Data Processing Security, Inc., states that of the companies surveyed that touted having recovery plans and that had experienced disasters, only 5 percent had workable plans. That's one in 20. Most of the plans failed because they had not been adequately updated and maintained. The problem is that so many firms are engaged in round-the-clock operations that there is little time to stage computer outages to test plans.

—*Exerpted from Alan Alper,* Computerworld, *May 12, 1986, 50.*

AT A GLANCE

Every new system must undergo testing. The user puts the system to the final test. A test procedure checks for quick response, how well the system performs under stress, and how quickly it recovers from failure. The test verifies that the system as a whole will meet user requirements. The success of testing has a great deal to do with a well-thought-out plan that specifies the steps and procedure for program, system, and user acceptance testing.

For a system to be effective, controls must be incorporated to ensure performance. Quality assurance must be provided in each phase of the system life cycle, especially during conversion. Quality assurance specialists validate a system through alpha and beta testing for certification. Quality assurance and EDP auditing are closely interrelated processes. It is the auditor's job to develop controls to ensure reliability, which promotes user confidence in the new system.

A crucial phase in the SDLC is implementation—a process of converting a new system into operation. This includes copying files from one system format to another, preparing test files, incorporating audit control procedures, parallel processing, and planning for postimplementation review.

In system implementation, user training takes on special priority. A successful training program promotes user acceptance and ensures system success. User-friendly manuals and help screens encourage the user to try out the system and use it on a regular basis. Postimplementation review involves checking to see if the system has met a standard. This phase also includes software maintenance and enhancements that are customary with most systems.

By the end of this chapter, you should know:

1. The steps taken in system testing
2. The role of quality assurance and EDP auditing in system testing and implementation
3. The importance of user training for minimizing resistance to change
4. The activities that make up system conversion
5. The makeup of postimplementation review
6. Disaster planning

Introduction

In Chapter 15, we discussed the process of system design and the features surrounding input, output, and file design. A new system should have all the parts working together. Before it becomes operational, the system is put to the test to make sure it meets user requirements. Testing attempts to force-fail or push the system to its limits. It is a tedious but necessary step for a new system installation.

After testing comes system *implementation,* which simply means putting the new system design into operation. This includes user training as well as installation of hardware, terminals, and a telecommunication network. System implementation actually goes beyond the mechanics of converting from one system to another. First, in any approach used the goal of implementation is to introduce benefits through use. Systems developed through prototyping show their impact early—as early as information requirements analysis. Any systems where end users develop their own applications and generate their own reports usually have an immediate impact. Finally, applications developed through the SDLC emphasize benefits that occur later in the implementation process. The reason is that these applications are complex, involve many people, and require an extensive procedure before they become operational. Imagine a large commercial bank with sixty tellers, eighty-five bookkeepers, and new equipment—all working together to be fully implemented by a specific deadline. It can take weeks, sometimes months, before full benefits are realized.

This chapter examines the activities and steps taken to prepare the system and the end user for implementation along with the overall impact of implementation on people and their organization. Following conversion, we evaluate system performance against criteria set in advance. Software maintenance and enhancements fall under postimplementation. They are discussed later in the chapter.

The Nature of Testing

Poor testing or no testing is a risky business. Errors that may appear later can prove to be too costly to correct. The main purpose of testing is to see if the new system produces accurate information. Assuming an on-line system, a variety of tests are used:

1. *Response time to inquiries.* The system is loaded with as much data through terminals as would be used during peak hours to estimate its peak load response time. (Example: Measure how long it takes for an inquiry when the system is loaded with operational data.)

2. *Stress testing.* A **stress test** is a verification procedure that measures how a system functions under peak loads. Unlike volume testing, where time is not a consideration, stress testing subjects the system to high workloads over a short timeframe. (Example: Run all terminals at the same time and observe out of the ordinary deviations.)

3. *Recovery testing.* We force-fail a system or enter invalid data to see how quickly it rebounds, detects the errors in time, or resorts to a backup

procedure to ensure maximum uptime. (Example: Load a backup file and continue processing without loss of data or data degradation.)

4. *Human factor testing.* During system testing, environmental factors (air conditioning, lighting, etc.) are evaluated to accommodate the human comfort. In addition, this test checks for the way the user uses the system when processing data. (Example: Determine what happens when the system does not properly respond to user inquiries.)

The Test Plan

We start a system test with a test plan. A well-thought-out plan improves communication between users and the design group and specifies the number of test runs to be executed, the portion of the program to be tested on each run, the data to be used, and the staff that will do the test. It also identifies:

1. *Criteria for user acceptance testing* and an agreement on the test and duration.
2. *Program test data* taken from the user's files or artificially generated for the test.
3. *User training procedure* and provisions for training material. A user training manual and the hardware to be used in training are also identified.
4. *Program documentation,* including the name of the programmer and program flowcharts (see Figure 17.1).
5. *Program and system test.*
6. *Completion* of system *documentation.*
7. *User acceptance test.*

Test Methodology

After a test plan has been developed, the next stage is a testing methodology with emphasis on program, system, and user acceptance testing.

Figure 17.1
System testing procedure.

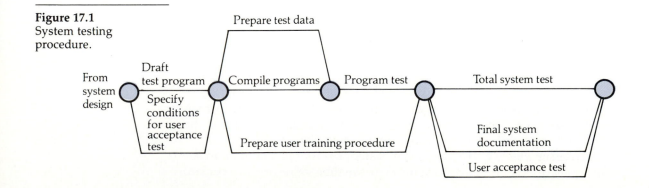

Program Testing   Program testing is a procedure for detecting and correcting syntax and logic errors. **Syntax errors** violate the rules of the language in which the program is written. For example, in dBASE III Plus programming, failing to place a numeric variable in quotes signals a syntax error. **Logic errors** are deviations from a range of acceptability. For example, a payroll program that processes 100 hours a week for employees who work no overtime would be committing a logic error.

In structuring program testing, each program module is checked individually (called *stub testing*) and then with every other module in a bottom-up approach until the whole program is verified. If errors are detected in a final test, it is easier to check modules for errors than to go over the whole program.

System Testing   This phase ensures that the whole set of programs work together properly where one program accepts as inputs the information generated from other programs. **System testing** checks for logic changes in the program and uncovers errors that slipped by in program testing.

User Acceptance Testing   Unlike a system test that was performed by programmers using test data, this test is performed by users using real data over an extended time period. It is the final test before the system is taken over (or rejected) by the end user (see Table 17.1).

There are several levels of acceptance testing. They address questions such as:

1. How adequate is the response time to meet a typical processing workload?
2. How easy is it to learn and use the new system?
3. How well does the system handle peak workloads?
4. How self-instructional is the user's manual?

As users try out the system, "bugs" are discovered and corrected under system maintenance. A well-trained maintenance programmer can do much to satisfy the user and ensure final acceptance at this stage.

Table 17.1   Test Methodology: A Summary Method

Test Type	Method
Program testing	Each module is tested individually and then with every other module in the program.
System testing	The whole set of programs is tested to make sure they work together properly. Here, programmers use test data.
User acceptance testing	The user uses real data to test the system over an extended period of time.

Quality Assurance

Quality assurance is the development of controls to ensure a quality system. During system testing, programmers take steps to ensure error-free software. Actually, quality assurance is emphasized in every stage of the system development life cycle. It is crucial that all programs be as error free and as reliable as possible.

System designers often compromise quality for the sake of productivity. Software quality is judged by various capabilities:

1. *Access control:* degree of control and audit of system access.
2. *Correctness:* level of completeness in input editing, calculations, and output. This implies reliability—how accurately the system performs to standards.
3. *Expandability:* how well the software can be modified to meet a user's changing requirements.
4. *Maintainability:* locating and correcting program errors, modularity, and simplicity.
5. *Portability and reusability:* running a program on different hardware configurations.
6. *Reliability:* the extent to which a system performs accurately according to standards.

Each factor can be monitored during the SDLC. For example, quality assurance in software testing evaluates the overall software and how well it meets the software requirements document. In postimplementation, quality assurance is concerned with reliability problems and ways of improving system performance. It also ensures that all errors are corrected and the system conforms to standards.

In quality assurance, then, the goal is to eliminate program errors. This is often achieved through a "force-fail" procedure to determine what it will take to make the system fail. For example, in one installation in a commercial bank, seventeen tellers were asked to tap information in a new database located 1500 miles away. They entered a variety of transactions—deposits, withdrawals, placed accounts on hold, etc. as quickly as they could. Some tellers staggered the same transactions to check for accuracy. After the 134th transaction, the mainframe began to respond more slowly to successive inquiries. The response time dropped from 2 to 17 seconds. The bank found out later that when sixty-four other banks tapped their respective databases on a busy Friday morning, response time dropped considerably. At that time, the system essentially failed the test on the response time criterion of system acceptability.

The information system is further validated through alpha and beta tests. An **alpha test** verifies that the system meets user requirements. Programmers use test data to test the system before it is released for user acceptance testing. A **beta test** is a user-run acceptance test to try out the new software for the first time on the user's site.

Software products in general average several defects in every thousand lines of code. These defects are so costly to modify that it is often cheaper to rewrite the whole program. The cost of detecting and correcting errors rises geometrically the closer they are found toward the end of the SDLC cycle. Thus, true quality assurance incorporates methods to detect flaws early in the development process. The goal is to speed the development of software that is error free, maintainable, and reliable.

The Role of the EDP Auditor   Controls are a part of system design. They are tested independently of the design staff. Much like the "force-fail" test, in an **audit trail** the auditor tests a system by introducing data that specifically violate the controls. At a minimum, the auditor should see the additions, deletions, and changes to the files. An audit trail should also document all changes made in the files.

It is the auditor's role to build controls into new systems to ensure system reliability and data integrity. Having the auditor on the system development team makes it convenient to review testing activities and enforce the controls that have been embedded during the testing phase.

System Implementation

Implementation means converting a new system into actual operation. **Conversion** is a major step in implementation. The other steps are post-implementation review and software maintenance.

Conversion

No conversion is ever a straightforward procedure. It is probably the busiest phase of the installation, especially when it is behind schedule. Conversion includes several activities. They are:

1. Review test documentation and the implementation plan.
2. Copy the files from one hardware to another.
3. Incorporate audit control procedures for file integrity.
4. Initiate a processing routine. There are three such routines:
   a. *Parallel processing,* or running the new system along with the old. Disconnect the old system when the new system has proven its reliability. This approach is costly, but it promotes security.
   b. *Pilot processing,* or testing the new system in one department or one area. If it runs to standards, then apply the system to the whole organization. The problem here is deciding what department should be chosen to test the new system. The benefit is cutting losses just in case there are serious bugs in the system.

Figure 17.2
Conversion procedure.

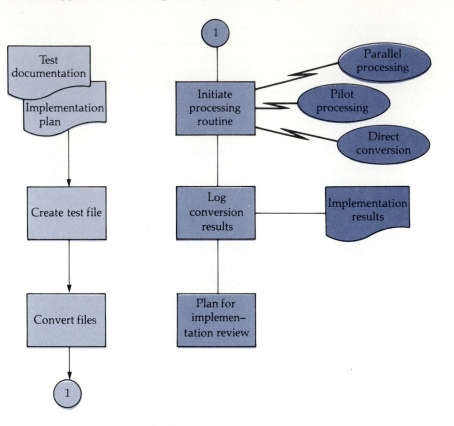

c. *Direct conversion,* or cutting off the old system and applying the new system immediately. It is a "go for broke" approach usually carried out with first-time users or organizations that require everyone to try to make the new system work.

5. Log the results for reference.
6. Plan for postimplementation (see Figure 17.2).

During conversion, the user is tempted to make last-minute changes as an afterthought. Changes at such time are risky. They should be left for postimplementation under software maintenance.

File Conversion   The goal of file conversion is to prepare files that are compatible with the new system configuration and format. Copying the "old" files intact is a primary concern during conversion. It is a hectic procedure, especially when there is a change in vendor hardware and specifications require major reformatting of file records.

Before the newly converted files are loaded, a test procedure is used to verify the conversion. This is a convenient opportunity to have user participation. A good test file should demonstrate how well the new system handles complex transactions. An automobile insurance file, for example, would include insurers with all possible types of coverage: comprehensive, no-fault, liability, medical, etc.

Conversion Guidelines   File conversion is more than dealing with new files. There are several pointers to consider in conversion.

Role of the User   For a new system to be successful, the user must ultimately assume responsibility for it. Getting the user to cooperate during conversion makes the job easier and the results better for the project team. The likelihood of success in conversion also increases substantially if there is a strong user commitment to lead in the conversion process.

The File Conversion Procedure   The first step in conversion is to decide on the information that will load the installation. A key point is to specify how each record field value will be generated. A translation table should be provided to convert a customer type, for example, from "14" in the old system to "D" in the new. In more complicated cases, a new field value may depend on one or more fields in the old system. For example, a 25-character field may have been compressed into 16 characters or partitioned into two 15-character fields. In either case, a conversion rule is needed.

Be Selective in the Conversion   Converting everything just because it is in the file does not make sense and can be dangerous. For example, when only 5 out of 13 field types in a record are active, then it may be that the remaining 13 fields are obsolete. Conversion is a time when unused fields are deleted and replaced by new ones. Therefore, loading data directly from the old files into the new ones is generally not recommended. A summary of conversion guidelines is:

1. Secure user commitment. User involvement is important.
2. Decide on the information that will load the system.
3. Discourage major changes.
4. Be selective in the conversion.

In this aspect of conversion, the role of the project team includes cleaning up data, monitoring the loading of files, and scheduling computer time. The user's functions include entering new data and participating in the overall conversion. The thrust of this whole procedure is to give the user properly converted files as they are the foundation of the user's information system.

User Training

A major component of system implementation is training the user on the new system. The level and duration of training depend on the user's knowledge level and the system's requirements. Users range from novices to experts. A *novice* is generally a casual user with limited knowledge of computers. An *expert* is someone with prior experience and who keeps abreast of the technology.

The requirements of the system also range from simple and user friendly to advanced. A user-friendly system is almost self-instructional, with menu-driven features and easy-to-use manuals. The duration of training, even for the novice user, is usually measured in hours to days. Advanced systems requiring knowledge of computer-based commands could take days to weeks even for the experienced user. From this, we can conclude that the level of training depends on:

1. The user's knowledge of computers
2. The complexity of the system and how well it accommodates the average user
3. The trainer's skill
4. The environment in which training is carried out

In any case, training must be geared to the specific user based on capabilities, experience, and system complexity. In situations where both the user and the system are new, basic training procedures are usually introduced first. For example, training first-time users on personal computers involves instruction in how to turn on the PC, how to format, how to copy data from one diskette to another, when to remove a diskette, and what procedure to use for shutting off the system. Once completed, the second step is to show the user how to enter data, load files, access information, update records, and so on.

Successful training is supported by a well-written user manual, easy-to-use help screens, and job aids. *User manuals* can be invaluable training documents, especially when the user is geographically isolated. A well-written user manual is well organized, highly illustrated, and contains an index for reference. Graphics, photographs, and templates for quick reference can be invaluable teaching aids for the user.

HELP *screens* are a part of virtually every software package. Used with a menu, the software offers the user a HELP option to help the user correct syntactic errors. For example, in dBASE III Plus, all the user needs to do is answer Y (yes) to the software-generated question:

```
"SYNTAX ERROR
DO YOU NEED HELP(Y,N)?"
```

The system loads the portion of the HELP package that describes the command in question and what it does.

Job aids help the user follow a procedure or diagnose basic problems. For example, color is used to identify hardware, schematics to illustrate procedures, and flowcharts to diagnose problems.

To sum up, successful user training relies on:

1. A well-written and highly illustrated user manual.

2. Availability of graphics, templates, and other tools for quick reference or as teaching aids.
3. HELP screens to guide in correcting syntactic errors.
4. Job aids and schematics to diagnose problems.

In cases where system implementation brings with it a change in hardware and software, conversion includes an alteration of the physical environment. Conversion of physical facilities, for example, could mean installing new terminals, replacing furniture, redesigning lighting, modifying air conditioning to standards, and providing communication and security networks for the new system.

Combating Resistance to Change   Regardless of what is being converted or how well conversion takes place, implementation means change and people in general resist change. People become anxious when they do not know what a new system will do, how it will affect their jobs, and the system's impact on career plans. The result is stress and resistance to change. Resistance is displayed in the following personal reactions:

1. *Projection:* Hostility toward peers
2. *Avoidance:* Withdrawal from the scene (calling in sick)
3. *Aggression:* Sabotage of the system, because they are unsure of its operation or use.

A psychological element that explains resistance to change is the value users place on information. In most organizations, information means power to those who hold it. While systems analysts develop systems that increase the availability of information through databases, users who stand to lose their information monopoly as a result may resist the new system. Much of this is a matter of attitude and perception of how the new system will affect their status in the firm. Certain people will resist any change. Resistance also has much to do with the individual personality, the organizational structure in which people work, and the group relations of the area in which the new system will be installed. Courses, user education and training, and participation in the development process can help reduce resistance to change.

A second resistance category comes from the system itself rather than people. Some systems have poor interface with the user and extensive training requirements for mastering them. Recent MIS literature supports the development of user-friendly software as a way of overcoming resistance to system implementation. Yet it is not enough to have a user-friendly technology. What is needed is a user that is friendly to the system. Overconcentration on technology and overlooking behavioral problems have resulted in system failure.

There are various methods of easing change that are appropriate for system implementation. They include:

• User attitude survey

- Communication training
- Training sessions
- Role negotiation technique

In a *user attitude survey,* we collect opinions from users to find out how well they like the system and how close it comes to meeting their initial requirements. Most users have difficulty communicating their requirements, more because of a lack of good communication skills than an inability to identify their needs. *Communication training* can be invaluable for improving user-analyst relationships as well as the quality of the system installation.

Training sessions are normally run by information system specialists. Here it is important for the trainer to have a clear impression of the user's training needs and the pace of training. For example, some users easily pick up system operation in one day; others might take a week.

Resistance to change becomes obvious when users perceive a change in their job. An interesting technique, called *role negotiation,* attempts to clarify what the user expects the altered job to offer in terms of authority and power. Once understood, users have been known to accept their role in the light of the change.

In summary, it seems obvious that for a new system to get user support, designers and users must improve communication channels and jointly discuss the new system's features and how the change will improve the quality of work. Users also need to participate in all phases of the conversion. Sensitivity to user relations and expectations is a step toward "conversion without tears."

Postimplementation Review

After the system is completely converted and the operation is "up and running," the effect of the new system on the organization should be carefully evaluated. The system's impact must be analyzed in terms of its effects on people, procedures, and the overall performance of the business. More specifically, the main areas of concern are quality of information and decision making, attitudes of end users, and costs of information processing. For example, the postimplementation study may show that a new bank customer service application has reduced the time it takes to open a customer's checking account by 60 percent. It may also show that data entry errors have been reduced to zero.

A number of key questions are asked in the postimplementation stage:

1. How have information systems changed the accuracy and timeliness of information?
2. Has the information system caused organizational changes? How constructive have they been?
3. Has the information system changed the attitudes of the end users affected by the system?

4. How has the information system affected the number of users that access data from the database?
5. How has the new system changed the cost of operating the business?
6. Has the new system affected the organization's decision making process?
7. In what way has the new system affected the relationships among end users in the organization?
8. How does the information from the new system justify the cost of investment?
9. How has the new system changed the way various operations are performed?

The goal is to evaluate the system against standards and determine how well it meets user requirements. The user initiates the review, which prompts a procedure for maintenance or enhancement.

Software Maintenance   **Software maintenance** accounts for up to 80 percent of total system development. Most systems require it. Programmers detest it. It is boring because it deals with the ongoing features of the system, not the discrete begin-end orientation of a project. As with any system, however, maintenance is a necessity.

Maintenance is classified as corrective or perfective. In *corrective* maintenance, programmers work on problems that were in the initial design. *Perfective* maintenance deals with the changes that users require as a result of their experience with the system. The problem with maintenance in general is that it is labor intensive and errors can also crop up. Coding is a manual job. Making a change in one program module often means changes in several other modules. Missing one change could create system integrity problems.

A successful program maintenance is a reflection of the programmer's skills and motivation. Because maintenance demands more training than any other programming activity, the MIS department must reward maintenance engineers in line with their contributions. This includes attractive salaries and benefits and, most important, recognition before peers and supervisors.

Security Considerations

Safeguarding information against unauthorized access is an important MIS issue. One aspect of user training is ensuring that passwords and security procedures are consistently observed by end users.

At a minimum, the new system should provide password protection so that only users with the correct password will be able to log onto the system. This is an elementary precaution. Beyond that, we need to decide to what extent the files on the system are worth protecting further by using additional passwords to restrict access. To illustrate, in constructing a software package for a church the board of elders decided to allow the minister access to all information except the pledge fund, which required another password. Likewise, church members could access the membership information file, but not the general ledger, pledge file, or the church's budget. These files have separate passwords that were given only to the treasurer. This procedure slows access but ensures system security and integrity.

End users become complacent when passwords have been assigned. Passwords must be changed immediately every time an employee with access to the system has left the firm. We also need to consider the weakness of most password systems, namely, the ease of cracking the system. One time an auditor was able to determine the password for over 75 percent of the users in a few hours by guessing at things like employee names, addresses, or department codes. Passwords should not be chosen because they are easy to remember. If they are, then they are not difficult to crack. A more secure way of preventing access to files is by hiding the files on disk. This is done by changing file attributes to "Hidden" or "Read only." Unfortunately, the more security conscious the software, the longer it takes the end user to access it.

Disaster Recovery

Security precautions serve the needs of management provided the database is available. What security steps must be taken to recover from a disk crash? A system failure, or other disaster? Planning for recovery from a disaster is becoming extremely important as more and more organizations become dependent on corporate databases for decision making.

Imagine the unthinkable taking place: A hurricane destroys the MIS center of a $10 billion bank. To make things worse, fire breaks out later that Monday evening on the first day after Christmas. During the first 24 hours of this catastrophe, the bank loses interest income because it is unable to get credit for outgoing cash letters. Check processing comes to a halt, which means no accounts are up to date. The general ledger is inoperative. The problem gets worse during the second 24 hours, forcing the bank to borrow emergency funds at a high interest rate to stay open. By the third day, files are off balance. Customers, employees, and federal agencies are losing faith in the bank's ability to stay afloat. Massive withdrawals begin with rumors that the bank is on the verge of collapse.

Our scenario sounds farfetched, but it could happen. Several studies have found that an organization's survival is threatened within 48 hours after its computer center fails. Financial losses can be excessive. Indirect losses such as loss of customers and uncollected receivables can be devastating. To protect against losses, disaster recovery planning has been introduced.

Disaster/recovery planning means a quick response to recovery, no matter what the disaster. An effective plan identifies potential threats, prioritizes applications, and devises safeguards to minimize losses in the event of a disaster.

There are several approaches to disaster/recovery. The two primary ones are fortress and backup plans. In the *fortress* plan, the entire computer facility is housed on one site. This means a full complement of hardware and tight physical security. The drawback is maintenance cost and the vulnerability of the site to floods, tornados, or other natural disasters.

In the *backup* plan, a service bureau is under contract to process applications during disaster. Quick availability and the security of a backup are the main advantages. The drawbacks, however, are high processing fees, problems of hardware/software compatibility, and turnaround time.

Regardless of the approach, it is important for an organization to devise a disaster plan that can be implemented on call. The plan must identify the priority of each user. Users are expected to assume responsibility for:

1. Identifying the key applications, their levels of importance, and the damage that may result from system failure.
2. Approving system and file protection procedures.
3. Financing the cost of the backup in the event of a disaster.

In developing a disaster/recovery plan, several questions are worth considering:

1. How long would it take to rebuild the facility?
2. How dependable is the backup facility?
3. What information must the company have to keep it afloat?
4. What personnel must be available in such an emergency?
5. What electric power source can be secured during a disaster?

Electric backup is perhaps the most critical. To illustrate, on May 17, 1985, this author's flight landed in Miami at a time when the city had just had a blackout. The airport was virtually shut down and traffic lights were inoperable. Every facility that depended on electricity was down. A major bank's computer facility, however, had its own electric power supply that automatically replaced the city's public utility. This allowed the computer to operate without loss of data or processing time. Such a backup is called an **uninterruptible power supply (UPS)** system.

Since computer systems are vulnerable to extended power outages, they must have an alternative power source for backup and a feature that ensures steady electric flow. A UPS has from 15 to 20 minutes of reserve power. In major installations, a diesel generator provides a backup power supply after the UPS supply is spent. In some systems, this can be as long as there is fuel to run the generator.

A disaster/recovery plan is developed in three steps:
1. *Appoint a competent team* of representatives of users and designers.

The team's main function is to set up the recovery plan and oversee its development. Specifically, it looks into backup sites, supplies, working copies of application programs, and communication facilities.

2. *Prepare planning tasks* in a cycle similar to that of the SDLC. This includes setting objectives for disaster/recovery, evaluating applications and potential vendors against objectives and choosing the final plan. In testing and implementation, the team checks out the backup system and verifies the procedures and prepares the site for the installation.

3. *Draft a disaster/recovery manual* with copies given to team members and users.

In summary, we can sense the importance and impact of the computer on the organization's operation. Without this marvelous machine and the software that supports its operation, today's organization cannot survive. Incorporating a backup for the hardware, software, electric, and personnel provides the cushion to absorb the shock, making it possible to continue functioning when a disaster occurs. Without such a plan, the whole organization is doomed. Such, unfortunately, is the cost of automation.

Implications for MIS

System testing and conversion are the most crucial steps in the SDLC. In taking this step, the MIS department is fulfilling several objectives:

1. To produce a tested system ready for user acceptance testing
2. To complete the acceptance test procedure
3. To prepare reports to management

User-MIS communication has a great impact on the success of an installation. In reviewing this interface, several questions should be considered:

1. Do analysts really *ask* the user to be involved? Or do they assume that the user does not want to be involved, so they provide input for him? If the user were not involved in the design, it is probably too late now.
2. Does the analyst *understand* the user's area of operation, the problem, or point of view? How much should they spend on the user site before they get into design?
3. Does the analyst *listen* long enough to give the user the benefit of the doubt?
4. Do analysts *write* things down while it is fresh in their mind? Do they also *review* completed work with the user?

Clearly, communication problems can be identified and corrected. It is the MIS manager's goal, then, to facilitate effective communication between the MIS personnel, especially those doing the design, and the user for a successful installation. The managerial aspects of information systems are discussed in Chapter 18.

Summary

▫ A newly designed system should have all its components working together. System testing evaluates every variation and pushes the system to its limits. It is a necessary step in system development.

▫ The first step in system testing is to develop a test plan that specifies conditions for user acceptance testing, requires test data for program testing, lays out user training procedures, content, and duration, provides the program(s) for testing, and finalizes system documentation before user acceptance testing.

▫ After the test plan, a testing procedure is carried out, focusing on program testing, system testing, and user acceptance testing. Program testing checks for syntax and logic errors. System testing uncovers weaknesses that were not found in earlier tests. This includes force-fail testing and recovery from failure. User acceptance testing is the user's own test of the system, using manuals and guidelines prepared for it. This is the final test before the system is placed in operation.

▫ Quality assurance ensures that the user adopts a system tailored to predefined requirements. In system testing, quality assurance seeks elimination of program errors by putting the system through a force-fail cycle to determine what will make it fail.

▫ The EDP auditor should be involved in various phases of the SDLC. A good audit control trail can be effective in detecting fraud and tracking problem-prone activities. It is the auditor's role to devise controls for the new system to ensure reliability and integrity, which promote user confidence in the system.

▫ Implementation is converting a new system design into actual operation. The conversion phase entails several steps:
  1. Create test files for program testing.
  2. Review test documentation and the implementation plan.
  3. Copy files from one system to another.
  4. Incorporate audit control procedures for file integrity.
  5. Initiate parallel processing.
  6. Log the results for verification and reference.
  7. Discontinue the old system.
  8. Plan for postimplementation.

▫ A serious concern in conversion is copying the files into a format acceptable to the new system. Test files are developed for determining how well the new system handles complex transactions.

▫ Several guidelines for the conversion phase are:
  1. Make sure the user is involved.
  2. Develop a conversion procedure.
  3. Discourage major changes in the program or implementation.
  4. Use a selective approach to file conversion.

▫ A major component of conversion is user training. Users range from the novice (casual) to the expert who has prior experience in the area. The duration of training is measured in hours to days; advanced systems take longer. In any case, user training has to be geared to the specific user based on his/her capabilities, experience, and the system's complexity.

▫ To ensure successful training, various aids are available: a well-documented user manual, HELP screens, and job aids that communicate vital information about the new system. They also help in reducing the user's resistance to change. Various behavioral techniques are also employed to alleviate certain behavioral problems encountered in system implementation. They include survey feedback, training sessions, and role negotiation technique.

▫ A postimplementation review makes it possible to evaluate a system against standards. This review encompasses software maintenance and enhancements. A major problem with maintenance is its labor-intensive nature and the likelihood of errors. Therefore, programming skill and training are crucial.

▫ An important factor to consider in system development is to provide a procedure for disaster recovery. This means quick recovery, no matter what the disaster is. When a disaster/recovery plan is drafted, several factors must be considered: the amount of time it takes to rebuild the facility, the availability of a backup installation and qualified staff, and the nature of the utility to be used during a disaster.

▫ To safeguard against future disaster, it is important to develop a plan that begins with a team that prepares planning tasks and drafts a disaster/recovery manual.

Key Terms

Alpha test
Audit trail
Beta test
Conversion
Disaster/recovery planning
Logic error
Quality assurance

Software maintenance
Stress test
Syntax error
System testing
Uninterruptible power supply
  system (UPS)

Review Questions

1. Why are systems tested? What does a test check for?

2. Elaborate on the makeup and importance of the test plan.

3. Distinguish between:
   a. Quality assurance and EDP audit
   b. Alpha and beta tests
   c. Maintainability and reusability
   d. Maintenance and enhancement

4. How does system testing differ from program testing? Explain.

5. In what respect is quality assurance important? Where is it initiated?

6. What features represent software quality? Which do you consider the most crucial to system security? Why?

7. Review the literature and write an essay on the role of the DP auditor in system design.

8. Contrast and compare the relationship between implementation and conversion in system development.

9. Elaborate on the major activities in conversion. Which activity is the least important? Why?

10. "A good test file should demonstrate how well it can handle basic tasks." Do you agree? Explain.

11. Suppose you were asked to develop a user training plan for training a novice user to interface with a database package on a recently installed microcomputer. What design considerations are involved in such a plan?

12. As long as the new system design meets user specifications, why should there be a fuss about resistance to change? Discuss.

13. Several behavioral techniques are appropriate for implementing system development. Explain briefly the major techniques.

14. Discuss in detail the role and implications of software maintenance in postimplementation.

15. What is disaster recovery? How does it relate to system development? Specify steps in planning for disaster recovery.

Application Problems

Arnold & Arnold, Inc. is a large multinational software development company in Reston, Virginia. Several years ago, a group of women programmers charged that the company was reluctant to promote women to the position of systems analyst. The company settled their class action suit by promising to set up several training programs that would promote female programmers for systems analyst positions. Those who had been with the firm for at least three years before the lawsuit had one year of college or more, and were senior programmers would be eligible. To make good on their promise, the firm offered a bonus of $2000 to any woman programmer who successfully completed the training.

The six-month training program included advanced college courses in systems design, software engineering, database management systems, and management theory. Most of the women soon found out that they had to work nights and weekends to catch up.

The Eastern Region division that was planning to absorb the newly trained analysts lost two bids on major government software contracts. A sudden surge of off-the-shelf software packages also severely hampered the firm's ability to expand. Consequently, management now is unsure what to do with the surplus of qualified women analysts. Of the forty-one who started the training, twenty-seven finished and were looking forward to the new assignments. They had worked very hard to earn the promotion. Most of them are in their late thirties and view the training as a big step in their career.

QUESTIONS
a. Since the training program took place before the loss of the government contracts, what can management do to solve this dilemma?
b. Do you think the bonus to go through the training was too attractive? Elaborate.
c. How do you evaluate a six-month versus a longer or a shorter training program in systems design work?

Selected References

Bronsewa, Gloria S. and Keen, Peter G. W. "Education Intervention and Implementation in MIS." *Sloan Management Review,* Summer 1983.

Cohen, Jeff M. "Disaster Recovery: Are You Really Prepared?" *Financial Computing,* September/October 1984, 15ff.

Connel, John and Brice, Linda. "Practical Quality Assurance." *Datamation,* March 1, 1985, 106–108ff.

DeSantis, Gerardine and Courtney, James F. "Toward Friendly User MIS Implementation." *Communications of the ACM,* October 1983, 732–738.

Markus, M. Lynne. "Power, Politics, and MIS Implementation" *Communications of the ACM,* June 1983, 430–444.

Parish, Girish. "Software Maintenance: Penny Wise, Program Foolish." *Computerworld,* September 23, 1985, ID/11–12ff.

Podolsky, Joseph L. "The Quest for Quality." *Datamation*, March 1, 1985, 119–120.

Seddon, John G. *Package Installation Handbook.* Englewood Cliffs, N.J.: Prentice-Hall, 1985.

Wood, Michael. "Converting Systems Requires a 'Common Ground' Approach." *Data Management*, January 1985, 16ff.

Zveqintzov, Nicholas. "Software Maintenance: Building Tomorrow on Today." *Data Management*, March 1984, 33.

PART V

MANAGERIAL CONSIDERATIONS

Managing MIS Personnel

Chapter Contents

Managing Your Boss

ONE OF THE BEST-KEPT secrets in business is how to manage up—a subject never taught in business schools. Nevertheless, the process of managing up is a fact of corporate life. Those who handle it effectively find that the road to success is smoother. Those who ignore the managing-up process find their career path filled with detours. Managing up is the process by which a person influences his or her boss. It's that simple.

The care and feeding of one's boss has long been recognized by management consultant William Oncken, Jr. as one of the keys to career growth. According to Oncken, managing up boils down to the "golden rule": The person who has the gold makes the rules. This means that your boss controls your destiny.

Consider this scenario. You decide to spend Sunday afternoon getting yourself organized. You set priorities, put things into piles and get fired up to take on the new week. You arrive at work early Monday morning raring to go. At 8:30 a.m., your boss calls to tell you that *he* had some free time on Sunday afternoon, which he used to get organized. As a result, he knows exactly what he wants you to do for the week. In fact, he has a list of activities that will keep you busy for the next month. How do you handle such a change of plans?

Oncken feels that you should quickly take your to-do list and throw it in the wastebasket. Because you know that no one in your organization was ever fired for saying, "Yes, sir" or "Yes, ma'am." Also, you have grown accustomed to a comfortable lifestyle that you would dislike giving up. Nevertheless, there is another way out of this dilemma. It involves the techniques of One Minute Management, including One Minute Goal Setting and One Minute Praising. The use of One Minute Goals can be very helpful in managing up because, with this process, both the boss and employee are involved in identifying and establishing goals. There is no manipulation. One Minute Management is not something you do *to* people; it is something you do *with* them.

Apply this process to the above scenario. If your boss presented you with a whole new list of objectives, you would refer to the goals you and your boss had set together at an earlier time. Then,

you would ask if those goals had changed. By managing up in such a way, you don't unilaterally abandon your existing projects for new responsibilities. Rather, you involve your boss in determining which duties have the greatest priority. By working this out together, you don't end up falling behind in your work and neglecting some duties in order to perform other assigned jobs. If you and your manager can work together to target priorities, you will have been effective in managing up.

The second key to managing up is knowing how and when to praise the boss. Many people don't give their boss much praise. That's unfortunate—especially if they want to effectively manage up. Usually, if a boss does something right, subordinates will say nothing: They figure that is what the boss is paid to do. If a manager makes a mistake, many people will comment on the error. Yet these same people dislike it when their manager does the same thing to them. Instead of emphasizing the positive with praising, people say nothing; then they gleefully point out mistakes.

Every time you give negative feedback, you take something away from a relationship. If you don't have much to start with in your human-relations account with that person, you are drawing on very weak resources.

Some people resist praising their boss because they believe that their praise will be thought insincere. If you remember that One Minute Praisings must be for some specific action, no one will mistake your praise for idle flattery. If you tell your boss, "Every night, I tell my wife how lucky I am to work for such a smart person," your sincerity will be in question. After a successful presentation, however, you might say to your boss, "Your report on productivity was really useful. I learned a great deal." In such a situation, your remarks will be accepted as being genuine.

One key factor in managing up is to develop a strong enough relationship with your boss so that you can engage in a dialog without seeming to be a threat to him or her. Don't forget the golden rule. Then take the time to begin managing up.

—Excerpted from Ken Blanchard, Today's Office, *September 1987, 88ff.*

AT A GLANCE

The managerial aspect of MIS focuses on the organization of the MIS department and selecting, training, motivating, and determining the career paths of information systems personnel. The information systems structure should be designed to accommodate rapidly changing directions of the 1980s and beyond.

The key components of information resources are data processing, end user computing, voice communication, and data communication. Given this environment, the MIS manager has responsibility for managing the operation of data processing and data communication activities, implementing guidelines for system applications, maintaining a talent base ready to undertake new applications, and ensuring the viability of the MIS area at all times.

The issue of centralization-decentralization of information resources continues, each alternative having advantages and drawbacks. Using system development and operations as the two major areas of the MIS department, either or both may be centralized or decentralized, depending on the organization's structure, the demand for complex applications, and the caliber of the MIS personnel.

There are several managerial and technical positions representing a functional information systems structure. Each job has unique skills and background requirements. In managing the information systems function, the MIS manager must specify the jobs and job requirements and secure qualified personnel. Staffing means selecting better, not more, people, fitting the job to the skills, developing communication skills, and making prompt selection decisions.

Selection of information systems personnel is a four-phase process: development of job descriptions and job specifications, screening of candidates, company visits and interviews, and final selection. The personnel involved in the selection process must have proper training and experience.

It is not enough to match people with jobs. Personnel must be motivated and their career paths set within the framework of the MIS division. Understanding personality types in addition to knowledge of personal skills, abilities, and vocational needs is a prerequisite of the career planning and development field.

By the end of this chapter, you should know:

1. How the MIS function is organized
2. The key occupational positions in the MIS department
3. The procedure for selecting candidates
4. How MIS personnel are motivated
5. The elements of career path planning

Introduction

Previous chapters have focused on the conceptual and practical foundations of MIS—structure, analysis, design, and implementation. This chapter addresses managerial issues related to MIS personnel. The primary interest is learning how to organize the MIS department and select, train, motivate, and determine the career paths of information systems personnel.

The term *management* refers to the planning, organizing, leading, motivating, and maintaining of work personnel. The management of information systems personnel lean heavily on the foundations of management. In this chapter, we discuss issues related to organizing the MIS department, how MIS jobs are filled, and the basics of career planning. With today's organization having to adapt to rapidly changing technology, the selection and management of MIS personnel are clearly important.

The Scope of MIS Management

Today's MIS goes well beyond the traditional mainframe and "bread and butter" applications. In large organizations, MIS plays a key role in managing data processing, data communication, and a variety of applications accessed by users when needed. The 1980s represent a trend toward managing integrated technologies. As shown in Figure 18.1, the scope of MIS management includes the following activities:

1. *Data processing.* In the broader scope of information systems management, data processing encompasses basic applications such as payroll along with managing the corporate database and preparing reports.

2. *Data communication.* This activity has been traditionally the responsibility of the data processing area. It also incorporates local area networks (LANs) and voice communication.

3. *End user computing.* Integration of word processing and spreadsheets with data processing via LANs provides a useful service to the end user.

The Role of the MIS Manager

This enlarged scope of activities has elevated the MIS manager from a departmental to an executive (VP) level, reporting to a senior vice president or a chief executive officer. The major tasks the MIS manager performs are:

1. Managing the operation of data processing and data communication projects.

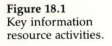

Figure 18.1
Key information
resource activities.

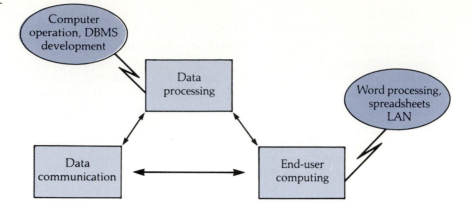

2. Developing and implementing guidelines for system applications and databases for the whole organization.
3. Coordinating and planning the use of information systems in the organization.
4. Maintaining a pool of skilled staff ready to undertake new applications or upgrade existing ones.
5. Acquiring and installing new technologies in line with the needs of the users.

The Organizing Function

As an organization grows in size and complexity, it is often necessary for the MIS department to adapt to the changing needs of its users and organize its personnel accordingly. In organizing the MIS function, there are several guidelines to consider:

1. The MIS function must be based on predefined *objectives* that set the performance level of the information system.

2. The MIS function should be organized with achievable outcomes and quality performance. This requires planning information resources and assigning personnel where they are most needed.

3. The design of the MIS activities requires sensitivity to the **span of control**, or the number of employees reporting to a supervisor. In organization design, the higher the level of the manager in the organization, the fewer the number of employees reporting to him or her and the greater the level of responsibility. For example, a programming supervisor has more employees reporting to him or her than the vice president of the MIS division. The authority relationship must be formalized so that control can be defined and the overall commitments of the MIS area to the organization can be clearly met.

4. The overall organization of the MIS area must allow for "give and take" in dealing with the external environment. There are actually two environmental layers. The immediate external environment is essentially the MIS-user interface and the external environment links the MIS division to the professional community and others outside the organization. The emphasis is on stability of operation and promoting viable interface on a regular basis.

A great deal is involved in managing the information resource function in an organization. There are issues of centralization versus decentralization, personnel management, planning and control issues, etc. In this chapter, we shall focus on the first two issues—whether to centralize or decentralize MIS operations and, consequently, how MIS personnel should be managed.

Centralization Versus Decentralization

An important question facing MIS managers is: "Should the MIS function be centralized or decentralized?" Why? Users in general have often vied for direct control over the database and their own information. The information center concept and the wide use of microcomputers to relieve backed-up user demands have created pressures favoring decentralization of information resources. There are other pressures, however, favoring centralization. The centralization/decentralization issue, then, is worth discussing.

Centralization is designed to serve the informational needs of the organization from a central location. **Decentralization** creates a functional information systems department within each operating unit in the organization. The MIS manager reports directly to the head of the operating unit. The main difference between centralization and decentralization is a decision on how authority, responsibility, and information resources must be allocated throughout the organization.

Reasons For and Against Centralization   The reasons favoring centralization are generally based on *efficiency* of operation and control, while those favoring decentralization are based on *effectiveness*. The pros and cons of each alternative are summarized in Table 18.1. The benefits of centralized control are:

1. *Better control of operations, databases, and procedures.* Centralization makes it possible to develop corporate databases and control data accessibility, integrity, and security at all times.
2. *More efficient approach to system development and programming.* A centralized facility can develop expertise, and provide challenging work and a pool of shared talent. This has implications for promoting career paths for MIS personnel.

Table 18.1   Centralized and Decentralized Control: Pros and Cons

	Centralized Control	**Decentralized Control**
Reasons For	· Better control of operations, databases, and procedures · More efficient approach to system development and programming · Reduction in duplication of resources and expertise · Capacity to handle large, complex applications	· Direct control of end user over operations · Data capture and error correction at the source · Lower total data communication costs · Lower overall costs, faster access to files, and more effective backup facility
Reasons Against	· Fewer accommodations for tailoring programs to user's needs · High backup costs · Slower access to files in a multiuser environment · End user has little control over chargebacks · High cost of data communication with the host computer	· High organizational costs due to duplication of efforts and equipment · Incompatibility between equipment and software · Restricted sophistication of applications due to restricted expertise · Limited career paths of MIS personnel, causing turnover · Duplication of operating procedures means inefficient operations

3. *Reduced duplication of resources and expertise.* This means a cost advantage to the organization.
4. *Capacity to handle large, complex applications.* Having a pool of shared talent makes it possible to develop large projects effectively.

In contrast to the benefits, centralized control has drawbacks:

1. There are limited accommodations for giving every user individualized attention.
2. High backup costs.

3. Slower access to centralized files in a multiuser environment, especially during peak hours.
4. End users are charged a portion of the total cost, but have little say about operating costs or control over information quality.
5. Data transmission costs between the user's workstation and the host computer tend to be excessive.

Reasons For and Against Decentralization   There are several reasons favoring decentralized control:

1. *The end user may have control over operations.* End users have been known to accept increased costs for direct control over computer operations. Direct control also means more frequent use of the computer and better support of new applications.
2. *Data input is captured at the user's level* and errors are corrected as soon as they are detected. This means the user is assured of file accuracy and reliability.
3. *Lower data communication costs.* Since the user files and programs reside in the decentralized information system, there are lower data communication costs between the user and the host computer.
4. *Faster access to local files and more effective backup facility.* The user also has a greater measure of control over total costs.

   The primary reasons against decentralization are:

1. Higher costs for the organization because of duplication of talent, files, hardware, and software.
2. Possible hardware/software incompatibility between the host computer and the user's information system.
3. Level of sophistication and complexity of applications are restricted due to limited expertise.
4. Career paths of MIS personnel are limited—therefore, tenure may be a problem.
5. Duplication of operating procedures that implies inefficient operation.

The Organizational Structure

The structure of a centralized MIS facility varies with the size of the organization and level of centralization. For the small firm, a typical centralized facility has analysts, programmers, data entry clerks, and one or more computer operators. The entire MIS function is the responsibility of a manager in charge of all personnel. The staff is usually less than ten employees (see Figure 18.2).

In a medium-sized organization, the jobs become more specialized, which tends to organize the MIS area by functional tasks. Figure 18.3 is a typical centralized MIS department for a medium-sized organization.

Figure 18.2
A typical centralized
MIS department for
a small firm.

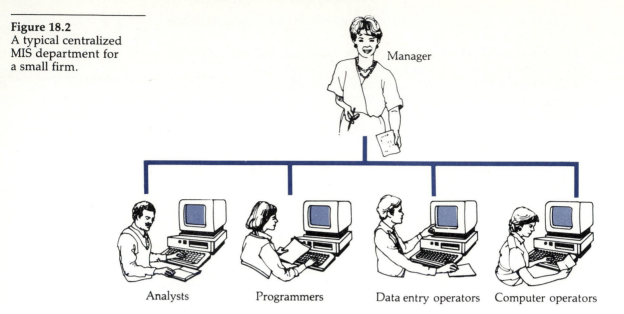

Manager

Analysts   Programmers   Data entry operators   Computer operators

Unlike the structure shown in Figure 18.2, the major areas of system development, programming, and operations are headed by supervisors reporting directly to the MIS manager. Management levels, though, are kept at a minimum.

A large organization requires greater sophistication in system development and work on long-term projects. This means hundreds of MIS personnel organized under two functional areas: system development and operations. The operations area is responsible for data entry and computer operations (see Figure 18.4).

The centralized structures in Figure 18.4 are based on functional areas. Personnel are grouped by functions such as system development, programming, and operations. The primary advantage of the functional approach is specialization of personnel.

An alternative structure is to organize by product. For example, a firm that has a chemical division, a food services division, and a film processing division would have an information systems department and support staff in each division. It is a form of decentralization that tends to be more responsive to the user's needs.

The issue of centralization-decentralization is not whether one design is better than the other. In some structures, it can be a combination of both. Using system development and operations as the two major areas of the MIS department, either or both may be centralized or decentralized, depending on the organization's structure, the nature of and demands for complex applications, and the caliber of the specialized personnel to make things happen in the MIS department.

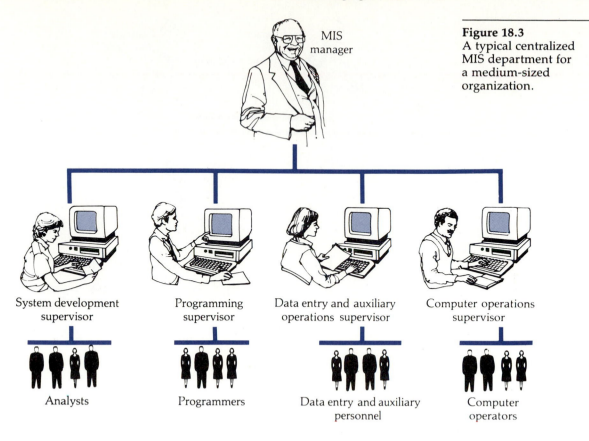

Figure 18.3
A typical centralized
MIS department for
a medium-sized
organization.

MIS
manager

System development
supervisor

Programming
supervisor

Data entry and auxiliary
operations supervisor

Computer operations
supervisor

Analysts

Programmers

Data entry and auxiliary
personnel

Computer
operators

Managing Information Systems Personnel

No matter what size the organization, MIS managers perform the functions of planning, organizing, directing, and controlling information systems activities and support personnel. One of the most critical responsibilities of MIS managers consists of attracting, motivating, and retaining
qualified personnel. Although more and more computing is assumed by
the end user, recruiting and retaining specialized staff continue to be
managerial roles for a centralized facility. In this section, we will review
key MIS positions, techniques for selecting and motivating systems personnel, and career path planning.

Occupational Positions

There are several managerial and technical positions in the MIS division.
At the supervisory level, the key positions are:

1. *Computer operations supervisor:* Responsible for maintaining the data

Figure 18.4
A large centralized MIS facility.

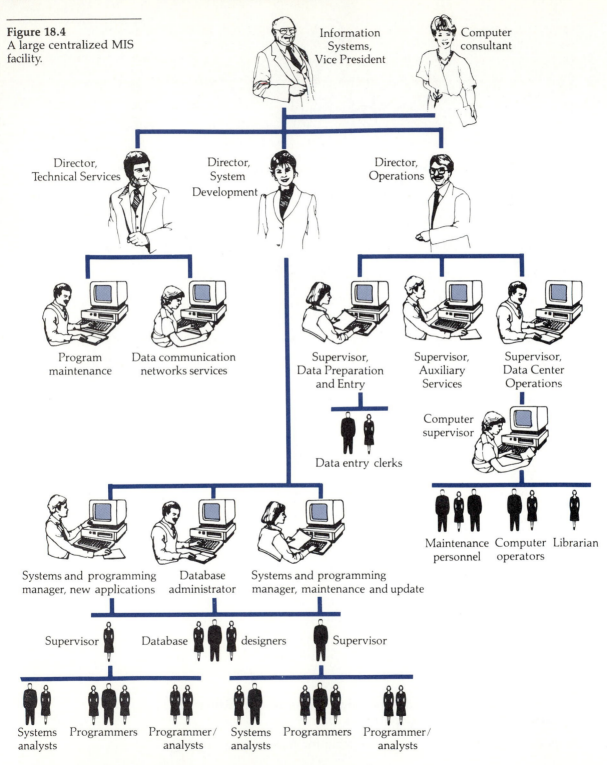

center's hardware, peripherals, and software. Knowledge of hardware/software is helpful. Ability to deal with people is required.

2. *Database administrator:* Manages, coordinates, and controls the corporate database. Sets standards for database security access and update. Technical skills in database structure and design are helpful.

3. *Data communications supervisor:* Works with systems analysts and the computer operations manager to evaluate, install, and operate communications systems or networks. Technical skills and knowledge of data communication hardware/software are required.

4. *Data entry manager:* Supervises data entry hardware and ensures adequate data entry staff at all times. Knowledge of data entry equipment and basic managerial skills is required.

5. *Operations director:* Responsible for computer operations, scheduling, peripheral devices, and quality control.

6. *Programming manager:* Directs and coordinates new applications and maintenance of existing programs. Technical and hiring skills are important.

7. *Project manager:* Administers systems analysts and programmers in new applications and maintenance of existing programs. Technical skills are required. Communication skills and knowledge of user's business are important.

8. *System development director:* Directs and coordinates the system development function, prioritizes projects, maintains adequate staffing and ensures that the organization's technical and computer-based needs are met at all times.

The technical positions include the following:

1. *Applications programmer:* Codes, debugs, tests, and documents programs based on system specifications. Technical programming skills and at least one high-level programming language are required.

2. *Database designer:* Designs database for mainframes and smaller computers. Requires working knowledge in DBMS and computer hardware. Communication skills are helpful.

3. *Data communication specialist:* Designs data communication networks for distributed systems. Has working knowledge of LAN. Background in data communication, hardware/software, and distributed data processing are required.

4. *Information analyst:* Works with end-user to define system requirements. Ability to deal with people, communication skills, understanding the user's business, and basic knowledge of information systems are important.

5. *Maintenance programmer:* Patching or enhancing application programs. Working skills in the programming language in use are required.

6. *Systems analyst/designer:* Evaluates existing systems, defines problem areas, and designs alternative systems to meet user requirements.

Technical knowledge is required. Knowledge of the organization and user environment are desirable.

7. *Systems programmer:* Programs and maintains computer-based or database software. Requires knowledge of hardware and programming skills.

8. *Quality assurance specialist:* Defines objectives of the project and ensures that the development process is free of errors, leading to a quality system. Communications skills and background in documentation, scheduling, and project procedures are required.

From these positions, we can see that each job requires certain skills and abilities. Systems analysts have different skill requirements than programmers. They deal more regularly with people than programs. Programmers work with programming languages and procedures and are more internally interfaced with the staff of the computer center than are the analysts.

It is important to remember that not all positions are available in every installation. Certain jobs (e.g., analysis and programming) are combined in a smaller MIS department, whereas they are full-time positions in other sites. Also, jobs such as database administrator and quality assurance specialist are unique to large corporate database installations, where such high-priced positions can be justified.

Selection Guidelines and Procedures

There is more to developing an MIS environment than making decisions on hardware and software. Selecting MIS personnel is the starting point in MIS services. To manage this vital function, each job must be properly defined and assigned to a qualified person. This is a personnel function that is often carried out by the MIS manager.

A crucial point in personnel selection is ensuring proper fit between what the candidate can do and the requirements of the position. Questions that haunt most personnel managers and job interviewers are: Does this candidate fit into the department? How do we know he/she will do an adequate job? If hired, how long would he/she stay? Likewise, a candidate might be wondering whether this job would be a satisfying job and whether it is a step in the right direction. It all comes down to a *job-person matching* that requires care, foresight, and adopting a procedure for effective selection.

Staffing Guidelines

There are five guidelines used in staffing MIS personnel. These can be useful both to the hiring organization as well as the applicants:

1. Use better, not more, people
2. Fit the job to the candidate's skills and motivation
3. Sharpen your interviewing skills
4. Develop communication skills
5. Make prompt selection decisions

Use better, not more, people. The wide productivity range among MIS personnel boils down to a small number of people producing most of the work. One study supports a similar concentration of productivity among authors, inventors, and other professionals. The top 20 percent of the people produce approximately 50 percent of the output, whereas the bottom 50 percent produce about 20 percent (see Figure 18.5). This emphasizes the importance of successful staffing and the need for a selection procedure that screens for the top talent.

Poor staffing assignments can increase project costs and turnover at all levels. Mismanagement is assigning the wrong people to jobs, providing poor working conditions, failing to reward performance, and using

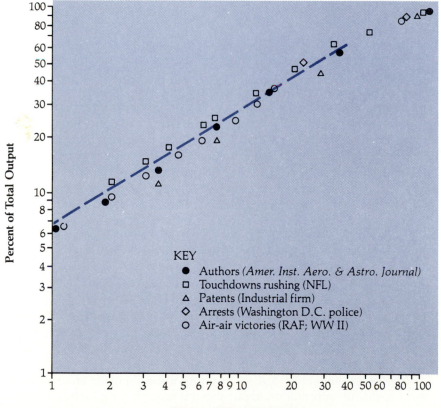

Figure 18.5
Concentration of productivity.

KEY
● Authors *(Amer. Inst. Aero. & Astro. Journal)*
□ Touchdowns rushing (NFL)
△ Patents (Industrial firm)
◇ Arrests (Washington D.C. police)
○ Air-air victories (RAF; WW II)

Percent of Total Output

Percent of Total Contribution

Figure 18.6
Comparative growth
needs and social needs.
(Cougar, Zawagki, 1978,
116–123.)

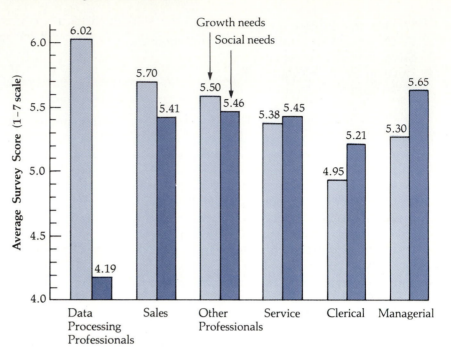

needed resources ineffectively. Conversely, effective management is promoting teamwork and coordinating projects at all levels of the information resources environment.

Fit the job to the skills and motivation of the candidate. A common violation of this guideline is the Peter principle: Employees tend to rise to their level of incompetence. For example, promoting skilled programmers to managerial positions has worked well in some organizations and was a disaster in others. One reason is illustrated by Couger and Zawacki's (1978) study that compared the relative growth need categories of various organizations. The data processing professional's social need is extremely low compared to his/her growth need. Those needs rank the opposite for managers. Therefore, rewarding good performance through promotion to managerial positions cannot be supported by making across-the-board decisions (see Figure 18.6).

Sharpen your interviewing skills. It has been known for some time that preliminary decisions on a candidate are made during the first 5 minutes of the interview. The reliability of the decision can be improved by asking the right question in the right sequence within the timeframe. The manager must prepare for the interview and decide on the structure and questions that best suit the person being interviewed. Interviewing and question construction have been covered in Chapter 14.

Develop communication skills. Obtaining information from a candidate and providing information about the job require an effective two-way exchange. One aspect of communication is the ability to listen and decide what information to offer, how much to offer, and what feedback to expect in return.

Make prompt selection decisions. Personnel directors know too well the cost of not making timely selection decisions. How long it should take between the interview and the job offer (or reject) depends on what information is available, the level of the position, the type of candidate, etc. Once all the necessary information becomes available, prompt decisions must be made.

Sources of Information Systems Personnel

Many of the selection decisions depend on where to look for applicants. Sources of personnel are sought either within or outside the hiring organization. Selecting company employees ranges from singling the person out to posting the position for all to apply, and there are many variations in between.

Applicants from outside the firm are recruited through universities, selective advertising, or employment agencies. In all options, state and federal employment guidelines must be observed, especially the **Equal Employment Opportunity Act (EEO)**, which prohibits discrimination against individuals because of their color, sex, age, or national origin.

There are three elements (the 3 Es) to be evaluated in selection: experience, education, and extracurricular activities. Ready-to-apply experience is a prime requirement if the company does not have a training program. The drawback is that sometimes applicants have had experience on the wrong system or come with experience in scientific rather than business computing. For entry-level jobs, an organization may prefer to hire applicants with hardly any experience to undergo special intensive training. In such an arrangement, experience may not be an attractive attribute.

College education is becoming an important prerequisite for most MIS jobs. A college degree in MIS or in a related field makes it easier to train the new employees. A college degree per se is not the goal. It is the maturation that coursework, group work, class presentations, and the like represent that recruiters look for in graduates. Personality, maturity, and aptitude are additional considerations for most jobs.

In addition to experience and education, an applicant's extracurricular activities are attractive for jobs in systems analysis, user liaison, and positions that require communication skills, selling change, and leadership. For systems development work, more and more organizations are attracted to well-rounded individuals rather than the automaton who can merely crank answers through the computer.

Procedure for Selection

Selection of MIS personnel is primarily a four-phase process:

1. Preparation of job descriptions and job specifications
2. Initial screening of candidates
3. Company visits and interviews
4. Final selection

Job Description and Specifications   A **job description** document defines the duties and responsibilities of the job, the reporting relationship, the work environment, and other job-related activities (see Figure 18.7). In contrast, a **job specification** document identifies the personal characteristics required to do the job. This includes the skills and abilities required, educational requirements (if any), years of experience, and the like.

Both documents must be available before initiating the job search. The manager must know in advance what the job offers and the type of person that best matches the job.

Initial Screening of Candidates   The purpose of initial screening is to weed out unsuitable candidates. This is done by reviewing the candidate's resume or application form. The interview is used to verify information about the candidate's abilities and skills. It is a "size-up" meeting that works both ways. The outcome is to reach a decision on whether to continue further with the selection process.

Company Visits and Interviews   If the candidate passes the initial screening test, he/she is invited to visit the firm for final interviews. During this time, the candidate is examined for the following character traits:

1. *Flexibility:* willingness to adapt to schedules and respond to emergencies.
2. *Initiative:* ability to suggest or attempt new approaches.
3. *Interpersonal skills:* ability to get along and work with peers, groups, and supervisors.
4. *Oral communication:* ability to express ideas and information clearly.
5. *Problem solving:* ability to work through and implement solutions.
6. *Coping with stress:* working satisfactorily under pressure and meeting deadlines under austere conditions.
7. *Work habits:* working out problems on one's own, but within company guidelines.

During the interview, several job-related questions may be asked regarding career, motivation, and experience. Sample interview questions are listed in Figure 18.8.

Figure 18.7
Sample job description.

JOB DESCRIPTION

Position title: Manager, systems analysis and design

Salary range: $28,000–34,000, depending on experience

Duties and responsibilities
1. Provide leadership and direction to three project leaders and two senior information analysts.
2. Plan system development work in consultation with the MIS vice president. This involves working closely with managers of departments requesting information systems services.
3. Recruit and maintain full-time analysts, designers, and support staff with proper training and experience. This involves working with the personnel department to develop a viable selection process and with its training center to secure a high-quality training program.
4. Chair an ad hoc committee to discuss the latest tools and techniques in system development and ways in which the systems staff can be successfully maintained.

Work Environment
The individual's office will be at the corporate headquarters in Charlottesville, Virginia. The systems analysis and design department is a part of the MIS division (23 analysts, 74 programmers, and 161 support staff), equipped with four IBM 3082s, extensive database management systems, and manages 174 IBM PCs distributed throughout the organization. The position of manager of systems analysis and design is a key position in the MIS division.

Job Relationships to MIS Division
Two other managers of programming and operations report to the MIS Vice President. These individuals work closely through weekly meetings to coordinate the work of the MIS division. The manager of systems analysis and design is expected to work closely with subordinates and maintain a work environment conducive to high performance at all times.

A company visit and the initial interviews help the organization make up its mind about the candidate. Unlike the first interview, the visit is a more intensive screening process that makes it possible for a number of managers to talk to the candidate before making a final decision.

Some organizations use tests in addition to interviews before making a final decision. The problem with most tests is their validity and reliability. Under equal opportunity employment legislation, a test should not be administered unless it measures something relevant to the job.

Figure 18.8
Sample interview
questions.

Career
1. Why are you applying for this position?
2. Why do you want to leave your present job?
3. What are your career goals? How will this job help you reach these goals?
4. What kind of a job or position do you see yourself holding five years from now?

Motivation
1. What do you enjoy most about being an analyst?
2. What would you like to accomplish if you got the job?
3. Most people have strong and weak points. Tell us about your strongest point. What area needs most improvement?
4. When you have been told about a problem in your area, what have you done? Give us an example.

Experience
1. Tell us a little about your duties and responsibilities on your last job.
2. Can you describe for us one or two of the most successful achievements in your career?
3. Tell us about something new or unique that you have done on your present job, like a program or a procedure you are really proud of.
4. What are some of the things you find frustrating in your present job?

Among the popular tests administered to programmers, for example, are:

1. *Berger Aptitude for Programming Test* (BAPT), distributed by Psychometrics, Inc. Santa Monica, Calif.
2. *Computer Programmer Aptitude Battery,* distributed by IBM's Subsidiary Science Research Associates, Inc., Chicago, Ill.
3. *Wolfe-Spence Programming Aptitude Test,* by Wolfe Computer Aptitude Testing, Ltd., Oradell, N.J.

Final Selection   This phase determines whether a job offer will be made to the candidate and what the terms of the offer will be. This is the culmination of interviews, reference check, tests (if any), and comparing one candidate against all others. In making a decision, there should be a first choice and a backup candidate. Should the first choice turn down the job, the backup would be the next person to contact. The terms of the offer should include a job description, starting salary, starting date, location of employment, relocation expenses (if any), conditions for employment (e.g., physical exams), and a deadline by which a candidate must respond.

The personnel department is expected to be familiar with state and federal employment regulations governing recruitment. All aspects of selection must also be monitored to ensure that they conform to the organization's policies and regulations.

Motivation of Information Systems Personnel

Research studies in MIS personnel have shown significant problems in **motivating** MIS personnel. For example, Baroudi's (1984) research concluded that turnover among information systems personnel is excessively high. Earlier studies have supported this finding. Systems analysts and other MIS personnel perceive themselves as professionals. They tend to identify with outside reference groups (e.g., professional associations) rather than the employing organization. This means commitment to the profession—more so than to the organization. The research by Couger and Zawacki (1980) also concluded that system personnel are committed to the computer area and expect challenging assignments in system development.

Another motivation problem is the variation between system design and system maintenance. To most analysts, there is a stigma attached to maintenance. It is perceived as mundane—lacking in creativity, ability utilization, and achievement. MIS personnel in general prefer to develop rather than maintain applications. Since over 70 percent of the work in MIS is maintenance, it is easy to anticipate motivation problems that need attention.

Another study (Couger, 1985) concludes that maintenance work has only one-half to two-thirds the motivating potential of the programming or analysis work. As shown in Figure 18.9, the job's motivating potential falls as the amount of maintenance increases and "fix-it" activities are especially demotivating.

With the high growth needs of MIS personnel and the low perceived status of maintenance, motivating MIS personnel is a challenge. Turnover can be reduced by evaluating employee vocational needs and what each job offers to satisfy those needs. Models have been developed to address the turnover issue. Although none has been successful at solving turnover, each model points out the need for employee satisfaction.

Career Path Planning

It is not enough to match people and jobs. People have to be motivated so that they can find meaning in their jobs. They expect to move upward

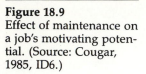

Figure 18.9
Effect of maintenance on a job's motivating potential. (Source: Cougar, 1985, ID6.)

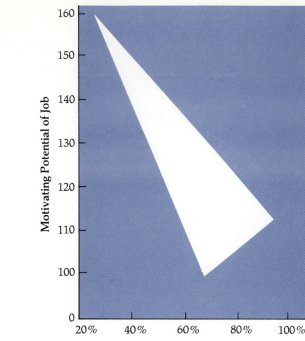

Percent of Maintenance

through promotions and advancements based on professional growth and performance. Therefore, planning a career path for employees serves to promote stability and commitment at work.

The Concept of "Career" and Career Planning

The term **career** implies an occupation that provides a clear pattern of systematic advancement—a career ladder or a path. In the traditional information systems department, the career path begins with programming and progresses to systems analysis and first-line management. On each rung of the ladder, it is necessary to develop the person's abilities and prepare him/her for the next higher position in the career plan.

In discussing careers, we should note that career per se does not imply success or failure. It describes a person's entire vocational life in a work environment. Career can satisfy a whole range of needs (social, physiological, ego, altruism, etc.). For this reason, learning about careers is important in motivating MIS personnel.

Career planning is basically an evaluation of the interaction between the individual and the employing organization over time. Figure 18.10 illustrates the major components in analyzing individual-organizational interaction. Careers are influenced by factors such as cultural values and

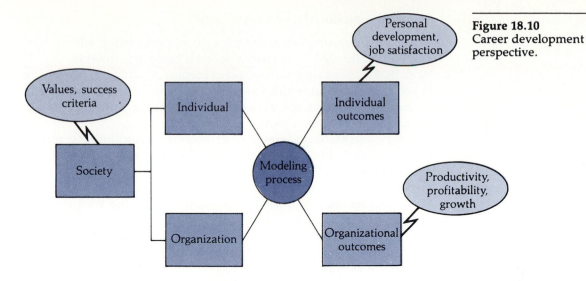

Figure 18.10
Career development
perspective.

success criteria that determine a path for a career. Society is governed
by laws governing individuals and organizations. For the *individual*, it
means balancing career plans with those for self-development. For the
organization, it means complying with equal employment opportunities
laws, the concepts of fairness, and health and safety.

The *matching* process is what brings the individual and the organization into a potentially rewarding relationship. This is accomplished
through selection, training, promotion, and the like. The matching process
is a success when both the individual and the organization benefit. Those
outcomes are manifest in organizational growth, personal development,
and job satisfaction.

From the career development view, it is important to recognize that
each person has a set of attitudes, skills, and personality characteristics
that reflect his/her job preferences. Related to the personality factor, Lyons
(1985) conducted a survey of the personalities and work preferences of
computer professionals in 100 organizations. The *Myers-Briggs Type Indicator* (MBTI) was used to assess the psychological types of MIS individuals. The resulting data revealed four personality preferences that determine one's psychological type:

Psychological type	*Meaning*
Extraversion (E)—Introversion (I)	Outward versus inward
Sensing (S)—Intuitive (N)	Practical, realistic versus creative
Thinking (T)—Feeling (F)	Impersonal analysis versus subjective analysis
Judging (J)—Perceiving (P)	Planned, orderly versus flexible, adaptive

The survey produced a number of results:

1. Not many extraverts relish the thought of performing solitary programming activities. This activity appeals more to introverts.
2. Work that involves maintaining and enhancing programs appeals more to sensing than intuitive MIS personnel. The analyst or designer with a strong intuitive preference may also have difficulty ending the design process and moving on to implementation.
3. The very successful programmer or analyst with a thinking preference (and probably also an introvert) has difficulty adjusting to a management position.
4. Persons with a strong perceiving preference are not good organizers. They tend to take deadlines less seriously than those with a strong judging preference.
5. An NF (intuitive, feeling) individual tends to be much happier as a systems analyst with direct user contact than developing program codes for a new application.
6. The ISTJs (intuitive, sensing, thinking, judging) are attracted to secure positions with well-defined procedures. They try to avoid areas like user liaison and training.

In summary, understanding personality types in addition to knowing the skills, abilities, and needs of personnel provides a basis for planning and developing their careers. The MIS manager who plans on integrating these specialized resources must understand that people differ in their career goals and must learn to use these differences to advantage.

Career Choice and Work Adjustment

Career choice takes place when the individual accepts a job. **Work adjustment** occurs after the individual becomes a member of the organization. Recognizing that a number of factors affect choice, various theories of career choice have been proposed in recent years. The one that has had much support is Holland's (1973) theory which is based on the old notion that "birds of a feather flock together." Individuals search for the organization that will allow them to exercise their abilities and assume an acceptable role. The outcome is that people who have similar personality patterns congregate and work in an environment that reflects the types they are. This forms the basis for person-job matching, training, career path development, and maintaining a stable work force.

The Career Planning Cycle

Career choice and work adjustment are followed by a career plan that specifies career goals, develops a strategy to meet the goals, evaluates

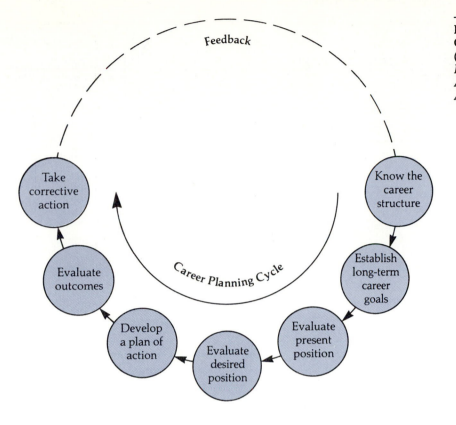

Figure 18.11
Career planning cycle.
(Cascio/Awad, *Human
Resources Management:
An Information Systems
Approach.* © 1981, p. 287.

actual progress, and makes adjustments accordingly. The career plan or cycle is illustrated in Figure 18.11. It represents several steps:

1. Understand the training and experience required for each position and the alternative paths available.
2. Establish realistic career goals.
3. Evaluate the person's present level of responsibility, experience, and skills in relation to his/her long-term goal(s).
4. Define the type of training and ability requirements to reach the desired career or job.
5. Develop an action plan to attain the new job.
6. Evaluate the results to take corrective action and keep the plan on target.

To illustrate, let us look at a single career path leading to the director of MIS. The positions representing a typical succession ladder are shown in Figure 18.12. At levels 1 and 2, career succession depends on the individual's level of technical knowledge. Level 3 is perceived to be the beginning of a systems analyst or a project leader having technical and managerial abilities. Here we see a shift in career emphasis from technical

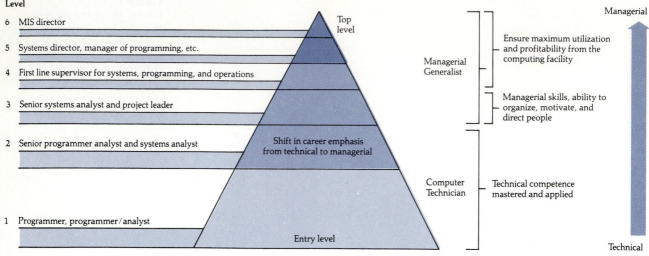

Figure 18.12
Succession ladder in MIS facility from entry level programming to MIS director. (Cascio/Awad, *Human Resources Management: An Information Systems Approach*, © 1981, p. 190. Adapted by permission of Prentice-Hall, Inc., Englewood Cliffs, N.J.)

to managerial. As the career develops further from levels 3 to 6, the managerial factor takes on increasing importance.

There are successive "windows" through which an individual must pass to reach higher levels. Not every one is expected to reach the top. Figure 18.13 illustrates the relationship between compensation and years of experience at each successive step. The key to vertical progression is to sense when it is time to go through the next "window." The shaded area represents the ideal pattern of career mobility in an MIS facility. Deviation from it means difficulty achieving career success.

To illustrate, individual A moved right along as planned. In contrast, individuals B, C, D, and E made errors. Individuals B and C had salaries higher than their marketable levels. Individual B switched early in his/her career, leading to a dead-end job, even though the salary continued to increase. He/she is presumed to be worth more to the present employer than to other organizations. This is often the case with overspecialization. Individuals D and E allowed themselves to simply stagnate, doing the same job. Individual E never made it to the first window.

Implications for MIS

Given the views on person-job matching, selection, the importance of motivation, and career path planning, we can draw several implications for MIS:

1. Each MIS area must have a set of job descriptions and job specifications before selection gets underway.

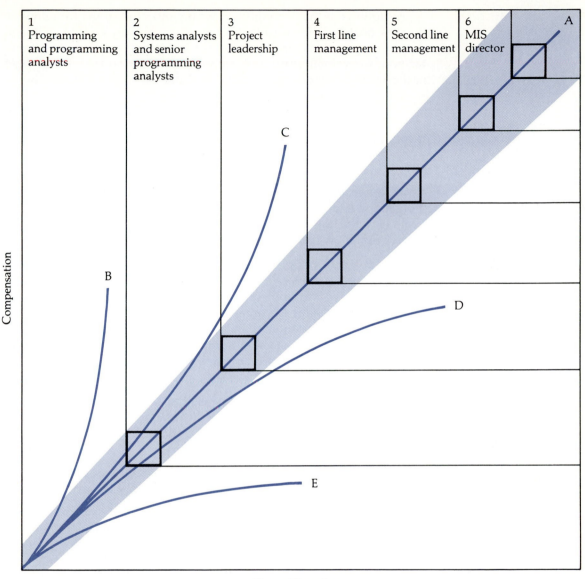

Figure 18.13
Career path chart for EDP personnel. (Source: EDP, Inc., n.d., 15.)

2. For MIS to secure a stable work environment, MIS managers must understand what kind of personality types match a given job and how one determines personality types.
3. Motivation of MIS personnel should be a continuing practice, not simply a reaction to turnover.
4. Developing a work environment that provides job reinforcers congruent with employees' vocational needs is an important consideration in securing competent staff.

Regardless of the procedure or the organization of the MIS division, it takes qualified, forward-looking management to foresee problems, develop a plan of attack, and succeed in finding solutions in a timely fashion. Coordination of the corporate MIS function can also be made easier through cooperation of MIS personnel at various levels. There is no alternative to effective performance.

Summary

□ Today's MIS area goes beyond the traditional mainframe and payroll-type applications. It now includes activities such as data communications and end user computing via LANs and networking. This trend has elevated the importance of MIS management and the role MIS plays in the organization's ability to make effective decisions.

□ The MIS executive performs several key functions:
  1. Managing the operation of the MIS center
  2. Developing and implementing guidelines for system applications and databases for the organization
  3. Coordinating, planning, and using information systems
  4. Maintaining qualified staff to undertake new applications
  5. Acquiring and disseminating new technologies that ensure the viability of the MIS area

□ Various pressures exist that favor centralization in some firms while favoring decentralization in others. The main difference is in determining how authority, responsibility, and information resources must be allocated throughout the organization.

□ The reasons favoring centralization are generally based on efficiency of operation, whereas those favoring decentralization are based on effectiveness.

□ The organization of a centralized structure varies with size and level of centralization. Personnel are organized according to the functional areas of information systems. An alternative structure is organizing by product, which tends to be more responsive to the user's needs.

□ There are several managerial and technical positions representing a functional information systems structure. The managerial positions range from computer operations supervisor to system development director. The technical positions include applications programmers, database designers, systems analysts, and quality assurance specialists.

□ There are five guidelines in staffing MIS personnel:
  1. Use better, not more, people
  2. Fit the job to the skills and motivation of the candidate
  3. Sharpen your interviewing skills

4. Develop communication skills
5. Make prompt selection decisions

□ The procedure for selection of information systems personnel involves a four-phase process:
1. Development of job descriptions and job specifications
2. Initial screening of candidates
3. Company visits and interviews
4. Final selection

During the interview, several questions may be asked regarding career, motivation, and experience. The questions must be job related. The final selection phase determines whether to offer the candidate the job and what the terms of the offer will be.

□ The high growth needs of MIS personnel and low perceived status of maintenance bring up the problem of motivation. Turnover may be reduced by providing means of satisfying vocational needs and job reinforcers.

□ The essence of career path planning is an evaluation of the interaction between the individual and the organization over time. A match between the employee and the job means a rewarding outcome for both and tenure on the job.

□ Understanding personality types in addition to knowledge of personnel's skills and vocational needs provides the basis for career planning and development. The result of this orientation is that people who have similar personality patterns congregate and work in an environment that reflects the types they are. This forms the basis for person-job matching, training, career path development, and stabilizing the work environment.

Key Terms

Career	Job description
Career choice	Job specification
Career planning	Motivation
Centralization	Span of control
Decentralization	Work adjustment
Equal Employment Opportunity Act (EEO)	

Review Questions

1. In what way(s) does today's MIS go beyond the traditional mainframe and "bread-and-butter" applications? Explain.

2. Explain in your own words the major tasks performed by the MIS manager.

3. What guidelines should be considered in organizing the MIS function? Would these guidelines differ with the size of the firm or the scope of MIS activities?

4. Discuss the pros and cons of centralization versus decentralization of the MIS function.

5. Distinguish between:
   a. Efficiency and effectiveness
   b. Centralization and decentralization
   c. Job description and job specification
   d. Programming manager and project manager

6. What issues are involved in organizing MIS personnel by product rather than by functional area?

7. "A crucial point in personnel selection is ensuring a proper fit between what the candidate can do and the requirements of the position." Do you agree? Elaborate.

8. What guidelines are useful in staffing MIS personnel? Explain.

9. How important is it for an MIS director to have strong interviewing skills? Be specific.

10. Discuss carefully the process for selecting MIS personnel. What phase in the selection process do you consider the most critical? Why?

11. When a candidate is invited to the firm for final interviews, what do interviewers look for? Elaborate.

12. What are some of the basic problems in motivating MIS personnel? How can these problems be handled?

13. Discuss the concept of "career" and career planning as it relates to MIS personnel. From what you know, how easy is it to plan a career in this area? Why?

14. Several steps make up the career planning cycle. Identify them.

15. What implications does career planning have for planning the activities of an MIS department? Elaborate.

Application Problems

1. The Andy Thompson Corporation (ATCO) is a large furniture manufacturer in North Carolina. In January 1987, the board of directors

authorized the company to adopt a distributed computing plan. This meant that each user division would be allowed to acquire its own computer hardware and software on condition that it justify investment through measurable improvements in the user division.

The MIS division was up in arms over the decision. Jack Holt, the MIS vice president, argued that managers and department heads do not have the experience necessary to make computer decisions, let alone proceed in applications programming. Within a four-month period, production, sales, marketing, and accounting divisions began to install personal computers using off-the-shelf spreadsheets, word processing, database, and special purpose packages. Each user division paid for the equipment out of its own budget, which had recently been adjusted to handle the acquisition.

A recent survey of the personal computer installation at ATCO revealed the following:

a. Installed hardware included twenty-seven Macintosh, forty-four IBM ATs, nineteen IBM PCs, four AT&T 6300s, two Wang PCs, and two COMPAQs.
b. Overall utilization of the PCs was under 19 percent.
c. Less than 40 percent of the software is installed and four out of ten users had only superficial understanding of the capabilities of the software. The remaining users had yet to learn the basics.

When several user departments approached MIS personnel for help, the staff was reluctant to participate, since it was bogged down with mainframe programming and maintaining over twenty major applications on a regular basis. Furthermore, since the MIS department had no control over purchases, they felt no obligation to bail out the end users.

The situation had come to a head. Sensing the severity of the situation, the board appointed a subcommittee to look into the matter.

QUESTIONS

a. What was wrong (if anything) with the initial decision to authorize the installation?
b. Do you think the MIS staff had an obligation to offer to help? Why?
c. If you were the chairperson of the subcommittee, how would you approach this problem? Be specific.
d. What solutions would you offer in this case? Elaborate and justify your answer.

2. You are a project manager in a large MIS division of a multinational firm. You have three systems analysts and eleven programmers reporting directly to you, each of whom enjoys a great deal of autonomy with end users in the firm. Last week, you received a complaint from the vice president of production that Neil Snyder, your senior analyst, is not doing his job effectively. Although the vice president was not explicit

about the nature of the problem, it was obvious that he is unhappy and that something has to be done to keep the project on course.

Snyder has been with the firm nine years. He has a master's degree from a prestigious school and has been known to be a performer in virtually all previous projects. He is a mentor for many of the junior analysts and programmers in the MIS division. But during the past two months, something has obviously gone wrong. He has been coming to work with a "chip on his shoulder," showing indifference to work and peers, and feeling low throughout the day. In fact, other end users resent his arrogance and find themselves uncomfortable working with him.

The news has already traveled to the top. As a project leader, you are under pressure to get to the heart of this problem quickly. The senior analyst obviously has the abilities and skills to do the job well, but he must be willing to use them.

QUESTIONS
a. As Snyder's immediate supervisor, how would you deal with this problem?
b. Is this an individual or a group problem? Why?
c. Which of the following approaches would you use in trying to solve the problem?
   (1) Make the decision yourself, using information available to you at that time.
   (2) Delegate the problem to Snyder, providing him with the information that you have. Give him responsibility for solving the problem alone; any solution that he decides on will receive your support.
   (3) Solve the problem in cooperation with Snyder, get his ideas and suggestions, then make the decision yourself.
   (4) Share the problem with Snyder, analyze the problem together, and arrive at a mutually acceptable solution.

3. You are the senior vice president of a computer consulting firm. Your firm has an opportunity to bid on a government contract pertaining to software development for a military satellite. You have written the document to accompany the bid, but you need to determine the dollar value that will represent the job. If you bid too low, you could lose money on the project; if you bid too high, you could lose it to a competitor.

In deciding on the dollar value, you must take into account costs and charges but there are also "unknowns." Of all your subordinates, Joan Anderson is the best to estimate the total costs of producing the software. She has an excellent accounting background, and her previous job estimates have been quite competitive. In the initial meeting with Joan, however, she was reluctant to participate in the project. From the nature of the argument, you inferred that her opposition is more ideological than economical. She is a member of a local church that opposes supporting warfare or weaponry that promotes war.

QUESTIONS
a. Is this an individual or a group problem?
b. As a senior vice president, what choices do you have?
c. How would you go about determining the bid? Be specific.
d. Which of the following approaches would you choose in solving this problem:
   1. Make the decision yourself, using information available to you at the time.
   2. Delegate the problem to Joan, providing her with the information you have. Give her a firm command for costing the job alone. Any figures she arrives at will receive your support.
   3. You solve the problem with Joan, trying to change her mind one way or another, then cost the job together.

Selected References

Augustine, N. R. "Augustine's Laws and Major System Development Programs." *Defense Systems Management Review,* 1979, 50–76.

Baroudi, J. J. "Job Satisfaction, Commitment, and Turnover Among Information System Development Personnel: An Empirical Investigation." Unpublished doctoral dissertation, New York University, 1984.

Cascio, W. and Awad, E. M. *Human Resources Management: An Information Systems Approach.* Reston, Va.: Reston, 1981.

Couger, J. D. "Motivating Maintenance Personnel." *Computerworld,* August 12, 1985, ID6–8ff.

Couger, J. D. and Zawacki, R. A. *Motivating and Managing Computer Personnel.* New York: John Wiley & Sons, 1980.

EDP, Inc. *Computer Salary Survey and* Career Path Planning Guide, n.d.

Ein-Dor, P. and Segev, E. "Information Systems: Emergence of a New Organizational Function." *Information and Management,* vol. 5 (1982), 279–286.

Holland, John L. *Making Vocational Choices.* Englewood Cliffs, N.J.: Prentice-Hall, 1973, 2–4.

Kline, Randall R. "The Beginnings of Modern Management." *Journal of Systems Management,* September 1985, 22–26.

Lyons, Michael L. "The DP Psyche." *Datamation,* August 15, 1985, 102–105ff.

Rifkin, Glenn. "Finding and Keeping DP/MIS Professionals." *Computerworld,* June 3, 1985, UP3–8.

Peter, L. J. and Hull, R. *The Peter Principle.* New York: Wm. Morrow & Co., 1969.

Salinger, Anthony W. "Leadership, Communication Skills Lift Projects to Success." *Data Management,* September 1985, 36–37.

MIS: Trends and Directions

Chapter Contents

Connectivity, Strategic DP Top User Concerns

ACROSS THE U.S., the distinctions between user and vendor are becoming increasingly blurred. The strongest evidence of the transition of the U.S. economy from being manufacturing based to information based comes from the large computer users themselves: A recent Arthur Andersen & Co. survey of information executives in Fortune 1000 companies found that the number 1 MIS issue is the use of information for competitive advantage.

"That is what is driving the hot technologies of communications, artificial intelligence, software engineering and computer-integrated manufacturing," says Melvyn E. Bergstein, Arthur Andersen's managing director of technology practices. "For many large users, the problem is understanding the concept of information for competitive advantage but not knowing how to implement it."

American Airlines' SABRE system and American Hospital Supply Corporation's (AHS) customer site terminals linking hospitals to the AHS data base are two of the most commonly cited examples, but many other firms are quietly planning what could be a stampede into the information business.

One company currently making the transition to information vendor is Agway, Inc. in Syracuse, N.Y., a $4 billion manufacturer and distributor of livestock feed and other farm products. Agway plans to add a bundled microcomputer and farm management software package to its product line, leveraging its strong presence in a large vertical market.

From feed grains to financial services, companies are beginning to study new uses of DP technology—with dramatic implications for MIS executives. "The MIS director today has to become a strategist," says David Keytes, an information technology management consultant with Booz Allen & Hamilton, Inc. "He has to understand the function of the company's business and bring his talents, the application of technology, to the table." The corporate stature of MIS still varies widely, however, and Keytes points out that more than 50 percent of his client companies do not house their MIS departments under the same roof as their corporate headquarters.

In the next few years, vendors will prosper by providing true solutions to the connectivity dilemmas facing virtually all users—particularly those trying to deliver information in the marketplace. Just about all the hot issues involving the processing and distribution of data come down to the same thing: networking.

—Excerpted from Clinton Wilder, Computerworld, *June 9, 1986, 49ff.*

AT A GLANCE

Information system technology is increasingly becoming the backbone of business. Today's achievements point to trends and potential progress in three key areas: office automation, personal computers, and languages. The future of office automation lies in the merging of voice, data, and image in compact, easy-to-use desktop units that are linked through telecommunications. Taking advantage of the advances in office automation is a challenge to managers and planners alike.

Trends in personal computers focus on increased use of microcomputer applications in the office and the changing attitude toward computer applications. The surge in personal computer acquisitions means a definite increase in the number of PC-based applications in the organization. This, in turn, improves user attitudes toward computer use on a regular basis.

The 1980s mark the advent of nonprocedural languages that require users only to define what they want the computer to do. The language processor does the rest, resulting in a significant increase in productivity. As the evolutionary process continues through the next decade, fourth-level language systems are expected to be replaced by fifth-generation systems—the more productive expert systems. Expert systems are setting the tone for what MIS will be in the twenty-first century.

By the end of this chapter, you should know:

1. Current trends in office automation
2. The future role of the personal computer
3. Future developments in computer language

Introduction

In this text we have reviewed the multifaceted aspects of MIS—the conceptual/structural view, the procedures for designing information systems, and the technology that supports applications. Information systems are everywhere. The computer industry is undergoing continuous change and is as volatile as a moving target. No one is certain where it is headed or even its potential for business. Undoubtedly, there will be problems as well as opportunities. In this chapter we will discuss some of the trends and likely directions for management information systems.

The Human Factor

End users in general are becoming increasingly computer literate. Their motivation or willingness to try out software and adapt to system requirements is a breakthrough in itself. Computer courses in high schools, evening schools, colleges and universities, industry seminars, and vendor-sponsored workshops all contribute to the end user's knowledge base.

Computer literacy begins in high school. A 1985 *New York Times* survey indicated that 52 percent of entering freshmen have more than mere familiarity with the computer. This suggests that as more students enter college with a basic computer background, the contents of information processing courses will also be more sophisticated. On the output end, college graduates, as future end users, will have a firmer grip on the use of the computer in decision making or for problem solving.

User Friendliness

A major obstacle in system development has been the communication gap between the end user and the system professional. Much of this has been corrected through user-friendly software and the changing role of the information supplier. Since the early 1980s, the computer and its accompanying software have become easier to use. Many software packages now require only that the user press any key on the keyboard to bring up the menu. The options are easy to understand and the instructions are straightforward. Software will become even more user friendly the closer we move toward natural languages. This area is covered later in the chapter.

Another important issue is the changing role of traditional computer-related jobs—systems analysts, programmers, and computer operators. Qualified professionals for some positions are in short supply and this shortage is expected to increase. For example, according to the Bureau of Labor statistics, in 1985 the demand for systems analysts jumped 30 percent compared to 1984. In contrast, the demand for programmers during the same period increased by only 5 percent.

Today's demand for both positions continues to be strong. A brief survey of computer jobs advertised five consecutive Sundays in the *Washington Post* and three Sundays in the *Los Angeles Times* revealed a strong demand for programmer/analysts and systems analysts (see Table 19.1). The majority of programming positions, however, were for COBOL programmers for mainframe-based applications (see Table 19.2).

A shortage of qualified professionals means that end users must wait to have their requests accommodated. The seriousness of this problem is compounded by the inability of colleges and universities to meet indus-

Table 19.1   Key MIS Positions: Selected Survey Results

Source	Position Date	Programmer/ Analyst	Systems Analyst	Data Entry	Computer Operator	Database Design	EDP Audit	Quality Assurance
Washington Post	5/5/85	93	36	32	27	5	0	0
	9/1/85	64	32	35	9	2	0	1
	9/8/85	109	40	23	28	8	3	5
	9/15/85	111	40	51	30	5	1	1
	9/22/85	105	26	47	23	15	0	2
Los Angeles Times	5/5/85	108	15	21	21	1	0	7
	9/1/85	85	18	14	30	0	7	3
	9/8/85	102	19	27	9	0	0	1

Table 19.2   Demand for Key Languages: A Brief Survey

Source	Languages Date	COBOL	CICS	FORTRAN	RPG	PASCAL	"C"	BASIC	Assembler
Washington Post	5/5/85	53	16	14	8	3	5	0	0
	9/1/85	30	0	11	1	3	4	4	3
	9/8/85	49	6	10	8	7	9	5	1
	9/15/85	7	2	7	3	0	0	2	1
	9/22/85	48	5	19	8	7	9	2	8
Los Angeles Times	5/5/85	31	13	5	13	3	6	5	4
	9/1/85	4	1	4	2	1	0	2	1
	9/8/85	29	16	3	5	2	1	3	3

try demand for computer professionals. Much of the dilemma is being corrected, however, by the fact that software houses have designed virtually maintenance-free software (that also requires users to compromise their information requirements).

Pairing Technology with People

Computers alone cannot get the job done. Take the case of General Motors, which automated through robotics without preparing its workforce to handle that kind of overreliance on technology. The result was constant production delays at the company's newest plants because of a badly equipped workforce. According to one report (Kumar Naj, 1986), roughly 15 percent of GM's hourly employees cannot read or write. Only 8 percent of its 425,000 hourly workers have college degrees. Obviously, the answer is securing a proper human-machine interface through training.

The goal of automation is to cut down on production workers. Because of the increasingly technology-based environment, those who remain part of the workforce need a background in computers. For example, when foulups occur with computer-aided robots, workers must intervene and determine the causes. They cannot simply pull the switch and stop the system.

The Office of the Future

American business has invested billions of dollars in computers and software to automate today's office. The current computerized office produces up to four times the productivity of the traditional office. Some reports estimate that we produce 370 million new documents, backed by about 2 billion pages of computer printouts, each day. For example, the IBM 3800 printer can generate 20,000 lines per minute or 376,000 pages a day—long enough to cover a 100-mile trail (Bleecker, 1986). The question is, how will such a volume enhance the profitability of the firm?

A key problem related to productivity relates to the classical view of office organization. Historically, the office has been organized like the factory. Since paper (documents) is the product of the office assembly line, office technologies have been designed accordingly. As shown in Table 19.3, the machine mentality of the industrial age—in which speed

Table 19.3 Technology's Changing Trends

Phase	Defining Technology	Strategic Resource	Transforming Resource	Product	Communication
Agricultural Age	Craftsman	Seeds, soil, manpower	Sun	Food (subsistence)	Local idea exchange
Industrial Age	Machine	Money	Electricity	Mass-produced products	Face-to-face conference (ideas transferred by transporting people)
Information Age	Intelligent system	Ideas (human mind)	Cooperative minds	Information	Teleconferencing (ideas transmitted electronically)

or beating the clock was the defining technology—has to be replaced with the requirements of today's information age—intelligent systems that use their power to create ideas.

Information technology relieves us from paper production chores to concentrate on ideas and information. To be freed from the constraints of the factory mentality, today's office must be organized around the flow of information rather than the flow of paper. Two persons no longer need to be near each other to improve a product that they can transmit in a flash anywhere around the globe.

Trends in Office Automation

As we have seen in Chapter 11, office automation is no longer a novelty. The majority of larger firms now use electronics and desktop technology as a way of life. From personal computers to smart phones and electronic mail, the advent of the intelligent machine has affected the job of almost every manager in business.

The future of office automation lies in the merging of voice, data, and image in compact, easy-to-use desktop units that are linked through telecommunication. The major users will be managers and executives at all organizational levels—and secretaries as well as professionals. The most obvious impact has been from word processors, which are fast replacing the typewriter, and from the electronic spreadsheet, which is replacing the ledger sheet.

Despite the benefits offered by office automation, over half of all managers have yet to use office computers. Among the reasons given are:

1. "They won't boost my productivity."
2. "They won't help me manage people better."
3. "They aren't appropriate for my job."

Before executives can derive real benefits from office automation, they must learn how to use it. Today's reluctance among senior management is perhaps understandable. Most senior executives are old business professionals whose training did not include computer literacy. Their attitudes differ dramatically from the newer managers who went through MBA programs during the past decade.

Another reason for the lack of support for office automation is the natural tendency to delegate sophisticated tasks to support staff as such tasks become computerized. Consequently, in 1986, over 74 percent of support staff have used office computers, compared to 55 percent of management and professional staff.

Since office automation and, in fact, today's personal computers are not designed for managers, executives continue to view computer-based

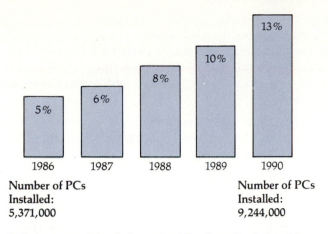

Figure 19.1
Percentage of business
personal computers con-
nected to local-area net-
works. (Adapted from
Network World, Novem-
ber 24, 1986, 13.)

Number of PCs
Installed:
5,371,000

Number of PCs
Installed:
9,244,000

Preliminary research done by International Data Corp., Framingham, Mass.

activity as boring and tedious. Except for software with HELP, ASSIST, and other "easy-to-learn" features, would-be users usually spend hours leafing through a not so user-friendly manual and other documentation before mastering the machine.

Despite these difficulties, the trend seems clear. Almost 75 percent of the Fortune 1000 companies already have LANs and use the telephone to carry voice and data. Over 60 percent currently use electronic mail. In terms of networking, over 5 million personal computers were connected to LAN in 1986. As projected in Figure 19.1, the number of connections is expected to double. Office automation, as represented by newer technologies, is definitely redefining white collar productivity.

Executive Use of Time

Making best use of executive time means focusing on the communication technology used by management and the activities that support such communication. According to one model, management generally spends up to 50 percent of the time in face-to-face meetings, 20 percent on the telephone, 19 percent on documentation, and 11 percent in administration. In enhancing productivity, it is helpful to look into the technology that improves the quality of the work as well as reduces the time spent on work activities. For example, videoconference technology has been known to improve management of executive time, despite its drawbacks.

For telephoning—managers' second most time-consuming activity—intelligent executive phones are making their appearance in the workplace. They perform many functions that were once handled by secretaries. The executive telephone has several features:

1. Speed dialing
2. The last number redial

3. Speakerphone capability
4. Automatic answering by voice alone
5. Display panel that supplies basic operating information such as the number being dialed, time of day, and so on
6. Voice mail that automatically records and replays messages to the person called

The most elaborate telephone enhancement is the voice and data workstation. It looks like a computer with a phone attached, offering two key features for management-level users:

1. Compactness, to fit in with the aesthetic features of the executive office.
2. Use of various functions simultaneously, including speaking on the phone, referring to displayed data, and calling up an electronic notepad or calendar.

The electronic notepad is a particularly convenient personal productivity aid. The user takes rough notes on a telephone conversation while using the voice/data workstation. The notes are filed for later retrieval.

Given these innovations, a challenge for advancing information technology is to control the demand for standardization. Integration of high-level tools is a strong measure of the vendor's ability to respond to standardization and the need for ease of use at the user's end. At the same time, management and support staff can benefit from an environment that is receptive to office automation tools. Information technology is already a necessary aspect of the management process. Taking advantage of the advances in office automation is a challenge to managers and planners alike.

Directions in Electronic Messaging

Since its introduction in 1980, **electronic messaging** has shown strong growth in the business office. Well over 400,000 electronic mail installations are in operation. Electronic messaging is easy to use, reliable, and cost effective. A recent study (Koladziej, 1985) found that while 62 percent of the Fortune 1000 corporate respondents already have long-distance messaging in place, that figure is expected to exceed 78 percent in 1987.

Electronic messaging is a natural for the business organization. It is often installed on a departmental rather than organizational basis and is successful with compatible equipment. In the field of personal computers, electronic messaging packages have been gaining in popularity since the early 1980s. Most of these packages sell in the $100–200 range.

Another messaging technology gaining corporate attention is **voice store-and-forward** (**VSAF**). Recent breakthroughs in digitizing and compression of voice suggest that VSAFs are on their way into the automated office. VSAF, however, is not cheap. Although prices are dropping, most small VSAFs cost over $5000. To make inroads, VSAF systems need to combine voice messaging with text and data applications in an integrated office environment. Ability to combine text and voice messages is a part of the integration emphasis.

Impact on Jobs

There is some concern that office automation tends to reduce the skill requirements of many clerical jobs. Published studies record the belief of the majority of office secretaries that word processing has improved their overall skills and made it possible for future advancement. However, few new career positions have actually been created as a result of this technology.

As information technology moves into the realm of professional work, it is expected that certain programmable tasks that require limited technical experience are candidates for automation—for example, the creation of a PERT chart by specialized packages such as "Harvard Project Manager."

Among the jobs that require professional skills but will see a reduction in the level of these skills is programming. High-level languages have simplified coding and debugging, and fourth-generation languages have further minimized programming altogether. The skills required to do programming have thus been drastically reduced.

In terms of the impact of office automation on managerial jobs, studies have shown that managers spend most of their time in verbal communications and meetings (Kelly Services, 1983; National Association of Working Women, 1984). Although office automation seems to have the capability of improving managerial productivity, the nature of the job seems to resist it. Most successes, however, have been in information tools that enhance communication capabilities, such as electronic messaging and voice store-and-forward message systems, that were cited earlier in the chapter.

Leveraging Information Technology Through Networks

We know from Chapter 7 that telecommunications and networking can promote employee productivity and improve working styles. Companies use communication as a great corporate resource—manipulating data on the competitive environment and creating new markets for their products and services. For example, think of Digital Equipment Corporation's internal network that uses 20,000 computers at 250 locations in 29 cities to reach over 65,000 users within seconds all over the world. Implications for performance are obvious.

As organizations compete for customers and productivity, the winners will be those who fully exploit the leverage provided by information systems to improve management. Those who incorporate information technology in strategic planning will apply new information technologies for competitive advantage. Those who do not seize these opportunities must simply operate with what others make available to them.

New networking technologies are in the works. For example, in a New Jersey office minutes west of New York City, an engineer from Bell Communications Research, Inc. is developing a phone system of the future. Your accountant Joe places a call and your phone rings. Before you answer, a phone computer announces the caller's name (Joe) in an electronic voice through a tiny speaker under the headset. You can push a button and answer the phone or simply ignore it and let it keep ringing as if no one is there.

This example is one of many feats on the horizon. A modernized network will change the way business communicates in many ways. Transmission speed through new fiber optic lines will increase up to ten times the current rates. A single integrated digital network could replace the several networks most organizations now need to handle data traffic and local area networks. The same network that makes it easier for businesses to communicate will also help phone company computers to avoid traffic jams by rerouting calls and pinpointing the source of breakdowns (Gorman, 1986).

The Role of the Personal Computer

Since the early 1980s, a number of changes have taken place that help us predict future developments in the office. The areas emphasized here focus on personal computer use in offices, daily personal computer-based applications, and changing attitudes toward computer applications.

Personal computer sales in 1985 were 3.4 million units and 4.7 million in 1986. Sales in 1987 are expected to exceed six million units.

Among the top industries using PCs are industrial conglomerates, life insurance, and general merchandise (see Table 19.4). The top three PC purchasers in 1986 were General Motors (31,000 units), General Electric (18,000 units), and Westinghouse (12,000 units).

The surge of PC acquisition means a definite increase in the number of PC-based applications in the organization. There were 11 million PCs in use in 1986, compared to 2.1 million in 1982. The number of PCs per 100 workers has also increased from four in 1982 to twenty-one in 1986. In banking, the nation's twenty-five $10 billion and over banks will add over 8000 microcomputers in 1987 (see Figure 19.2). In terms of the daily PC applications, the greatest use of the PC has been by professionals for analysis and planning. Over 14 percent of the professional's workday is devoted to PC use in analysis and planning (see Figure 19.3). Middle

Table 19.4 PC Industry Use (by units)

Industry Area	Unit
Electrical machinery manufacturing	350,000
Industrial conglomerates	335,000
Petrochemical firms	285,000
Life insurance	252,000
Grocery/drug/liquor	230,000
Industrial machinery manufacturing	225,000
Commercial banks	223,000
General merchandise	210,000
Food manufacturing and processing	205,000
Transportation equipment	166,000
Fabricated metals manufacturing	136,400
Lumber/wood/pulp/paper	133,500
Printing/publishing	130,500
Automobile dealerships	126,000
Durable goods wholesalers	120,000
Law firms	108,000
Casualty insurance	92,000
Accounting & bookkeeping	91,000
Engineering & architecture	85,000
Eating places	73,000
Lodging industry	63,200
Health services	62,000
Grocery wholesalers	52,000
Savings banks	48,000
Equipment leasing companies	44,300
Construction firms	41,000
Research and development labs	36,800
Advertising companies	26,000
Chemical and drug wholesalers	16,000

management follows professionals in PC use more closely than do top executives.

Because of the increased use and knowledge of the personal computer, we have experienced a comparable change in user attitudes toward PC applications. As shown in Figure 19.4, almost 60 percent of middle management support the use of the PC for data retrieval and manipulation. A favorable response also supports the spreadsheet, word processing, and messaging as viable applications. Professionals' attitudes follow those of middle management. Top executives' main interest focuses on data retrieval and messaging.

Among PC-based applications, the majority of organizations use financial analysis spreadsheets, accounting, and word processing appli-

Figure 19.2
Average number of PCs
added per bank in 1986,
estimated. (Adapted
from *Computers in Bank-
ing,* October 1985, 59.)

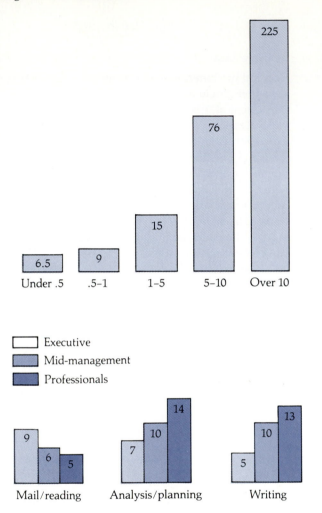

Figure 19.3
Percentage of workday
devoted to PC use,
by occupation level.
(Source: American Tele-
systems Corporation,
1985.)

cations. Database management and inventory control were moderately
supported (see Figure 19.5).

   With the relative increase in the number of PCs and applications during the first half of the 1980s, it seems likely that more managers will
learn present applications rather than selected managers adopting more
applications. As the quality of software improves and user friendliness
becomes a standard software feature, the viability of the personal computer in the MIS environment is expected to gain a lasting support.
Finally, as hardware technology makes the PC more price effective, and
as more PCs become workstations in a LAN environment, users are
expected to have easy access to decision support and, potentially, knowledge-based information for decision making. The latter outcome, however, is not likely to be common before the end of the 1990s.

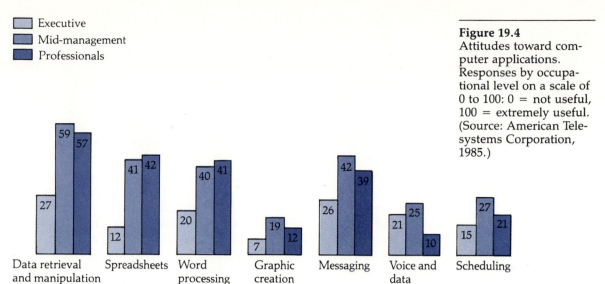

Figure 19.4
Attitudes toward computer applications. Responses by occupational level on a scale of 0 to 100: 0 = not useful, 100 = extremely useful. (Source: American Telesystems Corporation, 1985.)

The Role of the Executive

A top executive of a large firm pecking away at a computer keyboard somehow does not compliment the executive self-image. But a growing number of executives are finding important uses for the personal computer. An MIT study (Gottschalk, 1985) found that at thirty of forty-five randomly selected Fortune 500 companies, at least one senior executive had a computer terminal on his/her desk. By 1990, there should be routine use of computer terminals in the executive office.

It is obvious that computers are changing the way company information systems operate. Vital information is now available on the screen

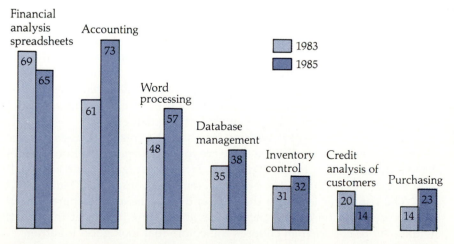

Figure 19.5
Percentage of surveyed companies using PCs for various applications. (From the *Dun's 5000 Survey*, prepared by the Economic Analysis Department. The Dun and Bradstreet Corporation, 1985.)

in numbers and graphs. Senior executives with minicomputer support systems think through critical issues and call up the information that is really important. There is no more waiting for what tradition or subordinates think they should see.

Micro-Mainframe Graphics Linkages

Nearly every organization recognizes the role of graphics as a competitive tool for marketing, planning, engineering, and financial management. Most of today's PC users have no access to high-quality graphics hard copy equipment. One major new development solves this problem by linking personal computers to mainframes for graphics. The link is accomplished by means of software or hardware extension to the personal computer. Charts are requested from the personal computer, previewed, and then routed to high-quality shared graphics equipment such as laser printers and continuous plotters.

The trend of personal computers as graphics terminals will be complemented by an attempt to link programs such as LOTUS 1-2-3 directly to mainframe graphics programs. When a LOTUS user, for example, makes a chart, the personal computer may be instructed to send the LOTUS worksheet to the mainframe, which, in turn, converts it into a high-quality slide or chart. We expect to see more and more high-quality graphics devices dedicated to individual PCs and on LANs. A "laserwriter" is actually fairly inexpensive and getting more so. The convenience and time savings of having immediately available output should not be underestimated.

Graphics performs a key role in project management. Project management systems determine the critical path. The new class of graphics project management software is being used more regularly than the older project management systems. New systems are capable of producing presentation-quality charts that show management the schedule and cost status of projects.

Software tools are also beginning to offer "pushbutton" graphics management for the executive. Traditional graphics packages served those who created charts rather than the executive who just wanted information displayed graphically. Today, new systems are becoming available that instantly deliver information in graphic formats. Referred to as *graphics decision support systems*, they consist of libraries of charts that are automatically updated with changes in underlying data.

Finally, graphics expert systems may soon be created to assist novice users in making charts. Such a software tool performs three knowledge-based functions: predesigned graphics, layout intelligence, and color palette selection. The user, for example, tells the computer, "Make chart 10." The computer looks up the data and then makes the chart. *Layout intelligence* relies on a database of facts about how to format the chart, while *color palette selection* chooses the colors that look good together.

The Future of Languages

Computer languages have one goal in common: allowing people to "talk" to the computer. As we have covered in Chapter 4, in three decades languages have passed from machine languages to assembler languages to procedural languages such as FORTRAN and COBOL. The 1980s mark the beginning of fourth-generation, nonprocedural languages. Unlike a **procedural language** that requires users to define how they want the computer to perform through the program's flow, **nonprocedural language** users define only what results they want. The language processor determines the program's flow. This division of labor results in a significant increase in productivity.

Other characteristics of natural language are user friendliness and interfacing a database with many integrated functions such as report preparation, spreadsheet analysis, and micro-mainframe communications. All of these features are menu driven, with extensive HELP and ASSIST facilities.

Several trends will affect fourth-generation development by the end of this decade (Cobb, 1985):

1. *Increased effort into adding functionality to products.* These include screen definition report generators that ferret information out of spreadsheets or statistical software. A key foundation facility is a workstation gateway that services the need for micro-mainframe links and data dictionaries that manage the information resource.

2. *Continuing shift of effort from people to computers.* People want to increase their personal productivity and are increasingly depending on the computer to achieve this goal. Productivity advantages of fourth-generation language across four key activities are shown in Table 19.5. For ad hoc inquiries, 89 percent of the respondents reported gaining a 10:1 productivity advantage or more. Thirty percent claimed 50:1 productivity advantage. A similar response was reported for report preparation. Even for data maintenance, 62 percent reported getting more than a 10:1 productivity advantage.

3. *Fourth-generation systems offer the user more than one way to do the same job.* This is expected to lead to *significant increases in personal productivity.*

Table 19.5 Productivity Improvements Using Fourth-Generation Language

Activity	Productivity Improvements (%)			
	5:1	*10:1*	*25:1*	*50:1 or more*
Ad hoc inquiries	11	25	34	30
Reports	17	37	31	15
Data maintenance	38	35	19	8
Building complete applications	38	33	20	9

Source: Cobb, 1985, ID41.

4. *A definite trend away from coding.* Productivity advantage includes the whole life cycle of a project and not just the coding phase. We are seeing the beginning of knowledge editors that know what the user is trying to do. This has direct bearing on productivity.

5. *Improvements in people-machine communications, with the computer to become largely verbal.* Voice recognition will be a strongly emerging reality during the next decade.

6. *The advent of natural language expert systems that produce applications automatically.* The user generates the specifications and code simply by making reference to the knowledge base that has the data. With such systems and for some applications, users direct the computer in common English rather than cryptic commands.

Person-machine interfacing, voice communication, and natural language understanding are likely to be delegated to the workstation that is linked to the mainframe. The end user will develop most of the applications through the workstation, some of which will run on the mainframe. This is *distributed processing.*

As the evolutionary process continues through the next decade, fourth-generation language systems will be surpassed by **fifth-generation languages**—the more productive expert systems. The fifth-generation project in Japan is developing a faster, denser circuitry to create new super-intelligent computers. These application systems will be capable of handling voice and video images as well as handwritten characters. They will learn from experience, associate between relationships, draw inferences, and make decisions. They may very well be the machine of the future information society.

Although they remain tools for designers and experienced users, the programs that expert systems create will soon penetrate the personal computer user base. The steady increase in the use of artificial intelligence is ushering in the new "intelligent" personal computer. That is just the trend that we may have to accept in the near future.

Ethical Issues*

Our society is truly an information society. Information (and thinking) is a means by which our mind expands its capacity to achieve better and higher goals. Millions of computers are now in operation and tens of millions of fiber optics and telecommunication wire link people and computers on a regular basis. These developments have generated a number of ethical issues. The three major issues are: accessibility, accuracy, and property.

*This discussion was adapted from Mason, 1986, 5–12.

In terms of *accessibility,* we ask: What information does a person or an organization have the right to obtain? Under what conditions can information become available? One powerful factor that is making information more accessible and economically attainable is the decreasing cost of computation. Large databases about all kinds of information can now be accessed via terminals and microcomputers. It is for society to determine what is *authorized* and the safeguards to prevent unauthorized access. Unfortunately, for every safeguard, there seems to be a violator who finds a way to break in.

Who is responsible for the *accuracy* of information? This issue is especially critical when people rely on it for matters of life and death. Consider the $3.2 million lawsuit charging the National Weather Service for failure to predict accurately a storm on the slopes of Georges Bank in 1980. Peter Brown steered his fishing boat out toward his lobster traps near Nova Scotia. The forecasts assured him that his destination was free of hurricane-like storms. He kept his course only to encounter 80-knot winds and 60-foot waves. Two of the crew washed overboard.

The source of the problem was a buoy—station 4403 Georges Bank—that was out of service, a fact that caused the computer to misforecast the storm trajectory by over 60 miles. The question for us is: How many fatalities result from inaccurate information? We are currently producing so much information about so many people and their activities that we have an enormous vulnerability to inaccuracy.

This trend in information raises the third ethical issue of *property.* Who owns information? Information per se is costly to produce in the first place. Yet once it is stored, information has the tempting attribute of being easy to copy and disseminate. Unlike real property, it is not so easy to protect.

Nowhere is the potential threat to ownership so severe as it is in expert systems. Designers proceed by extracting knowledge from experts and embed this knowledge into the computer software, where it is viewed as capital. Then the hardware transfers control of property to those who own the hardware and software. Is such an exchange warranted? Information systems should protect intellectual property from unauthorized dissemination or use.

In Retrospect

Today's knowledge workers thrive on spontaneity and exchange of ideas. They do not operate serially like machines. They process information in parallel. Chief executive officers, for example, consider several options simultaneously and do not decide in a structured way. Moreover, we should speak less of productivity and more of creative integration; less of processed energy and more of mental energy; less of strong back and more of strong mind. In the industrial age, people aided machines. In today's information age, machines aid people.

Given the structural and operational framework of the MIS environment, we cannot very well overlook social factors in information processing. Granted, these issues were not important in the early days of computer development. Today, MIS has become so all pervasive that it is a target for government intervention and surveillance. Individuals have dreaded the power of the computer via huge government databases that summon up the specter of the Big Brother society. The Privacy Act of 1974 provided safeguards by permitting individuals to examine their own records held by government and question certain data. Yet human vulnerability in the information age seems to produce anxieties and mistrust about organizations that support technology without adequate safeguards.

Finally, we must look at MIS not only as a technological and operational system but also as a human system. All three components must be integrated for MIS to be a viable contributor to business. The computer industry has already carved a niche in the technological area. Most end user requirements can now be met using existing technology. The operational component is the installation of a system in a specific business setting. But a system that is technologically and operationally sound will fail if the human factor has not been embedded in the design. For that reason, we consistently emphasize the importance of the human factor in the form of user participation and management support in MIS development. These three criteria form the triad that will determine how the world of MIS beyond the year 2000 will differ from ours.

Summary

- End users are becoming increasingly computer literate. Today's entering students have a basic familiarity with computers and, with additional training through college, are expected to be effective end users after graduation.

- The surge in user-friendly software and the changing role of the information supplier have done a great deal to improve the user-machine interface. This also makes up for the shortage of programmers. Increasing demand for system installations, however, continues to push upward the demand curve for systems analysts. Colleges and universities are under pressure to address the shortage problem.

- The future of office automation lies in the merging of voice, data, and image in easy-to-use desktop units that are linked to telecommunications. The major users will be managers at all organizational levels and secretaries as well as professionals. The most obvious impact has been from word processors that are fast replacing the typewriter and electronic spreadsheets that are replacing the ledger sheet.

□ Electronic messaging has shown strong growth in the business office. It is easy to use, reliable, and cost effective. A unique electronic messaging technology is voice store-and-forward (VSAF). To make inroads, VSAF must be able to combine voice messaging with text and data applications in an integrated office environment.

□ As information technology moves into the realm of professional work, it is expected that certain programmable tasks requiring limited technical experience are candidates for automation. Programming is predicted to be a job requiring reduced skill levels with the advent of fourth-generation languages.

□ The surge of personal computer acquisitions means a definite increase in the number of PC-based applications in business. Because of increased use and knowledge of the PC, we have experienced a comparable change in user attitudes toward PC applications.

□ A definite trend favoring use of the personal computer is linking the PC to the mainframe for graphics. This will be complimented by linking programs such as LOTUS 1-2-3 directly to mainframe graphics programs. Graphics also is fast performing a key role in project management.

□ The 1980s marked the introduction of fourth-generation, nonprocedural languages that request users to define only what they want the computer program to do. The language processor keeps track of the program's flow. This division of labor results in a significant increase in productivity.

□ As we learn more about language development through this decade, fifth-generation languages are fast appearing in the marketplace under the label of expert systems. As far as one can predict, expert systems will be the ultimate in the application of computers to problem solving.

Key Terms

Electronic messaging	Nonprocedural language
Fifth-generation language	Procedural language
Knowledge base	Voice store-and-forward (VSAF)

Review Questions

1. What contributions has the computer made to its end users? How do you foresee the future? Elaborate.

2. How likely is it that we can expect a decrease in the demand for traditional programmers during the next decade? Why? Discuss.

3. Recent advances in software have favored users rather than programmers. Do you agree? Why?

4. Discuss carefully the major trends in office automation. How important is telecommunication in such a trend? Why?

5. In what way(s) has the executive's time been changed or reallocated as a result of office automation?

6. What features do intelligent phones offer the business enterprise? Explain briefly.

7. Illustrate how electronic messaging plays a role in executive-to-executive communication.

8. "There is some concern that office automation tends to reduce the skill requirements of many clerical jobs." Do you agree? Discuss.

9. The text cites statistics on PC sales, applications, and user attitudes toward the PC. What do you conclude from this in terms of (a) the future PC impact on decision making, (b) the future role of programmers, and (c) the role of the mainframe in information processing?

10. Distinguish between procedural and nonprocedural languages. How do you foresee nonprocedural language being an improvement for high-level languages such as COBOL? Explain.

Application Problems

1. Many corporations are experiencing increasing pressure to replace or displace office workers whose skills are no longer required because of the capabilities offered by available office technologies. The implication is that advanced office systems will make it possible for organizations to distribute more responsibility downward. This downward movement will result in flattened organizational structures and, in turn, will provide opportunities to eliminate many middle-level management and professional positions.

At the same time, office technology will offer large organizations an opportunity to utilize more and more paraprofessionals in place of mid-level managers and professionals. Many of the paraprofessionals will be women returning to the workforce after raising families.

QUESTIONS
a. Do you agree with this assessment? Elaborate. Review the literature since early 1986 and report key changes or developments that support your position.
b. To what extent does office automation improve managerial performance? Explain.

2. In *The Third Wave,* Alvin Toffler describes the following scenario: In the morning of a not-too-distant year, a white-collar worker gets up, dresses, eats, and steps out of the house. Instead of driving the car to work, this worker walks a few blocks to a plain building in the neighborhood. In one room, there is a desk, a videophone, and a portable computer folded like a briefcase. Like other workers in rooms on either side, the worker sits down and begins similar work, using similar equipment. The main difference is that each worker is employed by a different organization. Their jobs have nothing in common.

QUESTIONS

a. How necessary is it for all workers of any organization to be situated within the same walls of a given location? Discuss.

b. Can remote networks of remote work sites be organized to promote productivity? What factors are involved? Discuss the pros and cons of such an "electronic cottage" concept.

Selected References

Anderson, Andy. "The Automated Office of the 1990s." *C&FM,* January–February 1985, 14–17.

Bleecker, Samuel. "Taking the Factory Out of the Office." *Computerworld,* June 16, 1986, 95–103ff.

Cobb, Richard. "Fourth-Generation Languages: From Backwater to Mainstream." *Computerworld,* October 14, 1985, ID 39–52ff.

Falce, Tom. "Changing Role of Management Information Systems and Office Automation." *Journal of Systems Management,* May 1985, 26–29.

Gorman, Roger. "The Rewiring of America." *Business Week,* September 15, 1986, 188–190ff.

Gottschalk Jr., Earl C. "Executive Computing." *Wall Street Journal,* September 16, 1985, 3-23.

Julian, Ken. "Defense Program Pushes Microchip Frontiers." *High Technology,* May 1985, 49–59.

Kelly Services. *The Kelly Reports on People in the Electronic Office.* Troy, Mi.: 1983.

Koladziej, Stan. "Where Is the Electronic Messaging Explosion?" *Computerworld,* October 16, 1985, Focus 21–23ff.

Kumar Naj, Amal. "The Human Factor." *Wall Street Journal,* November 10, 1986, 36D.

Mason, R. O. "Four Ethical Issues of the Information Age." *MIS Quarterly,* 10, 1 (March 1986), 5–12.

Morgan, Howard. "The Microcomputer and Decision Support." *Computerworld,* August 19, 1985, 39–40ff.

National Association of Working Women, National Survey on Women and Stress, *9 to 5*. Cleveland, Oh.: 1984.

Reeve, R. C. "Where Are the Robots?" *Computerworld*, June 10, 1985, ID 25ff.

Rifkin, Glenn. "Toward the Fifth Generation." *Computerworld*, May 6, 1985, UP3–6.

Weiss, Edmond. "The Next Wave of User Documentation." *Computerworld*, September 9, 1985, 15–19.

Glossary

Absolute address: The exact location of a record on a disk or in main memory.

Access method: In file organization, a way of accessing data in a file.

Acoustic coupler: A device connected to a terminal that enables the terminal to access a CPU, using a standard telephone.

Action planning: Planning that addresses a firm's key business directions.

Adaptability: The ease with which a software package can be extended.

Address: (1) An identification, as represented by a name, label, or number, for a register, location in storage, or any other data source or destination such as the location of a station in a communications network. (2) Loosely, any part of an instruction that specifies the location of an operand for the instruction.

Alpha test: Verifying and studying software errors and failures based on simulated user requirements.

Analog computer: A computer that represents variables by physical analogies. Thus, any computer that solves problems by translating physical conditions such as flow temperature, pressure, angular position, or voltage into related mechanical or electrical quantities and that uses mechanical or electrical equivalent circuits, such as an analog for the physical phenomenon being investigated. In general, a computer that uses an analog for each variable and produces analogs as output. Thus, an analog computer measures continuously, whereas a digital computer counts discretely.

Application generator: A prototyping tool that handles the full range of system development details.

Application software: Software that performs user-oriented functions as opposed to operating system functions.

Argument: In languages, the objects or values that functions or procedures operate on.

Arithmetic/logic unit (ALU):   The unit of a computing system that contains the circuits which perform arithmetic and logical operations.

Artificial intelligence (AI):   Doing on computers what, if done by humans, would be called intelligent; capability of a computer to learn from experience, understand natural language, access information, and draw conclusions.

ASCII: A coding scheme used for representation of characters in storage.

Assembler: Software that converts assembly programs into machine language instructions.

Assembly language: A computer language that converts binary digits of machine language into abbreviations to indicate processing operations.

Asynchronous transmission: An operation initiated by a signal that a preceding operation has been completed and a new one can begin. Also, one bit at a time of transmission.

Attribute: A data item that characterizes an object.

Audit trail: Using documents to retrace the processing of data by changing or modifying records in a file.

Backward iteration: Calculating backward in determining the parameter of the problem, given the parameters of the results.

Bar code: A special machine- and human-readable code adopted by the grocery and retail industries to automate data gathering and processing.

Baseband network: LAN transmission technique that is unique to telecommunications.

BASIC: *Beginner's All-Purpose Symbolic Instruction Code.* An interactive programming language that is easy to learn and use.

Baud: A unit of signaling speed that amounts to 1 bit per second.

Benchmark: In system testing, a test run on a candidate system to measure how long it takes to run a selected application.

Beta test: Subjecting modified software to the actual (live) user site environment.

Bidirectional: Used to describe a printer that prints lines in two directions.

Binary-coded decimal (BCD):   A decimal notation in which the individual decimal digits are each represented by a group of binary digits; for example, in the 8-4-2-1 binary-coded decimal notation, the number 23 is represented by 0010 0011, whereas in binary notation, 23 is represented as 10111.

Bit: (1) An abbreviation of binary digit. (2) A single character in a binary number. (3) A single pulse in a group of pulses. (4) A unit of information capacity of a storage device.

Boss module: A module that is not called on by any other module but calls on other modules to do work.

Bounded rationality: In data gathering, a concept that states that a person's ability to determine information requirements is bounded by a limited capacity for rational thinking as well as limited training and the person's attitude.

Brainstorming: A technique for generating new ideas; a participant is asked to define ideal solutions and then select the most feasible one.

Breakeven analysis: The point at which the cost of the candidate system and the present system are equal.

Broadband network: LAN transmission technique in which a large capacity cable is partitioned into several channels.

Bus network: LAN layout in which all functional devices are connected to a length of passive coaxial cable, called a bus.

Business systems planning (BSP):   Systematic way of analyzing an organization in terms of its data classes, data elements, business processes and functions, and relating them to the information needs of the organization; process that translates business strategy into MIS.

Byte: A set of consecutive binary digits (usually an 8-bit set) that operates as a unit.

Candidate system: A newly developed information system designed to replace a system currently in use.

Capacity planning: Projecting future volume (capacity) requirements based on current workload.

Career: An occupation that provides a clear pattern of systematic advancement, a career ladder, or path; people in any particular role or status; a person's job history, a series of positions held over an entire work life.

Career choice: The responses an individual makes in determining and adjusting to an occupation.

Career planning: An evaluation of the interaction between the individual and the employing organization over time.

Central processing unit (CPU): Major computer device containing the arithmetic/logic unit, main memory, and control unit.

Centralization: Designing an MIS area responsible for providing information processing services to all the organization's operating units.

Chain: A series of records connected by means of pointers.

Chained list: A field that holds the address of the next record in the sequence; used to keep records in logical order.

Channel: A parallel track on a magnetic tape, a band on a magnetic drum, or a path along which information flows.

Child: In a database, an owned entity.

Chip: A memory or processing device made from wafers of silicon that is wired externally and sealed in plastic for building the main memory of a computer.

Choice: Third phase of decision making; selecting and implementing a course of action.

Cladding: In fiber optics, the second layer that bounces the light waves back into the core of the fiber optics unit.

Closed question: A question in which the response(s) is presented as a set of alternatives.

COBOL: *COmmon Business Oriented Language.* A business-oriented programming language.

Coding: Writing coded program instructions that are later translated into a computer language.

Collision: See **synonym**.

Common carrier: A government-regulated organization that offers public telecommunication facilities such as telephone service.

Compatibility: The capability of additional software, hardware, or peripherals to fit in with an organization's existing computer system.

Compiler: A software package that prepares a machine language program from a computer program written in another programming language by making use of the overall logic structure of the program, generating more than the machine instruction for each symbolic statement, as well as performing the function of an assembler.

Computer-output microfilm (COM): Recording system output on microfilm or microfiche, usually for archival storage.

Concatenated key: Two or more keys linked together to identify or access a record.

Connection: A vector that links two modules.

Connective: Operator signal; in expert systems, used to link predicates into large expressions.

Connotational view: Concept of DSS as an evolutionary extension beyond MIS.

Consolidated computing: Second stage of technological change in computing, in the late 1960s. Characterized by a high demand for programmers and computer center facilities.

Consult mode: In expert systems, the mode in which facts and rules are entered.

Contagion: A stage of MIS growth characterized by heavy demand for computer use and a period of processing application backlogs.

Contention: A method of network control that allows the computer to sense a bid from a terminal and then authorize the terminal to begin transmission.

Contrived observation: An observation set up by the observer in a place outside the user environment, such as a lab.

Conversion: Process of changing from an existing system to a new one.

Couple: A connection between modules; a symbol representing data items moved from one module to another.

Critical success factors (CSF):   The limited number of areas (usually four to six) in which satisfactory results will insure successful performance for a business; a technique used to elicit the information requirements of managerial users.

CSMA/CD: A detection device that looks at the transmitting device for a signal on the line to avoid a collision with another device already transmitting.

Culture: The set of values, attitudes, and norms passed down from generation to generation to prescribe the behavior of a society.

DAM: See **direct access method**.

Data aggregate: See **entity**.

Data definition language (DDL):   For a database, the language used to describe how data are structured in the database.

Data dictionary: A structured repository of data about data; a list of terms and their definitions for all data items and data stores of a system.

Data element: The smallest unit of data where no further breakdown is provided. Also known as a **primitive**.

Data flow diagram (DFD):   Graphic representation of data movement, processes, and files (data stores) used in support of an information system.

Data independence: Changing hardware and storage procedures or adding new data without having to rewrite application programs.

Data manipulation language (DML):   In database—a language that specifies for the DBMS what is required; the techniques used to process data.

Data migration: Moving data from one device to another. For instance, transferring infrequently used data to archival storage.

Data model: For a database, a framework or mental image of how the user's view looks.

Data store: In a data flow diagram, a storage area usually representing a file; symbolized by an open rectangle.

Data structure: A logically related set of data that can be decomposed into lower-level data elements; a group of data elements handled as a unit.

Database: A store of integrated data capable of being directly addressed for multiple uses; it is organized so that various files can be accessed through a single reference based on the relationship among records in the file rather than the physical location.

Database management system (DBMS): The software that determines how data must be structured to produce the user's view; manages, stores, and retrieves data and enforces procedures.

Decentralization: Setting up a functional information systems department within each operating unit of an organization.

Decision criterion: A rational method or rule for choosing an alternative that will best meet the given objective.

Decision making: Process of evaluating, selecting, and implementing a course of action for problem solving.

Decision support system (DSS): A "what-if" approach that uses an information system to assist management in formulating policies and projecting the probable consequence of decisions.

Decision tree: Graphic representation of conditions and outcomes resembling the branches of a tree.

Delphi inquiry: Debating by questionnaire. Participants fill out forms and the results are given to them along with followup questions.

Descriptor: In a knowledge base, a node that provides descriptive information about a preceding or succeeding node. For example, the node "male" may be a descriptor of "John."

Design: Second phase of decision making; analyzing alternative courses of action to solve a problem.

Desktop publishing: Integrated software that generates near-typeset-quality publications quickly and cheaply.

Dialogue: A set of easy-to-use commands that allow communication between user and system.

Dichotomous question: A yes or no question; a question offering two answer choices.

Digital computer: A computer that operates on discrete data by performing arithmetic and logic processes on the data.

Direct access method (DAM): A method in which records in a file can be accessed directly.

Direct cost: Cost that is normally applied directly to the operation in question; for example, the purchase of a new tape for $40 is a direct cost.

Direct observation: A situation in which the analyst actually observes the subject or system at work.

Disaster/recovery planning: A procedure for identifying potential threats, prioritizing applications, and devising safeguards to minimize losses in the event of a disaster.

Disclaimer: Related to a warranty; means that the vendor makes no promise about the quality of the software.

Distributed data processing (DDP): Availability of a computerized environment at the user's level with control at the organization's host computer.

Dot matrix: An impact printer that forms characters by striking a ribbon, which then strikes the paper; the letters are made up of many small dots.

DSS builder: Person who assembles the necessary capabilities from the DSS generator to configure the specific DSS to meet user needs.

DSS generator: A package of related hardware/software that has the capability to build a specific DSS.

Dumb terminal: A terminal with no logic or intelligence capability.

EBCDIC: An 8-bit coding scheme used in data transmission.

Electronic funds transfer (EFT): A network or system that eliminates the need for a cash exchange of funds by transferring funds electronically from one account to another.

Electronic messaging: Electronic transmission of messages that are stored and forwarded from one site to another.

Embedded computing: Fourth stage of technological change in computing, in the mid- to late 1970s. Characterized by greater demand for computer professionals and a rising role of the user.

End user: Person who uses a computer (e.g., a manager entering an inquiry via a keyboard).

Entity: Something of interest to the user about which to collect or store data; represents a number of data elements.

EPROM: See Erasable Programmable **ROM** (**EPROM**).

Equal Employment Opportunity Act (EEO): Federal hiring procedure that prohibits discrimination against individuals on the basis of their color, sex, age, or national origin.

Erasable Programmable ROM (EPROM): Memory chips that can be modified through ultraviolet light, but must be removed from the computer to perform the process.

Ergonomics: The science of adjusting machine specifications to match human comfort.

Expandability: Ease of adding, deleting, or modifying the existing software to meet changing user requirements.

Expected value: A given outcome times the probability that the outcome will occur.

Expert system: An extension of artificial intelligence; a system that uses symbolic knowledge to mimic the decision-making and problem-solving thought processes of human experts.

Facilities management (FM): A company's computer facility managed by an outside agency under contract.

Feasibility study: A procedure that identifies, describes, and evaluates candidate systems and selects the best system for the job.

Fiber optics: A technique that uses light to carry information along a hair-sized plastic or glass fiber from one point to another.

Fifth-generation language: Generally refers to natural language; a nonprocedural language used in artificial intelligence applications.

Firmware: Prewired hardware that is programmed to perform specific functions.

Fitness: A principle that is grounds for litigation if a vendor sells a user a system that he knows will not be useful for the user's intended purpose.

Flowcharting: A design tool that shows a program's processing flow and the operations to be performed in a specific sequence.

Folding: Approach to addressing records in which the key is split into parts which are added and the sum is used as an address.

Form: A user-friendly tool for end users in which form layout is automatically followed by the program.

Formatted form: A fill-in-the-blank approach to data entry; a preformatted form is displayed on the screen, requesting the user to enter data in the appropriate locations.

Formula: In a spreadsheet, an instruction that describes the calculations to be performed on data.

FORTRAN (*FOR*mula *TRAN*slation):   A programming language used for writing scientific and engineering programs.

Fourth-generation language (4GL):   User-oriented, easy-to-learn, nonprocedural language.

Frame: A knowledge carrier that helps describe the syntax of a knowledge base; a set of slots and their associated entries; associates an object with facts, rules, or values.

Front-end processor: A computer that controls transmission between the main computer and remote terminals.

Full-duplex: A channel that facilitates simultaneous transmission in both directions.

Function key: Key on a keyboard dedicated to a special function such as HELP.

Functionality: A definition of the facilities, performance, and other factors that the user requires in the finished product.

Goal: General or ultimate end toward which effort is aimed in an organization.

Goal seeking: See **backward iteration**.

Half-duplex: Transmission channel that transmits in either direction, but in one direction at a time.

Hard copy: Permanent form of the information displayed on a computer screen or stored in memory.

Hardware: Physical equipment—for example, mechanical, magnetic, electrical, or electronic devices.

Hashing: An approach to addressing in which a hashing algorithm performs arithmetic operations on a given field and the result is used as an address.

HELP facility (also HELP screen):   Menu that allows a user to request additional information at any point during interface with the computer.

Heuristic: In expert systems—a rule of thumb, experiential reasoning, as opposed to textbook knowledge.

Hierarchical structure: Breaking down a large project into a series of successively smaller, manageable parts through iteration and according to a logical sequence.

High-level language: English-like programming language; a compiler translates the language into a machine language.

HIPO chart: (Hierarchy/Input/Process/Output). A documentation tool that graphically portrays functions in a chart from a general level down to detailed levels.

Hybrid computer: A computer that utilizes both digital and analog representation of data.

Icon: A picture of a function on a CRT, such as a wastebasket to stand for a delete function.

Indexed sequential access method (ISAM):   A method for accessing records in an indexed sequential file.

Indexed sequential file organization: Storing logical records in a file so that they are in sequential order with an index to the location of records.

Indirect cost: Overhead; results of operations not directly associated with a given system or activity; examples are insurance, maintenance, heat, and air conditioning.

Indirect observation: An observation that relies on mechanical devices such as cameras and videotapes to capture information.

Industry-specific software: Software that performs a specific function that can only be used in one type of industry, such as an airline reservation system.

Inference: In expert systems, the process of inferring new facts from current information.

Inference engine: Part of an expert system, it stands between the user and the knowledge base; contains the inference strategies and controls required for manipulating the facts and rules.

Information resource center (IRC):   A physical site providing hardware, software, and consulting support to allow rapid information retrieval.

Information resource management (IRM):   A concept that views information as a scarce resource; therefore, it must be managed effectively for a successful MIS.

Inheritance: In a semantic network, instances of one class are assumed to have all the properties of more general classes of which they are members.

Ink-jet printer: A low-speed nonimpact printer that employs a stream of electrostatically charged droplets that are used with the print head to produce the character matrix.

Input: The data to be processed; the process of transferring data from external storage to internal storage.

Instance: The value of an attribute for a specific occurrence.

Instantiate: To give a variable a specific value, an instance.

Integrated system: DSS software that provides word processing and database management along with basic tasks.

Intelligence: First phase of the decision-making process; searching the environment for conditions that call for a decision.

Intelligent terminal: A key terminal that performs such functions as editing and verifying keyed data, inserting standard information into keyed data, requesting particular pieces of data to be keyed, or requesting corrections to previously keyed data.

Interactive processing: An end user is able to carry on a dialog with the computer system.

Interview: A data-gathering or data-verification approach; talking with people in an organized manner and with a purpose.

Inverted list: A copy of a list that has been inverted into a given sequence; the duplicated data is replaced by pointers to the original list.

Isolated computing: First stage of technological change in computing, in the early 1960s. All organizational computing was done in an "isolated" quarter of the company.

Job description: Defines the duties and responsibilities of a job, the reporting relationship, the work environment, and other activities that the job entails.

Job specification: Identifies required personal characteristics, including the skills and abilities required for the job, educational requirements, years of experience, and the like.

Join: A relational operation that produces a new relation which includes all the combinations of tuples from two given relations that meet a specified condition.

Key: An attribute or set of attributes that identifies a record.

Knowledge base: A part of expert system architecture; contains an unstructured set of facts and inference rules for determining new facts.

Knowledge engineering: Building expert systems; replicating the behavior of a specific expert in solving a narrowly defined problem.

Knowledge worker: A manager, supervisor, or clerk who is actively involved in thinking, processing information, analyzing, and recommending procedures or changes based on the use of information.

Label: In a spreadsheet, a nonnumeric or alphabetic character that is preceded by a label prefix; also called a string.

Laser printer: A nonimpact printer in which a laser writes characters on a drum that are then given an electrostatic charge. The charge attracts pigments that stick to the paper around the drum to form characters.

Link: Symbolic reference in memory used to associate an object with other objects.

***LIS*t *P*rocessing language (LISP):**   A highly interactive AI language that combines symbols into basic shapes that are the equivalent of sentences or lists.

Local area network (LAN):   An electronic communication linkage where all sources and recipients are in one office, in a single building, or on a single work site, typically less than one mile in radius.

Logic: (1) The science dealing with the criteria or formal principles of reasoning and thought. (2) The systematic scheme that defines the interactions of signals in the design of an automatic data processing system. (3) The basic principles and application of truth tables and interconnection between logical elements required for arithmetic computation in an automatic data processing system.

Logic error: Deviation from a range of acceptability.

Logical design: In developing a system, laying down specifications and depicting its logical flow through a data flow diagram.

Logical view: What the data look like, regardless of how they are stored in the database.

Machine language: The lowest level of computer language; the format is a series of binary digits, 0 and 1.

Macro: A group of keystrokes to which a name is assigned; examples are labels, values, formulas, and commands.

Magnetic core: Main memory device in second- and some third-generation computers.

Magnetic ink character recognition (MICR):   Input method that codes and identifies checks, deposit slips, and documents preencoded with special magnetic ink.

Main memory: Also called primary storage; the internal storage within a computer.

Maintainability: Ease of locating and correcting program errors; modularity; simplicity.

Management information system (MIS):   An integrated approach to the design and use of computer-based information systems that provides summary information and highlights exception conditions for corrective decision making; a federation of subsystems.

Management science: The application of scientific methodology to management decisions.

Managerial information: Information of direct use to middle management or department heads whose focus is on tactical planning, decision making, and control.

Managerial planning: Process in which predefined functional plans are applicable to a range of years to show how strategies are implemented to achieve long-range plans.

Maximax criterion: Assumes that whatever alternative is chosen results in the best outcome.

Maximin criterion: Used to select the action that will have the highest (maximum) utility outcome if the worst (minimum) state of nature takes place.

Mean time between failure (MTBF):   The average time the system is available to users before breaking down.

Menu: A selected list of options that the user chooses from and then types an option for a computer operation.

Merchantability: An implied warranty ensuring that a system or a piece of software functions properly within realistic guidelines.

Microcomputer: Desk-sized computer consisting of a keyboard, a CPU, and a CRT.

Microfloppy: A microdiskette measuring 3½ inches used in leading microcomputer systems.

Microwave transmission: A process of transmitting signals line-of-sight through the atmosphere; relay stations must be positioned at fixed points to continue the transmission.

MIPS: Million instructions per second.

Mission: Well-defined roles in which an organization elects to concentrate its efforts; a long-run (global) vision of what the organization is trying to become.

Model: A logical or mathematical representation of a system that encompasses features of interest to the user.

Model generator: Comprehensive DSS software that has the capability of defining models, performing statistical analysis, linking the model to a database, and providing a user-machine dialog.

Modem: A device that converts analog to digital (and vice versa) between the user and a remote computer.

Modularity: In systems maintenance, when a system is constructed in modular units of a limited size to simplify maintenance when necessary; in software reliability, the ease with which a package can be modified.

Module: A group of instructions with a single entry point and a single exit point.

Modus ponens: In expert systems, a common rule for deriving new facts from existing rules and known facts; a rule of inference used in proof procedures and an intuitive way of conducting reasoning.

Monochrome monitor: A TV-like screen (monitor) that displays only one color (green, amber, etc.) on a black background.

Motherboard: A circuit board containing a collection of chips, including the CPU, RAM, and ROM chips.

Motivation: A process governing choices made by persons among alternative forms of voluntary activity.

Mouse: A hand-held device designed to draw graphs or select functions displayed on a screen.

Multiplexing: The simultaneous transmission of several messages over a single line through the use of predetermined frequencies or time intervals within the bandwidth.

Multipoint network: A nonswitched network configuration in which several terminals are linked to a single sending line.

Multiprocessing: A system involving more than one arithmetic and logic unit for simultaneous use.

Multiprogramming: Two or more programs run in the central processing unit at the same time. Program execution is interleaved so that each program is partly processed in a certain time slot; processing, then, is not simultaneous.

Multitasking: Running several jobs simultaneously from several terminals by more than one user. This feature is popular on new microcomputers such as the IBM System 2.

Narrow band: Low-speed transmission of up to 300 baud.

Natural language: Computer programs capable of reading, speaking, or understanding human language.

Natural observation: An observation in the user's place of work or surroundings.

Net advantage to leasing formula: The difference between the present value of after-tax cost of ownership and the present value of after-tax cost of leasing.

Net benefit analysis: Total benefits minus total costs.

Net present value: Discounted benefits minus discounted costs.

Network structure: Events and activities in PERT/CPM; in a database, a data structure that allows 1:1, 1:M, or M:N relationships between entities.

Node: In a database, an element; a part of a network structure.

Nonprocedural language: Requests users to define results; the language processor automatically keeps track of the program's flow.

Nonprocedurality: A procedure that allows the user complete freedom as to the order in which equations are entered into the computer.

Nonswitched network: A network system in which several terminals may be linked to a single line, but only one terminal can transmit at a time.

Normal form: A class of relational schemas that conform to some set of rules.

Normalization: A process of transforming relations to normal forms.

Normative model: Developed by management scientists; describes how consistent decision makers should act to make rational decisions.

Object: A representation of knowledge in symbolic form that can be efficiently used by an inference engine.

Object program: The program that is the output of a compiler. Often the object program is a machine language program ready for execution, but it may well be in an intermediate language.

Objective: As distinct from goal, management's intentions to accomplish its mission.

Office automation: The integration of computer and communication technology with human patterns of office work.

On-line, real-time: A system that receives input data, processes it, and returns results (output) fast enough to affect an ongoing process.

Open architecture: Making minor changes in the software so that it can run on different vendor hardware.

Operating system: A collection of programs that control and manage the activities of a computer system.

Operation code: A code that represents a specific operation. Synonymous with instruction code.

Operational planning: Process of devising programmed, short-range plans that focus on the day-to-day activities of the system.

Optical character recognition (OCR):   A technique that relies on electronic devices and light to detect, and convert into machine form, characters that have been printed or written on documents in human-understandable form.

Packed decimal: Two digits packed into one byte.

Parallel processing: A processing routine in which the new and the old information systems are run simultaneously for a designated time period.

Parameterized application package: A preprogrammed software package designed to run a specific application.

Parent: In a database, an owning entity.

Payback analysis: A method of determining how long it will take a system to generate enough savings to cover departmental costs.

Payoff: The result of choosing a given alternative. The definition of expected payoffs aids in the decision-making process.

Peer-to-peer network: A network in which users work with applications without involving services from another computer center.

Physical design: In system design, the stage after logical design that develops program software—the working system.

Physical view: What the data actually look like in storage.

Planning: Studying a projected course of action and determining what is to be done to meet stated goals.

Point-of-sale (POS):   A technique geared to automatic collection of source data through on-line computer systems.

Point-to-point network: A network with direct lines between terminals and computers in data communications.

Pointer: A data item in a record that contains the storage address of another record.

Policy: A generalization that prescribes what an organization ought to do.

Portability: Ability of software to be used on different hardware and operating systems.

Predicate: In logic programming, an expression with a true or false condition.

Premise: A situation; in expert systems, a premise is combined with a conclusion to form a rule.

Present value: Current value of money, determined by discounting future economic values backward in time to the present.

Primary key: An attribute that uniquely defines a record.

Primitive: See **data element**.

Problem-oriented language: A machine-independent language requiring only a statement of the problem (not the procedure) for proper solution.

Procedural language: Language that requires the user to provide the logical steps or procedures to the computer for problem solving.

Procedural specifications: Explicit specifications that state the module's function and the way to write the program instructions.

Processing: Transforming input into output; in a data flow diagram, indicated by a bubble or a circle.

Program: A procedure for solving a problem; loosely, a routine. As a verb: to devise a plan for solving a problem; loosely, to write a routine.

Program logical view: See **subschema**.

Project: A relational operation that selects specified attributes from a relation to produce a new relation with the new attributes.

Project planning: Response to lack of fit between user requirements and system performance; setting delivery schedules, identifying milestones, and periodic review of projects.

PROLOG: *PRO*gramming language for *LOG*ic; a logic programming dialect that is suitable as an implementation language for expert systems.

Prompt: A symbol on a computer screen that asks the user for a command or response.

Protocol: Refers to the rules that both the sender and the receiver use; a standardized use of certain characters for control of the communications procedure and error-handling rules.

Prototyping: A working system to explore implementation or processing alternatives and evaluate results.

Pseudocode: A design tool that produces a highly readable program design.

Quality assurance: Developing controls to ensure a quality product; defining factors that determine system quality and the criteria that the software must meet to contain these factors.

Query: A language used to specify characteristics of data to be retrieved from a database.

RAM: *Random Access Memory*. A type of main memory; where data and application programs are stored for processing.

Random file organization: A method whereby records are stored randomly throughout the file and are accessed via addresses that specify the disk locations.

Ranking scales question: A question that asks the respondent to determine preferences for the importance of a set of items.

Rating scales question: A multiple-choice item that offers a range of responses along a given dimension.

Rationality: Making choices based on known sets of alternatives with corresponding outcomes, a set of relations that orders the alternatives, and maximizations of something definitive such as cost, profit, or some utility.

Redundancy: A situation in which two or more pieces of information in a file are the same.

Regret criterion: Assumes that the true evaluation of decision-making performance is the amount of regret expressed for having taken one action when another action could have been chosen.

Relation: Two-dimensional table.

Relational algebra: A set of operations that acts on relations to produce new relations.

Relational structure: Data and relationships represented in a flat, two-dimensional table.

Relative address: The location of a record relative to the beginning of the file.

Reliability: Dependability or level of confidence; in systems work, the need to gather dependable information for use in making decisions about the system being studied; in software, refers to how well the software will perform for a given time period without failure.

Report generator: A software that allows the user to interactively define the data files and produce reports.

Request for proposal (RFP):   A report by the user requesting selected vendors to bid on a proposed system.

Resource planning: Focusing on the future and determining the hardware, software, and personnel needs to handle a growing number of computer applications.

Responsiveness: Relating to the time required by the computer between a user's request and receipt of the desired data.

Ring chain: A chain in which the last record points back to the first.

Ring network: LAN layout in which several processors or microcomputers are linked together to form the equivalent of a ring, so that data lines connect each unit to adjacent ones only.

Risk analysis: Making a decision when only the probabilities of the outcomes of each alternative are known.

ROM: The part of computer memory that contains prewired functions. The functions cannot be altered by programmed instructions.

Root: In database, a parent with no owners.

Rule: In forms design, a rule (line) that guides the human eye in reading and writing data groups and separates them on the form; in expert systems, a conditional statement that specifies an action to be taken, if a certain condition is true.

Schema: A map of the overall structure of a database.

Secondary storage: Storage media such as magnetic tape or magnetic disk.

Select: A relational operation that takes horizontal rows in a relation or identifies the tuples to be included in a new relation.

Sequential Access Method (SAM):   A method for locating records in a sequentially organized file.

Sequential list: Data that are listed sequentially on a given key; uses a sequential file organization format.

Sequential organization: Sorting in physical, contiguous blocks within files on tape or disk.

Serviceability: A criterion for software selection focusing on documentation and vendor support.

Servicer: A computer service bureau.

Sibling: In database, the relationship of the children of one parent.

Simplex: Transmission of information in one direction only.

Slot: Part of a frame where facts and values related to a specific object are stored.

Soft copy: A temporary copy of the output such as display of the output on the screen.

Software: (1) The collection of programs and routines associated with a computer; for example, compilers, library routines. (2) All the documents associated with a computer; for example, manuals, circuit diagrams.

Software maintenance: A preventive procedure designed to ascertain that the software continues to function to standards.

Source program: A procedure or format that allows enhancements on a software package.

Span of control: The number of employees that a supervisor can handle effectively.

Specific DSS: The hardware/software that allows a user or decision maker to deal with a specific set of related problems.

Spreadsheet software: A generalized program that allows the user to create models for handling a variety of problems.

Star network: LAN layout in which each terminal is linked by a separate line to a central host computer.

State of nature: A future event that is beyond the control of the decision maker; affects the decision-making process.

Stored program concept: A series of instructions in storage to direct the step-by-step operation of the computer.

Strategic information: Information used by upper management in long-range policy planning.

Strategic planning: In system planning, establishing relationships between the organization plan and the plan for a candidate system.

Strategy: A possible alternative in a decision situation.

Stress testing: Subjecting the new system to a high volume of data over a short time. The purpose is to ensure that the system does not malfunction under peak loads.

Structure chart: Graphic representation of the control logic of processing functions or modules representing a system.

Structured analysis: A set of techniques and graphic tools that allow the analyst to develop a new kind of system specification that is easily understandable to the user.

Structured decision: A decision made through a routine procedure, primarily used by lower management.

Structured English: Formal English statements used for communicating processing rules or describing the structure of a system.

Structured interview: Also called a directive interview; an approach in which the questions and the alternative responses are fixed.

Structured question: A question that is presented with the same wording to all respondents.

Structured walkthrough: A design procedure that helps systems analysts recognize various errors in system design.

Subschema: A map of the programmer's view of data he or she uses; derived from the schema.

Switched network: A network configuration in which all sending lines funnel into a switching center that links the designated station until the message has been transmitted.

Symbolic code: A program code that uses mnemonics. For example, the character W stands for Write (print), S for Subtract, and R for Read.

Symbolic programming: Symbolically structured knowledge base in a macro working memory, maintained by knowledge engineers and experts.

Synchronous transmission: Occurring concurrently with a regular time relationship; transmission of a burst of data at a time.

Synonym: A hashed address that is not unique.

Syntax error: A program statement that violates one or more rules of the language in which it is written.

System design: Detailed concentration on the technical and other specifications that will make the new system operational.

System development life cycle (SDLC): A structured sequence of phases for implementing an information system.

System flowchart: A graphic representation of a system showing the overall flow of control in processing at the job level; specifies what activities must be done to convert from a physical to a logical model.

System software: Software designed to control system operations and implementation as opposed to user oriented functions.

System specifications: Key information for programming, testing, and implementing the project.

System testing: Testing of the whole system by the user after major programs and subsystems have been tested.

Telecommunication: The movement of information by an electrical transmission system among multiple sites; a long-haul network system linking the organization with its branches and the outside world.

Term: In logic, the name of an object.

Theoretical view: View of DSS that defines it as being a subset of MIS.

Timesharing: Sharing of a computer by two or more users in the same time interval. Each user has the impression that he or she is the sole user of the system.

Token passing: A procedure that allows a terminal to transmit only while it holds a logical "token" that is passed from one terminal to another in a predefined manner.

Toolsmith: Person concerned with developing technological components for the DSS, a new language, and how they can be integrated to form a DSS generator with the requisite capabilities.

Transaction support system: A low-level information system that provides detailed operational information to lower management.

Tree network: Also called a hierarchical structure; a hierarchy of groups of data such that the highest in the hierarchy has only one group called a root, and all groups except the root are related to only one group on a higher level than themselves.

Tuning: Adjusting a database to improve its performance.

Tuple: A group of related fields.

Tutorial: An easy-to-use program for teaching first-time users how to work with a specific software package.

Unbundling: The acquisition of hardware components, software, training, or supplies as separate entities. The system can be comprised of software and peripherals from a number of different vendors.

Uninterruptible Power Supply **(UPS)** An electric power supply that automatically replaces that of the local public utility in the event of a power outage. This allows an organization's computers to operate without loss of data or processing time.

Union: A relational algebra operation that combines the tuples of one relation to the tuples of another relation to form a third relation.

Unstructured decision: A decision whose nature is more judgmental than computational, primarily used by upper management.

Unstructured interview: An approach in which the questions and the alternative responses are open ended.

Unstructured questionnaire: An approach that allows respondents to freely answer questions in their own words.

User friendliness: Concerned with tools and features designed to break down barriers between the end user and the computer.

User friendly: Relates to computers that accept languages or are designed to interact with the end user in a human-oriented language or one understandable to the user.

User manual: A manual written to serve the user of a computer system.

User's view: The perspective that the user brings to an MIS system.

Utility software: A set of programs that perform common tasks such as copying disk files to tape for backup.

Validity: Determining how well a question asked is worded as to elicit the information sought.

Value-added network (VAN): Packed switched network based on the Advance Research Projects Agency Communication Network of the U.S. Department of Defense.

Very large scale integration (VLSI): A fourth-generation development; a chip with circuit densities approaching 100,000 components.

Voice band: Medium-speed transmission of between 4,800 and 9,600 bauds; used for communicating human voice.

Voice mail: A computer-based system capable of storing messages digitally.

Voice store-and-forward: A relatively new telecommunication messaging technology.

Warnier/Orr diagram: A hierarchy chart used in the modular design of a system program.

Wide band: High speed transmission of 9,600 to 50,000 bauds over private-line channels.

Window: A screen divided into a number of rectangular areas, making up a split screen.

Word: An ordered set of characters that occupy one storage location and are treated by the computer circuits as a unit and transferred as such. Ordinarily, a word is treated by the control unit as an instruction and by the arithmetic unit as a quantity. Word lengths may be fixed or variable depending on the particular computer.

Work adjustment: The correspondence between the individual and the work environment.

Worker module: A module that contains a subroutine and is called on by another module.

Workstation: An area set aside for users, equipped with office furniture, a "smart" terminal, voice transfer devices, and other computer oriented equipment; a man-machine interface—a device through which a user can communicate with an office system.

CREDITS

TEXT CREDITS: p. 53, Driving by the Glow of a Screen. © 1987 Time Inc. All rights reserved. Reprinted by permission from *TIME*. p. 95, Developers pick Basic for High Productivity. © 1987 by Infoworld Publishing, Inc., a subsidiary of IDG Communications, Inc. Reprinted from *Infoworld*, 1060 Marsh Road, Menlo Park, CA 94025. p. 134, Hard Disks. Reprinted from *PC Week*, July 8, 1986. © 1986 by Ziff Communications Company. p. 163, Designing a Database Application. Reprinted from *PC Week*, April 29, 1986. © 1986 by Ziff Communications Company. p. 195, Send It By Satellite. Reprinted from *Datamation*, May 1, 1986. © 1986 by Cahners Publishing Company. p. 233, Litton Resources Solution: Cullinet. © 1986 by CW Communications, Inc., Framingham, MA 01701. p. 262, Planning and Building a DSS. Reprinted from *Datamation*, March 15, 1986. © 1986 by Cahners Publishing Company. p. 293, DSS at Phillips Gusher Strategic Information. From *Data Management* Magazine. Copyright and reprint permission granted. Data Processing Management Association. All rights reserved. p. 320, Computer-Based Training Tutors Ensure Quality Education. From *Data Management* Magazine. Copyright and reprint permission granted. Data Processing Management Association. All rights reserved. p. 352, Purdue System Aids Farmers. Reprinted by permission of Texas Instruments Inc., Austin, TX. p. 385, Planning Amid Change. © 1985 by CW Publishing, Inc., Framingham, MA. Reprinted from *Computerworld*. p. 457, Accelerated Design Speeds the Application Development Cycle. From *Data Management* Magazine. Copyright and reprint permission granted. Data Processing Management Association. All rights reserved. p. 485, Who's Responsible for the Bugs? Reprinted from *PC Week*, May 27, 1986. © 1986 Ziff Communications Company. p. 511, Holiday Fire Puts Firm's Disaster Plan to the Test. © 1986 by CW Publishing, Inc., Framingham, MA. 01701. Reprinted from *Computerworld*. p. 535, Managing your boss. Excerpted from *Today's Office* by permission of Dr. Kenneth Blanchard. p. 567, Connectivity, Strategic DP Top User Concerns. © 1986 by CW Publishing, Inc., Framingham, MA. 01701. Reprinted from *Computerworld*.

ILLUSTRATION CREDITS: Fig. 1.1—Reprinted with permission of Unisys Corporation. Fig. 1.5—Courtesy Texas Instruments Data Systems Group. Photo, p. 53—Photo courtesy of Etak. Fig. 3.1—Contact Press/Louis Psihoyos, © 1986. Fig. 3.2—Courtesy of International Business Machines Corporation. Fig. 3.3—Courtesy of International Business Machines Corporation. Fig. 3.4—Courtesy of Cray Research, Inc. and Amdahl Corporation. Fig. 3.5—Intel Corporation. Fig. 3.10—Courtesy of International Business Machines Corporation. Fig. 3.12—Courtesy of International Business Machines Corporation. Fig. 3.14—Courtesy of Apple Computer, Inc. Fig. 3.17—Reprinted with permission from the May 1984 issue of *Popular Computing* magazine. © McGraw-Hill, Inc. Fig. 3.23—Recognition Equipment Inc. Fig. 3.25—Reprinted with permission of Unisy Corporation. Fig. 3.27—Photo courtesy NCR. Fig. 3.28—Courtesy of Hewlett-Packard Company. Fig. 3.31—Wayland Lee, Addison-Wesley Publishing Company, Inc., Menlo Park, CA. Fig. 6.1—James Martin, *Principles of Data-Base Management*, © 1976, p. 37. Reprinted by permission of Prentice-Hall, Inc., Englewood Cliffs, NJ. Fig. 6.2—Adapted from Awad, E.M.: *Systems Analysis and Design*, 2nd edition, p. 234. © 1985, Richard D. Irwin, Inc., Homewood, IL. Fig. 7.5—Courtesy International Business Machines Corporation. Fig. 7.7—Reprinted with permission of Unisys Corporation. Fig. 7.12—Kessler Marketing Intelligence, Newport, RI, 1987. Table 9.1—From *Data Management* Magazine. Copyright and reprint permission granted. Data Processing Management Association. All rights reserved. Table 9.4—From *Data Management* Magazine. Copyright and reprint permission granted. Data Processing Management Association. All rights reserved. Fig. 9.4—Sprague/Carlson, *Building Effective Decision Support Systems*. © 1982, p. 14. Adapted by permission of Prentice-Hall, Inc., Englewood Cliffs, NJ. Fig. 9.5—Adapted from *Datamation*, May 1, 1987. © 1986 by Cahners Publishing Company. Fig. 9.9a—Courtesy of International Business Machines Corporation. Fig. 9.9b—Microsoft Corporation. Table 9.3—Adapted from "Computer-Based Decision Aids: The Evaluation Problem" by P.G.W. Keen, *Sloan Management Review*, Spring 1975, p. 28, by permission of the publisher. © 1975 by the Sloan Management Review Association. All rights reserved. Fig. 11.1—Photo courtesy of INMAC, Santa Clara, CA. Fig. 11.2—Courtesy Xerox Corporation. Fig. 11.7—Courtesy of International Business Machines. Fig. 11.8a—Courtesy of Apple Computer, Inc. Fig. 11.8b—Courtesy of Apple Computer, Inc. Fig. 11.9—Courtesy of Hewlett-Packard Company. Table 11.1—© 1982 Hunter Publishing Co., Inc. Reprinted with permission of *Systems/3X World*, formerly *Small Systems World*. Table 12.4—© 1984 by CW Publishing, Inc., Framingham, MA. 01701. Reprinted from *Computerworld*. Fig. 12.1—© 1983 by CW Publishing, Inc., Framingham, MA. 01701. Reprinted from *Computerworld*. Fig. 12.3—© 1985, Association for Computing Machinery, Inc. Fig. 12.4—Adapted from "Texas Instruments: A Progress Report," Texas Instruments, Dallas, TX. Fig. 13.1—From Massie/Douglas, *Managing: A Contemporary Introduction*, 4th edition, © 1985, p. 113. Reprinted by permission of Prentice-Hall, Inc. Englewood Cliffs, NJ. Fig. 13.6—Reprinted from *Datamation*, July, 1981 by Cahners Publishing Company. Fig. 13.7—Adapted from *Business Systems Planning*, 1981. Courtesy International Business Machines Corporation. Fig. 13.8—Adapted from *Business Systems Planning*, 1981. Courtesy International Business Machines Corporation. Fig. 14.4—Adapted from *Structured Analysis and System Specification* by Tom DeMarco. © 1979, p. 26 (A Yourdon Book). Adapted by permission of Prentice-Hall, Inc., Englewood Cliffs, NJ. Table 14.9—Awad, E.M. *Systems Analysis and Design*, 2nd edition, p. 244, 249. © 1985, Richard D. Irwin, Inc., Homewood, IL. Fig. 15.5—Courtesy of Apple Computer, Inc. Fig. 18.6—Reprinted from *Datamation*, September, 1978, by Cahners Publishing Company. Fig. 18.9—© 1985 by CW Publishing, Inc., Framingham, MA. 01701. Reprinted from *Computerworld*. Fig. 18.11—Wayne F. Cascio/Elias M. Awad, *Human Resources Management: An Information Systems Approach*. © 1981, p. 287. Adapted by permission of Prentice-Hall, Inc., Englewood Cliffs, NJ. Fig. 18.12—Wayne F. Cascio/Elias M. Awad, *Human Resources Management: An Information Systems Approach*,© 1981, p. 190. Adapted by permission of Prentice-Hall, Inc., Englewood Cliffs, NJ. Fig. 19.5—From the *Dun's 5000 Survey*, prepared by the Economic Analysis Department. The Dun and Bradstreet Corporation, 1985.

Index